PSYCHOLOGICAL EVALUTION AND
TESTING SERVICE (P.E.T.S.)
DEPARTMENT OF PSYCHIATRY
EVANSTON HOSPITAL
2650 RIDGE AVENUE
EVANSTON, ILLINOIS 60201
(312) 492-4518

Attention Deficit Disorder
Clinical and Basic Research

edited by

Terje Sagvolden
University of Oslo, Norway

Trevor Archer
*Astra Alab AB, Södertälje, and
University of Umeå, Sweden*

LEA LAWRENCE ERLBAUM ASSOCIATES, PUBLISHERS
Hillsdale, New Jersey   London

Lawrence Erlbaum Associates, Inc., Publishers
365 Broadway
Hillsdale, New Jersey 07642

Library of Congress Cataloging-in-Publication Data

Attention deficit disorder : clinical and basic research / edited by
Terje Sagvolden and Trevor Archer.
    p. cm.
Dased on a conference of the European Brain and Behaviour Society
held July 21-24, 1987 in Oslo, Norway.
Bibliography: p.
Includes indexes.
ISBN 0-8058-0098-0
1. Attention deficit disorders--Congresses. I. Sagvolden, Terje.
II. Archer, Trevor. III. European Brain and Behaviour Society.
RJ496.A86A875 1989
618.92'8589--dc19   88-12113
                           CIP

Printed in the United States of America
10 9 8 7 6 5 4 3 2 1

Contents

Preface

This book grew out of an European Brain and Behaviour Society Workshop on Attention Deficit Disorder, Minimal Brain Dysfunction, Hyperkinetic Syndrome, and related dysfunctions held in Oslo, Norway in 1987.

Virtually millions of children and adults suffer from problems variously described as attention deficit disorder (ADD), minimal brain dysfunction (MBD), hyperkinetic syndrome, or, most recently, attention- deficit hyperactivity disorder (ADHD). In these related disorders there are interactions between brain functioning and the psychological environment. In recent years, we have seen a virtual explosion of knowledge within the neurosciences. There was an urgent need to bring about a rapprochement between the neurosciences and the behavioral sciences. The major purpose of the conference and this book is to unite clinical and basic researchers in order to improve our understanding of ADD and related dysfunctions. Thus, hopefully, this book will aid both clinicians and researchers in the neurosciences interested in allieviating these problems.

A main conclusion of the conference was that the attention problems of ADD children might be secondary to basic motor-control problems. Although sensory and motor processes interact, by placing the problems more on the motor side, one might be closer to the heart of the hyperkinesis problem. Another conclusion was that ADD might be related to dysfunctions in the central catecholaminergic systems.

We would like to acknowledge the help of the following individuals in organizing and running the conference: Jan Blegeberg, Hans M. Borchgrevink, Halvor Dahl, Knut Klippenberg, Hallgrim Kløve, Edvard I. Moser, May-Britt Moser, Michael Rutter, Espen Sagvolden, Geir Sagvolden, Liv Sagvolden, Yvonne Wade, Boaz Wultz, Ester Wultz, and finally, Torbjørn Danielsen and his students.

The conference was supported by: European Brain and Behaviour Society (EBBS), International Brain Research Organization (IBRO), The Norwegian Research Council for Science and the Humanities (NAVF), University of Oslo, The Norwegian Directorate of Health (Ministry of Health and Social Affairs), Astra Alab AB, Bik Bok, Christian Berner, Ciba Geigy Norway, Den Norske Creditbank, Norsk Kollektiv Pensjonskasse, Postgiro, and Smith, Kline, and French. Terje Sagvolden has in part been supported by a Senior Fulbright Scholar Fellowship.

Terje Sagvolden
Trevor Archer

Attention Deficit Disorder/ Hyperkinetic Syndrome: Conceptual and Research Issues Regarding Diagnosis and Classification

Michael Rutter
MRC Child Psychiatry Unit
Institute of Psychiatry
University of London

CONCEPT OF MINIMAL BRAIN DYSFUNCTION

Current concepts of hyperkinetic and attentional deficit disorders have several historical roots (Rutter, 1982; Schachar, 1986; Weiss & Hechtman, 1986). However, much of the earlier literature was based on the notion that the disorder was synonymous with "minimal brain dysfunction" or MBD (Wender, 1971; Clements, 1966). This idea derived from the writings of Strauss and his colleagues (Strauss & Lehtinen, 1947) regarding behavioural syndromes supposedly due to brain damage in mildly mentally handicapped individuals; from the studies of Pasamanick and his colleagues (Pasamanick & Knobloch, 1966) linking a "continuum of reproductive casualty" with hyperactive behaviour; and most of all from Bradley's (1937) discovery of the therapeutic effect of amphetamines in the treatment of behavioural and educational problems. Much of the argument in favour of the concept of "minimal brain dysfunction" was based on circular reasoning of various types and it has not stood the test of time (Rutter, 1983). The hypothesis of a single characteristic MBD syndrome that takes the form of hyperactivity no longer warrants serious scientific consideration.

Because the diagnostic term 'MBD' continues to be used by some clinicians and a few researchers, it is perhaps important to make explicit what is, and is not, being rejected. There is, of course, no doubt that there can be substantial brain disease or damage without this being evident in abnormalities on the clinical neurological examination (Rutter, 1983; Rutter, Chadwick & Schachar, 1983). It cannot therefore be doubted that some psychiatric syndromes for which there is no clinical evidence of neurological disorder at present will ultimately turn out to have a basis in organic brain pathology. As our understanding of brain

1

function improves and as our tools to investigate brain malfunction develop so the range of psychiatric disorders known to have an organic basis is likely to increase (Rutter, 1986). It also cannot be doubted that child psychiatric disorder has important associations with neurodevelopmental immaturities, so-called "neurological soft signs" (Shaffer et al., 1983), and with developmental delays in functions such as language (Howlin & Rutter, 1987). In these instances the conceptual difficulty stems from the uncertainty as to what the "soft signs" or developmental delays reflect (Shafer et al., 1983; 1986). As such, they cannot be taken as unambiguous indicators of organic brain dysfunction, although sometimes this will be the case. A further difficulty, moreover, with respect to consideration of hyperkinetic or attention deficit syndromes, is that the neurodevelopmental associations are by no means confined to this type of behavioural problem. Thus, Shaffer and his colleagues (1985) found that neurological soft signs were most strongly associated with anxiety disorders in adolescence. Accordingly, one of the key features of the MBD concept that must be rejected is the idea that brain damage or dysfunction gives rise to a uniform behavioural picture. It does not (Rutter, 1981). Indeed, the presence of brain damage or dysfunction is associated with an increase in the risk for a wide range of psychiatric disorders of which attention deficit disorders are by no means the most prominent.

It should be added that the idea that MBD syndromes were largely explicable on the basis of perinatal complications must also be rejected. There are, at best, only very weak associations between such complications and any of the features said to characterize MBD and the presence of reproductive abnormalities does not serve to delineate any type of behavioural syndrome (Nichols & Chen, 1981). To an important extent, this negative finding is a function of the fact that in most cases perinatal complications do not in fact give rise to brain damage and it is possible that conclusions may need to be modified once there has been a more adequate follow up into middle childhood of children in whom perinatal complications have been associated with brain damage as identified by modern imaging techniques (Stewart, 1983; Stewart et al., 1987). However, it seems dubious whether this will give rise to a specific association with attention deficit or hyperkinetic disorders. All in all, biological findings fail to establish the nosological validity of an MBD syndrome (Ferguson & Rapoport, 1983; Taylor, 1986b). How, then, is this dismissal of the MBD notion to be reconciled with the claim a few years ago by Gillberg and his colleagues (1982, 1983) that "about a third of children diagnosed according to strict criteria as suffering from 'minimal brain dysfunction' show generalized hyperkinesis" (p.245)? The claim derives from a systematic and large scale epidemiological study. The flaw is that similar problems in attention were used to define both MBD and the hyperkinetic syndrome. Accordingly, the association was to a large extent tautological. As used by these investigators, MBD was defined in part by the very attentional deficits that it is supposed to explain. That point is recognized by Gillberg (this volume). His data are of very considerable interest in their own right but they do not help with syndrome definition. Of course, there is nothing wrong with an hypothesis that specifies that a syndrome is defined in terms of a constellation or combination of features. However, validation must be obtained by demonstration that such a constellation differs from other behavioural syndromes in terms of features that are external to the diagnostic criteria (Rutter, 1978). It is in that validating criterion, which is crucial to the whole of diagnosis and classification, that the MBD concept falls down. The concept of minimal brain dysfunction need preoccupy us no longer and I will not consider it further.

CONCEPT OF ATTENTION
DEFICIT/HYPERACTIVITY SYNDROME

Let me turn now to the related, but somewhat different, concept of a behavioural syndrome that is defined in terms of the presence of hyperactivity and attentional problems, without reference to any particular aetiological hypothesis, organic or otherwise. There is now a vast literature of empirical investigations on children suffering from these behavioural problems. This has been well summarized in detailed reviews, several of which are book length, by researchers in North America, Europe and the Antipodes (Barkley, 1981; Prior & Griffin, 1985; Ross & Ross, 1982; Safer & Allen, 1976; Taylor, 1986 a & b). I will make no attempt to evaluate this whole literature again but will instead draw attention to some of the key conceptual and research issues that remain. Although some earlier reviews had cast serious doubt on the validity of any syndrome defined in terms of overactivity or inattention (Shaffer & Greenhill, 1979), most commentators today accept that it is highly likely that there is such a valid syndrome, although important doubts remain on exactly how to define it. I agree with both the likelihood of validity and also the doubts on definition.

The problem in definition begins with the heterogeneity and diffuseness of the behaviours that are supposed to characterize the syndrome. Thus, overactivity may be seen in the restlessness of anxiety, the psychomotor agitation of depression, the excessive energy and talkativeness of mania, and in the hyperkinesis of autism, as well as in that associated with hyperkinetic syndromes. The phenomenon also varies somewhat with age; hyperactivity tends to diminish as the children grow older, although a tendency to increased activity levels continues in many cases (Weiss & Hechtman, 1986).

A further problem, albeit one that is common to many psychiatric phenomena in childhood, is that there is no clear dividing line between normal and abnormal levels of activity. Children vary greatly in their activity level and, indeed, activity level is usually accepted as one of the main features of temperamental variation in childhood (Buss & Plomin, 1975, 1986). An added complication is that, ordinarily, younger normal children are more active than older ones so that a child's age needs to be taken into account in judging what is abnormal. Finally, it is obvious that activity levels vary enormously from situation to situation. Is it the overall level of activity that matters or, rather, is it the inappropriateness in relation to the context of the activity? I will return to some of these issues but let me note for the moment that dissatisfaction with overactivity as the unifying feature of the syndrome led to a shift of focus to problems of inattention - a shift reflected in the American Psychiatric Association (1980) re-naming the syndrome attention deficit disorder or ADD. Two years earlier, the World Health Organization (1978) had similarly stated that a short attention span was an essential feature of the hyperkinetic syndrome, implying that it was actually a more constant manifestation than overactivity. For a while this consensus was thought by many to have solved a lot of problems. However, it is now clear that that is far from the case. Both Douglas (1983) and Taylor (1980, 1986b) have noted the many different meanings of attention; Sergeant (1981) cast doubt on the selective attention deficit hypothesis as an explanation for hyperkinesis (see also Sergeant and van der Meere, this volume); and Prior (Draeger et al., 1986; Prior & Griffin, 1985; Prior & Sanson, 1985; Prior et al., 1985) has even questioned whether children with the hyperkinetic syndrome do have any intrinsic problem in attention.

Several rather different aspects of attention create difficulties in its use as a diagnostic feature. Firstly, there is the major difficulty of how to infer attention from what one observes of the child's behaviour. Is the child who is looking out of the window watching what is going on in the fields outside or is he in fact seeking to work out in his head the mathematical problem with which he is preoccupied? Similarly, is the child who is staring at the book in front of him processing what he is reading or is he reading at all? Perhaps his mind is fully engaged with thinking about what he will be doing when he gets out of school. Psychological tests of attention do not suffer from this problem but they have a rather different limitation. That is, a poor performance on any given test may mean that the child was unable to perform well or it may simply mean that he wasn't trying. Of course, that is a problem with any test but it is an especial problem with assessments of attention, which frequently use very boring, apparently meaningless, tasks.

As with overactivity, another difficulty is that inattention in one form or another is an extremely common feature of psychiatric disturbance in childhood. In the Isle of Wight studies (Rutter, Tizard & Whitmore, 1970) poor concentration was reported by both parents and teachers as a feature of the majority of children with psychiatric disorder, irrespective of diagnosis. Poor attention in itself is not a useful differentiating characteristic for different types of psychiatric syndrome. But, this does not mean that all these problems of attention are the same. A distinction must be drawn between the behaviours involved in paying attention to a task and the processing of incoming information by the brain once that behavioural engagement has taken place.

Also, of course, the central processing involves a variety of different functions (Douglas, 1983; Taylor, 1980). For different tasks it may be necessary to focus on some stimuli to the exclusion of others (selective attention); for other tasks it may be necessary to divide attention in order to integrate different sources of information; in other cases the key issue is maintenance of attention in spite of boredom, frustration or distraction; other tasks require efficient exploration of the environment and systematic sampling of stimuli; and concentration may also vary in its intensity. Children's task performance will, in addition, be influenced by strategies that involve processes other than attention as such. Thus, it is generally thought that hyperactive children are impulsive in the sense that they do not adequately consider what they should do before they act (although the notion that this means that they act faster than other children has not been supported by empirical findings). Also, hyperactive children appear to seek stimulation more than other children, they find it difficult to inhibit when that is necessary and they are not good at accepting delayed gratification. It should be added that, as with overactivity, children's ability to attend effectively increases as they grow older. Difficulties in attention may therefore be a reflection of cognitive immaturity and, in the assessment of attention deficits, it is necessary to take children's mental age into account.

VALIDATION OF ATTENTION DEFICIT/HYPERACTIVITY SYNDROME

All of these problems in concept and in measurement make for difficulties in the use of either overactivity or inattention as the essential defining features of the syndrome that we are considering. Nevertheless, there are a variety of ways in which these difficulties may be overcome and the validity of the hypothesized syndrome tested. For that purpose, we need to turn to studies that have compared the syndrome (however defined) with other psychiatric disorders in terms of some criterion that is external to the behavioural definition of the diagnostic groups being examined. In this connection, the numerous studies that have contrasted hyperkinetic children with normal controls are of no value. They have shown innumerable differences in all manner of features but the issue is not the differentiation of the syndrome from normality but rather the differentiation of the syndrome from other psychiatric conditions. This is a particularly crucial issue because all general population and clinical studies have underlined the very high frequency with which overactivity and inattention are associated with other psychiatric problems. In particular, there is a very major overlap with conduct disturbances and with learning disabilities.

The requirement, therefore, is for a search to find non-symptomatic characteristics that divide up the large overall group of children with disruptive, overactive, inattentive, and antisocial behaviour. In view of what has been said about the generality of the symptoms of overactivity and inattention, it is not surprising that such studies have failed to find that the mere presence of either symptom in itself provides any useful diagnostic differentiation. However, equally, such research has indicated that meaningful differentiations can be identified. The evidence may be considered briefly under the headings of drug response, cognitive correlates and developmental delays, long term follow up, "organic" features, and family correlates.

Drug Response

At one time it was widely thought that the response of hyperactive children to stimulant medication was paradoxical in that they were calmed by these drugs. It is clear from the work of Rapoport and her colleagues that this is a mistaken notion (Rapoport, 1983). Stimulants such as methylphenidate or dextroamphetamine tend to improve attention and reduce activity level in all people, children and adults, irrespective of whether or not they are hyperactive. There does seem to be a difference between children and adults with respect to side effects in that dysphoria is more frequent in childhood and euphoria in adult life. But in so far as that is so, it seems to be more a function of age than hyperactivity. Severe depressive reactions may be more frequent in children with organic brain disease or who are mentally retarded but again this does not seem to be a function of hyperactivity or inattention as such. However, although qualitative differences in people's responses to stimulant medication are not a feature, there are important quantitative differences that help in syndrome definition.

The recent study by Taylor and his colleagues (1986a & b, 1987) used a double-blind, placebo-control, cross-over trial of methylphenidate and placebo as a diagnostic discriminator in a group of boys referred to a psychiatric clinic for antisocial, disruptive, or overactive behaviour. A good response (as defined by a difference between reactions to methylphenidate and placebo) was predicted by higher levels of inattentive and restless behaviour, impaired performance on tests of attention, clumsiness, younger age and by the absence of overt anxiety as shown at school. Interestingly, neither DSM-III nor ICD-9 diagnoses of ADD/Hyperkinetic Syndrome were good predictors. DSM-III was not a good predictor because the ADD diagnostic category included many children who responded poorly to medication and ICD-9 was poor for the opposite reason; namely, that it failed to include many children who responded well to drugs. It should be emphasized that the findings are not due to statistical regression to the mean (because response measures were based on a difference between drug and placebo period).

Several points are relevant for syndrome definition. First, the symptoms of overactivity and inattention are useful discriminators, thus providing justification for their use as defining features of the syndrome. However, in spite of arguments that teachers are better judges of overactivity (Rapoport et al., 1986), drug response was predicted better by hyperactivity at home than at school, although both were associated with a good drug response. The findings suggested that the syndrome may be best conceptualized in terms of both the severity and pervasiveness of hyperactivity and inattention. A further important feature was that a good drug response was predicted by the absence of marked anxiety.

This is not a criterion that is included in either the DSM-III or ICD-9 syndrome definitions and the evidence suggests that perhaps it should be. The presence of disruptive behaviour or conduct disturbance did not differentiate responders and non-responders to stimulants. The implication is that it may not be useful to subdivide the syndrome according to the presence or absence of conduct disturbance.

Cognitive Correlates and Developmental Delays

An early small scale clinical study by Sandberg and her colleagues (1978) showed that pervasive hyperactivity (meaning that shown on observation during psychological testing as well as on parent and teacher questionnaires) served to pick out children who were of lower IQ and, having controlled for IQ, who had a higher rate of neurodevelopmental immaturities and who showed more errors on the Matching Familiar Figures Test. In all but one of the seven children with this pervasive pattern, the onset was before the age of 5 years (compared with only 1 out of the 7 children with other psychiatric disorders).

Schachar et al. (1981) used the Isle of Wight data to compare situationally hyperactive and pervasively hyperactive children (defined solely in terms of parent and teacher questionnaire scores). The situationally hyperactive children did not differ from controls on cognitive measures, whereas the pervasively hyperactive were much more likely to show cognitive deficits.

Both these studies were limited in the quality of the measures available but similar comparisons were made by Taylor et al. (1986b) in a much more detailed study with standardized interview measures as well as psychological testing. A cluster analysis served to identify a group of pervasively hyperkinetic children who were characterized by hyperactivity that had an onset before the age of 5 years, a lower IQ, more neurodevelopmental abnormalities, a high frequency of language impairment or other forms of developmental delay, accident prone behaviour and markedly poor peer relationships, as well as a good response to stimulant medication. It is clear that the evidence from all three studies points in the same direction. Moreover, the association with cognitive impairment serves to divide up the group in much the same way as does response to stimulants. In both cases the pervasiveness and early onset of hyperactivity is crucial.

Long-Term Outcome

Several studies have now shown the importance of hyperactivity as an indicator of a poor prognosis in children who have conduct disturbances. This was evident, for example, in the Isle of Wight data reanalyzed by Schachar et al. (1981), where the outcome at 14 to 15 years was worse for children with pervasive overactivity at 10 than with those who showed situational overactivity or no overactivity. Magnusson (1987) in the Stockholm Longitudinal Study also showed that adult crime was most strongly predicted by the combination of hyperactivity, inattention, and aggression in middle childhood. This combination was a better predictor than either aggressiveness or hyperactivity alone. McGee et al. (1984 a & b), in their epidemiological study, also found that the combination of high aggression and hyperkinesis was more strongly associated with a poor outcome in middle childhood than was the case with either pure aggression or pure hyperactivity. The worse outcome associated with the combination of hyperactivity and aggression was evident for both cognitive performance (with a higher rate of specific reading retardation) and behavioural disturbance. Offord et al. (1979) found that hyperactive delinquents showed both more antisocial symptoms than non-hyperactive delinquents and also an earlier onset of delinquent behaviour. Loeber's (1986) longitudinal study has also shown that the presence of hyperactivity is associated with an increased likelihood of recidivist delinquency. It was not known in these studies when the hyperactivity problems began but the longitudinal study from age 3 to 8 years undertaken by Richman et al. (1982) showed that overactivity in the preschool years was a strong predictor of later psychiatric disturbance in boys. We may consider that hyperactivity and inattention with an early onset is predictive of continuing psychiatric problems but also that it is the combination of these features with aggressiveness that is most strongly predictive.

Organic Brain Dysfunction

There is a difficulty in assessing the role of organic brain dysfunction in the definition of a hyperkinetic or attention deficit disorder syndrome in view of the lack of unambiguous indicators of organic brain dysfunction. The studies that have already been mentioned are in agreement in showing that pre- and peri-natal complications are not a defining feature. However, as already noted, they are also in agreement in showing that children with pervasive hyperactivity of early onset tend to have more neurodevelopmental immaturities and have a high frequency of delays in language or motor development, as well as a lower mean IQ. The findings are certainly consistent with the notion that some form of organic brain dysfunction may play a role in aetiology, although such an inference does not flow unambiguously from the data. On the other hand, the alternative suggestion that the cognitive impairment associated with hyperactivity in Taylor's research was experientially determined seems less likely in view of the finding that there was no difference in social class between children in the hyperkinetic cluster and those in other diagnostic clusters (Taylor et al., 1986b). Indeed, although the difference fell short of statistical significance, the hyperkinetic children were somewhat less likely to be socially disadvantaged or to come from large families. We may conclude that a relatively high rate of neurodevelopmental problems is differentially associated with pervasive hyperactivity of early onset and that the possibility that this is due to some identifiable form of organic brain dysfunction remains a hypothesis well worthy of more systematic investigation using modern methods.

Family Correlates

The only study with really adequate family measures to examine diagnostic differences is that by Taylor et al. (1986a & b; 1987). No psychosocial measures, either by their presence or their absence, served to differentiate children in the hyperactive cluster. The same applied in the New Zealand general population study of McGee et al. (1984a & b). Their negative result however, is greatly weakened by the fact that they excluded boys who had been hyperactive at age three, thereby removing the group of most interest in terms of diagnostic differentiation. The only finding that stands out from this generally negative pattern is the association between an institutional upbringing and overactivity at school. This has been evident in two studies of institution-reared children (Roy, 1983; Tizard & Hodges, 1978) and it was also apparent in Taylor et al.'s (1986a & b) study of psychiatric clinic attenders. The finding is potentially important in its suggestion that a lack of continuity in parenting may impair development of the normal modulation of activity and attention. However, in all three studies the association with institutional rearing applied only to hyperactivity at school, and not at home. Also, institutional rearing did not form part of the pervasive hyperactivity diagnostic cluster. Accordingly, it doesn't help in syndrome definition although it does underline the strong possibility that patterns of rearing may be associated with some forms of overactive, inattentive behaviour.

Provisional Conclusions on Syndrome Delineation

The empirical findings relevant to syndrome definition are rather sparse but, nevertheless, they are reasonably consistent in what they show. They suggest that neither the ICD-9 nor the DSM-III classification is satisfactory. This is not only because the former is too narrow and the latter too broad but also because neither includes all the crucial dimensions. Taylor (1986b) has argued that the findings suggest that the most useful approach to definition of an hyperkinetic (attention deficit) disorder syndrome in the light of present knowledge requires the presence of severe problems in attention together with severe overactivity that is present in several situations, that is independently confirmed by direct observation, that has been present from the pre-school years, that is not part of autism or any other pervasive developmental disorder, and that is not associated with marked anxiety or depression. He added that the last criterion is debatable and requires further evidence but it derives from the response to medication. The presence of developmental delays or neurodevelopmental immaturity should not form part of the definition but when the disorder is defined as indicated above it is likely that these will often be present. A good response to medication is also expected. Most children with such a syndrome will show problems of conduct disturbance and the presence or absence of conduct disturbance should not be a defining feature (although it might constitute a reason for further subdivision). Barkley's (1981) criteria are closely similar. It should be added that the evidence is fairly consistently against the validity of the broader concept of ADD as exemplified in the DSM-III criteria. Werry et al. (1987) have reviewed much of the available evidence and their own study (Reeves et al., 1987) provides some of the most systematic data (based on diagnoses generated from the DISC structured interview). Few diagnostic differentiations were found and those that were mainly applied to the contrast between anxiety disorders and the rest. It should be noted that their diagnostic approach resulted in the great majority of children (83 out of 108) being diagnosed as suffering from an attention deficit disorder. Werry et al. argued for keeping DSM-III as it is until it has been more thoroughly tested but, at least so far as ADD is concerned, my own view is that we know enough already to conclude that the approach does not work adequately and that it requires substantial modification. The same applies to the ICD-9 definition.

REMAINING CONCEPUTAL
AND RESEARCH ISSUES

If we accept this tentative conclusion for the moment, we need to go on to consider the various conceptual and research issues that remain, for there are many. Let me begin by focusing on those aspects of my tentative conclusion on syndrome definition that remain controversial before turning to a few of the many other crucial issues that it side-steps or by-passes.

Pervasiveness of Hyperactivity/Inattention

As already discussed, the evidence from our own studies has been consistent in showing the importance of pervasiveness in picking out children who have a disorder that is meaningfully different from other psychiatric conditions. This has been evident in both the general population and clinical studies and is shown by the findings on cluster analysis, response to stimulant medication, and long-term outcome. Various other studies have also shown differences between pervasively and situationally hyperactive children, although the differences found have varied from minor to major (Campbell et al., 1977a & b; 1981; Firestone & Martin, 1979; Cohen & Minde, 1983). Rapoport et al. (1986) compared children with hyperactive behaviour on teacher reports according to whether or not the parent questionnaire score also showed hyperactivity (there being just eight children in each group). The continuous performance test, actometer counts, and neurological examination findings were available only on some of the children in both groups but, for those, the findings did not differentiate the pervasively and situationally overactive. The only difference found was that half of the children with hyperactivity at school only, were not reared by their biological parents (being fostered or adopted, etc.) whereas this was so for none of the pervasive group. On this basis, Rapoport argued that the pervasive-situational distinction is not a useful one and that diagnosis should be mainly based on teacher reports.

The study is based on an unusual sample (all were in-patients in a very specialized research unit), the sample size was very small with data missing for some children, and the variables studied did not include either reponse to medication or long-term outcome, which have been found to be important differentiators in our own research. Moreover, the suggestion that teacher reports should constitute the main diagnostic criterion is out of keeping with the evidence from Taylor et al.'s study showing that hyperactivity at home was a better predictor of drug response. However, it should be noted that the latter finding is based on systematic interviewing of the parents and not from a questionnaire score. There are too few studies to make a confident assertion on the importance of pervasiveness but the evidence generally suggests that it may be a useful discriminator. It should be emphasized, however, that the designation of pervasiveness in the studies of clinic populations does not depend just on questionnaire scores. It is preferable that it be based on more systematic and intensive data gathering than is possible by questionnaire; moreover it should include observational data as well as reported findings. It is likely, of course, that the situational hyperactivity group is a heterogeneous one. Some of the children will show problems similar to those found in the pervasive group but, because of measurement error, they just have not been detected. On the other hand, some will be showing problems that are reactive to environmental determinants present only in one situation. Insofar as the latter is the case, it would seem likely that they constitute a somewhat different type of disorder to that conceptualized as reflecting a basic problem in attention and activity that has been present from the pre-school years and which, on the whole, tends to persist into adolescence or even adult life. While further research is needed on the question, it would seem desirable to use the pervasiveness criterion as one of the diagnostic differentiators and that, in any case, measures should be taken in several different situations and circumstances.

That suggestion naturally raises the question of which situations are the ones most likely to tap the forms of overactivity and inattention that are relevant to the diagnosis. Regrettably little is known on this important topic. Porrino et al. (1983) used twenty-four hour actometers to compare twelve hyperactive boys with normal controls. The greatest differences between the groups were found in classroom activity levels and no differences were found during playtimes and during physical education. Barkley (1982) reported that hyperactive boys are more likely to display problems (not necessarily overactivity as such) when they might be required to inhibit behaviours (such as when their parents are on the phone or when with visitors or in public places) and least likely to do so when on their own. Sleator and Ullman (1981) noted that hyperactive children were less likely to misbehave in the paediatrician's office than in more familiar situations. The data are inadequate for firm conclusions, but they provide useful guidelines.

Overlap with Other Diagnoses

Because hyperactivity so often overlaps with other forms of psychiatric disturbance, it is crucial to consider how diagnosis should deal with the question of overlapping symptomatology. The usual approach in DSM-III has been to ignore the issue and simply make multiple diagnoses in most cases (although exclusion criteria are employed for some diagnoses). ICD-9 follows the opposite path in its emphasis on using the predominant pattern to make a diagnosis (although multiple diagnoses can be made in some circumstances). The ICD-9 approach is to be preferred in theory in that it is more plausible that children usually have one condition rather than several (that is if one is to make diagnoses in condition terms rather than according to dimensions). However, it has many limitations in practice just because we lack the knowledge on how to decide whether to give preference to one set of symptoms or another.

DSM-III has the advantage that it does not force the clinician to make unjustified assumptions about symptom precedence but it complicates syndrome differentiation in that so often the same children appear in each of several diagnostic groups. What then is one to do in the case of hyperactivity and attention deficit syndromes? There would be general agreement that children who show autism or some other pervasive developmental disorder should not be given the additional diagnosis of ADD simply because the overall behavioural pattern includes overactivity and inattention. That is both because autism constitutes a well-validated syndrome (Rutter & Schopler, 1988) with a characteristic course that is quite different from that of ADD (Rutter et al., 1967), and because such evidence as there is suggests that hyperactivity that is part of autism tends to be replaced by underactivity in adolescence whereas overactivity in ADD tends to persist in the same (although diminished) form (Weiss & Hechtman, 1986).

It is also usual not to make the diagnosis of ADD in children with mental retardation, at least when the retardation is of severe degree. It is less clear whether this exclusion is justified, although there are pointers suggesting that it is. Stereotyped, repetitive movements are common in overactive retarded children, whereas these are almost never seen in hyperactive children of normal intelligence (Taylor, 1986b). The Menkes et al. (1967) follow-up suggested that some intellectually dull hyperactive children developed psychoses in early adult life and Thorley's (1984) follow-up of severely hyperactive children seen at the Maudsley Hospital, many of whom were also intellectually retarded to some degree, found that they were more prone to develop epileptic fits than were children with other forms of psychiatric disorder. A discriminant function analysis showed that mentally retarded children with a hyperkinetic syndrome differ markedly from retarded children with either autism or an unsocialized conduct disorder. Evidence from other studies suggests that mentally handicapped hyperactive children do not respond well to stimulant medication (Aman & Singh, 1982); also it is in this group that severe depressive reactions following stimulants may occasionally be seen. It seems that, at least for the moment, it would be prudent to treat this as a separate diagnostic group whose nosological validity has yet to be established.

I have already noted briefly the evidence suggesting that highly anxious children should not be included in the hyperkinetic syndrome. The evidence is quite limited so far in that the issue has been systematically investigated only in the study by Taylor and his colleagues. There are, however, two additional reasons for supposing that this exclusion might make sense. Firstly, it is well recognized that high anxiety in people without ADD is often associated with restlessness and poor concentration. It would seem likely that, provided this could be adequately assessed, this form of anxious restlessness would be different from the hyperactivity that first becomes evident during the pre-school years and which is associated with an increased risk of anti-social behaviour that persists into adult life. Moreover, low physiological reactivity has been associated with recidivist criminality (Rutter & Giller, 1983) and in some studies, with hyperactivity. Too much should not be made of this in that the physiological findings are inconsistent (but so are the groups that have been studied). However, it seems well worth separating off highly anxious overactive children in order to see whether or not they do differ from children with pervasive hyperactivity that is unassociated with high anxiety. Also, the possible importance of the association between hyperactivity and low physiological responsiveness warrants further investigation.

The Meaningfulness of "Pure" Hyperactive and Inattentive Syndromes

The other side of the diagnostic overlap problem is the meaningfulness, or other wise of so-called pure groups in which either hyperactivity or inattention are seen in isolation without other forms of problem behaviour. The evidence on the validity of such a pure category of hyperactivity is weak. Factor analyses of questionnaire data have often, but by no means always, shown a hyperactivity dimension that is distinct from a conduct disorder dimension (Trites & Laprade, 1983). However, such studies are limited by the crudity of rater differentiations on questionnaires. Thus, Schachar et al. (1986) found that teacher ratings of overactivity and inattention agreed moderately well with direct observations of the same behaviours by a trained observer using a timed sampling procedure. However, it was also found that teacher ratings of hyperactivity were biased by the presence of defiance. The result is that there is more overlap between hyperactivity and defiance on teacher ratings than is in fact the case in the childrens' actual behaviour.

Taylor et al. (1986a) used more systematic detailed measures and found that a factor of restless, inattentive, impulsive behaviour was differentiated from one of non-compliance and tempers (as well as for one of overtly anti-social behaviour). Moreover, the hyperactivity dimension differed from the defiance dimension in its correlates. Hyperactivity was associated with poorer cognitive performance and abnormalities on a developmental/neurological examination, whereas defiance was associated with impaired family relationships and psychosocial adversity. It may be concluded that the behaviours of overactivity and inattention can be reliably differentiated from those of defiance and disruptive behaviour and that these dimensions differ in their associations with external features. On the other hand, the finding that the dimensions differ does not necessarily mean that syndromes cluster in the same way. As already noted, in our own data they did not coincide exactly. A hyperkinetic syndrome did indeed differ from a syndrome of conduct disorder but the hyperactive cluster was characterized by the presence of pervasive hyperactivity rather than by the absence of defiant behaviour. Nevertheless, it did differ from the conduct disorder group in it's correlates with lower IQ and developmental delays. August and Stewart (1982) similarly found that purely hyperactive children were generally similar to those with both hyperactivity and defiance or aggression. Only a small group of children with pure pervasive hyperactivity without conduct disturbance could be defined and they tended to have a low IQ. So far, then, it is clear that the main hyperkinetic syndrome concept should not be defined in terms of an absence of conduct disturbance but, equally, we know rather little about children with pure hyperactivity problems. It remains quite uncertain whether or not they will prove to be a meaningful group. I think that the balance of evidence suggests that they will not, but this remains most uncertain at present.

DSM-III includes a diagnosis of attention deficit without hyperactivity although its validity has been questioned (Lahey et al., 1984). Carlson (1986) has recently reviewed the evidence on this sub-group. The limited available findings suggest that children in this sub-group display poor academic functioning and peer relationship problems; are perceived as drowsy and apathetic; do not have conduct disorders; and may appear anxious, shy and socially withdrawn. This picture suggests that the disorder is very different from that associated with hyperactivity. Not enough is known on external correlates to draw any conclusions about the validity or otherwise of this "pure" attention deficit category. However, it does seem that the starting point should be that it is likely to be different from hyperactivity rather than that both should be included under the same broad category. Studies by Sergeant and Scholten (1985a & b) suggest that the attentional problems shown by "distractable" children without hyperactivity may differ from those that accompany hyperactivity.

Attention Deficits, Low IQ, and Developmental Delays

The notion of an underlying attention deficit has a central place in the concept of a hyperkinetic syndrome. The evidence suggests that this is justified in part but also misleading in part. It is justified in so far as repeatedly hyperactive behaviour has been shown to be associated with problems in attention as measured in various different ways - both by report and by psychological test performance.

This is a relatively specific association as the same correlates are not found with defiant or aggressive behaviour (Taylor et al., 1986a). There is, therefore, good reason for grouping inattention and hyperactivity together. What is potentially misleading is the idea that the inattention is necessarily due to some specific abnormality in the central processing of information and that this causes the hyperactivity. In the first place, the association is not just with inattention; it is also with lower IQ levels and delays in the development of language and motor function. It could be argued on this basis that the underlying disorder concerns a generalized delay or abnormality in development that gives rise to a range of associated difficulties including inattention, hyperactivity, language impairment and lower IQ. In other words, inattention could be one of several features of developmental immaturity, rather than the basic deficit *per se*.

On the other hand, that is clearly not the whole story as shown by several different bits of evidence. Thus, many studies have shown abnormalities in attention in hyperactive children of normal IQ. Also, inattention shows some association with hyperactivity even after IQ has been taken into account. Furthermore, psychological test measures of attention deficit in a study by Taylor et al. (1987) predicted a specific drug effect on hyperactivity above and beyond the effects of IQ. Clearly, there is something specific about the association with inattention. What is less certain is whether this reflects a specific abnormality in central processing of information. Hyperkinetic children tend to make rather high rates of errors in various tasks requiring attention or reaction to stimuli. This does not seem to be a function of an undue distractability (Douglas, 1983). Also it is not because they react more quickly than other children. In part it seems to be a function of their difficulty in inhibiting responses. Rapport et al. (1986) showed that hyperactive children differed from controls in being less able to delay gratification and McCulture and Gordon (1984) showed that hyperactive children differed from non-hyperactive emotionally disturbed children in being less able to refrain from responding when required to inhibit reactions to stimuli; and Draeger et al. (1986) found that attentional difficulties in hyperactive children were most evident when the experimenter was absent and therefore not imposing external controls. On this basis it has been argued that much of the problems in attention derive from impulsivity or disinhibition or non-compliance rather than from a defective control filter mechanism for incoming stimuli.

The findings are broadly in keeping with Douglas and Peters' (1979) review that concluded that the major feature is the inability to sustain attention and to inhibit impulsive responding. Exactly what mechanism this reflects is uncertain, but it seems to be different from the over-selectivity of attention associated with mental retardation and autism (Lovaas et al., 1979) or the signal detection abnormality thought to be associated with schizophrenia (Nuechterlein, 1985). Further studies designed to delineate the precise nature of attentional problems in the hyperactive syndrome are clearly warranted but so far the evidence does not allow any firm conclusion that the condition is due to some specific abnormality in central processing.

Temperamental Dimension or Psychiatric Disorder?

So far, I have discussed hyperactivity in terms of its conceptualization as a psychiatric syndrome. It remains to consider whether or not that is the most appropriate approach to the issue. The alternative is to regard hyperactivity as the extreme of a temperamental dimension. According to this view the presence of hyperactivity would create a psychiatric risk factor that influenced the onset and course of psychiatric disorder, perhaps also helped shape its symptomatic features, but did not in itself constitute a syndrome. The apparent separateness of hyperactivity and conduct disturbance dimensions of behaviour would be consistent with that view. However, it is important to emphasize that the question is not whether activity is a dimension or a syndrome but rather which concept works best in clinical practice. Thus, for example, IQ is obviously a dimension and it functions as such in a whole range of situations. On the other hand, the categorical differentiation of severe mental handicap serves to identify a group of individuals who stand out in terms of the almost universal presence of organic brain dysfunction, a high frequency of single gene abnormalities, severely restricted fecundity and markedly limited life expectancy (Rutter & Gould, 1985). In that group, IQ functions dimensionally with respect to predictions of educational attainment and social functioning in adult life but yet an IQ below 50 also serves categorically to pick out a medically distinctive diagnostic group.

The same possibility applies with respect to hyperactivity. There can be no doubt that activity level does indeed operate as a temperamental dimension. The question is whether or not the extreme pattern that has been described as characteristic of the syndrome does something different. That it may do so is indicated by the association with neurodevelopmental impairment and developmental delays, as well as by the increased predictive power that stems from the joint presence of hyperactivity and conduct disturbance or aggression. However, the matter has not been put to systematic test and further research into this issue is needed.

In that connection, genetic evidence might be helpful in showing whether the main familial association or twin concordance pattern is for an activity attribute or a psychiatric syndrome. The evidence available so far is inconclusive as a result of a host of methodological limitations (McMahon, 1980). There is evidence that activity levels show greater concordance in monozygotic than dizygotic twin pairs but it is not clear what relevance this has to the disorder for hyperkinesis. Equally, it is clear that children with the hyperkinetic syndrome show an increased familial loading for various psychiatric disorders but it is not clear whether this is a function of their hyperactivity or their associated conduct disturbance. The research strategies that might help in this connection are available but so far they have not been used with maximum efficiency. Again, another research task that is waiting to be undertaken.

CONCLUSION

In this review of conceptual and research issues, I have concentrated on those that apply to the hypothesis of a valid diagnostic entity characterized by hyperactivity and problems in attention. Of course, these are by no means the only, or even necessarily the most important, issues that face us in dealing with the clinical problems presented by hyperkinetic children. In particular, I have not discussed the important research examining the possible pathophysiology of the disorder or the biochemical changes that underlie beneficial drug responses. These have been well reviewed by Zametkin and Rapoport (1986). I have also not discussed the many issues involved in deciding the most appropriate therapeutic strategies involved in both the short term and the long term. These have been reviewed several times with the usual conclusion that, although stimulant medication is the most effective short term treatment, long term management requires a combination of treatment strategies of which medication is only one, and not necessarily the most important (Prior & Griffin, 1985; Taylor, 1986b). We know little about the long term benefits of medication and we do know that family adversities and maladaptive patterns of parent-child interaction play an important part in the course of the disorder irrespective of whether they play any role in initial aetiology (Weiss & Hechtman, 1986). It appears that drugs may bring about a short term improvement in the family functioning (see Gittelman Klein, 1987; Schachar et al., submitted) and it may be that greater use needs to be made of this initial response in building up a therapeutic strategy. Because of this it would seem that the combination of behavioural and pharmacological approaches might be most beneficial but the evidence that this is so is largely lacking. On the other hand, the studies have mainly been of relatively short term responses and it could well be that the long term effects are different. The posing of this question, together with a similar posing of questions on the interconnections over time between the different facets of the hyperkinetic syndrome as the children grow up, emphasizes that the issues that I have considered on diagnosis also have implications for our understanding of treatment and prognosis.

Let me end by noting some of the research tasks for the future. The first point that I would wish to emphasize is that there should be no premature closure on the issue of diagnosis and classification. Neither DSM-III nor ICD-9 provide satisfactory definitions and it is clear that we must look to research to provide for improvements. The research already undertaken indicates the direction to go but many problems are as yet unresolved. There is a need to compare the advantages and disadvantages of different diagnostic groupings in terms of their power to provide a differentiation from other psychiatric disorders in relation to external validating criteria. This underlines the importance of comparing children with the hyperkinetic syndrome with those suffering from other psychiatric disorders. There are situations in which it may be useful to make comparisons with normal children but for the most part inter-diagnostic comparisons are likely to be more fruitful. If we are to progress in the development of more satisfactory diagnostic criteria, it is also crucial that we have sensitive and discriminating measures of behaviour. This means that questionnaires and highly structured interviews requiring "yes" or "no" answers to closed questions are of limited value. It is clear that naive raters are not very good at making the kind of discriminations that are crucial in the understanding of the hyperkinetic syndrome. Instead, there needs to be greater reliance on investigator-based standardized interviews that require descriptions of actual behaviour, on standardized observational methods, on mechanical means of recording, and on psychological testing.

The one diagnostic concept that I suggest that we abandon is that of minimal brain dysfunction. It suffers from the severe limitation that is conflates behaviour and hypothesized aetiological mechanisms, thereby making it impossible to study connections between the two. In other words, it is the portmanteau diagnosis that requires unwarranted assumptions that should be rejected, but there is much value in the search for a possible specific biological basis to the syndrome (or, rather, possible bases as the condition may well prove to be heterogeneous). In that connection there is a need for systematic genetic studies, for the use of non-invasive brain imaging techniques that can study active brain function and for computerized EEG studies studying brain functioning in relation to task performance, to mention but three examples. I think, too, that there is a place for further psychophysiological studies in which the aim is to examine the value of behavioural/psychophysiological composites. This seems to be a useful approach to the study of behavioural inhibition (Kagan et al., 1987) and it may well also prove to be fruitful in the examination of hypothesized linkages between physiological underreactivity, aggressiveness, and hyperkinesis.

It should be added that there is a need, too, to study specific factors that may be important for subgroups of hyperactive children although unlikely to account for the syndrome as a whole. This applies, for example, to dietary sensitivities (Egger et al., 1985) and to foetal alcohol damage (Steinhausen & Spohr, 1986)

The value of further studies of attentional behaviour and attentional processes is obvious. Several features of much current work are most encouraging here. Again, it is most important to compare the attentional problems associated with hyperactivity with those that accompany other psychiatric disorders. But also it is crucial to do so with careful attention to the use of comparable measures and test procedures. It is clear that results are much influenced by apparently minor variations in how tests are given. Most of all, however, I think that it is crucial to use ingenuity in devising approaches that allow direct comparison of competing hypotheses regarding the mechanisms that underlie deficits in attentional performance. Very frequently, such approaches require the devising of variations in test procedure or conditions that will alter bad performance to good (see Sergeant and van der Meere this volume). One of the problems in the interpretation of failure on any task is the difficulty of knowing why the child failed. The answer will often be found in delineation of the variations that transform failure into success.

One valuable but so far little used research strategy concerns the comparison of males and females with the hyperkinetic syndrome. Because the syndrome is so much less common in girls than boys the comparison should be fruitful. For example, if genetic factors operate within a multifactorial framework, and if the same genetic factors are responsible for the sex difference, there are clear expectations on what should be found in family studies.

The role of family influences in the hyperkinetic syndrome remains obscure. On the one hand, although it often accompanies the syndrome, psychosocial adversity is *not* particularly associated with the dimension of overactivity/inattention. On the other hand, such adversity is associated with a less good outcome. Further research is needed to delineate the mechanisms involved. Several distinctions need to be drawn. First, shared and non-shared nonenvironmental factors need to be differentiated (Plomin & Daniels, 1987). Perhaps hyperactivity is associated more with the latter than the former; for example with scapegoating or focused negative emotion rather than with general family discord. In that connection it will be important to determine whether the syndrome usually affects just one child in the family or several, as is often the case with delinquency and conduct disorders (Shields, 1977). Second, factors specific to the syndrome need to be distinguished from those that operate as risk factors for a wider range of psychiatric disorders. Third, family influences that act experientially should be differentiated from those that reflect genetic mechanisms. Fourth, family disturbances that are a consequence of the child's disorder need to be separated from those that are a cause of the child's problems. Fifth, those that influence the course of the disorder need to be differentiated from those that act as initiators or causes. In that connection, of course, family problems that were first brought about by the child's disorder may still influence the course of that disorder. It should be added that, as with other studies of possible causative influences, the possibility that the syndrome is aetiologically heterogeneous needs to be considered, and tested whenever possible.

Finally, much is to be gained by the use of longitudinal research strategies. We need to determine not only the basis of the hyperkinetic syndrome but also the reasons why this form of overactive inattentive behaviour constitutes a serious risk factor for poor peer relationships, antisocial behaviour, and personality difficulties in adolescence and early adult life. How do the risks associated with the factors in the child combine or interact with psychosocial adversities and family influences to produce adaptive or maladaptive outcomes? One key issue that forms an important part of that broad question is the query as to whether hyperkinesis is most usefully considered in dimensional or categorical terms.

Let me conclude by stating simply that I think that we have reached a most exciting point in the history of this fascinating syndrome. We have had to reject some of the myths and dogmas that prevailed in years gone by. However, this rejection has been accompanied by a growing body of evidence that there is indeed something of considerable importance in the diagnostic concept of a syndrome of hyperkinesis and inattention. We are not yet at a stage where there can be a consensus on precisely how this concept should be operationalized, nor do we adequately understand the mechanisms involved. But we do have a much better appreciation of many of the points that were matters of controversy a mere decade or so ago. Our concepts have been sharpened and developments in our investigative tools have opened up important new avenues of research.

REFERENCES

Aman, M.E. and Singh, N.N (1982). Methylphenidate in severely retarded residents and the clinical significance of stereotypic behavior. *Applied Research in Mental Retardation, 3*, 345–358.

American Psychiatric Association (1980). *Diagnostic and statistical manual of mental disorders (DSM-III)*. Washington DC: A.P.A.; Author.

August, G.J. and Stewart, M.A. (1982). Is there a syndrome of pure hyperactivity? *British Journal of Psychiatry, 140*, 305–311.

Barkley, R.A. (1981). *Hyperactive children: A handbook for diagnosis and treatment*. New York: Guilford Press.

Barkley, R.A. (1982). Guidelines for defining hyperactivity in children: Attention deficit disorder with hyperactivity. In B.B. Lahey and A.E. Kazdin (Eds.), *Advances in clinical child psychology, Vol. 5* (pp. 137–180). New York: Plenum Press.

Bradley, C. (1937).The behavior of children receiving Benzedrine. *American Journal of Psychiatry, 94*, 577–585.

Buss, A.H. and Plomin, R. (1975). *A temperament theory of personality development*. New York: John Wiley.

Buss, A.H. and Plomin, R. (1986). The EAS approach to treatment. In R. Plomin and J. Dunn (Eds.), *The study of temperament: Changes, continuities and challenges* (pp. 67–80). Hillsdale, NJ: Lawrence Erlbaum.

Campbell, S.B., Endman, M.W., and Bernfeld, G. (1977a). Three year follow up of hyperactive preschoolers into elementary school. *Journal of Child Psychology and Psychiatry, 18*, 239–249.

Campbell, S.B., Gluck, D.S. and Ewing, L.J. (1981). Hyperactivity in toddlers: Behavioral and developmental differences between pervasive and situational subgroups. Paper presented at the Meeting of the Society for Research in Child Development, Boston.

Campbell, S.B., Schleifer, M., Weiss, G. and Perlman, T. (1977b). A two year follow up of hyperactive preschoolers. *American Journal of Orthopsychiatry, 47*, 149–162.

Carlson, C.L. (1986). Attention deficit disorder without hyperactivity: A review of preliminary experimental evidence. In B.B. Lahey and A.E. Kazdin (Eds.), *Advances in clinical child psychology, Vol. 9* (pp. 153–175). New York: Plenum Press.

Clements, S.D. (1966). *Minimal brain dysfunction in children* (NINCDS Monograph No 3, U.S. Public Health Service Publication, No 1415). Washington DC: US Government Printing Office.

Cohen, N.J. and Minde, K. (1983). The 'hyperactive syndrome' in kindergarten children: Comparison of children with pervasive and situational symptoms. *Journal of Child Psychology and Psychiatry, 24*, 443–455.

Douglas, V. (1983). Attentional and cognitive problems. In M. Rutter (Ed.), *Developmental neuropsychiatry* (pp. 280–329). New York: Guilford Press.

Douglas, V. and Peters, K.G. (1979). Towards a clearer definition of the attentional deficit of hyperactive children. In G.A. Hale and M. Lewis (Eds.), *Attention and Cognitive Development* (pp. 173–247). New York: Plenum Press.

Draeger, S., Prior, M. and Sanson, A. (1986). Visual and auditory attention performance in hyperactive children: Competence or compliance. *Journal of Abnormal Child Psychology, 14*, 411–424.

Egger, J., Carter, C.M., Graham, P.J., Gumley, D. and Soothill, J.F. (1985). Controlled trial of oligoantigenic treatment in the hyperkinetic syndrome. *Lancet, 1*, 540–545.

Ferguson, B.H. and Rapoport, J. (1983). Nosological issues and biological validation. In M. Rutter (Ed.), *Developmental neuropsychiatry* (pp. 369–384). Edinburgh: Churchill Livingstone. New York: Guilford Press.

Firestone, P. and Martin, J.E. (1979). An analysis of the hyperactive syndrome: A comparison of hyperactive, behaviour problem, asthmatic, and normal children. *Journal of Abnormal Child Psychology, 7*, 261–273.

Gillberg, C., Carlstrom, G. and Rasmussen, P. (1983). Hyperkinetic disorders in seven-year-old children with perceptual, motor and attentional deficits. *Journal of Child Psychology and Psychiatry, 24*, 233–246.

Gillberg, C., Rasmussen, P., Carlstrom, G., Svenson, B. and Waldenstrom, E. (1982). Perceptual, motor and attentional deficits in six-year-old children. Epidemiological aspects. *Journal of Child Psychology and Psychiatry, 23*, 137–144.

Gittelman Klein, R. (1987). Pharmacotherapy of childhood hyperactivity: An update. In H. Y. Meltzer (Ed.), *Psychopharmacology: The third generation of progress* (pp. 1215–1224). New York: Raven Press.

Howlin, P. and Rutter, M. (1987). The consequences of language delay for other aspects of development. In W. Yule and M. Rutter (Eds.), *Language development and disorders*. Clinics in Development Medicine, No 101/102. London: MacKeith Press.

Kagan, J., Reznick, J.S. and Snidman, N. (1987). The physiology and psychology of behavioral inhibition in children. *Child Development, 58*, 1459–1473.

Lahey, B.B., Schaughency, E.A., Strauss, C.C. and Frame, C.I. (1984). Are attention deficit disorders with and without hyperactivity similar or dissimilar disorders? *Journal of the American Academy of Child Psychiatry, 23*, 302–309.

Loeber, R. (1986). Behavioral precursors and accelerators of delinquency. Paper presented at the conference Explaining Crime, University of Leiden, Leiden, Holland, June 1986.

Lovaas, O.I., Koegel, R.I. and Schreibman, L. (1979). Stimulus overselectivity in autism: A review of research. *Psychological Bulletin, 86*, 1236–1254.

Magnusson, D. (1987). *Individual development in an interactional perspective* (Vol 1. Series: Paths through Life, Ed., D. Magnusson). Hillsdale, NJ: Lawrence Erlbaum.

McCulture, F.D. and Gordon, M. (1984). Performance of disturbed hyperactive and nonhyperactive children on an objective measure of hyperactivity. *Journal of Abnormal Child Psychology, 12*, 561–571.

McGee, R., Williams, S. and Silva, P.H. (1984a). Behavioral and developmental characteristics of aggressive, hyperactive and aggressive-hyperactive boys. *Journal of the American Academy of Child Psychiatry, 23*, 270–279.

McGee, R., Williams, S. and Silva, P.H. (1984b). Background characteristics of aggressive, hyperactive, and aggressive-hyperactive boys. *Journal of the American Academy of Child Psychiatry, 23*, 280–284.

McMahon, R.F. (1980). Genetic etiology in the hyperactive child syndrome: A critical review. *American Journal of Orthopsychiatry, 50*, 145–149.

Menkes, M., Rowe, J. and Menkes, J. (1967). A 25 year follow-up study on the hyperactive child with minimal brain dysfunction. *Pediatrics, 39*, 393–399.

Nichols, P.L. and Chen, T.C. (1981). *Minimal brain dysfunction: A prospective study*. Hillsdale, NJ: Lawrence Erlbaum.

Nuechterlein, K.H. (1985). Childhood precursors of adult schizophrenia. *Journal of Child Psychology and Psychiatry, 27*, 133–144.

Offord, D.R., Sullivan, K., Allen, N. and Abrams, N. (1979). Delinquency and hyperactivity. *The Journal of Nervous and Mental Disorders, 167*, 734–741.

Pasamanick, B. and Knobloch, H. (1966). Retrospective studies on the epidemiology of reproductive casualty: Old and new. *Merrill-Palmer Quarterly of Behavior and Development, 12*, 7–26.

Plomin, R. and Daniels, D. (1987). Why are children in the same family so different from one another? *The Behavioral and Brain Sciences, 10*, 1–15.

Porrino, C.J., Rapoport, J., Behar, D., Sceery, W., Ismond, D.R. and Bunney, W.E. (1983). A naturalistic assessment of the motor activity of hyperactive boys: I. Comparison with normal boys. *Archives of General Psychiatry, 40*, 681–687.

Prior, M. and Griffin, M. (1985). *Hyperactivity: Diagnosis and management.* London: Heinemann Medical.

Prior, M. and Sanson, A. (1986). Attention deficit disorder with hyperactivity: A critique. *Journal of Child Psychology and Psychiatry, 27*, 307–319.

Prior, M., Sanson, A., Freethy, C. and Geffen, G. (1985). Auditory attentional abilities in hyperactive children. *Journal of Child Psychology and Psychiatry, 26*, 289–304.

Rapoport, J. (1983). The use of drugs: Trends in research. In M. Rutter (Ed.), *Developmental neuropsychiatry* (pp. 385–403). New York: Guilford Press.

Rapoport, J.L., Donnelly, M., Zametkin, A. and Carrougher, J. (1986). 'Situational hyperactivity' in a U.S. clinical setting. *Journal of Child Psychology and Psychiatry. 27*, 639–646.

Rapport, M.D., Tucker, S.B., DuPaul, G.J., Merlo, M. and Stoner, G. (1986). Hyperactivity and frustration: The influence of control over and size of rewards in delaying gratification. *Journal of Abnormal Child Psychology, 14*, 191–204.

Reeves, J.C., Werry, J.S., Elkind, G.S. and Zametkin, A. (1987). Attention deficit, conduct, oppositional, and anxiety disorders in children: II. Clinical characteristics. *Journal of the American Academy of Child and Adolescent Psychiatry, 26*, 144–155.

Richman, N., Stevenson, J. and Graham, P.J. (1982). *Pre-school to school: A behavioural study.* London: Academic Press.

Ross, D.M. and Ross, S.A. (1982). *Hyperactivity: Theory, research and action (2nd ed.).* New York: Wiley.

Roy, P. (1983). Is continuity enough? Substitute care and socialization. Paper presented at the Spring Scientific Meeting, Child and Adolescent Psychiatry Specialist Section, Royal College of Psychiatrist, London, March, 1983.

Rutter, M., Greenfeld, D. and Lockyer, L. (1967). A five to fifteen year follow up study of infantile psychosis: II Social and behavioural outcome. *British Journal of Psychiatry, 113*, 1183–1199.

Rutter, M. (1978). Diagnostic validity in child psychiatry. *Advances in Biological Psychiatry, 2*, 2–22.

Rutter, M. (1981). Psychological sequelae of brain damage in children. *American Journal of Psychiatry, 138*, 1533–1544.

Rutter, M. (1982). Syndromes attributed to 'minimal brain dysfunction' in childhood. *American Journal of Psychiatry, 139*, 21–33.

Rutter, M. (Ed.). (1983). *Developmental neuropsychiatry.* New York: Guilford Press.

Rutter, M. (1986). Child psychiatry : Looking 30 years ahead. *Journal of Child Psychology and Psychiatry. 27*, 803–840.

Rutter, M., Chadwick, O. and Schachar, R. (1983). Hyperactivity and minimal brain dysfunction: Epidemiological perspectives on questions of cause and classification. In R.E. Tarter (Ed.), *The Child at Psychiatric Risk* (pp. 80–107). New York: Oxford University Press.

Rutter, M. and Giller, H. (1983). *Juvenile delinquency: Trends and perspectives.* Harmondsworth, Middx: Penguin Books.

Rutter, M. and Gould, M. (1985). Classification. In M. Rutter and L. Hersov (Eds.), *Child and adolescent psychiatry: Modern approaches* (2nd ed.) (pp. 304–321). Oxford: Blackwell Scientific

Rutter, M. and Schopler, E. (1988). Autism and pervasive developmental disorders: Concepts and diagnostic issues. In M. Rutter, A.H. Tuma, and I. Lann (Eds.), *Assessment and classification in child psychopathology.* New York: Guilford Press.

Rutter, M., Tizard, J. and Whitmore, K. (Eds.), (1970). *Education, health and behaviour.* London: Longmans. (Reprinted, 1981, Melbourne, Florida: Krieger).

Safer, D.J. and Allen, R.P. (1976). *Hyperactive children: Diagnosis and management.* Baltimore: University Park Press.

Sandberg, S., Rutter, M. and Taylor, E. (1978). Hyperkinetic disorder in psychiatric clinic attenders. *Developmental Medicine and Child Neurology, 20,* 279–299.

Schachar, R. (1986). Hyperkinetic syndrome: Historical development of the concept. In E.A. Taylor, (Ed.), *The overactive child* (pp. 19–40). London: SIMP/Blackwell Scientific, Philadelphia: J B Lippincott Co.

Schachar, R., Rutter, M. and Smith, A. (1981). The characteristics of situationally and pervasively hyperactive children: Implications for syndrome definition. *Journal of Child Psychology and Psychiatry, 22,* 375–392.

Schachar, R., Sandberg, S. and Rutter, M. (1986). Agreement between teachers' ratings and observations of hyperactivity, inattentiveness and defiance. *Journal of Abnormal Child Psychology, 14,* 331–345.

Schachar, R., Taylor, E., Wieseberg, M., Thorley, G. and Rutter, M. (submitted for publication). Effect of methylphenidate on family function and relationships.

Sergeant, J.A. (1981). *Attentional studies in hyperactivity.* Groningen: Veenstra Visser Offset.

Sergeant, J.A. and Scholten, C.A. (1985a). On resource strategy limitations in hyperactivity: Cognitive impulsivity reconsidered. *Journal of Child Psychology and Psychiatry, 26,* 97–109.

Sergeant, J.A. and Scholten, C.A. (1985b). On data limitations in hyperactivity. *Journal of Child Psychology and Psychiatry, 26,* 111–124.

Shafer, S.Q., Shaffer, D., O'Connor, P.A. and Stokman, C.J. (1983). Hard thoughts on neurologic "soft signs". In M. Rutter (Ed.), *Developmental neuropsychiatry* (pp. 133–143). New York: Guilford Press.

Shafer, S.Q., Stokman, C.J., Shaffer, D., Ng, S.K-C., O'Connor, P.A. and Schonfeld, I.S. (1986). Ten-year consistency in neurological test performance of children without focal neurological deficit. *Developmental Medicine and Child Neurology, 28,* 417–427.

Shaffer, D. and Greenhill, L. (1979). A critical note on the predictive validity of "the hyperkinetic syndrome." *Journal of Child Psychology and Psychiatry, 20,* 61–72.

Shaffer, D., O'Connor, P.A., Shafer, S.Q. and Prupis, S. (1983). Neurological "soft signs"; their origins and significance for behavior. In M. Rutter (Ed.), *Developmental neuropsychiatry* (pp. 144–163). New York: Guilford Press.

Shaffer, D., Schonfeld, I. O'Connor, P.A., Stockman, C., Trautman, P., Shafer, S. and Ng, S. (1985). Neurological soft signs: Their relationship to psychiatric disorders and intelligence in childhood and adolescence. *Archives of General Psychiatry, 42,* 342–351.

Shields, J. (1977). Polygenic influences. In M. Rutter and L. Hersov (Eds.), *Child and adolescent psychiatry: Modern approaches* (pp. 22–46). Oxford: Blackwell Scientific.

Sleator, E.K. and Ullman, R.K. (1981). Can the physician diagnose hyperactivity in the office? *Pediatrics, 67,* 13–17.

Steinhausen, H-C. and Spohr, H-L. (1986). Fetal alcohol syndrome. In B.B. Lahey and A.E. Kazdin (Eds.), *Advances in Clinical Child Psychology, Vol. 9.* (pp. 217–243). New York: Plenum Press.

Stewart, A. (1983). Severe perinatal hazards. In M. Rutter (Ed.), *Developmental neuropsychiatry.* New York: Guilford Press.

Stewart, A.L., Reynold, E.O.R., Hope, P.L., Hamilton, P.A., Baudin, J., Costello, A.M.de L., Bradford, B.C. and Wyatt, J.S. (1987). Probability of neurodevelopmental disorders estimated from ultrasound appearance of brains of very preterm infants. *Developmental Medicine and Child Neurology, 29,* 3–11.

Strauss, A.A. and Lehtinen, L.E. (1947). *Psychopathology and education of the brain injured child.* New York: Grune and Stratton.

Taylor, E. (1980). Development of attention. In M. Rutter (Ed.), *Scientific foundations of developmental psychiatry* (pp. 185–197). London: Heinemann Medical.

Taylor, E. (1986a). Childhood hyperactivity. *British Journal of Psychiatry, 149,* 562–573.

Taylor, E. (Ed.) (1986b). *The overactive child.* Clinics in Developmental Medicine No.101/102. London/Oxford: MacKeith Press/Blackwell Scientific.

Taylor, E., Everitt, B., Thorley, G., Schachar, R., Rutter, M. and Wieselberg, M. (1986a). Conduct disorder and hyperactivity: II. A cluster analytic approach to the identification of a behavioural syndrome. *British Journal of Psychiatry, 149*, 768–777.

Taylor, E., Schachar, R., Thorley, G. and Wieselberg, M. (1986b). Conduct disorder and hyperactivity: I. Separation of hyperactivity and antisocial conduct in British child psychiatric patients. *British Journal of Psychiatry, 149*, 760–767.

Taylor, E., Schachar, R., Thorley, G., Wieselberg, H.M., Everitt, B. and Rutter, M. (1987). Which boys respond to stimulant medication? A controlled trial of methylphenidate in boys with disruptive behavior. *Psychological Medicine, 17*, 121–143.

Thorley, G. (1984). *Clinical characteristics and outcome of hyperactive children*. PhD thesis. University of London.

Tizard, B. and Hodges, J. (1978). The effect of early institutional rearing on the development of eight-year old children. *Journal of Child Psychology and Psychiatry, 19*, 99–118.

Trites, R.L. and Laprade, K. (1983). Evidence for an independent syndrome of hyperactivity. *Journal of Child Psychology and Psychiatry, 24*, 573–586.

Weiss, G. and Hechtman, L.T. (1986). *Hyperactive children grown up*. New York: Guilford Press.

Wender, P. (1971) *Minimal brain dysfunction in children*. New York: Wiley.

Werry, J.S., Reeves, J.C. and Elkind, G.S. (1987). Attention deficit, conduct, oppositional, and anxiety disorders in children: I. A review of research on differentiating characteristics. *Journal of the American Academy of Child and Adolescent Psychiatry, 26*, 133–143.

World Health Organization. (1978). *International Classification of Diseases, 9th Revision*. Geneva: World Health Authority.

Zametkin, A.J. and Rapoport, J.L. (1986). The pathophysiology of attention deficit disorder with hyperactivity. In B.B. Lahey and A.E. Kazdin (Eds.), *Advances in clinical child psychology, Vol. 9.* (pp. 177–216). New York: Plenum Press.

Attention Deficit Disorder:
Clinical Issues

Terje Sagvolden
Institute of Neurophysiology
University of Oslo
Norway

Trevor Archer
Department of Behavioural Pharmacology
AB Astra Alab, Södertälje
Sweden

The clinical aspects of attention deficit disorder (ADD) covered in this volume range from diagnostic and classification considerations to problems concerning treatment. In this introduction we will try to point out some of the topics treated and indicate which of the chapters offer important and necessary treatises of those particular topics. In particular, we will try to relate clinical questions and problems to relevant findings of basic research reported in the chapters.

There have been a wide variety of terms used to describe the children we now refer to as suffering from attention deficit disorder (ADD). The original minimal brain dysfunction, MBD, concept of Clements and Peters (1962) has evolved to the behavioral description ADDH (American Psychiatric Association's DSM-III (1980) and revised to ADHD in DSM-III-R from 1987. Professor Michael Rutter summarizes this history in the introductory chapter (see also Shaywitz & Shaywitz, this volume).

A person suffering from ADD often fails to finish things started, often does not seem to listen, is easily distracted, has difficulty concentrating on tasks requiring sustained attention, has problems with sticking to an activity, often acts before thinking, has difficulty awaiting turn, shifts excessively from one activity to another, has difficulty organizing work; and, may be hyperactive. These behavioral categories are to some extent overlapping and the symptoms vary from person to person.

Although the disorder may best be conceptualized in terms of both the severity and the pervasiveness of inattention and hyperactivity, it is not easy to reach a unified definition. This is partly reflected in differences between the two commonly used diagnostic schemes: DSM-III and ICD-9 (Ninth Revision of the World

Health Organization's International Classification of Disease) and partly in the cross-cultural differences in diagnostic practice as discussed by Eric Taylor (this volume). Both Rutter and Taylor, as well as Sergeant and van der Meere (this volume), and Sally and Bennett Shaywitz (this volume), argue that the formulation of the diagnostic schemes need to be reconsidered. Such nosological problems hamper, of course, basic research on the extrapolation and evaluation of animal models which, in general, may be of vital importance for the advancement of medical knowledge and clinical therapy.

Rutter (this volume) discusses in great detail why the MBD concept should be abandoned. His point is partly that brain damage does not give rise to a uniform behavioral picture and that there is no strong association between the diagnosis of MBD and generalized hyperkinesis. It is important to notice that this is not the same as saying that the disorder might not have an organic basis, or bases. Although computer tomographic (CT) brain scans of ADD children do not show any pathology (Shaywitz, Shaywitz, Byrne, Cohen & Rothman, 1983), considerable evidence support the hypothesis put forth by Wender in 1971 that central catecholaminergic mechanisms may play a role in the genesis of ADD. For example, urinary MHPG, a noradrenaline metabolite, is reduced in ADD children (Shaywitz & Shaywitz, this volume; Shekim, DeKirmenjian & Chapel, 1977; Yu-cun & Yu-feng, 1984).

There are several chapters in the present volume dealing with possible organic bases of ADD (e.g., Robbins, Jones & Sahakian; Shaywitz & Shaywitz). These new findings and arguments are far more refined than the notion of a "simple" MBD. These arguments should be related to the chapters on model experiments (Archer; Beninger; Oades; Sagvolden, Wultz, Moser, Moser & Mörkrid) as well as the chapters on mechanisms of drug action (Normile, Altman & Gershon; Robbins, Jones & Sahakian; Seiden, Miller & Heffner, all this volume). These chapters underline the role of the catecholamines.

With the current change in terminology from MBD to ADD, the primary focus has in recent years been on the inattention problem rather than upon the hyperactivity that need not be present. Issues concerning the definition of ADD are discussed in several chapters. The problems are summarized and introduced by Michael Rutter and followed up by Eric Taylor, by Sally and Bennett Shaywitz advocating a new nosology (ADD versus ADD-Plus), and by Joseph Sergeant and Jacob van der Meere in thoroughly investigating the concept attention itself and the attentional problems of these children. Sergeant and van der Meere raise the question of whether ADHD children have primary attention problems. Their conclusion is in accordance with several other studies (Draeger, Prior & Sanson, 1986; Prior & Sanson, 1986; Prior, Sanson, Freethy, & Geffen, 1985). Thus, we might be in the situation where both the Minimal Brain Dysfunction term as well as the Attention Deficit Disorder term might be on its way out.

Some chapters (Robbins, Jones & Sahakian; Sagvolden & Archer; Sagvolden, Wultz, Moser, Moser & Mörkrid; Sergeant & van der Meere, all this volume) put a new perspective on the attention problems of ADD children by suggesting that at least some of these may be secondary to response control processes. The implications of this view are elaborated and analyzed in terms of reinforcement mechanisms and catecholaminergic dysfunctions by Sagvolden, Wultz, Moser, Moser and Mörkrid (this volume) and in the final chapter of this volume.

The relevance of neurological "soft signs" is discussed by Taylor, by Gillberg and by Borchgrevink in their chapters. It might be that the "soft signs" simply reflect developmental lag since they sometimes disappear with age (see also Gittelman Klein & Mannuzza, this volume). In order to understand neural mechanisms behind acquisition of motor skills, Richard F. Thompson's studies (this volume) are highly relevant as well as Richard Beninger's chapter (this volume). It is our impression, however, that the clinical significance of neurological "soft signs" is declining.

ADD may not solely be associated with learning disabilities, but can also be found in individuals with extreme degrees of giftedness and above average learning capacity (Shaywitz & Shaywitz, this volume; Shaywitz, Shaywitz, Jamner, Towle & Barnes, 1986). This group of gifted children with ADD showing neither hyperactivity nor aggressivity may be frequently overlooked.

Already a long time ago, it was suggested that hyperactive children might be physiologically underaroused (Satterfield & Dawson, 1971). When both baseline and fluctuations of the skin conductance level are used as indices of arousal, it is shown that depending upon clinical and other criteria, there are both hyperaroused as well as hypoaroused children with suspected ADD (Klöve, 1987; Mörkrid, Qiao & Reichelt, 1987). Studies on physiological arousal are presented in the chapters of Brand and van der Vlugt, and Klöve. Arousal seems to be closely connected to catecholaminergic functions and may now be subdivided into systems with different functions (Robbins, 1984; Robbins, Jones & Sahakian, this volume). The changed-arousal data should be related (i) to the chapters on model experiments systematically investigating the roles of catecholaminergic neurons and thereby producing attention and activity problems, and (ii) to the chapters on basic mechanisms of drug action. But Sergeant and van der Meere (this volume) present data and arguments that question arousal as an explanatory concept of ADD.

The therapeutic effect of amphetamine was originally described by Bradley (1937). This effect is now, at least partly, understandable since we now know that neurochemically, central stimulants to a large extent act on the catecholamines. The entire section on basic mechanisms of drug action, as well as the chapter by Sally and Bennett Shaywitz, updates our knowledge on effects of central stimulants. In this connection, their debrisoquin study is clinically of central importance because it shows that methylphenidate (Ritalin) and d-amphetamine differ in their effects on brain catecholaminergic systems, which, in turn, are important for understanding not only side effects, but also the mechanisms of action of these drugs (but see also Sagvolden et al., this volume). It seems now to be established beyond doubt that ADD children do not respond paradoxically to central stimulants (Gittelman Klein & Abikoff, this volume; Rapoport, 1983; Robbins, Jones & Sahakian, this volume; Rutter, this volume).

A rate-dependency principle has frequently been used in order to describe the behavioral consequences of administering central stimulants like amphetamines and methylphenidate. This principle states that the effect of the drug is inversely related to the frequency of behavior under control conditions: Low-rate behavior tends to increase while high-rate behavior tends to decrease following drug administration (Dews, 1955; Dews & Wenger, 1977). This phenomenon has frequently been attributed to the motor-stimulatory, gradually stereotyping effects of these drugs as originally suggested by Lyon and Robbins (1975; see Robbins, Jones & Sahakian, this volume, for a detailed discussion). It is important to notice that rate dependency dealing with the vigoration of behavior is a completely different phenomenon from state dependency dealing with discrimination (see also Sagvolden & Archer, the final chapter of this volume).

Rutter's chapter introduces the very important topic of treatment. Rachel Gittelman Klein and Howard Abikoff's chapter summarizes the role of psychostimulant and psychosocial treatment and concludes that a combination of treatment strategies, methylphenidate and behavioral modification, is most effective. The choice of methylphenidate is significant and should be related to Sally and Bennett Shaywitz' debrisoquin study (this volume). Treatment is also discussed in several of the other chapters (e.g., Klöve; Robbins et al.; Shaywitz & Shaywitz, all this volume, as well as in the final chapter).

As reviewed by Philip Graham (this volume), dietary control has been tried as a possible therapeutic tactic for children with ADD. Several workers have suspected that particular food antigens and/or other compounds ingested could contribute to at least some of the behavioral problems. Among the better-known arguments are those of Feingold (1975) suggesting synthetic dyes and preservatives as the culprits. But up to now it has been difficult to localize the crucial agents in the diet. However, the data presented in this volume provide some guidelines for future research on the role of foods and food related substances. These arguments are presented in the final chapter.

The long-term outcome of the disorder is discussed in the chapter by Rachel Gittelman Klein and Salvatore Mannuzza, but see also the chapters by Eric Taylor and Christopher Gillberg describing longitudinal studies going on in this field. The information provided by these authors may clarify many puzzles and shed new light upon various aspects of ADD and other similar conditions that constitute the majority of children and youths referred to outpatient mental health care centers. In addition, such knowledge is important for our understanding of the disease state. Gittelman Klein and Mannuzza present data showing that a substantial proportion of ADD children retain symptoms of the original disorder in adulthood and demonstrate conduct disorder and antisocial personality type disturbances.

REFERENCES

American Psychiatric Association (1980). *Diagnostic and Statistical Manual of Mental Disorders (DSM III)*. Third edition, Washington DC; Author.

American Psychiatric Association (1987). *Diagnostic and Statistical Manual of Mental Disorders (DSM III)*. Third edition - Revised edition, Washington DC; Author.

Bradley, C. (1937). The behavior of children receiving benzedrine. *American Journal of Psychiatry, 94*, 577–585.

Clements, S.D., & Peters, J.E. (1962). Minimal brain dysfunctions in the school-aged child. *Archives of General Psychiatry, 6*, 185–187.

Dews, P.B. (1955). Studies on Behavior. III. Effects of pentobarbital, methamphetamine and scopolamine on performances in pigeons involving discriminations. *Journal of Pharmacology and Experimental Therapeutics, 115*, 380–389.

Dews, P.B., & Wenger, G.R. (1977). Rate-dependency of the behavioral effects of amphetamine. In T. Thompson & P.B. Dews (Eds.), *Advances in Behavioral Pharmacology* Vol. 1 (pp. 169–227). New York: Academic Press.

Draeger, S., Prior, M., & Sanson, A. (1986). Visual and auditory attention performance in hyperactive children: Competence or compliance. *Journal of Abnormal Child Psychology, 14*, 411–424.

Feingold, B. (1975). Hyperkinesis and learning disabilities linked to artificial food flavors and colors. *American Journal of Nursing, 75*, 797–803.

Klöve, H. (1987). Activation, arousal, and neuropsychological rehabilitation. *Journal of Clinical and Experimental Neuropsychology, 9*, 297–309.

Lyon, M., & Robbins, T.W. (1975). The action of central nervous system stimulant drugs: A general theory concerning amphetamine effects. In: W. Essman & L. Valzelli (eds.). *Current Developments in Psychopharmacology*. New York: Spectrum, pp. 79–163.

Mörkrid, L., Qiao, Z.-G., & Reichelt. K.L. (1987). Effect of methylphenidate on skin conductance in hyperactive children and its relationship to urinary peptides. *Journal of Oslo City Hospital, 37*, 35–40.

Prior, M., & Sanson, A. (1986). Attention deficit disorder with hyperactivity: A critique. *Journal of Child Psychology and Psychiatry, 27*, 307–319.

Prior, M., Sanson, A., Freethy, C., & Geffen, G. (1985). Auditory attentional abilities in hyperactive children. *Journal of Child Psychology and Psychiatry, 26*, 289–304.

Rapoport J. (1983). The use of drugs: Trends in research. In M. Rutter (Ed.), *Developmental neuropsychiatry* (pp. 385–403). New York: Guilford Press.

Robbins, T.W. (1984). Cortical noradrenaline, attention and arousal. *Psychological Medicine, 14*, 13–21.

Satterfield, J.H., & Dawson, M.E. (1971). Electrodermal correlates of hyperactivity in children. *Psychophysiology, 8*, 191–198.

Shaywitz, B.A., Shaywitz, S.E., Byrne, T., Cohen, D.J., & Rothman, S. (1983). Attention deficit disorder: Quantitative analysis of CT. *Neurology, 33*, 1500–1503.

Shaywitz, S.E., Shaywitz, B.A., Jamner, A.H., Towle, V.R., & Barnes, M.A. (1986). Heterogeneity within the gifted: Higher IQ boys exhibit increased activity, impulsivity and parenting problems. *Annals of Neurology, 20*, 415-416.

Shekim, W.O., DeKirmenjian, H., & Chapel, J.L. (1977). Urinary catecholamine metabolites in hyperkinetic boys treated with d-amphetamine. *American Journal of Psychiatry, 134*, 1276-1279.

Wender, P.H. (1971). *Minimal Brain Dysfunction in Children*. New York, Wiley.

Yu-cun, A., & Yu-feng, W. (1984). Urinary 3-methoxy-4-hydroxyphenylglycol sulfate excretion in seventy-three school children with minimal brain dysfunction syndrome. *Biological Psychiatry, 19*, 861-870.

On the Epidemiology
of Hyperactivity

Eric Taylor, FRCP, MRCPsych
Institute of Psychiatry
University of London

INTRODUCTION

The idea of an attention deficit disorder has often been powerfully and destructively criticised (e.g. Shaffer, 1980; Sandberg, 1981; Rutter, 1983; Prior & Sanson, 1986). No behavioural syndrome of "minimal brain dysfunction" has been reliably identified. The DSM-III definition of "Attention Deficit Disorder with Hyperactivity" (ADDH) suggests a common, broad syndrome (American Psychiatric Association, 1980); but in fact this cannot be sustained as a biological entity (Taylor, 1986a). ADDH is not coherent in its symptomatology (Koriath et al., 1985); it is not reliably diagnosed in practice (see below); it has not been shown to have predictive value separately from the antisocial conduct problems which frequently coexist (Ferguson & Rapoport, 1983; Werry et al., 1987); and its associations are with psychosocial adversity as much as with biological disadvantage (Taylor, 1986a). It does predict a poor outcome (Gittelman et al., 1985; Weiss & Hechtman, 1986); but this could be because hyperactivity is a marker to severity of antisocial conduct rather than a separable disorder. The response to amphetamines is not different in kind in children with hyperactivity and those without (Taylor, 1983).

While the notion of a broad syndrome has many weaknesses (detailed by Rutter in this symposium) the narrower idea of hyperkinetic syndrome continues to be of research interest (Taylor, 1986b). What sort of disorder should be recognised, and what is its nature? Epidemiological approaches are an essential set of tools in answering the question because of the likelihood that clinic-based cases will be highly selective. The artefacts of referral can make symptoms appear to be associated even when they do not go together in the population of disturbed children. Many arguments go on about nosology between investigators whose real difference is only that they work in different clinical settings. Often paediatric assessment centres will see groups of children with major developmental and physical problems and more minor behavioural problems. They may see cases of uncomplicated, mild ADDH and overestimate the biological causes. By contrast, psychiatrists in tertiary referral centres may be exposed to severe cases with multiple forms of psychiatric pathology—and therefore doubt whether separable forms of disorder exist at all. By contrast again, primary care workers will see very many cases of mildly disruptive behaviour, based upon psychosocial problems, and could be in danger of forgetting the importance and existence of severe and uncommon neuropsychiatric disorders.

There are yet other reasons for taking an epidemiological approach to the disorders related to hyperactivity. To begin with, a survey can indicate prevalence and need for services. This is especially relevant when one community has evolved a system of assessment and treatment that is of interest to other societies, that then need to determine how far that system will be relevant to their own population. In North American child psychiatry, hyperactivity is a frequent diagnosis among children referred because of disruptive behaviour. Treatment of such children is often directed toward the hyperactivity itself, with stimulant drugs being the most common mode of intervention, and with behavioural and cognitive approaches playing an increasingly important role in treatment. By contrast, the disparate traditions of British and French psychiatry have led to the treatment of the problems of schoolchildren with disruptive behaviour in rather different ways. Hyperactivity is seldom diagnosed, and stimulants are rarely prescribed; clinics and schools focus their intervention on different aspects of the children's problems; psycho-social and intra-psychic factors are more commonly invoked in formulations of the problem. Since most societies are dissatisfied with their achievements in helping the social adjustment of their young people, it is reasonable for them to consider how far they should direct their efforts to the recognition of biological determinants and the modification of hyperactivity. This will require surveys of the problems as they exist in each society.

Major scientific gains can accrue from planning the study of population-based samples in such a way that national differences can be included. It allows for the possibility of disentangling what aspects of a condition are universal and fundamental, and what are accidental or culturally determined. If, for example, it were to appear that impairments of the ability to concentrate were equally common and equally linked to developmental delays in the U.S.A. and China, yet that activity levels were lower and impulsiveness less marked in the Chinese group, then it would be possible seriously to study the notion that there is a basic condition of disordered attention whose manifestation in behaviour varies according to the actions and expectations of other people.

Comparison of rates of a disorder across areas is a classic tool for one of the major purposes of epidemiology: the discovery of the causes and pathogenesis of psychiatric conditions. If one can find the reasons for differences in rates, then one is likely to have determined one part of the aetiology. Furthermore, the study of cases found in a setting in which the condition is usually rare is likely to throw etiological factors into sharp relief. For example, the ninth revision of the World Health Organization's International Classification of Disease (ICD-9) contains a rarely diagnosed category of "hyperkinetic syndrome". Girls are even less likely than boys to show this severe syndrome. I have reported elsewhere upon some of the characteristics of severely hyperkinetic girls (Taylor, 1986a). The affected girls were much more likely than affected boys to show developmental delays, especially in language, suggesting an aetiological role for the neurodevelopmental disabilities.

Finally, the way a disorder develops may vary from one part of the world to another. If so, then the reasons for this variation deserve study. Such variations might be, for example, the result of some protective factor, enjoyed by children in certain settings, that could be transferred to children in another. There is much to be said for attempting to project the longitudinal and developmental dimensions from the beginning of a survey.

All these reasons call for the development of epidemiological surveys of the disorders of activity, attention, and conduct. Such surveys encounter major obstacles of methodology. A crucial difficulty is that with which we began: the problems in answering the question "What is a case?" This chapter examines some of the issues involved, suggests a way of answering the question, and considers what lessons can be drawn from epidemiological correlates for the nature of the hyperkinetic disorder. Particular reference is made to the development of a programme of combined clinical and epidemiological studies, at London University's Institute of Psychiatry, that has involved many colleagues (especially Drs. Sandberg, Rutter, Thorley, and Schachar).

Methodological issues

1. What sort of problem is to be defined?

The history of the hyperkinetic syndrome has been outlined elsewhere (Schachar 1986, Taylor 1986b). For the purposes of this symposium, I should emphasize the degree to which early accounts (Still, 1902; Kahn & Cohen, 1934; Strauss & Lehtinen, 1947) were attempting to delineate a brain dysfunction syndrome, but failed to provide a description at the psychiatric level that could delineate the disorder from other psychiatric conditions. Levin's (1938) paper did not receive the attention it deserved: he distinguished between common, mild restlessness that was linked to upbringing; and severe restlessness stemming from cerebral disorder.

The great expansion of the diagnosis of ADDH took place under the spur of amphetamine therapy (Laufer et al., 1957; Clements, 1966). In countries such as the U.K. and France which preferred to restrict amphetamine use, the diagnosis did not catch on and it remained a restricted concept. This narrow form of the hyperkinetic syndrome is linked to brain dysfunction. When neurologically disabled children are surveyed, they show not only a high prevalence of hyperkinesis but also a disproportionately high rate expressed as a percentage of all diagnoses made (Taylor, 1986b). This is in some contrast to the category of ADDH, and suggests that neurological models may be of interest for the study of hyperkinesis.

Unfortunately, the lack of clear diagnostic criteria makes it uncertain whether these clinically based studies reflect anything other than the diagnostic beliefs of clinicians. Further development of criteria is required.

2. *What level of definition should be taken?*

Ratings of behaviour make it clear that hyperactivity is continuously distributed in the population, with progressively smaller numbers at higher levels of severity, and no indication of a separable pathological group (Taylor, 1986a). No validated cutoff yet exists; the cutoffs chosen vary from study to study; so no prevalence estimate based upon such scales yet has a scientific basis.

This need not be a crucial problem: arbitrary levels of case definition have been needed in many fields of medicine. However, it would make serious difficulty for biological investigations if social and familial factors dominated the aetiology at less severe levels of disturbance, while biological factors were only significant at extreme levels. It would also be damaging to clinical practice if conclusions drawn from research populations with high levels of disorder were inapplicable to the milder problems seen in everyday clinical work. The significance of milder and more severe degrees of hyperactivity therefore needs to be compared.

3. *Is diagnosis adequate for case identification?*

Unfortunately, clinical diagnosis is not strong enough to sustain either epidemiological enquiry or neurobiological research. Different sets of diagnostic criteria are in operation, and even when a single scheme is applied by several clinicians, diagnoses may not agree very well.

This is a disappointing conclusion. It suggests that difficult and expensive procedures will be necessary. In most fields of medicine, the systematic gathering of clinical data on morbidity and mortality has been strong enough at least to generate useful ideas and hypotheses to test. I shall therefore describe some of the studies that have addressed the reliability of the diagnosis of hyperactivity and its international variations (see Table I).

"Diagnosis," of course, means many different things. The confusion is apparent as soon as one starts to compare the approaches of different traditions of psychiatry. For example, Lefevre et al. (1983) criticised the DSM-III scheme for its superficiality in describing symptoms only, rather than the psychological disorders that gave rise to them. Their criticism, from a French psychoanalytic perspective, emphasises how many functions diagnosis is expected to bear. The function of describing dynamic pathology is opposed to that of making epidemiological comparisons, because the degree of inference involved is bound to militate against the reliable reproduction of diagnosis in different places.

The DSM-III scheme has been assessed in the U.S.A. and the U.K. for its suitability as an instrument for reliable case-finding. The "field trials" of DSM-III, conducted by the APA, were not designed to give useful reliability figures. Participants rated their cases and checked them against colleagues' ratings. The selection of rater pairs and of cases probably led to an inflated estimate of reliability. The overall kappa of .68 is therefore of very limited value. In general, one would expect clinicians working together to have a similar diagnostic practice and to show high reliability. The important scientific question is whether clinicians in different centres are adequately reliable, and this must involve a systematic comparison of raters' judgements on the same group of cases.

Some studies (e.g., Strober et al., 1981; Werry et al., 1983) have described the DSM-III agreement between two psychiatrists, either with one examining the child and the other observing the examination, or with both listening to the same case presentation. These naturalistic studies are in some contrast to the more controlled investigations of Mattison et al. (1979) and Mezzich et al. (1985), in which a wider group of clinicians rated a series of prepared case summaries. In the latter and more standardised studies, diagnostic agreement was rather low. These figures are more relevant to epidemiological and international comparisons than the agreement between closely cooperating diagnosticians, and imply that accurate replicability of psychiatric diagnosis has not yet been achieved.

The ICD-9 diagnostic scheme, which differs in several respects from the DSM-III scheme, might at first sight seem a more suitable means of comparing nations, precisely because it was set up by the World Health Organization as an international classification. However, it is not as explicit as the DSM-III scheme and may therefore be vulnerable to idiosyncrasies of interpretation. It also differs in expecting a single psychiatric diagnosis rather than encouraging several.

Reliability studies of ICD-9 have been carried out in the U.K. (Gould et al., 1984) and in West Germany (Remschmidt, 1984). Both used the same group of case histories; in each instance the cases were rated by a panel of experienced clinicians. The overall figures for inter-rater agreement were similar, and quite low. The diagnosis of hyperkinetic syndrome was not at all common. "Hyperkinetic syndrome" accounted for only 3.6% of all the diagnostic judgements made; by comparison with "conduct disorder" (25.7% of all diagnoses), it was a rare condition in the study by Gould et al. On the other hand, the category of hyperkinetic syndrome was quite reliably distinguished from conduct disorder. The kappa for that single diagnosis was .63, while for "Disturbance of Conduct," it was .48.

TABLE 1
Reliability of child psychiatric diagnosis
in studies of Axis I of DSM-III and ICD-9

DSM-III STUDIES

Study	Material rated	N of cases	N of raters	Kappa	(% agreement)
Mattison et al	Case histories	24	20	not given	(54%)
American Psychiatric Association	Joint evaluations of unstandardized information	126	app. 84 (2–4 per case)	0.68 (Phase 1) 0.52 (Phase 2)	
Strober et al	Joint psychiatric interviews and reports	95	2	0.74	
Werry et al	Clinical case presentation	195	6 (2–4 per case)	0.71	
Mezzich et al	Case histories	27 (3 per rater)	134	0.37	

ICD-9 STUDIES

Study	Material rated	N of cases	N of raters	Kappa	(% agreement)
Gould et al	Case histories	28	52	0.38	(59%)
Remschmidt et al	Case histories	28	21	not given	(58%)

The low rate of the diagnosis in the ICD-9 studies might merely be a quirk of the way that the cases were selected. A recent collaborative investigation between NIMH and the Institute of Psychiatry in London is therefore relevant (Prendergast et al., 1988). In this study, a bank of some 40 cases was established. Half the cases were from American clinics, half from English. Every case had a summary of clinical findings prepared in standard format, and for half the cases there was also a videotaped interview between the child and a psychiatrist. All the cases were diagnosed by a panel of U.S. clinicians, a panel of U.K. clinicians, a U.S. research team and a U.K. research team. All the diagnosticians made both DSM-III and ICD-9 diagnoses on every case.

The cases involved only normally intelligent boys between the ages of 6 and 10. A group had therefore been selected in which both hyperactivity and conduct disorder were common, and in which diagnostic distinctions were likely to be uncertain. Research teams achieved a substantial degree of agreement between the U.S. and the U.K., comparable with or better than that found in studies of more securely differentiated conditions. The two schemes as applied by the research team generated a modest difference in the numbers of cases of hyperactivity. For the U.S. team, ICD-9 gave 27 cases (of hyperkinetic syndrome) and DSM-III, 33 (of ADDH); for the U.K. team, ICD-9 gave 23 cases and DSM-III, 35.

Panels of clinicians were much less reliable. The U.S. panel obtained a kappa of 0.32 for overall DSM-III diagnosis, 0.26 for ICD-9; the U.K. team had 0.34 for DSM-III and O.29 for ICD-9. Diagnostic rates were also more at variance. The U.S. panel generated a total of 398 diagnoses of ADDH in DSM-III and 335 of hyperkinetic syndrome in ICD-9 : for the U.K. panel the corresponding figures were 425 and 251. In other words, there was an interaction between the scheme used and the nationality of the diagnostician using it. When multiple diagnoses were in use, clinicians in both countries recognised the presence of hyperactivity with similar frequency. When a single diagnosis was required, hyperactivity was given less weight by U.K. clinicians than by U.S.

Routine diagnostic practice is evidently not comparable across countries. From one point of view, DSM-III is preferable to ICD-9 in that the use of multiple diagnoses probably removes one source of systematic disagreement between cultures (i.e., the issue of which diagnosis carries priority). However, the superiority of DSM-III in inter-diagnostician agreement is negligible.

Biological investigations of hyperactive children should not be based on groups defined only by a physician's diagnosis, nor even by two physicians. Special training of diagnosticians might be considered; but a better route would be through the use of scored, reliable measures of behaviour.

4. *Are there adequate measuring instruments?*

The manifold problems associated with using diagnostic schemes have led many to prefer formalised rating scales, yet the detailed psychometric properties of these are seldom examined. Neither are they necessarily suitable for countries other than those (usually North American) where they have been introduced. Even when they have been expertly translated and back-translated, investigators cannot assume that they measure the same thing. This is all the more so since the items that compose questionnaire scales are not usually tied to precise behaviours. They are high-level ratings of behavioural styles. A rating of "impulsiveness," for example, may mean different things to adults in cultures where children's development is thought of in different terms.

"Impulsiveness" means, to some, a reckless and hurried style of decision-making. To others it signifies the uncontrolled expression of instinctual impulses. The latter might therefore use the term very much more inclusively, for all forms of rule-breaking, including those motivated by resentment or fear. The former would presumably have in mind only the thoughtless kind of rule-breaking, but might also include some behaviour that did not involve any transgression of major social rules.

There is also the possibility that a measure of behaviour may be confounded with the social response to it. In structured interviews, for instance, the severity of antisocial behaviour is commonly gauged by asking for the child's recall of whether he or she has been in trouble because of certain behaviours (e.g., the teacher shouting in response to a specific behaviour). Even leaving aside the problem of the validity of this judgement by children, it is evident that the answer will be determined by qualities of the teacher as well as the child. It is quite possible that a "low-hyperactivity" culture contains an expectation for control of activity that is met by most children within it. Minor degrees of restlessness may then constitute just as great an infraction of social norms as would severe degrees in a "high-hyperactivity" culture. Very different children would consequently be rated as identical.

Rather similarly, raters are likely to adjust their rating standards in response to the cultural expectations to which they are exposed. A judgement of what is pathological is likely to depend upon what is expected. For example, hyperactivity in teachers' ratings does not seem to be related to the age of the child (Goyette et al., 1978; Taylor & Sandberg, 1984). This would be odd if true, considering the dependence of activity upon age in several observational settings (Routh & Schroeder, 1976). One likely explanation is simply that teachers adjust their expectations and ratings in the light of their knowledge of other children of the same age. A similar process of adaptation might very well obscure cultural variations. Multiple measures will therefore be required, to attempt with at least some measures, to transcend subjective impression.

The rating of a symptom on a scale is not likely by itself to index a particular pathology. For example, reviewers have repeatedly pointed out that the rating of "attention problem" is very common in all kinds of psychiatric disorders (e.g., Shaffer, 1980). Indeed, children may behave inattentively for all kinds of different reasons - dreaminess, boredom, finding their tasks too difficult, preoccupation - and subclassification is essential. To capture the different quality of a "hyperactive" lack of attention (if such there be) then more detailed and precise measures of attentive behaviour will be necessary than mere global ratings.

Raters should obviously be asked to describe the child's behaviours in the setting in which they see it, not to guess at what other raters would say. Any single rating is therefore bound to be a partial account. The differences between (for example) one teacher and another are not likely to be all attributable to error in the senses of random fluctuations in scores or bias on the part of raters. Some of it will derive from the interaction between the qualities of the child and of the setting that determines the situation specificity of behaviour. The idea of a deficit in attention seems to imply that it should be manifest to some degree in several different settings, and indeed empirical evidence favours the predictiveness of a category of hyperactivity that is defined by pervasiveness across settings over a category which includes setting-specific behaviours (as Rutter has argued in this symposium).

For all these reasons, multiple measures are necessary. Researchers could draw upon multiple raters to identify either pervasive hyperactivity (Sandberg et al., 1978) or a calculated latent dimension of behavioural disturbance (Ferguson & Horwood, 1987). They might use mechanical measures of activity, or laboratory tests of the ability to concentrate (though this ability should not be equated to the behaviour called attentiveness). They might draw upon direct observation of behaviour (with the attendant problems of the observer altering the situation) or the psychiatric interview with the child as a source of expert ratings of (possibly unrepresentative) mental state and behaviour; or they could use standardised interview techniques in which one source of rater bias is reduced by having the informant remember particular episodes and types of behaviour, while the rating of abnormality is made by a trained research interviewer. All these techniques have their merits and none is free of drawbacks; all have been used (as described below) at one stage or another of the investigation to be described.

Development of Measures in a Clinical Setting

The need to establish both convenient measures, which could be used as the screening stage of a population survey, and reliable measures, which could be used for secure case identification, gave rise to a phase of refining instruments. Rating scales by teachers were examined in population samples for their inter-rater agreement, test-retest stability, and factor structure (Taylor & Sandberg, 1984); for their construct validity in the sense of ability to predict significant associations of disorder and longitudinal course (Sandberg et al., 1980, Schachar et al., 1981); and for their ability to predict the results of direct observation of children's behaviour and interactions in the classroom. The Rutter and modified Conners scales were taken as useful. Parents' rating scales seem particularly likely to reflect attitudes and projections by the raters as well as observations and recall; and need to be interpreted with appropriate caution.

Direct observation of off-task behaviour relies upon a trained observer watching a child who is engaged in a task requiring persistence and concentration. "Off-task" behaviour would of course mean little unless there were a specified task, incompatible with interest in irrelevant features of the environment. We have used the task of doing a 17-minute automated continuous performance test that requires sustained attention on a video screen. The observer uses an interval-sampling scheme to code whether particular behaviours have occurred during 10-second periods, and different observers show good agreement (Sandberg et al., 1978). The advantages of the method are its reliability and simplicity; the disadvantage is of course the artificial laboratory setting in which it is conducted.

Standardised psychiatric interview also relies upon the training of the observer for adequate reliability. A child psychiatrist conducts a conversational interview with the child. Play materials are available, the atmosphere is relatively relaxed, and no schedule of specific questions is prescribed. However, the general course of the interview and the areas of conversation are specified. On this basis, the psychiatrist rates a number of different possible symptoms and behaviours according to prestated definitions. The scheme is described by Rutter and Graham (1968). The most relevant ratings for the present studies are those of poor attention span, distractibility, overactivity in moving around the room, fidgetiness and disinhibition in relationship to the examiner.

Videotapes of children being interviewed in this way can also be used as the raw material for the direct observation of specific behaviours. Luk has developed an interval-sampling measure for the frequency of occurrence of a range of different behaviours (Luk, 1984). The most attention-related of these are 'exploration' (when children change activity and move to a new toy or new part of the room) and 'distractibility' (when children orient themselves to stimuli that are extraneous to the interview). Others are related to hyperactivity: 'fidgetiness' refers to limb movements that are not part of play or task activity, 'disinhibition' to cheekiness or personal questioning towards the examiner, 'non-compliance' to disobeying a request or instruction from the examiner, and 'overactivity' to moving around the room. All these give high inter-rater reliability, and all are associated with hyperactivity (rather than emotional disorder) from a psychiatrist's independent judgement (Taylor, 1986a).

The Parental Account of Children's Symptoms (P.A.C.S.) is a standardised interviewing method intended to provide more detailed and reliable information about home behaviour than can be obtained from parental questionnaires (Taylor et al., 1986a).

Parents do of course know far more about their children than anybody else, and their view of children's behaviour is not distorted by the artificial context that is generated when a professional observer enters the home. Accordingly, the P.A.C.S. is based upon a trained interviewer enquiring into details of behaviour in a whole range of situations. The parent provides the recall of what actually happened; the interviewer provides the judgements about frequency and severity of the behaviour problems described. These judgements are reliable in the sense that there is good inter-rater agreement on the scoring of an interview

(Taylor et al., 1986a). A wide range of behaviour is covered, and resulting scales of attention span, distractibility, fidgetiness and activity level are themselves averaged to give a hyperactivity scale. The other main scales from the P.A.C.S. are defiance (antisocial and aggressive items) and emotional disorder (symptoms of anxiety, phobias, obsessions and depression). There is also a number of items—including somatic symptoms, clumsiness, enuresis and proneness to accidents—that are not included in the main scales.

Attention, in the sense of particular kinds of test performance, also needs to be measured in several ways (Taylor, 1980). Sustained attention, selective attention, new learning, and impulsiveness of style all enter into the notion. They required a combination of tests, whose stability over time proved adequate in preliminary studies. The tests include: *Continuous Performance Test*, which is designed to measure sustained attention over a 17-minute period on a task requiring vigilance. Children sit in front of a video screen on which a microcomputer program presents 640 representations of playing cards, each lasting 500 msecs, with an interval of 1000 msecs between each pair. The task is to detect when two identical pictures are presented one after the other. This happens on 80 occasions during the test, randomly interspersed among the other stimuli. When it happens, and only then, the subject presses a button. Errors are of two kinds: missing an identical pair; and pressing the button when the two previous pictures were non-identical. Two patterns of errors are derived: observer sensitivity (which is low when the observer cannot distinguish 'signal' from 'noise'); and observer criterion (which is low when the observer sets a low threshold for responding). The effect of distracting stimuli on test scores is assessed separately.

Digit Repetition Test: this is a test of selective listening. Digits are recorded on tape, spoken by two distinct voices (a man's and a woman's). Six numbers, three from each voice, are played back at a time. After each 6-digit presentation the child has to repeat those digits which have been spoken by one of the voices only. There are two conditions, given in randomised order. In the first the subjects know in advance which voice to listen to; in the second they are told only after they have heard the digits. The score is based on the improvement of performance achieved in the first condition by comparison with the second.

Paired Associate Learning Test: this is a task requiring persistence and use of strategies for memorising. The children are shown pictures of animals on a screen; their task is to learn from which of four zoos each animal comes. The difficulty of the task is manipulated by varying the number of animals, between four and ten. The score for each child is then taken from the errors made at the appropriate level of difficulty for him (i.e., on the shortest list that he fails to learn in ten presentations).

Porteus Mazes Test: this measures both visuospatial ability and a quality of impulsive and poorly-organised performance (Porteus, 1967). Children are asked to trace paths through a set of mazes of increasing difficulty. One measure is that of the number of mazes correctly solved. The other measure is taken from a count of impulsive and inefficient ways in which the path is drawn.

Digit Span: this, the simplest and quickest of the tests given, is a standardised version of the familiar clinical test that measures the greatest number of digits that children can repeat forwards (the "digit span") and backwards.

Wechsler Intelligence Scales for Children (Revised): this battery of standardised tests taps a variety of problem-solving abilities, and yields an overall IQ score that places individuals relative to others of their own age.

Matching Familiar Figures uses the MFF-20 revision (Cairns & Cammock, 1978) of Kagan's well-known test of impulsiveness versus reflectiveness.

Weighted scores from all the attentional tests are summed to yield a summary scale of "attention performance", which is high when performance is good.

Taxonomy of Disorder in Clinically Referred Boys

The next step of the research programme was to apply these reliable and independent measures of children's behaviour and performance to clinically referred cases. Results have been described for a series of 64 boys aged from 6 to 10 years who were referred to any one of three clinics in South London because of disruptive or antisocial behaviour (Taylor et al., 1986a). Separate symptom dimensions could be inferred from factor analysis, corresponding to inattentive-restless behaviour ("hyperactivity") and to defiant, oppositional, aggressive conduct; as well as dimensions of overt affective symptomatology. Extreme cases on the dimension of hyperactivity showed a significant increase in signs of developmental delay, including clumsiness and language problems. Extreme cases on the dimension of defiant conduct showed an increase in signs of problems in family relationships, including high levels of negative expressed emotion by parents and relatively weak coping skills. This was compatible with previous studies that had used case history record information, recorded by the clinicians themselves (Taylor, 1980b) or by trained researchers (Loney et al., 1978). Most cases showed a mixture of both problems, and pure forms of either were uncommon.

The majority of boys in this diagnostic study received a clinical diagnosis of ADDH when DSM-III criteria were applied, but one of conduct disorder when ICD-9 was used. The large groups so defined appeared to be heterogeneous, but the best way of further classification was not so obvious. Accordingly, we applied the techniques of cluster analysis, which seek to order individual cases into groups on the basis of their similarities to one another. However, they are not based on any single theoretical approach; the different techniques are diverse; spurious groupings can be created; there is no accepted way of deciding how many clusters should be chosen to describe a given set of cases. These difficulties have meant that rather few investigators have chosen to use the techniques. Those who have employed them to generate typologies have obtained rather conflicting results (Taylor et al., 1986b).

Nevertheless, some of the weaknesses relate to details of studies rather than to the whole approach. They are certainly arguments against its blind, mechanical application to error-laden and single-source data in the hope that a good classification will somehow emerge from the machine. However, the approach may be more valid when used with reliable data to address a specific question. We therefore used it, with reliable and independent measures obtained on clinic-referred boys, to test the idea that there is a natural subgroup of hyperkinetic children among children with overactive and disruptive behaviour problems (Taylor et al., 1986b).

Nine key measures were taken of the current psychological state of the children. From the domain of home behaviour, indexed by the Parental Account of Children's symptoms (P.A.C.S.), we chose the scales of hyperactivity, defiance, and emotional disorder. From the Conners' Teacher Rating Scale (TRS), we took the subscales of hyperactivity, defiance and anxiety. From the standardised psychiatric interview with the child, we took a scale of hyperactivity and one of depression. From the neuropsychological tests, we took the composite scale of "attention performance". The four different sources of information were independent and blind to other assessments; all scales were acceptably reliable. Two different kinds of cluster analysis were performed: Ward's method and the method of complete linkage. The reason for doing it in two different ways was so that we could detect spurious groupings resulting from quirks of an analysis rather than the structure of the data.

In fact, both kinds of analysis gave very similar results, with 90% of cases classified into the same four-cluster solution. One of the clusters showed high levels of hyperactivity at home, school and clinic and poor performances on attentional tests. It made up a quarter of the whole group of boys with disruptive behaviour. It was not simply a severely affected group, for it was characterised also by low scores on measures of affective disturbance. The degree of conduct disorder was not different from that in the other boys in the series.

This subgrouping did not give total support either to the ICD-9 or the DSM-III clinical diagnosis; but it gave partial support to both. The ICD-9 diagnosis of "hyperkinetic syndrome" was made on only 7 children. All 7 emerged in the "pervasively hyperactive" cluster. The other 8 in the cluster were similar in their test scores, but had all been diagnosed as "conduct disorder" in the ICD-9 scheme. By contrast, the DSM-III diagnosis of "attention deficit disorder with hyperactivity" was much more common (40 children). Of the 15 children in the "pervasively hyperactive" cluster, 13 had been identified by clinical diagnosis as ADDH. The remaining ADDH children were scattered evenly over the other clusters.

This analysis suggested the classificatory value of a subgroup of children with pervasive hyperkinesis and poor test performance. It did not support the distinction into "pure hyperactive", "pure conduct disorder" and "mixed" subtypes. We should therefore not assume that the best categorical ordering will simply be by the two dimensions of hyperactivity and conduct disorder - though the significance of those two dimensions will need further study in the population.

The emergence of a cluster does not by itself establish a useful classification. Cluster membership would need to predict other important features of the cases defined. The hyperactive subgroup was therefore compared with the other children. To begin with, they were younger when they were first seen at a psychiatric clinic; and younger when their problems first started. The earlier referral probably reflected the earlier onset; but it is also possible that problems changed with the passage of time and presented in a different way if referral was deferred. Epidemiological and longitudinal strategies will be needed to make clear which alternative applies.

Another characteristic of the pervasively hyperactive, as defined by this clustering procedure, was their relatively low IQ (mean 84.5, compared with approximately 100 for the others). This was presumably a result of their initial definition on the basis (in part) of poor neuropsychological test scores. In line with this finding - though less immediately predictable - was the motor clumsiness of the severely and pervasively hyperactive children, and the frequency of language delay. They showed a significantly higher score (more abnormal) on a developmental neurological exam, with a mean score three times that obtained by boys with non-hyperactive conduct disorder. Analysis of covariance, with age as covariate, showed that the difference between the groups was still significant after allowing for the relative youth of the hyperactives.

Some characteristics of the hyperactive cluster reflected severity of problems: they showed particularly unsatisfactory peer relationships and a high frequency of minor accidents.

An important distinction between the clusters was their response to treatment. Thirty-eight of the 60 children went on to complete a trial of stimulant medication (11 from the pervasively hyperactive group and 27 others). Each of the 38 had three weeks of methylphenidate treatment and three weeks of placebo in a double-blind crossover design with random allocation to which treatment was given first. Most children, in all groups, showed some reduction on hyperactivity, but a child from the hyperactive group was very much more likely than the others to be judged as showing a marked response to methylphenidate (and not to placebo). This finding was not dependent upon the clinical judgement of the raters. A more objective criterion of response was also taken: a reduction of symptoms by methylphenidate (as compared to placebo) of at least 50% on either the teacher rating scale or the parent (P.A.C.S.) measure of hyperactivity. This criterion was also significantly more likely to be reached by the hyperactive children. Furthermore, the size of response to treatment in the hyperkinetic was not just a consequence of their being younger. The strongest predictors of response were hyperactive behaviour, inattention on tests, and lack of emotional symptoms; and in a multiple regression analysis these were significant even after allowing for age and IQ.

This prediction of the response to treatment is interesting for both theory and practice. The separation of the groups is sharp enough to be useful to clinical decisions about which children should be given a trial of drug and which should not. More theoretically, it is an independent validation of a classification approach that includes a restricted definition of hyperkinesis. It is in marked contrast to the weakness of ADDH, a broader diagnostic definition, in predicting treatment response.

The results of this classificatory clinic study suggest the discriminative value of a category based upon the severity and pervasiveness of inattentive and restless behaviour, the presence of cognitive impairment (whose exact nature needs more study) and the absence of affective syndromes. They suggest rather than establish it because the validity of such a categorisation needs to be checked in a sample other than that which generated it.

I have reviewed the results of epidemiological studies from several countries elsewhere (Taylor, 1987); and they have been reviewed by Professor Rutter in this symposium. They have not yet given clear answers to our questions of case definition; and the lack of a solid foundation for this step makes progress very insecure. I shall therefore describe preliminary findings from the next phase of the research programme: a population survey in East London.

An Epidemiological Study in East London

We surveyed the 6- and 7-year old boys in a school system, and obtained Rutter's B(2) scales and Conners' Classroom Rating Scales, completed by the teachers of 3,107 boys (representing more than 98% of all the boys in the age group on school rolls). Parents completed Rutter's A(2) scale for 2,433 of them.

Factor analysis confirmed the familiar pattern of separable dimensions of "defiance" and "hyperactivity", as well as the factors of overt emotional disturbance.

The children were divided into groups on the basis of their questionnaire scores. The first division separated those with the presence of pervasive hyperactivity from those who did not meet criteria for hyperactivity. Pervasive hyperactivity was defined, in the same way as by Schachar et al. (1981), as a score of 3 or greater on both scales. The second division was by the presence or absence of antisocial conduct disorder (defined by the same cutoffs as in the original studies by Rutter et al., 1970). A random sample from each group was then taken for the second stage of intensive investigation of behavioural patterns, cognitive abilities, neurological status, and family relationships.

In the second stage, a DSM-III diagnosis of the presence or absence of ADDH was made by a child psychiatrist. Since the DSM-III manual gives explicit instructions that the diagnosis should be founded on teacher reports (which should be given priority when evidence conflicts), the behavioural information was taken from a standardised interview between psychiatrist and teacher, in which the teacher was asked for detailed descriptions of the child's behaviour in a range of specified classroom situations. The P.A.C.S. interview scales were also measured (see above). Operational criteria for "hyperkinetic syndrome" were taken as a score above 1.0 on the P.A.C.S. hyperactivity scale and above 1.5 on the Conners C.R.S. hyperactivity factor. This level of definition corresponded to the "hyperkinetic" group from the clustering study above (Taylor, 1986a).

The relationships between the different levels of definition are set out in Figure 1. The criteria for the DSM-III diagnosis were met more than four times as often in children who had been screened into one of the two "hyperactivity" groups, than in normally active children. This may seem like a very good correspondence between independent measures, but in fact it is not. The diagnostic rate of 12% in the "normal" group is unmanageably high, and implies that the vast majority of children meeting these ADDH criteria would be drawn from the group screened as "normal". The high rate is not likely to be simply a quirk of this research team. Other researchers making DSM-III diagnoses of ADDH on the basis of structured interviews have also found very high rates in populations screened as behaviourally normal (Gittelman et al. 1985). The DSM-III definition of ADDH probably needs rethinking. The classroom behaviours on which it is founded are very common and the resulting category is too inclusive.

Hyperkinetic syndrome is a narrower category, a subgroup both of pervasive hyperactivity and ADDH.

Comparisons of Questionnaire-Defined Groups

The original division into the pervasively hyperactive and the non-hyperactive can now be broken down again by a division into those with and without conduct disorder (see Figure 2).

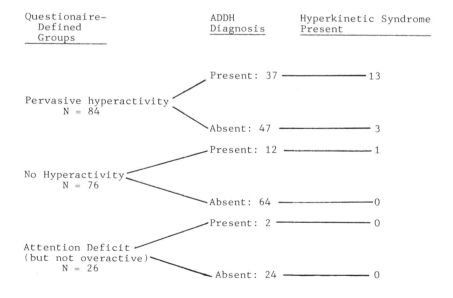

FIGURE 1.   BEHAVIOR PROBLEMS IN CASES SELECTED FOR INTENSIVE STUDY

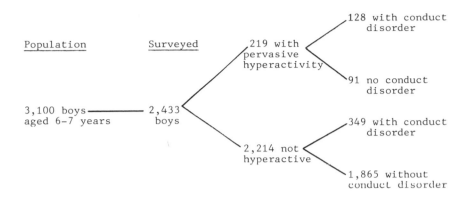

FIGURE 2. BEHAVIOR PROBLEMS IN A LONDON POPULATION OF SCHOOLBOYS

From those who show neither problem a fifth group can be separated : those who show inattentiveness of behaviour but are neither restless nor defiant. Do any of these show evidence of neurodevelopmental delays?

The fifth group, of "pure attention deficit" can be dealt with first. They are, by comparison with normal controls, clumsy and perform poorly on psychometric tests. However, their test deficit can completely be accounted for by their low IQ, and when this is allowed for statistically, they show no further impairment on tests of attention. The finding is comparable with that of Goldstein (1987) in a large American cohort studied with IQ tests and teacher questionnaires: inattentiveness was associated with a lower IQ, hyperactivity was not. It may indicate that inattentive behaviour causes learning difficulties; or that inattentiveness at this age reflects a general immaturity of development. If the former, one would expect that inattentiveness will predict increasing cognitive impairment at followup.

When the "pure inattentives" are excluded, then the remaining four groups do not differ in IQ. However, both the "pure" and "mixed" hyperactivity groups are characterised by a lower test performance, more motor incoordination, and more frequent histories of language delay.

Comparisons of Groups at Different Levels of Definition

The differences between the questionnaire-defined groups are not large and could be due solely to their containing a few cases of more strictly defined syndromes.

Accordingly, Table 2 shows the developmental associations of groups at different levels of definition of disorder, comparing (a) controls (b) those identified as pervasively hyperactive by teacher and parent rating scales, but not meeting ADDH or hyperkinetic disorder criteria; (c) those meeting ADDH criteria, but not hyperkinetic syndrome (d) those meeting operational criteria for hyperkinesis.

Analysis of variance shows that the groups differ on all these variables. Scheffe tests between pairs of groups indicate that the only significant differences are those found between hyperkinetics and controls, and, for some measures such as the neurological examination, those between the hyperkinetics (d) and the other "hyperactive" groups (b and c).

Conclusions

The study confirms that a rigorously defined syndrome of hyperkinesis is uncommon by comparison with other forms of disruptive activity; but that it is a valid subgroup in that it is associated with the kinds of neurodevelopmental dysfunction on which this symposium concentrates.

The weight of evidence against the DSM-III definition of ADDH suggests that it is not an adequate way of defining groups for biological study. Simple clinical diagnosis of hyperkinesis (ICD-9) is unreliable and generates systematic differences between nations; it cannot be recommended either. Questionnaire scales have some value, but contain much error variance from several sources.

Clinical studies have suggested, and epidemiological evidence has supported, a diagnosis along the following lines:

(a) A pattern of markedly inattentive, restless behaviour (not just antisocial, impulsive, or disruptive acts) that is excessive for the child's age and IQ, and a handicap to development

(b) presence of this pattern in two or more situations, such as home, school, and clinic

(c) evidence of inattention, restlessness, or social disinhibition, from direct observation or testing by the diagnostician (i.e., not solely by unconfirmed ratings from a child's caretakers)

TABLE 2

	IQ	Neurological signs	Attention scale	Lanugage delay previously queried
Not hyperactive	104	6.8	14	33%
Pervasive hyperactivity	101	10.2	5.3	29%
A.D.D.H.	99	9.9	0.1	39%
Hyperkinetic syndrome	87*	16.3*†	-10.3*†	64%

*Different from controls, p < .05
† p < .05 after covarying IQ

Developmental correlates of different categories.

(d) absence of childhood autism, other pervasive developmental disorders, or affective disorders (including depression, anxiety states, and mania)

(e) onset before the age of six years and duration of at least six months

All of the above should be present, and for research purposes (a), (b) and (c) can be translated into scores on standardised instruments. Learning disabilities, conduct disorder, neurological impairment and drug responsiveness do not come into the definition, which is behavioural rather than aetiological. The definition should be useful for comparisons across areas as well as for biological research; but for purposes of planning services it should be remembered that most cases of behavioural disturbance warranting therapy will not be included. Future epidemiological research should seek to make comparisons between high- and low-prevalence populations; to use crosscultural strategies to determine influences on course; and to describe more clearly the nature of the neuropsychological processes involved in hyperactivity, in pure attention deficit and in other disor ders.

The hyperkinetic syndrome should repay the study of neuroscientists. They should remember that hyperkinesis in the intellectually retarded is often associated with stereotypies, does not respond well to stimulants, and may be a different condition entirely (Taylor, 1986a). They should also remember that the cognitive basis of hyperkinesis is not established, and that it is essentially a behavioural concept. Inattentive behaviour without hyperactivity is a different kind of problem again, and attempts to study it should take careful account of general developmental maturity.

Finally—though I have not laboured the point in this article—epidemiological and clinical findings from several countries emphasise the psychosocial as well as the neurodevelopmental correlates of hyperkinetic disorder (Taylor, 1986a). We are not examining a fixed neurological condition, but an interaction between brain function and psychological environment. Two major developmental transitions need to be addressed: one in early childhood, as temperamental variations in attention span and activity are translated into different levels of cognitive impairment and hyperactivity through close personal relationships; and one as hyper activity in 6 - 9 year old children evolves into differing levels of conduct disorder in adolescence. The way forward is through a rapprochement between the neurosciences, investigating the likely basis of dysfunction, and the behavioural and social sciences, addressing the links between brain function and simple forms of behaviour and the reciprocal interactions between the individual and the surrounding world. Administrators of research should be aware of the urgent need to create centres of study that combine sophistication in neurological, behavioural and social sciences; and of the high scientific promise of these collaborations.

ACKNOWLEDGMENTS

Epidemiological research quoted in this article was carried out jointly with Dr. S. Sandberg and Professor M. Rutter and supported by the Medical Research Council. Clinical research was carried out with Dr. R. Schachar, Dr. G. Thorley and Dr. H. M. Wieselberg; supported by CIBA and the Medical Research Council of Canada. Diagnostic research was carried out jointly with Dr. J. Rapoport, Dr. M. Prendergast and other colleagues and supported by Bethlem/Maudsley Research Fund and the Grant Foundation. The support of the MacArthur Foundation is gratefully acknowledged.

REFERENCES

American Psychiatric Association. (1980). *Diagnostic and statistical manual of mental disorders* (3rd ed.).Washington, DC: Author.

Cairns, E., & Cammock, T. (1978). Development of a more reliable version of the Matching Familiar Figures Test. *Developmental Psychology, 14*, 555–560.

Clements, S. D. (1966). *Minimal brain dysfunction in children: Terminology and identification. Phase one of a three-year project.* (NINDB Monograph No. 3). Washington, DC: U.S. Department of Health Education and Welfare.

Ferguson, H. B., & Rapoport, J. L. (1983). Nosological issues and biological validation. In M. Rutter (Ed.), *Developmental neuropsychiatry* (pp. 369–384). New York: Guilford Press.

Fergusson, D. M., & Horwood, L. J. (1987). The trait and method components of ratings of conduct disorder - Part II. Factors related to the trait component of conduct disorder scores. *Journal of Child Psychology and Psychiatry, 28*, 261–272.

Gittelman, R., Mannuzza, S., Shenker, R., & Bongura, N. (1985). Hyperactive boys almost grown up: I. Psychiatric status. *Archives of General Psychiatry, 42*, 937–947.

Goldstein, H. S. (1987). Cognitive development in low attentive, hyperactive and aggressive 6 through 11 year-old children. *Journal of the American Academy of Child Psychiatry, 26*, 214–218.

Goyette, C. H., Conners, C. K., & Ulrich, R. F. (1978). Normative data on revised Conners' parent and teacher rating scales. *Journal of Abnormal Child Psychology, 6*, 221–236.

Gould, M. S., Shaffer, D., Rutter, M., & Sturge, C. (1984). *UK/WHO Study of ICD-9: Issues of classification.* Paper presented at Research Workshop on Psychopathology. Washington, DC: Center for Studies of Child and Adolescent Psychopathology, Clinical Research Branch, NIMH.

Kahn, E., & Cohen, L. H. (1934). Organic drivenness: a brain-stem syndrome and an experience with case reports. *New England Journal of Medicine, 210*, 748–756.

Koriath, U., Gualtieri, C. T., van Bourgondien, M. E., Quade, D., & Werry, J. S. (1985). Construct validity of clinical diagnosis in pediatric psychiatry: Relationship among measures. *Journal of the American Academy of Child Psychiatry, 24*, 429-436.

Laufer, M., Denhoff, E., & Solomons, G. (1957). Hyperkinetic impulse disorder in children's behavior problems. *Psychosomatic Medicine, 19*, 38-49.

Lefevre, M., Lebovici, S., & Jeammet, P. L. (1983). L'application de la nouvelle classification americaine dite DSM-III a la psychiatrie de l'enfant et de l'adolescent. *Psychiatrie de l'Enfant, 26*, 459-505.

Levin, P. M. (1938). Restlessness in children. *Archives of Neurology and Psychiatry, 39*, 764-770.

Loney, J., Langhorne, J., & Paternite, C. (1978). An empirical basis for subgrouping the hyperkinetic/minimal brain dysfunction syndrome. *Journal of Abnormal Psychology, 87*, 431-441.

Luk, S. L. (1984). *Direct observation of grossly overactive child psychiatric patients.* M.D. Thesis. Hong Kong: University of Hong Kong.

Mattison, R., Cantwell, D. P., Russell, A. T., & Will, L. (1979). A comparison of DSM-II and DSM-III in the diagnosis of childhood psychiatric disorders. II. Inter-rater agreement. *Archives of General Psychiatry, 36*, 1217-1222.

Mezzich, A. C., Mezzich, J. E., & Coffman, G. A. (1985). Reliability of DSM-III vs. DSM-II in child psychopathology. *Journal of the American Academy of Child Psychiatry. 24*(3), 273-280.

Porteus, S. (1967). *The Porteus Maze Test Manual*. London: Harrap.

Prendergast, M., et al. (1988). The diagnosis of childhood hyperactivity: A U.S.-U.K. cross-national study of DSM-III and ICD-9. *Journal of Child Psychology and Psychiatry*, in press.

Prior, M., & Sanson, A. (1986). Attention deficit disorder with hyperactivity: A critique. *Journal of Child Psychology and Psychiatry, 27*, 307-320.

Remschmidt, H. (1984). *Multiaxial classification in child psychiatry: Results of some empirical studies.* Paper presented at Research Workshop on Assessment, Diagnosis, and Classification in Child and Adolescent Psychopathology. Washington, DC: Center for Studies of Child and Adolescent Psychopathology. Clinical Research Branch, NIMH.

Routh, D. K., & Schroeder, C. S. (1976). Standardised playroom measures as indices of hyperactivity. *Journal of Abnormal Child Psychology, 4*, 199-207.

Rutter, M. (1983). Introduction: Concepts of brain dysfunction syndromes. In M. Rutter (Ed.), *Developmental neuropsychiatry* (pp. 1–11). New York: Guilford Press.

Rutter, M., Graham, P., & Yule, W. (1970). *A neuropsychiatric study in childhood.* London: Spastics International Medical Publications/Heinemann.

Rutter, M., & Graham, P. (1968). The reliability and validity of the psychiatric assessment of the child: I. Interview with the child. *British Journal of Psychiatry, 114*, 563-579.

Sandberg, S. T. (1981). The overinclusiveness of the diagnosis of hyperkinetic syndrome. In R. Gittelman (Ed.), *Strategic interventions for hyperactive children.* New York: M. E. Sharpe.

Sandberg, S. T., Rutter, M., & Taylor, E. (1978). Hyperkinetic disorder in psychiatric clinic attenders. *Developmental Medicine and Child Neurology, 20*, 279-299.

Sandberg, S. T., Wieselberg, M., & Shaffer, D. (1980). Hyperkinetic and conduct problem children in a primary school population: Some epidemiological considerations. *Journal of Child Psychology and Psychiatry, 21*, 293-311.

Schachar, R. J. (1986). Hyperkinetic syndrome: Historical development of the concept. In E. A. Taylor (Ed.), *The Overactive Child.* Clinics in Developmental Medicine No. 97. London: MacKeith Press/Blackwell.

Schachar, R., Rutter, M., & Smith, A. (1981). The characteristics of situationally and pervasively hyperactive children: Implications for syndrome definition. *Journal of Child Psychology and Psychiatry, 22*, 375-392.

Shaffer, D. (1980). An approach to the validation of clinical syndromes in childhood. In S. Salzinger., J. Antrobus, & J. Glick (Eds.), *The ecosystem of the "sick" child.* London: Academic Press.

Still, G. F. (1902). The Coulstonian lectures on some abnormal psychical conditions in children. *Lancet, i*, 1008-1012, 1077-1082, 1163-1168.

Strauss, A., & Lehtinen, L. (1947). *Psychopathology and education of the brain-injured child.* New York: Grune & Stratton.

Strober, M., Green, J., & Carlson, G. (1981). Reliability of psychiatric diagnosis in hospitalized adolescents: Interrater agreement using DSM-III. *Archives of General Psychiatry, 38*, 141-145.

Taylor, E. (1980a). Development of attention. In M. Rutter (Ed.), *Scientific foundations of developmental psychiatry.* London: Heinemann.

Taylor, E. (1980b). Brain damage: Evidence from measures of neurological function in children with psychiatric disorder. In E. F. Purcell (Ed.), *Psychopathology of children and youth: A crosscultural perspective.* New York: Josiah Macy Jr. Foundation.

Taylor, E. (1983a). Measurement issues and approaches. In M. Rutter (Ed.), *Developmental neuropsychiatry.* New York: Guilford Press.

Taylor, E. (1983b). Drug response and diagnostic validation. In M. Rutter (Ed.), *Developmental neuropsychiatry* (pp. 348–368). New York: Guilford Press.

Taylor, E. A. (Ed.) (1986a). *The overactive child.* Clinics in Developmental Medicine No. 97. London: MacKeith Press with Blackwell Scientific. Philadelphia: J. B. Lippincott.

Taylor, E. A. (1986b). Childhood hyperactivity. *British Journal of Psychiatry, 149*, 562-573.

Taylor, E. A. (1987). Cultural differences in hyperactivity. *Advances in Developmental and Behavioral Pediatrics, 8*, 125–150.

Taylor, E., & Sandberg, S. (1984). Hyperactive behavior in English schoolchildren: A question-naire survey. *Journal of Abnormal Child Psychology, 12*, 143–156.

Taylor, E., Schachar, R., Thorley, G., & Wieselberg, M. (1986a). Conduct disorder and hyperac-tivity: I. Separation of hyperactivity and antisocial conduct in British child psychiatric patients. *British Journal of Psychiatry, 149*, 760–767.

Taylor, E., Everitt, B., Thorley, G., Schachar, R., Rutter, M., & Wieselberg, M. (1986b). Conduct disorder and hyperactivity: II. A cluster analytic approach to the identification of a behavioural syndrome. *British Journal of Psychiatry, 149*, 768–777.

Weiss, G., & Hechtman, L. T. (1986). *Hyperactive children grown up.* New York: Guilford Press.

Werry, J., Methuen, R. J., Fitzpatric, J., & Dixon, H. (1983). The interrater reliability of DSM-III in children. *Journal of Abnormal Child Psychology, 11*, 341–354.

Werry, J. S., Reeves, J. C., & Elkind, G. S. (1987). Attention deficit, conduct, oppositional and anxiety disorders in children: I. A review of research on differentiating characteristics. *Journal of the American Academy of Child Psychiatry, 26*, 133–143.

4

Critical Issues
in Attention Deficit Disorder

Sally E. Shaywitz, M.D.
Bennett A. Shaywitz, M.D.
Departments of Pediatrics, Neurology and Child Study Center
Yale University School of Medicine

INTRODUCTION

Attention deficit disorder (ADD) represents what many believe to be one of the most frequent and serious neurobehavioral disorders of childhood, affecting children from their earliest infancy, through school age and into adolescence and adult life. While ADD has captured the imagination of investigators and clinicians alike for almost 50 years, the past decade has witnessed an explosion in the number of investigations examining every conceivable facet of ADD. In this report we have limited our discussion to what we believe represent two of the most critical issues in ADD, problems fundamental to our understanding of ADD and central to the development of more precise and effective strategies for identification and, eventually, intervention in affected children. The specific areas we have chosen to focus on are:(1) The Search for a Biological Marker; (and 2) The Development of a Nosology.

Although for presentation purposes we have discussed these as separate issues, in fact, the two are inextricably linked. Thus, it is obvious that any search for a biological marker presupposes the identification of a clinically homogeneous cohort that different observers would all diagnose as having ADD. Furthermore, the development of a nosology for ADD not only has important implications for investigators attempting to determine a biological marker, but the development of a nosology, itself, will have a significant impact on many other areas of research. In particular, what may not be appreciated is that what we decide to call ADD in research studies may have a powerful impact on the clinician's

53

view of the disorder. Thus, if particular groups of children are never included in research studies as among those identified as having ADD, it will become increasingly difficult for both clinicians and investigators to then include these particular groups within the ADD diagnosis. Ultimately, such research studies which provide the basis for definition and identification will have a significant impact on public policy regarding the provision of services for children.

THE SEARCH FOR A BIOLOGICAL MARKER

Historical Perspective

As we will describe below, the belief that biological factors are central to the development of the symptoms of ADD had its origins in the late 19th century when physicians first observed the association of behavioral symptoms following an insult to the brain. Throughout the early part of this century, specific kinds of insults, for example, head injury (Goldstein, 1936; Meyer, 1904) and infections of the central nervous system (Bender, 1942; Hohman, 1922), had been linked to a constellation of behaviors termed the *brain damage* syndrome. By the late 1930's and 1940's, Strauss and his associates (Strauss & Lehtinen, 1947; Werner & Strauss, 1941) had promulgated the notion that these behavioral manifestations could themselves be evidence of brain damage, and thus, rather than starting with known brain injury causing a particular constellation of behaviors, the abnormal behaviors, in and of themselves, were considered indicative of brain damage. Over time, the occurrence of the behavioral symptoms without a history of a brain insult were termed minimal brain damage, and then *minimal* brain *dysfunction* (Clements & Peters, 1962).

By the 1960s the term MBD was used to designate children not only with a particular constellation of behaviors (primarily hyperactivity) but with learning deficits and minor neurologic signs. Those children whose primary problems related to learning deficits came to be called specific learning disabilities (Kirk, 1962), while those children with primarily behavioral disturbances were usually labeled as hyperactive (Laufer & Denhoff, 1957), a term codified in a diagnostic manual published in 1968 (DSM II). The 1970's witnessed the emergence of classification systems for behavioral disorders, systems employing specific criteria to either include or exclude particular patients. A later version of the diagnostic manual noted above (termed DSM III rather than DSM II) was published in 1980 and provided even more specific criteria to be used in identifying children with what this new diagnostic manual now termed ADD.

Brain Anatomy in ADD

The belief that the symptoms of ADD are related to disturbances in brain function and that such disturbances might be reflected in abnormalities of brain structure has provided the basis for a number of investigations relating to the pathogenesis of ADD. Not surprisingly, such studies have utililized a range of techniques to examine brain structure and function; furthermore, as each new diagnostic procedure was unveiled, investigators have attempted to employ the newest methodology to attempt to document CNS abnormalities in children with ADD. Since the last century, neuropathologic studies have classically been used to examine a variety of CNS disorders in both adults and children. However, it is rare that the opportunity for such an examination would arise. While convincing reports of anatomic disturbances have been noted for dyslexia (Gallaburda et al., 1985; Gallaburda & Kemper, 1979), to date, no pathological reports have appeared for children with ADD. Studies of CT scans in such children have been performed however. Although an initial study suggested abnormalities in as many as 30% of cases, more recent studies employing double-blind evaluations and control groups have indicated that CT scans are indistinguishable between children with ADD and non-ADD contrasts (Shaywitz et al., 1983; Harcherak et al., 1985).

Positron emission tomography (PET) provides a unique opportunity to examine metabolic factors in vivo in a variety of disorders. Such a procedure involves adminstration of radioactive products to patients, and is not permitted by NIH regulations to be used in children. However, results are available from such studies performed in Sweden by Lou et al. (1984) on 13 children with learning and attention problems. The clinical profiles are not detailed, but measures of regional cerebral blood flow (rCBF) by PET scanning indicate regions of hypoperfusion in the periventricular white matter and in watershed areas between major cerebral vessels. Methylphenidate increased perfusion in mesencephalon and basal ganglia while decreasing perfusion in cortical areas. The authors suggest that their findings represent sequelae of hypoxic-ischemic encephalopathy. Most recently, Zametkin et al. (1986) examined glucose utilization by PET in 9 parents of children with ADD. The parents, who themselves satisfied Wender Utah critieria for ADD residual type, were compared to 27 age matched controls. Whole brain glucose utilization was reduced significantly in the ADD group, etiology decreased in right frontal areas but increased in posterior medial orbital areas. Clearly, such studies need to be replicated.

Neurochemical Studies in ADD

Evidence from several lines of investigation has converged to suggest that brain monoaminergic (primarily catecholaminergic) systems play a central role in the pathogenesis of Attention Deficit Disorder (ADD). In this section we examine this evidence. The compounds that have received most attention are the monoamines, comprising the catecholamines (dopamine and norepinephrine) and the indoleamine, serotonin. While it is clearly beyond the scope of this report to comprehensively review the neurochemistry and neuropharmacology of the monoamines (the interested reader is referred to Cooper, Bloom and Roth's, 1986, text for details) we have chosen to provide a brief outline of their basic biochemistry and pharmacology.

Monoamines: Basic Neuropharmacology

Catecholamines in the brain originate from the precursor amino acid l-tyrosine which is transported to brain via blood and concentrated within neurons. Dopamine (DA) formation proceeds via the enzyme tyrosine hydroxylase acting on tyrosine and resulting in the formation of l-dihydroxyphenylacetic acid (l-DOPA) which is then decarboxylated to DA. Norepinephrine (NE) formation proceeds from DA via dopamine - β - hydroxylase (DBH). Nerve stimulation or stimulation by drugs results in release of the neurotransmitter into the synaptic cleft with subsequent inactivation by reuptake mechanisms and metabolism. The catecholamines are metabolized by two enzyme, monoamine oxidase (MAO) and catechol - o - methyltransferase (COMT). In brain the principal metabolite of DA is homovanillic acid (HVA) and for NE is 3-methoxy-4-hydroxyphenylglycol (MHPG). The indoleamine, serotonin, originates from the amino acid l-tryptophan which in a series of metabolic steps analogous to those for the catecholamines forms serotonin (5HT). This is metabolized by monoamine oxidase to 5-hydroxyindoleacetic acid (5-HIAA).

Monoamines and ADD

Historically, the earliest evidence linking monoamines and ADD was derived from the observation that stimulants produce an often remarkable ameliorative effect on the symptoms of ADD. Thus, a stimulant, d-amphetamine, was the first agent found to be effective in the treatment of hyperactivity (Bradley, 1937) and since that initial report abundant evidence from many investigative groups supports the belief that stimulants (amphetamine, methylphenidate, pemoline) are effective in reducing activity levels and improving attention in 60-70% of children with ADD (Barkley, 1977; Conners & Werry, 1979; Gadow, 1983; Kavale, 1982; Ottenbacher & Cooper, 1983; Rosenthal & Allen, 1978; Weiss, 1985; Whalen and Henker, 1976).

Investigations employing continuous monitoring of truncal activity recorded automatically for 24 hours per day, for seven days (Porrino et al., 1983) indicate that this reduction in activity levels occurs during academic studies in structured on-task activities, and activity during physical education was actually increased. Furthermore, the reduction in activity appears to be related to a reduction in perceived intensity of activity (Henker et al., 1986; Whalen et al., 1979; Whalen et al., 1981), a finding consonant with the observations of Barkley et al. (1985) that stimulants enhance appropriate or rule governed behavior, i.e., result in a general increase in improving compliance of ADD children to their mothers' commands or in the duration of this compliance.

Considerable evidence supports the belief that stimulant agents affect central catecholaminergic mechanisms. Investigations in animals (Kuczenski, 1983) demonstrate that stimulants such as d-amphetamine and methylphenidate act via central monoaminergic systems to: (1) inhibit reuptake, (2) increase release of amine, and (3) to some extent inhibit monoamine oxidase activity (MAO), all actions that serve to increase the concentration of catecholamine (both dopamine and norepinephrine) at the synaptic cleft. The actions of pemoline are not nearly as well studied, though it is now clear that the early suggestion that pemoline preferentially stimulates dopamine synthesis is not supported by more recent studies. These indicate that pemoline reduces catecholamine turnover and may inhibit catecholamine uptake (Fuller et al., 1978; Molina & Orsingher, 1981).

This commonality between the effects of stimulants on the symptoms of ADD and their known mechanism of action suggested that brain catecholaminergic mechanisms could be influential in the genesis of ADD (Wender, 1971). A further corollary is that it is reasonable to believe that alterations in plasma and urinary concentrations of either catecholamines, their metabolites or compounds believed mediated by catecholamines may provide an index of the function of that particular catecholamine system.

Animal models, too, provide evidence for a relationship between brain catecholamines and ADD. Thus, utilizing the neurotoxin 6-hydroxydopamine, it is possible to produce a selective depletion of brain dopamine in the neonatal rat (Shaywitz et al., 1976a). The behavior of these animals is remarkably similar to those observed in children with ADD including hyperactivity which abates with maturity and learning deficits which persist. Administration of amphetamine (Shaywitz et al., 1976b) or methylphenidate (Shaywitz et al., 1978) reverses the hyperactivity. Selective depletion of brain norepinephrine results in performance deficits but normal activity (Shaywitz et al., 1984).

More direct evidence is provided by examination of monoamines, their metabolites and related enzymes in blood, urine and CSF of children with ADD. Further evidence is provided by pharmacological studies termed pharmacological probe studies. These are discussed here.

Dopaminergic (DA) Mechanisms. Abnormalities in central dopaminergic systems have been suggested by reports of reduced concentrations of homovanillic acid (HVA), the principal metabolite of dopamine in CSF of children with ADD (Shaywitz et al., 1977), suggesting an abnormality in DA turnover. Pharmacological studies, using a dopamine agonist (DOPA) indicate a weak effect (Langer et al., 1982). More recent studies have employed methylphenidate as a pharmacological probe, and the hormone prolactin as an index of central dopaminergic activity. Prolactin increases activity of tuberoinfundibular DA neurons. These neurons, in turn, release DA which inhibits prolactin. Methylphenidate acts to release DA and NE. DA inhibits prolactin, resulting in reduction in prolactin levels. Results of this study suggest significant relationships between the symptoms of ADD and alterations in prolactin concentration (Shaywitz et al., 1985).

Noradrenergic (NE) Mechanisms. Considerable evidence supports the belief that central noradrenergic mechanisms play a role in the genesis of ADD. Good evidence indicates that 60% of urinary MHPG is derived from brain (Maas, 1983) and thus, it is reasonable to believe that determination of urinary MHPG in children will provide an index of brain NE. In fact, urinary MHPG is reduced in children with ADD compared to controls (Shekim et al., 1977; 1979; Yu-cun & Yu-feng, 1984). The pressor response to standing is greater in ADD children, suggesting to Mikkelson et al. (1981) increased alpha 2 receptor sensitivity. Pharmacological studies, too, suggest a role for NE mechanisms. Thus amphetamine reduces urinary MHPG in ADD children (Brown et al., 1981; Shekim et al., 1977; 1979; Zametkin et al., 1984), a reduction observed primarily in those who responded positively to the agent (Shekim et al., 1983). Administration of the tricyclic antidepressant agent desmethylimipramine (DMI) results in decreases in both plasma and urinary MHPG, decreases correlated with behavioral improvement (Donnelly et al., 1986). Support, too, derives from examination of the behavioral effects of different monoamine oxidase inhibitors. Two types of MAO are now recognized, differentiated on the basis of their substrate specificity. MAO A acts on NE and 5HT while MAO B acts on DA (as well as phenylethylamine). Chlorgyline (primarily an MAO A inhibitor) and tranylcypromine (an inhibitor of both MAO A and MAO B) are both effective in ADD (Zametkin et al., 1985). However, deprenyl (an MAO B) inhibitor is not effective in ADD (Donnelly, personal communication, cited by Zametkin and Rapoport, in press).

Serotonergic Mechanisms. To date, there is little evidence to suggest a role for serotonin in ADD. No changes have been noted in 5-HIAA concentrations in cerebrospinal fluid (Shaywitz et al., 1977; Shetty & Chase, 1976), or platelets (Irwin et al., 1981; Rapoport et al., 1974). Fenfluramine, an agent which reduces brain serotonin, has no effect on behavior, though chemical measures of serotonin were reduced (Zametkin & Rapoport, in press).

Other Points of View. Despite the relatively strong evidence suggesting a role for central catecholaminergic mechanisms in ADD, questions still remain. Thus, some studies have not found decreases in urinary MHPG in ADD (Rapoport et al., 1978) while others report decreased 5HT in blood (Coleman et al., 1971). Furthermore, tricyclics are more specific for NE yet they are not as effective as the stimulants in the treatment of ADD. Finally, there is often a dissociation between the biochemical and the behavioral effects. For example, cessation of stimulants (or an MAO inhibitor) results in an abrupt worsening in behavior yet urinary MHPG continues reduced (Zametkin et al., 1985). In addition to its effects on serotonin noted above, fenfluramine results in reduction in MHPG, but with no concomitant behavioral effects. Newer methodologies, described below, may circumvent some of these problems.

Pharmacologic Probe Strategy. As noted above, a number of investigators have employed stimulants such as amphetamine and methylphenidate as well as other drugs with well characterized mechanisms of action as pharmacological probes to examine the role of brain catecholamines in children with ADD. This strategy, termed the pharmacological probe method, is predicated on the belief that administration of the pharmacologic probe will result in alterations in the particular neurotransmitter systems affected by the agent. In previous studies investigators have measured concentrations of neuroendocrine related compounds, for example, growth hormone and prolactin, which appear to be mediated by central catecholaminergic systems. We utilized a double-blind, drug-placebo design to examine growth hormone and prolactin response to oral administration of methylphenidate in 14 boys (ages 10-12.4 years) with ADD. Four conditions, representing three different methylphenidate doses (0.3 mg/kg O.D., 0.3 mg/kg B.I.D., 0.6 mg/kg O.D.) and placebo were compared in each subject, each condition lasting for a period of 3 weeks. Growth hormone and prolactin response were measured both as maximum peak (growth hormone) or nadir (prolactin) as well as area under the curve for the first four hours after methylphenidate administration. Prolactin response was significantly increased after methylphenidate compared to placebo. Significant correlations were observed between the improvement in reaction time on Kagan's Matching Familiar Figures Test and both growth hormone and prolactin response. We also found significant correlation between improvement in attention (as measured by a teachers behavior rating scale) and growth hormone response.

Despite these findings, it was clear to us that the relationship between these neuroendocrine measures and brain monoamine function was rather tenuous. Thus, while prolactin is a relatively specific measure of DA effect, its decrease after methylphenidate or amphetamine is limited by a "floor effect." No such effect is noted for growth hormone (which will *increase* after stimulant administration). However, growth hormone response is less specific since it is mediated by DA, NE and 5HT. Thus, it is necessary to develop a strategy that will permit not only the more precise delineation of the specific CA system involved, but one which will permit examination of brain (central) rather than peripheral CA systems.

A New Strategy: Pharmacologic Probe Coupled with Debrisoquin. Recent advances for the first time offer the possibility of stimulating specific central (brain) catecholaminergic systems in children, measuring the effects of this stimulation on compounds present in plasma and urine, and differentiating the effects in brain from those occurring in the peripheral nervous system. The first is technological: it is now possible, utilizing a combination of gas chromatography coupled with mass fragmentography to measure catecholamines and their metabolites in blood at concentrations as low as 10-50 fematomoles (10^{-15}M)! Furthermore, high performance liquid chromatographic techniques coupled with electrochemical detection provide a relatively inexpensive assay of monoamines and their metabolites in the low picogram range.

The second major advance is the development of strategies to differentiate peripheral from central catecholaminergic systems, a problem considerably more troublesome in the DA than in NE systems. Thus, brain NE is metabolized preferentially to MHPG, while NE in the peripheral nervous system is metabolized to vanillylmandelic acid (VMA). Furthermore, urinary NE is derived almost exclusively from peripheral NE, since NE under normal circumstances does not cross the blood brain barrier. Thus, plasma and urinary MHPG is a useful marker of brain NE while urinary VMA and NE reflect peripheral NE metabolism. In the DA system we are not so fortunate. Here, both brain DA and DA originating in the peripheral nervous system are metabolized to HVA which appears in blood and urine. The discovery of a compound that blocks the peripheral nervous system contribution to plasma and urinary HVA provides a unique opportunity to examine brain DA systems in man. The agent, debrisoquin, is a weak MAO inhibitor which does not cross the blood brain barrier and, thus, acts only on peripheral CA. Evidence suggests that pre debrisoquin, 33% of plasma HVA is derived from brain, but post debrisoquin this rises to 75% (Swann et al., 1980). Thus, the measurement of HVA in blood and urine pre debrisoquin will yield measures reflecting both central+peripheral DA systems. The elimination of HVA from the peripheral nervous system by the administration of debrisoquin means that urinary and plasma HVA concentrations post debrisoquin reflect primarily brain DA activity.

To date we have employed this strategy to investigate 20 children with ADD (19 boys, 1 girl) ages 5-14 years. Children received either D-amphetamine (.25 mg/kg, 7 children) or methylphenidate (0.5 mg/kg, 13 children) or placebo as a single oral morning dose for 7 days as outpatients and were then admitted to our Children's Clinical Research Center for debrisoquin loading. Debrisoquin resulted in significant reductions in plasma homovanillic acid (HVA) between baseline predrug levels and those observed 18 hours following debrisoquin in the placebo (43.3), d-amphetamine (42.8) and methylphenidate (38.2) conditions. In contrast to placebo and methylphenidate which produced minimal effects from this nadir (reductions of 9.4% and 17.6%, respectively), d-amphetamine resulted in increases in plasma HVA (54.4). Similar changes were observed for urinary dopamine which was similar for the placebo and methylphenidate condition but was increased 64.8% in d- amphetamine treated children compared to placebo. This contrast between stimulants was not observed for 3-methoxy 4-hydroxy phenylethylene glycol (MHPG) where the initial decline in metabolite 18 hours following debrisoquin averaged 57.5%, 53.7% and 52.1% for placebo, d-amphetamine and methylphenidate, respectively. Subsequent declines averaged 13.2%, 3.2% and 21.4%. No significant changes were observed for urinary norepinephrine or epinephrine. These findings suggest that despite their clinical similarity, d-amphetamine and methylphenidate differ in their effects on brain catecholaminergic systems with d-amphetamine influencing brain dopaminergic mechanisms, perhaps by increasing turnover of brain dopamine. Though such studies are just in their infancy, this study as well as others (Riddle et al., 1986; Shaywitz et al., 1986) demonstrate that, as predicted, administration of debrisoquin results in significantly reduced concentrations of HVA and MHPG in plasma. Together with the pharmacologic probe strategy described previously, the debrisoquin strategy provides the investigator with a "window" on brain CA systems, for the first time offering a unique opportunity to examine the relationships between particular behaviors in ADD and brain DA and NE functioning.

THE DEVELOPMENT OF A NOSOLOGY

Overview of Problem

We turn now to still another critical issue, the development of a nosology for ADD. Within this obviously very broad arena we have chosen to examine two particular but intimately related questions: 1) the influence of selective referral patterns on the representativeness of the sample chosen for any research study; and 2) recognition and identification of children with ADD without hyperactivity.

Selective Referral Patterns

As we have noted previously (vide supra), what we today term ADD evolved most recently from the hyperactive child syndrome. Rather than hyperactivity, the primary focus was now on inattention, and hyperactivity need not be present. This change in focus has had a number of significant influences on how we view ADD. For example, when hyperactivity was the major focus, behavioral disturbance was considered to be the prime symptom and hyperactive children were likely to be referred to psychiatrists and mental health centers. With the change in focus to attentional deficits, poor school work and learning difficulties were often the principal reasons for referral. Furthermore, children with inattention were more likely to be referred to pediatricians, child neurologists, or learning disorders units rather than to mental health centers.

It is becoming increasingly apparent that selective referral patterns insure that significant biases are built in to any study of ADD employing children referred to mental health settings. For example, Loney and Milich (1982) found aggressive symptoms in 2/3 of children diagnosed as hyperactive in a mental health clinic, compared to aggressive symptoms in only 18% of hyperactive children in a classroom sample. In another study, this time from Dunedin, New Zealand (McGee et al., 1984), three groups of hyperactive children were identified by parents and teachers: hyperactivity only, aggression only or hyperactivity in association with aggression. Those with hyperactivity alone were judged to be least severely affected while those with hyperactivity in association with aggression were the most severely affected, with the referral rate for the most severe group six times that in the less severe groups.

Implications

Consideration of the bias that results from these selective referral patterns has significant implications both for research and public policy. One consequence of this selective referral bias is that non-representative associations may emerge that are not typical of most children with ADD, for example the association of conduct disorder and aggression in children with ADD derived from mental health settings. Any generalizations from studies of these mental health center populations of ADD children to ADD children in the general population may not be appropriate. Thus, rather than regarded as prototypal of ALL children with ADD, children referred to a mental health center may represent the *extreme of the continuum*.

Still another consequence is that the number of affected children may be seriously underestimated. ADD children who are inattentive and who have learning problems but who are not hyperactive or aggressive may be overlooked and underrepresented in study samples. Thus, children described as ADD in mental health clinics may represent the *"tip of the iceberg"* and not the entire spectrum of ADD.

ADD without Hyperactivity (ADDnoH)

In fact, many of the children who might be overlooked would be diagnosed as exhibiting ADD without hyperactivity (ADDnoH). Currently, three subtypes of ADD are recognized by DSM III. ADD without hyperactivity (ADDnoH) is used to describe children with inattention and impulsivity, while the term ADD with hyperactivity (ADDH) describes those with inattention, impulsivity and hyperactivity. ADD residual type (ADDRT) indicates older adolescents with a history of ADDH at a younger age but who no longer exhibit hyperactivity though the inattention and impulsivity persist.

Not only are there significant differences between ADD children and normal control children, but there are significant differences within the groups of ADD children themselves. For example ADDH and ADDnoH children differ in terms of behavioral, academic, and social patterns, though both groups exhibit inattention. Children with ADDH demonstrate what are referred to as externalizing behaviors, behaviors such as hyperactivity that are obvious to observers external to the child. In contrast, ADDnoH children tend to have symptoms not as obvious to an observer, though the symptoms may be as or more disabling to themselves than the symptoms found in ADDH children. For example, ADDnoH children are more anxious and often have poor school performance. One study (Lahey et al., 1984) found 72% ADDnoH children were retained for a year in the same grade compared to only 17% of ADDH children.

ADDnoH and Learning Disabilities

Although it is not our primary purpose to review the entire topic of learning disabilities (LD), we digress in the interests of providing a perspective on the relationship between ADD (in particular, ADDnoH) and learning disabilities (LD).

Good evidence indicates a significant overlap between the two, yet the relationship is unclear, with co-occurrence rates varying, in no small measure because of the inconsistent criteria used to diagnose both ADD and LD. However, two recent studies (Halperin et al., 1984; Shaywitz, 1986) have found that approximately 10% of children diagnosed as ADD also demonstrate LD. There is considerably more variation in the percentage of children diagnosed as LD who also can be defined as ADD, with rates varying from 33 (Shaywitz, 1986) to 41 (Holobrow & Berry, 1986) to 80% (Safer & Allen, 1976).

What is clear however, is that many ADD children have significant academic achievement problems, performing below expectations in reading and arithmetic, falling significantly behind in academic subjects, and more academic subjects than controls. One recent study found that ADD children are seven times more likely to experience "very much difficulty in all academic areas" (Holobrow & Berry, 1986).

A recent study (Sandoval & Lambert, 1985) showed that not only reading achievement but hyperactivity and particularly hyperactivity in association with aggression was significantly related to referral for special education, and, in fact, twice as many hyperactive as control children who were not LD were receiving special education services.

The implications of these findings are very important for research studies because they demonstrate that subject selection for LD that is based on children selected by an educational system, (referred to as system identified) carry an inherent bias: criteria for selection employ behavioral criteria, not necessarily those of LD. This means that any data derived from such studies will by necessity be biased and inaccurate as well and will tend to show that hyperactivity and aggression are common in LD children.

This is particularly important because, as we (Shaywitz et al., 1986) and Trites (1979) have shown, hyperactivity may also be associated with extreme degrees of giftedness or above average learning capacity.

Still another implication is significant as well: The child with ADDnoH is far less visible and less likely to come to the attention of either parents, educators or other professionals, but at the same time may be at much greater risk for school failure and social failure than children with ADDH. Therefore, it is not only reasonable, but imperative that research should focus on a clearer delineation of this group of children, particularly in terms of the relationship between ADDnoH and learning disability. In the future, any investigation must recognize first, that LD and ADD are related but the nature of the relationship is not well defined. Such studies must employ well-defined, non-system identified children, where the diagnosis of both LD and ADD is made on the basis of rigorous criteria. It is only through such studies that we will be able to learn about not only the prevalence of the co-occurrence of ADD and LD but about the mechanism of their interaction and the expression and course of one on the other. Such studies are fundamental if we are to develop more effective intervention strategies for both ADD and LD.

Toward a New Nosology: ADD vs ADD - Plus

Thus, at the present time the term ADD has come to encompass a wide range of symptoms involving both behavioral and cognitive domains. In particular, the association of the symptoms of conduct disorder (or what DSM III-R terms Oppositional Defiant Disorder, ODD) with ADD has created significant problems for any investigator attempting to define a clinically homogeneous cohort. As a first approach, we suggest utilization of the term ADD, indicating ADD alone, without any other complicating feature; and ADD-Plus, a term indicating that ADD is present in association with some other complicating factor, for example, ADD in association with conduct disorder, affective disorder, mental retardation or oppositional disorder. In this way, the reader of a report on ADD will have a much more precise picture of exactly which group of ADD children has been studied.

SUMMARY

In this report we have examined two critical areas in ADD: The search for a biological marker and the development of a nosology. Identification of a biological marker continues to intrigue investigators and recent advances in imaging and neuropsychopharmacology for the first time offer the hope of reliably documenting biological abnormalities in children with the disorder. Our investigative group has focused on the examination of central catecholaminergic mechanisms in children with ADD. Most recently, we have coupled the use of a pharmacologic probe (d-amphetamine) with the agent debrisoquin. The former is known to alter both central catecholaminergic systems as well as the symptoms of ADD while the latter, a weak monoamine oxidase inhibitor which acts peripherally, differentiates central from peripheral catecholamines. Together, the pharmacologic probe and debrisoquin represent a strategy that provides a "window" on central catecholaminergic mechanisms.

The issue of a more precise and reliable nosology for ADD represents the second area we believe is critical if advances in the field are to continue. Thus, it is clear that any attempt to define a biological marker in children with ADD mandates that such research efforts identify clinically homogeneous groups of children. More than simply wanting to identify children for purposes of establishing a biological marker, a nosology represents the basic descriptive characteristics that form the core of epidemiological and outcome studies as well. We have shown how historically the disorder was described by the psychiatric community. In fact, because the psychiatric literature has provided the foundation for the description of the disorder, it is not surprising that the characteristic symptoms have, in a sense, been dictated by this psychiatric bias. Thus, children referred to mental health centers or child psychiatric units exhibit considerably more disruptive behaviors than children referred to developmental pediatricians or child neurologists primarily for poor academic performance in school. As we have indicated, considerable evidence supports the belief that at the present time many children with ADD are going unrecognized, a state of affairs we have attributed, in part, to bias in the referral patterns of affected children.

Recognizing such differences in symptomatology that to a large extent reflect referral bias, we offer the concept of ADD-Plus as a term that acknowledges the already well recognized clinical heterogeneity observed between investigative groups. Thus, utilization of the term ADD is taken to indicate ADD alone, without any other complicating feature. ADD-Plus represents ADD in association with some other complicating factor, for example, oppositional defiant disorder, conduct disorder, affective disorder, or mental retardation. Learning disability, however, could be associated with either ADD or ADD-Plus.

Finally, a plea to all investigators to recognize that the development of a nosology has significant implications for public policy and the decisions about whether particular groups of children receive the kinds of educational services they require. Thus, the all too common practice of identification of ADD on the basis of hyperactive and aggressive behaviors overlooks the quiet, non-hyperactive, non-aggressive child with ADD, that is those with ADDnoH. Thus, this group of children falls between the cracks and are presently often not identified. The first stage of treatment is identification and those children who are never identified as having a problem can never be treated. These children (ADDnoH) need greater visibility. They may have high intelligence but may not function up to their ability, not because of conceptual reasons, but because of inattention, carelessness with details and problems monitoring their work. Because these children may not have externalizing signs, they are faulted for poor motivation, for not trying hard enough. Because they have good intelligence, this leads to the assumption that if only they tried harder when, indeed, they are trying harder than anyone else. It is not surprising, therefore, that the most rapidly accumulating data indicates that this group of children is at the highest risk for academic difficulties and poor self concept.

We must recognize that the spectrum of ADD must encompass variation according to intellectual ability. For example, children falling into this underidentified, underserved category of ADDnoH have been found even at the highest levels of intelligence, and sometimes these are the children penalized the most. Thus, recent evidence recognizes ADD in several important populations:

a) most highly gifted
b) students in selective colleges

Often, these children who have the highest potential are penalized the most, not because of conceptual limitations, not because they don't understand, but because educators often fail to recognize the symptom complex and make the small modification that would allow for success, modification which could include such simple strategies as allowing extra time on tests, or allowing the child to type. The educational effort must extend from the primary grades, through college and even graduate school.

The focus has so much been on the "tip of the iceberg." You know that 90% of the iceberg is not visible. We now have to expand our view, to look for and identify those children presently underidentified, who are most needy and most overlooked. Many of these children are now succeeding through intelligence and hard work - but many more could.

REFERENCES

American Psychiatric Association (1968). *Diagnostic and Statistical Manual of Mental Disorders, Second Edition (DSM II).* Washington, DC; Author.

American Psychiatric Association (1980). *Diagnostic and Statistical Manual of Mental Disorders, Third Edition (DSM III).* Washington, DC; Author.

Barkley, R. A. (1977). A review of stimulant drug research with hyperactive children. *Journal of Child Psychology and Psychiatry, 18,* 137-165.

Barkley, R. A., Karlsson, J., Pollard, S., & Murphy, J. V. (1985). Developmental changes in the mother-child interactions of hyperactive boys: Effects of two dose levels of ritalin. *Journal of Child Psychology, 26,* 705-715.

Bender, L. (1942). Post encephalitic behavior disorders in childhood. In L. Bender (Ed.), *Encephalitis: A clinical study.* New York: Grune & Stratton.

Bradley, C. (1937). The behavior of children receiving benzedrine. *American Journal of Psychiatry, 94,* 577-585.

Brown, G. L., Ebert, M. H., Hunt, R. D., & Rapoport, J. L. (1981). Urinary 3-methoxy-4-hydroxyphenylglycol and homovanillic acid response to d- amphetamine in hyperactive children. *Biological Psychiatry, 16,* 779- 787.

Clements, S. D., & Peters, J. E. (1962). Minimal brain dysfunctions in the school-aged child. *Archives of General Psychiatry, 6,* 185-187.

Coleman, M. (1971). Serotonin concentrations in whole blood of hyperactive children. *Journal of Pediatrics, 78,* 985-990.

Conners, C. K., & Werry, J. S. (1979). Pharmacotherapy. In H. C. Quay & J. S. Werry (Eds.), *Psychopathological disorders of childhood.* New York: John Wiley & Sons.

Cooper, J. R., Bloom, F. E., & Roth, R. H. (1986). The *biochemical basis of neuropharmacology.* New York: Oxford University Press.

Donnelly, M., Zametkin, A. J., Rapoport, J. L., Ismond, D. R., Weingartner, H., Lane, E., Oliver, J., & Linnoila, M., Potter,W.Z. (in press). Treatment of childhood hyperactivity with desipramine: Plasma drug concentrations, cardiovascular effects, plasma and urinary catecholamines and clinical response. *Journal of Pharmacology and Experimental Therapeutics.*

Fuller, R. W., Perry, K. W., Bymaster, F. P., & Wong, D. T. (1978). Comparative effects of pemoline, amfoelic acid, and amphetamine on dopamine uptake and release in vitro on brain 3,4-dihydroxyphenylacetic acid concentration on spiperone-treated rats. *Journal of Pharmacy and Pharmacology, 30,* 197-198.

Gadow, K. D. (1983). Effects of stimulant drugs on academic performance in hyperactive and learning disabled children. *Journal of Learning Disabilities, 16,* 290-299.

Galaburda, A. M., & Kemper, T. L. (1979). Cytoarchitectonic abnormalities in developmental dyslexia: A case study. *Annals of Neurology, 6,* 94- 100.

Galaburda, A. M., Sherman, G. F., Rosen, G. D., Aboitiz, F., & Geschwind, N. (1985). Developmental dyslexia: Four consecutive patients with cortical anomalies. *Annals of Neurology, 18(2),* 222-233.

Goldstein, K. (1936). Modification of behavior consequent to cerebral lesion. *Psychiatric Quarterly, 10*, 539-610.

Halperin, J. M., Gittelman, R., Klein, D. F., & Rudel, R. G. (1984). Reading-disabled hyperactive children: A distinct subgroup of attention deficit disorder with hyperactivity? *Journal of Abnormal Child Psychology, 12*, 1-14.

Harcherik, D. F., Cohen, D. J., Ort, S., Paul, R., Shaywitz, B. A., Volkmar, F. R., Rothman, S. L. G., & Leckman, J. F. (1985). Computed tomographic brain scanning in four neuropsychiatric disorders of childhood. *American Journal of Psychiatry, 142*, 731-737.

Henker, B., Astor-Dubin, L., & Varni, J. W. (1986). Psychostimulant medication and perceived intensity in hyperactive children. *Journal of Abnormal Child Psychology, 14*, 105-114.

Hohman, L. B. (1922). Post encephalitic behavior disorders in children. *Johns Hopkins Hospital Bulletin, 380*, 372-375.

Holborow, P., & Berry, P. S. (1986). Hyperactivity and learning difficulties. *Journal of Learning Disabilities, 19*, 426-431.

Irwin, M., Belendink, K., McCloskay, K., & Freedman, D. X. (1981). Tryptophan metabolism in children with attention deficit disorder. *American Journal of Psychiatry, 138*, 1082-1085.

Kavalc, K. (1982). The efficiency of stimulant drug treatment for hyperactivity: A meta-analysis. *Journal of Learning Disabilities, 15*, 280-289.

Kirk, S. A., & Bateman, B. (1962). Diagnosis and remediation of learning disabilities. *Exceptional Children, 29*, 73-78.

Kuczenski, R. (1983). Biochemical actions of amphetamines and other stimulants. In I. Crease (Ed.), *Stimulants: neurochemical, behavior and clinical* (pp. 31–63). New York: Raven Press.

Lahey, B. B., Schaughency, E. A., Strauss, C. C., & Frame, C. L. (1984). Are attention deficit disorders with and without hyperactivity similar or dissimilar disorders? *Journal of the American Academy of Child Psychiatry, 23*, 302-309.

Langer, D. H., Rapoport, J. L., Brown, G. L., Ebert, M. H., & Bunney, W. E. Jr. (1982). Behavioral effects of carbidopa/levodopa in hyperactive boys. *Journal of the American Academy of Child Psychiatry, 1*, 8-10.

Laufer, M., & Denhoff, E. (1957). Hyperkinetic behavior syndrome in children. *Journal of Pediatrics, 50*, 463 474.

Loney, J., & Milich (1982). Hyperactivity, inattention, and aggression in clinical practice. *Advances in Development and Behavioral Pediatrics, 3*, 113-147.

Lou, H. C., Henriksen, L., & Bruhn, P. (1984). Focal cerebral hypoperfusion in children with dysphasia and/or attention deficit disorder. *Archives of Neurology, 42*, 825-829.

Maas, J. W., & Leckman, J. F. (1983). Relationships between central nervous system functioning and plasma and urinary MMPG and other metabolites. In J. Mass (Ed.), *MMPG: Basic mechanisms and psychopathology* (pp. 33-43). New York: Academic Press.

McGee, R., Williams, S., & Silva, P. A. (1984). Background characteristics of aggressive, hyperactive, and aggressive-hyperactive boys. *Journal of the American Academy of Child Psychiatry, 23*, 280-284.

Meyer, A. (1904). The anatomical facts and clinical varieties of traumatic insanity. *American Journal of Insanity, 60*, 373-441.

Mikkelson, E., Lake, C. T., Brown, G. L., Ziegler, M. G., & Ebert, M. H. (1981). The hyperactive child syndrome. Peripheral sympathetic nervous system function and the effect of d-amphetamine. *Psychiatry Research, 4*, 157-169.

Molina, V. A., & Orsingher, O. A. (1981). Effects of Mg-pencoline on the central catecholaminergic system. *Archives International Pharmadynamic, 251*, 66-79.

Ottenbacher, K. J., & Cooper, M. M. (1983). Drug treatment of hyperactivity in children. *Developmental Medicine and Child Neurology, 25*, 358-366.

Porrino, L. J., Rapoport, J. L., Behar, D., Sceery, W., Ismond, D. R., & Bunney, W. E., Jr. (1983). A naturalistic assessment of the motor activity of hyperactive boys I. Comparison with normal controls. *Archives of General Psychiatry, 40*, 681-693.

Rapoport, J. L., Mikkelsen, E. J., Ebert, M. H., Brown, G. L., Weise, V. L., & Kopin, I. J. (1978). Urinary catecholamine and amphetamine excretion in hyperactive and normal boys. *Journal of Neurology and Mental Disease, 166,* 731-737.

Rapoport, J. L., Quinn, P. O., Scribanic, N., & Murphy, D. L. (1974). Platelet serotonin of hyperactive school age boys. *British Journal of Psychiatry, 125,* 138-140.

Riddle, M. A., Leckman, J. F., Cohen, D. J., Anderson, M., Ort, S. I., Caruso, K. A., & Shaywitz, B. A. (1986). Assessment of central dopaminergic function using plasma-free homovanillic acid after debrisoquin administration. *Journal of Neural Transmission, 67,* 31-43.

Rosenthal, R. H., & Allen, T. W. (1978). An examination of attention, arousal, and learning dysfunctions of hyperkinetic children. *Psychological Bulletin, 85,* 689-715.

Safer, D. J., & Allen, R. D. (1976). *Hyperactive children: Diagnosis and management.* Baltimore: University Park Press.

Sandoval, J., & Lambert, N. M. (1984-85). Hyperactive and learning disabled children: Who gets help? *The Journal of Special Education, 18,* 495-503.

Shaywitz, B. A., Cohen, D. J., & Bowers, M. B. (1977). CSF monoamine metabolites in children with minimal brain dysfunction-evidence for alteration of brain dopamine. *Journal of Pediatrics, 90,* 67-71.

Shaywitz, B. A., Shaywitz, S. E., Byrne, T., Cohen, D. J., & Rothman, S. (1983). Attention deficit disorder: Quantitative analysis of CT. *Neurology, 33,* 1500-1503.

Shaywitz, B. A., Shaywitz, S. E., Gillespie, S. M., Anderson, G. M., Riddle, M. A., Leckman, J. F., Cohen, D. J., & Jatlow, P. (1986). Effects of methylphenidate during debrisoquin loading on plasma and urinary concentrations of monoamines and their metabolites in children with attention deficit disorder. *Annals of Neurology, 20,* 416.

Shaywitz, S. E. (1986). Prevalence of attentional deficits in an epidemiologic sample of school children (unpublished raw data).

Shaywitz, S. E., Shaywitz, B. A., Jamner, A. H., Towle, V. R., & Barnes, M. A. (1986). Heterogeneity within the gifted: Higher IQ boys exhibit increased activity, impulsivity and parenting problems. *Annals of Neurology, 20,* 415-416.

Shekim, W. O., DeKirmenjian, H., & Chapel, J. L. (1977). Urinary catecholamine metabolites in hyperkinetic boys treated with d-amphetamine. *American Journal of Psychiatry, 134,* 1276-1279.

Shekim, W. O., DeKirmenjian, H., & Chapel, J. L. (1979). Urinary MHPG excretion in minimal brain dysfunction and its modification of d- amphetamine. *American Journal of Psychiatry, 136,* 667-671.

Shekim, W. O., Javaid, J., Dans, J. M., & Bylund, D. B. (1983). Urinary MHPG and HVA excretion in boys with attention deficit disorder and hyperactivity treated with d-amphetamine. *Biological Psychiatry, 18,* 707-714.

Shetty, T., & Chase, T. N. (1976). Central monoamines and hyperactivity of childhood. *Neurology, 26,* 1000-1002.

Strauss, A. A., & Lehtinen, L. E. (1947). *Psychopathology and Education in the Brain-injured Child.* New York: Grune & Stratton.

Swann, A. C., Maas, J. W., Hattox, S. E., & Landis, D. H. (1980). Catecholamine metabolites in human plasma as indices of brain function: Effects of debrisoquin. *Life Sciences, 27,* 1857-1861.

Trites, R. L. (1979). Prevalence of hyperactivity in Ottawa, Canada. In R. L. Trites (Ed.), *Hyperactivity in Children* (pp. 29-52). Baltimore: University Park Press.

Weiss, G. (1985). Hyperactivity. Overview and new directions. *Psychiatric Clinics of North America, 8,* 737-753.

Wender, P. H. (1971). *Minimal brain dysfunction in children.* New York: Wiley–Interscience.

Werner, H., & Strauss, A. A. (1941). Pathology of the figure-background relation in the child. *Journal of Abnormal and Social Psychology, 36,* 236-248.

Whalen, C. K., & Henker, B. (1976). Psychostimulants and children: A review and analysis. *Psychological Bulletin, 83,* 1113-1130.

Whalen, C. K., Henker, B., Collins, B. E., McAulliffe, S., & Vaux, A. (1979). Peer interaction in a structured communication task: Comparisons of normal and hyperactive boys and of methyl-phenidate (Ritalin) and placebo effects. *Child Development, 50*, 388-401.

Whalen, C. K., Henker, B., Dotemoto, S., Vaux, A., & McAuliffe, S. (1981). Hyperactivity and methylphenidate: Peer interaction styles. In K. D. Gadow & J. Loney (Eds.), *Psychosocial aspects of drug treatment for hyperactivity* (pp. 381-415). Boulder, Colorado: Westview Press.

Yu-cun, A., & Yu-feng, W. (1984). Urinary 3-methoxy-4-hydroxyphenylglycol sulfate excretion in seventy-three school children with minimal brain dysfunction syndrome. *Biological Psychiatry, 19*, 861-870.

Zametkin, A., Nordahl, T., Gross, M., Semple, W., Rapoport, J. L., & Cohen, R. (1986). Brain metabolism in hyperactive parents of hyperactive children. *American Academy of Child and Adolescent Psychiatry Annual Meeting, abstracts.*, 23.

Zametkin, A., Rapoport, J. L., Murphy, D. L., Linnoila, M., & Ismond, D. (1985). Treatment of hyperactive children with monoamine oxidase inhibitors. *Archives of General Psychiatry, 42*, 962-966.

Zametkin, A. J., Karoum, F., Linnoila, M., Rapoport, J. L., Brown, G. L., Chuang, L. W., & Wyatt, R. J. (1985). Stimulants, urinary catecholamines and indoleamines in hyperactivity: A comparison of methylphenidate and dextroamphetamine. *Archives of General Psychiatry, 42*, 251-255.

Zametkin, A. J., & Rapoport, J. L. (In press). The neuropharmacology of attention deficit disorder with hyperactivity.

5

The Long-Term Outcome of the Attention Deficit Disorder/ Hyperkinetic Syndrome

Rachel Gittelman Klein, Ph.D.
Salvatore Mannuzza, Ph.D.
New York State Psychiatric Institute and
Long Island Jewish Medical Center

Our understanding of psychopathology is greatly enhanced by longitudinal studies. These facilitate diagnostic refinements, improve therapeutic developments, and enable proper interpretation of influential events, whether social or biological. The notion that long-term outcome reveals important clinical features in psychopathology is not new. It was responsible for the distinction made by Kraepelin between dementia praecox and manic depressive psychoses in the late 19th century. More recently as well, developmental aspects of psychopathology have been influential in guiding the investigation of adult disorders. We now know of rapid cycling bipolar illness, of multiple versus infrequent relapsers in recurrent unipolar depressions, and of deteriorating and periodic schizophrenias.

The long-term study of psychopathology is especially pertinent to children since they undergo many changes that raise questions regarding the ultimate significance of dysfunction. The relevance of early symptomatology to adult functioning may be especially ambiguous in the case of the hyperkinetic syndrome[1] since the signs are not qualitatively peculiar, as in infantile autism or schizophrenia for example, but represent excessive rates of ordinary childhood behaviors. Moreover, because inattention, impulsivity, and activity level diminish with time in normal children, the ultimate importance of their early deviant manifestations is all the more likely to be minimized in the absence of proper investigation. Historically, this is what occurred, and clinical lore held for a long time that hyperkinetic children suffered from a maturational lag whereby the timing of inhibitory processes was delayed, and behavior could be expected to normalize during adolescence.

A knowledge of the long-term outcome of Attention Deficit Hyperactivity Disorder (ADHD) (APA, 1987) is especially important since the disorder probably

71

represents the most common reason for referral to outpatient care centers in the United States. Understandably, parents are interested in knowing what likely fate awaits their children. If only for this clinical goal, the evaluation of later functioning in children with ADHD is important. Inevitably, longitudinal research provides other scientific and clinical advances (Nicol, 1985).

Recent publications (Brown & Borden, 1986; Thorley, 1984; Weiss & Hechtman, 1986) have reviewed follow-up studies of hyperactive children published until 1985. To avoid redundancy, we discuss overlapping topics briefly, and emphasize findings that either were not included or not detailed previously.

METHODOLOGICAL CONSIDERATIONS[1]

The quality of the information generated by longitudinal studies is constrained by methodological issues; some are summarized below.

Prospective and Retrospective Studies

The terms, prospective and retrospective, have been used inconsistently. For example, Dykman and Ackerman (1980) and Weiss (1985) classify studies by Mendelson, Johnson, and Stewart (1971) and Menkes, Rowe, and Menkes (1967) as retrospective, whereas Brown and Borden (1986) describe them as prospective.

The retrospective-prospective distinction is based on when the syndrome was diagnosed, as well as on the quality of the information obtained. Retrospective studies, in general, have serious limitations. In studies that rely on old records to identify suitable cases, even if hyperkinetic syndromes were diagnosed in childhood, the selection of a homogeneous clinical sample is dubious since the standards for diagnosis are likely to have been inconsistent (e.g., Mendelson et al., 1971). This problem is compounded when the diagnosis was not made in childhood (e.g., Borland & Heckman, 1976), but is inferred from clinical notes. Finally, retrospective studies that rely on the recollections of informants at "follow-up" are susceptible to selective forgetting, selective recall, memory distortions, and a host of other factors.

In this review, a study is considered prospective if:

(1) The diagnosis of a hyperactivity syndrome was made in childhood, and
(2) The diagnosis was based on relatively uniform clinical standards for assessment or on specified clinical criteria.

Selection Criteria

A closely related issue to the retrospective-prospective distinction concerns the

---

[1]In this chapter we refer to the hyperkinetic syndrome, hyperactivity, Attention Deficit Disorder with Hyperactivity (ADDH) (APA, 1980), and Attention-Deficit Hyperactivity Disorder (ADHD) (APA, 1987) interchangeably.

criteria applied to the selection of the original patient group. In his review of follow-up studies of hyperactive children, Thorley (1984) states:

> One of the most difficult problems facing this review is that it is not certain that similar groups of children—hyperactives or controls—are being studied. This arises because detailed selection criteria are either not used or not reported. (p.117)

The majority of the follow-up studies shown in Table 1 stipulate inclusion and exclusion selection criteria; most studies that did not were retrospective. Among the prospective studies, all used information obtained from parents. However, only about half (Ackerman, Dykman, & Peters, 1977; August, Stewart, & Holmes, 1983; Gittelman, Mannuzza, Shenker, & Bonagura, 1985; Huessy, Metoyer, & Townsend, 1973, 1974; Mannuzza & Gittelman, 1984, in press; Satterfield, Hoppe, & Schell, 1982) obtained information from teachers.

Sample Size and Attrition

The number of individuals evaluated at follow-up varies widely across studies (see Table 1). In general, prospective studies tend to have larger follow-up samples (most over 50 cases) than retrospective studies (most under 30 cases).

Perhaps a more significant factor in the quality of data is attrition rate. A substantial proportion of the studies achieved less than 70% retrieval. The greater the attrition rate, the lower the likelihood that outcome findings are representative of the original group. There is no satisfactory way to establish that the subjects evaluated at follow-up do not differ systematically from those who were not. Cox, Rutter, Yule, and Quinton (1977) report that in epidemiological studies, cases with "missing" data had more pathology than obtained cases, i.e., more behavioral deviance on teacher questionnaires, higher rates of childhood conduct disorder, and greater marital discord. If these findings are true of hyperactive samples as well, they suggest that studies with high rates of attrition may generate misleading findings. Therefore, investigators who obtain no differences between probands and controls, with greater attrition rates in probands, are particularly problematic.

Sex Composition and Control Groups

As shown in Table 1, with few exceptions (Morrison, 1979, 1980), the overwhelming majority of cases in follow-up studies are males. [The 12 females studied by Mannuzza and Gittelman (1984, in press) were part of a larger sample consisting of 89% males.] As Thorley (1984) notes, since males (vs. females) in the general population are at an increased risk for antisocial behavior, follow-up studies of hyperactive boys would be expected to show relatively high rates of conduct problems. Therefore, sex-matched controls are necessary to enable

TABLE 1
Follow-Up Studies of Hyperactive Children

Study	No. Studied	% of Cohort	% Males	Age Mean	Age Range	Follow-Up Interval (Years)	Controls	"Blind"
Retrospective Studies								
Blouin et al. (1978)	23	55	87	14	N.I.	5	Poor Students	No
Borland & Heckman (1976)	20	54	100	30	N.I.	20-25	Siblings	No
Gomez et al. (1981)	100	87	95	40	20-65	—	Normals	N.A.
Laufer (1971)	66	66	N.I.	20	15-26	12	None	N.A.
Loney et al. (1981)	124	92	100	14	12-18	5	None	No
Loney et al (1983)	22	11[x]	100	N.I.	21-23	N.I.	Siblings	No
Mendelson et al. (1971)[+]	83	59	90	13	12-16	2-5	None	No
Menkes et al. (1967)	14	78	79	31	22-40	25	None	No
Morrison (1979, 1980)	48	—	56	30	N.I.	—	Psychiatric Cases	No
Stewart et al. (1973)	81	58	89	13	12-16	2-5	None	No
White et al. (1979)	12	—	100	N.I.	13-16	N.I.	Psychiatric Cases / Normals	N.A.
Prospective Studies								
Ackerman et al. (1977)	23	79	100	14	13-14	4	Hypo & Normoactive Learning Disorders Normals	No
August et al. (1983)	52	68	100	14	9-16	4	(Hyperactives with and without Conduct Disorder)	Yes
Butter (1977)	13	41	85	13	10-16	4	Normals	No
Charles & Schain (1981)	62	63	79	12	10-16	4	None	No

Study								
Cohen et al. (1972)*	20	31 (Random Selection)	100	15	13-16	5	Normals	No
Gittelman et al. (1985)	101	98	100	18	16-23	9	Normals	Yes
Hechtman & Weiss (1986)*	61	59	90	25	21-33	15	Normals	Yes
Hechtman, Weiss, & Perlman (1984)*	53	51	86	21	19-26	12	Normals	Yes
Hechtman et al. (1981)*	75	72	91	19	17-24	10	Normals	No
Hopkins et al. (1979)*	70	67	N.I.	19	17-24	10	Normals	No
Hoy et al. (1978)*	15	23	100	15	N.I.	5	Normals	N.A.
Huessy et al. (1973, 1974)	75	89 (Random Selection)	N.I.	15	9-24	9	None	No
Mannuzza & Gittelman (1984, in press)	12	100	0	17	16-18	9	Hyperactive Males Normal Males	Yes
Minde et al. (1972)*	91	88	89	13	11-17	5	Normals	No
Riddle & Rapoport (1976)	72	95	100	10	N.I.	2	Normals	No
Satterfield et al. (1982)	110	73	100	17	14-21	8	Normals	N.A.
Weiss et al. (1971)*	64	91	92	13	10-18	5	Normals	No
Weiss et al. (1979)*	75	72	91	19	17-24	10	Normals	No
Weiss et al. (1985)*	51-63	49-61	90	25	21-33	15	Normals	Yes
Zambelli et al. (1977)	9	100	100	14	12-16	N.I.	Normals	Yes

*Same sample as Weiss et al.

⁺Same sample as Stewart et al.

ˣOf total sample, 63% of those with brothers

N.I.—Not Indicated.

N.A.—Not Applicable. Follow-up assessments limited to measures unaffected by investigator bias, e.g., criminal records, questionaires, etc.

proper interpretation of results. However, as shown in Table 1, a number of studies (most retrospective) had no controls.

Age and Follow-Up Interval

Particularly among the prospective studies, mean age at follow-up interval tends to be 15 years or younger, and follow-up interval is 4 or 5 years. Since most hyperactive children are referred during elementary school years, their status at an early age does not provide information relevant to outcome much beyond the peak of the age-risk period for diagnosis. The follow-up age ranges in Table 1 indicate that, in some longitudinal studies, some children are as young as 9 when reevaluated.

Follow-Up Measures and Sources of Information

Follow-up measures and data collection procedures have varied widely: e.g., arrest records (Satterfield et al., 1982), semi-structured interviews with parents and subjects (Gittelman et al., 1985; Mannuzza & Gittelman, 1988), questionnaires sent to subjects (Laufer, 1971), psychophysiological assessments (Butter, 1977), self-rating inventories completed by subjects (Gomez, Janowsky, Zetlin, Huey, & Clopton, 1981), interviews with mothers (Mendelson et al., 1971), projective psychological tests (Riddle & Rapoport, 1976), interviews with subjects (Weiss, Hechtman, Perlman, Hopkins, & Wener, 1979), etc. The majority of studies employed open-ended interviews—evaluation procedures that are susceptible to investigator biases. With few exceptions, assessments were conducted with full knowledge of the person's childhood status (see Table 1), and the degree to which this knowledge may have influenced the evaluators' judgments cannot be determined.

The psychiatric literature, in general, has indicated poor agreement between parent and child on the reporting of childhood symptoms, and consequently of mental disorders in the child (Kashani, Orvaschel, Burk, & Reid, 1985; Cohen, O'Connor, Lewis, Puig-Antich, & Malachowski, 1984). Similarly, investigators who have examined the agreement between parent and offspring on discrete problems have reported marked inconsistencies (Herjanic & Reich, 1982; Stewart, Mendelson, & Johnson, 1973). To assess adjustment of cases between 16 and 23 years of age, we administered semi-structured psychiatric interviews to adolescents, formerly hyperactive children and normal controls, ages 16 to 23, and to their parents (Mannuzza & Gittelman, 1986). Interviewers were blind to the group membership of the parents and the adolescents. Reliability estimates showed that parents and adolescents achieved good agreement on the diagnosis of Conduct Disorder, but poor agreement on ADHD. The data were also analyzed with respect to the discriminant validity of each type of informant, that is, the ability of parents and offspring to differentiate between probands and controls if one source of information was accounted for. In other words, we examined whether either informant (parent or adolescent) added a significant increment over the other in the ability to distinguish the controls and probands. For ADDH, both parent reports and self-reports discriminated between probands and controls even after controlling for diagnoses based on the other informant (parent or self). However, for Conduct Disorder, parent diagnoses, but not self-diagnoses, provided an increment in discriminant validity between the former patients and controls. The findings on reliability and validity, taken as a whole, suggest that, optimally, information from both parents and subjects should be obtained, at least for adolescents and young adults (Mannuzza & Gittleman, 1986).

CONCLUSION

Many methodological shortcomings are directly or indirectly associated with retrospective studies, which were summarized by Brown and Borden (1986), Dykman and Ackerman (1980), Thorley (1984), and Weiss (1985). Since ample research now exists, this review focuses on controlled, prospective studies, because of their obvious superiority. In addition, we emphasize information obtained in hyperkinetic children reevaluated at age 15 or later, to restrict the overview to a developmental period which is, without doubt, beyond the modal age for case identification.

OVERVIEW OF OUTCOME

The summary of outcome covers two broad domains of dysfunction. The first consists of aspects of adjustment that are relevant to the functioning of all individuals, such as academic achievement, cognitive skills, and occupational status. The second major outcome is the frequency of symptomatology and diagnosable mental disorders. Although the presentation of adjustment measures and psychiatric diagnoses provides a very full picture of the long-term adjustment of hyperactive children, we feel that it is incomplete. Not surprisingly, not every hyperactive child has been found to have disability or maladjustment in later life. Therefore, in addition to summarizing the rate of dysfunction and of psychiatric diagnoses in hyperactive children at maturity, we also discuss the adjustment of cases who do not receive psychiatric diagnoses at follow-up.

A. AREAS OF DYSFUNCTION

The major aspects of adaptation that have been studied in follow-ups of hyperkinetic children include cognitive function, academic performance, social functioning, and occupational status.

Cognitive Function

The Montreal group, headed by Dr. Gabrielle Weiss, has been the only one so far to report systematic assessments of the cognitive performance of hyperactive children in later life. In their first reports, significant differences in cognitive performance were found between the index adolescents and controls (Cohen, Weiss, & Minde, 1972; Hoy, Weiss, Minde, & Cohen, 1978). The once hyperactive youngsters performed more poorly on the Matching Familiar Figures Test, with shorter latencies and more errors, with slower performance on the Embedded Figures Test, greater errors on a vigilance task and on a visual motor integration test. Because only a very partial sample of the original cohort was tested, interpretation of these data is problematic, though they have been quoted widely as documenting continued impairment in cognitive performance in former hyperactive children. In a much larger sample of the same cohort evaluated at average age 20, in late adolescence and early adulthood, 10 years after referral, the former patients were significantly worse than controls on the same tests given earlier (Hopkins, Perlman, Hechtman, & Weiss, 1979). These results seemingly give strong support to the maintenance of compromised cognitive functioning in grown hyperactive children. However, negative findings were obtained in the same subjects in adulthood (Weiss & Hechtman, 1986), suggesting normalization of cognitive performance as time goes on.

In our own study, a variety of tests were selected because of their putative relationship to attentional processes. Contrary to the findings reported by the Montreal group, we found no significant differences between the former hyperactive group and controls after controlling for I.Q., except for only one difference out of 10, showing a significant disadvantage for the former patients (Piacentini, Mannuzza, & Klein, 1987). Unfortunately, our test battery differed from others, and the only test in common with the Montreal group was the Matching Familiar Figures Test, on which we obtained no group differences. Our sample represented the same proportion of cases as these investigators', and to the extent that it included only 70% of the cohort it is unsatisfactory. Nevertheless, it is difficult to reconcile the two sets of data and difficult to assert that there is clear disadvantage in cognitive processing in former hyperactive children. The inconsistent results are all the more striking since other findings from these two samples are congruent (these are discussed below).

Academic Performance

It is generally assumed that inefficient cognitive performance places children at risk for relatively poor academic achievement. In the five year follow-up of the Montreal group, the subjects were rated as performing more poorly by teachers than IQ matched controls, but there were no differences in their rate of being held back in school (Minde, Weiss, & Mendelson, 1972). Thus, it appears that the magnitude of academic dysfunction is not such as to incur institutional action. In a further assessment at age 15, the former patients obtained significantly worse scores on two measures of language performance. The ten year follow-up, when the youngsters were 20 years of age on the average, yielded results that indicated significant academic disadvantage for the index group (Weiss et al., 1979). They had received lower grades, had failed more frequently, had completed fewer years of education, and had been expelled from school more frequently, than controls.

In our own follow-up study, in spite of not obtaining differences on specific cognitive measures, the subjects had worse scores on standardized achievement tests than controls (after controlling for I.Q.), and had significantly more academic problems consisting of being held back, failing grades. In addition, more had been expelled (Klein & Mannuzza, unpublished data).

Social Functioning

Although social functioning, including peer and family relationships, is undoubtedly related to many other important aspects of adjustment, such as job performance, self-esteem, etc., its investigation is hampered by a lack of adequate means of assessment. Reliance has been mostly on self-assessments which are probably unsatisfactory, due to the strong likelihood that young individuals' self-ratings are influenced by social desirability. Therefore, special interest is generated by those studies that report significant decrements in social functioning in previously hyperactive children.

In a subgroup of the Montreal sample, the former patients rated themselves as having less peer contact than controls; no other differences in social functioning were detected (Hoy et al., 1978). In adulthood, worse social skills were reported in former patients than controls, but only when judgments were derived from interview measures, and not from self-ratings (Hechtman, Weiss, & Perlman, 1980). This discrepancy may reflect the inadequacy of self-ratings in assessing behaviors that are influenced by the tendency to shape one's responses to be congruent with social expectations.

Occupational Status

The Montreal investigators are unique in reporting objective assessments of occupational functioning. Remarkably, ratings from employers for subjects and controls were obtained. Strikingly, at age 20, employer ratings of occupational performance for the former hyperactives and normals did not differ (Weiss, Hechtman, & Perlman, 1978). The former hyperactive children appeared to have selected work settings that enabled adequate performance in spite of continued inattention or restlessness; in fact, hyperactives had less sedentary jobs (Weiss & Hechtman, 1986). In the subsequent follow-up in adulthood (ages 21-33), only a very partial sample of the cases could be evaluated since most would not allow contact with their employers (this reluctance was not found in the controls). A different pattern of job performance emerged. This time, employers reported that the hyperactive cases were worse than controls on adequacy and completion of performance, independent work, and relationships with supervisors. Moreover, there was a trend for them to be less likely to be rehired than controls. Social relationships with co-workers and punctuality were not different between the two groups. Self-reports indicated less stability in employment among hyperactives, and, as adults, they had inferior occupational adjustment. The inconsistent findings in occupational adjustment at the two time periods are difficult to reconcile due to the inequality of the groups.

B. MENTAL STATUS

ADD Symptoms

Short-term (4 to 5 year) follow-up studies, at ages 13 to 14, consistently have shown that inattention, impulsivity, and hyperactivity persist. This has been demonstrated with interview data (August et al., 1983) and with laboratory measures of attention (Butter, 1977; Zambelli, Stamm, Maitinsky, & Loiselle, 1977). Minde et al. (1972) reported that, although measures of hyperactivity, distractibility, aggressivity, and excitability showed significant decreases from initial (childhood) evaluation to follow-up assessment, all symptoms were more prevalent in hyperactive adolescents than in controls. Also, distractibility replaced hyperactivity as the chief complaint made by mothers (Weiss, Minde, Werry, Douglas, & Nemeth, 1971).

In their 10-year follow-up (ages 17 to 24), Weiss et al. (1979) found that hyperactivity and restlessness persisted, as estimated by self-reports and direct observations. There was also convergent, suggestive, evidence of continued impulsivity. Probands exhibited more impulsive life styles (more car accidents, more changes of residence) and were judged to have impulsive personality traits (Weiss et al., 1979). Moreover, they had relatively elevated scores on psychological tests presumed to reflect impulsivity (Hopkins et al., 1979). No findings were reported on inattention.

In our study (Gittelman & Mannuzza, 1985), inattention, impulsivity, and hyperactivity, were more common in probands than in controls, regardless of whether rates were derived from parent or self reports. Prevalence rates for probands ranged from 16 to 21% from self reports, and 32 to 41% from parents'; in contrast, rates for controls were 0 to 4%.

Weiss, Hechtman, Milroy, and Perlman (1985), the only investigators to have followed hyperactive children into adulthood (ages 21 to 33) in a controlled, prospective design, found that many more probands (66%) than controls (7%) reported that at least one of the above symptoms was mildly to severely disabling. Also, consistent with their 10-year follow-up findings, more probands than controls complained of feeling restless, and were observed to be restless during the interview. However, as Weiss et al. (1985) acknowledge, these judgments were not made blind to group membership. These authors conclude that, "In general, the findings indicate that about half of our hyperactive adults had not outgrown all aspects of the syndrome" (p. 218).

Substance Use and Abuse

Follow-up findings on substance use and abuse (both alcohol and other compounds) have not been consistent (Weiss & Hechtman, 1986). A partial listing of potential reasons for these inconsistencies includes differences in geographic study locations (e.g., New York vs. Montreal), the birth years of subjects, attrition rates, data collection procedures, definitions of use and abuse, and varying degrees of co-morbidity (e.g., ADD symptoms and conduct problems) across studies.

Conduct Problems/Antisocial Behavior

Conduct problems in the early adolescence of hyperactive children have been found in most studies. Weiss et al. (1971) reported that, at follow-up (mean age 13 years), 25% of formerly hyperactive subjects showed a history of antisocial behavior, 16% were referred to juvenile court, and 3% (2 of 64 subjects) were placed in a reform school. Also, teachers reported that hyperactives exhibited more conduct problems than controls. Ackerman et al. (1977) compared hyperactive, hypoactive, and normoactive learning-disabled boys and controls in a 4-year follow-up (mean age 14 years), and found a three to sixteen fold increase in fairly serious behavioral problems in the hyperactive group. Examples included breaking and entering, aggressive acts in school, and serious incorrigibility.

Outcome in late adolescence and young adulthood is less clear. In an 8-year prospective study (mean age, 17), Satterfield et al. (1982) reported that, depending on social class, 36% to 58% of former patients, compared with 2% to 11% of controls, had been arrested for serious offenses (i.e., grand theft, robbery, and assault with a deadly weapon).

In their 10-year prospective study, Hechtman, Weiss, and Perlman (1984) reported a different pattern. At age 19 years, there was only a tendency for former patients to have more court referrals than controls during the five years preceding the evaluation (47% vs. 32% $p < .07$), and there was no difference for the year before the interview. Also, the groups were not different in the number and seriousness of offenses. Furthermore, the number of hyperactives and controls who reported stealing did not differ. However, more hyperactives were involved in major thefts in high school. Strikingly, in this study, the rate of serious criminal activity in the grown hyperactive children is lower than it is among the controls studied by Satterfield et al. (1982).

Several factors might have contributed to these discrepant findings (Satterfield et al., 1982; Hechtman, Weiss, and Perlman, 1984). Satterfield et al. obtained arrest records, whereas the Hechtman study relied on self-reports. Perhaps subjects lied and underreported antisocial behavior. Also, there may have been more antisocial children in the original cohort of Satterfield et al.

In their follow-up study into adulthood (mean age, 25 years; range, 21 to 33), Hechtman and Weiss (1986) found a trend for more court appearances in former patients than controls in the previous three years (18% vs. 5%, p < .09). However, most involved auto-related offenses, such as speeding, that are usually not considered antisocial activities. When antisocial acts were categorized by subsequent consequences (police involvement, no police or court involvement), probands and controls did not differ. All those who displayed antisocial behavior in adulthood had exhibited previous conduct problems earlier either in childhood, or in adolescence, at the previous follow-ups. This antisocial behavior never appeared *de novo* in adulthood. These observations are consistent with those found in studies of conduct disorder (Robins, 1966).

Psychiatric Diagnosis

Relatively little attention has been paid to the occurrence of diagnosable psychiatric illness in the long-term outcome of hyperactive children. The Montreal group reported that Antisocial disorder was the only DSM-III diagnosis that was more common to the former hyperactive group than controls at the average age of 25 (23% vs. 2.4%, respectively) (Weiss et al., 1985).

Loney and associates (Loney, Whaley-Klahn, Kosier, & Conboy, 1983) examined the prevalence of diagnoses of antisocial personality, and substance use disorders in 22 cases, and their brothers, ages 21 to 23, from rural areas of Iowa. Antisocial disorders were more prevalent in the cases than brothers (45% and 18%, respectively), but the two groups did not differ in rates of alcohol or drug use disorders.

In our follow-up study in the New York area, we found that about 30% of the cases at average age 18 (range 16 to 23) were diagnosed as having the full DSM-III ADDH syndrome versus only 3% of the controls (p < .000) (Gittelman et al., 1985). In addition, the former hyperactive youngsters had more conduct/antisocial personality disorders, and more substance use disorders.

There was no difference between the groups on any of the other diagnoses (e.g., affective or anxiety disorders). The three disorders that characterized the outcome of the probands (ADDH, conduct/antisocial, personality, and substance use disorders) overlapped greatly and aggregated in the same individuals. Those who had retained the ADDH syndrome were much more likely to go on to have antisocial disorders than those without ADDH at follow-up; moreover, substance use disorders occurred almost exclusively among those who had developed an antisocial disorder. Thus, the maintenance of the original symptoms was a critical clinical feature in the prediction of serious impairment at follow-up due to antisocial behavior and drug abuse.

The diagnostic discrepancies across the three studies are likely to be due, in part, to different interview practices. The New York study is the only one that inquired systematically about ADDH symptomatology as defined in DSM-III, whereas the Montreal and Iowa groups did not, thereby precluding formal diagnoses of ADDH. The difference in rates of substance use disorder is more problematic. In all studies, the former patients had a marked increase in Antisocial disorder, which is regularly associated with drug abuse. Therefore, it is surprising that drug use was not more prevalent in the hyperactive than control groups of the Montreal and Iowa studies. It is conceivable that the loss of half the sample in the Montreal diagnostic study led to an unusual pattern in clinical results.

C. ADJUSTMENT OF UNDIAGNOSED INDIVIDUALS

As noted above, there has been very little attention paid to psychiatric diagnosis in the study of outcome. It is only in their final report that the Montreal group used formal diagnostic assessments. In their absence, the picture generated from reports on school adjustment, and social and occupational functioning, is difficult to interpret since the dysfunctions could be accounted for entirely by cases who qualified for psychiatric diagnoses. However, the inclusion of psychiatric diagnoses does not inform as to the level of functioning in those who do not receive a diagnosis. The undiagnosed cases do not experience dysfunction severe enough to warrant a diagnosis, but they may have difficulties associated with some functional impairment.

It is possible for different models of pathology to account for the greater prevalence of mental disorder in probands than controls. If degree of functional impairment is continuous, then one possible model would place proband and control distributions of dysfunction along a continuum, with the proband distribution shifted to the right. This model predicts that undiagnosed probands, namely those below the "diagnosis threshold," will have higher rates of dysfunction than undiagnosed controls.

Another model of outcome posits that the distributions of dysfunction for probands and controls differ in shape; the distribution for probands is bimodal, but the distribution for controls is unimodal. Accordingly, the distribution of dysfunction for the controls and the left mode of the probands' distribution overlap, whereas the right mode of the probands' distribution is located to the right of the controls' distribution, above the "diagnosis threshold." This model predicts that, if diagnosed cases are removed (those above the "diagnosis threshold"), the undiagnosed probands and controls will not differ.

To examine which model applied, we compared cases from the proband and control groups who had not received a psychiatric diagnosis at follow-up. We compared the undiagnosed cases of former hyperactives and their controls at follow-up on outcome measures of school adjustment, conduct problems in and out of school, rate of substance use, and temper dyscontrol. In addition, ratings of overall adjustment were examined to determine whether overall clinical judgments of quality of adjustment differentiated the probands and controls who were not judged to have a mental disorder at follow-up (Mannuzza, Klein, Bonagura, Konig, & Shenker, 1988). Contrary to our expectations, we found no disadvantages for the probands in occupational adjustment, social functioning, temper dyscontrol, alcohol and drug use or abuse, and no group difference on a multitude of antisocial activities. The results suggest that psychiatric diagnosis had accounted for most of the behavioral deviance at follow-up.

There is an important clinical exception to the above pattern; the undiagnosed youngsters continued to be rated as having worse overall academic achievement, and worse comportment in high school. Therefore, it appears that, in adolescence, the academic setting is especially problematic for hyperactive children; it is associated with worse performance and adjustment even in those who do not meet criteria for a diagnosis.

We conclude that reports of single measures of outcome are inadequate to the task of describing eventual status, since it is likely that outcome measures that have been found to disfavor grown hyperactive children are accounted for by cases who continue to meet criteria for a clinical diagnosis. The findings indicate that the multiple dysfunctions found in grown hyperactive children are not randomly distributed across the group, but aggregate within a subgroup that is dysfunctional. It is probable that the youngsters who score poorly on cognitive tests, those who have specific school impairment, and those with significant social impairment, are the same individuals who would have been diagnosed as continuing to have ADHD if the follow-up had included diagnostic assessments.

Clinically, the findings are important since they indicate that ultimate functioning of hyperactive children is not regularly poor. There is a subgroup for whom it clearly is, but the rest can be expected to do as well as unaffected children, except with regard to the school environment. It is common nowadays to find disclaimers of the original maturational lag theory of ADHD. Yet, the view may not be altogether inaccurate. There appears to be a subgroup of hyperactive children whose adjustment normalizes with age, typically around ages 15 to 16. Until then, the functioning of the hyperactive youngsters continues to be deviant in the great majority of cases. It is difficult to project a specific rate of recovered cases. The rate we obtained (about 50% at average age 18) may be particular to our sample, and different rates of recovery might be observed in groups from different social backgrounds.

DIFFERENTIAL OUTCOME OF BOYS AND GIRLS

Studies of clinical samples as well as population surveys have shown that boys are greatly overrepresented among hyperactive children (Gittelman-Klein, Klein, Katz, Saraf, & Pollack, 1976; Lambert, Sandoval, & Sassone, 1978; Trites, Dugas, Lynch, & Ferguson, 1979; Werry, 1968). Most investigators who report on ''hyperactive'' girls have studied non-clinical groups of children (Battle & Lacey, 1972; Huessy & Cohen, 1976; Pelham & Bender, 1982; Prinz & Loney, 1974) and it is not clear whether such results are applicable to diagnosed groups.

To our knowledge, there is only one controlled prospective follow-up study of a clinical sample of hyperactive boys and girls (Mannuzza & Gittelman, 1984, in press). A complete cohort (i.e., 0% attrition) of 12 hyperactive girls was compared to 24 hyperactive and 24 normal boys matched for age and social class. At follow-up (ages 16-18), there were no significant differences between the formerly hyperactive males and females on measures of academic, behavioral, and social adjustment, in junior high school or in high school, and on rate of mental disorder. Yet, compared to normal male controls, the female probands were worse on measures of academic, behavioral, and social functioning. The use of normal males as controls for the female sample is very stringent since males are expected to display higher rates of conduct problems. The fact that the former hyperactive girls were worse than the normal males is therefore revealing of continued deviance in the girls.

In summary, the behavior and functioning of hyperactive girls and boys matched for age and social class are similar in early and late adolescence. The findings are inconsistent with genetic multiple threshold and social learning theories which predict a less favorable outcome in hyperactive girls (Mannuzza & Gittelman, 1984). Finally, the results of case-control comparisons in disfavor of hyperactive girls (as well as boys, see Gittelman et al., 1985) suggest that ADHD does not regularly ''disappear'' with age but continues to impair affected girls in a variety of settings.

CHILDHOOD PREDICTORS OF LATER OUTCOME

In view of the variability in outcome, the identification of early predictors of later functioning is of great interest. However, conclusions from reports concerning the prediction of outcome are complicated by interpretational problems.

It is known that there is often overlap between ADHD and conduct disorders. The stability of conduct disorders is also well documented. Therefore, it is important to identify the diagnostic composition of the original ADHD samples. If they included a significant proportion of conduct disorders, which are associated with other disadvantages such as family instability and pathology, the predictors identified might be related to the presence of conduct disorders, rather than to the independent influence of the predictors. The interpretation of the predictive outcome literature is complicated by uncertainty regarding the possible co-occurrence of conduct disorders in the original groups. Moreover, one of the studies (Hechtman, Weiss, Perlman, & Amsel, 1984) used statistical methods (discriminant function analysis) that require replication in independent samples. The information summarized should be viewed with these cautions in mind.

Clinical Characteristics

Loney, Kramer, and Milich (1981) found that age of onset predicted poor course, with inattention and drug use being prominent outcome features. In our study, age at referral was not related to outcome; however, age of onset and referral are not identical and it is more meaningful to examine onset as a potential contributor to course rather than age of referral, since the latter may be a reflection of opportunity for treatment rather than an indicator of severity.

Loney and her associates were the first to report a relationship between childhood aggression and poor outcome in early adulthood (Loney et al., 1981). Hechtman and associates (Hechtman, Weiss, Perlman, & Amsel, 1984) reported that aggression in childhood was predictive of poor academic standing, but not number of legal offenses, and of extent of alcohol use in early adulthood. Early aggression was unrelated to later emotional or work adjustment.

Our study used psychiatric ratings of aggressive behavior, and distinguished between impulsive, eruptive aggression reflecting poor frustration tolerance, and deliberate aggression. The two overlap: usually children with deliberate, antisocial aggression also have eruptive aggression, but the reverse is not true. Many hyperactive children lash out when frustrated, but do not also engage in deliberate fighting. The above clinical distinction was a meaningful one. Eruptive aggression, alone, did not predict later conduct disorder, but antisocial aggression did (Klein et al., unpublished data).

Another important clinical finding emerged. Nonaggressiveness in childhood, or "pure hyperactivity," did not preclude an antisocial adolescent outcome. Thus, 22% of the pure hyperactive cases had a diagnosis of conduct disorder at follow-up vs. 8% of the controls, (p = .000). Our definition of aggression differed from Loney and her colleagues' since these investigators included a broad range of conduct problems and antisocial behavior in the concept of aggression. Our standards were narrower, and included only specific aggressive behavior.

Social Factors

Social class has not been observed to be a consistent predictor of later adjustment (Weiss & Hechtman, 1986). More subtle parental characteristics have been reported to contribute to good outcome in adolescence, but a major handicap to the study of familial characteristics is the unavailability of established, satisfactory, measures.

In our sample, family stability (rated by a social worker) was significantly but weakly related to a good outcome. Loney et al. (1981) reported that poor family organization was associated with a negative outcome. However, neither study systematically excluded cases of mixed conduct disorders and hyperactivity. The presence of disrupted families correlates highly with the occurrence of childhood conduct disorders, and the association between family status and outcome may be confounded by the contribution of conduct disorders to the relationship. Our sample had been screened to exclude obvious conduct disorders, but this was not done with objective standards. It may be that family organization is not a contributing factor independently of the presence of conduct disorders in the children. The study of young adults by Hechtman, Weiss, Perlman, and Amsel (1984) found that early socioeconomic status predicted poor academic and work functioning, as well as police involvement. In addition, a number of measures reflecting quality of family interaction in childhood related to later emotional adjustment, academic performance, antisocial outcome, and drug use.

Cognitive/Neuropsychological Factors

One study reported that childhood I.Q. was negatively correlated with alcoholism, but not with drug abuse, in adulthood (Loney et al., 1981). These investigators also found that I.Q., but not academic achievement, in childhood was a predictor of antisocial behavior and of antisocial personality disorder diagnosis.

In the Canadian study (Hechtman, Weiss, Perlman, & Amsel, 1984), I.Q. was significantly related to a number of outcome measures in early adulthood, i.e., friendships, school performance, work adjustment, and legal offenses. In our sample, childhood I.Q. and achievement were not associated with diagnosis at follow-up. However, we obtained a trend for early decrements in academic test performance to be associated with the later diagnosis of ADD or antisocial personality disorder (p's = .06).

Neurological Factors

In the predictive study by Loney et al. (1981), perinatal complications were positively associated with the presence of hyperactivity in adolescence. In contrast, delinquency was negatively correlated with neurological impairment. This pattern of findings is extremely puzzling in the context of our results wherein antisocial behavior was uncommon among those who did not continue to have hyperactive symptomatology. Therefore, if both sets of results are correct, it would lead to the expectation that there are significant differences in the rate of childhood perinatal complications among those who retain ADDH but do not develop conduct disorders, and those who have both ADDH and conduct disorders (CD) at follow-up. The rate of perinatal complications should be significantly higher in the pure ADDH group than in the mixed ADDH/CD group.

Two studies have examined the relationship between childhood EEG and later outcome (Hechtman, Weiss, & Metrakos, 1978; Klein et al., unpublished data). Hechtman et al. did not find an association between childhood EEG findings and outcome at about age 20. We reanalyzed these authors' data; by combining mild and moderate EEG abnormalities, a trend between the EEG findings and outcome emerges (p = .09, two-tailed). In our larger sample, we found a significant relationship between abnormal childhood EEG and the presence of a DSM-III diagnosis at follow-up (p < .05). The association is weak, and non-contributory to individual prediction, but it is of theoretical interest. These results are consistent with other reports of EEG abnormality in adult antisocial disorders (Petersen, Matousek, Mednick, Volavka, & Pollock, 1982; Volavka, Mednick, Gabrielle, Matousek, & Pollock, 1984). The definition of abnormality in EEG's varies across studies. Atypically, our data included 14 and 6 spiking as an abnormal EEG finding. Because this is a controversial interpretation, others may not have included it; when it is omitted, we obtain no relationship between EEG and outcome.

SUMMARY

This chapter summarizes the results obtained from prospective longitudinal studies of hyperkinetic children. Several methodological limitations are noted, the most problematic consisting of relatively large attrition rates (Table 1). The adolescent status of hyperkinetic children is characterized by impaired cognitive test performance and poor scholastic achievement. However, studies in adulthood do not reveal continued cognitive disadvantage, but work functioning seems negatively affected. Consistently, a substantial proportion of hyperkinetic children retains symptoms of the original disorder, and go on to conduct and antisocial disorders. Contradictory results have been obtained with regard to drug abuse; some investigations report an excess, whereas others do not.

Psychiatric diagnosis appears to account for much of the maladjustment found in the outcome of the cases, since those undiagnosed at follow-up have not been found to have more problematic behavior than controls.

Little is known about differential natural histories in males and females, but the evidence so far appears to indicate similar outcomes in the two genders.

The major predictor of poor outcome appears to be childhood aggression; its absence reduces the likelihood of later developing antisocial disorders, but does not eliminate it. However, interpretation of these data is complicated by the lack of information regarding the possibility that some of the hyperactive children already had conduct disorders. Other predictors of outcome include social factors, I.Q., neurological findings (including EEG), but none is sturdy.

ACKNOWLEDGMENT

This chapter was supported, in part, by Public Health Service Grant MH 18579, and by Mental Health Clinic Research Center Grant MH 30906.

REFERENCES

Ackerman, P.T., Dykman, R.A., & Peters, J.E. (1977). Teenage status of hyperactive and non-hyperactive learning disabled boys. *American Journal of Orthopsychiatry, 47*, 577-596.

American Psychiatric Association. (1980). *Diagnostic and statistical manual of mental disorders* (3rd. ed.). Washington, DC: Author.

American Psychiatric Association. (1987). *Diagnostic and statistical manual of mental disorders*, (3rd ed. - rev. ed.). Washington, DC: Author.

August, G.J., Stewart, M.A., & Holmes, C.S. (1983). A four-year follow-up of hyperactive boys with and without conduct disorder. *British Journal of Psychiatry, 143*, 192-198.

Battle, E.S., & Lacey, B. (1972). A context for hyperactivity in children, over time. *Child Development, 43*, 757-773.

Blouin, A.G.A., Bornstein, R.A., & Trites, R.L. (1978). Teenage alcohol use among hyperactive children: A five year follow-up study. *Journal of Pediatric Psychology, 3*, 188-194.

Borland, B.L., & Heckman, H.K. (1976). Hyperactive boys and their brothers: A 25-year follow-up study. *Archives of General Psychiatry, 33*, 669-675.

Brown, R.T., & Borden, K.A. (1986). Hyperactivity at adolescence: Some misconceptions and new directions. *Journal of Clinical Child Psychology, 15*, 194-209.

Butter, H.J. (1977). Attention, sensory reception, and autonomic reactivity of hyperkinetic adolescents: A follow-up study. *The Psychiatric Journal of the University of Ottawa, 2*, 103-111.

Charles, L., & Schain, R. (1981). A four-year follow-up study of the effects of methylphenidate on the behavior and academic achievement of hyperactive children. *Journal of Abnormal Child Psychology, 9*, 495-505.

Cohen, N.J., Weiss, G., & Minde, K. (1972). Cognitive styles in adolescents previously diagnosed as hyperactive. *Journal of Child Psychology and Psychiatry, 13*, 203-209.

Cohen, P., O'Connor, P., Lewis, S., Puig-Antich, J., & Malachowski, B. (1984, October). *A comparison of lay and clinician administered psychiatric diagnostic interviews of an epidemiological sample of children.* Paper presented at the Annual Meeting of the American Academy of Child Psychiatry, Toronto.

Cox, A., Rutter, M., Yule, B., Y Quinton, D. (1977). Bias resulting from missing information: Some epidemiological findings. *British Journal of Preventive and Social Medicine, 31*, 131-136.

Dykman, R.A., & Ackerman, P. (1980). Long-term follow-up studies of hyperactive children. *Advances in Behavioral Pediatrics, 1*, 97-128.

Gittelman, R., & Mannuzza, S. (1985). Diagnosing ADDH in adolescents. *Psychopharmacology Bulletin, 21*, 237-242.

Gittelman, R., Mannuzza, S., Shenker, R., & Bonagura, N. (1985). Hyperactive boys almost grown up: I. Psychiatric status. *Archives of General Psychiatry, 42*, 937-947.

Gittelman-Klein, R., Klein, D.F., Katz, S., Saraf, K., & Pollack, E. (1976). Comparative effects of methylphenidate and thioridazine in hyperkinetic children: I. Clinical results. *Archives of General Psychiatry, 33*, 1217-1231.

Gomez, R.L., Janowsky, D., Zetin, M., Huey, L., & Clopton, P.L. (1981). Adult psychiatric diagnosis and symptoms compatible with the hyperactive child syndrome: A retrospective study. *Journal of Clinical Psychiatry, 42*, 389-394.

Hechtman, L., & Weiss, G. (1986). Controlled prospective fifteen year follow-up of hyperactives as adults: Non-medical drug and alcohol use and anti-social behavior. *Canadian Journal of Psychiatry, 31*, 557-567.

Hechtman, L., Weiss, G., & Metrakos, K. (1978). Hyperactive individuals as young adults: Current and longitudinal electroencephalographic evaluation and its relation to outcome. *Canadian Medical Association Journal, 118*, 919-923.

Hechtman, L., Weiss, G., & Perlman, T. (1980). Hyperactives as young adults: Self-esteem and social skills. *Canadian Journal of Psychiatry, 25*, 478-483.

Hechtman, L., Weiss, G., & Perlman, T. (1984). Hyperactives as young adults: Past and current substance abuse and antisocial behavior. *American Journal of Orthopsychiatry, 54*, 415-425.

Hechtman, L., Weiss, G., Perlman, T., & Amsel, R. (1984). Hyperactives as young adults: Initial predictors of adult outcome. *Journal of the American Academy of Child Psychiatry, 23*, 250-260.

Hechtman, L., Weiss, G., Perlman, T., Hopkins, J., & Wener, A. (1981). Hyperactives as young adults: Prospective ten-year follow-up. In K.D. Gadow & J. Loney (Eds.), *Psychosocial aspects of drug treatment for hyperactivity* (pp. 417- 442). Boulder, Colorado: Westview Press.

Herjanic, B., & Reich. W. (1982). Development of a structured psychiatric interview for children: Agreement between child and parent on individual symptoms. *Journal of Abnormal Child Psychology, 10*, 307-324.

Hopkins, J., Perlman, T., Hechtman, L., & Weiss, G. (1979). Cognitive style in adults originally diagnosed as hyperactives. *Journal of Child Psychology and Psychiatry, 20*, 209-216.

Hoy, E., Weiss, G., Minde, K., & Cohen, N. (1978). The hyperactive child at adolescence: Cognitive, emotional, and social functioning. *Journal of Abnormal Child Psychology, 6*, 311-324.

Huessy, H.R., & Cohen, A.H. (1976). Hyperkinetic behaviors and learning disabilities followed over seven years. *Pediatrics, 57*, 4-10.

Huessy, H., Metoyer, M., & Townsend, M. (1973). Eight-ten year follow-up of children treated in rural Vermont for behavioral disorder. *American Journal of Orthopsychiatry, 43*, 236-238.

Huessy, H.R., Metoyer, M., & Townsend, M. (1974). 8-10 year follow-up of 84 children treated for behavioral disorder in rural Vermont. *Acta Paedo-Psychiatrica, 40*, 1-6.

Kashani, J.H., Orvaschel, H., Burk, J.P., & Reid, J.C. (1985). Informant variance: The issue of parent-child disagreement. *Journal of the American Academy of Child Psychiatry, 24*, 413-428.

Lambert, N.M., Sandoval, J., & Sassone, D. (1978). Prevalence of hyperactivity in elementary school children as a function of social system definers. *American Journal of Orthopsychiatry, 48*, 446-463.

Laufer, M.W. (1971). Long-term management and some follow-up findings on the use of drugs with minimal cerebral syndromes. *Journal of Learning Disabilities, 4*, 519-522.

Loney, J., Kramer, J., & Milich, R. (1981). The hyperkinetic child grows up: Predictors of symptoms, delinquency and achievement at follow-up. In K. Gadow & J. Loney (Eds.), *Psychosocial aspects of drug treatment for hyperactivity* (pp. 381-415). Boulder, Colorado: Westview Press.

Loney, J., Whaley-Klahn, M.A., Kosier, T., & Conboy, J. (1983). Hyperactive boys and their brothers at 21: Predictors of aggressive and antisocial outcomes. In K.T. Van Dusen & S.A. Mednick (Eds.), *Prospective studies of crime and delinquency* (pp. 181-206). Boston: Kluwer-Nijhoff Publishers.

Mannuzza, S., & Gittelman, R. (1984). The adolescent outcome of hyperactive girls. *Psychiatry Research, 13*, 19-29.

Mannuzza, S., & Gittelman, R. (1986). Informant variance in the diagnostic assessment of hyperactive children as young adults. In J.E. Barrett & R.M. Rose (Eds.), *Mental disorders in the community* (pp. 243-254). New York: Guilford Press.

Mannuzza, S., & Gittelman, R. (in press). Childhood characteristics and adolescent outcome of hyperactive girls and boys. In K.R. Merikangas (Ed.), *Psychopathology in Women: Risk Factors in Course*.

Mannuzza, S., Klein, R.G., Bonagura, N., Konig, P.H., & Shenker, R. (1988). Hyperactive boys almost grown up: II. Status of subjects without a mental disorder. *Archives of General Psychiatry, 45*, 13-18.

Mendelson, W., Johnson, N., & Stewart, M.A. (1971). Hyperactive children as teenagers: A follow-up study. *Journal of Nervous and Mental Disease, 153*, 273- 279.

Menkes, M.M., Rowe, J.S., & Menkes, J.H. (1967). A twenty-five year follow-up study on the hyperkinetic child with minimal brain dysfunction. *Pediatrics, 39*, 393-399.

Minde, K., Weiss, G., & Mendelson, N. (1972). A 5-year follow-up study of 91 hyperactive school children. *Journal of the American Academy of Child Psychiatry, 11*, 595-619.

Morrison, J.R. (1979). Diagnosis of adult psychiatric patients with childhood hyperactivity. *American Journal of Psychiatry, 136*, 955-958.

Morrison, J.R. (1980). Childhood hyperactivity in an adult psychiatric population: Social factors. *Journal of Clinical Psychiatry, 41*, 40-43.

Nicol, A.R. (1985). *Longitudinal studies in child psychology and psychiatry.* New York: John Wiley.

Pelham, W.E., & Bender, M.E. (1982). Peer relationships in hyperactive children: Description and treatment. In K.D. Gadow & I. Bialer (Eds.), *Advances in learning and behavioral disabilities* (Vol. 1, pp. 365-436). New York: JAI Press.

Petersen, K.G.I., Matousek, M., Mednick, S.A., Volavka, J., & Pollock, V. (1982). EEG antecedents of thievery. *Acta Psychiatrica Scandinavica, 65*, 331- 338.

Piacentini, J., Mannuzza, S., & Klein, R.G. (1987, August). *Cognitive functioning of young adult males previously diagnosed as hyperactive.* Paper presented at the annual meeting of the American Psychological Association, New York City.

Prinz, R., & Loney, J. (1974). Teacher-rated hyperactive elementary school girls. *Child Psychiatry and Human Development, 4*, 246-257.

Riddle, K.D., & Rapoport, J.L. (1976). A 2-year follow-up of 72 hyperactive boys. *Journal of Nervous and Mental Disease, 162*, 126-134.

Robins, L.N. (1966). *Deviant children grown-up.* Baltimore. Williams & Wilkins

Satterfield, J.H., Hoppe, C.M., & Schell, A.M. (1982). A prospective study of delinquency in 110 adolescent boys with attention deficit disorder and 88 normal adolescent boys. *American Journal of Psychiatry, 139*, 795-798.

Stewart, M.A., Mendelson, W.B., & Johnson, N.E. (1973). Hyperactive children as adolescents: How they describe themselves. *Child Psychiatry and Human Development, 4*, 3-11.

Thorley, G. (1984). Review of follow-up and follow-back studies of childhood hyperactivity. *Psychological Bulletin, 96*, 116-132.

Trites, R.L., Dugas, E., Lynch, G., & Ferguson, H.B. (1979). Prevalence of hyperactivity. *Journal of Pediatric Psychology, 4*, 179-188.

Volavka, J., Mednick, S.A., Gabrielle, W.F., Matousck, M., & Pollock, V.E. (1984). EEG and crime: Evidence from longitudinal perspective studies. *Advances in Biological Psychiatry, 15*, 97-101.

Weiss, G. (1985). Follow-up studies on outcome of hyperactive children. *Psychopharmacology Bulletin, 21*, 169-177.

Weiss, G., & Hechtman, L.T. (1986). *Hyperactive children grown-up.* New York: Guilford Press.

Weiss, G., Hechtman, L., Milroy, T., & Perlman, T. (1985). Psychiatric status of hyperactives as adults: A controlled prospective 15-year follow-up of 63 hyperactive children. *Journal of the American Academy of Child Psychiatry, 24*, 211-220.

Weiss, G., Hechtman, L, & Perlman, T. (1978). Hyperactives as young adults: School, employer and self-rating scales obtained during 10-year follow-up evaluation. *American Journal of Orthopsychiatry, 48*, 438-445.

Weiss, G., Hechtman, L., Perlman, T., Hopkins, J., & Wener, A. (1979). Hyperactives as young adults: A controlled prospective ten-year follow-up of 75 children. *Archives of General Psychiatry, 36*, 675-681.

Weiss, G., Minde, K., Werry, J.S., Douglas, V., & Nemeth, E. (1971). Studies on the hyperactive child: VIII. Five-year follow-up. *Archives of General Psychiatry, 24*, 409-414.

Werry, J.S. (1968). Developmental hyperactivity. *Pediatric Clinics of North America, 15*, 581-599.

White, J., Barratt, E., & Adams, P. (1979). The hyperactive child in adolescence: A comparative study of physiological and behavioral patterns. *Journal of the American Academy of Child Psychiatry, 18*, 154-168.

Zambelli, A.J., Stamm, J.S., Maitinsky, S., & Loiselle, D.L. (1977). Auditory evoked potentials and selective attention in formerly hyperactive adolescent boys. *American Journal of Psychiatry, 134*, 742-747.

Six-Year-Old Children with Perceptual, Motor, and Attentional Deficits: Outcome in the 6-Year Perspective

Christopher Gillberg, M.D.
I. Carina Gillberg, M.D.
Department of Child and Adolescent Psychiatry
University of Göteborg, Sweden

INTRODUCTION

The long-term outcome for children diagnosed as suffering from Attention Deficit Disorder (ADD), Hyperactivity and so called Minimal Brain Dysfunction (MBD) syndromes has not been well documented, despite the considerable investment that has gone into writing and saying something about it. Only a very limited number of papers have been published which have anything at all substantial to say about the natural outcome for such children (Blouin et al., 1978; Dykman & Ackerman, 1980; Feldman et al., 1979; Huessy, 1967; Huessy et al., 1972; Kohler et al., 1979; Laufer, 1971; Laufer & Denhoff, 1957; Mendelson et al., 1971; Menkes et al., 1967; Milich & Loney, 1979; Minde et al., 1972; O'Neal & Robins, 1958; Riddle & Rapoport, 1976; Ross & Ross, 1982; Shelley & Riester, 1972; Weiss et al., 1971; White et al., 1979; Wood et al., 1976). These studies (cited in these articles) differ with regard to subjects, treatment given, follow-up methods and whether or not outcome was assessed retrospectively or on the basis of prospective longitudinal studies. It should be no surprise, therefore, that conclusions vary from one extreme to the other, viz., that children with Deficits in Attention, Motor control and Perception (henceforth referred to as DAMP) have a poor prognosis (Menkes et al., 1967) to that, given time, they will mature and grow out of severe problems almost without fail (Laufer & Denhoff, 1957).

In this chapter we present briefly the outcome results in the rather short-term perspective from pre-school age to the early teens in groups of children with and without DAMP. The details have been or are being published in a series of papers

(Gillberg, 1985; 1987; Gillberg & Gillberg, 1983, Gillberg et al., 1983b; Gillberg & Gillberg, 1987a, 1987b; Gillberg et al., 1987) the major findings of which are summarized here.

METHOD

Subjects

Seventy-two percent of the entire Göteborg population of six-year-olds (n = 5114) were screened by their pre-school teachers in 1977 using a 34-item questionnaire pertaining to areas of fine motor functions, gross motor functions, perception, speech and language, attention and overall behaviour (Figure 1). Factor analysis by varimax rotation was performed. This analysis formed the basis for selecting groups of children with the combination of attention deficit signs and motor perception dysfunction and children without such signs.

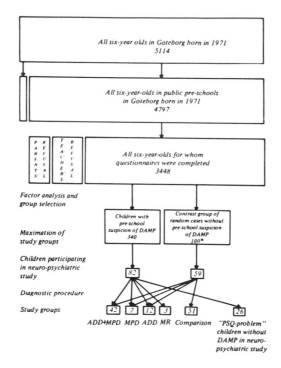

* 8 cases in random contrast group of 100 were found in the "PSQ-problem" group of 340 as well. These cases were excluded from the contrast group, leaving 92 for further selection.

FIG. 1.   Screening for MBD in public pre-schools of Göteborg

Altogether 340 (c.10%) of all the children showed that combination of problems according to their teachers. One hundred random children out of that group and one hundred random children from the remaining group without the combination of problems referred to were selected for further study. After setting the maximum number of cases to 140 (financial limitations) and after some attrition (15-22) there were 82 index and 59 comparison cases left. These were then examined blind as to the pre-school evaluation by two child psychiatrists (home visits), a child neurologist, a physiotherapist, and a child psychologist.

Comprehensive neurodevelopmental diagnoses were made on the basis of neurological and psychological assessments and psychiatric diagnoses were formulated without knowledge of these.

Study groups—neurodevelopmental diagnoses

The following groups were formed

(1) *ADD* (Attention Deficit Disorder); (n = 12, 10 boys and 2 girls) in children showing cross situational signs of attention deficit *but no* motor-perception dysfunction.

(2) *MPD* (Motor Perception Dysfunction); (n = 7, 4 boys and 3 girls) in children showing signs of motor-perception dysfunction (scores exceeding the mean +2 standard deviations (SDs) of the original comparison group) *but no signs* of ADD.

(3) *ADD + MPD* (n = 42, 33 boys and 9 girls) in children showing *concomitant* ADD and MPD.

None of the children in groups (1)-(3) had cerebral palsy or IQ <70.

(4) *MR* (Mental Retardation); (n = 3, all boys) who fulfilled clinical and psychometric criteria for mental retardation.

(5) *Comparison group*; (n = 51, 27 boys and 24 girls) who constituted the original Comparison group of 59 children less those who showed ADD, MPD or MR.

(6) *'PSQ-problem/NPS-healthy' group*; (n = 26, 21 boys and 5 girls) i.e., those children receiving high dysfunction scores according to the pre-school questionnaire (PSQ) but who were said to be without problems at the neuropsychiatric examination (NPS).

Generalized hyperkinesis (n = 18, 13 boys and 5 girls) was diagnosed in cases recruited from any of the above groups if they showed hyperkinetic symptoms in 3 out of 3 possible examinations. A majority of these cases also belonged in groups (1) and (2)(Gillberg et al., 1983).

In Table 1, some of the epidemiological data from the diagnostic study at age 7 years are presented. It needs emphasizing that ADD, MPD and generalized

TABLE 1
Prevalence data relating to original DAMP diagnostic study
at age 6-7 years

	Prevalence /Ratio
Population frequency	
ADD + MPD total	7.1%
severe cases	1.2%
Boy:girl ratio ADD + MPD (population corrected)	2.3:1
severe cases	10.5:1
Marked psychiatric abnormality	
ADD + MPD total	69%
severe cases	79%
Comparison group blindly examined	10%
Generalized hyperkinesis regardless of concomitant motor-perception dysfunction or not (population rate)	0.9-3.6%

hyperkinesis were considered neurodevelopmental rather than psychiatric diagnoses. Subcategories within the main category of marked psychiatric abnormality were used. Very briefly, autistic features (i.e. stereotypies, ritualistic behaviour, language problems reminiscent of those seen in autism and severely disturbed peer relations) and depressive symptoms were fairly common, especially in the severe cases, whereas conduct problems occurred in a substantial minority of the mild-moderate cases (Gillberg, 1983; Gillberg & Rasmussen, 1982a; Gillberg & Rasmussen, 1982b; Gillberg et al., 1982; Gillberg et al., 1983a).

Methods used

A range of different evaluation tools were used in the study of the children. In the original neuropsychiatric diagnostic study at age 7 years, all children were subjected to an extremely thorough examination including the taking of a medical and developmental history encompassing more than 1000 items. Two major follow-up examinations were then performed at the ages of 10 and 13 years. At all three ages (a) attentional, (b) psychiatric/behavioural, (c) perceptual/school achievement, and (d) neurological/developmental items were included in the follow-up assessments.

(a) *Attentional Assessment*

Attention variables were studied in accordance with structured manuals at all three ages. The details are presented in Gillberg (1987).

b) *Psychiatric/behavioural assessment*

At age 7 years, 2 psychiatrists made home visits and interviewed mother and child separately for about 2 hrs. 'Marked psychiatric abnormality' was diagnosed in cases with a long-standing psychic problem causing handicap to the child or his environment.

At age 10 and 13 years, a number of self-report and parent and teacher-questionnaires were used; the Birleson depression inventory (1980), the Conners teacher scale (1969), and the Rutter teacher (1970) and parent (1967) scales. 'Definite behavioural abnormality' was diagnosed in cases scoring above the mean plus 2 standard deviations of the comparison group for any composite or sub-score on any of the four scales. Finally, a child psychiatrist made a clinical interview in an out-patient setting at age 10 and 13 years.

(c) *Perceptual/school achievement evaluation*

'Perceptual dysfunction' at age 7 years was diagnosed on the basis of results obtained at testing with the SCSIT (Southern California Sensory Integration Tests) (Ayres, 1972). At ages 10 and 13 years, a special teacher questionnaire designed to tap achievement problems in various school subjects was used (Gillberg et al., 1983). 'Obvious school achievement problems' was the diagnostic term used in children showing either severe reading/writing difficulties according to the teacher, or who had been awarded the lowest mean mark for reading/writing and spelling on a 5-point scale, or who had failed at least one grade of primary school because of achievement problems.

(d) *Neurological/developmental assessment*

Modified versions of the Touwen (1979) neurodevelopmental examination method were used in all 3 studies. 'Minor Neurological Dysfunction' (MND) was diagnosed in cases showing composite abnormality scores surpassing the mean +2 standard deviations of the comparison group (Rasmusen et al., 1983).

Finally, the Swedish national registers reporting on hospital treatment were searched in order to identify all children in the study who, before age 13 years had been admitted as in-patients, either for physical or psychiatric disorders. Also, the local registers of all relevant Child Guidance and Child Psychiatric Clinic registers were searched in order to trace all cases who, before that age had applied for out-patient help.

Statistical methods

For univariate analyses, Fisher's non-parametric permutation test was mostly used. Chi-square tests (with Yates' correction whenever appropriate) were applied to some contingency tables. The one-sample-case method was used for comparing intraindividual scores at different ages.

RESULTS

The major results are shown in Figures 2-6. Boys and girls within the study group usually showed similar results and so group frequencies for the two sexes are presented together.

The ADD + MPD group (Figures 2 and 3) by definition had motor control and attention problems in 100% of the cases at age 7 years. In this group motor control problems dropped to 55% at age 10 years and to 30% at age 13 years ($p < .01$, and $p < .05$ when compared with "previous" age). Attention problems also subsided in many cases, whereas behavioural and school achievement problems persisted in two thirds or more of the cases throughout the follow-up period. Cases with severe problems in the original study had much higher rates of dysfunction at follow-up than did those who had shown mild-moderate difficulties at age 7 years. The differences between the ADD + MPD group and the Comparison group were all statistically significant at or below the .1% level.

Cases with only ADD (Figure 4) or only MPD (Figure 5) had a much better outcome in all respects and the Comparison group (Figure 6) had rates less than 10% for all variables studied except behavioural abnormality.

Generalized hyperkinesis (regardless of concurrence of DAMP or not) persisted at age 10 years in 73% of cases with this diagnosis at age 7 years and in 40% of cases at age 13 years. Conduct problems had been prevalent at age 7 years in this group, but tended to subside markedly over the years.

DISCUSSION

This intermediate-term follow-up study of children diagnosed in the early latency years as suffering from DAMP is probably the first-ever population-based controlled prospective natural outcome study in the field. Most previous studies have either examined the outcome for stimulant-treated children, or have not made use of a Comparison group or have been of a retrospective nature. Therefore, the results cannot be readily compared with those from previous investigations.

Also, other authors have usually focused on children described as 'hyperactive' who may or may not have shown concomitant motor-perceptual problems, whereas this research has been geared to studying children with a combination of attentional and motor-perceptual problems. In the light of recent developments in classification, this presents a problem. However, when the study was started in the mid 1970s, the clinical concept of a syndrome defined on the basis of both attention deficit and motor-perceptual problems was very common in the Scandinavian countries and this influenced the original design of the study.

One of the major advantages of our study is that the groups of children followed have been drawn from the general population on the basis of screening examinations. A disadvantage is the relatively small number of children actually

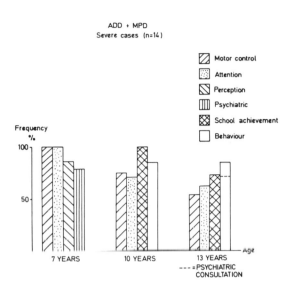

FIG. 2.   Rates of abnormalities at age 7, 10, and 13 years. ADD + MPD. Severe cases.

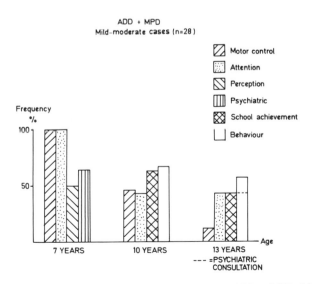

FIG. 3.   Rates of abnormalities at age 7, 10, and 13 years. ADD + MPD. Mild-moderate cases.

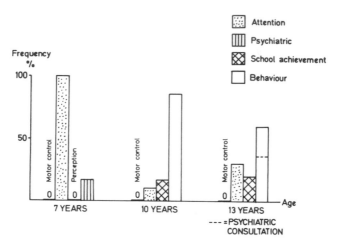

FIG. 4. Rates of abnormalities at age 7, 10, and 13 years. ADD.

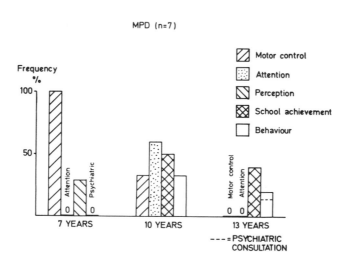

FIG. 5. Rates of abnormalities at age 7, 10, and 13 years. MPD.

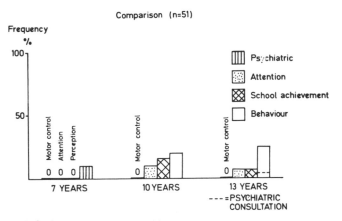

FIG. 6.   Rates of abnormalities at age 7, 10, and 13 years. Comparison

included in each study group. Therefore, in spite of the groups probably being representative, generalized conclusions cannot be drawn.

Our studies have not contributed to diagnostic issues in the field, but our ADD + MPD group is similar to the currently delineated hyperkinetic syndrome group (Taylor, 1986).

The results do allow for some well-founded speculation. It appears that motor control problems in children with DAMP have a fair prognosis in the six-year period from age 7 to 13 years, although some doubt remains because more subtle handicaps representing persistent problems may not have been detected by the measures we used. In the fields of perceptual functions and school achievement, outcome is nothing near so favourable, and behavioural problems seem to be extremely prevalent throughout the latency years.

The results might be taken to indicate that some of the more 'neurological-type' problems have a relatively good prognosis, whereas the 'psychiatric-type' problems increase in frequency or remain at extremely high rates in children diagnosed at age 7 years as suffering from the combination of ADD and MPD. This, in turn might be interpreted in at least two rather different ways. First, one might posit that the results mirror the course of a developmental disorder with varying biological manifestations at different ages, the neurological and psychiatric problems representing but various aspects of the same underlying biological dysfunction. The other possibility would be that the neurological problems are at the root of the disorder and that school achievement and behavioural consequences are seen as secondary phenomena. The latter perspective would suggest that intervention strategies aimed at increasing the awareness in the child and others of the nature of the basic handicap condition might help to prevent the development of behaviour problems.

To sum up, this study has shown the latency age development of children who showed DAMP in pre-school to be markedly different from that of children without such deficits. Normal development during this phase is highlighted by intellectual consolidation, acquisition of important academic skills, gradual sophistication in the control of body movements, relative behavioural stability and positive growth of self-confidence.

Children with DAMP instead have problems in all these fields during the period up to the early teens. Low self-esteem might turn out to be one of the most important consequences. To what extent such a consequence will be carried forward into adolescence and adult life, can only be borne out by further follow-up. The children in this research are currently being examined at age 16 years, one of the aims being to shed some light on this issue.

REFERENCES

Ayres, A.J. (1972). *Southern California sensory integration tests*. Los Angeles: Western Psychological Services.

Birleson, P. (1981). The validity of depressive disorder in childhood and the development of a self-rating scale: A research report. *Journal of Child Psychology and Psychiatry, 22*, 73-88.

Blouin, A., Bornstein, R., & Trites, R. (1978). Teenage alcohol use among hyperactive children: A 5-year follow-up study. *Journal of Pediatric Psychology, 3*, 188-194.

Conners, C.K. (1969). A teacher rating scale for use in drug studies with children. *American Journal of Psychiatry, 126*, 884–888.

Dykman, R., & Ackerman, P. (1980). Long-term follow-up studies of hyperactive children. In B.W. Campbell, (Ed.), *Advances in behavioural pediatrics, Vol. 1*. Greenwich, Connecticut: JAI Press. ticut: JAI Press.

Feldman, S., Denhoff, E. & Denhoff, J. (1979). The attention disorders and related syndromes: Outcome in adolescence and young adult life. In E. Denhoff & L. Stern (Eds.), *Minimal brain dysfunction: A development approach*. New York: Masson.

Gillberg, C. (1983). Perceptual, motor and attentional deficits in Swedish primary school-children. Some child psychiatric aspects. *Journal of Child Psychology and Psychiatry, 24*, 377-403.

Gillberg, C., & Rasmussen, P. (l982a). Perceptual, motor and attentional deficits in six-year-old children. Screening procedure in pre-school. *Acta Paediatrica Scandinavica, 71*, 121-129.

Gillberg, C., & Rasmussen, P. (1982b). Perceptual, motor and attentional deficits in seven-year-old children. Background factors. *Developmental Medicine and Child Neurology, 24*, 752-770.

Gillberg, C., Rasmussen, P., Carlstrom G., Svenson, B., & Waldenström, E. (1982). Perceptual, motor and attentional deficits in six-year-old children. Epidemiological aspects. *Journal of Child Psychology and Psychiatry, 23*, 131-144.

Gillberg, C., Carlström, G. & Rasmussen, P. (1983a). Hyperkinetic disorders in seven-year-old children with perceptual, motor and attentional deficits. *Journal of Child Psychology and Psychiatry, 24*, 233-246.

Gillberg, I.C. (1985). Children with minor neurodevelopmental disorders. III. Neurological and neurodevelopmental problems at age 10. *Developmental Medicine and Child Neurology, 27*, 3-16.

Gillberg, I.C. (1987). Six-year follow-up of seven-year-old children with minor neurodevelopmental disorders. Behavioural outcome. *Develomental Medicine and Child Neurology*. Submitted for publication.

Gillberg, I.C., & Gillberg, C. (1983). Three-year follow-up at age 10 of children with minor neurodevelopmental disorders. I. Behavioural problems. *Developmental Medicine and Child Neurology, 25*, 438-449.

Gillberg, I.C., Gillberg, C., & Rasmussen, P. (1983b). Three-year follow-up at age 10 of children with minor neurodevelopmental disorders. II. School achievement problems. *Developmental Medicine and Child Neurology, 25*, 566-573.

Gillberg, I.C., & Gillberg, C. (1987a). Six-year follow-up at age 13 of children with minor neurodevelopmental disorders. School achievement outcome. *Developmental Medicine and Child Neurology.* Submitted for publication.

Gillberg, I.C., & Gillberg, C.(1987b). Generalized hyperkinesis: Follow-up from age seven to thirteen years. *Journal of the American Academy of Child Psychiatry.* Submitted for publication.

Gillberg, I.C., Gillberg, C., & Groth, J. (1987). Children who had 'DAMP' (Deficits in Attention, Motor control and Perception) at age 7. Neurological and neurodevelopmental profile at age 13. *Developmental Medicine and Child Neurology.* Submitted for publication.

Huessy, H. (1967). Study of the prevalence and therapy of the choreatiform syndrome or hyperkinesis in rural Vermont. *Acta Paedopsychiatrica, 37,* 194-199.

Huessy, H., Marshall, C., & Gendron, R. (1972). Five hundred children followed from grade 2 through grade 5 for the prevalence of behaviour disorder. *Acta Paedopsychiatrica, 39,* 301-309.

Köhler, E.M., Köhler, L., & Regefalk, C. (1979). Minimal Brain Dysfunction in pre-school age - risk for trouble in school? *Paediatrician, 8,* 219-227.

Laufer, M. (1971). Long-term management and some follow-up findings on the use of drugs with minimal cerebral syndromes. *Journal of Learning Disabilities, 4,* 55-58.

Laufer, M., & Denhoff, E. (1957). Hyperkinetic behaviour syndrome in children. *Journal of Pediatrics, 50,* 463-475.

Mendelson, W., Johnson, H., & Stewart, M. (1971). Hyperactive children as teen-agers: A follow-up study. *Journal of Nervous and Mental Disease, 153,* 273-379.

Menkes, M., Rowe, J., & Menkes, J. (1967). A 25-year follow-up study on the hyperkinetic child with minimal brain dysfunction. *Paediatrics, 39,* 393-399.

Milich, R., & Loney, J. (1979). The role of hyperactive and aggressive symptomatology in predicting adolescent outcome in hyperactive children. *Journal of Paediatric Psychology, 4,* 93-112.

Minde, K., Levin, D., Weiss, G., & Mendelson, N. (1972). A five-year follow-up study of 91 hyperactive school children. *Journal of the American Academy of Child Psychiatry, 11,* 595-610.

O'Neal, P., & Robins, L. (1958). The relation of childhood behaviour problems to adult psychiatric status. *American Journal of Psychiatry, 114,* 961-969.

Rasmussen, P., Gillberg, C., Waldenström, E., & Svenson, B. (1983). Perceptual, motor and attentional deficits in seven-year-old children. Neurological and neurodevelopmental aspects. *Developmental Medicine and Child Neurology, 25,* 315-333.

Riddle, K., & Rapoport, J.L. (1976). A two-year follow-up of 72 hyperactive boys. *Journal of Nervous and Mental Disease, 162,* 126-234.

Ross, D.M., & Ross, S.A. (1982). *Hyperactivity: Theory, research, and action* (2nd ed.) New York: Wiley.

Rutter, M. (1967). A children's behaviour questionnaire for completion by teachers: Preliminary findings. *Journal of Child Psychology and Psychiatry, 8,* 1-11.

Rutter, M., Graham, P., & Yule, W. (1970). A neuropsychiatric study in childhood. *Clinics in Developmental Medicine, Nos 35/36.* London: SIMP with Heinemann Medical.

Shelley, E., & Riester, A. (1972). Syndrome of minimal brain damage in young adults. *Diseases of the Nervous System, 33,* 335-338.

Taylor, E.A. (Ed.) (1986). *The overactive child.* Clinics in Developmental Medicine, No. 97. Oxford and Philadelphia: SIMP.

Touwen, B.C. (1979). *Examination of the child with minor neurological dysfunction.* Clinics in Developmental Medicine, No 71., London: SIMP with Heinemann Medical.

Weiss, G., Minde, K., Werry, J., Douglas, V., & Nemeth, E. (1971). Studies of the hyperactive child - VIII. Five-year follow-up. *Archives of General Psychiatry, 21,* 409-414.

White, J., Barrat, E., & Adams, P. (1979). The hyperactive child in adolescence: A comparative study of physiological and behavioural patterns. *Journal of the American Academy of Child Psychiatry, 18,* 154-159.

Wood, D., Reimherr, F., Wender, P., & Johnson, G. (1976). Diagnosis and treatment of minimal brain dysfunction in adults. *Archives of General Psychiatry, 33,* 1453-1460.

Cerebral Processes Underlying Neuropsychological and Neuromotor Impairment in Children with ADD/MBD

H.M. Borchgrevink, MD BA
Laboratory of Audiology
Ulleval Hospital
University of Oslo, Norway

INTRODUCTION

Attention Deficit Disorder (ADD), hyperkinetic syndrome (ADDH) and Minimal Brain Dysfunction (MBD) refer to children with deviant behaviour characterized by impaired or fluctuating attention and concentration; increased distractibility, impulsivity, aggression; and, restless motor or mental activity - most often accompanied by slight motor, memory, and speech/language impairment. The constellation, predominance, severity, and pervasiveness of these symptoms may vary (see for example Gillberg, Rasmussen, Carlström, Svenson, & Waldenström, 1982; Shaywitz & Shaywitz, this volume).

Corresponding symptoms are frequently associated with slight encephalopathy in general, e.g., in patients surviving meningococcal disease (Borchgrevink, Aanonsen & Gedde-Dahl, paper presented at the EBBS Workshop on Attention Deficit Disorder and Hyperkinetic Syndrome, Oslo, 1987). However, as many of these symptoms are characteristic of the young normal child, and also may be found to some extent in otherwise "normal" adolescents and adults, there is obviously a continuum towards normal behaviour with abating degree of symptoms. Consequently, to select the individuals who need special care or training, the diagnostic approach must be based partly on knowledge of cerebral processing and characteristic manifestations of minor brain pathology—and partly on definite, age-related criteria for symptoms that should be considered pathological; that is, symptoms which represent a significant deviation from normal development and behaviour.

Diagnosis of organic etiology must be considered crucial for choice of optimal therapeutic intervention. In an organic *sensory* disorder (e.g., deafness, or blindness), *compensatory stimulation* via the best intact perceptual channels combined with compensatory modes of expression/response is generally considered the best and only accepted pedagogical strategy. The same should logically be true in case of organic brain damage. For example, the perception of a given stimulus will be impaired regardless of whether stimulus analysis fails at the sensory level or at some higher level of stimulus processing. However, in case of perception and expression disorders, specific training of the impaired function is the rule, e.g. in speech/language disorder or in motor dysfunction, even though the effect of training may well be questioned (e.g., Taylor-Sarno, 1980; Hallahan & Cruickshank, 1973). The logical as well as the empirical basis for this change of training strategy is puzzling. If environmental stimulation was the only factor of influence, increased adequate stimulation should always lead to improved development, learning or skill. Children with delayed or deviant function/behaviour would then be expected to catch up with, and pass, the performance level of normal children due to the additional training given. Empirically this is not the case (Hallahan & Cruickshank, 1973). Besides, if the function of a child does develop during training, this will not necessarily imply that the ongoing stimulation is effective. The improvement of function may, e.g., reflect the rate of cerebral maturation (see below). Thus, to prove efficient, stimulation should induce a significant change in the rate of development. Gradual development at pre-stimulation rate during training rather indicates that training has no effect, or is redundant, which logically should lead to reconsideration of the strategy applied.

Brain damage characteristically leads to loss of, e.g., specific language functions (Benson & Geschwind, 1976) with subsequent permanent impairment and failure to show normal response to training, in adults (Taylor-Sarno, 1980) as well as in children (St. James Roberts, 1979). The clinical evidence thus clearly demonstrates that brain damage tends to be permanent and lead to permanent impairment of function, even though the effects may vary somewhat with localization, age onset and severity of the disease (Woods & Carey, 1979). The existence of reports claiming that children may fail to show functional impairment (some years) after confirmed brain damage (emphasised by Rutter, 1984a) may well be expected, and does neither exclude organic cerebral damage in the reported cases, nor weaken the relevance of a neuropsychological approach in observed functional impairment. The damaged area may for instance not be essential for the control of functions examined. Or, the symptoms of brain damage may not be recognised due to poor sensitivity and specificity of the clinical examination applied. In children, the symptoms may also be concealed (even though the damage is not necessarily healed) by functional improvement in the course of childhood cerebral maturation (see Gillberg et al., 1982; Gillberg, this volume). In rare cases, normal function may even be due to shift of cerebral lateralisation; e.g. right hemisphere speech perception and production in a right-handed boy with left temporal lobe agenesy (Borchgrevink, 1982). The few patients who show unexpected right hemisphere control of speech in spite of long-standing fronto-temporal epilepsy (Rasmussen & Milner, 1977) indicate that, in general, shift of speech lateralisation is rather infrequent.

Thus, behaviour should be regarded a response to environmental stimulation—*within the limits set by the person's (brain's) capacity for perception, processing, and response to stimulation.* In case of organic cerebral impairment the main principle would then logically be to give sufficient, "good enough," stimulation via the intact, accessible, *best perceptive channels*—rather than focusing on training of the poor functions—and adjust any stimulation to what is just within the child's capacity. Further, one should allow, and urge, the child to respond in his best expressive mode (that inhibits his responses least). The training, or "stimulation profile", should thus be adjusted to the "profile of function" along with functional development (Borchgrevink, 1979, 1980, 1981, 1986a; Gjaerum & Borchgrevink, 1985, 1987a; paper presented at the EBBS Workshop on Attention Deficit Disorder and Hyperkinetic Syndrome, Oslo, 1987b).

Accordingly, in behavioural disorders, one of the most essential diagnostic tasks is to sort out whether the symptoms are due to impaired brain capacity for perception, processing or response to stimulation; disadvantageous environment and stimulation—or combinations thereof. The aim is to define the child's potentials as well as the factors delimiting development and behaviour, as basis for the planning of treatment and training.

ASPECTS OF CEREBRAL PROCESSING— DIAGNOSTIC IMPLICATIONS

In principle, the rather strictly "programmed" subcortical centers largely give automatic reflex response to specific stimulation, mostly related to fundamental body functions. The cerebral cortex appears to exert control partly by inhibiting, or not inhibiting, these reflex responses. Besides, the cortex is essential for flexible voluntary behaviour in general (Towbin, 1981; Cavada & Goldman-Rakic, 1987). Selective cortical damage may accordingly lead to impaired inhibition (e.g., epilepsy, hyperreflexia) and may affect advanced, integrative and voluntary function in general (Towbin, 1981). Further, impaired inhibition may increase impulsive behaviour (cf. the so-called "disinhibition" hypothesis of ADD and hyperkinetic disorder discussed by Douglas, 1984). To some extent, different parts of the brain have specific transmitter systems. Certain chemical agents (drugs) may therefore have effects on specific brain areas and may thus modify specific functions, e.g., attention (cf. Beninger; Shaywitz & Shaywitz, both this volume).

The frontal lobes seem to be largely responsible for the processing of motor and expressive response *output:* voluntary inhibition, activation, initiation, plan/programme and execution of behaviour (Luria, 1973; Luria & Homskaya,

1970; Kirschner, 1986; Kelly & Kirschner, 1986; Freund, 1984; Ito, 1986). Salmaso and Denes (1982) found that the frontal lobes had a critical role in the maintenance of attention. Recent findings indicate that the frontal cortex may play a major role in the "act" of performance in general, included the "act" of perception (= the act of processing sensory input) and the controlled integration of other centers in the functionally advanced association cortex (cf. Milner & Petrides, 1984; TINS, 1984; Cavada & Goldman-Rakič, 1987). Attention deficit might thus be due to impairment of frontal lobe "top-down" processing, in accordance with the results of Beninger (this volume), rather than the "bottom-up" hypo-arousal deficit discussed by Klöve (this volume).

Infant psychomotor development as reference for neuropsychological evaluation

The subcortical centers that control fundamental reflex body functions (e.g., respiration, sucking), and the sensory functions appear to be rather well developed at birth, whereas the cortex is relatively immature (according to neuropathological findings, Towbin, 1981). Infant behaviour is accordingly dominated by standardised and automatic reflex responses to stimulation, and is characterised by poor coordination and poor voluntary response control. Postnatal cerebral maturation, which seems to takes place largely in the cortex (Towbin, 1981; Bourgeois, Goldman-Rakič & Rakič, 1987), gradually increases cortical efficiency and integration capacity. Together with environmental stimulation this leads to gradually improved control of function with age—as reflected in the child's psychomotor development.

The different stages of psychomotor development are reached at amazingly constant age levels—and in a characteristic order—for children growing up under different environmental stimulation. This is illustrated by the fact that schemes of psychomotor development largely hold also for children of other societies and across race and different socio-economic populations. Compare, e.g., Denver Developmental Scale (Frankenburg & Dodds, 1967) with the Danish study by Holle, Kemp, Boennelycke, and Mortensen (1977) and the Swedish Standardisation of the Griffith Scale (Nordberg & Alin-Aakerman, 1982). The failure to show significant psychomotor differences related to socio-economic state in the culturally heterogeneous U.S. population (Knobloch, Stevens, & Malone, 1980) does in a way compensate for the lack of scales from the third world. Socio-economic differences were only reflected for speech/language function from the age of 18 months, and for adaptive behaviour from 3 years. A certain tendency for earlier physical, and thus cerebral/psychomotor maturation has though been registered, as between the original and revised Gesell and Amatruda Developmental Scales (Knobloch et al., 1980). This implies that under reasonably normal conditions, environmental stimulation is not likely to be the factor limiting early psychomotor development. Or, put another way, despite the apparent cultural and socio-economic differences in infant nursing regimes, these environmental variables generally do not seem to be sufficient to have significant influence on early psychomotor development. Psychomotor—and more specifically motor development—must therefore largely reflect the degree of cerebral (cortical) maturation reached.

As most parameters of perinatal infant evaluation (e.g., respiration, and the other parameters recorded in the Apgar score) focus on functions controlled by subcortical centers, the poor correlation between perinatal symptoms and later neurological/behavioural dysfunctions (Graziani, Mason, & Cracco, 1981) is hardly amazing. Fetal and infant pathological studies show that cerebral pathology at or after birth tends to have greatest impact on the cerebral cortex (Towbin, 1981). In infants with peri- or postnatal cerebral damage, the cortical coordination and inhibition potential will therefore tend to be even poorer than in normal infants. Consequently more time will be needed for the brain to reach the level of processing needed for control of a certain skill. Psychomotor development will be correspondingly delayed, and should thus be a sensitive indicator of infant brain pathology. Accordingly, *significant psychomotor delay signals organic brain damage.* By statistical criteria for significant psychomotor delay, selected developmental measures might therefore be useful both as screening criteria for the detection of children at risk, and as references for neuropsychological evaluation in small or poorly cooperating children—e.g., in ADD children that, because of inconsistent responses, often cannot be examined by conventional methods. The child's "profile of function": the level/quality of each function relative to the other functions in the same child, can be expressed in terms of developmental age, implicitly compared with the normal population.

Criteria for detection and evaluation of children who need special care, should be chosen to correspond roughly to the group where "normal" care/intervention has proved insufficient - whether the etiology is environmental, genetic, or due to acquired organic brain pathology. The use of so-called "soft signs," or functional impairment and behavioural criteria for the diagnosis of brain damage, are often criticised. One frequent argument is that such "soft signs" are not diagnostically significant as they appear at a high rate in the normal population (Schaffer, O'Connor, Shafer, & Prupis, 1984; Ferguson & Rapoport, 1984). For instance, there are reports claiming that up to 16 percent of normal children may show up to five "soft signs" of brain damage without other evidence of brain disorder (Rutter, Graham, & Yule, 1970). However, one might as well argue that this should rather be taken as an indication of the inadequacy of the applied "soft" criteria, than lead to the conclusion that behavioural "soft sign" criteria have proved inadequate for the diagnosis of organic brain damage.

Used as selection criterion for those who need special intervention or care, the cut-off-point for statistically significant psychomotor delay should hardly be in the order of 16 percent. For the so-called normal (Gaussian) distribution, 2.3 percent fall beyond (=develop later than) mean plus 2 standard deviations. In the British National Child Developmental Study 2.3 percent were considered to be in need of special schooling because of educational backwardness (Davie, Butler, & Goldstein, 1975). In the Swedish Standardisation of the Griffith Scale (Nordberg & Ajin-Aakerman, 1983) which did *not* exclude those with delayed/deviant development, the developmental age for mean plus 2 standard deviations, corresponding to the 97.7 percentile, for most items could only be poorly defined, simply because the age/acquisition relation at that point is almost parallel to, and hardly approaching, the 100 percent level—because a given skill will never be reached by all individuals of a society. Eliminating the children with developmental delay from the sample, which has been done in several other developmental scale studies, would however be inappropriate if the scale should later be used for establishing criteria for screening of children in terms of psychomotor delay (but perhaps relevant for the establishment of the diagnostically useless mean age for acquisition of a certain skill). However, the age/acquisition relation was most often well defined up towards 90-95 percent level.

Brain damage in infancy and early childhood tends to be of rather diffuse character (Towbin, 1981) and will accordingly lead to psychomotor delay for more than one item. For diagnostic purposes the constellation of functional delay will be essential. As the same children would not be expected to show delay on exactly the same functional items, the percentage of children showing more than 95 percentile delay for more than one item, will always be lower than the 5 percent showing such delay for one single parameter only—thus approaching the mean plus 2 standard deviation level.

The relevance of the above reasoning is supported by epidemiological findings. In their large epidemiological study, Gillberg et al. (1982), Gillberg, Gillberg and Rasmussen (1984) found that 3-6 percent of all children showed mild to moderate motor-perceptual disorder, depending upon the applied criteria, and 93 percent of the MBD group showed severe behavioural and/or achievement problems and were in need of special intervention at a three-year follow-up. For the clinical diagnosis, percentiles in the 90-95 percent region should therefore be appropriate. In accordance with this, Holle et al. (1977) used the 93 percent level as the "upper normal cut-off" whereas the Denver scale gives the 90 percent level.

Using a previously standardised reference background may thus "harden" the claimed "soft" character of behavioural signs of brain damage and prove adequate for the distinction of children who need special care or training. Besides, for practical purposes it reduces the need for a control group in clinical studies. Despite their apparent subtle character, the inter-rater reliability for evaluation of behavioural parameters in children is generally found to be high (Rutter, 1984c). The same is true for evaluation of developmental scale parameters (Knobloch et al., 1980). Test-retest reliability is characteristically somewhat lower (Rutter, 1984c). This may be due to cerebral maturation in case of long test-retest intervals. For short test-retest intervals, less than 3 weeks, combined inter-rater and test-retest reliability was found to be around 90 percent in children with developmental disorders and mental age less than 8 years (Gjaerum & Borchgrevink, paper presented at the EBBS Workshop on Attention Deficit Disorder and Hyperkinetic Syndrome, Oslo, 1987).

Consequently, psychomotor delay observed longitudinally in one area of function, or a simultaneous constellation of findings compatible with known neurological syndromes, expected from knowledge of brain construction and function, or present in other family members, would be a strong indication of underlying inherited or acquired organic brain pathology. In case the dysfunctions also have proved to be resistant to training, this would further increase the probability of organic brain etiology. Objective measures like EEG and CT often fail to detect the slight organic damage that give impairment of complex functions only (cf. Shaywitz, Shaywitz, Byrne, Cohen, & Rothman, 1983; and Table 1). Accordingly, a functional evaluation based on the constellation of consistent, reproducible neurological "soft signs" and significant psychomotor delay, resistant to therapeutic intervention, expected from knowledge of brain function, and compatible with symptoms seen in more severe cases of confirmed brain lesion, must be regarded a reliable and reasonably valid indication of underlying organic cerebral impairment of acquired or inherited origin—and at present might be the most adequate diagnostic approach to the diagnosis of minor brain dysfunction.

Hemisphere anaesthesia may simulate symptoms due to diffuse cortical damage

The cerebral lateralisation of speech and handedness are genetically determined by polygenic factors (Annett, 1976). Language lateralisation is manifested anatomically in the fetus (Chi, Doolling, & Gilles, 1977), and electrophysiologically (Molfese, 1977) as well as behaviourally (Entus, 1977) in the infant. Of the total population (100%), practically all right-handers (85–90%), 2/3 off the left-handers (7%) and the ambidextrous (0–5%) have speech controlled by the left hemisphere; only 1/3 of the left-handers (3%) show right hemisphere speech control (discussed by Steffen, 1975). Left hemisphere damage will thus be likely to produce combined impairment of both the control of speech and the right hand, leaving the subject with impaired speech and genetically unexpected left-handedness.

However, speech and articulation also require advanced motor coordination. In case of predominantly left fronto-sagittal damage, general pre-motor programme impairment including motor speech disorder, and impaired foot control (balance) rather than unexpected handedness, would be expected to be associated with motor speech disorder. All these functions are closely located in the fronto-sagittal area and therefore would be expected to be affected by the same damage, which also might produce attention deficit. (Fig. 1).

Hemisphere specialization (summarized in Fig. 2) may be studied directly by testing of which functions are conserved and which are lost during selective temporary anaesthesia of one hemisphere after the other in the same individual by intracarotid amytal barbiturate injection (Wada & Rasmussen, 1960; Rasmussen & Milner, 1977; Borchgrevink, 1982, 1986a, 1987a, 1987b; for reviews, see Springer & Deutsch, 1981; Kolb & Whishaw, 1985).

As the functional impairment temporarily induced by this diffuse unilateral cortical anaesthesia would be expected to resemble impairments produced by diffuse cortical brain damage, it might be relevant for the choice of strategy in the "soft-sign" functional diagnosis of ADD/MBD to take a closer look at characteristic functional effects of such anaesthesia. Which functions that are impaired, and the order, as well as the manner or characteristics of how functions are lost and regained, gives unique, direct information on the underlying cerebral processing and indications of which symptoms to look for. For instance, complex or marginal capacities that are first lost and last regained during anesthesia, would be expected to be first lost in case of diffuse brain damage.

Recovering from hemisphere anaesthesia, contralateral distal dynamic motor coordination (e.g., finger wiggle, articulation) are gradually and simultaneously regained, and are generally among the last elements to be restored. In cases where memory span is unilaterally controlled by the speech hemisphere, digit span is characteristically around 3 items as soon as speech is regained, and is gradually restored to pre-anaesthetic normal level along with the parallel regain of contralateral distal dynamic motor coordination (e.g., finger wiggle, articulation). Amnesia for early per-anaesthetic events is often found: the patient may fail to recall, and even fail to recognise, objects that were shown 20-30s earlier even

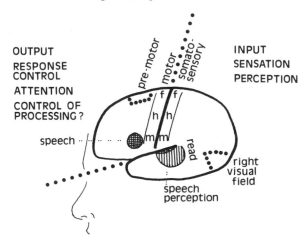

FIG. 1   Functional organisation of the left (speech) hemisphere cortex in the normal right-hander. For references: see text. Codes: In the post-central *somato-sensory* area, and in the pre-central *motor* area, are indicated the control areas for mouth (*m*), hand (*h*) and foot (*f*, on the medial surface). The planum temporale area essential for phonetic reading is indicated by *read*.

though he can name them, and named them correctly in the first place. Impaired memory span, distal dynamic motor disorder, motor speech disorder, and impaired memory storage (''learning'') would therefore be symptoms expected in diffuse cortical brain damage.

Occasionally, carotid angiography shows that intracarotid injection also leads to transient filling of the contralateral anterior cerebral artery, producing in effect a bilateral prefrontal and fronto-sagittal anaesthesia in addition to the ipsilateral hemisphere anaesthesia. The patient is then characteristically unable to initiate any response what-so-ever, even though the previously raised ipsilateral arm is kept raised. Correspondingly, bilateral damage to the fronto-sagittal supplementary motor programme area leads to loss of motor initiation (Freund, 1984). Initially, the anaesthetized patient may be inattentive, not responding to objects shown. The focusing of objects, followed by ability to initiate clumsy, simple movements of the ipsilateral hand, are then characteristically regained before speech. Simultaneous singing or motor prompt may facilitate speech initiation —much in the same way as in Melodic Intonation Therapy (Sparks & Holland, 1976) and in transcortical motor aphasia (Benson & Geschwind, 1976). Facilitation phenomena indicate that when a function is impaired, but close to threshold, *simultaneous* stimulation of specific and related functional areas may provide the additional excitation needed to reach threshold level. Last regained are ipsilateral followed by contralateral distal dynamic motor coordination. Long-term memory recall and recognition are mostly unaffected throughout (Borchgrevink, 1982; 1987 a,b; Borchgrevink, unpubl.). Accordingly, diffuse prefrontal and fronto-sagittal cortical brain damage would most likely lead to impaired attention accompanied by motor programme disorder including speech and articulation.

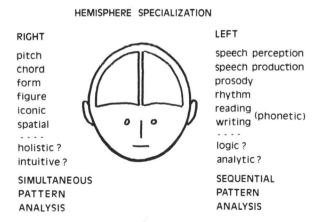

FIG. 2.   Hemisphere specialization in the normal right-hander. For references: see text.

Toward a Neuropsychological Assessment of ADD/MBD Children

The developing child may be regarded to operate at the margins of his capacity, using most of his potential to master a recently acquired skill. Even minor dysfunction that would have no significant effect on adult function may therefore be expected to give developmental deviation and consequent delay in the child, e.g., delayed articulation in neurologically normal Kindergarten children with small (mean 12 dB) and fluctuating mechanical hearing loss (blind study by Helland, Hemsen, & Borchgrevink, 1983). To be sensitive enough, the diagnostic reference should therefore be continuously adjusted to what is just mastered by the child, which again speaks in favour of using significant psychomotor developmental delay as reference for diagnosing of "soft signs" in ADD/MBD. For instance, memory span is gradually increased from 2 to 6 or 7 ($+/-1$) in the 2-7 year old child (Elliott, Murray, & Pearson, 1978). Adult function is reached at 7 years of age, which largely also is the case with speech. Impairment of speech and memory span would therefore be expected to be more frequent, more severe, and thus be more sensitive diagnostic parameters in preschool children than in older children and adults for corresponding brain damage. Indeed, in a controlled blind study, adult patients surviving meningococcal disease showed ADD/MBD-like symptoms with high correlation ($R=0.87$) between impaired concentration and pathological score on Benton Visual Retention Test (Borchgrevink, Aanonsen & Gedde-Dahl, paper presented at the EBBS Workshop on Attention Deficit Disorder and Hyperkinetic Syndrome, Oslo 1987). However, they had only slight impairment of digit span and articulation, compared with the ADD/MBD children of the present study.

Attention requires the ability to focus selectively on characteristic stimulus features. Decoding of *sequential* information (e.g., speech) implies sustained attention over time while simultaneously storing and continuously analysing the elements presented (cf., Borchgrevink, 1986b). Analysis of simultaneous events (e.g., figures), will draw more heavily on the number of elements focused at a time. Different "attention profiles" might therefore be expected both among ADD children, and versus children with other impairments, e.g., in terms of memory span, speech and utterance length versus visuocognitive skill (cf. Fig. 2 and Borchgrevink, 1987a). It might even be appropriate to look for differences in scores on visuocognitive tasks that include discrimination of many simultaneous elements at a time (complex matching tasks), as opposed to visuocognitive tasks where only one cognitive principle is involved. Such information would be crucial for the choice of optimal training, for example in which manner cognitive stimulation should be presented. The traditional discrimination between verbal and performance IQ would not be expected to detect these differences in attention and cognitive profiles, as they both imply sequential and integrative motor coordination. Indeed, verbal and performance IQ do generally not show very different scores in ADD children, as demonstrated by Gittelman Klein, and Mannuzza (this volume). The diagnostic assessment should therefore include a nonverbal visuocognitive test (e.g., Leiter Visual Performance Scale, Arthur, 1949) as opposed to sequential or motor integration tasks like memory span, speech, balance, motor coordination, bicycling, and drawing. In case of predominantly sagittal damage, the sagittally controlled foot/ankle coordination (balance) would be expected to be affected more than e.g. hand/fingers and handedness, and being accompanied by relative impairment of speech, drawing and cycling according to the degree of pre-motor "programme" disorder (cf. Fig. 1).

For motor coordination it should therefore be relevant to distinguish between *proximal* (e.g., arm) versus *distal* (e.g., finger) impairment, *static* (e.g., balance) versus dynamic (e.g., running, bicycling) integration, comparing the degrees of such impairments for different organs (foot/ankle, hand/fingers, mouth/lips/ tongue), rather than making the conventional distinction between "gross motor" and "fine motor" performance. Further, for all functions one should look for systematic motor execution impairment (always present) versus non-systematic motor programme impairment present mostly for advanced static and dynamic control, and with non-systematic error pattern due to poor programme command.

The study of perceptual function should correspondingly include tests relevant for the various stages of stimulus processing:

- sensation (task: is the stimulus present or not?)
- discrimination (task: similar or not?)
- identification (task: recognise target stimulus among others, requires discrimination as well as memory storage and recall)
- signal decoding (task: understand simple concept-reference relations)
- symbol (language) decoding (task: more advanced, abstract understanding of concept-reference relations).

For the examination of speech and language function it would be considered relevant to distinguish between impairments of naming/decoding and utterance length. Figure 3 summarizes stages of speech/language and visuocognitive processing.

By studying attention deficit disorder and accompanying symptoms in *all* children referred to the author for the diagnosis of therapy-resistant communication disorder during a certain time period, the potential bias in a group selected on beforehand as ADD/MBD children (cf. Douglas, 1984; Shaywitz & Shaywitz, this volume) might be avoided.

METHODS

Fifty-six children with chronological age (CA) 2-15 years (mean 4.5 years, median 4 years) referred for therapy-resistant communication disorder went through

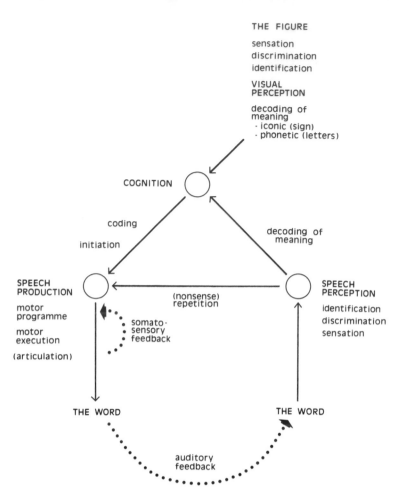

FIG. 3. Stages of speech/language and visuocognitive processing. For references: see text. Correlate also with Figures 1 and 2.

Language may be defined as a code for communication of ideas. Verbally: The auditory reference for a concept or idea, *THE WORD* (bottom right) goes through the auditory sensation, discrimination and identification processing required for *SPEECH PERCEPTION*. By *decoding of meaning* the message reaches the concept level (*COGNITION*). Verbal response implies *coding* the concept to *SPEECH PRODUCTION*. *Initiation*, *motor programme* and *motor execution* produces *articulation* of *THE WORD* (bottom left), controlled by listening (*auditory feedback*) as well as *somatosensory feedback*. Alternatively, the (nonsense) sound pattern may be directly transferred from *SPEECH PERCEPTION* to *SPEECH PRODUCTION* via a *(nonsense) repetition* pathway, without decoding of meaning - e.g., as in nursery rhymes.

Visually: The visual reference for a concept or idea, *THE FIGURE* (top right) goes through the visual *sensation*, *discrimination* and *identification* processing required for *VISUAL PERCEPTION*. By *decoding of meaning*, *iconic* or *phonetic*, the message reaches the concept level (*COGNITION*). Visual response implies coding the concept to, e.g., sign language (not shown in Figure 3).

a detailed neuropsychological and neuromotor evaluation based largely on the above reasoning (Gjaerum & Borchgrevink, 1985; 1987; and paper presented at the EBBS Workshop on Attention Deficit Disorder and Hyperkinetic Syndrome, Oslo 1987). Against the well-defined background of developmental scale statistics, this method combines

- anamnestic data on gestation, delivery, psychomotor development, heritage, family handedness, environment, response to previous treatment and training
- systematic observation of spontaneous behaviour
- response to developmental, neuropsychological, neuromotor, verbal and visuocognitive tests

registering which of selected functions that are significantly chronologically delayed (in the order of 90-95 percent, or mean plus 2SD), the level of function in each area, as well as the qualitative characteristics of neuropsychological and behavioural function. The constellation of findings describes the child's "profile of function": the developmental level and quality of function in each area relative to other areas in the same child, and serves as basis for the neuropsychological evaluation. In another study the same procedure yielded combined inter-rater/test-retest reliability of 88.6 percent (mean) agreement (SD=3.9), and concurrent criterion validity around 90 percent (mean) for the 1/3 of items available (Gjaerum & Borchgrevink, paper presented at the EBBS Workshop on Attention Deficit Disorder and Hyperkinetic Syndrome, Oslo 1987).

Each of the 56 children (33 boys and 23 girls) was examined by the author according to the above procedure in one 2 hr session including the structured anamnestic interview of the accompanying mother, father or therapist, who also were asked to confirm whether the functions observed during the examination were representative for the child. The results of the examination were progressively evaluated for each child in the random order of referral. All scoring, as well as the calculation of the mean results for the total group, were performed before the sample was split into subgroups. The children were referred for evaluation of therapy-resistant communication disorder from a Kindergarten for hearing and communication disorders (n=24), hospital audiology departments (n=13), paedagogical/psychological outpatient centers (n=12) and child psychiatry units (n=7).

RESULTS AND DISCUSSION

All of the 56 children referred for therapy-resistant communication disorder showed symptoms compatible with organic cerebral impairment, both in terms of statistically significant developmental delay and in terms of characteristic deviant function and constellation of findings. Details and the mean profiles for subgroups of children are given in Table 1. Practically all could have been referred at or before the age of 2 years for statistically significant developmental delay according to simple psychomotor criteria. In most cases the mother had suspected pathology well before that age. All showed predominantly distal motor control impairment, most expressed for speech and foot/ankle (impaired balance) coordination. Problems were frequently reported in connection with delivery (75 percent) and gestation (30 percent). Related disorder in the family was claimed for 46 percent of the children.

In case of psycho-social etiology, impaired balance would not be expected to be found in every child referred for communication disorders. Combined with the other findings, this demonstrates that therapy-resistant communication disorder is likely to be of brain organic etiology. Accordingly, the applied psycho*motor* criteria and "soft signs" seem appropriate as criteria for the diagnosing and early selection of "risk children" who need special training or care. Besides, the results call for a neuropsychological and neuromotor diagnostic assessment as basis for choice of optimal treatment and training in children with communication disorders.

Of the total group, 84 percent of the children were evaluated as having attention deficit disorder (ADD), defined as poor or fluctuating attention for age considered to require special intervention, both from the child's performance during the examination and according to anamnestic information. With corresponding criteria, 57 percent showed increased distractibility, 38 percent reduced impulse control, 29 percent hyperkinesis and 21 percent impaired concentration. Memory span was impaired in 73 percent whereas only 5 percent showed long term memory impairment.

In terms of developmental age, different subgroups of children showed different (mean) profiles of function (Table 1). The children (n = 14) with even slight degree of *cognitive impairment* (defined as the mental age (MA) for the child's "best" cognitive function being less than 80 percent of that expected from chronological age (CA)—showed an even, "flat" profile of function—with relatively poor language production in spite of the relatively advanced motor performance. Their cognitive profile was significantly different from the rest of the group (n = 42), (Chi sq. = 22.83, p<0.001), with reference to the total group median for

$$\frac{\text{visuocognitive MA}-1/2 \text{ (language comprehension MA + play \& social MA)}}{\text{CA}}$$

Relative to the total group, the *cognitive impairment* group showed low memory span, matching their language production level. Attention deficit matched the frequency of impaired memory span. Distractibility and hyperkinesis were increased. Low self-esteem or increased anxiety were infrequent. Motor impairment was most expressed for dynamic distal impairment in foot/ankle, and relatively good for hand/fingers and dynamic proximal tasks, with increased frequency of static proximal dysfunction with predominantly systematic articulation and motor *execution* problems. Of the group 46 percent were lefthanded, and 23 percent showed non-established/mixed handedness. Late delivery, hyper-reflexia, pathological foot-vault tone/strength, epilepsy and EEG/CT pathology were more frequent.

TABLE 1

Mean cognitive profiles, and per cent of children with observed and reported impairment, given for subgroups of children—and for the total group. M:F = male-to-female ratio. MA:CA < 0.8 see text for definition. Patients p05 and p45 excluded from small subgroups because of influence of high chronological age on the group mean age.

	Total Group		With ADD, Without Cognitive Impairment MA:CA > 0.8	Walked Before Crawled	With Cognitive Impairment MA:CA < 0.8 p45 excl.	With ADD	Without Add p05 + p45 excluded
	n = 56 M:F = 1.3		n = 36 M:F = 1.6	n = 13 M:F = 2.3	n = 13 (14) M:F = 1.3	n = 47 M:F = 1.5	n = 7(9) M:F = 1.3
	median	mean	mean	mean	mean	mean	mean
Cognitive Profiles							
Chronological age (CA) in ys.	4	4.8	4.8	4.1	2.7	4.5	4.0
Mental age (MA) in ys.					%		
- visuocognitive (Leiter)		4.4	4.9	4.5	1.7	4.2	4.5
- play/social		3.4	3.5	3.0	1.7	3.1	3.7
- language comprehension		3.4	3.4	3.3	1.7	3.1	3.6
- drawing/construction		3.8	3.6	3.2	1.7	3.5	4.2
- motor		3.1	3.3	3.0	2.0	3.0	3.0
- language production		2.1	2.1	1.9	1.0	1.8	2.4
Memory span		2.4	2.6	2.7	1.2	2.3	2.7
Mother suspected pathology at age (ys.)		1.6					
Psychomotor Delay		%	%	%	%		
> 2 ys 2 word utterance		93	92	85	100		
> 3 ys cycles 3-wheel bike		77	79 (n = 33)	100	100 (n = 11)		
> 16 m walk		66	58	54	85		
> 4.5 ys hop on one foot		63	79 (n = 19)	31 (n = 5)	100 (n = 7)		
> 3 ys jump		50	52 (n = 33)	62	73 (n = 11)		
> 8 m sit		43	50	46	85		
> 0 m sucking impaired		32	28	46	38		

(Continued)

TABLE 1
(Continued)

	Total Group n = 56 M:F = 1.3		With ADD, Without Cognitive Impairment MA:CA > 0.8 n = 36 M:F = 1.6	Walked Before Crawled n = 13 M:F = 2.3	With Cognitive Impairment MA:CA < 0.8 p45 excl. n = 13 (14) M:F = 1.3	With ADD n = 47 M:F = 1.5	Without Add p05 + p45 excluded n = 7(9) M:F = 1.3
	median	mean	mean	mean	mean	mean	mean
> 8 m differentiated babble	32		31	23	31		
> 16 m dribble persists	30		36	54	38		
> 0 m poor gaze/contact	27		28	8	31		
walked before crawled	21		33	100	8		
1 or more of the above features < 4.5 y	98						
1 or more of the above features < 2.0 y	98						
2 or more of the above features < 4.5 y	96						
2 or more of the above features < 2.0 y	95						
Motor Coordination, General		%	%	%	%		
Motor coordination, any impairment		100	100	100	100		
- dynamic distal impairment		100	100	100	100		
- static distal impairment		96	97	92	100		
- dynamic proximal impairment		70	69	100	69		
- static proximal impairment		5	3	0	15		
- motor programme disorder, non-systematic		55	78	92	38		
- motor execution disorder, systematic		84	92	92	92		
- articulation disorder		95	100	100	100		
programme disorder, non-systematic		57	67	88	100		
execution disorder, systematic		77	67	77	100		
- speech, reduced utterance length		95	100	92	100		

	%	%	%	%
Motor Coordination, Organ Specific				
foot/ankle: "balance" impairment	100	100	100	100
mouth/lips/tounge impairment	91	89	100	92
hand/fingers impairment	84	89	100	77
Somato-Sensory	11	14	8	8
Attention Deficit				
Attention (poor or variable)	84	100	85	70
Memory span impairment (words, digits or pointing)	73	75	62	70
Distractibility (by environmental events)	57	58	23	77
Impulse control (impaired)	38	42	38	46
Hyperkinetic (restless shifting of activity)	29	22	31	54
Concentration (activity not maintained even for favourite tasks)	21	22	31	23
Long term memory impairment	5	3	8	8
Low Self Esteem or Performance Limited by Anxiety tries to avoid testing of weak functions	46	53	62	23
Speech Perception limited by utterance length	54	61	46	31
Delivery (any of below features)	75	78	77	77
- rapid	32	33	15	23
- early > 28 days	13	14	23	15
- late > 14 days	23	17	8	31
- complications	46	53	62	38
- jaundice (light-treated)	14	11	23	8
Gestation, e.g. bleeding, hypertension	30	28	31	31
Family, related disorder in 1. or 2. relative	46	47	77	46
Left-Handedness				
- in family, 1. or 2. relative	16	11	23	15
- in the patient	29	22	23	46
- mixed/non-established	13	11	8	23
- expected in population	<10			

(Continued)

121

TABLE 1
(Continued)

	Total Group n = 56 M:F = 1.3		With ADD, Without Cognitive Impairment MA:CA > 0.8 n = 36 M:F = 1.6	Walked Before Crawled n = 13 M:F = 2.3	With Cognitive Impairment MA:CA < 0.8 p45 excl. n = 13 (14) M:F = 1.3	With ADD n = 47 M:F = 1.5	Without Add p05 + p45 excluded n = 7(9) M:F = 1.3
	median	mean	mean	mean	mean	mean	mean
Left-Foot Preference							
- in the patient, balance left > right	16		22	2	8		
Epilepsy/Convulsion history	18		22	15	31		
EEG/CT Pathology reported	10		8	8	23		
Neurology (any of below features)	95		92	92	100		
- hyper-reflexia ankle/knee	48		44	54	54		
- hypo-reflexia ankle/knee	34		39	38	23		
- spasticity-reflexia ankle/knee	36		39	54	31		
- Babinsky inverted/indiff.	36		39	38	23		
- foot-vault tone/strength	57		53	38	73		

Birth complications and rapid delivery were less frequent. The mean chronological age was generally lower (except patient p45), probably reflecting that more severe symptomatology is likely to lead to early referral.

The "flat" profile of function—and the increased rate of lefthandedness, predominant systematic motor-execution problems, and motor performance being more advanced than cognitive capacity—indicates that in case of even slight general cognitive impairment, the brain's general developmental potential and processing capacity is the limiting factor, rather than the specific frontal lobe act of initiating and controlling the process. The lack of superior visuocognitive function combined with high rate of left-handedness indicate that the left hemisphere is essential for analytic cognitive processing in general.

In contrast, the children (n = 36) with *attention deficit and normal cognitive function* (defined as MA/CA > 80 percent) showed an uneven profile of function with specifically impaired language production and poor motor performance relative to the visuocognitive function, which was age adequate or beyond. Memory span was low, matching the language production level. Attention deficit was more frequent than memory-span impairment. The scores on multifactorial detailed visuocognitive matching tasks were characteristically poorer than for tasks solved according to a single principle. Their cognitive profile was significantly different from the cognitive impairment group in terms of the above parameter (Chi sq. = 14.69, p < 0.001). Hyperkinesis appeared less frequently. Low self-esteem or increased anxiety were more frequent. Motor impairment was less organ specific, though most expressed for dynamic distal impairment in foot/ankle, with relative increase of non-systematic articulation and generalised motor programme disorder, and low frequency of static proximal dysfunction. Drawing performance was poor. Lefthandedness and mixed handedness were relatively infrequent, though somewhat above expected for the population, whereas lefthandedness in the family was as expected for the population. Leftfoot preference appeared as infrequent as lefthandedness, and the two were not well correlated. Birth complications and rapid delivery were increased, with relative increase of *hypo*reflexia and a pathological Babinski reflex, whereas epilepsy and EEG/CT pathology were more infrequent.

This profile of function with preserved visuocognitive capacity combined with impaired attention, increased distractibility and impaired impulse control, impaired language comprehension, language production, memory span, drawing and dynamic distal motor coordination in general - with only slight increase of left-hand and left-foot preference, is in accordance with pure or predominantly symmetric sagittal frontal cortex impairment (cf. the above discussion). In ADD the "top-down" processing of activation, attention, motor programme, and the sequential control thus seem to be the limiting factors. In contrast, in case of cognitive impairment the cognitive capacity as such, not the act of using it, seems to be delimiting.

The children with specific impairment of proximal integrative motor function ("walked before crawled") showed "ADD-like" profile of function, but with more advanced visuocognitive function, higher anxiety level and greater impairment of dynamic motor coordination. Low self esteem and increased anxiety was thus increasing with relative increase of mental to chronological age. The children without attention deficit also showed "ADD-like" profile of function, but with drawing/construction ability being age adequate or beyond, significantly different from that of the ADD group (Chi sq. = 12.66, p < 0.001) in terms of group median for

$$\frac{\text{visuocognitive MA - drawing \& construction MA}}{\text{CA}}$$

EEG and CT generally failed to detect cerebral pathology. The rate of speech perception utterance length covaried with the rate of memory span impairment for all but the cognitive impairment group.

Given the arbitrary selection of the referred patient sample, all children being examined with the same diagnostic procedure by the same examiner in the order of referral, the selection of subgroups being performed after scoring, and the high combined test-retest/inter-rater reliability and concurrent criterion validity demonstrated for the examination procedure (see Methods), the above findings should be reasonably representative. The high rate of speech disorders would be expected in the period of language acquisition (cf. the above discussion), especially in case of motor coordination impairment and reduced memory span. From the above findings one would expect continuous variation and combination of types and degrees of impairment, depending upon the type and degree of brain damage on top of the premorbid genetic potential. Indeed, predominant motor initiation, balance and integration impairment on top of mental retardation without attention deficit was found e.g. in patient p45—an unexpected lefthander with severe stuttering. Speech was facilitated by simultaneous motor prompt and rhythmic motion, indicating predominantly fronto-sagittal damage (cf. above). Patient p21, right-handed and diagnosed as autistic, showed visuocognitive function beyond what was expected for age, but had severely impaired response initiation and increased response latency (in the order of 20 s)—leading to apparent "attention deficit" combined with general motor programme and coordination problems and hardly no speech capacity - compatible with fronto-sagittal damage. The profile of function for this autistic child thus resembles the "ADD- profile" in principle, but is more exaggerated.

CONCLUSION

The results indicate that attention deficit disorder is an activation deficit caused by prefrontal and/or sagittal frontal pathology, probably predominantly cortical ("top-down"). Most likely, there is a continuum between ADD and autism - as well as with other cerebral damage. The continuum character speaks in favour of regarding ADD as a separate descriptive *symptom* rather than as a syndrome with multiple subspecifications, as has been proposed by Shaywitz and Shaywitz (this volume).

Considering the above results, and that reports claim that 3/4 of referred children may show signs of MBD (Gross & Wilson, 1974), Rutter's rejection of the MBD syndrome as too vague (Rutter, 1984a, b; this volume), should not imply rejection of the MBD concept as such. Brain damage is associated with increased risk for psychiatric and behavioural disorders - including ADD - (Rutter, this volume). As organic brain damage will have major implications for the child's developmental potential, and consequently for the choice of therapeutic approach (see above), MBD should perhaps rather be preserved as a reference for minor encephalopathy in general, and lead to increased diagnostic effort in the search for specific organic etiology underlying impaired function or behaviour. Reconsideration of organic versus environmental etiology proved relevant for autism (Rubinstein, 1985) with major consequences for choice of therapeutic strategy.

Birth complications were most frequent for the ADD-group. Hypoxia is the most frequent cause of fetal and neonatal brain damage, and tends to give diffuse cortical pathology when occurring at birth (Towbin, 1981). Pathology will only be registered for the function(s) where trauma, disease, premorbid marginal, or subnormal genetic potential - or their combined influence - bring cerebral capacity below the potential required for normal performance. Thus, in case of diffuse cerebral damage, impairment may be expected to occur first for the most advanced cerebral functions and lead to impairment of functions that draw heavily upon integrative cortical coordination and control. If the frontal cortex plays the major role in activation and advanced integration of other parts of the brain, the pathophysiological mechanism might well be that diffuse cortical damage is likely to cause predominantly frontal lobe symptoms, with or without additional impairment. In patient p52, CT showed diffuse dilatation of the left lateral ventricle, supporting this reasoning. The perfect correlation between impaired balance and ADD might thus reflect that attention, as well as the act of continuous maintenance and regain of balance, are most complex and thus extremely vulnerable functions depending upon frontal cortex control.

On the other hand, the pathophysiological mechanism might be that hypoxia causes cerebral edema leading to elevated intracranial pressure. Hypothetically, the pressure would then be expected to be higher when distributed over the smaller medial (sagittal) cortical surfaces than when spread over the hemisphere convexities, which might lead to more severe sagittal than lateral damage. A corresponding pressure distribution would also be expected in case of rapid delivery, which was most frequently reported for the ADD group. In another patient sample, NMR showed left fronto-sagittal infarcted area in a three-year-old girl with fronto-sagittal profile of function, previously diagnosed as showing autistic behaviour (Borchgrevink, unpublished).

Although speculative, either of these two mechanisms, alone or combined, might lead to the above ADD profile of function compatible with predominant "top-down" fronto-sagittal cortical impairment—"pure" or in association with genetic and/or acquired damage to other brain areas. Stimulants might then improve attention by improving the frontal cortex potential for activation and integration of complex behaviour, in line with the findings of Beninger, and of Sergeant and van der Meere (both this volume). As no reliable diagnostic index seems to be available, blind placebo-controlled drug trial against a sufficiently sensitive and specific reference will at present be required to decide whether drug therapy is indicated in a given child. Regardless of etiology or underlying mechanism, whenever the profile of function is changed, e.g., due to drug therapy, the stimulation profile should be adjusted accordingly.

SUMMARY

The cerebral processing assumed to be relevant for the diagnostic assessment of children with ADD/MBD is discussed, followed by a report of a clinical study based on the diagnostic principles developed. The diagnostic assessment should aim to reveal whether the observed behaviour is due to organic brain disorder, focusing on the child's potentials as well as the factors limiting normal development and behaviour. This "profile of function" then may serve as basis for the neuropsychological evaluation, and for the choice of optimal training. As in sensory disorders, one should rather seek to compensate for therapy-resistant organic brain disorder by use of the best alternative perceptive and expressive functions.

Fifty-six children with chronological age (CA) 2-15 years (mean 4.5 years, median 4 years) referred for therapy-resistant communication disorder went through a detailed neuropsychological and neuromotor evaluation according to Gjaerum and Borchgrevink (1987). This assessment aims to indicate the type, degree, level and localization of organic cerebral impairment from the constellation of anamnestic data, neurological findings and a thorough "mapping" of motor-perceptual and cognitive profiles - against a reference of statistically significant psychomotor developmental delay (in the order of 90-95 percent, or mean plus 2 SD).

All of the children showed symptoms compatible with organic cerebral impairment - indicating that therapy-resistant communication disorder is likely to be of organic etiology. Practically all of them could have been referred by or before the age of 2 years according to simple criteria of statistically significant psychomotor delay. 84% had attention deficit.

The results indicate that attention deficit disorder (ADD) is compatible with predominant frontal cortex pathology, prefrontal and/or premotor (sagittal). This leads to impaired "top-down" activation of voluntary behaviour and poor integration of complex sequential functions including motor, speech and memory span impairment. The results indicate a continuum between ADD and autism - as well as with other cerebral damage. The continuum character speaks in favour of regarding ADD as a separate descriptive symptom rather than as a syndrome with multiple subspecifications.

REFERENCES

Annett, M. (1976). Handedness and the cerebral representation of speech. *Annals of Human Biology, 3*, 317-28.

Arthur, G. (1949). The Arthur adaption of the Leiter international performance scale. *Journal of Clinical Psychology, 5*, 345-349.

Benson, D.F. & Geschwind, N. (1976). The aphasias and related disturbances. In A.B. Baker & L.H. Baker (Eds.), *Clinical Neurology, 1*, chap. 8, 1-28. Hagerstown: Lippincott/Harper & Row.

Borchgrevink, H.M. (1979). Tests for central auditory function. *Proceedings of the VIII. Congress of the Union of European Phoniatricians* (pp.29-31). Köszeg, Hungary,

Borchgrevink, H.M. (1980). Improving auditory perception diagnosis by considering the cerebral lateralisation of speech and musical stimuli. In D. Ingram, F.C.C. Peng & Ph. Dale (Eds.), *Proceedings of the first international congress for the study of child language* (pp.317-322). Lanham: University Press of America.

Borchgrevink, H.M. (1981). Speech, language and brain function - diagnostic and therapeutic implications. *HNO-Praxis, 3*, 222 (abstract).

Borchgrevink, H.M. (1982). Prosody and musical rhythm are controlled by the speech hemisphere. In M. Clynes (Ed.), *Music, mind and brain. The neuropsychology of music* (pp.151-157). New York: Plenum Press.

Borchgrevink, H.M. (1986a). The brain behind the therapeutic potential of music. In E. Ruud (Ed.), *Music and health* (pp.63-96). Oslo/London: Norsk Musikforlag.

Borchgrevink, H.M. (1986b). Concept-reference coherence in speech perception: Consequences for native and second language speech comprehension in noise. In R.J. Salvi, D. Henderson, R.P. Hamernik & V. Colletti (Eds.), *Basic and applied aspects of noise induced hearing loss* (pp.357-367). New York: Plenum Press.

Borchgrevink, H.M. (1987a). Left hemisphere: Sequential analysis, right hemisphere: Simultaneous/instantaneous analysis? Right (non-speech) hemisphere anaesthesia affects pitch in singing, while prosody (pitch in speech) and musical rhythm is preserved. *The Second World Congress of Neuroscience (IBRO). Neuroscience, 22* (Suppl.). S755. Oxford/New York: Pergamon Press (abstract).

Borchgrevink, H.M., Aanonsen, N.O. & Gedde–Dahl, T.W. (1987). Patients surviving meningococc-events, while preserving long term memory recall and recognition. Transient findings recorded in some patients recovering from induced intracarotid amytal anaesthesia of the left (speech) hemisphere. *The Second World Congress of Neuroscience (IBRO), Neuroscience, 22* (Suppl.), S508. Oxford/New York: Pergamon Press (abstract).

Borchgrevink, H.M., Aanonsen, N.O. & Gedde–Dahl, T.W. (1987). Patients surning meningococcal disease report and exhibit neurological/neuropsychological symptoms of the types found in children with ADD/MBD - a controlled, "blind" study in young men. *European Brain and Behaviour Society. Workshop on attention deficit disorder and hyperkinetic syndrome*. Oslo (abstract).

Bourgeois, J.P., Goldman-Rakič, P.S. & Rakič, P. (1987). Synaptogenesis in the prefrontal cortex of the macaque monkey. *The Second World Congress of Neuroscience (IBRO), Neuroscience, 22* (Suppl.), S211. Oxford/New York: Pergamon Press (abstract).

Cavada, C. & Goldman-Rakič, P.S. (1987). Parcellation of primate posterior cortex based on connections with frontal, sensory and limbic areas. *The Second World Congress of Neuroscience (IBRO), Neuroscience, 22* (Suppl.), S116. Oxford/New York: Pergamon Press (abstract).

Chi, J.G., Doolling, E.C., & Gilles, F.H. (1977). Left-right asymmetries of the temporal speech areas in the human fetus, *Archives of Neurology, 34*, 346-348.

Davie, R., Butler, N., & Goldstein, H. (1975). *From birth to seven*. London: Longman.

Douglas, V. (1984). Attentional and cognitive problems. In M. Rutter (Ed.), *Developmental Neuropsychiatry* (pp.280-347). London: Churchill–Livingstone.

Elliott, C.D., Murray, D.J., & Pearson, L.S. (1978). *British Ability Scales. Recall of digits. Manual 3+4*. Windsor: NFER Publ. Co.

Entus, A.K. (1977). Hemispheric asymmetries in processing of dichotically presented speech and non-speech stimuli by infants. In S.J. Segalowitz & F.A. Gruber (Eds.), *Language development and neurological theory* (pp. 63–73). London: Academic Press.

Ferguson, H.B., & Rapoport, J.L. (1984). Nosological issues and biological validation. In M. Rutter (Ed.), *Developmental Neuropsychiatry* (pp.369-384). London: Churchill-Livingstone.

Frankenburg, W.K., & Dodds, J.B. (1967). The Denver developmental screening test, *Journal of Pediatrics, 71,* 181-91. See also the Swedish standardisation of the Denver developmental screening test: Egnell-Sundquist, G., Ingevald, B., Loven, K., Frantzich, I., Werner, S. & Zander, B. (1980) *Denverskalan.* Stockholm: Psykologiförlaget.

Freund, H.J. (1984). Premotor areas in man. *Trends in Neurosciences, 7,* 481-483.

Gillberg, C., Rasmussen, P., Carlström, G., Svenson, B., & Waldenström, E. (1982). Perceptual, motor and attention deficits in six-year-old children. Epidemiological aspects. *Journal of Child Psychology and Psychiatry, 23,* 131-144.

Gillberg, C., Gillberg, I.C., & Rasmussen, P. (1984). MBD-problematik bland Göteborgsbarn: Epidemiologi, etiologi och prognos. *Nordisk Psykiatrisk Tidsskrift, 38,* 115-121. (Summary in English pp. 120-121).

Gjaerum, B. & Borchgrevink, H.M. (1985). Neuropsychological and neuromotor profiles for the planning of treatment and training in mental retardation. *Progress through knowledge in mental retardation. The VII. World Congress of the International Association for the Scientific Study of Mental Deficiency* (p.32). New Dehli (abstract).

Gjaerum, B. & Borchgrevink, H.M. (1987a). *Neuropsychological and neuromotor assessment procedure. Manual.* Second edition: Oslo: Institute of Child Psychiatry, University of Oslo, Norway. (Unpublished).

Gjaerum, B. & Borchgrevink, H.M. (1987b). Neuropsychological assessment of children 8 years with ADD and other development disorders—principles of a new assessment procedure. *European Brain and Behaviour Society. Society workshop on attention deficit disorder and hyperkinetic sydnrome.* Oslo (abstract).

Graziani, L.J., Mason, J.C., & Cracco, J. (1981). Neurological aspects and early recognition of brain dysfunction in children: Diagnostic and prognostic significance of gestational, perinatal and postnatal factors. In P. Black (Ed.), *Brain dysfunction in children* (pp.131-170). New York: Raven Press.

Gross, M. & Wilson, W.C. (1974). *Minimal brain dysfunction: A clinical study of incidence, diagnosis and treatment in over 1000 children.* New York: Brunner/Mazel.

Hallahan, D.P., & Cruickshank, W.M. (1973). *Psychoeducational foundations of learning disabilities.* Englewood Cliffs, N.J.: Prentice Hall.

Helland, S., Hemsen, E., & Borchgrevink, H.M. (1983). Phonetic/phonemic disabilities and hearing threshold levels in preschool children. In M. Edwards (Ed.), *XIX. Congress of the IALP* (pp.508-513). Edinburgh/London.

Holle, B., Kemp, E., Bönnelycke, K., & Mortensen, L.T. (1977). *Motorisk-perceptuell udvikling 0-7 år.* Copenhagen: Munksgaard.

Ito, M. (1986). Neural systems controlling movement. *Trends in Neurosciences, 9,* 515-518.

Kelly, M.P. & Kirschner, H. (1986). Syndromes of the frontal lobes. In H. Kirschner (Ed.), *Behavioral neurology. A practical approach*, pp.101-120. New York/London: Churchill-Livingstone.

Kirschner, H. (1986). (Ed.), *Behavioral neurology. A practical approach.* New York/London: Churchill-Livingstone.

Knobloch, H., Stevens, F. & Malone, A.F. (1980). *Manual of developmental diagnosis. The administration and interpretation of the revised Gesell and Amatruda developmental and neurological examination.* Hagerstown: Harper & Row Publishers.

Kolb, B. & I.Q. Whishaw (1985). *Fundamentals of human neuropsychology.* San Francisco: Freeman.

Luria, A.R. (1973). *The working brain.* Harmondsworth: Penguin Books.

Luria, A.R. & Homskaya, E.D. (1970). Frontal lobes and the regulation of arousal processes. In D.I. Mostovsky (Ed.), *Attention: Contemporary theory and analysis* (pp.303-330). New York: Appleton-Century-Crofts.

Milner, B. & Petrides, M. (1984). Behavioural effects of frontal-lobe lesions in man, *Trends in Neurosciences, 7*, 403-407.

Molfese, D.L. (1977). Infant cerebral asymmetry. In S.J. Segalowitz & F.A. Gruber (Eds.), *Language development and neurological theory* (pp. 21–35). London: Academic Press.

Nordberg, L. & Alin-Akerman, B. (1983). *Standardisering av Griffiths utvecklingsskala for aldrarna 2–8 å.* Stockholm: Psykologiforlaget.

Rasmussen, T. & Milner, B. (1977). The role of early left-brain injury in determining lateralization of cerebral speech functions. In S.J. Dimond & D.A. Blizard (Eds.) *Annals of the New York Academy of Sciences, 299*, 355-369. New York.

Rubinstein, B. (1985). Organicity in child psychiatry. *Psychiatric Clinics of North America 8*(4), 755-777.

Rutter, M. (1984a). Introduction: concepts of brain dysfunction syndromes. In M. Rutter (Ed.) *Developmental Neuropsychiatry* (pp.1-11). London: Churchill-Livingstone.

Rutter, M. (1984b). Issues and prospects in developmental neuropsychiatry. In M. Rutter (Ed.) *Developmental Neuropsychiatry* (pp.577-598). London: Churchill-Livingstone.

Rutter, M. (1984c). Behavioural studies: questions and findings in the control of a distinctive syndrome. In M. Rutter (Ed.) *Developmental Neuropsychiatry* (pp.259-279). London: Churchill-Livingstone.

Rutter, M., Graham, P., & Yule, W. (1970). *A neuropsychiatric study in childhood. Clinics in developmental medicine*, Nos. 35-36. London: Spastics International Medical Publications/Heinemann Medical Books.

Salmaso, D. & Denes, G. (1982). Role of the frontal lobes on an attention task: A signal detection analysis. *Perceptual and motor skills, 54*, 1147-1150.

Schaffer,D., O'Connor, P.A., Schafer, S.Q. & Prupis, S. (1984). Neurological "soft signs": their origin, and significance for behavior. In M. Rutter (Ed.) *Developmental Neuropsychiatry* (pp.144-163). London: Churchill-Livingstone.

Shaywitz, B.A., Shaywitz, S.E., Byrne, T., Cohen, D.J. & Rothman, S. (1983). Attention deficit disorder: Quantitative analysis of CT. *Neurology, 33*, 1500-1503.

Sparks, R.W. & Holland, A.L. (1976). Method: Melodic intonation therapy for aphasia, *Journal of Speech and Hearing Disorders, 41*, 287.

Springer, S.P. & Deutsch, G. (1981). *Left brain, right brain.* San Francisco: Freeman.

Steffen, H. (1975). Cerebral dominance: The development of handedness and speech. *Acta Paedopsychiatrica, 41*(6), 223-235.

St. James Roberts, I. (1979). Neurological plasticity, recovery from brain insult, and child development. In H.W. Reese & L.P. Lipsitt (Eds.), *Advances in child development and behavior*, Vol. *14* (pp. 253–319). New York: Academic Press.

Taylor-Sarno, M. (1980). Review of research in aphasia: Recovery and rehabilitation. In M. Taylor Sarno & O. Höök (Eds.), *Aphasia: Assessment and treatment* (pp.15-32). Stockholm: Almquist & Wiksell.

TINS (1984). The frontal lobes - uncharted provinces of the brain. *Trends in Neurosciences.* Special issue, 7(11).

Towbin, A. (1981). Neuropathological aspects. II. Perinatal brain damage and its sequels. In P. Black (Ed.), *Brain dysfunction in children* (pp.47-78). New York: Raven Press.

Wada, J. & Rasmussen, T. (1960). Intracarotid sodium amytal for the lateralization of cerebral speech dominance. *Journal of Neurosurgery, 17*, 266.

Woods, B.T. & Carey, S. (1979). Language deficits after apparent clinical recovery from childhood aphasia. *Annals of Neurology, 6*, 405-407.

The Hypoarousal Hypothesis:
What is the Evidence?

Hallgrim Klöve
Department of Clinical Neuropsychology
University of Bergen, Norway

INTRODUCTION

This chapter addresses the hypoarousal hypothesis as a model of explaining the effects of central stimulants in improving hyperactive behavior. Arousal is a rather vaguely defined concept and is often used synonymously with other terms such as activation, awakeness, emotions, drive, and similar concepts as discussed by Eysenck (1970) in his book, "The biological basis of personality." One could relate the concept to an "intensity dimension" of behavior as visualized by Duffy (1962) in a neurological context, it may represent the degree of cortical activation, which again may reflect the degree of activity in the central activating system which is also often known as the Reticular Activation System (RAS) (Moruzzi & Magoun, 1949). Netter (1975) has skillfully described and illustrated some of the important features of RAS, and basic features will be reviewed here.

AROUSAL

If a normal person receives a certain level of stimulation, by extraneous or internal events, he will ordinarily remain awake and conscious of his environement, provided he is not overwhelmed by fatigue. When cortex receives sufficient afferent impulses, it is said to be aroused or activated. That is when a critical number of cortical neurons are brought into the proper pattern of activity characterizing a state of conciousness and alertness. Such changes in activity can be recorded electroencephalographically. The arousal or activation pattern evoked by a stimulus of a certain minimum intensity is called desynchronization and has cognitive and emotional problems of hyperactive children (Barkley & Jackson, 1977). There is, however, no evidence that the effects of central stimulants are paradoxical or act in way which is special for hyperactive children. All evidence indicate that central stimulants pharmacologically and behaviorally act similarly

131

in hyperactive children as it does in normal children (Rapoport, 1978). It is probably also fair to say that many animal studies in regard to the effects of central stimulants have been in part misunderstood, and in part been used for very simplistic analogies in regard to human problems (for critical discussions see Robbins, Jones, & Sahakian; and Sagvolden, Wultz, Moser, Moser, & Mörkrid; both this volume). In reviewing the clinical literature it appears that both inclusion and exclusion criteria differs considerably from study to study. Nevertheless there low voltage, high frequency potentials. Thus, the great afferent systems are important for promoting cortical activation and wakefulness. However, at relatively low levels of stimulation this is not enough and the ascending reticular activating system of the brain, which terminates rostrally in the posterior hypothalamus and lower thalamus, becomes important and serves as an amplifier. The reticular system has a generalized influence on the cortex. Thus, when we in this context are talking about activation or arousal, we are talking about the generalized, undifferentiated, central-activation-system response. This response has two important dimensions, namely the general activation of neocortex and the general activation of the autonomic nervous system, notably the sympathetic part. The pathways from its rostral part to the neocortex are not well understood. Collaterals from the great afferent pathways feed into RAS and, theoretically, if it receives enough impulses it will discharge into the cortex and produce cortical wakefulness even if the activity of the afferent system in itself is not strong enough to do so. RAS is thus able to maintain wakefulness at levels of visceral and somatic stimulation which would not ordinarily activate the cortex.

RAS is sometimes regarded as a non-specific sensory system, because in some experiments, it has been possible to stimulate the structure alone and produce the cortical and behavioral effects of arousal. The evidence is overwhelming that the reticular system in the brain stem is a necessary prerequisite for activation. When it is damaged by accident, disease, or experiments, the organisms behavior will change.

THE HYPOAROUSAL HYPOTHESIS

That hypoarousal is a feature of hyperactivity is a very attractive idea from the point of view of being able to explain the effect of central stimulants. The idea that the beneficial effect of central stimulants represents a so-called "paradoxical effect," is not very well substantiated at all, and there is no well substantiated neither theoretical nor empirical evidence of the relevance of the paradoxical effect hypothesis. The idea has, however, developed on the basis of the fact that stimulants do indeed modify in a positive direction, the hyperkinetic as well as the cognitive and emotional problems of hyperactive children (Barkley & Jackson, 1977). There is, however, no evidence that the effects of central stimulants are paradoxical or act in a way which is special for hyperactive children. All evidence indicate that central stimulants pharmacologically and behaviorally act similarly in hyperactive children as it does in normal children (Rapoport, 1978). It is probably also fair to say that many animal studies in regard to the effects of central stimulants have been in part misunderstood, and in part been used for very simplistic analogies in regard to human problems (for critical discussions, see Robbins, Jones & Sahakian; and Sagvolden, Wultz, Moser, Moser & Mør-krid; both this volume). In reviewing the clinical literature it appears that both inclusion and exclusion criteria differs considerably from study to study. Nevertheless there has been a clear tendency to compare studies in spite of quite obvious differences in the criteria used for composing groups. For example, Virginia Douglas (1979) has in several of her studies deliberately excluded children with brain injury. On the other hand, other studies have deliberately excluded children in whom one could reasonably explain the deviant behavior on the basis of psychological problems such as anxiety or depression or on the basis of medication such as barbiturates or certain antihistamines (Klöve & Hole, 1979).

Ferguson and Pappas (1979) have made a very comprehensive review of the psychophysiological research on hyperactivity. In reviewing this article, it is interesting to notice that while there is rather consistent evidence that groups of hyperactive children with considerable consistency show evidence of hypoarousal, the conclusion in Ferguson and Pappas' review, is formulated so that it is easy to come to a different conclusion: "Despite large numbers of investigations carried out and the wide variety of measures used, we can make no certain conclusion regarding the arousal state of the CNS of hyperactive children. We are faced with conflicting findings from studies examining both peripheral and central indecies of arousal. There are a number of easy scapegoats for this failure to find reliable differences on any single index of arousal. First, careful scrutiny would allow us to fault almost every study on one or another methodological point: Such specifics as electrode placement, electrode jelly, interstimulus intervals, stimulus intensity, instructions, and details of data analysis provide fertile ground for questioning individual studies" (Ferguson & Pappas, 1979, p. 70-71). In reviewing in detail the studies on basis of which Ferguson and Pappas drew their conclusions, it is quite obvious that the situations is very confusing. As Ferguson and Pappas point out, there are two or three main reasons for the inconsistencies in data. Obvious problems are the criteria used in composing the groups, and, the psychophysiological recording techniques. Design problems are also listed as relevant in many instances. Since many studies used repeated measures, a cross-over design should be a standard feature in this type of research.

The heterogeneity of subject population used is certainly a problem. The subjects have been labeled variously as "learning disabled," "minimal brain damage," "minimal brain dysfunction," "hyperkinetic," and "hyperactive." The screening for brain damage, emotional and psychiatric problems and low intelligence varied from study to study, and in additon as mentioned, the recording techniques have also been inconsistent. However, in a review of the available evidence there is actually only one study (Laufer, Denhoff, & Solomons, 1957) that supports the overarousal hypothesis. It is clear at this point that although many crucial variables change from study to study, those differences that have been described between hyperactives and normal controls strongly favor the underarousal hypothesis. In regard to indeces of central arousal, as for instance in studies using EEG, the results are no more consistent that those having used electrodermal measures.

On the basis of observations on the relationship between centrally stimulating drugs and arousal level, it has been only natural that psychologists have turned their attention towards psychophysiological reaction patterns in hyperactive children. Studies by Boydstun (1968), and by Satterfield and Dawson (1971) do indeed suggest that hyperactive children are hypo-aroused from a central nervous system reactivity point of view. Satterfield and Dawson found that hyperactive children had a higher skin resistance level and fewer spontaneous skin resistance responses than control children.

In general, we have found that there is a high correlation between tonic and phasic response in the sense that without a minimal tonic level, there can be no phasic response. EEC has also been used, and some interesting studies (e.g., Grünewald- Zuberbier, Grünewald, & Rasche, 1975) have demonstrated that hyperactive children have specific changes in several EEC variables. There seems to be higher percentage of alpha activity. There seems to be a higher threshold for desynchronizing the EEC in hyperactive children, and once this desynchronizating is achieved, return to baseline alpha activity is more rapid than in controls. All these findings tend to support the hypoarousal hypothesis. Finally, the brainstem evoked-potential technique should be mentioned, but the lack of standardized equipment and procedures has been a barrier in comparing results between laboratories.

The problem of the definition of hyperactivity is amply demonstrated by Ferguson and Pappas (1979). Our concept of hyperactivity has been operationally defined as those hyperactive children who were not anxious and neurotic, depressed, exhibited marked situational coping problems, or who were on drugs known to induce hyperactive behavior (Klöve & Hole, 1979). In other words, a number of conditions which are known to cause hyperactive behavior, restlessness, concentration problems, and affective control problems were excluded. Applying those criteria in several independent studies on different patient samples, we have been able to show that the hyperactive groups have lower Skin Conductance Level (SCL) and a more rapid habituation rate to auditory stimuli than control children and children with behavioral problems which could be explained psychologically or on the basis of taking drugs such as barbiturates and other antiepileptics. These results have been published earlier (Klöve & Hole, 1979).

In this study, SCL were obtained before and one hour after administration of 10 mg of methylphenidate (Ritalin). The premedication levels were significantly lower than for the control groups, while after medication SCL changed in direction of the control groups. It is our contention that children who demonstrate a clear psychophysiological response to methylphenidate or dextro-amphetamine are also behaviorally good responders to the drug. It should be mentioned that there also are children who do not show clear psychophysiological responses to stimulants who appear to be good responders behaviorally.

With background in Bradley's (1937) observation that dextro-amphetamine had a positive effect on undesired behavior, and a large number of subsequent studies on the effect of centrally stimulating drugs (Barkley, 1977), we have formulated two hypotheses, namely (1) Since in some patients the hyperactive behavior improves after administration of centrally stimulating drugs, the drug is most likely stimulating a *hypoactive* central nervous system. The idea of a paradoxical effect of centrally stimulating drugs is in other words rejected. It is felt that the theoretical basis for this concept never has been demonstrated, and the use of the "paradoxical effect" explanation developed as a result of lack of understanding of the pharmacological actions of centrally stimulating drugs. (2) If the centrally stimulating drugs indeed are acting upon a *hypo*functional nervous system, there ought to be independent evidence supporting the hypothesis of a dysfunctional nervous system. With this in mind the developmental history of the patients in our studies were analyzed in detail with an idea of revealing deviations in early development. As I just indicated, our hypothesis relating to a hypoaroused central nervous system seem to be supported by our findings. In regard to these childrens' early development, a rather striking finding was that after having obtained the data on the birth weight and gestation period ratio, it was found that about 50% of the hyperactive children with abnormally low autonomic reactivity fell below or above two standard deviations from the mean, thus representing a group with an unusual large proportion of dysmature children.

CONCLUSION

In conclusion, there is ample evidence to support the hypoarousal hypothesis in hyperactive children. Theoretically, it may be difficult to explain the positive effects of central stimulants in hyperaroused cases and both empirically and clinically it appears doubtful if central stimulants are indicated in these cases.

Footnote: The author acknowledges the support of the Norwegian Research Council for Science and the Humanities.

REFERENCES

Barkley, R.A. (1977). A review of stimulant drug research with hyperactive children. *Journal of Child Psychology and Psychiatry and Allied Disciplines, 18*, 347-165.

Barkley, R.A., & Jackson, Jr., T.L. (1977). Hyperkineses, automatic nervous system activity and stimulant drug effects. *Journal of Child Psychology and Psychiatry and Allied Disciplines, 18*, 347-357.

Boydstun, J.A. (1968). Physiologic and motor conditioning and generalization in children with minimal brain dysfunction. *Conditional Reflex, 3*, 81-104.

Bradley, C. (1937). The behavior of children receiving benzedrine. *American Journal of Psychiatry, 94*, 577-585.

Douglas, V.I. (1979). Discussion of "The Hyperkinetic Syndrome". In R.L. Trites (Ed.), *Hyperactivity in children* (p. 137). Baltimore: University Park Press.

Duffy, D.E. (1962). *Activation and behavior.* New York: Wiley and Sons.

Eysenck, H.J. (1970). *The biological basis of personality.* Springfield: Charles C. Thomas.

Ferguson, H.B., & Pappas, B.A. (1979). Evaluation of psychophysiological, neurochemical and animal models of hyperactivity. In R.L. Trites (Ed.), *Hyperactivity in children* (pp. 61-92). Baltimore: University Park Press.

Grünewald-Zuberbier, G., Grünerwald, G., & Rasche, A. (1975). Hyperactive behavior and EEC arousal reactions in children. *Electroencephalography and Clinical Neurophysiology. 38*, 149-159.

Klöve, H., & Hole, K. (1979). The hyperkinetic syndrome: Criteria for diagnoses. In R. L. Trites (Ed.) *Hyperactivity in children* (pp. 121-136). Baltimore: University Park Press.

Laufer, M.W., Denhoff, E., & Solomons S. (1957). Hyperkinetic impulse disorder in children's behavior problems. *Psychosomatic Medicine, 19*, 38-49.

Moruzzi, G., & Magoun, H.W. (1949). Brain stem reticular formation and activation of the EEG, *Electroencephalography and Clinical Neurophysiology, 1*, 455-473.

Netter, F.H. (1975). *Nervous system, Vol. I.* The Ciba collection of medical illustrations. Basel: Ciba.

Rapoport, J.L., Buchsbaum, M.S., Zahn, T.P., Weingartner H., Ludlow, C., & Mikkelsen, E.J. (1978). Dextroamphetamine: Cognitive and behavioral effects in normal prepubertal boys. *Science, 199*, 560-562.

Satterfield, J.H., & Dawson, W.E. (1971). Electrodermal correlates of hyperactivity in children. *Psychophysiology, 8*, 191-198.

Activation: Base-Level and Responsivity
A Search for subtypes of ADDH Children by Means of Electrocardiac, Dermal and Respiratory Measures

Eddy Brand
Harry van der Vlugt
Department of Psychology
Tilburg University
The Netherlands

INTRODUCTION

ADDH in relation to ECR-patterns

The present study is designed to investigate the specificity of the traditional diagnostic procedures to identify ADDH children by means of psychophysiological assessment procedures. Outcomes obtained from traditional questionnaires like the Kendall's Self Control Rating Scale were compared with some psychophysiological measures. The current view on ADDH is that at least two subtypes of this syndrome do exist: One subtype that benefits from stimulant-treatment and another that does not benefit. Based upon his research with the Galvanic Skin Level (GSL), Klöve (1987) suggests a hyperaroused subtype and a hypoaroused subtype. The last subtype apparently responds favorably to stimulant drug treatment.

During a previous study of ADDH (Brand, 1985) three groups (N = 10) of 11-year old boys (ADDH boys; non-ADDH Learning Disabled boys; and a control group) were subjected to a short screening battery (mainly cognitive tests) and the Continuous Performance Task (CPT). During the CPT, Electro Cardiac Activity (ECG) was recorded. The Inter-Stimulus-Interval (ISI) time of 4 s was too short to return to a stable baseline level of the ECG making it impossible to analyse the contribution of the stimuli to the ECG variables. However, the discriminative power of the screening battery in combination with the outcomes of the CPT enabled us to discriminate the three groups at a highly significant level (83% correct). The present study was done at the Pedological Institute Nijmegen to (a) improve the methods and add neurophysiological measures and (b) in order to detect perhaps the two proposed subtypes of hyperactivity. The heart-rate data are compared with data we collected in normal controls one year earlier.

Activation, Arousal

Cohen and Douglas (1972) demonstrated that the responses and habituation to nonsignal stimuli are the same for hyperactive and non-hyperactive children. When a reaction-time type of task is used, the non-hyperactive children outperform the hyperactives. Hyperactive children do not show such a profound orientation response (OR), they do not perform as well and seem to profit less from the warning signal, and they seem to be less well prepared for the task; their alertness does not increase as much.

Zentall (1975) was among the first to suggest that hyperactive children were underaroused. He based his theory mainly upon the fact that hyperactive children perform better after stimulant medication. He also indicated that a stimulus-rich environment improved the performance of hyperactive children, the so-called "optimal-stimulation theory."

The fact that amphetamines have a positive effect on hyperactive children could also be interpreted in a different way: Most of these alternative interpretations do suggest that amphetamines have a paradoxical effect on hyperactive children. The proposed different brain mechanisms were:

1) stimulantia do affect those nuclei that stimulate or regulate behavior more for hyperactive children than for normal children.
2) stimulantia affect the impulse-inhibiting nuclei more in hyperactive children.
3) stimulantia activate those nuclei where information is filtered more in hyperactive children.

In a review, Hastings and Barkley (1978) concluded that hyperactives do not differ in their autonomic nervous system (ANS) *baseline* level of activity. (Although subgroups do show signs of underarousal on some ANS measures.) On *phasic* ANS measures consistent group differences between hyperactive and non-hyperactive children are found (Hastings & Barkley, 1978). According to these authors hyperactive children are less responsive to stimulation; they appear to be underaroused. Studies using EEG measures show similar effects, although in a more complex way. It is clear that hyperactive children do not constitute a homogeneous group. Recent research suggests that stimulantia do not have a paradoxical effect upon hyperactive children, but works just the same way as it does for non-hyperactive children.

Because activation cannot be considered a unitary construct, but as a collection of activation levels, hyperactivity must not be seen any longer as a homogeneous phenomenon. Reality is better reflected when one speaks of specific activation and specific responsivity: Specific in the sense that every dimension of activation, like heart rate, skin conductance etc., show different responses. Specific also in the sense that hyperactive children do demonstrate a different evoked-response pattern than non-hyperactive children (Hastings & Barkley, 1978).

Measuring Heart Rate

Psychophysiological responses are extremely sensitive to changes in psychological states, often more sensitive than behavioral ratings (Campos, 1976). Studies of heart rate (HR) response have been demonstrated to be one of the most sensitive and reliable responses to be measured. HR responses can be useful in the detection of the perceptual and the emotional reactions of the child. Test-retest reliability of individual HR responses are sufficient to justify HR-studies. HR can decrease or increase (bidirectional nature) as a response to a stimulus.

Directional Fragmentation

According to Lacey, Kagan, Lacey, and Moss (1963), the autonomous nervous system does not respond with all dimensions in the same direction, does not respond either with sympathetic or parasympathetic nervous system activation throughout the entire organism. Almost all organs are innervated by both; there is a balance between the two systems. Lacey talks about sympathetic-like and parasympathetic-like reactions, when it is too difficult to determine if a physiological reaction is caused by an increase in one part or a decrease in the other part of the autonomic system. The Evoked Cardiac Response (ECR-pattern) is a reflection of the balance between the sympathetic and parasympathetic nervous system. Both the cardiac acceleration and deceleration are under primary control of the parasympathetic (vagal) nervous system. When the vagal nerve is activated, the heart rate decreases and sympathetic effects are masked (Siddle & Turpin, 1980). The vagal-mediated HR effects are directly related to somato-motor activity; the activity of the striped muscles like the muscles around the mouth, muscles of gross motor activity and body position. All these phenomena are adaptations of the central nervous system to the environmental demands.

Evoked Cardiac Response and Reaction Time

Sroufe (1971) states that in a Simple Reaction Time task (SRT) with a fixed foreperiod, the HR deceleration preceding the Reaction Signal (RS) correlates significantly with the speed of responding. He thought that this deceleration reflects attention. This is particularly important as hyperactive children in general have attention problems. Sergeant (1981), and Sergeant and Kalverboer (1985) however demonstrated that hyperactive children perform as well as normal children on tasks that were self-paced or are of short duration. The hyperactive children's attention problems were only to be seen when sustained attention was required.

The Effect of Age on the Evoked Cardiac Response

By using the ECG data from a study by Blankers and Hamers (1986) we were able, by means of a regression analysis, to demonstrate an effect of age on the DECLEV variable. The variable DECLEV was computed; it compares the magnitude of the first and second deceleration in the typical triphasic WS-RS deceleration-acceleration-deceleration complex, where WS stands for warning stimulus and RS stands for reaction signal. Normal children show the following development: the response on the RS becomes relatively larger than on the WS, by increasing age. Analysing the ECR pattern of young children, they apparently do not respond differently on the WS and the RS. Although the WS and RS do have a different informative value and especially the WS should elicit an orienting reflex, the older children (11 years and above) respond relatively little on the WS, but strongly on the RS, which seems to be more important to them. Sroufe (1971) demonstrated, by means of a simple reaction time task, that:

1. With increasing age there is an increase in the D2 response, and
2. There is a correlation between a shorter reaction time and a larger D2 response using an ISI time of 5 s, but not with a 10 s ISI time.

Effect of Respiration on Heart Rate (HR)

The questions we asked ourselves were:

- are there any systematic differences in the Electro Cardiac Response (ECR) pattern between hyperactives and normoactives on a Simple Reaction Time task (SRT)?
- are residential children from a Pedological Institute different from normal school children with regard to ECR-measures?
- does the age-effect on the ECR-pattern found in normal children also occur in the ECR-pattern of the interns of the Pedological Institute?
- are there any differences in the phasic GSR-pattern and tonic GS-levels during a SRT task between hyperactive and non-hyperactive children?

Hypothesis concerning the possible relationship between ADDH and Cardiac Activity:

- The magnitude of the D2 in the ECR pattern is smaller in hyperactive children than in non-hyperactive children because the D2 may reflect attention (Lacey et al., 1963; Sroufe, 1971).

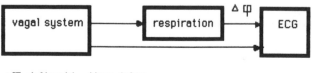

Δφ delta phi = time delay

FIG. 1.   Interactions between the vagal system, respiration and heart rate as measured by the electrocardiogram (ECG). For details see text.

- The autonomous activation level of hyperactive children is reduced (Zentall,1975), Hyperactive children may react positively to stimulantia. Hyperactive children are underaroused and less responsive to stimuli. They have a smaller score on the ECREAC variable (Fig. 2).
- Hyperactive children are more impulsive, and will respond more to the WS than to the RS (DECLEV score).
- About 75% of the hyperactive children will show a clear somatic/autonomic hypoarousal effect. These hyperactive children will respond favorably to stimulantia.
- The balance between the sympathetic and parasympathetic nervous system might be different between hyperactive and non-hyperactive children, which might be reflected in the ECR pattern.

METHOD

Subjects

All 40 subjects, mostly boys, were residents of the Pedological Institute at Nijmegen. They were between 7 and 13 years. An important feature one should be aware of is that the children from the Pedological Institute are compared with each other. This means that controls were severely learning-disabled children also institutionalized at the Pedological Institute. All children participating in this study had serious developmental problems.

Procedure

The various dimensions (signals from heart, skin, respiration, reaction time) were recorded on an instrumentation recorder (Hewlett Packard) to be analyzed off line. The analog-digital conversion took place on a DEC PDP 11/10 computer.

All children who are residents of the Pedological Institute Nijmegen were examined with:

a) the Dutch translation of the Kendall questionnaire, the Self Control Rating Scale (SCRS), translated into Dutch by Oosterbaan (1986).
b) a neuropsychological screening battery by Berndsen-Peeters & van der Vlugt (1986).
c) Recordings of the ECG and GSR during SRT. The SCRS's were completed by the teachers and the group-leaders of the children. Data obtained from the above-mentioned measurements was compared with heart-rate data (evoked-cardiac-response patterns) collected from a normal population at Tilburg University in 1986 (Brand, van der Vlugt, & Oosterbaan, 1987).

After the child was accustomed to the testing situation, the testing procedures were explained to the child and the experimental task was practiced until the child knew the simple reaction time task (SRT). A 3000 Hz, 70 dB tone, lasting 50 ms was used as a warning signal (WS). The response signal (RS) was a light-flash. The fore-period was 16 s, the inter-stimulus interval (ISI) was 4 s. The total duration of each trial was 20 s. Responses on the WS were recorded as 'false alarms', responses occurring more than 650 ms after the RS were recorded as 'late' responses, and responses more than 3 s after the RS were counted as omissions. In both of the last-mentioned cases, a penalty tone (feedback) was given. During the 20 min test session, all signals were recorded on magnetic tape. The signals were: ECG, GSL, GSR, Respiration, RT, WS, and RS. All signals were also monitored on two oscilloscopes. Simultaneously, peculiarities like falling from the chair, gliding, unexpected visitors etc., were recorded.

The Kendall SCRS were filled in by the teachers and the group-workers. The test scores were corrected for age and intelligence. The physiological data were registered as follows: The heart activity signal was recorded by means of three Ag-AgCl electrodes placed according to the Leidse triangle system (One electrode on the sternum, and the other two electrodes right and left on the lowest rib of the chest).The heart signals went through a preamplifier to the magnetic tape recorder. The amplifier had a cutoff frequency of 40 Hz (high). The GSL and the GSR were measured with a skin conductance recorder (Conductron 330). Two small lead electrodes, which were adjusted to the finger with adhesive tape were used.

Operationalizing the ECG-activation: the "Anchor-Points" of the Evoked Cardiac Response (ECR). For the statistical analysis we divided the ECR pattern into the following parts (1) a 16 s fore-period terminating with the Warning Signal (WS) (2) a 4 s block-period between WS and Reaction Signal (RS) (see Fig. 3).

Data were analyzed off line on a DEC VAX cluster (two 785's and later a VAX 8700), using programs written in FORTRAN and statistics from the SPSS-X package. We used the Kolmogorow Smirnow test and the Mann Whitney U-test for the analysis of the paper-and-pencil test data, and a t-test for the psychophysiological data. Because age effects are demonstrated for HR and the magnitude of the ECR, age was used as a covariate in the regression. For most variables a clear regression line could be computed. If necessary the test scores were corrected for age. The studentized residuals are used for all of the variables.

RESULTS AND DISCUSSION

The population of the Pedological Institute is a heterogeneous group. The small number of children (N=37) and the large age-range (7-13 years) posed us with an extra difficulty. During the interpretation of the outcomes one should be aware of the small number of hyperactive children. This leads us to the first problem we encountered with a population like this. How does one identify the typical hyperactive child? The teacher ratings showed a high correlation with the test-results of the neuropsychological screening battery, while the ratings of the group-workers showed a high correlation with the psychophysiological data. Maybe the teachers are better observers of the cognitive consequences of hyperactivity. Also the ratings given by the teachers were systematically lower than those of the group-workers. The ratings given by the teachers were calculated relative to the mean SCRS of the class. The most reliable rating of hyperactivity was obtained by averaging the relative teacher SCRS and the relative group-worker SCRS. Differences in the SCRS in the school situation and the SCRS in the housing situation can be caused by the fact that these hyperactive children demonstrated more hyperactive behavior in the school than in the housing situation. (For the differentiation between pervasive versus situational hyperactivity see Rutter, this volume; Taylor, this volume). Also, the teacher may score the Kendall questionnaire from a different point of view than the group-worker.

Based on the average SCRS's a cutoff score was calculated in order to assign the children to the hyperactive and the non-hyperactive groups. The SCRS's were also used as a continuum in order to allow for the calculation of correlations between the SCRS's and the psychophysiological variables. Although some questions remain to be solved, there seems to be a relation between HR deceleration and attention (Kagan, 1965; Lewis, Kagan, Campbell, & Kalafat, 1966). Based on recent research findings, the previously accepted explanation is in question again. Even neonatals do show a cardiac orienting response when presented a visual stimulus (Sameroff & Chandler, 1975).

In Figure 3 one can see two decelerations (D1 and D2) and two accelerations (A1 and A2). One can also see the latencies of the extremes (LD1, LA1, LD2, LA2). One can also measure the top-top differences, for instance between A1 and D2 (A1D2). In the present study, we used a heart-responsivity score suggested by Lyytinen (1984) where the summation of the absolute values of the decelerations and the accelerations were as explained in Figure 2.

The mean level of the fore-period (16 s) is used as the base-line or Mean Heart Rate (MHR). This level differs from person to person. The eight 0.5 s intervals (the 4 s between WS and RS) are considered as block-period. There are two ways to analyze the ECR: In the first way, all measurements are taken from fixed points, for example the base-line or the WS. In the second way, all variables are measured as individual top-top differences, so that both time and amplitude are mea-

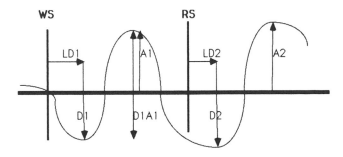

FIG. 2.   ECREAC = D1 + D1A1 + A1D2 + D2A2. For explanation see text.

sured from non-prefixed points. Both ways (fixed and non-fixed) were used in the present study.

The Heart-Rate Data

The results of the HR data are partially a replication of results obtained from hyperactive children attending special schools for the learning disabled (Brand, 1985). The ECR pattern is emerging later after the WS, the difference in latency increasingly lagging behind over time. The whole pattern seems to be stretched. Besides that, the overall ECR pattern (Fig. 3) after the first deceleration is increasingly debased, resulting in a pattern below the base-line.

The present study showed a larger reactivity (ECREAC) in the hyperactive children. At first sight these results seem to be contrary to the prediction that hyperactive children are hypoaroused. But when we consider that the ECR-pattern is totally controlled by the parasympathetic nervous system (PNS) a system that in all other cases only inhibits processes—the results might make sense. The PNS is responsible for the slowing down of somatic processes, such as heart rate, perspiration, etc. The PNS seems to be more active in hyperactive children than in non-hyperactive children, resulting in a more intense cardiac response in hyperactive children. We also examined the difference between the first and the second deceleration (the DECLEV variable), and compared hyperactive children with non-hyperactive children. In contrast to normal children, hyperactive children do not show an age effect on the DECLEV variable.

Although the D2 is supposed to be related to attention, we did not find that the relative magnitude of the D2 is smaller for the hyperactive children. Again a PNS effect was demonstrated (e.g., a lower ECR-pattern for the hyperactive children) but not an attention effect (e.g., no smaller D2 for the hyperactive children).

The mean heart rate is the same for hyperactive and non-hyperactive children. For hyperactive children, the responsivity of the heart is greater, the ECR-pattern falls below the base-line and is delayed as is shown in Figure 3.

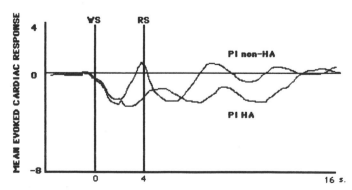

FIG. 3.   Evoked cardiac responses (ECR) in hyperactive (PI HA) and Control (PI non-HA) Children. For details see text.

Galvanic Skin Measures
Galvanic Skin Level

According to several theories (e.g., Zentall & Zentall, 1975) and in conjunction with the results of Klöve (1987; this volume), hyperactive children are supposed to be hypoaroused. With regard to the variable Galvanic Skin Level we can agree with this notion. The Galvanic Skin Conductance Level is lower for hyperactive children than for non-hyperactive children.

Galvanic Skin Response

For the Galvanic Skin Response there is supposed to be less responsivity. Only the evoked skin responses in the block-period were considered in our analysis. In the present study, the recording of the GSR has a fairly large number of missing values due to intermittent problems with the apparatus during the experiment. In contrast, the other signals (ECG, respiration, etc.) were always recorded. The GSRs in the hyperactive children were approximately as frequent as in the non-hyperactive children. The magnitudes of the responses were smaller for the hyperactive children (Fig. 4). The latency of the responses cannot be compared directly due to variable spontaneous response activity in the fore-period, but in hyperactive children the mean latency of the GSR seems to be shorter than in non-hyperactives. However the mean amplitude was smaller, so it is quite understandable that the skin response reaches its maximum earlier. It was predicted that the responses were smaller and slower. Only the first prediction was confirmed.

At first the skin responses were analysed in another way than by Lyytinen (1984). We computed the cumulative frequencies of responses in short time intervals instead of detecting and computing the tops of the skin responses, the latencies and the magnitudes of the tops. In an additional analysis we used Lyytinen's method. The conclusion of the electrodermal activity is that for the three most hyperactive children there is a clear lower skin level baseline, and the mean skin response is smaller.

Respiration

There were no differences between hyperactives and non-hyperactives in terms of respiration data. The variance was large in the total Pedological Institute group. (We did find a small, non significant, difference: The hyperactive children showed faster respiration-rates before the WS, after the WS no difference was noticed.)

Reaction Time Task

All the children from the Pedological Institute had longer reaction times than children attending regular schools (Fig. 5). Previous research by Van Zomeren (1980) demonstrated that brain-damaged children and adults had longer reaction times. Although the children of the Pedological Institute had normal or near-normal intelligence levels, they suffer from severe learning and/or behavioral problems. It is possible that most of these children, at a neurological level, function differently from regular school-children. The slow reaction times and current extensive neuropsychological assessment indicate cerebral dysfunction.

Reaction-speed, attention, and motivation are positively correlated with the magnitude of the D2 (Sroufe, 1971; Lewis et al., 1966). The mean reaction time for the most-hyperactive children (H) is even slower than the mean reaction time of the other Pedological Institute children (O) (Figure 5). The hyperactive children also do show much more false alarms (p < .03) and more omissions (p < .02). Previous studies by Douglas (1972) and Czudner and Rourke (1972) also showed more false alarms and omissions for hyperactive children. They also showed the longer mean reaction-times for hyperactive children. Hyperactive children can sometimes respond as fast as non-hyperactive children, but their capacity for sustained attention is lower and the reaction-times do show more fluctuations than normals. (Czudner & Rourke, 1972). Many of these variables are influenced by age.

In general, the older the child gets, the better he can perform on a task and the less errors he makes. A developmental effect is even true for the evoked cardiac response. The most remarkable finding is that all residents of the Pedological Institute showed a delayed evoked cardiac response pattern and that they responded as intensely to the WS as to the RS.

Other variables

There were no group differences in terms of respiration, cardiac-arhythmia and some relative-score variables. Neither the habituation of the ECR nor the GSR discriminated between the groups.

The variable D1 of the psychophysiological data in Figure 6 shows that children number 1 and 3 do have the greatest deceleration following the WS. Also the latency of the acceleration following the RS is longer for these two children. They also do show the fastest habituation. Klove (1987) reported that hyperac-

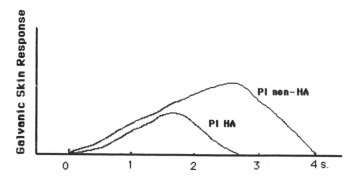

FIG. 4.   Galvanic Skin response (GSR) in hyperactive (Pi HA) and control (Pi non-HA) Children.

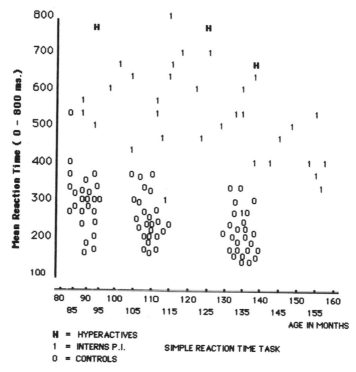

FIG. 5. Reaction Times in hyperactive (H), interns of the Pedological Institute (1) and Controls (0) as measured by the Simple Reaction Time Task.

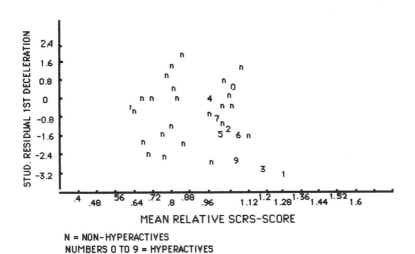

FIG. 6. The non-hyperactive children are drawn as 'n' and the 10 children with the highest SCRS do have the symbols 1 through 9, werein the child with number 1 has the highest SCRS.

Studentized Residual of the first deceleration in the cardiac orienting response plotted against mean relative Self Control Rating Scale score.

tives are not only less responsive to stimuli, but they also show a faster habituation to stimuli (Klöve, 1987). The plot containing the mean reaction times does, not show consistent group results; only the three most hyperactive children are different (Fig. 5). We see the three most hyperactive children as H's in Figure 5. The amount of hyperactivity, operationalized in the SCRS score, correlated with the latency of the decelerations and accelerations of the evoked cardiac response pattern. The entire pattern had a longer latency in the hyperactives compared to the non-hyperactive children (Fig. 3). The entire population of the Pedological Institute (hyperactives and non-hyperactives) show a delayed cardiac-response pattern compared to a normal control group.

Figure 6 shows that the evoked cardiac response is as large to the WS as to the RS for the Pedological Institute children. The normal control group shows a developmental effect: the older the child gets, the bigger the response is on the RS compared to the response on the WS. The magnitude of the two decelerations is not the same for all the children in the normal control group. For the hyperactive as well as the non-hyperactive Pedological Institute children, the D1 and the D2 are equally big. The developmental effect on the relative response-intensity on WS and RS, as demonstrated for normal children by Blankers and Hamers (1986), was not reproduced. Hyperactive children showed more false alarms and omissions then the controls. All of the children of the Pedological Institute responded slower on the RT task than normal controls of the same age.

CONCLUSION

Research on hyperactivity (ADDH) in a group of residential severely-disturbed children is quite a challenge. Trying to select the top 10 or 20% hyperactive children based upon the Self Control Rating Scale by Kendall turned out to be very problematical. Teachers and groupleaders apparently used different criteria.

Electrocardiac, dermal, respiratory, and reaction time measures appear to play an important role in the identification of those hyperactive children that will benefit from stimulant treatment. Comparison on these variables within the Pedological Institute group was seriously confounding. Comparison with an external regular school demonstrates clear differences between children at the Pedological Institute and regular school children.

This study demonstrates again the need for "absolute standardized measures," instead of the relative value of the questionnaire approach. The validity of the psychophysiological measures like EEG, ECR, GSL, GSR require further exploration.

Standardization of the criteria, recording procedures, and an interdisciplinary (psychophysiological, neuropsychological, psychiatrical, etc.) approach might be a first step towards our understanding of the *hyperactive(s)*.

REFERENCES

Berndsen-Peeters, K., & van der Vlugt, H. (1986). Development and application of a screening battery for the detection of hyperactive and learning-disabled children. [Summary]. Proceedings of the ninth European Conference of the International Neuropsychological Society, 1986. *Journal of Experimental and Clinical Neuropsychology, 8*, 122.

Blankers, A., & Hamers, J. (1986). *Ontwikkelingsaspecten van fasische hartslagveranderingen in een WS-RS paradigma* [Developmental aspects of phasic heart rate changes in a WS-RS paradigm]. Unpublished doctoral dissertation, Tilburg University. The Netherlands.

Brand, E. (1985). Hartslagregistratie en Aandachtstaken bij hyperactieve, leergestoorde, en controle groep kinderen. [Heart rate registration and attention tasks in hyperactive, learning disabled, and control group children]. Unpublished doctoral dissertation, Tilburg University, The Netherlands. [Summary]. Proceedings of the European Conference of the International Neuropsychological Society, 1986. *Journal of Experimental and Clinical Neuropsychology, 8*, 122.

Brand, E., van der Vlugt, H., & Oosterbaan, H. (1987). Evoked cardiac responses in residential children.[Summary]. Proceedings of the Tenth European Conference of the International Neuropsychological Society, *Journal of Clinical and Experimental Neuropsychology, 9*, 277.

Campos, J. J. (1976). Heart rate: A sensitive tool for the study of emotional development in the infant. In L. P. Lipsitt (Ed.), *Developmental psychobiology: The significance of infancy* (pp. 1–31). Hillsdale, New Jersey: Erlbaum.

Cohen, N. J., & Douglas, V. I. (1972). Characteristics of the orienting response in hyperactive and normal children. *Psychobiology, 9*, 238 245.

Czudner, G., & Rourke, B. P. (1972). Age difference in visual reaction time of "brain-damaged" and normal children under regular and irregular preparatory interval conditions. *Journal of Experimental Child Psychology, 13*, 516–526.

Douglas, V. I. (1972). Stop, look, listen: The problem of sustained attention and impulse control in hyperactive and normal children. *Canadian Journal of Behavioral Science, 4*, 259–282.

Hastings, J. E., & Barkley, R. A. (1978). A review of psychophysiological research with hyperkinetic children. *Journal of Abnormal Child Psychology, 6*, 413–447.

Kagan, J. (1965). Reflection, impulsivity and reading ability in primary grade children. *Child Development, 36*, 609–628.

Klöve, H. (1987). Activation, arousal and neuropsychological rehabilitation. *Journal of Clinical and Experimental Neuropsychology, 9*, 297 309.

Lacey, J. I. , Kagan, J., Lacey, B. C., & Moss, H. A. (1963). Situational determinants and behavioral correlates of autonomic response patterns. In P.H. Knopp (Ed.), *Expression of emotions in man* (pp. 161–196). New York: International University Press.

Lewis, M., Kagan, J., Campbell, H., & Kalafat, J. (1966). The cardiac response as a correlate of attention in infants. *Child Development, 37*, 63–72.

Lyytinen, H. (1984). *The psychology of anticipation and arousal.* Unpublished doctoral dissertation. University of Jyväskylä, Finland.

Oosterbaan, H. (1986). *Dutch version of the Kendall's Self Control Rating Scale.* Unpublished Report, Nijmegen, The Netherlands.

Sameroff, A. J., & Chandler, M. J. (1975). Reproductive risk and the continuum of caretaking casualty. In F. D. Horowitz, (Ed.), *Review of child development research, 4* (pp. 187–244). London. University of Chicago Press.

Sergeant, J. A. (1981). *Attentional studies in hyperactivity.* Unpublished doctoral dissertation, Groningen University, Groningen, The Netherlands.

Sergeant, J. A., & Kalverboer, A. F. (1985, June). Hyperactivity: A scientific challenge. Unpublished symposium report. Groningen, The Netherlands.

Siddle, D. A. T., & Turpin, G. (1980). Measurement, quantification, and analysis of cardiac activity. In I. Martin & P. Venables. (Eds.), *Techniques in psychophysiology* (pp. 139–240). Chicester: Wiley and Sons.

Sroufe, L. A. (1971). Age changes in cardiac deceleration within a fixed foreperiod RT task: An index of attention. *Developmental Psychology, 5*, 338–343.

Van Zomeren, A. H. (1981). *Reaction time after closed-head injury.* Unpublished doctoral dissertation. Groningen University, Meppel, Krips, The Netherlands.

Zentall, S.S. (1975). Optimal stimulation as a theoretical basis of hyperactivity. *American Journal of Orthopsychiatry, 45*, 549–563.

The Diagnostic Significance of Attentional Processing: Its Significance for ADDH Classification—A Future DSM

Joseph Sergeant
Department of Clinical Psychology
University of Amsterdam
The Netherlands

Jaap J. van der Meere
Laboratory of Experimental
Clinical Psychology
University of Groningen
The Netherlands

DIAGNOSING ATTENTION DEFICITS

Psychodiagnostics is concerned with the classification, the explanation of how a disorder is caused, and with indicating an appropriate mode of remedy for a psychological disorder. In order to achieve the goals of psychodiagnostics, it is necessary to have a theoretical conception of the nature of the disorder(s) which is (are) the object of study. In this chapter, the object of study is a child who is unanimously described as being overboisterous at inappropriate settings, has apparently average intellectual abilities but is found to be a poor academic performer, which is associated with seemingly distractible and impulsive behaviour. The children which are being referred to have gone under various names: Minimal Brain Damage/Dysfunction (MBD), hyperkinetic, hyperactive, and currently: Attentional Deficit Disorder with Hyperactivity (ADDH). It would seem obvious that, if a child is called by the title of the diagnosis, i.e., suffering from Attentional Deficit Disorder, that the theoretical underpinnings for the diagnosis would be modern attentional theory. It will be argued here that the evidence supporting an attentional-process dysfunction in ADDH children is seriously open to question. Rather, it will be suggested, unless there is structural damage, the experimental evidence would favour the interpretation that the boisterous difficult-to-manage child whom we all recognise, is suffering from a disorder in energetical regulation mechanisms. In this chapter we will first consider what current diagnostics require in determining the diagnosis. We then proceed to examining strict process models of attention and then consider the evidence in support and against attention both as a process and as an energetical mechanism.

CURRENT CLASSIFICATION

As noted above, there have been a wide variety of terms used to describe the children which are currently being referred to as ADDH. The original conceptions of a brain dysfunction either of slight or minimal nature (Clements & Peters, 1962) passed to a behavioural description of hyperactivity (Stewart et al., 1966). The architects of the term ADDH avoided neurological assumptions and placed the symptomatology which would positively identify children squarely in the behavioural domain. With hindsight, it can be said the that term ADDH was generated by the then available research which suggested that sustainment of attention was poor in hyperactive children (Sykes et al., 1973) and that behavioral impulsivity could be found in cognitive measures of impulsivity such as the Matching Familiar Figures Test (Cohen et al., 1972; Campbell et al., 1977). Thus, apart from activity, the Diagnostic and Statistical Manual III (APA, 1980) defines the two crucial areas inattention and impulsivity as follows:

Inattention

Often fails to finish things he or she starts,

Often doesn't seem to listen,

Easily distracted,

Has difficulty concentrating on schoolwork or other tasks requiring sustained attention,

Has difficulty sticking to a play activity.

It is easy to see that one of the problems with this definition of inattention is the use of higher order and undefined terms such as distraction and sustained attention.

While it is easy to be critical of the efforts of the committee which assembled this definition, it is much harder to arrive at a consensus of terms which can be considered a well-operationalized set of research diagnostic criteria. The inattention cluster seems to be attempting to tell the diagnostician that the controlled maintenance of concentration both in terms of selective and sustained abilities is lacking in the ADDH child. As has been argued elsewhere, the description is imprecise and does not indicate which of the many cognitive processes associated with selective attention that may be disturbed (Sergeant, 1987).

The approach described here uses a well-defined model of attentional processing which is clearly linked to measurable parameters of attention.

Impulsivity

For the present purposes, it is necessary at this point to consider the concept of impulsivity. This term can be used to refer to unexpected, sudden and often inappropriate behaviour. DSM III catches this aspect of behaviour in its definition of impulsivity:

Often acts before thinking,

Frequently calls out in class,

Has difficulty awaiting turn.

The description becomes more heterogeneous with:

Shifts excessively from one activity to another,

Has difficulty organizing work,

Needs a lot of supervision

Again we note the idea of lack of control in modulating and organizing behaviour. In this sense, it is easy to understand that early research on the impulsivity of hyperactive children examined the cognitive control required by the child when both the speed and the accuracy of processing is demanded. This was operationalized in a task in which speed of processing and decision making often led to inaccurate responding. This was the well known Matching Familiar Figures Test developed by Kagan et al., (1964). In the earlier studies (Campbell et al., 1971; Cohen et al. 1972), the emphasis in interpretation seemed to be placed on the speed factor rather than on the inaccuracy parameter of processing. Possibly this emphasis can be explained by the apparent assumption that impulsivity is associated with haste. Later studies indicated the accuracy variable to be the more discriminative of these two variables in hyperactive children (Homatidis & Konstantareas, 1981; Schleifer et al., 1975; Sergeant et al., 1979). Indeed, follow-up of previously diagnosed hyperactives indicated that the accuracy of performance and not the speed of performance distinguished the hyperactives from controls (Hopkins et al., 1979).

An important issue to consider at this point is whether tests of attention such as the Stroop or attentional performance tasks are then truly reflecting a dysfunction in attention or are being confounded by how the subject is prepared to trade accuracy for the sake of speed. The subtle balance between how fast one may perform a test or task and the accuracy with which it is performed is a common human experience. In cognitive psychology this is referred to as the strategy of performance (Pachella, 1974). Clearly, before one may diagnose an attentional process disorder in any group of patients, one must be certain that the observed results are not due to the strategy which is being employed by the subjects. This is a point often missed by clinical researchers: a task can discriminate between the patient and control group but whether the task is tapping only the process, the strategy of the subject, or a combination of both has to be identified. In particular, it can be shown that the strategy employed by the subject in such tasks is dependent on the instructions which the researcher administers to the subjects (Pachella, 1974).

This has implications for the validity of the diagnostic terms used in DSM III to describe ADDH children. Can we be certain that: "acting before thinking" and "has difficulty awaiting turns" are reflecting stable personality traits or some subtle interaction between impulsivity control and the induced strategy evoked by a particular social situation? One consequence of this would be that instead of impulsivity and inattention being presented as separate factors in ADDH behaviour, they would be linked in a single list which describes failures of cognitive control.

The following section describes the operationalization of attention as a controlled process in terms of the division, sustainment and energetic qualities. These terms will be linked to a model of human information processing.

TOWARD A FUTURE CLASSIFICATION

Attention and Human Information Processing

Attention is a higher order construct, which when undefined can be used in a wide variety of different and sometimes conflicting ways (Rosenthal & Allen, 1978). The first concept of attention as used here is the division of attention, a process requiring controlled information processing. A second use of attention refers to the energetical aspects of the information processing system. This is commonly operationalized in clinical studies in terms of the sustainment of attention. More recently, it has also come to include the effort which a subject brings to bear in a task (Kahneman, 1973). In the present chapter, attention is defined as the rate at which controlled information processing occurs in human short term memory.

Before proceeding to inform the reader of the details of the model, it may be useful to commence with a general overview. This overview is provided schematically in Figure 1, which is derived from Sanders (1983). Basically, one may say that there are two aspects of the model: the micro-structural and the energetical features. Sanders (1983) martialled an impressive body of studies in which he showed that the concept of arousal, as distinguished from activation (Pribram & McGuiness, 1975), could be linked to the input and the output phases of the information processing chain.

In addition, he postulated that the task of the energy pool effort was to modulate or enhance the arousal, and activation system. Consequently, the information processing demands placed on the organism do not reflect only abstract, computational mechanisms but also the energetical aspects of the system. Thus, requiring a child to perform an attentional task necessarily involves both the computational mechanism required to perform the task and at the same time places

PROCESS–ENERGY MODEL

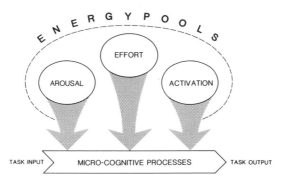

FIG. 1

demands on the effort, arousal, and activation pools. The significance of this for diagnostic purposes is that results from a particular study may reflect either of these two features or a combination of both. In order to achieve construct validity in ADDH research, careful definition and operationalization of task variables is required. It is this requirement which is the strength of the controlled processing model proposed by Schneider and Shiffrin (1977) and Shiffrin and Schneider (1977).

The primary distinction in the model of Shiffrin and Schneider is that attention demands are sometimes met by working in a controlled mode of processing and sometimes they are met by operating in the automatic mode of processing. Controlled processing requires time, is slow, can be inaccurate, and requires effort. This is to be distinguished from automatic processing which is fast, highly accurate, and costs little effort. By defining the central limitation of attention as being localized in the speed at which working memory could function, demands upon controlled processing became operationalized in the rate at which search in working memory could take place. When the demands of a task were able to be met by automatic processing, this would be manifested by an extremely short search time. This relationship is shown in Figure 2.

In the left hand panel of Figure 2, controlled processing is demanded by the task. This in manifested by a linear increase in reaction time as task demands increase. In the right hand panel, as the task demands increase, reaction time remains constant. Hence, the concepts control and automatic processing are operationalized in terms of the slope of reaction time in relation to the demands of a task.

The task which Schneider and Shiffrin used for their research was a variation of the paradigm developed by Sternberg (1969). In this paradigm, the subject is required to retain a number of targets in working memory. The number of targets to be held in memory may vary. This is called the load variable. The fea-

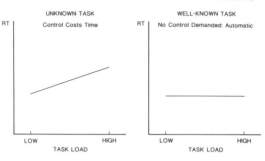

TASKS REQUIRING CONTROLLED AND AUTOMATIC PROCESSING

FIG. 2

ture which was added to this paradigm by Schneider and Shiffrin was variation or constancy in the target set. They found that, when the target set was varied from one trial to another, even after many thousands of trials, reaction time increased as a function of load. This was not the case when targets were kept constant. After practice with a constant set of targets, the reaction time gradually parallels the x axis. This was assumed to indicate that load no longer required controlled processing and hence the subject was using an effortless, fast, and automatic mode of processing.

The logic of the additive factor method (AFM) was used in establishing this model as well as that proposed by Sanders (1983). Sternberg (1969) proposed that a taxonomy of information processing variables could be derived by showing which task variables remained independent of one another and which variables interact with one another. He suggested that the micro or computational process of the information processing system could be discovered by showing that two task variables which were independent would be assumed to influence two independent stages of processing. When two task variables were found to interact, it would be said that these two variables operated on the same stage or process. This led to the microstructure of stages shown in Figure 3. As may be seen from Figure 3, there is an encoding stage followed by the serial comparison and decision stages. The two central stages: search and decision reflect the microstructures which are required for controlled processing. The final stage is a motor or output stage of the system.

Armed with this model, it may in principle be possible to determine what is

MICRO-COGNITIVE PROCESSES

FIG. 3

the nature of ADDH children's defect in controlled and automatic processing and thus to localize the dysfunction. Alternatively, as mentioned above, the dysfunction may not be related to the degree of control-automaticity of processing but be found to be linked to one or more of the energetical pools: arousal, activation, or effort. The following sections attempt to provide a summary of the results obtained so far in this endeavour.

Controlled Processing and ADDH

Several studies have now emerged which indicate that, when controlled processing demands are placed on the ADDH child, this child can be successfully distinguished from the control child (Sergeant & Scholten, 1983, 1985; van der Meere & Sergeant, 1987a). Although the two groups differ from one another in a controlled processing search task, the groups did not exhibit a differential effect with respect to increasing the amount of controlled processing demands. That is to say, both groups differed from one another and remained clearly separable from one another throughout the task but this difference was not a function of the load which was required to be processed. The conclusion then is, following the logic of the additive factor method, that the deficit in processing is not accounted for by a divided attention task.

Since the groups did differ from one another at the beginning of the task, one might think that the differences observed through manipulation of the two central stages, search and decision, were already present and possibly caused by the preceding input stage: encoding. Manipulation of this process through stimulus degradation failed to explain why ADDH children were slower and less accurate than controls (Sergeant & Scholten, 1985b).

At this point, it should be noted that there is clear evidence of differences between ADDH and control children. Further, the lack of an explanatory factor at this stage was not due to the fact that the task variables did not operate, since they clearly did. Thus, the explanation has to be sought elsewhere. As indicated previously, the strategy which a subject uses to perform a task may be considered a form of strategic control. Given that the subject may choose to emphasize speed at the cost of accuracy, one may speak of a trade-off between the two parameters of performance.

Trade-offs in performance measures have been widely cited in the hyperactivity literature reviewed above. The novelty that was introduced by Sergeant and Scholten (1985a) was to manipulate actively the variable known to influence strategy control, namely, instruction set. Strategy is influenced by the emphasis given to the accuracy or the speed of performance in the instruction set. The control change, however, is not a process control change such as when load is increased. Rather, the control change which is occurring is the allocation of energy through the speed instruction set. When speed is demanded, considerable energy will be allocated. When accuracy is emphasized, speed has to be reduced. In the manipulation of speed and accuracy, it was found that distractible and control children followed the expected curve of the speed-accuracy trade-off. ADDH children obeyed the trade-off for accuracy and "normal" instruction sets. They clearly differed from controls and distractibles in the speed condition not only by remaining slower than these two groups but actually by becoming slightly slower in this condition than they were in the "normal" condition. This result appeared at first counter-intuitive. How is it possible that, when speed is emphasized, the ADDH children can become less accurate, just as controls, but fail to speed-up? The explanation is to be sought in the variances of the speed condition. The range of fast and slow responses increases for the ADDH in the speed condition. This means that the ADDH child can show fast responding in this condition but fails to be able to maintain this speed. This was the first hint that the explanatory factor in the attentional processing of ADDH children was concerned more with an energetical than a process factor.

The results of this study clearly questioned the suggestion that cognitive impulsivity was a discriminating factor in the ADDH. The control children showed that they were able to a greater extent to trade accuracy for speed. When this trade-off was encouraged by instruction, the ADDH encountered difficulty in maintaining the trade-off. Thus, while the ADDH child can be impulsive, the degree and maintenance of cognitive strategies associated with impulsivity is limited.

From Controlled to Automatic Processing in ADDH Children

While previous studies had shown that controlled processing of information did not lead to identifying the locus of the deficit, it occurred to us that the deficiency in ADDH children could be in the transition of controlled to automatic processing. Douglas (1983) has suggested that a possible discriminating characteristic between the ADDH child and normal child is that the former acquire more slowly the cognitive sets required to gain new information. This could be interpreted to imply that controls would acquire efficient automatic processing more swiftly than hyperactives.

Recently the rate of acquisition of automatic processing was studied by van der Meere and Sergeant (1988a). This is done by presenting a consistent set of targets over blocks of trials. In the first instance, the effect of load upon reaction was observed: load led to substantial increases in reaction time. However, with the consistent presentation of targets over time, the subject was able to learn the target set and process this information extremely efficiently. This led to less time being demanded for processing the target load. Thus the slope of the reaction time curve can become virtually parallel with the x axis. In the study conducted by van der Meere and Sergeant (1988a), it was found that the degree and the rate of acquisition of automatic processing did not differentiate between the hyperactive and the control group. Hence, acquisition of a cognitive skill is not impaired in the ADDH group.

Sustained Allocation of Energy

Probably one of the most significant set of studies in hyperactivity and attention is that conducted by the Montreal group (Sykes et al., 1971; Sykes et al., 1973). This group used the Continuous Performance Test (CPT) developed by Rosvold et al. (1956). In this task the subject is required to monitor a continuous train of stimuli usually over a period of 15 min. The subject's task is to determine when, for example, the letter X is preceded by the letter A. When this occurs, he is instructed to press a key. Thus his task is a signal detection task: the combination A-X to be detected against the background of noise stimuli. Sykes et al. (1971) reasoned that failures to detect such signals would be "due to momentary lapses in attention" which are engendered by having to sustain attention over a period of time.

When the published figures of that study are examined carefully, one notes that the error rate of the hyperactive group increased from the first to the second block and remained constant until the third and final block of trials. Controls, in contrast, remained constant over time in the efficiency with which they performed the task. The point is that contrary to failing to maintain the level of performance as a function of time, the hyperactive group exhibited an initial decline in performance, which was *maintained* with time. In other studies, the CPT has been varied and the level of performance by hyperactives improved through the administration of ritalin (Klorman et al., 1979). In passing, it should be noted that poorer CPT performance is not specific to the ADDH child. Friedman et al. (1982) showed that this task could discriminate between controls and children at high-risk for schizophrenia.

In order to provide a convincing demonstration of the failure of ADDH children to sustain energetical allocation over time, a number of demands should be placed on a study. The task should be long. It should clearly demand the child's attentional control (Fisk & Schneider, 1981). This should be apparent both for the ADDH and the control children and not simply for the ADDH group. This requirement is necessary in order to demonstrate that the task has functional validity. Finally, the performance deficit of the ADDH children should increase more with time than that of the controls.

Recently van der Meere and Sergeant (1987) reported a divided attention study. The data from that study were reanalysed (Sergeant, 1988). The children had to maintain their attention on tasks lasting 15 min for more than 2 hours. The tasks placed a high level of cognitive load upon the children: a load of 16 units. That is, they had to retain four potential targets in memory and search a display of four letters (load = display × memory). The data were reanalysed by plotting the mean reaction time results using a moving window. In this procedure a fixed number of trials (say five) are averaged and a point plotted. Thus, trials 1-5 are averaged and a point plotted. The window is moved and trials 2-6 are averaged and this point plotted. The window moves to 3-7 and the process repeated until all trials have entered the window. The data showed that the ADDH and control children were indistinguishable in terms of maintaining their performance over time.

This study can be criticised on the grounds that the tasks, although summing to a continuously long period of performance, actually had discrete blocks, hence children could rest themselves between blocks. If this is true, it is of interest that ADDH children can restore their energy reserves during the few minutes between tasks. Thus, their allocation of energy may equal that of controls, even without having to be given a drug. A second criticism of this task is that the children were required to learn a new target set each trial. This would imply that as opposed to having a boring, repetitive task to do, the children had to perform a more interesting task, thus a vigilance deficit could not emerge. It is interesting that this argument shifts the weight of the criticism away from maintenance of attention to explaining failures of sustained attention as due to problems of boredom. If this is the case, the fact that ADDH children were able to maintain their sustained allocation of energy through constantly changing memory demands is not only of theoretical interest (Parasuraman & Davies, 1977; O'Dougherty et al., 1984) but also of practical therapeutic interest. It is, nevertheless, clear that these points of criticism will have to be met.

In designing a sustained attention task, an essential distinction has to be made between two classes of tasks. One class of task loads on the sensitivity parameter: d'. This is the statistic for distinguishing signal with noise versus noise alone. The second parameter is the response bias or confidence parameter which is referred to as beta: β. Tasks can be designed which load on one rather than the other parameter of sustained attention. A recent study investigated the sensitivity parameter (van der Meere & Sergeant, 1988b). The task required that a constant stimulus be detected and the task duration was 36 min. While clearly able to show that performance declined for both groups with the duration of the task and that the ADDH children were less efficient than controls, these authors were unable to find any evidence of a differential deficit in the sustainment of performance in the hyperactive group.

These data suggest that another diagnostic interpretation is required for the ADDH syndrome than a dysfunction in sustained attention. Task duration is apparently not the critical diagnostic variable in ADDH children. Since such tasks operate primarily on the arousal energetical pool (Sanders, 1983), it would seem that the arousal of the ADDH child is equally questionable as a diagnostic, explanatory concept. Thus, the research effort is forced to examine the other energy pool: activation, as defined by Pribram and McGuiness (1975).

Performance Activation and ADDH

A few years ago, a study of hyperactive children was published using event related potentials in which the CPT and variants thereof was employed with hyperactive children (Loiselle et al., 1980). This study is undeservedly seldom cited. Its crucial feature lay in the fact that the same type of task could be shown to substantially increase in its diagnostic power when the event rate or speed of signal presentation was manipulated. A fast event rate tends to influence the arousal energy pool and a slow event rate requires that the activation level be increased to maintain performance. Up to this point, the research program has used only performance measures to arrive at diagnostic conclusions. Clearly, convergent evidence from another domain would considerably bolster our confidence, if it could be shown that both performance and physiological measures tapped the same energetical pools.

Since the term effort was introduced into the attention literature by Kahneman (1973), there has only gradually appeared evidence that effort may be measured electrophysiologically and could be related to the concept of effort. Mulder (1980) demonstrated that power spectral analysis of cardiological data could meet this demand. The research conducted by our group suggested that a scalp electrocortical measure might be suitable for monitoring the activation and effort of subjects. This measure is the time locked power (voltage squared) of the electroencephalogram and is referred to as event related desynchronization (ERD), since the power which is measured is localized in the alpha rhythm of the EEG (van Winsum et al., 1984). It was shown in that study that the increase in cognitive effort to meet the cognitive load of memory search, such as used in our studies of ADDH children, was independent of the effect that event rate had upon ERD. Event rate is known to influence the activation pool (Sanders, 1983). Thus load and event rate influenced two independent energy pools in this study. Furthermore, it could be shown that this measure, while paralleling considerably the event related potential P300, differed primarily in its sensitivity for event rate, an activation variable (Sergeant et al., 1987). It is important to realize that both the performance and the electrophysiological variables converged by showing that the central stages of the system and the output side of the system, as predicted by the model, were independent. This suggested that the succeeding study with ADDH children should be one in which event rate should be manipulated.

In this most recent study in our series, the rate at which stimuli were presented had three levels: fast, medium, and slow. The reaction time data indicated that in this particular task, at a fast event rate, it is virtually impossible to distinguish between the ADDH and control child. With a slow event rate, both controls and ADDH children slowed down but the ADDH children suffered a greater performance deficit. This is precisely the diagnostic task demands which were set out by Rosenthal and Allen (1978): tasks which showed no difference between groups at one level but when the stimulus presentation was systematically varied produce interactive effects. This result suggests that the output and probably the activation pool is the key to defining ADDH children's dysfunction.

DISCUSSION AND CONCLUDING REMARKS

The diagnostic significance of any piece of clinical research rests on two points: its technical and criterion validity. In the research reported here, the technical validity of a task has been shown through predicting what from the model of human information processing is to be expected and by showing that the task met predictions. The second demand of concept validity is much more difficult, which in practice boils down to showing the criterion validity of the groups used. Schachar et al. (1981) indicated that one of the most important points in deciding on the criterion validity of ADDH children would be the pervasiveness of the hyperactivity. In this conception, an ADDH child is not simply a child who is hyperactive in one setting but is so in multiple settings. The early research reported by our group employed children who were rated as ADDH by teachers and observers. Many pointed to the fact that this could hardly be called pervasiveness, since the ratings all took place in the same school setting, although independent of one another. It was decided to amend this weakness by employing multiple sources in later studies. For this purpose, teachers, parents, test assistants, and psychologists were used as sources of ratings. From a large sample of nearly 1500 children only a very small proportion of children (N = 15) met the criterion of pervasive hyperactivity. These children were used as subjects in the later studies. There would seem sufficient criterion validity for this group.

What has the attentional research conducted thus far taught us? The diagnostic criteria of DSM III for ADDH suggest that the energetical aspect of attention be the primary target. The specific variant of attention is sustained attention. From the research reported here and elsewhere, it is clear that sustainment of attention is not the primary diagnostic criterion. ADDH children who are undrugged can maintain attention. It is not in the late part of a task which such children distinguish themselves most, but in the early phase of a task. It would then seem more useful to employ this information in creating a future DSM IV, rather than maintaining that sustainment of attention is crucial to such children.

The ability to divide attention, even under considerable levels of cognitive load, has repeatedly been shown to be intact. Thus controlled search in working memory is not defective in the ADDH child. Likewise, when controlled demands are shifted to more automatic processing this occurs in ADDH children at about the same rate as that of control children. This is not only theoretically significant but gives confidence that therapies which are directed towards acquisition of skilled behaviour are well-founded. A further, but not immediately obvious, point should be made from the finding that automatic behaviour is acquired at the same rate in control and ADDH children. If controlled processing could not be shifted to automatic processing in such children, the energetical deficiency of ADDH children could then have been explained as due to the debilitating effect of having to maintain high levels of control. This explanation is ruled out by our findings.

Following these negative indications of what hyperactivity or ADDH is not, what can be said of what it is? The data which are currently available suggest that the activation and output systems should be the primary candidates for future experimental diagnostics. It is at the present time too premature to suggest a full model of the dysfunction. Nevertheless, fairly clear contours are beginning to emerge. The clear interaction of ADDH children with a slow event rate suggests that the allocation of activation is particularly sensitive to task demands. This could explain a number of difficult theoretical puzzles in the literature. For example, one study shows a clear-cut difference between hyperactives and controls while a subsequent study, using the same type of task, finds no difference between the groups. This effect can be explained by the activation hypothesis. The first study used an event rate which placed demands on the activation of the ADDH children and the second did not. The fact that activation and not arousal would seem to be implicated assists in understanding why speed instructions lead to a slowing in the mean and an increase in the variance of responding. The speed instruction activates the arousal pool which meets the demands. The activation pool fails to be able to continue the supply in the motor output system and leads eventually to highly variable responding. A further prediction to be derived from the activation hypothesis is that activation and a typical motor control variable such as stimulus-response compatibility should be found to interact in ADDH children. Positive experimental results of this kind would considerably bolster our theoretical knowledge and improve our diagnostics of the hyperactive child.

SUMMARY

The diagnostical significance of the term Attention Deficit Disorder with Hyperactivity (ADDH) is examined in this chapter. It is argued that the DSM III definition is conceptually heterogeneous in terms of the type of attentional mechanism which has been thought to be responsible for ADDH behaviour.

The chapter examines how the term attention is defined in modern cognitive psychology. This term is defined here as the rate at which controlled information processing occurs in human short term memory. The term attention is operationalized in memory search tasks, since the limitations of attention can be most clearly shown as a restriction in the rate of processing.

Studies of ADDH children are reviewed. It is concluded that the limitation of information processing of ADDH children is not due to a defective attentional mechanism, as defined here. Two areas are indicated where ADDH children can be specifically shown to differ from controls and other subgroups of children: The first is in the strategy of information processing. The second is in the energetical allocation which such children use to meet task demands. It is argued that it is this factor which is crucial for the understanding and diagnostics of ADDH children.

REFERENCES

American Psychiatric Association. (1980). *Diagnostic and statistical manual of mental disorders.* (3rd ed.). Washington, DC: Author.

Campbell, S.B., Douglas, V.I., & Morgenstern, G. (1971). Cognitive styles in hyperactive children and the effect of methylphenidate. *Journal of Child Psychology and Psychiatry, 12,* 55–67.

Campbell, S.B., Endman, M.W., & Bernfeld, G. (1977). A three-year follow-up of hyperactive preschoolers into elementary school. *Journal of Child Psychology and Psychiatry, 18,* 239–249.

Clements, S.D., & Peters, J. (1962). Minimal brain dysfunction in the schoolaged child. *Archives of General Psychiatry, 6,* 185–197.

Cohen, N.J., Weiss, G., & Minde, K. (1972). Cognitive styles in adolescents previously diagnosed as hyperactive. *Journal of Child Psychology and Psychiatry, 13,* 203–209.

Douglas, V.I. (1983) Attentional and cognitive problems. In M. Rutter (Ed.), *Developmental psychiatry* (pp. 280–329). Guilford, New York.

Fisk, A.D., & Schneider, W. (1981). Control and automatic processing during tasks requiring sustained attention: A new approach to vigilance. *Human Factors, 23,* 737–750.

Friedman, D., Erlenmeyer-Kimling, L., & Vaughan, H.G. (1982). Cognitive brain potentials in children at risk for schizophrenia: Progress, problems and prospects. In: A. Rothenberger (Ed.), *Event-related potentials in children* (pp. 365–377). Amsterdam: Elsevier.

Homatidis, S., & Konstantareas, M.M. (1981). Assessment of hyperactivity: Isolating measures of high discriminant ability. *Journal of Consulting and Clinical Psychology, 49,* 533–541.

Hopkins, J., Perlman, T., Hechtman, L., & Weiss, G. (1979). Cognitive style in adults originally diagnosed as hyperactives. *Journal of Child Psychology and Psychiatry, 20,* 209–216.

Kagan, J. Rosman, B.L., Albert, J., & Phillips, W. (1964). Information processing in the child, significance of analytic and reflective attitudes. *Psychological Monographs* (Whole no. 578).

Kahneman, D. (1973). *Attention and effort.* Englewood Cliffs, NJ: Prentice Hall.

Klorman, R., Salzman, L.F., Pass, H.L., Borgstedt, A.D., & Dainer, K.B. (1979). Effects of methylphenidate on hyperactive children's evoked response during passive and active attention. *Psychophysiology, 16,* 23–29.

Loiselle, D.L., Stamm, J.S., Maitinsky, S., & Whipple, S., (1980). Evoked potential and behavioural signs of attentive dysfunctions in hyperactive boys. *Psychophysiology, 17,* 193–201.

Meere, J.J. van der, & Sergeant, J.A. (1987). A divided attention experiment in pervasively hyperactive children. *Journal of Abnormal Child Psychology, 15,* 379–391 (a).

Meere, J.J. van der, & Sergeant, J.A. (1988). Acquisition of attention skill in pervasive hyperactives. *Journal of Child Psychology and Psychiatry. 29*, 301–310.

Meere, J.J. van der, & Sergeant, J.A. (1988). Sustained attention deficit hypothesis in pervasively hyperactive children reconsidered. Journal Abnormal Child Psychology, in press.

Mulder, G. (1980). *The heart of mental effort.* Thesis. University of Groningen.

O'Dougherty, M., Neuchterlein, K.H., & Drew, B. (1984). Hyperactive and hypoxic children: Signal detection, sustained attention and behaviour. *Journal of Abnormal Psychology, 43*, 178–191.

Pachella, R.G. (1974). The interpretation of reaction time in information processing research. In B. Kantowitz (Ed.), *Human information processing: Tutorial in performance and recognition* (pp. 41–82). Hillsdale, N.J.: Lawrence Erlbaum Associates.

Parasuraman, R. & Davies, D.R. (1977). A taxonomic analysis of vigilance performance. In. R.R. Makie (ed.), *Vigilance: Theory, operational performance and physiological correlates* (pp. 559–574). New York: Plenum.

Pribram, K.H., & McGuinness, D. (1975). Arousal, activation and effort in the control of attention. *Psychological Review, 83*, 116–149.

Rosenthal, R.H., & Allen, T.W. (1978). An examination of attention, arousal and learning dysfunctions of hyperkinetic children. *Psychological Bulletin, 85*, 689–715.

Rosvold, H.E., Mirsky, A.F., Sarason, I., Bransome, E.D., & Beck, L.H. (1956). A continuous performance test of brain damage. *Journal of Consulting Psychology, 20*, 343–350.

Sanders, A.F. (1983). Towards a model of stress and human performance. *Acta Psychologica, 53*, 61–97.

Schachar, R., Rutter, M., & Smith, A. (1981). Characteristics of situationally and pervasively hyperactive children: Implications for syndrome definition. *Journal of Child Psychology and Psychiatry, 22*, 375–392.

Schleifer, M., Weiss, G., Cohen, N., Elman, M., Cvejic, H., & Kruger, E. (1975). Hyperactivity in preschoolers and the effect of methylphenidate. *American Journal of Orthopsychiatry, 45*, 38–50.

Schneider, W., & Shiffrin, R.M. (1977). Controlled and automatic human information processing: I. Detection, search & attention. *Psychological Review, 84*, 1–66.

Sergeant, J.A., Velthoven, R. van, & Virginia, A. (1979). Hyperactivity, impulsivity and reflectivity. An examination of their relationship and implications for clinical child psychology. *Journal of Child Psychology and Psychiatry, 20*, 47–60.

Sergeant, J., & Scholten, C.A. (1983). A stages-of-information approach to hyperactivity. *Journal of Child Psychology and Psychiatry, 24*, 49–60.

Sergeant, J.A., & Scholten, C.A. (1985). On resource strategy limitations in hyperactivity: Cognitive impulsivity reconsidered. *Journal of Child Psychology and Psychiatry, 26*, 97–109.(a)

Sergeant, J.A., & Scholten, C.A. (1985). On data limitations in hyperactivity. *Journal of Child Psychology and Psychiatry, 26*, 111–124 (b).

Sergeant, J.A. (1988). From DSM attentional deficit disorder to functional defects. (in press). In: L.F.M. Bloomingdale & J.A. Sergeant (Eds.) *Attention deficit disorder* V (pp. 183–198). N.Y.: Pergamon.

Sergeant, J.A., Geuze, R., & Winsum, W. (1987). Event related desynchronization and P 300. *Psychophysiology, 24*, 272–277

Shiffrin, R.M., & Schneider, W. (1977). Controlled and automatic human information processing: I. Detection, search and attention. *Psychological Review, 84*, 1–66.

Sternberg, S. (1969). Discovery of processing stages: Extensions of Donder's method. In W.G. Koster (Ed.), *Attention and Performance II*, Noord-Holland, Amsterdam.

Stewart, M.A., Pitts, F.N, Craig, A.G., & Dieryf, W. (1966). The hyperactive child syndrome. *American Journal of Orthopsychiatry, 36*, 861–867.

Sykes, D.H., Douglas, V.I., & Morgenstern, G. (1973). Sustained attention in hyperactive children. *Journal of Child Psychology and Psychiatry, 14*, 213–220.

Sykes, D.H., Douglas, V.I., Weiss, G., & Minde, K.K. (1971). Attention in hyperactive children and the effect of methylphenidate (Ritalin). *Journal of Child Psychology and Psychiatry, 12,* 129–139.

Winsum, W. van, Sergeant, J.A., & Geuze, R. (1984). The functional significance of event related desynchronization of alpha rhythm in attentional and activating tasks. *Electroencephalography and Clinical Neurophysiology, 58,* 519–524.

The Role of Psychostimulants and Psychosocial Treatments in Hyperkinesis

Rachel Gittelman Klein
New York State Psychiatric Institute, New York

Howard Abikoff
Long Island Jewish Medical Center, New York

It will not come as a surprise to anyone that there is no perfectly effective treatment for hyperkinesis.[1] Therefore, the quest for new interventions is not only justified, but highly deserving, Yet, much of the effort that has been invested in the development of novel therapies has not stemmed from a realistic, sober appraisal of the merits and demerits of existing treatments, but often from ideological views that were in conflict with practice. The treatment of hyperkinesis, like much of the rest of psychological and psychiatric practice, has been polarized between those amenable to the use of medication and those unsympathetic, if not hostile, to it. Fortuitously, the conflictual climate that has characterized the therapeutics of hyperkinesis has had a remarkably positive effect because it has stirred the profession into action. As a result, the treatment of hyperkinesis is among the best studied of all psychiatric disorders.

This review emphasizes controlled investigations. Uncontrolled studies are noted only if they have heuristic value, and single-case reports are not presented.

PHARMACOTHERAPY

A number of compounds have established efficacy in hyperkinesis, including neuroleptics (chlorpromazine, thioridazine, and haloperidol), tricyclics (imipramine),

---

[1]Hyperkinesis, and Attention Deficit Disorder with Hyperactivity (ADDH) (APA, 1980), which is now called Attention-Deficit Hyperactivity Disorder (ADHD) (APA, 1987) are used interchangeably in this chapter.

and psychostimulants (dextroamphetamine, magnesium pemoline and methylpheni-date); the latter group is the most effective (for a review of drug effects, see Klein, Gittelman, Quitkin, & Rifkin, 1980). Since methylphenidate is the compound of choice, we focus on recent research concerning its impact in hyperkinetic children.

Though the overall efficacy of stimulants on hyperactive behaviors has been well documented since the 1970's, the magnitude of its clinical effect was questioned. Investigations comparing the comportment of stimulant treated ADDH children and normal children in the classroom have indicated that much of the problematic behavior of hyperkinetic children is normalized by methylphenidate so that it no longer differs from normal children (Abikoff & Gittelman, 1985b; Loney, Weissenburger, Woolsen, & Lichty, 1979; Pelham, Bender, Caddell, Booth, & Moorer, 1985; Pelham, Schnedler, Bologna, & Contreras, 1980; Por-rino, Rapoport, Behar, Ismond, & Bunney, 1983; Whalen et al., 1978; Whalen, Henker, Collins, Finck, & Dotemoto, 1979). However, this level of efficacy does not occur reliably across all deviant behaviors (Abikoff & Gittelman, 1985b). A fair appraisal of the drug's efficacy is that many but not all aspects of symptomatic behaviors are normalized by stimulant treatment.

The response to stimulant medication on more subtle aspects of difficulty have been examined as well. The original belief that social behavior was compromised in the course of treatment has not been documented. On the contrary, enhanced peer interaction is part of the overall drug effect (Whalen et al., 1987). In addition, the social interaction of children with their mother is benefited by the medication. Not only do the children's behaviors directed to the mothers improve, but the mothers' behavior toward the child is also positively affected (Barkley & Cunningham, 1979, 1980; Barkley, Karlsson, Strzelecki, & Murphy, 1984; Humphries, Kinsbourne, & Swanson, 1978). Similar effects have been found in teachers (Whalen, Henker, & Dotemoto, 1980, 1981).

Because many hyperkinetic children have relatively deficient academic performance, much concern has been expressed regarding the lack of effect of stimulants on scholastic performance over time. In spite of this often raised concern, only one systematic study has appeared. Enhanced performance on arithmetic and language tasks was obtained with methylphenidate treatment (Douglas, Barr, O'Neill, & Britton, 1986).

A provocative study (Brown & Sleator, 1979; Sprague & Sleater, 1977) reported that the doses of methylphenidate that were optimal for inducing clincial change impaired cognitive performance as measured by a rote visual memory task. In contrast, lower doses enhanced performance but had little impact on hyperactive behaviors. A serious issue was thereby raised concerning the possibility of compromising learning in children treated with stimulants. Several studies have investigated the dissociation between learning and behavioral effects of methylphenidate, and have failed to replicate the early reports (Ballinger, Varley, & Nolen, 1984; Charles, Schain, & Zelniker, 1981; Conners & Solanto, 1984; Gan & Cantwell, 1982; Pelham et al., 1985; Rapport, DuPaul, Stoner, & Jones,

1986; Rapport, Stoner, DuPaul, Birmingham, & Tucker, 1985; Solanto & Conners, 1982; Walker, 1982).

In summary, recent research has broadened our knowledge of the nature of stimulant effects in ADDH children. Not only are the cardinal symptoms of the disorder ameliorated, but they are often to a remarkable degree since they may be reduced often to normal levels; in addition, other important social behaviors are improved as well. This broad range efficacy has not been found to occur at the cost of impaired learning.

Other than stimulants, newer compounds, such as MAO inhibitors, clonidine and buproprion, have been studied in small trials. These are beyond the scope of this chapter [they are summarized elsewhere (Klein, 1987)].

PSYCHOSOCIAL THERAPIES

Although the short-term efficacy of stimulant medication in ADDH is one of the best established treatments in child psychiatry, stimulant treatment is not always a panacea. For example, while medication may increase academic productivity in some children, it is not evident that it facilitates the acquisition of academic skills. Further, there is little evidence that long-term stimulant treatment substantially alters the eventual outcome of these children, because deficient learning and social skill and poor academic performance are still present in adolescence and young adulthood. Moreover, the positive behavior changes associated with stimulants are not maintained following termination of medication, necessitating long-term stimulant treatment in many cases. Finally, a proportion of youngsters are either nonresponders, demonstrating little or no benefit from medication, or experience side effects which preclude drug treatment.

The often noted reservations concerning stimulant treatment are exemplified in Achenbach's text (1982):

> Reducing overt behavior problems does not automatically bring improvement in other areas, such as school work. Drugs offer an easy way to reduce behavioral problems under natural conditions, but additional effort is needed to promote the academic and social skills needed for long-term adaptation. (p. 386)

Given the limitations of stimulant treatment, there is considerable clinical importance attached to alternative and adjunctive interventions that attempt to provide hyperkinetic children with skills and tactics that enable them to cope more efficaciously.

Among non-medical treatment modalities, behavioral treatment, an umbrella term that encompasses behavior management, behavior modification, behavior therapy, operant conditioning, and contingency based reinforcement procedures, was viewed at first as a competitor to stimulant medication. Evidence for efficacy rested initially on single-subject studies, although subsequent small, controlled investigations provided some statistical support for treatment efficacy (for reviews, see Mash & Dalby, 1979; Prout, 1977; Wolraich, 1979).

Behavior Therapy

There are few investigations of behavior therapy in hyperkinetic children. The early studies, from which the efficacy of this treatment was surmised, had short-comings. For one, they did not include a control condition for the professional attention given to those receiving behavioral treatment; second, they did not obtain independent assessments of the children's response to treatment (O'Leary, Pelham, Rosenbaum, & Price, 1976; Rosenbaum, O'Leary, & Jacob, 1975). A recent small study (Pelham et al., in press) includes a comparison of behavior training and social skills training, but does not include an attention control.

The issue of the relative efficacy of behavior therapy and pharmacotherapy has engendered much polemic, but little systematic investigation. The largest study comparing behavior therapy with methylphenidate is our own which also included the combination of behavior therapy with methylphenidate (partial reports appeared in Gittelman-Klein et al., 1976, and Gittelman et al., 1980). Completed, the study included a total of 86 children who received behavior therapy alone (with a placebo), or methylphenidate (mean dose, 38 mg/d, range 10 to 60 mg/d), or the combination of the two treatments. Behavior therapy was implemented at home and in school. All members of the family were involved if they were judged to be important to the treatment goals. Behavioral management included positive and negative reinforcements, which were tailored individually, as were behaviors targeted for modification. Treatment lasted two months. Multiple assessments were made, including teacher, parent, and psychiatric ratings, as well as direct classroom observations. It is important to emphasize that although medication and placebo conditions were double-blind, there could be no blind for behavior therapy in the case of teachers, parents, and clinic staff except for classroom observers. Methylphenidate alone was superior to behavior therapy alone on all teacher ratings, including global improvement ratings (80% vs. 40% improved, respectively). On the direct classroom observations, which included measures of motor activity, inattention, and impulsive behaviors, children on methylphenidate had markedly superior outcomes than those who had received behavior therapy alone. This latter group changed little, if at all, on objective behavioral measures. Improvement with behavior therapy was obtained only on measures rated by individuals who were involved in the treatment process, and who were inevitably biased in their evaluation. All results indicated that behavior therapy was much less effective than medication.

The Combination of Stimulants and Behavior Therapy

Because of the very different nature and clinical effect of pharmacological and psychotherapeutic approaches, the reasonable expectation has been held that by combining the two, clear advantage would accrue in the management of hyperactive children. In a recent review, Pelham and Murphy (1986) reiterate this view, and claim that ''each of these treatment modalities has something to offer that can improve the other's effectiveness'' (p. 115). A large clinical report of combined treatments suggests that it may be the case (Satterfield, Satterfield, & Cantwell, 1981). Systematic investigations of this premise have been conducted by combining methylphenidate with behavior modification (Gittelman et al., 1980; O'Leary & Pelham, 1978; Pelham et al., 1985; Wolraich, Drummond, Salomon, O'Brien, & Sivage, 1978), with parent training in behavior management (Firestone, Kelly, Goodman, & Davey, 1981), and with cognitive training (Abikoff & Gittelman, 1985a; Brown, Wynne, & Medenis, 1985; Bugental, Whalen, & Henker, 1977; Cohen, Sullivan, Minde, Novak, & Helwig, 1981). [Much of the literature on behavior therapy was reviewed by Rapport and Sprague in 1983 (Rapport, 1983; Sprague, 1983), and little new data have appeared since.] In our study mentioned above, the two drug treated groups (drug alone and drug combined with behavior modification) did not differ on directly observed classroom behavior, both treatments induced marked reductions in impulsive, disruptive and inattentive behaviors. On teacher ratings, the combination of behavior therapy and methylphenidate was superior to the drug alone on measures of hyperactivity, but not on those of inattention and conduct problem.

In a small cross-over study (N = 8), the combination of methylphenidate and behavior therapy was not superior to methylphenidate alone in spite of a relatively lengthy treatment period of 13 weeks (Pelham et al., 1980). Another study of combined behavior therapy and medication, conducted recently, includes only 40 children in a six-group design; therefore, as few as five cases are included in some treatments (Pelham, et al., in press). This is a very low power situation that is unlikely to be reliably informative regarding treatment differences. Furthermore, the study did not include a group receiving only medication, so that the merit of adding different types of behavioral interventions to drug alone is not clarified.

In view of findings concerning the efficacy of behavior therapy versus methylphenidate, the clinically relevant question is not whether behavior therapy is an alternative treatment strategy to methylphenidate, but whether the addition of behavior therapy to medication leads to accrued improvement. The answer appears to be yes, sometimes. On the majority of measures, there seems to be no difference between medication alone and medication with behavior therapy. On some, there is. Therefore, the results suggest that behavior therapy cannot be recommended routinely for children receiving methylphenidate, but should be considered among those who continue to have residual behavior problems while receiving medication.

Cognitive Training

The initial enthusiasm for behavior therapy has been tempered because of several problems associated with it. First, treatment effects, if they occur, invariably fail to affect settings outside the ones in which treatment is instituted, and effects are maintained only as long as treatment is in place. Further, the clinical impact of behavioral treatment with ADDH children is limited, since classroom behavior is not normalized with treatment (Abikoff & Gittelman, 1984).

In the 1970s, based largely on the work of Meichenbaum (1977) and Douglas (1975), cognitive training was promoted as a promising intervention for ADDH children. A number of different treatment procedures and approaches fall under the cognitive training rubric, including self-instructional training, cognitive modeling, attentional training, self-regulation, cognitive problem-solving, strategy training, social problem-solving, and cognitive behavior modification. The central goal of this treatment approach is the development of self-control skills and reflective problem-solving strategies, both of which are presumed deficient in ADDH children. These deficiencies are purported to account for difficulties in regulating attentive and impulsive behaviors. The expectation is that the enhancement and internalization of self-regulating cognitive skills should provide the ADDH child with the means for more appropriate behavioral regulation, thereby facilitating generalization and maintenance of treatment effects.

Unfortunately, the clinical efficacy of cognitive training in ADDH children has not been documented (Abikoff, 1985, 1987). Except for scattered instances of improved test performance, there is no evidence that cognitive training enhances attentional or memory processes.

Support for the efficacy of cognitive training in ameliorating academic functioning has been minimal. Neither reading achievement nor productivity have been shown to improve with training. The effect on math performance is somewhat better. Two uncontrolled reports (Cameron & Robinson, 1980; Varni & Henker, 1979), as well as a small controlled study (Kirby & Grimley, 1986) found gains in children who received cognitive behavioral training. However, in the controlled investigation this was so because the controls became worse. There is no indication that self-instruction procedures, a cornerstone of most cognitive training studies, facilitate academic performance.

Finally, improvement in parent ratings of self-control is reported by Kirby and Grimley (1986) for children receiving cognitive behavioral training. However, the data were not analyzed appropriately, and clear interpretation of treatment effects is problematic.

So far, there is no evidence from controlled studies indicating that the behavior of ADDH children, either in school or at home, improves with cognitive training. In spite of the limited evidence for the value of cognitive training, it has been held as an alternative treatment to methylphenidate; it has also been hoped that its combination with psychostimulants might be advantageous, because the improved behavior and attention resulting from medication should facilitate the learning of problem-solving and and self-control skills (Horn, Chatoor, & Conners, 1983).

The Relative Efficacy of Cognitive Training and Methylphenidate Alone and Combined

Studies of stimulants compared to and in combination with cognitive training vary in a number of critical features, including length of training, and training procedures. Assessment of the scope of treatment efficacy also differs across studies. Some evaluate change in only one sphere of functioning (cognitive, academic, or behavioral), whereas others assess the impact of treatment on various domains. Follow-up assessment is not common to all studies either. Moreover, the studies address different clinical issues. Some have examined the advantage of adding cognitive training to methylphenidate, and provide information regarding the efficacy of drug alone versus drug with cognitive training. Others have examined whether the combination is superior to cognitive training alone, but do not examine whether medication alone differs from training alone. Since the literature reviewed above has failed to demonstrate efficacy for cognitive training in ADDH, a comparison of it alone and combined with medication appears to have little rationale. Nevertheless, we review each type of study.

Cohen et al. (1981) examined the impact of cognitive-behavior modification, methylphenidate, the combination of both treatments, and no treatment, in hyperactive kindergartners. The cognitive-behavior treatment was a 20-week "total push" program that used sensorimotor, cognitive, and social tasks, and included parent and teacher involvement. At the end of treatment, no differential treatment effect was obtained on cognitive performance and behavior problems. The children continued to be regarded by parents and teachers as significantly more problematic than normal peers. As noted by the authors and others (Loper, 1980), the immature cognitive development of 5- and 6-year olds may restrict the efficacy of cognitive training. This possibility as well as the relative value of cognitive training and methylphenidate are not clarified by the study since the small group sizes (N's = 4, 6, and 8) preclude meaningful treatment comparisons.

Two studies by Brown and his colleagues evaluated the efficacy of cognitive training and methylphenidate on cognitive, academic, and behavioral functioning. Brown et al. (1985) employed a 4 group design: 1) cognitive training alone, 2) methylphenidate alone, 3) the treatment combination, and 4) a no treatment control. Training lasted 3 months and focused exclusively on psychoeducational tasks; no social or academic material was included. Regrettably, the study does not provide differential treatment efficacy since between-group comparisons were not conducted. Significant changes within groups are reported on various measures, but academic functioning did not improve. Inspection of the results suggests that improvement in the combined medication/cognitive training group was a function of medication, because equal or greater behavioral improvement was found in children treated with medication alone.

In a subsequent study, Brown, Borden, Wynne, Schleser, and Clingerman

(1986) evaluated academically deficient ADDH youngsters assigned either to 1) cognitive training, 2) methylphenidate, 3) the treatment combination, or 4) attention control groups. Unlike the previous study, which did not include academic or social tasks, there were 6 training sessions devoted to academics, as well as 6 social problem-solving sessions. Nevertheless, there was no evidence for differential treatment efficacy on a host of cognitive, academic, or behavioral measures. Given that the children were all at least 1 year behind in arithmetic, reading, or spelling, it is not especially surprising that the brief amount of training devoted to academic skills failed to have a meaningful impact on academic performance.

Cognitive training as an adjunct to maintenance stimulant treatment has been investigated by Abikoff and colleagues. In the largest study with elementary school-aged ADDH children, Abikoff and Gittelman (1985a) evaluated a 4-month program which emphasized cognitive and interpersonal problem-solving skills. Children who received cognitive training in combination with methylphenidate showed no superiority in the multiple cognitive and academic measures obtained, when compared to children who remained on methylphenidate alone. Similar negative results were obtained on all behavioral ratings tapping adjustment at home and in school. Not a single trend in favor of cognitive training was obtained, but some potential negative treatment effects were found. Children who received cognitive training were significantly slower in their performance in situations requiring speed, leading to significantly worse Performance IQ's. Further, cognitive training did not facilitate performance following stimulant termination, as the groups did not differ in cognitive, academic, or behavioral functioning one-month after treatment termination. Moreover, during a one-month placebo follow-up phase, the behavior of children in all groups deteriorated markedly, necessitating remediation in most cases. Therefore, a lengthy exposure to cognitive training did not protect children against relapse when stimulants were withdrawn.

Rather than attempting to modify ADDH children's cognitive style in the hope that generalized change would ensue, Abikoff (1983) carried out a pilot study that was aimed at instructing ADDH youngsters who were methylphenidate responders on how to approach academic tasks in an optimal fashion. The results of the 10 week study were encouraging, as significant improvements were found in decoding and reading comprehension. However, a subsequent controlled investigation with academically deficient ADDH boys failed to validate these results (Abikoff, Ganeles, Reiter, Blum, Foley, & Klein, in press). A combination of methylphenidate with a 16-week academically oriented cognitive training program, focused exclusively on academic skills and the strategies to apply them, was compared to remedial tutoring plus medication, and to medication alone. No evidence for differential treatment efficacy in academic achievement or teacher ratings of academic functioning was obtained immediately after treatment and at 6-month follow-up.

None of the studies has generated results to indicate, or even suggest, that cognitive training is a competitor to stimulants, or that it enhances their beneficial effects.

Comparisons of Cognitive Training to Treatments Other than Stimulants

Some have addressed whether cognitive behavioral treatment has a specific impact by comparing it to other psychotherapeutic approaches. A study by Bugental et al. (1977) is unique because it is the only one to have examined the interaction of subject and treatment variables in ADDH children. The study evaluated interaction of locus of control, medication, and type of behavioral treatment (cognitive training or social reinforcement). A high level of internal control, as defined by attribution of school success to personal effort, was predictive of improvement in maze performance for children receiving either cognitive training or placebo, but not for those on medication or social reinforcements. In contrast, low perception of self-control over school performance was related to improved maze performance with social reinforcement, and medication. No treatment differences were obtained in teacher rated hyperactivity. A 6-month follow-up of a subsample indicated that both groups maintained their improvement in maze performance, and a trend remained of the interaction effects (Bugental, Collins, Collins, & Chaney, 1978). Follow-up findings were consistent with the expectation that the cognitively trained children would show greater attributional shifts in the direction of more perceived control over school success and failure. Contrary to prediction, teachers rated the children who had received social reinforcement as more improved than those cognitively trained. The authors suggest that the combination of cognitive training and social reinforcement might maximize treatment efficacy.

The results provide some evidence for treatment generalization for cognitive training, because improved maze performance resulted from training on other tasks. However, training did not affect classroom behavior. Further, the obtained interaction needs to be interpreted cautiously, since teacher ratings (which are sensitive to drug effects) did not differentiate between the medicated and unmedicated children before the study, suggesting that the groups were not equivalent in the type of children included (Mash & Dalby, 1979).

In 120 clinically medicated and unmedicated children, Brown (1980) compared three treatments: 1) a cognitive modeling group observed a 7-minute tape of a youngster displaying reflective behavior while working on the Matching Familiar Figures Test (MFFT); 2) an instruction group was given specific directions regarding reflective performance on the Matching Familiar Figures Test and was also required to memorize a Stop, Look, Listen strategy; 3) untreated controls. The MFFT, WISC-R Coding subtest, and a copying task were administered before, and one week after, treatment, In both training groups, only medicated youngsters reduced WISC-R Coding errors, and time on the copying task. Since the children were exposed to a total of 7 minutes of training, perhaps it is surprising that any treatment effects were expected, let alone obtained.

A small study by Hinshaw, Henker, and Whalen (1984a) investigated whether adding stress inoculation in children receiving cognitive training affected response to taunting and teasing. In addition, the additive effect of methylphenidate to the two cognitive procedures was studied. The combination of stress inoculation and cognitive training was superior to cognitive training alone on 2 of 11 responses (self-control and coping strategies) to a 45 second peer provocation. There was no accrued advantage for the combination of medication with either form of cognitive training. Unfortunately, the small group sizes limit a full test of the respective treatments and their combination.

Moreover, in spite of its elegance, aspects of the study limit its clinical utility, as noted by the authors. First, the data were collected in experimental classrooms; therefore, the generalizability of the results to real-life settings is unknown. Second, because only immediate treatment effects were assessed, maintenance over time was not established. Finally, the assessment of anger control was done ''on cue'' during very brief time periods; it is not known how the youngsters reacted to usual forms of social provocation.

Hinshaw, Whalen, and Henker (1984b) evaluated the effects of reinforced self-evaluation procedures on the social behaviors of 8- to 13-year-old ADDH boys attending a summer school research project. The four treatment conditions consisted of methylphenidate or placebo, combined with reinforced self-evaluation (RSE) or extrinsic reinforcement alone (RA). During four weeks of cooperative and competitive playground games, boys were trained to monitor their behavior, compare it to a behavioral criterion, and estimate or match the trainer's ratings of their behavior. Observations of the youngsters' positive and negative social behaviors were subsequently collected over 2 days. Half the boys were assigned to RSE on day 1 and RA on day 2; the remaining half followed the reverse order. Medication status was constant during the 2 days. Medication plus RSE was most effective in reducing negative and increasing positive social behaviors. Further, only this treatment combination reduced negative social behavior to levels of normal controls.

Conclusions

The early expectations of the potential clinical utility of cognitive training, either as an alternative or adjunct to stimulant medication in ADDH children, have been tempered by a decade of research. The notion that the development of internalized self-regulation skills is relevant to the clinical behavior problems and facilitates cognitive functioning of ADDH children is questionable, and when some improvement is found, generalization and maintenance have not been realized. In studies where transfer effects have been evaluated, the results have been disappointing. However, some of the studies included too few children or used short treatment periods.

SUMMARY

The major treatment modalities for hyperkinetic children include psychostimulant medication (especially methylphenidate), behavior therapy, and cognitive training. The effects of methylphenidate have been broadened to encompass improvement in social interaction with peers, with mothers, and with teachers. There is now evidence that some aspects of academic performance also are ameliorated. Furthermore, many clinical behavioral signs of the syndrome drop to a level that makes the treated children indistinguishable from normal children.

Behavior therapy and cognitive training have not been shown to induce clinically meaningful behavioral changes. The hope that these interventions would be superior to medication in providing learning strategies that would facilitate the acquisition of academic and social skills in ADDH children has not materialized.

The addition of behavior therapy to a regimen of medication offers incremental therapeutic benefit. But this advantage is not consistent, and the combination cannot be recommended as a routine intervention, but is better viewed as a useful option when behavior problems remain.

Cognitive training has not been shown to provide significant behavioral or academic improvements. Its addition to medication appears to offer no clinical advantage. Based on current evidence, this treatment is of little relevance, if any, to the management of hyperkinetic children.

REFERENCES

Abikoff, H. (1983, August). *Academic cognitive training and stimulants in hyperactivity: A pilot study.* Paper presented at the annual meeting of the American Psychological Association, Anaheim, CA.

Abikoff, H. (1985). Efficacy of cognitive training interventions in hyperactive children. *Clinical Psychology Review, 5,* 479–512.

Abikoff, H. (1987). An evaluation of cognitive behavior therapy for hyperactive children. In B. B. Lahey & A. E. Kazdin (Eds.), *Advances in clinical child psychology,* (Vol. 10, pp. 171–216). New York: Plenum Press.

Abikoff, H., Ganeles, D., Reiter, G., Blum, C., Foley, C., & Klein, R. G., (in press). Cognitive training in academically deficient ADDH boys receiving stimulant medication. *Journal of Abnormal Child Psychology.*

Abikoff, H., & Gittelman, R. (1984). Does behavior therapy normalize the behavior of hyperactive children? *Archives of General Psychiatry, 41,* 449–454.

Abikoff, H., & Gittelman, R. (1985a). Hyperactive children treated with stimulants: Is cognitive training a useful adjunct? *Archives of General Psychiatry, 42,* 953–961.

Abikoff, H., & Gittelman, R. (1985b). The normalizing effects of methylphenidate on the classroom behavior of ADDH children. *Journal of Abnormal Child Psychology, 13,* 33–44.

Achenbach, T. M. (1982). *Developmental psychopathology.* New York: John Wiley.

American Psychiatric Association. (1980). *Diagnostic and statistical manual of mental disorders* (3rd ed.). Washington, DC: Author.

American Psychiatric Association. (1987). *Diagnostic and statistical manual of mental disorders* (3rd ed.–rev. ed.). Washington, DC: Author.

Ballinger, C. T., Varley, C. K., & Nolen, P. A. (1984). Effects of methylphenidate on reading in children with attention deficit disorder. *American Journal of Psychiatry, 141,* 1590–1593.

Barkley, R. A., & Cunningham, C. E. (1979). The effects of methylphenidate on the mother-child interactions of hyperactive children. *Archives of General Psychiatry, 36*, 201–208.

Barkley, R. A., & Cunningham, C. E. (1980). The parent-child interactions of hyperactive children and their modification by stimulant drugs. In R. M. Knights & D. J. Bakker (Eds.), *Treatment of hyperactive and learning disordered children* (pp. 219–236). Baltimore: University Park Press.

Barkley, R. A., Karlsson, J., Strzelecki, E., & Murphy, J. V. (1984). Effects of age and Ritalin dosage on the mother/child interactions of hyperactive children. *Journal of Consulting and Clinical Psychology, 52*, 750–758.

Brown, R. T. (1980). Impulsivity and psychoeducational intervention in hyperactive children. *Journal of Learning Disabilities, 13*, 249–254.

Brown, R. T., Borden, K. A., Wynne, M. E., Schleser, R., & Clingerman, S. R. (1986). Methylphenidate and cognitive therapy with ADD children: A methodological reconsideration. *Journal of Abnormal Child Psychology, 14*, 481–497.

Brown, R. T., & Sleator, E. K. (1979). Methylphenidate in hyperkinetic children: Differences in dose effects on impulsive behavior. *Pediatrics, 64*, 408–410.

Cameron, M. I., & Robinson, V. M. J. (1980). Effects of cognitive training on academic and on-task behavior of hyperactive children. *Journal of Abnormal Child Psychology, 8*, 405–420.

Charles, L., Schain, R., & Zelniker, T. (1981). Optimal dosages of methylphenidate for improving the learning and behavior of hyperactive children. *Journal of Developmental Behavioral Pediatrics, 2*, 78–81.

Cohen, N. J., Sullivan, J., Minde, K., Novak, C., & Helwig, C. (1981). Evaluation of the relative effectiveness of methylphenidate and cognitive behavior modification in the treatment of kindergarten-aged hyperactive children. *Journal of Abnormal Child Psychology, 9*, 43–54.

Conners, C. K., & Solanto, M. V. (1984). The psychophysiology of stimulant drug response in hyperkinetic children. In L. N. Bloomingdale (Ed.), *Attention deficit disorder: Diagnostic, cognitive and therapeutic understanding* (pp. 191–204). New York: Spectrum Publications.

Douglas, V. I. (1975). Are drugs enough? To treat or train the hyperactive child. *International Journal of Mental Health, 4*, 199–212.

Douglas, V. I., Barr, R. G., O'Neill, M. E., & Britton, B. G. (1986). Short term effects of methylphenidate on the cognitive, learning and academic performance of children with attention deficit disorder in the laboratory and the classroom. *Journal of Child Psychology and Psychiatry, 27*, 191–211.

Firestone, P., Kelly, M. J., Goodman, J. T., & Davey, J. (1981). Differential effects of parent training and stimulant medication with hyperactives. *Journal of the American Academy of Child Psychiatry, 20*, 135–147.

Gan, J., & Cantwell, D. P. (1982). Dosage effects of methylphenidate on paired-associate learning: Positive/negative placebo responders. *Journal of the American Academy of Child Psychiatry, 21*, 237–242.

Gittelman, R., Abikoff, H., Pollack, E., Klein, D. F., Katz, S., & Mattes, J. A. (1980). A controlled trial of behavior modification and methylphenidate in hyperactive children. In C. K. Whalen & B. Henker (Eds.), *Hyperactive children: The social ecology of identification and treatment* (pp. 221–243). New York: Academic Press.

Gittelman-Klein, R., Klein, D. F., Abikoff, H., Katz, S., Gloisten, A. C., & Kates, W. (1976). Relative efficacy of methylphenidate and behavior modification in hyperkinetic children: An interim report. *Journal of Abnormal Child Psychology, 4*, 361–379.

Hinshaw, S. P., Henker, B., & Whalen, C. K. (1984a). Self-control in hyperactive boys in anger-inducing situations: Effects of cognitive-behavioral training and of methylphenidate. *Journal of Abnormal Child Psychology, 12*, 55–77.

Hinshaw, S. P., Henker, B., & Whalen, C. K. (1984b). Cognitive behavioral and pharmacologic interventions for hyperactive boys: Comparative and combined effects. *Journal of Consulting and Clinical Psychology, 52*, 739–749.

Horn, W. F., Chatoor, I., & Conners, C. K. (1983). Additive effects of Dexedrine and self-control training: A multiple assessment. *Behavior Modifications, 7*, 383–402.

Humphries, T., Kinsbourne, M., & Swanson, J. (1978). Stimulant effects on cooperation and social interaction between hyperactive children and their mothers. *Journal of Child Psychology and Psychiatry, 19,* 13–22.

Kirby, E. A., & Grimley, L. K. (1986). *Understanding and treating attention deficit disorder.* New York: Pergamon Press.

Klein, D. F., Gittelman, R., Quitkin, F., & Rifkin, A. (1980). *Diagnosis and drug treatment of psychiatric disorders: Adults and children.* Baltimore: Williams & Wilkins.

Klein, R. G. (1987). Pharmacotherapy of childhood hyperactivity: An update. In H. Y. Meltzer, W. Bunney, J. Coyle, K. Davis, I. Kopin, C. R. Schuster, R. I. Shader, & G. Simpson (Eds.), *Psychopharmacology: The third generation of progress* (pp. 1215–1224). New York: Raven Press.

Loney, J., Weissenburger, F. E., Woolson, R. F., & Lichty, E. C. (1979). Comparing psychological and pharmacological treatments for hyperkinetic boys and their classmates. *Journal of Abnormal Child Psychiatry, 7,* 133–143.

Loper, A. B. (1980). Metacognitive development: Implications for cognitive training. *Exceptional Education Quarterly, 1,* 1–8.

Mash, E. J., & Dalby, J. T. (1979). Behavioral interventions for hyperactivity. In R. L. Trites (Ed.), *Hyperactivity in children: Etiology, measurement, and treatment implications* (pp. 161–216). Baltimore: University Park Press.

Meichenbaum, D. H. (1977). *Cognitive-behavior modification: An integrative approach.* New York: Plenum Press.

O'Leary, K. D., Pelham, W. E., Rosenbaum, A., & Price, G. H. (1976). Behavioral treatment of hyperkinetic children: An experimental evaluation of its usefulness. *Clinical Pediatrics, 15,* 274–279.

O'Leary, S. G., & Pelham, W. E. (1978). Behavior therapy and withdrawal of stimulant medication with hyperactive children. *Pediatrics, 61,* 211–217.

Pelham, W. E., Bender, M. E., Caddell, J., Booth, S., & Moorer, S. H. (1985). Methylphenidate and children with attention deficit disorder: Dose effects on classroom academic and social behavior. *Archives of General Psychiatry, 42,* 948–952.

Pelham, W. E., & Murphy, H. A. (1986). Attention deficit and conduct disorders. In M. Hersen (Ed.), *Pharmacological and behavioral treatment: An integrative approach* (pp. 108–148). New York: John Wiley.

Pelham, W. E., Schnedler, R. W., Bologna, N. C., & Contreras, J. A. (1980). Behavioral and stimulant treatment of hyperactive children: A therapy study with methylphenidate probes in a within-subject design. *Journal of Applied Behavioral Analysis, 13,* 221–236.

Pelham, W. E., Schnedler, R. W., Miller, J., Ronnei, M., Paluchowski, C., Budrow, M., Marks, D., Nilsson, D., & Bender, M. (in press). The combination of behavior therapy and psychostimulant medication in the treatment of hyperactive children. In L. Bloomingdale (Ed.), *Attention deficit disorders.* New York.

Porrino, L. J., Rapoport, J. L., Behar, D., Ismond, M. A., & Bunney, M. D., Jr. (1983). A naturalistic assessment of the motor activity of hyperactive boys: II. Stimulant drug effects. *Archives of General Psychiatry, 40,* 688–693.

Prout, H. T. (1977). Behavioral intervention with hyperactive children: A review. *Journal of Learning Disabilities, 10,* 141–146.

Rapport, M. D. (1983). Attention deficit disorder with hyperactivity: Critical treatment parameters and their application in applied outcome research. In M. Hersen, R. Eisler, & P. Miller (Eds.), *Progress in behavior modification* (Vol. 14, pp. 219–298). New York: Academic Press.

Rapport, M. D., DuPaul, G. J., Stoner, G., & Jones, J. T. (1986). Comparing classroom and clinic measures of attention deficit disorder: Differential, idiosyncratic, and dose-response effects of methylphenidate. *Journal of Consulting and Clinical Psychology, 54,* 334–341.

Rapport, M. D., Stoner, G., DuPaul, J., Birmingham, B. K., & Tucker, S. (1985). Methylphenidate in hyperactive children: Differential effects of dose on academic, learning, and social behavior. *Journal of Abnormal Child Psychology, 13,* 227–244.

Rosenbaum, A., O'Leary, K. D., & Jacob, R. G. (1975). Behavioral intervention with hyperactive children: Group consequences as a supplement to individual contingencies. *Behavioral Therapy*, *6*, 315–323.

Satterfield, J. H., Satterfield, B. T., & Cantwell, D. P. (1981). Three-year multimodality treatment study of 100 hyperactive boys. *Behavioral Pediatrics*, *98*, 650–655.

Solanto, M. V., & Conners, C. K. (1982). A dose response and time-action analysis of autonomic and behavioral effects of methylphenidate in Attention Deficit Disorder with Hyperactivity. *Psychophysiology*, *19*, 658–667.

Sprague, R. L. (1983). Behavior modification and educational techniques. In M. Rutter (Ed.), *Developmental neuropsychiatry*. New York: Guilford Press.

Sprague, R. L., & Sleator, E. K. (1977). Methylphenidate in hyperkinetic children: Differences in dose effects on learning and social behavior. *Science*, *198*, 1274–1276.

Varni, J. W., & Henker, B. (1979). A self-regulation approach to the treatment of three hyperactive boys. *Child Behavior Therapy*, *1*, 171–192.

Walker, M. A. (1982). Stimulant drugs. In S. E. Breuning & A. D. Poling (Eds.), *Drugs and mental retardation* (pp. 235–266). Springfield, IL: C. C. Thomas.

Whalen, C. K., Collins, B. E., Henker, B., Alkus, S. R., Adams, D., & Stapp, J. (1978). Behavior observations of hyperactive children and methylphenidate (Ritalin) effects in systematically structured classroom environments: Now you see them, now you don't. *Journal of Pediatric Psychology*, *4*, 177–187.

Whalen, C. K., Henker, B., Collins, B. E., Finck, D., & Dotemoto, S. (1979). A social ecology of hyperactive boys: Medication effects in structured classroom environments. *Journal of Applied Behavioral Analysis*, *12*, 65–81.

Whalen, C. K., Henker, B., & Dotemoto, S. (1980). Methylphenidate and hyperactivity: Effects on teacher behaviors. *Science*, *208*, 1280–1282.

Whalen, C. K., Henker, B., & Dotemoto, S. (1981). Teacher response to the methylphenidate (Ritalin) versus placebo status of hyperactive boys in the classroom. *Child Development*, *52*, 1005–1014.

Whalen, C. K., Henker, B., Swanson, J. M., Granger, D., Kliewer, W., & Spencer, J. (1987). Natural social behaviors in hyperactive children: Dose effects of methylphenidate. *Journal of Consulting and Clinical Psychology*, *55*, 187–193.

Wolraich, M. L. (1979). Behavior modification therapy in hyperactive children. *Clinical Pediatrics*, *18*, 563–569.

Wolraich, M., Drummond, T., Salomon, M., O'Brien, M., & Sivage, C. (1978). Effects of methylphenidate alone and in combination with behavior modification procedures on the behavior and academic performance of hyperactive children. *Journal of Abnormal Psychology*, *6*, 149–161.

Practical Aspects of Dietary Management of the Hyperkinetic Syndrome

Philip J. Graham, FRCP, FRCPsych.
Department of Child Psychiatry,
Institute of Child Health,
Hospital for Sick Children, London

INTRODUCTION

The extent of food intolerance in the child population is unknown, but a high proportion of UK children are restricted in their dietary intake by their parents in the belief that a particular food or class of foods is harmful to them. Rona and Chinn (1987) found that about 3% of parents of UK children aged 5 to 11 years were regarded as food intolerant in 1984, and other children were restricted from foods even though no evidence of harm was reported. Orange squash (4%) and nuts were the foods most often restricted. Most children restricted from particular foods were thought to suffer allergic illness if they were exposed, but unfortunately no specific enquiry was made concerning hyperactivity. Irritability was present in 17% of food-intolerant children compared to 2% of food-tolerant children.

Information on the number of children on diets for hyperactivity is unknown, but, in the UK at least, it must be substantial. Whenever an article is published on the subject in the popular press, and the address of the Hyperactive Children's Support Group is given, several hundred letters are received, mainly from mothers who believe they have a hyperkinetic child who might benefit (Colquhoun, personal communication). The main information provided by this Group concerns the use of diet. Even if only a fraction of those who enquire from the Support Group about the diet actually use it, and even if the use of diet is not maintained for more than a few weeks, the number of children on additive-free diets must nevertheless be considerable. In order to comply with new legislation, and to meet popular demand, all food manufacturers now label their products with a description of their composition, and many products such as fruit squashes now almost invariably carry a conspicuous statement that they are free from colourings and preservatives.

There has probably been a corresponding decline in the number of children in the UK receiving stimulant medication. The number of children receiving stimulants for the hyperkinetic syndrome was never very great and indeed the number of child psychiatrists who ever used them was always limited. Now, in addition, parents appear to be more cautious in accepting that their children might benefit from stimulants and indeed, even in those cases of severe, pervasive disorder where stimulants might well play a most helpful part, it is now not at all uncommon for parents to refuse the use of medication. Methylphenidate is now only available in the UK if special request is made to the manufacturing company.

Ironically, bearing in mind the difference in their popular usage, in contrast to the situation with stimulants, scientific information regarding the effectiveness of dietary manipulation in the hyperkinetic syndrome is still very inadequate. Stimulants are well evaluated and have a small but definite place in therapy: the proper place of diet remains uncertain. Current popular interest in diet as a means of controlling hyperactivity was stimulated in relatively recent times by Feingold (1975) who incriminated synthetic dyes and preservatives as well as naturally occurring salicylates and claimed behavioural benefit by their exclusion. It is difficult to exaggerate the impact of Feingold's views in the 1970s and early 1980s on the dietary management of children whom their parents thought to be difficult or ''overactive.'' National organizations such as the UK Hyperactive Children's Support Group were set up, and local branches proliferated. The popularity of the approach probably depended on its simplicity, on the fact that it absolved parents from the responsibility for their children's behaviour, and on the fact that family practitioners and child psychiatric services were inadequate to deal with the problem. It is, as yet, uncertain whether the successes claimed were mainly due to psychophysiological changes induced by the change of diet, or to more non-specific effects, such as increased parental attention or more effective parental control of undisciplined behaviour.

The scientific evidence suggests that non-specific effects of the Feingold diet are likely to be of much greater importance than specific effects. Double-blind trials in which children who are supposed to be affected by additives and colourings are introduced to the substances inserted into their diet in an experimental manner with placebo controls, suggests that specific effects are unusual (Connors, Goyette, Southwick, Lees, & Andrulonis, 1976, Harley, Ray, Tomasi, Eichman, Matthews, Chun, Cleeland, & Traisman, 1978). Recently, in a rather striking study, David (1987) admitted to a hospital twenty-four children claimed by parents definitely to respond adversely to tartrazine and benzoic acid. In no patient was any change in behaviour noted either by parents or nursing staff after the administration of placebo or active substances. Twenty-two of these children returned to a normal diet without problems, though a number continued to receive conventional psychiatric treatment. On the other hand, single case studies have, on occasions, demonstrated positive results (Mattes & Gittelman-Klein, 1978, Weiss, Williams Margen, Abrams, Caan, Citron, Cox, McKibben, Ogar, & Schultz, 1980). These findings suggest that additives and colourings alone are probably a rare cause of behaviour disturbance.

Feingold's focus on additives and colourings may however have distracted attention from a more general phenomenon. There is no particular reason why children should respond adversely to these substances rather than a whole range of naturally occurring foodstuffs. Indeed allergies and idiosyncratic responses are well recognized in pediatric practice to occur in response to a whole range of foods including cows' milk, fish, and chocolate.

At the Institute of Child Health, London, over the last ten years, Soothill has therefore pioneered a more thoroughgoing dietary approach. On confirmation of a diagnosis, children are put on a "few foods" diet, consisting of a highly restricted range of foodstuffs. These might consist of one meat (e.g., lamb), a carbohydrate (rice), a vegetable, water, calcium, and vitamins. The diet must be acceptable to the child. If children do not respond to the diet they are offered an alternative but equally restricted diet with a non-overlapping range of foods (Carter et al., 1985). Further non-response is taken to indicate the child is unlikely to respond to dietary measures. However, if the child appears to benefit, foods are gradually introduced one by one over the following three to four months. If the reintroduction of a food is followed by a worsening of behavioural symptomatology, it is withdrawn and another food substituted. Ultimately the child is receiving as wide a range of foodstuffs as possible. During the development of the method, the child was then subjected to an experiment using a double-blind design to ensure that the responsiveness of the child could be confirmed scientifically.

Soothill and his colleagues have been able to demonstrate the effectiveness of this approach in eczema and severe childhood migraine. Subsequently in a study of 76 children with the hyperkinetic syndrome, or with a behaviour disturbance in which hyperactivity was a prominent feature, it was found that 82% responded in the open phase of the trial. Twenty-eight children entered the double-blind phase and in over 80% of these subjects, parents and the pediatrician found the child's behaviour less disturbed in the placebo than in the active phase. These results were highly significant statistically (Egger et al., 1985). Independent observations made by a psychologist confirmed these findings, though the differences found on standardized psychological tests were largely statistically non-significant. Colourings and additives were the most common ingestants incriminated, but 43 naturally occurring foods were also apparently responsible. In no child were colourings and additives the only substances identified to have an adverse effect. Usually two, three or four naturally occurring foods were identified in addition (Egger et al., 1985).

Caution must be expressed before these findings (Egger, Carter, Graham, Gumley, & Soothill, 1985) are generalized. The group of children investigated in this study were not typical of hyperkinetic children in the general population. They were attending a highly specialized children's hospital. They suffered from a very high rate of associated physical symptoms and many had allergic disorders. The rate of atopy in children with the hyperkinetic syndrome is about the same as that in the general population. There is considerable need to replicate the work described in the study to children without such marked evidence of atopy and indeed such work is in progress.

There is also a need to investigate further the mechanisms whereby ingestion of particular foods might affect behaviour. The apparently higher rate of responsiveness in allergic subjects suggests an immunological mechanism, but other possibilities exist, and Brostoff (1987) has summarized evidence relating to non-immunological food reactions, especially those that might arise from enzyme deficiency. There are a number of ways in which these non-immunological mechanisms might link to the established abnormalities of catecholamine metabolism identified in children with ADD and described elsewhere in this book. The existence of neuropeptides in the gut similar to brain neuropeptides might provide one clue, but we have little idea how particular foods might release gut neuropeptides, nor how catecholamine secretion would be affected if such release occurred. A possibly relevant finding is that of Littlewood et al. (1982) who have shown that patients with dietary migraine have low levels of platelet phenolsulphotransferase, as this enzyme is known to inactivate monoamines including tyramine. Tyramine acts both directly as a sympathomimetic amine, and is indirectly responsible for release of noradrenaline. Clearly however there is a need for much further scientific work in this field.

THE DIETARY APPROACH: RESERVATIONS

It could perhaps be argued that, if parents believe their children respond adversely to certain foods or certain food additives, and choose to restrict their children's diets accordingly, there is little harm done and no particular reason why professionals should wish to intervene. There is in fact much to be said for this view. Most dietary restriction used by parents with children is practiced either as a preventive against the development of possible behaviour disturbance, or as a treatment for mild behaviour disturbance that is not severely disabling and for which alternative modes of management are of doubtful value. In these circumstances, dietary restriction is used rather unsystematically and does not involve significant social disability, particularly now that dietary restriction is so widespread that many of the child's friends are likely to be experiencing similar constraints. There is no reason why minor forms of dietary restraint or variation should require professional approval.

Unfortunately there are reasons why this tolerant professional approach may have limitations and indeed, in some circumstances, be dangerous. Evidence is provided by David (1987) and is merely summarized here. First there are well recorded instances (e.g., Warner & Hathaway, 1984) when children have been literally starved of essential nutrients on the grounds of false parental beliefs that they are disturbed and responding adversely to certain essential foods. The testing and, as it has turned out, disconfirmation of such beliefs, has sometimes required children to be taken into care. Such severe abuse is probably neither common, nor rare. A much more common, though less serious form of abuse occurs when children's lives are severely limited socially because of an unsubstantiated belief that the child is responding adversely to certain foods, and is consequently not allowed to go into shops selling food, or visit other children's homes in case the diet the child is on might be broken. A second problem arises when children are subjected to severe environmental stress, and parents attribute disturbed behaviour to food responsiveness without appropriate evidence, and are unable to contemplate the possibility that stresses may be affecting the child. Now it is perfectly possible that children under stress may, in addition, be responding adversely to certain foods and indeed there is some evidence that this may sometimes be the case (Egger, Carter, Graham, Gumley, & Soothill, 1985), but it must surely be an unsatisfactory situation when parents cannot at least examine the possibility that stressful circumstances, as well as the food they eat, are affecting their children adversely. Again this is a not uncommon situation. Thirdly, dietary treatments, when appropriately applied, can be expensive in professional time, and can involve the use of professionals, such as dietitians, who are in very short supply. Fourthly, dietary treatments usually require considerable motivation on the part of parents and, if the child has reached school age, of the child. It is not easy, for example, to restrict a child from eating junk foods and confectionary when other children are unrestricted, and it may be almost impossible if the child is difficult, self-willed, and capable of taking himself to the local shops. Fifthly, the diets may be financially expensive to apply. Some aspects of dietary treatment are quite unnecessarily expensive. For example, in the UK, parents may be charged significant sums by private laboratories undertaking expensive analyses of hair, skin testing, and carrying out various provocation tests, when there is no satisfactory scientific evidence for the value of such investigations. Certain expensive dietary treatments, such as the use of Efamol, are similarly unsupported by scientific evidence. However, even those treatments such as restriction of additives and the use of a few foods diet, where some positive scientific evidence does exist, are more expensive than unrestricted diets. Sixthly, worrying reports, though admittedly very few in number, have been made of children experiencing severe reactions such as anaphylactic shock, when they have been restricted from certain foods for some time and then suddenly been re-exposed. It must therefore be recognized that professional tolerance should have its limits, and there are times when it is very appropriate to express concern at the unsupervised use of dietary treatments.

PRACTICAL ASPECTS OF DIETARY MANAGEMENT

In the light of the information provided above, pediatricians, family doctors, psychiatrists, psychologists, and other professionals will find themselves faced with a number of practical clinical problems concerned with diet and behaviour.

For example, a situation quite commonly arises when a child reported by a parent to have been overactive is placed on a diet. The child's behaviour is reported to have improved with the diet, and the referral may be motivated in a variety of ways. The parents may be requesting that laboratory tests be carried out to confirm the diagnosis of "food allergy" and, if possible, to identify more precisely the specific foods to which the child is "allergic". In these circumstances one can confidently say that there are no laboratory tests of proven scientific value that can be used for this purpose (Cant, 1986). However one's duty to the child may not end there, for it is quite possible that the child has been inappropriately placed on a diet in the first place. The evidence for hyperactivity may be weak, and unconfirmed by independent observers such as the child's teachers. In these circumstances, while it is not helpful to confront parents with one's doubts about the need for the diet, it may well be appropriate to discuss with parents the use of a more experimental approach aimed towards the gradual reintroduction of the foods from which the child has been withdrawn.

In other circumstances, a child may be referred because there is serious concern that abuse of the child by restriction of diet is occurring. A small number of children are referred to pediatric departments in a malnourished state because of dietary restriction resulting in under nutrition. When parents are unwilling to allow relaxation of diet with the use of a more experimental approach, child-protection procedures may need to be invoked. In the light of current knowledge it would never be appropriate for children to be placed for behavioural reasons on a diet that restricted their growth and development.

Finally, a child may be referred for a behaviour problem in which hyperactivity is one of the main features. The value of diet is raised as one of a number of therapeutic possibilities. Approach to management in these circumstances has been described in more detail elsewhere (Graham, 1987) but will be summarized here.

First steps in management must involve assessment of nature of the problem. Assessment will vary depending on the time available, the orientation of the practitioner and the reason for referral. It will, however, always be important to obtain a clear idea of the nature of the behaviour problems, their severity, and the circumstances in which they occur. Actual examples of difficult behaviour should be obtained. For how long, for example, can the child settle to an activity such as drawing or doing a puzzle? For how long can he sit at the table for a meal? Does the difficult behaviour occur both at home and at school, playgroup, or merely in one setting? What seems to make the behaviour better or worse? These descriptions will be supplemented by the practitioner's own observations of the behaviour of the child. Some children who are described as constantly overactive will appear to the observer to be quiet, calm, and able to concentrate well. Parents may comment on how atypical the child's behaviour is while in the consulting room. It is, of course, not uncommon for a child's behaviour to be variable, but inevitably the practitioner will have more confidence in parental statements about difficult behaviour that he has been able to verify for himself.

Parents should be asked for any evidence concerning food responsiveness that they have already noted. Variability of behaviour may be one indication of food responsiveness. Parents may have observed episodes of tension, explosiveness, and over-excitement after ingestion of particular foods. If there are associated physical changes, such as pallor, flushing, skin rashes, or blotching of the skin, this is also indicative of responsiveness to a toxin or an allergic reaction.

Finally, the presence of evidence of allergy in the past history of the child or in a close member of the family should be noted. An early history of feeding difficulties with vomiting and diarrhea may be suggestive of cow's milk allergy. A past or family history of asthma, eczema, or other allergic disorder may also be relevant.

TREATMENT

This will depend on whether the behaviour problem is mildly or severely disabling. The "few foods" diet with its restriction/reintroduction approach is not justified when a child is able to attend school and lead an active social life even if mildly handicapped by a generally high level of overactivity, distractability, and poor concentration. A preliminary judgment therefore needs to be made concerning the level of the child's disability. A severe disability may be considered to exist when a child, by virtue of overactivity and associated deficits, is unable to relate to his peers, is failing educationally, and/or is showing disruptive behaviour at school or at home to an extent that is attracting frequent rejection and hostility.

It needs to be emphasized that conventional approaches to the management of overactivity are also, to some degree, dependent on the severity of the disability. Most clinicians would agree that formal behaviour modification, stimulant medication, and the use of special educational facilities should be reserved for the more severely disabled child, whereas parental counselling emphasizing the recognition and acceptance of individual characteristics, and the need for consistent discipline should be applied in cases of mild disability. Severity of disorder can similarly guide the use of dietary treatments.

Mild overactivity (see Figure 1). If the child is already on an additive-free diet and the parents claim this is effective, it seems appropriate not to suggest changes in dietary management. The diet the child is receiving may in fact not be necessary, but if it is likely not to limit the child socially, little harm will be done. Parental counselling along the lines described above may be helpful, and parents should be encouraged to attempt de-restriction of the diet every three to four months to check whether the child is still apparently responding adversely.

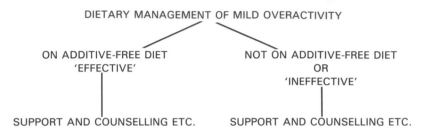

FIGURE ONE

DIETARY MANAGEMENT OF MILD OVERACTIVITY

ON ADDITIVE-FREE DIET   NOT ON ADDITIVE-FREE DIET
'EFFECTIVE'   OR
                                      'INEFFECTIVE'

SUPPORT AND COUNSELLING ETC.   SUPPORT AND COUNSELLING ETC.

It is helpful to explain that, just as children normally "grow out" of allergic conditions such as asthma and eczema, so they may be expected to "grow out" of food allergies. Parents can also be counselled about behavioural management along the lines described above.

In children with mild problems who have not been placed on an additive-free diet, it seems sensible not to suggest a dietary approach, but instead to apply more conventional lines of treatment. Parental counselling with emphasis on behavioural management techniques is often effective.

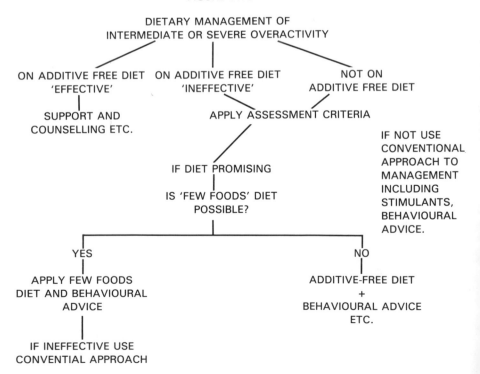

FIGURE TWO

DIETARY MANAGEMENT OF
INTERMEDIATE OR SEVERE OVERACTIVITY

ON ADDITIVE FREE DIET   ON ADDITIVE FREE DIET   NOT ON
'EFFECTIVE'   'INEFFECTIVE'   ADDITIVE FREE DIET

SUPPORT AND   APPLY ASSESSMENT CRITERIA
COUNSELLING ETC.   IF NOT USE
                                                       CONVENTIONAL
                                                       APPROACH TO
                         IF DIET PROMISING   MANAGEMENT
                                                       INCLUDING
                         IS 'FEW FOODS' DIET   STIMULANTS,
                         POSSIBLE?   BEHAVIOURAL
                                                       ADVICE.

YES   NO

APPLY FEW FOODS   ADDITIVE-FREE DIET
DIET AND BEHAVIOURAL   +
ADVICE   BEHAVIOURAL ADVICE
                                                ETC.

IF INEFFECTIVE USE
CONVENTIAL APPROACH

Intermediate or severe levels of overactivity (see Figure 2). If the child is on an "additive-free" diet that appears to be controlling the situation, there is probably no indication for further dietary interference. Parental guidance and other conventional measures can be applied as in the case of mild problems. If however an additive-free diet has been found to be ineffective or no dietary measures at all have been applied, then existing scientific evidence would suggest that is appropriate to try the effects of a "few-foods" restriction re-introduction approach. However, not all children will be found suitable. In particular, if the child is of school age but unmotivated, or if discussion with the parents reveals they would probably not be able to cope with the very demanding regime, the "few-foods" diet is contra-indicated. Further, if the clinical assessment provides no indication of food responsiveness or an allergic disorder, i.e., if the parents have noticed no reaction to specific foods, and there are no associated physical symptoms and no family or past history of allergic disorder, then scientific evidence for the effectiveness of the "few foods" diet does not exist. Consequently it may be thought more appropriate to use conventional methods of treatment—parental guidance, formal behaviour modification, stimulants and possibly special educational treatment. Parental preference for treatment should be taken into account in these circumstances.

If however the positive implications already described for a more rigorous dietary approach do exist, the "few-foods" diet should be undertaken. Brief details have been described in this chapter, and further accounts published elsewhere (Carter, Egger, & Soothill, 1985). An at least partially successful outcome of the application of the "few-foods" diets may be expected in the majority of cases where the indications are positive. If, however, the treatment is ineffective, recourse may be made to more conventional forms of treatment. These should, in any case, be applied when positive indications for the use of diet are lacking or where the family would not be able to cope with its demands.

Finally, it must be emphasized that the dietary approach described here is based on flimsy scientific evidence. There is, above all, need for further research in two main areas: The underlying mechanisms, be they immunological or toxicological, whereby foods produce behavioural responses, are very poorly understood at this point in time. Further research, both in humans and animals, is required to elucidate these mechanisms. Secondly, there is a need to conduct further trials of the "few-foods" restriction/re-introduction approach in children without physical symptoms and with no strong past or family history of allergic disorder. The value of the "few-foods" treatment in such children is quite unknown.

REFERENCES

Brostoff, J. (1987). Non-immunological food reactions. Effects of enzyme deficiency and neuropeptides in food sensitive patients. In J. J. Dobbing (Ed.), *Food intolerance* (pp. 32-55). London: Bailliere Tindall.

Cant, A. (1986). The diagnosis and management of food allergy. *Archives of Diseases in Childhood*, *61*, 730-731.

Carter, C. M., Egger, J., & Soothill, J. F. (1985). A dietary management of severe childhood migraine. *Human Nutrition: Applied Nutrition*, *39*, 294-303.

Conners, C. K., Goyette, C. H., Southwick, D. A., Lees, J. M., & Andrulonis, P. (1976). Food additives and hyperkinesis. *Pediatrics*, *58*, 154-166.

David, T. (1987). Reactions to dietary tartrazine. *Archives of Diseases in Childhood*, *62*, 119-122.

David, T. (1987). Unhelpful recent developments in the diagnosis and treatment of allergy and food intolerance in children. In J. Dobbing (Ed). *Food intolerance* (pp. 185-214). London: Bailliere Tindall.

Egger, J., Carter, C. M., Graham, P. J., Gumley, D., & Soothill, J. F. (1985). Controlled trial of oligoantigenic treatment in the hyperkinetic syndrome. *The Lancet, i*, 540-545.

Feingold, B. F. (1975). Hyperkinesis and learning disabilities linked to artificial food flavors and colors. *American Journal of Nursing*, *75*, 797-803.

Graham, P. (1986). *Child psychiatry: A developmental approach*. London: Oxford University Press.

Harley, J. P., Ray, R. S., Tomasi, L., Eichman, P. L., Matthews, C. G., Chun, R., Cleeland, C. S., & Traisman, E. (1978). Hyperkinesis and food additives: Testing the Feingold hypothesis. *Pediatrics*, *61*, 818-828.

Littlewood, J., Glover, V., & Sandler, M. (1982). Platelet sulphotransferase deficiency in dietary migraine. *Lancet, i.* 983-986.

Mattes, J. A., & Gittelman-Klein, R. (1978). An intensive cross-over study of the effects of artificial food colourings in a hyperkinetic child. *American Journal of Psychiatry 135*, 987-988.

Rona, R. J., & Chinn, S. (1987). Parents perceptions of food intolerance in primary school children. *British Medical Journal*, *294*, 863-866.

Warner, J. D., & Hathaway, M. J. (1984). Allergic form of Meadow's syndrome (Munchausen Syndrome by Proxy). *Archives of Diseases in Childhood*, *59*, 151-6.

Weiss, B., Williams, J. H., Margen, S., Abrams, B., Cann, B., Cirron, L., Cox, C., McKibben, J., Ogar, D., & Schultz, S. (1980). Behavioural response to artificial food colors. *Science*, *207*, 1487-1489.

13

Basic Mechanisms of Drug Action: Catecholaminergic Issues

Trevor Archer
Department of Behavioural Pharmacology
AB Astra Alab Södertälje and Department of Psychology University of Umeå, Sweden

Terje Sagvolden
Institute of Neurophysiology University of Oslo Norway

Although it is essentially impossible to cover adequately the topic on *Basic mechanisms of drug action* in Attention Deficit Disorder and Hyperkinetic Syndrome, the three chapters offer a formidable coverage from a neuropharmacological perspective of the problem under consideration. James McGaugh introduced the central theme of memory enhancement (for details, see McGaugh, Introini-Collison, Nagahara, & Cahill, 1988). The choice of this problem was indeed fortunate since the contribution by Normile, Altman and Gershon (this volume) is built upon the 'global' strategy of evolving 'cognition enhancers' with potential efficacy for a range of cognitive dysfunctions, including ADHD and dementia of the Alzheimer's type. Trevor Robbins, G.H. Jones, and Barbara Sahakian discuss the possible 'paradoxical' effects of the psychomotor stimulants, methylphenidate and d-amphetamine, upon ADHD children in order to develop an understanding of the neuropharmacological mechanisms of these drugs in behavioral procedures. The mediatory effects of the mesolimbic dopamine (DA) projections to the nucleus accumbens and associated structures of the ventral striatum are delineated in the context of the several behaviors stimulated by d-amphetamine. These behaviors and their interactions with the stimulants and the neuroanatomical sites are defined with a careful pursuance of their mechanistic action. This chapter also discussed indications that the hyperactivity and the attention disorder may arise from functional changes in relatively independent catecholaminergic systems and describes the neurobehavioral effects of rearing. Lewis Seiden's chapter provides a comprehensive review of the successful application of the neonatal 6-hydroxydopamine (6-OHDA) intracerebroventricular procedure, which produces

191

a very drastic, but selective, DA depletion in forebrain areas, to analyse the functional changes produced by extreme hyperactive juvenile and adult rats. Seiden indicates most succinctly the actions of the stimulant drugs on the hyperactivity and performance deficits of neonatally DA depleted rats.

Besides those covered by the following chapters, there are other avenues of research to investigate mechanisms of drug action that may be related to the ADHD disorder. Neurochemical analyses performed about fifteen years ago demonstrated that the DA containing neurons in rats developed functionally during the first week after birth (Kellogg & Lundborg, 1972). In a subsequent series of experiments, Ahlenius et al. (Ahlenius, Brown, Engel, & Lundborg, 1973; Ahlenius, Engel, & Lundborg, 1975; Engel & Lundborg, 1974) showed that the offspring of nursing mothers administered the neuroleptic drugs, pimozide or penfluridol, during the first postnatal week showed marked deficits of conditioned avoidance responding and brightness discrimination responding when tested at juvenile ages (i.e., about four weeks after birth). These findings confirmed the earlier results of Hoffeld and Webster (1965, rats) and Ordy, Samorajski, Collins, and Rolsten (1966, mice) who found learning deficits in the offspring of mice administered chlorpromazine during the gestation period. Interestingly, it was also found by Ahlenius et al. (1975) that the administration of d-amphetamine to the offspring of the neuroleptic-treated dams, prior to testing in the learning task, significantly improved the performance of these animals; but however it was shown also that d-amphetamine failed to reverse the hyperactivity shown by rats following neonatal haloperidol treatment (Schechter, & Concannon, 1982). Subsequent investigations (Ahlenius, Engel, Hård, Larsson, Lundborg, & Sinnerstedt, 1977) have demonstrated that early postnatal administration of neuroleptic compounds to nursing mothers produced a marked hyperactivity in the offspring of these dams. Another recent study involving neonatal exposure to nomifensine, a catecholamine uptake inhibitor, demonstrated increases in motor activity and brain monoamine levels (Hilakivi, Hilakivi, Ahtee, Haikala, & Attila, 1987) at adult ages. This evidence does not necessarily mean that monoamine uptake inhibitors generally produce this effect since both elevations, reductions and no changes in spontaneous motor activity have been obtained following neonatal administration of various different compounds (e.g., Broitman & Donoso, 1978; Coyle, 1975; Cuomo, Cortese, Cagiano, Renna, & Racagni, 1984; Drago, Continella, Alloro, & Scapagnini, 1985). The consensus of these and other lines of evidence, i.e., those results pertaining to hyperactivity and/or learning deficits following treatments affecting DA neurotransmission neonatally, rather than monoaminergic systems in general, lend much support to the neurochemical and behavioral findings presented in the Seiden chapter of this volume. It appears that the behavioural deficits (encompassing cognitive performance and a state of hyperactivity which relates to basic assumptions concerning ADHD) shown by the offspring of pregnant or nursing mothers treated with neuroleptic drugs, are due to some developmental disturbance of the central catecholamine neurons.

Although probable facilitatory effects of various "cognition enhancers" on measures of cognitive performance have been reported (e.g., Gamzu, 1985; Giurgea & Salama, 1977; Sara & David-Remacle, 1974), it would be unwise to draw any clear interpretation of these results with regard to the efficacy of these compounds upon measures of learning and memory. This point may be illustrated through consideration of two compounds that have been studied fairly extensively with a view to obtaining some form of memory improvement. Some evidence suggest an improvement in the performance of certain tasks following administration of nootropic drugs like piracetam (Giurgea, Greindl, Preat, & Puigdevall, 1982; Nicolaus, 1982; Schindler, Rush, & Fielding, 1984), but generally the real effectiveness of piracetam remains difficult to access (Buresova & Bures, 1982; Crook, 1985; Goodnick & Gershon, 1984; Means, Franklin, & Cliett, 1980; Oglesby & Winter, 1974; Wolthuis, 1971). The same uncertainty regarding effects on learning and memory applies to the muscarinic agonist, choline (e.g., Bartus, 1980; Johns, Greenwald, Mohs, & Davis, 1983; Thal, Rosen, Sharpless, & Crystal, 1981), although the combined administration of choline and piracetam has been found to be clearly more efficacious than each drug administered separately (Bartus, Dean, Sherman, Friedman, & Beer, 1981; Platel, Jalfre, Pawelec, Roux, & Porsolt, 1984; Reisberg, Ferris, Schneck, Corwin, Mir, Friedman, Sherman, McCarthy, & Bartus, 1982). But, at least one failure to obtain this "combination effect" exists (Ennaceur & Delacour, 1987). Much of the uncertainty regarding the "cognition enhancers" stems from a failure to distinguish between measures of working memory (cf., Olton, 1978, 1983) and other measures of performance, e.g., avoidance. Thus, while choline may not consistently affect performance on active avoidance learning tasks, a clear facilitatory effect on delayed alternation learning has been shown (Ennaceur & Delacour, 1987). On the other hand, piracetam may produce beneficial effects on animal amnesic models and on aged animal and human subjects (Atanackovic, Simonic, & Roganovic, 1984; Bartus, Dean, & Beer, 1984; Valzelli, Bernasconi, & Sala, 1980; Vincent, Velderese, & Gamzu, 1984). Thus, the consensus of these and other diverse investigations appears to be that the viable prospects for "cognition enhancers" in the problems of the aged may prove to be effective in certain aspects of ADHD.

Another tactic for investigating mechanisms of drug action relating to ADDH is to assess the performance of some learning task (whether of an instrumental or classical conditioning nature) by animals under the influence of either a psychomotor stimulant (essentially as pursued by Robbins, Jones, & Sahakian, this volume) or a direct acting DA agonist, e.g., apomorphine. Using the latent learning phenomenon (Tolman, 1932, 1949; Tolman & Honzik, 1930) by which rodents can acquire an instrumental task, like maze learning, if they have previous experience in the environment, Ahlenius, Engel and Zöller (1977) demonstrated that it was possible to study the consequences of a drug treatment on the ability of mice to learn a maze task at a later period, i.e., when in a nondrugged state.

They found that mice injected with the DA agonist apomorphine failed to show latent learning, possibly due to an overactivation of DA receptors resulting in a loss of stimulus control in the maze learning task during the preexposure phase.

A phenomenon related to latent learning is the one termed latent inhibition (Lubow, 1965; Lubow & Moore, 1959) by which the initial unreinforced presentation of a Conditioned Stimulus (CS), followed by trials during which the CS precedes an unconditioned stimulus (US), retards the subsequent learning about the consequences of CS presentation. In a typical latent inhibition experiment the CS (e.g., light) is presented in the absence of the US (e.g., shock) for a number of trials, for one group but not another. Following this, conditioning trials consisting of light-shock pairings (in this case) are presented. During testing of response suppression, or conditioning, to the light it is found that the amount of suppression evoked by the light CS is less in the case where light had been presented without shock (during pre-exposure) than in the case where light had not been presented without shock (during pre-exposure) than in the case where light had not been presented until the conditioning phase (e.g., Lubow, 1973). Latent inhibition has proven to be a useful procedure for analysing attentional processes (e.g., Mackintosh, 1985) and it is in this capacity that Weiner, Feldon and coworkers (e.g., Weiner, Lubow, & Feldon, 1984) have applied the technique to study the involvement of dopaminergic receptors. d-Amphetamine, for example, was shown to disrupt the developement of latent inhibition whereas haloperidol facilitated the effect (Weiner & Feldon, 1987; Weiner, Lubow, & Feldon, 1981). The rearing of rats in social isolation, which produces a hyperactive state accompanied by learning deficits (Mohammed, Jonsson, & Archer, 1986; Smith, 1972), caused marked disruption of the latent inhibition effect (Feldon, Weimer, & Avnimelech-Gigus, 1987).

Weiner (personal communication) has summarized several important points regarding the use of the latent inhibition phenomenon: (1) It assesses the rat's capacity to ignore irrevelant stimuli and is essentially an attentional process. (2) It appears to be uniquely sensitive to dopaminergic manipulation, i.e., haloperidol facilitation and amphetamine disruption. The effects of both drugs appears to be not upon the animal's ability to respond *per se*, but the subsequent capacity to ignore (not respond to) the irrelevant stimulus as such. Their effect is dependent upon presence of the drugs during both the preexposure and conditioning stages. (3) It is sensitive to manipulations of the juvenile animals, i.e., nonhandling or isolation disrupt the phenomenon although isolation reverses the effects of early nonhandling in males. Weiner and her associates imply a strong dopaminergic involvement in attentional processes, at least with regard to straightforward latent inhibition since noradrenaline does not seem to affect the basic procedure (Archer, 1982). However, basic latent inhibition can be modulated by the introduction of contextual variables and under these conditions a clear noradrenergic involvement can be observed (Archer, Mohammed, & Järbe, 1983). Taken together, these findings further implicate some involvement of catecholaminergic transmission in the attentional deficits of adult and juvenile rats and serve to indicate other avenues of research to facilitate the search for improved therapeutic agents effective in the alleviation of ADDH.

REFERENCES

Ahlenius, S., Brown, R., Engel, J., & Lundborg, P. (1973). Learning deficits in 4 weeks old offspring of the nursing mothers treated with the neuroleptic drug penfluridol. *Naunyn-Schmiedeberg's Archives of Pharmacology, 279*, 31–37.

Ahlenius, S., Engel, J., & Lundborg, P. (1975). Antagonism by d-amphetamine of learning deficits in rats induced by exposure to antipsychotic drugs during early postnatal life. *Naunyn-Schmiedeberg's Archives of Pharmacology, 288*, 185–193.

Ahlenius, S., Engel, J., Hård, E., Larsson, K., Lundborg, P., & Sinnerstedt, P. (1977). Open field behaviour and gross motor development in offspring of nursing rat mothers given penfluridol. *Pharmacology, Biochemistry and Behavior, 6*, 343–347.

Ahlenius, S., Engel, J., & Zöller, M. (1977). Effects of apomorphine and haloperidol on exploratory behavior and latent learning in mice. *Physiological Psychology, 5*, 290–294.

Archer, T. (1982). DSP4(N-2-chloroethyl-N-ethyl-2-bromobenzylamine), a new noradrenaline neurotoxin, and stimulus conditions affecting acquisition of two-way active avoidance. *Journal of Comparative and Physiological Psychology, 96*, 476–490.

Archer, T., Mohammed, A. K., Järbe, T. U. C. (1983). Latent inhibition following systemic DSP4: Effects due to presence and absence of contextual cues in taste-aversion learning. *Behavioral and Neural Biology, 38*, 287–306.

Atanackovic, D., Simonic, A., & Roganovic, J. (1984). Influence of piracetam on active avoidance behavior in rats. *Acta Pharmacologica Jugoslavia, 34*, 139–142.

Bartus, R. T. (1980). Cholinergic drug effect on memory and cognition in animals. In L. W. Poon (Ed.), *Aging in the 1980s: Psychological issues* (pp. 163-180). Washington, DC.: APA.

Bartus, R. T., Dean, R. L., & Beer, B. (1984). Cholinergic precursor therapy for geriatric cognition: Its past, its present and a question of its future. In J. M. Ordy, D. Harman, & R. Alfin-Slaten (Eds.), *Nutrition in gerontology* (pp. 191-225). New York: Raven Press.

Bartus, R. T., Dean, R. L., Sherman, K. A., Friedman, E., & Beer, B. (1981). Profound effects of combining choline and piracetam on memory enhancement and cholinergic function in aged rats. *Neurobiology of Aging, 2*, 105–111.

Broitman, S. T., & Donoso, A. O. (1978). Effects of chronic imipramine and clomipramine oral administration on maternal behavior and litter development. *Psychopharmacology, 56*, 93–101.

Buresova, O., & Bures, J. (1982). Radial-maze as a tool for assessing the effect of drugs on the working memory of rats. *Psychopharmacology, 77*, 268–271.

Coyle, J. T. (1975). Changes in developing behavior following prenatal administration of imipramine. *Pharmacology, Biochemistry and Behavior, 3*, 799–807.

Crook, T. H. (1985). Clinical drug trials in Alzheimer's diseases. *Annals of the New York Academy of Sciences, 444*, 428–436.

Cuomo, V., Cortese, I., Cagiano, R., Renna, G., & Racagni, G. (1984). Behavioral changes in rats after prenatal administration of typical and atypical antidepressants. In P. L. Chambers, P. Preziosi, & C. M. Chambers (Eds.), *Disease, metabolism and reproduction in the toxic response to drugs and other chemicals. Archives of Toxicology, 7*, 504–507.

Drago, F., Continella, G., Alloro, M. C., & Scapagnini, U. (1985). Behavioral effects of perinatal administration of antidepressant drugs in the rat. *Neurobehavioral Toxicology and Teratology, 7*, 493–497.

Engel, J., & Lundborg, P. (1974). Regional changes in monoamine levels in the rate of tyrosine and tryptophan hydroxylation 4 weeks old offspring of the nursing mothers treated with the neuroleptic drug penfluridol. *Naunyn-Schmiedeberg's Archives of Pharmacology, 282*, 327–334.

Ennaceur, A., & Delacour, J. (1987). Effect of combined or separate administration of piracetam and choline on learning and memory in the rat. *Psychopharmacology, 92*, 58–67.

Feldon, J., Weiner, I., & Avnimelech-Gigus, N. (1987). The effects of early handling and isolation on attentional processes in male rats. Paper presented at the *Workshop on Attention Deficit Disorder and Hyperkinetic Syndrome*, Oslo.

Gamzu, E. (1985). Animal behavioral models in the discovery of compounds to treat memory dysfunction. *Annals of the New York Academy of Sciences, 444*, 370–393.

Giurgea, E. C., & Salama, M. (1977). Nootropic drugs. *Progress Neuropsychopharmacology, 1*, 235–247.

Giurgea, E. C., Greindel, M. G., Preat, S., & Puigdevall, J. (1982). Piracetam compensation of MAM-induced behavioral deficit in rats. *Aging, 19*, 281–286.

Goodnick, P., & Gershon, S. (1984). Chemotherapy of cognitive disorders in geriatric subjects. *Journal of Clinical Psychiatry, 45*, 196–209.

Hilakivi, L. A. Hilakivi, I., Ahtee, L., Haikala, H., & Attila, M. (1987). Effect of neonatal nomifensine exposure on adult behavior and brain monoamines in rats. *Journal of Neural Transmission, 70*, 99–116.

Hoffeld, D. R., & Webster, R. L. (1965). Effect of injection of tranquillizing drugs during pregnancy of offspring. *Nature, 205*, 1070–1072.

Johns, C. A., Greenwald, B. S., Mohs, R. C., & Davis, R. L. (1983). The cholinergic treatment in strategy in aging and senile dementia. *Psychopharmacological Bulletin, 19*, 185–197.

Kellogg, C., & Lundborg, P. (1972). Ontogenic variations in response to L-Dopa and monoamine receptor-stimulating agents. *Psychopharmacologia* (Berl.), *23*, 187–200.

Lubow, R. E. (1965). Latent inhibition: Effect of frequency of nonreinforced preexposure of the CS. *Journal of Comparative and Physiological Psychology, 60*, 454–457.

Lubow, R. E. (1973). Latent inhibition. *Psychological Bulletin, 79*, 398–407.

Lubow, R. E., & Moore, A. V. (1959). Latent inhibition: The effect of nonreinforced preexposure of the CS. *Journal of Comparative and Physiological Psychology, 52*, 415–419.

Mackintosh, N. J. (1985). Contextual specificity or state dependency of human and animal learning. In L. G. Nilsson & T. Archer (Eds.), *Perspectives on learning and memory* (pp. 223–242). Hillsdale, N.J.: Lawrence Erlbaum Associates.

McGaugh, J. L., Introini-Collison, I. B., Nagahara, A. H., & Cahill, L. (1988). Involvement of the amygdala in hormonal and neurotransmitter interactions in the modulation of memory storage. In T. Archer, & L. G. Nilsson (Eds.), *Aversion, avoidance and anxiety: Perspectives on aversively motivated behavior*. Hillsdale, N.J.: Lawrence Erlbaum Associates.

Means, L. W., Franklin, R. D., & Cliett, C. E. (1980). Failure of piracetam to facilitate acquisition or retention in younger or older rats. *Experimental Aging Research, 6*, 175–180.

Mohammed, A. K., Jonsson, G., & Archer, T. (1986). Selective lesioning of forebrain noradrenaline neurons at birth abolishes the improved maze learning performance induced by rearing in complex environment. *Brain Research, 398*, 6–10.

Nicolaus, B. J. R. (1982). Chemistry and pharmacology of nootropics. *Drug Development Research, 2*, 463–474.

Oglesby, M. W., & Winter, J. C. (1974). Strychnine sulfate and piracetam: Lack of effect on learning in the rat. *Psychopharmacologia, 36*, 163–173.

Olton, D. S. (1978). Characteristics of spatial memory. In S. H. Hulse, H. F. Fowler & W. K. Honig (Eds.), *Cognitive aspects of animal behavior* (pp. 342–373). Hillsdale, N.J.: Lawrence Erlbaum Associates.

Olton, D. S. (1983). Memory functions and the hippocampus. In W. Seifert (Ed.), *Neurobiology of the hippocampus* (pp. 335–373). New York: Academic Press.

Ordy, J. M. Samorajski, T., Collins, R. L., & Rolsten, C. (1966). Prenatal chlorpromazine effects of liver, survival and behaviour of mice offspring. *Journal of Pharmacology and Experimental Therapeutics, 151*, 110–125.

Platel, A., Jalfre, M., Pawelec, C., Roux, S., & Porsolt, R. (1984). Habituation of exploration activity in mice: Effects of combination of piracetam and choline on memory processes. *Pharmacology, Biochemistry and Behavior, 21*, 209–212.

Reisberg, B., Ferris, S. H., Shneck, M. K., Corwin, J., Mir, P., Friedman, E., Sherman, K. A., McCarthy, M., & Bartus, R. T. (1982). Piracetam in the treatment of cognitive impairment in the elderly. *Drug Development Research, 2*, 475–480.

Sara, S. J., & David-Remacle, M. (1974). Recovery from electroconvulsive shock-induced amnesia by exposure to the training environment: Pharmacological enhancement by piracetam. *Psychopharmacologia, 36*, 59–66.

Schechter, M. D., & Concannon, J. T. (1982). Haloperidol-induced hyperactivity in neonatal rats: Effect of lithium and stimulants. *Pharmacology, Biochemistry and Behavior, 16*, 1–5.

Schindler, U., Rush, D. K., & Fielding, S. (1984). Nootropic drugs: Animal models for studying effects on cognition. *Drug Development Research, 4*, 567–576.

Smith, H. W. (1972). Effects of environmental enrichment on open-field activity and Hebb-Williams problem solving in rats. *Journal of Comparative and Physiological Psychology, 80*, 163–186.

Thal, L. J., Rosen, W. G., Sharpless, N. S., Crystal, H. A. (1981). Choline chloride fails to improve cognition in Alzheimer's disease. *Neurobiology of Aging, 2*, 205–208.

Tolman, E. C. (1932). *Purposive behavior in animals and men*. New York: Century.

Tolman, E. C. (1949). There is more than one kind of learning. *Psychological Review, 56*, 144–155.

Tolman, E. C., & Honzik, C. H. (1930). Introduction and removal of reward, and maze performance in rats. *University of California Publications in Psychology, 4*, 257–275.

Valzelli, L., Bernasconi, S., & Sala, A. (1980). Piracetam activity may differ according to the age of the recipient mouse. *International Pharmacopsychiatry, 15*, 150–156.

Vincent, G., Velderese, A., & Gamzu, E. (1984). The effects of aniracetam (Ro 13–5057) and piracetam on the enhancement of memory in mice. *Society for Neuroscience Abstracts, 10*, 258.

Weiner, I., & Feldon, J. (1987). Facilitation of latent inhibition by haloperidol in rats. *Psychopharmacology, 91*, 248–253.

Weiner, I., Lubow, R. E., & Feldon, J. (1984). Abolition of the expression but not the acquisition of latent inhibition by chronic amphetamine in rats. *Psychopharmacology, 83*, 194–199.

Weiner, I., Lubow, R. E., & Feldon, J. (1981). Chronic amphetamine and latent inhibition. *Behavioural Brain Research, 2*, 285–286.

Wolthuis, O. L. (1971). Experiments with UCB 6215, a drug which enhances acquisition in rats: Its effects compared with those of methamphetamine. *European Journal of Pharmacology, 16*, 283–297.

14

Central Stimulants, Transmitters and Attentional Disorder: A Perspective from Animal Studies

Trevor W. Robbins, G.H. Jones
Department of Experimental Psychology,
University of Cambridge

Barbara J. Sahakian
Institute of Psychiatry,
University of London

The syndrome of childhood hyperactivity and attentional disorder poses several interesting questions. Its aetiology is not known, although many contributing factors have been advanced. The causal relationships existing between its major symptoms of hyperactivity and distractibility remain obscure, and their neural basis even more so. Treatment of hyperactive children with psychomotor stimulant drugs such as amphetamine and methylphenidate (Ritalin) appears paradoxical, but in view of our, by now, considerable understanding of the neurochemical and neural mechanisms by which these drugs act in animals, this link may provide us with a possible clue about the neural systems contributing to childhood hyperkinesis. This article: (i) reviews what is known about the neural mediation of the behavioural effects of psychomotor stimulant drugs; (ii) describes some of the recent evidence suggesting that hyperactivity and attentional disorder can result from altered function in relatively independent catecholaminergic systems; (iii) describes the behavioural and neurochemical effects of rearing rats in social isolation, a treatment which mimics some of the behavioural effects of stimulant drugs; and (iv) considers the possible relevance of this work for childhood attentional disorder.

NEURAL BASIS OF THE BEHAVIOURAL EFFECTS OF PSYCHOMOTOR STIMULANT DRUGS

There is considerable evidence that the majority of the behavioural effects of psy-

199

chomotor stimulants in adult animals are mediated by the forebrain dopamine (DA) systems, particularly the 'mesolimbic' projection to the nucleus accumbens and associated structures of the ventral striatum. The predominant unconditioned effects of amphetamine in rats are, with increasing dose, locomotor hyperactivity and stereotyped behaviour. The latter can be defined as repetition in an invariant sequence of behaviour and has been observed in all mammalian species studied, including man. In the rat, the behaviour is often manifested as focused sniffing in one location with repetitive head movements (see Robbins & Sahakian, 1983; Robbins, Mittleman, O'Brien, & Winn, 1988 for reviews).

Amphetamine hyperactivity is blocked by dopamine depletion from the region of the nucleus accumbens produced by the selective catecholamine neurotoxin 6-hydroxydopamine, but this treatment leaves the stereotyped behaviour comparatively unaffected (Kelly, Seviour, & Iversen, 1975). By contrast, dopamine depletion from the caudate-putamen blocks the expression of the stereotyped behaviour (Creese & Iversen, 1975; Kelly et al., 1975), although amphetamine locomotor hyperactivity may be increased (Joyce & Iversen, 1984), probably as a result of the reduced competition that normally occurs between these responses (Lyon & Robbins, 1975). Microinfusions of amphetamine into the nucleus accumbens produce a locomotor stimulation (Pijnenberg, Honig, Van der Heyden, & van Rossum, 1976), which is greater than that observed following systemic injection (J.R. Taylor & T.W. Robbins, unpublished). Similar infusions into the caudateputamen have been reported to produce stereotyped behaviour, but the responses are weak, and not on the same scale as those seen following systemic treatment with the drug (see Robbins et al., 1988, for a review).

Many of the effects of amphetamine seen in more structured situations, such as occur under schedules of reinforcement or following discrimination training, are also attenuated by forebrain dopamine depletion, particularly from the nucleus accumbens. It is important to realize that not all of these effects are stimulatory in nature. Amphetamine often suppresses or disrupts certain forms of behaviour, perhaps as a result of its overall stimulatory action (Lyon & Robbins, 1975). For example, the effects of amphetamine and other stimulants on operant behaviour depend upon the baseline rate of responding seen in control conditions. Thus, whereas low rates of responding are elevated by amphetamine, high control rates (as may occur for example under fixed ratio schedules) may exhibit reductions. This inverse dependence of the drug effect upon the control level of responding has been termed "rate-dependency" (Dews & Wenger, 1977: Robbins, 1981). Such rate-dependent effects of amphetamine on responding under a fixed interval schedule of food presentation were attenuated by mesolimbic dopamine depletion (see Fig. 1) (Robbins, Roberts, & Koob, 1983). In the same situation, excessive levels of drinking occur in the interval between each presentation of food. This behaviour, which may be a laboratory analogue of displacement activity, is called schedule-induced polydipsia (Falk, 1971) and is very susceptible to disruption by amphetamine. Mesolimbic dopamine depletion blocked these suppressive effects of the drug (Robbins et al., 1983).

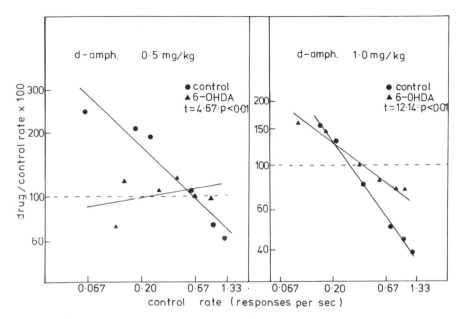

FIG. 1.   Attenuation of rate-dependent effects of d-amphetamine performing
under a fixed-interval schedule of reinforcement in groups of rats receiving either
6-OHDA lesions of the nucleus accumbens or a sham control procedure. The data
are from Robbins et al. (1983) but have been re-analysed and re-plotted. Abscissa:
control rate of responding. Ordinate: Drug effect, expressed as percentage change
and plotted on logarithmic axes. The lines were fitted by linear regression and the
t values are for statistical comparisons of their slopes.

Recent evidence has shown that the disruptive effects of amphetamine on a
discrimination task in which rats were trained to indicate which of two stimuli
terminated first, are also attenuated by mesolimbic dopamine depletion (Robbins
et al., 1986). The pattern of results in this experiment suggested that amphetamine may have two separate disruptive effects: one caused by the induction of
competing activities which distract the animal from the task requirements and
another more direct effect upon attentional switching. The former of these two
effects was most susceptible to mesolimbic dopamine depletion.

The results with the discrimination task are theoretically important because
they suggest that some of the disruptive effects of amphetamine upon discrimination performance simply result from drug-induced hyperactivity. Other evidence
also suggests that impairments in discrimination performance can arise indirectly from the effects of the drug upon response output. Koek and Slangen (1983)
showed that impaired accuracy in an auditory discrimination task resulted indirectly
from the effect of the drug to increase the tendency to repeat the last response:
this might perhaps be considered as a higher-order example of stereotyped behaviour.

Amphetamine can also exert facilitatory effects on performance which similarly may depend indirectly upon its stimulant action. Weiner, Feldon and Ben-Horin (1987) have recently confirmed the results of some older work (e.g., Kulig & Calhoun, 1972) suggesting that, in certain circumstances, amphetamine can improve reversal learning. Carr and White (1984) have also shown that intra-caudate infusions of amphetamine following training in a one-trial passive avoidance paradigm can apparently facilitate retention. It is significant in this latter case that the degree of facilitation was related to the intensity of stereotyped behaviour produced by the drug. An example from our own work (Evenden & Robbins, 1985) concerns the apparent facilitation of tracking performance shown by rats following doses of amphetamine. In this experiment, animals were trained to track a visual stimulus which moved between two levers. Responding on one of two levers was only reinforced if the light above the lever was illuminated. Amphetamine appeared to increase the efficiency of tracking the light, but a closer analysis showed that this was due to the overall effects of the drug on response switching. Thus, the drug increased the tendency to switch away from, as well as towards, the light. The former tendency was, of course much lower as a result of training, and so the net effect was an improvement in performance. Such results indicate the need to analyze performance improvements following stimulant drugs with great care.

There is also considerable evidence that the effects of amphetamine on reward-related processes are also mediated by mesolimbic dopamine. Rats will self-administer amphetamine, thus confirming its reinforcing actions. This self-administration is blocked by dopamine depletion from the nucleus accumbens (Lyness, Friedle, & Moore, 1979). Furthermore, the place preference that can be conditioned to the effects of the drug is also blocked by such lesions (Spyraki, Fibiger, & Phillips, 1982). Perhaps the most dramatic demonstration is the self-administration of amphetamine in minute quantities directly into the region of the nucleus accumbens (Hoebel et al., 1983). This evidence shows that the reinforcing effect of the drug depends upon the integrity of the mesolimbic dopamine system, but does not answer the question of why the drug has rewarding effects. The phenomenon of conditioned place preference suggests that the rewarding effects of the drug might depend upon an interaction of its effects with features of the environment. Taylor & Robbins (1984, 1986) have provided further evidence for this by showing that intra-accumbens amphetamine can apparently increase the control over behaviour exerted by stimuli paired with rewards such as water. Rats treated in this way exhibit large increases in responding for a stimulus previously associated with water, but no effects if there has been no positive correlation (Taylor & Robbins, 1984). This effect is blocked by dopamine depletion from the nucleus accumbens, but not the caudate nucleus (Taylor & Robbins, 1986). Lesions of the ascending noradrenergic systems have no effects (M. Cador and T.W. Robbins, unpublished). A related piece of evidence suggests that the discriminative properties of amphetamine are also mediated by dopamine receptors in the nucleus accumbens. Nielsen and Scheel-Krüger (1986) were able to show that rats discriminate doses of intra-accumbens amphetamine as low as $1\mu g$, when using the cue to mediate a food-reinforced discrimination.

The results described above show that the reinforcing, appetitive, and discriminative effects of amphetamine depend upon the integrity of dopamine neurons in the nucleus accumbens. It is likely that these operationally defined effects reflect the mood-altering, euphoriant, and subjective effects of psychomotor stimulants. The results suggest several important questions. For example, to what extent do the subjective and cognitive effects depend upon the activational effects of the drug, as manifested for example by behavioral hyperactivity? Swerdlow and Koob (1984) have argued that the conditioned place preference for amphetamine crucially depends upon the hyperactivity produced by the drug. If the animals were restrained on the drug-paired side so that they could not exhibit hyperactivity, the normal conditioned place preference was abolished. Such results indicate that the primary action of the drug might be to increase the rate and probability of behaviour which has some minimal tendency, and that this increased activation indirectly helps to determine the cognitive and subjective effects of the drug.

The involvement of the nucleus accumbens in the behavioural effects of amphetamine also leads to several interesting questions about the functions of this structure. Previously, the nucleus accumbens has been considered to be an interface between limbic and motor systems, in view of its connections with limbic system structures such as the prefrontal cortex, amygdala, and hippocampus, and its status as a basal ganglia structure (see Kelley & Domesick, 1982). In considering the effects of amphetamine, it would appear that this drug can influence information processed by the limbic system via its dopaminergic actions in the ventral striatum. However, the drug might also be able to modulate information processed neocortically, by affecting dopaminergic activity in the rest of the striatum, which receives predominantly neocortical inputs.

Despite this evidence that psychomotor stimulants exert most of their behavioural effects via dopamine receptors in the ventral striatum, there is a limited amount of evidence to suggest that the behavioural expression of their effects may be modulated by their action on noradrenergic neurons. Early evidence of the effects of 6-OHDA lesions of the ascending noradrenergic systems failed to find any effects upon amphetamine-induced locomotor activity or stereotyped behaviour (Creese & Iversen, 1975; Roberts, Zis, & Fibiger, 1975). However, noradrenergic depletion using 6-OHDA or DSP-4 enhances amphetamine-induced perseveration in an 8-arm maze (Bruto, Beauchamp, Zacharko, & Anisman, 1984) and appears to reduce aspects of amphetamine-induced locomotor activity over a certain dose range (Archer et al., 1986). Interpreting such results depends to a large extent upon evolving theories of the functions of the central catecholamine systems.

CONTRASTING FUNCTIONS OF
THE CENTRAL CATECHOLAMINE NEURONS

A strong case can be made that the major symptoms of childhood attentional disorders would be likely to depend upon different projections of the central catecholamine systems. In the rat, we have already seen that there is strong evidence to support the hypothesis that psychomotor stimulation depends upon the dopaminergic input to the ventral striatum. This section will develop this notion further by showing how this hyperactivity can be related to deficits in impulsive behaviour, produced by amphetamine or by distracting sources of arousal. These behavioural traits may be related to, but also be distinct from, deficits in selective attention which may result from changes in function in other forebrain catecholamine projections, including, for example, the coeruleo-cortical noradrenergic system. Previous attempts to model the hyperactivity syndrome in developing rats by manipulations of the catecholamine systems have perhaps failed adequately to encompass both the impulsive behaviour and selective attentional impairments, and more particularly, the relationship between them. This has been hindered to some extent by conceptual problems of the nature of attention.

Although selective attention can be defined as that process by which an animal ignores irrelevant stimuli, this may occur at any of several stages of processing beginning at the level of stimulus input and including output mechanisms such as the preparation and selection of responses. Separating such diverse aspects of attention and distinguishing them from global changes in activity is difficult in animal studies and this has considerably complicated the investigation of the involvement of central dopaminergic systems in selective attention (see for example, Carli, Evenden, & Robbins, 1985; Robbins et al., 1986; and the above discussion of the results of Evenden & Robbins, 1985). Whereas alterations in dopaminergic function readily alter levels of motor output, this does not occur significantly following neurotoxic lesions of the central noradrenergic systems: for example, 6-OHDA-induced lesions of the dorsal or ventral noradrenergic bundles do not affect spontaneous locomotor activity or its habituation (Robbins et al., 1982).

Study of the behavioural functions of the coeruleo-cortical noradrenergic system received some impetus from electrophysiological discoveries and led to a theory that this system was involved in selective attention (Mason & Iversen, 1979). The main evidence advanced to support this theory has come from predictions about changes in attentional processes that can be made from paradigms used in animal learning theory, such as latent inhibition, blocking and non-reversal shift (see Mason & Lin, 1983). However, early reports of results favouring this hypothesis have not been fully borne out (see Robbins, Everitt, Cole, Archer, & Mohammed, 1985) and it seems unlikely that dorsal noradrenergic bundle (DNAB) lesions alter stimulus associability or salience *per se*. This chapter summarizes some work on the attentional hypothesis carried out using a different behavioural approach, where it is also possible to measure the speed and impulsivity of responding. A version of the 5-choice serial reaction task devised by Leonard for examining attentional efficiency in humans operating in the presence of different stressors (Eysenck, 1982) has been modified to study the effects of central catecholaminergic manipulations in the rat. Hungry rats are trained to earn their food in a continuous performance test programmed in an apparatus which has a bank of five holes, monitored by infra-red beams, and behind which visual stimuli can be presented (see Carli, Robbins, Evenden, & Everitt, 1983).

In the basic form of the 5-choice reaction task, rats are trained to discriminate the location of spatially unpredictable, brief visual stimuli by responding in the hole behind which the stimulus has occurred. Each stimulus (0.2 s) is presented 5 s after a correct or incorrect trial is terminated by a visit by the rat to the food magazine. Following training to a stable, high level of accuracy ($>80\%$ correct) rats received either 6-OHDA lesions of the dorsal noradrenergic bundle (DNAB) resulting in a profound ($>90\%$) depletion of neocortical and hippocampal noradrenaline, or sham surgery.

Post-operatively, performance was unaffected by DNAB lesions, even if the visual stimuli were dimmed systematically in order to degrade discrimination performance. There was an equivalent, monotonic decline in discrimination accuracy in the two groups, showing that DNAB lesions failed to affect the normal sensory and visual attentional processes by which the task is mediated. However, deficits were evident when the task was altered in various ways. For example, the interpolation of bursts of loud (100dB) white noise at various points during a trial impaired the DNAB lesion group to a greater extent than the sham controls. There was no disruption evident when the noise occurred at the same time as the visual discriminanda. When the noise occurred just prior to the expected visual target, there was an enhanced incidence of premature responses which was, however, again equivalent in the lesion and sham groups. Despite this equivalent activational or disinhibitory effect of the noise, the two groups were differentially affected in terms of accuracy, the DNAB group being significantly worse than the sham controls (see Carli et al., 1983). In fact, although the white noise clearly disturbed the controls by increasing premature responses, these rats were nevertheless able to maintain high levels of discriminative accuracy. Therefore, it appears that under conditions where impulsive responding occurs as a result of disruption of the external stimulus control of performance, discriminative deficits can be observed in rats with DNAB lesions.

A recent experiment (B.J. Cole & T.W. Robbins, unpublished) has replicated and extended this result by examining the combined effects of dimming the visual stimuli and interpolations of white noise on some trials, just before the occurrence of the visual discriminanda. The results showed no additive effects of dimming the stimuli and presenting white noise in the DNAB group. This lack of a significant interaction, and hence lack of potentiation of deficits, implies that white noise is not acting in the same way as dimming the visual discriminanda, but at some point subsequent in the processes by which an appropriate action is prepared and selected in response to the visual signal.

As the visual stimuli follow the previous trial at a predictable time, the rat has an adequate opportunity to prepare an appropriate orienting response to scan the array of holes for the occurrence of the visual stimulus. The interpolated white noise is maximally effective just prior to the time of presentation of the visual event and so it seems possible that the deficit results from some disruption of the orienting and motor responses preparatory to the discriminative response at one of the five holes. One way of testing this hypothesis is to make the visual events temporally, as well as spatially, unpredictable. In the first series of experiments, the intertrial interval (ITI) was varied unpredictably from 0 to 4.5s (Carli et al., 1983; B.J. Cole & T.W. Robbins, unpublished). In a second series of experiments, the ITI was varied unpredictably to include longer intervals. In both experiments, these manipulations impaired the accuracy of the DNAB group more than that of the sham controls, supporting the hypothesis that some form of an attentional deficit may be present in the DNAB group, operating probably at the level of response preparation and selection. It is insufficient to argue that the deficit results merely from the more 'difficult' demands made by altering the task parameters, as the manipulation of dimming the discriminanda produced equivalent decrements in performance, but failed to separate the two groups.

The experiment with white noise suggests that conditions of elevated activation (where the probability, and perhaps also speed, of responding are enhanced) are especially effective in impairing discriminative accuracy in the DNAB group, and so it is of particular interest to compare its effects with those of d-amphetamine. Previously, it has been shown that this drug, over a wide dose range (0.2-1.6 mg/kg), produces similar effects in normal rats to those of white noise; it increases the incidence of premature responses, but does not significantly impair discriminative accuracy (Robbins & Sahakian, 1983). As described in an earlier section, most of the behavioural effects of amphetamine are known to depend on the integrity of the forebrain dopaminergic systems, and this would suggest that the increased activational effects of both white noise and amphetamine depend upon the integrity of these systems. Evidence for this has been obtained in unpublished studies of B.J. Cole and T.W. Robbins of the effects of mesolimbic dopamine depletion following 6-OHDA lesions of the nucleus accumbens and ventral striatum. Such treatment reduces dopamine concentrations by about 80% in the nucleus accumbens, while depleting the anterior head of the caudate nucleus by only about 20-30%. By themselves, such lesions produce a completely different pattern of results to those of DNAB lesions. Rats with mesolimbic dopamine depletion are no less accurate than controls, but are slower to respond and make more errors of omission, especially over the first few post-operative test days (Robbins et al., 1982; B.J. Cole & T.W. Robbins, unpublished). This is the opposite pattern to that seen with d-amphetamine, and may be viewed as an activational impairment. Unlike rats with DNAB lesions, animals with mesolimbic dopamine depletion have more problems with speed of responding than accuracy. These lesions also block the disruptive effects of both d-amphetamine and white noise, suggesting that these two different forms of disruption may share some common neural effects. Further evidence for the mediation of the effects of d-amphetamine by dopaminergic mechanisms within the nucleus accumbens comes from the demonstration that the peripheral effects of the drug can be reproduced by infusions of d-amphetamine directly into the region of the nucleus accumbens, via permanently implanted cannulae. These effects were blocked by peripheral injections of the neuroleptic drug alpha-flupenthixol, and so were presumably dopaminergic in nature (Cole & Robbins, 1987a).

If the effects of white noise and d-amphetamine are indeed comparable, then it would be expected that rats with DNAB lesions should also be impaired in terms of discriminative accuracy following treatment with d-amphetamine at doses sufficient to produce activational effects (as indicated by elevations in premature responses). Bilateral infusions of the drug into the region of the nucleus accumbens (3-30 $\mu g/\mu l$) produced large increases in premature responses that were similar in the DNAB lesion and sham groups. However, once again, the DNAB lesioned rats exhibited dose-related reductions in discriminative accuracy as they had also shown following white noise (Cole & Robbins, 1987a). Thus, the DNAB group was susceptible not only to the exteroceptive activation produced by white noise, but also to the interoceptive activating effects of d-amphetamine. The difference between the two groups was abolished by the neuroleptic drug alpha-flupenthixol, thus suggesting that it arises from a dopaminergic action. These results have been interpreted to support the view that the coeruleo-cortical NA system becomes active under conditions when dopaminergic activity increases, with the effect of preserving attentional selectivity at such times of increased arousal (and perhaps stress, see Robbins, 1984; Robbins & Everitt, 1987).

In behavioural terms, the results agree with the hypothesis that arousal produces changes in several different sub-cortical ascending transmitter systems, including the catecholaminergic forebrain projections, which have overlapping, but separable, functions. The present results have shown a functional interaction between two of these systems in which overactivity in the mesolimbic dopamine system exposes a deficit in rats with impaired coeruleo-cortical NA transmission. Other lines of evidence certainly support the view that deficits in function following DNAB lesions depend markedly upon the precise nature of the testing conditions. Thus, for example, rats with DNAB lesions do not show learning impairments in simple appetitive conditioning situations, but are impaired at learning complex conditional discriminations. (Everitt, Robbins, Gaskin, & Fray, 1983). They are also deficient in the acquisition, but not performance, of aversive conditioned suppression (Cole & Robbins, 1987b). Perhaps of most significance for the present hypothesis, DNAB lesions have been found to impair the learning of a spatial water maze, but only if the rats are tested in the more stressful circumstances of cold, rather than warm, water (B. J. Cole & T.W. Robbins, unpublished). The cold water induced faster swimming than the warm water, but this effect was equivalent in the lesion and control groups. Thus, as in the experiments on selective attention, although the DNAB lesion did not affect the activation of behaviour, there was a concomitant impairment of selective attention and learning. These results imply that behavioural activation need not lead to a disruption of stimulus control of behaviour, as some mechanisms, which include activity in the coeruleo-cortical projection, normally appear to protect the organism from the potentially deleterious effects of overarousal. However, if there is some malfunction in this compensatory or protective mechanism, then behavioural activation will lead to cognitive failure.

BEHAVIOURAL AND NEURAL EFFECTS
OF ISOLATION-REARING IN RATS

Many animal models of the hyperactivity syndrome have been proposed, based on toxicological, pharmacological, neural, and environmental manipulations (see reviews by Robbins & Sahakian, 1979; Mailman, Lewis, & Kilts, 1981). In the absence of any strong evidence concerning the aetiology of the attentional deficit syndrome, and in view of the strong possibility that the syndrome is of multifactorial origin (see Robbins & Sahakian, 1979) it would be wise at this point to consider a broad range of possibilities. In this chapter, we do not attempt a systematic comparison of the various models, but it is probably worth considering a few guiding principles for their design. Perhaps the most important considerations are that the model should take into account developmental variables, encompass both hyperactivity and cognitive disorder, and attempt to elucidate the so-called 'paradoxical' effect of psychomotor stimulants in hyperactive children. For several years, we have intermittently studied the behavioural and neurochemical effects of rearing rats in social isolation, as this produces a behavioural syndrome which at least partially satisfies these criteria and also has interesting implications for defining the functions of central transmitter systems, including the catecholamines.

When rats are separated from their mothers and peers at 17 days of age (but are still allowed to hear and smell other rats), they quickly become hyperactive. Fig. 2 shows the effects of repeated testing of socially reared and isolated female rats in photocell activity cages in 30 min sessions over a number of days. This hyperactivity persists into adulthood, but may eventually decline. Control experiments have shown that the hyperactivity is an effect of rearing and not isolation-housing per se; if rats at 50 days of age are isolated, they do not subsequently become hyperactive (Einon & Morgan, 1976).

The hyperactivity may reflect an enhanced reactivity to exteroceptive stimuli. The hyperactivity is often only present in brief tests in novel environments and is less evident over 24 hr tests (Sahakian, Burdess, Luckhurst, & Trayhurn, 1982). Isolates show enhanced exploration of novel objects and environments, an effect

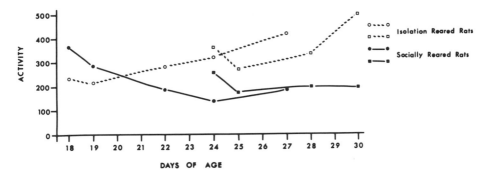

FIG. 2.   Development of photocell cage hyperactivity in different groups of rats isolated from 17 days of age. (Sahakian, 1977).

which is probably not merely the result of impaired habituation (Sahakian, Robbins, & Iversen, 1977). Paradoxically, isolates may take longer to emerge in a neophobia test, although this effect may result from isolation-housing rather than isolation-rearing. Isolates are also more responsive to tail-pinch stimulation, showing an enhanced incidence of oral behaviour such as licking and biting (Sahakian & Robbins, 1977a). There is also evidence of enhanced food intake and weight gain in such animals (see Sahakian et al., 1982).

In terms of learning, attention, and schedule-controlled behaviour, isolates are known to be slow to extinguish (Morgan, Einon, & Morris, 1977) and to reverse (Morgan, 1973; Rosenzweig, 1971). They also make many more errors in a spatial memory task (radial maze), an effect also shown to be dependent on rearing, rather than housing, variables (Einon, 1980). Recent work has also shown that isolation-reared, but not isolation-housed, rats are impaired in the acquisition of schedule-induced polydipsia (Jones, Hernandez, & Robbins, 1987).

In addition to effects on spontaneous behaviour, isolation also has profound effects on responses to drugs. Isolates exhibit enhanced stereotyped behaviour in response to a variety of stimulant drugs, including d-amphetamine, but no exaggeration of its locomotor stimulant effects (Sahakian, Robbins, Morgan, & Iversen, 1975). The enhanced stereotypy is an effect of rearing rather than housing and occurs early in development (Sahakian, 1977). A more detailed analysis of the time course of response to the drug indicates differences between the isolates and socially-reared animals. Figure 3 shows that the isolates are actually significantly less active in their initial response to 2 mg/kg d-amphetamine; evidence at this and other doses suggests that there is a shift in the response towards later time periods, perhaps because of enhanced stereotyped behaviour which competes with the locomotor stimulation (G.H. Jones & T.W. Robbins, unpublished). The probable competition between the hyperactivity and stereotypy is underlined by the effects in isolates of the anti-cholinergic drug scopolamine, which produces hyperactivity in the absence of stereotypy. When administered soon after isolation between 20 and 30 days of age, scopolamine produces a huge potentiation

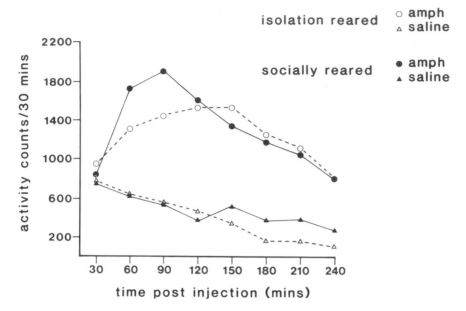

FIG. 3.   Time course of locomotor activity in isolation- and socially (or group-) reared rats in response to an i.p. dose of 2mg/kg of d-amphetamine, or saline control, immediately before the test session. (unpublished data of G.H. Jones and T.W. Robbins). The isolation-reared rats were hyperactive compared with the socially-reared animals in a 30 min habituation test, preceding the test session.

in the hyperactivity of isolates as compared with effects of d-amphetamine (Sahakian, 1977; see Fig. 4).

Isolates also show reduced responses to the hypnotic effects of barbiturates (Einon, Stewart, Atkinson, & Morgan, 1976) and to the effects of the neuroleptic drug, alpha-flupenthixol on tail-pinch-induced oral behaviour (Sahakian & Robbins, 1977a). The difference in susceptibility to barbiturates most probably reflects an effect of housing in isolation rather than effect of rearing (Einon et al., 1976). The origin of the differential response to the neuroleptic is not known, but is consistent with the heightened stereotyped response to amphetamine, in suggesting elevated central dopaminergic activity in isolates.

There has been much research into the neurochemical effects of social isolation, but there has not always been sufficient attention paid to variables such as species, time of isolation, and establishment of the importance of the developmental variable, rather than the effects of housing *per se*. In addition, it has often been difficult to interpret the changes seen because of their small size and because of problems of interpretation imposed by technical limitations. For example, Stolk, Conner, and Barchas (1974) showed that rats isolated at 70 days of age for three or four weeks, showed evidence of a higher basal rate of turnover of noradrenaline in the brain stem but no effects on serotonin metabolism, in contrast to that previously seen in mice. Weinstock, Speiser, and Ashkenazi (1978)

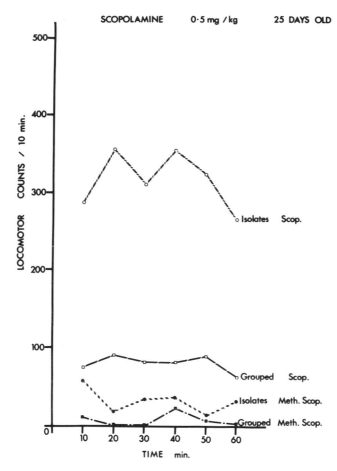

FIG. 4. Hyperactive response of isolation-reared rats to i.p. scopolamine at 25 days of age, by comparison with group- (or socially-) reared rats, and with the effects of the centrally inactive anti-muscarinic methylscopolamine, as control treatment. (Sahakian, 1977)

extended these results by finding that rats reared in isolation from 6-8 weeks following isolation showed significantly lower dopamine and noradrenaline turnover in the home-cage, but apparently greater noradrenaline turnover than that of group-reared rats when exposed to an open field. Blanc et al., (1980) suggest that long-term isolation reduced measures of dopamine turnover in the mesocortical projections. These results encourage the view that some of the hyperactive and attentional disorders of the isolated rat may be correlated with changes in central catecholamine function.

Our own psychopharmacological results described above suggest that isolated rats may exhibit changes in central dopaminergic function, perhaps both pre- and post-synaptically. One brief communication has reported changes in striatal D2 receptors in rats reared in isolation over long periods (Guisado, Fernandez-Tome, Garzon, & Del Rio, 1980). We now report preliminary evidence of changes in presynaptic striatal DA function, using the *in vivo* dialysis technique developed by Ungerstedt and his colleagues (Ungerstedt et al., 1982) for measuring changes in extracellular dopamine concentration. Figure 5 shows the response of groups of socially- and isolation-reared rats to a dose of 2mg/kg of d-amphetamine. There is a marked increase (and shift in time) of the peak DA concentration, which parallels the altered behavioural response seen in Figure 3 (G. H. Jones, T. D. Hernandez, & T. W. Robbins, unpublished). These results have to be extended to samples from other regions, including the ventral striatum, but they do indicate that it may be possible to correlate the altered behavioural responses seen in isolation-reared rats to changes in central transmitter function. It will be important to establish which behavioural responses are associated with central noradrenaline and dopamine function, and how these systems interact. The results described earlier would suggest crudely that, whereas the enduring spontaneous hyperactivity and enhanced drug-induced stereotypy may result from changes in dopamine activity, the cognitive deficits of isolation rearing will depend on alterations in central noradrenergic function.

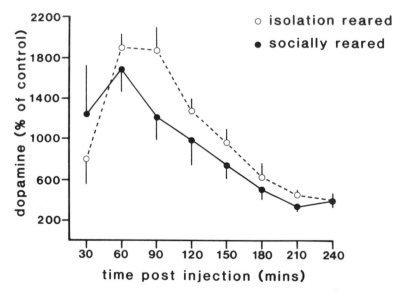

FIG. 5.   Striatal dopamine concentration as a function of time in halothane anaesthetized isolation- or socially-reared rats, following a dose of 2mg/kg of d-amphetamine, as measured using *in vivo* dialysis. The data are expressed as a percentage change from control measurements made during a 2 hour period before the drug treatment (isolates, 0.14 pmol, social, 0.21 pmol/60 μl dialysate). The perfusion rate was 2ul Ringer's solution/min.

IMPLICATIONS OF FINDINGS FOR CHILDHOOD HYPERACTIVITY AND ATTENTIONAL DISORDER: EXPLAINING THE 'PARADOXICAL' RESPONSE TO STIMULANT DRUGS

Specification of the behavioural and neural mechanisms by which amphetamine affects behaviour in animals may be of value in beginning to explain the so-called 'paradoxical' effects of psychomotor stimulant drugs in hyperactive children (for review, see Aman, 1982). There are several plausible hypotheses for explaining such effects.

Hypothesis 1 suggests that there may be some change in the central nervous system in hyperactive children producing a qualitatively different response to the drug, which may even be opposite in direction to normal. This class of hypothesis depends upon finding evidence of neurochemical or organic pathology in hyperactive children which could explain an altered response to the psychomotor stimulants. Hypotheses 2 and 3 both suggest that the response to the drug is not, in fact, paradoxical. Hypothesis 2 depends on the fact that low doses of stimulants can occasionally benefit human cognitive performance (Weiss & Laties, 1962), and this is assumed to be the basis of the therapeutic effect in children. This is supported by evidence showing that the apparently "beneficial" effects of such drugs in hyperactive children can also be seen in normal children (Rapoport et al., 1980), but this account is unable easily to explain why hyperactivity is reduced, and indeed, to specify the mechanisms underlying the beneficial effects. Hypothesis 3 suggests that the reduction in activity may in fact be predicted from the fact that hyperactive children have high baselines of activity, and, according to an extension of the rate-dependency principle to between-subject effects, will show reductions in activity at doses that may stimulate activity if at a low baseline level (Robbins & Sahakian, 1979). According to this hypothesis, any high level of activity, however it is generated, will be susceptible to rate-reducing effects of the drug. A corollary to this hypothesis is that one possible reason for the reduction in activity is not due to a sedative effect of the drug, but to competing behaviour which may be stereotyped and focused in nature. This view is prompted by the theoretical ideas about the behavioural effects of amphetamine in animals expressed in the article by Lyon and Robbins (1975). Applied to the case of the response to amphetamine by hyperactive children, this view would suggest that performance may be improved in terms of simple tasks requiring attentional focusing, but may be deficient in more complex situations, especially for example where a child has to shift attentional set (Sahakian & Robbins, 1977b). Thus, the latter view endorses the principle that there will be cognitive costs, as well as benefits, of medication with psychomotor stimulant drugs, in line with the comments made earlier about the facilitatory effects of these drugs on cognitive performance in animals.

This chapter concentrates on tests of Hypothesis 3. The rate-dependency hypothesis was developed from studies of individual animals trained in operant procedures, but there seems to be no good reason for not extending the principle to between-subject analyses of unconditioned behaviour (Dews & Wenger, 1977). To illustrate the principle here, consider Figure 6, which replots the data shown in Figure 3 to show on an individual basis the log effect (drug/control) of amphetamine over the entire test period relative to log baseline activity measured in the saline control session (see Robbins & Sahakian, 1979, for a more detailed explanation of these plots). For both the isolation-reared and the socially-reared groups, it is clear that those animals exhibiting the largest response to the drug had the lowest baseline levels of activity. As it stands, Figure 6 does not show an entirely unequivocal effect of rate-dependency because the apparent lack of effect in animals with higher baseline rates might arise from a ceiling effect which constrains further increments in activity. A more convincing demonstration would show *reductions* in activity from high baseline rates. This result is clearly predicted from the regression slope shown in Figure 6; but no animal shows a sufficiently high level of baseline activity for reductions to be seen. This type of evidence, however, has been found in studies of spontaneously hypertensive rat strain (SHR). These animals are also hyperactive in the open field (Knardahl & Sagvolden, 1979) and in photocell activity cages (Myers, Musty, & Hendley, 1982). The latter

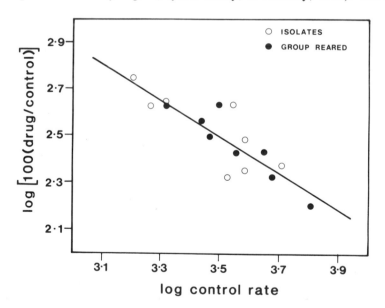

FIG. 6.   Rate-dependent plot of data shown in Fig. 3 for the effects of amphetamine. The control rates of activity (abscissa) are obtained from the saline control data shown in Fig. 3. Each point represents one rat. The ordinate shows the log drug effect. The data for the group- (or socially-) reared and isolation-reared rats fall along a single line, fitted by linear regression and the value of r is -0.85.

authors have shown that the SHR rats exhibit *reductions* in activity following amphetamine, at doses causing behavioural stimulation in a normotensive, 'control' WKY strain. These effects were shown by Myers et al. (1982) to be clearly rate-dependent; the two strains did not differ *qualitatively* in their response to the drug, the difference observed was almost entirely attributable to their different baseline levels of activity. In the context of this chapter, it is also important that reductions in activity also occur in the SHR strain following infusioin of low (1 μg) doses of the drug into the nucleus accumbens (Musty, Myers, Forgays, & Hendley, 1979). Furthermore, the SHR strain exhibit alterations in catecholamine utilization in several regions, including the frontal cortex (Myers, Whittemore, & Hendley, 1980).

In an earlier article (Robbins & Sahakian, 1979) we plotted individual data for spontaneous activity of hyperactive children treated with a stimulant or placebo, kindly supplied to us by investigators in this field. These plots all indicated that there was a negative relationship between baseline activity and drug effect, with those children with the highest baseline levels of activity showing the greatest reductions in activity. By way of illustration, we have plotted data reported by Millichap and Johnson (1974) in this way, for the purposes of this article. Figure 7 shows a rate-dependent plot of the response to methylphenidate in a group of 28 children. Two of the points shown in the figure were statistical outliers and

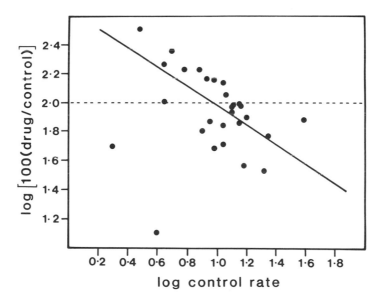

FIG. 7. Rate-dependent plot of individual data reported by Millichap and Johnson (1974) for the effects of methylphenidate. Each point represents the response of one child. The control data were taken from a placebo baseline session. The line was fitted by linear regression and the value of r is −0.74. The hashed line indicates no effect of drug (i.e. the log value of 100% of control values = 2.00).

excluded from the analysis of the clear inverse relationship ($r = -0.74$) between the drug effect and the baseline rate.

The question remains whether the clear inverse dependence of baseline activity shown in the hyperactive children in the Millichap and Johnson (1974) study represents a normal rate-dependent effect of the drug which extends over the whole population of normal, as well as hyperactive, children, or whether the evident rate-dependency in the hyperactive children is nevertheless different from what would be observed in normal children. A partial answer to this question is provided by a plot of individual data from a remarkable study by Rapoport et al., (1980) which compared the response to d-amphetamine of hyperactive children, normal children and normal adults. Unsurprisingly, these three groups differed in their baseline levels of activity and this is reflected in the individual data plotted in Figure 8. What also seems evident from this figure is that the response to amphetamine in the three groups can be predicted from a single regression line which shows the inverse relationship between baseline control activity and response to amphetamine. Clearly, more analyses of this type are needed to establish the reliability of this finding, but the result suggests that the response to stimulants in

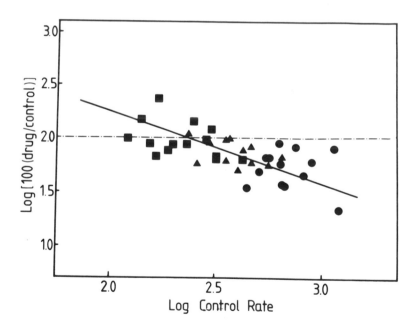

FIG. 8.   Rate-dependent plot of individual data from the study of Rapoport el al. (1980). The data are plotted similarly to those of Fig. 7. Each square represents activity of a normal human adult, each triangle that of a normal child and each circle that of a hyperactive child. The line through all the points was fitted by linear regression and the value of r is -0.62. For further details, see the article by Robbins and Sahakian (1979), from which this figure was taken, with permission from the publishers, Pergamon Press.

hyperactive children is not 'paradoxical', but can be predicted from the effects of the drug in normal populations as a continuous function of baseline levels of activity (Robbins & Sahakian, 1979).

Other analyses of rate-dependency in the effects of stimulants in hyperactive children have concentrated on the operant paradigm, and within-subject analyses of rate-dependent effects, in the tradition of those studies in animals which first analyzed drug effects in this way (see Dews & Wenger, 1977). Weber (1985) found in a sample of hyperactive boys that methylphenidate did not have the rate-increasing effects on low rates of responding engendered by DRL schedules or rate-reducing effects on the high rates of responding under an FR schedule that would have been expected from animal studies. However, for performance under the FR schedule, there was a greater stimulant effect in subjects with lower baseline rates. Rapport, DuPaul and Smith (1985) also found some discrepancies in effects of methylphenidate in schedule-controlled responding in hyperactive boys compared with what might have been expected from animal studies. However, rate-dependent effects were found within both reinforcement schedules. These results are interesting in showing some of the constraints of extrapolating studies of operant behaviour in animals to children. It will be important in further studies to compare the effects of stimulants in normal, as well as hyperactive children in schedule-controlled responding and also to compare the effects seen in this type of situation with measures of spontaneous activity. Some of the analyses of spontaneous activity in children in the Robbins and Sahakian (1979) paper were of measures of the collateral activity shown by children while performing cognitive tasks. Thus, they complement the types of operant measure used in the recent studies of Weber (1985) and Rapport et al. (1985) and it would be useful to obtain both types of measure in the same study.

We have used the principle of rate-dependency to test the hypothesis of a paradoxical response to stimulant drugs in hyperactive children, but it should be made clear that this is only an empirical generalization that can be made about drug effects and sheds no light on the precise mechanisms by which rate-dependent effects arise. Detailed discussion of the possible mechanisms underlying rate-dependent effects is beyond the scope of this article (see instead, Robbins, 1981), but it should be pointed out that many biological systems perform according to the principle of the Law of Initial Values, and apparent rate-dependent effects can occur at the neuronal level, when for example, the effects of iontophoresed dopamine appear to depend upon baseline firing rates for their direction of response (see Groves & Tepper, 1983).

One interpretation of the reduced spontaneous activity following medication with stimulant drugs is that the child becomes more focused in his or her behaviour (Sahakian & Robbins, 1977b, and see above). This effect will possibly lead to apparent improvements in simple tasks requiring concentration (e.g., responding under the FR schedules mentioned above). But if this increased focusing is a mild expression of a stereotyped mode of responding, then deficits will emerge for example if the child is required to switch attention. There is some suggestive evidence of such deficits from some studies in the literature. Of particular interest is the study of the cognitive effects of methylphenidate on a small sample (n = 5) of children reported by Dyme, Sahakian, Golinko and Rabe (1982). These authors found that, whereas performance on Coding tests from the WISC, and the Visual Search and Color Naming components of the Lafayette Clinic Repeatable Battery showed improvement over placebo, there were seious impairments in 4/5 cases in performance on the Wisconsin Card Sorting Test. This latter test has been commonly used to test adult patients with injury to the frontal lobes and can be seen as a test of attentional switching or cognitive flexibility (Milner, 1982). Three of the five children tested with the drug showed more perseverative errors in this task, continuing to sort cards according to an old category. This result urgently needs replication with a larger sample and a wider range of doses, but it does provide suggestive evidence for the hypothesis that the apparently 'paradoxical' effect of the drug could have been predicated from animal studies and for the view that improvements' in performance following drugs in some situations may be offset by decrements in performance in others.

CONCLUSIONS

This article has described some recent advances made in understanding possible functions of the central catecholamines in animals, and the ways in which these systems interact to control behaviour. We know of no strong direct evidence which links childhood hyperactivity *specifically* to central catecholamine dysfunction, but it seems reasonable to postulate some involvement, especially given that drugs used to modify the behaviour of hyperactive children exert many of their actions via these systems. Three major points can be made. First, through such studies, we are beginning to understand the complex interaction between impulsivity and selective attention and their underlying neural mechanisms. Second, it appears from some of the preliminary evidence provided here that variations in early social experience in animals can lead to characteristic behavioural changes, correlated with measurable changes in central transmitter function. Third, studies of the behavioural effects of stimulants in animals have led to some working hypotheses about how such drugs may affect behaviour in children.

ACKNOWLEDGMENTS

Portions of the experimental work were supported by a Project Grant from the Medical Research Council to B.J. Everitt and T. W. Robbins (G8323331N).

REFERENCES

Aman, M. G. (1982). Stimulant drug effects in developmental disorders and hyperactivity—toward a resolution of disparate findings. *Journal of Autism and Developmental Disorders*, *12*, 385–398.

Archer, T., Fredrikson, A., Jonsson, G., Lewander, T., Mohammed, A., Ross, S., & Soderberg, U. (1986). Central noradrenaline depletion antagonizes aspects of d-amphetamine-induced hyperactivity in the rat. *Psychopharmacology*, *88*, 141–146.

Blanc, G., Hervé, D., Simon, H., Lisoprawski, A., Glowinski, J., & Tassin, J. P. (1980). Response to stress of mesocortical-frontal dopaminergic neurones rats after long-term isolation. *Nature*, *284*, 265–267.

Bruto, V., Beauchamp, C., Zacharko, R., & Anisman, H. (1984). Amphetamine-induced perserverative behaviour in a radial arm maze following DSP-4 or 6-OHDA pretreatment. *Psychopharmacology*, *83*, 62–69.

Carli, M., Evenden, J. L., & Robbins, T. W. (1985). Depletion of unilateral striatal dopamine impairs initiation of contralateral actions and not sensory attention. *Nature*, *313*, 679–682.

Carli, M., Robbins, T. W., Evenden, J. L., & Everitt, B. J. (1983). The effects of lesions to ascending noradrenergic neurones on performance of a 5-choice serial reaction task in rats: Implications for theories of dorsal noradrenergic function based on selective attention and arousal. *Behavioural Brain Research*, *9*, 361–380.

Carr, G. D., & White, N. M. (1984). The relationship between stereotypy and memory improvement produced by amphetamine. *Psychopharmacology*, *89*, 340–346.

Cole, B. J., & Robbins, T. W. (1987a). Amphetamine impairs the discriminative performance of rats with dorsal noradrenergic bundle lesions on a 5-choice serial reaction time task: New evidence for central dopaminergic-noradrenergic interactions. *Psychopharmacology*, *91*, 458–466.

Cole, B. J., & Robbins, T. W. (1987b). Dissociable effects of cortical and hypothalamic noradrenaline on the acquisition, performance and extinction of aversive conditioning. *Behavioral Neuroscience*, in press.

Creese, I., & Iversen, S. D. (1975). The pharmacological and anatomical substrates of the amphetamine response in the rat. *Brain Research*, *83*, 419–436.

Dews, P. B., & Wenger, G. R. (1977). Rate-dependency of the behavioural effects of amphetamine. In T. Thompson & P. B. Dews (Eds.), *Advances in behavioral pharmacology Vol. 1* (pp. 169–227). New York: Academic Press.

Dyme, I. Z., Sahakian, B. J., Golinko, B., & Rabe, E. (1982). Perseveration induced by methylphenidate in children: Preliminary findings. *Progress in Neuropsychopharmacology and Biological Psychiatry*, *6*, 269–273.

Einon, D. F. (1980). Spatial memory and response strategies in rats: Age, sex and rearing differences in performance. *Quarterly Journal of Experimental Psychology*, *32*, 473–489.

Einon, D. F., & Morgan, M. J. (1976). A critical period for social-isolation in the rat. *Developmental Psychobiology*, *10*, 123–132.

Einon, D. F., Stewart, J., Atkinson, S., & Morgan, M. J. (1976). Effect of isolation on barbiturate induced anesthesia in the rat. *Psychopharmacology*, *50*, 85–88.

Evenden, J. L., & Robbins, T. W. (1985). Effects of d-amphetamine, chlordiazepoxide and alphaflupenthixol on food-reinforced tracking of a visual stimulus by rats. *Psychopharmacology*, *85*, 361–366.

Everitt, B. J., Robbins, T. W., Gaskin, M., & Fray, P. J. (1983). The effects of lesions to ascending noradrenergic neurones on discrimination learning and performance in the rat. *Neuroscience*, *10*, 397–410.

Eysenck, M. W. (1982). *Attention and arousal*. Berlin: Springer-Verlag.

Falk, J. L. (1971). The nature and determinants of adjunctive behavior. *Physiology and Behavior*, *6*, 577–588.

Groves, P. M., & Tepper, J. M. (1983). Neuronal mechanisms of action of amphetamine. In I. Creese

(Ed.), *Stimulants: Neurochemical, behavioral, and clinical perspectives* (pp. 81–129). New York: Raven Press.

Guisado, E., Fernandez-Tome, P., Garzon, J. & Del Rio, J. (1980). Increased dopamine receptor binding in the striatum of rats after long-term isolation. *European Journal of Pharmacology, 65*, 463–464.

Hoebel, B. G., Monaco, A. P., Hernandez, L., Aulisi, E. F., Stanley, B. G., & Lenard, L. (1983). Self-injection of amphetamine directly into the brain. *Psychopharmacology, 81*, 158–163.

Jones, G. H., Hernandez, T. D., & Robbins, T. W. (1987). Isolation-rearing impairs the acquisition of schedule-induced polydipsia in rats. *Society for Neuroscience Abstracts*.

Joyce, E. M., & Iversen, S. D. (1984). Dissociable effects of 6-OHDA lesions of the neostriatum on anorexia, locomotor activity and stereotypy: The role of behavioural competition. *Psychopharmacology, 83*, 363–366.

Kelley, A. E., & Domesick, V. (1982). The amygdalostriatal projection in the rat—an anatomical study by anterograde and retrograde tracing methods. *Neuroscience, 7*, 615–630.

Kelly, P. H., Seviour, P., & Iversen, S. D. (1975). Amphetamine and apomorphine responses in the rat following 6-OHDA lesions of the nucleus accumbens and corpus striatum. *Brain Research, 94*, 507–522.

Koek, W., & Slangen J. L. (1983). Effects of d-amphetamine and morphine on discrimination: Signal detection analysis and assessment of response repetition in the performance deficits. *Psychopharmacology, 80*, 25–128.

Knardahl, S., & Sagvolden, T. (1979). Open field behaviour of spontaneously hyperactive rats. *Behavioral and Neural Biology, 27*, 187–200.

Kulig, B., & Calhoun, W. (1972). Enhancement of successive discrimination reversal learning by methamphetamine. *Psychopharmacologia, 27*, 233–240.

Lyness, W. H., Friedle, N. M., & Moore, K. E. (1979). Destruction of dopaminergic nerve terminals in nucleus accumbens: Effect on d-amphetamine self-administration. *Pharmacology, Biochemistry and Behavior, 11*, 553–556.

Lyon, M., & Robbins, T. W. (1975). The action of central nervous system stimulant drugs: A general theory concerning amphetamine effects. In W. Essman and L. Valzelli (Eds.), *Current developments in psychopharmacology. Vol 2* (pp. 79–163). New York: Spectrum.

Mailman, R. B., Lewis, M. H., & Kilts, C. D. (1981). Animal models related to developmental disorders: Theoretical and pharmacological analyses. *Applied Research in Mental Retardation, 2*, 1–12.

Mason, S. T., & Iversen, S. D. (1979). Theories of the dorsal bundle extinction effect. *Brain Research Reviews, 1*, 107–137.

Mason, S. T., & Lin, D. (1983). Dorsal noradrenergic bundle and selective attention. *Journal of Comparative and Physiological Psychology, 94*, 819–832.

Millichap, J., & Johnson, F. K. (1974). Methylphenidate in hyperkinetic behaviour: Relation of response to degree of activity and brain damage. In C. K. Conners (Ed.), *Clinical use of stimulant drugs in children* (pp. 130–140). Amsterdam: Excerpta Medica.

Milner, B. (1982). Some cognitive effects of frontal lobe lesions in man. *Philosophical Transactions of the Royal Society London, B298*, 211–226.

Morgan, M. J. (1973). Effects of post-weaning environment in the rat. *Animal Behaviour, 21*, 429–442.

Morgan, M. J., Einon, D. F., & Morris, R. G. (1977). Inhibition and isolation rearing in the rat: Extinction and satiation. *Physiology and Behavior, 18*, 1–6.

Musty, R. E., Myers, M. M., Forgays, J. A., & Hendley, E. (1979). Systemic or intracerebral administration of d-amphetamine decreases activity in hyperactive, spontaneously hypertensive rats. *Society for Neuroscience Abstracts, 5*, 658.

Myers, M. M., Musty, R. E., & Hendley, E. (1982). Attenuation of hyperactivity in the spontaneously hypertensive rat by amphetamine. *Behavioral and Neural Biology, 34*, 42–54.

Myers, M. M., Whittemore, S. R., & Hendley, E. (1980). Changes in catecholamine neuronal uptake and receptor binding in the brain of the spontaneously hypertensive rat (SHR). *Brain Research, 220*, 325–338.

Nielsen, E. B., & Scheel-Krüger, J. (1986). Cueing effects of amphetamine and LSD: Direct elicitation by microinjections into the nucleus accumbens. *European Journal of Pharmacology, 125,* 85–92.

Pijnenberg, A. J. J., Honig, W. M. M., Van der Heyden, J. A. M., & Van Rossum, J. M. (1976). Effects of chemical stimulation of the mesolimbic dopamine system upon locomotor activity. *European Journal of Pharmacology, 35,* 45–58.

Rapoport, J. L., Buchsbaum, M. S., Weingartner, H., Zahn, T. P., Ludlow, C., & Mikkelsen, E. J. (1980). Dextroamphetamine—its cognitive and behavioral effects in normal and hyperactive boys and normal men. *Archives of General Psychiatry, 37,* 933–943.

Rapport, M. D., DuPaul, G. J., & Smith, N. F. (1985). Rate-dependency and hyperactivity: Methylphenidate effects on operant responding. *Pharmacology, Biochemistry and Behavior, 23,* 77–83.

Robbins, T. W. (1981). Behavioural determinants of drug action: Rate-dependency revisited. In S. J. Cooper (Ed.), *Theory in Psychopharmacology Vol. 1* (pp. 1–63). London: Academic Press.

Robbins, T. W. (1984). Cortical noradrenaline, attention and arousal. *Psychological Medicine, 14,* 13–21.

Robbins, T. W., & Everitt, B. J. (1987). Psychopharmacological studies of arousal and attention. In S. M. Stahl, S. D. Iversen & E. Goodman (Eds.), *Cognitive Neurochemistry.* London: Oxford University Press, in press.

Robbins, T. W., & Sahakian, B. J. (1979). ''Paradoxical'' effects of psychomotor stimulant drugs from the standpoint of behavioural pharmacology. *Neuropharmacology, 18,* 931–950.

Robbins, T. W., & Sahakian, B. J. (1983). Behavioral effects of psychomotor stimulant drugs: Clinical and neuropsychological implications. In I. Creese (Ed.). *Stimulants: Neurochemical, behavioral and clinical perspectives.* (pp 301–338). New York: Raven Press.

Robbins, T. W., Roberts, D. C. S., & Koob, G. F. (1983). Effects of d-amphetamine and apomorphine upon operant behavior and schedule-induced licking in rats with 6-hydroxydopamine-induced lesions of the nucleus accumbens. *Journal of Pharmacology and Experimental Therapeutics, 222,* 662–673.

Robbins, T. W., Mittleman, G., O'Brien, & Winn, P. (1988). Neuropsychological significance of stereotypy induced by stimulant drugs. In S. J. Cooper & C. Dourish (Eds.), *The neurobiology of stereotypy.* London: Academic Press, in press.

Robbins, T. W., Everitt, B. J., Cole, B. J., Archer, T., & Mohammed, A. (1985). Functional hypotheses of the coeruleal-cortical noradrenergic projection: A review of recent experimentation and theory. *Physiological Psychology, 13,* 127–150.

Robbins, T. W., Evenden, J. L., Ksir, C., Reading, P., Wood, S., & Carli, M. (1986). The effects of d-amphetamine, alpha flupenthixol and mesolimbic dopamine depletion on a test of attentional switching in the rat. *Psychopharmacology, 90,* 72–78.

Robbins, T. W., Everitt, B. J., Fray, P. J., Gaskin, M., Carli, M., & de la Riva, C. (1982). The roles of the central catecholamines in attention and learning. In M. Y. Speigelstein & A. Levy (Eds.), *Behavioural models and the analysis of drug action* (pp. 109–134). Amsterdam: Elsevier.

Roberts, D. C. S., Zis, A., & Fibiger, H. C. (1975). Ascending catecholamine pathways and amphetamine-induced locomotor activity: Importance of norepinephrine. *Brain Research, 93,* 441–454.

Rosenzweig, M. R. (1971). Effects of environment on development of brain and behavior. In E. Tombach, L. R. Aronson, & E. Shaw (Eds.), *Biopsychology of development.* New York: Academic Press.

Sahakian, B. J. (1977). *The effects of isolation on unconditioned behaviour and response to drugs in rats.* Unpublished Ph.D. thesis, University of Cambridge.

Sahakian, B. J., Burdess, C., Luckhurst, H., & Trayhurn, P. (1982). Hyperactivity and obesity: The interaction of social isolation and cafeteria feeding. *Physiology and Behavior, 28,* 117–124.

Sahakian, B. J., & Robbins, T. W. (1977a). Isolation-rearing enhances tail-pinch-induced behavior in rats. *Physiology and Behavior, 18,* 53–58.

Sahakian, B. J., & Robbins, T. W. (1977b). Are the effects of psychomotor stimulant drugs on hyperactive children really paradoxical? *Medical Hypotheses, 3,* 154–158.

Sahakian, B. J., Robbins, T. W., & Iversen, S. D. (1977). The effects of isolation on exploration in the rat. *Animal Learning and Behavior*, *5*, 193–198.

Sahakian, B. J., Robbins, T. W., Morgan, M. J., & Iversen, S. D. (1975). The effects of psychomotor stimulants on stereotypy and locomotor activity in socially deprived and control rats. *Brain Research*, *84*, 195–205.

Spyraki C., Fibiger H. C., & Phillips A. G. (1982). Dopaminergic substrates of amphetamine-induced place conditioning. *Brain Research*, *253*, 185–193.

Stolk, J. M., Conner, R., & Barchas, J. D. (1974). Social environment and brain biogenic amine metabolism in rats. *Journal of Comparative and Physiological Psychology*, *87*, 203–207.

Swerdlow, N. R., & Koob, G. F. (1984). Restrained rats learn amphetamine-conditioned locomotion but not place preference. *Psychopharmacology*, *84*, 163–166.

Taylor J. R., & Robbins, T. W. (1984). Enhanced behavioral control by conditioned reinforcers following microinjections of d-amphetamine into the nucleus accumbens. *Psychopharmacology*, *84*, 405–412.

Taylor, J. R. & Robbins, T. W. (1986). 6-hydroxydopamine lesions of the nucleus accumbens but not of the caudate nucleus, attenuate enhanced responding with reward-related stimuli produced by intra-accumbens d-amphetamine. *Psychopharmacology*, *90*, 390–397.

Ungerstedt, U., Herrara-Marschitz, Stahle, L., & Zetterstrom, T. (1982). Models for studying synaptic mechanisms—correlative measurements of transmitter release and drug-altered behaviour. In M. Y. Speigelstein & A. Levy (Eds.), *Behavioural models and the analysis of drug action* (pp. 57–70). Amsterdam: Elsevier.

Weber, K. (1985). Methylphenidate: Rate-dependent drug effects in hyperactive boys. *Psychopharmacology*, *85*, 231–235.

Weiner, I., Feldon, J., & Ben-Horin, E. (1987). Facilitation of discrimination transfers under amphetamine: The relative control by S+ and S− and general transfer effects. *Psychopharmacology*, in press.

Weinstock, M., Speiser, Z., & Ashkenazi, R. (1978). Changes in brain catecholammine turnover and receptor sensitivity induced by social deprivation. *Psychopharmacology*, *56*, 205–209.

Weiss, B., & Laties, V. G. (1962). Enhancement of human performance by caffeine and the amphetamines. *Pharmacological Reviews*, *14*, 1–36.

15

Neurotransmitters in Attention Deficit Disorder

Lewis S. Seiden
*Department of Pharmacological
and Physiological Sciences
University of Chicago*

Frederick E. Miller
*Department of Psychiatry
University of Illinois*

Thomas G. Heffner
*Pharmaceutical Research Division
Department of Pharmacology
Warner-Lambert/Parke-Davis*

Research to date indicates that the monoamine neurotransmitter systems play an important role in the expression of attention deficit disorder with hyperkinesis (ADDH). In this chapter we review briefly the clinical evidence for this assertion. We then describe in detail an animal model for ADDH which involves early life damage to central dopaminergic transmitter pathways.

The primary pharmacologic treatment of ADDH is sympathomimetic drugs such as d-amphetamine, methylphenidate and pemoline (Brunstetter & Silver, 1975). The fact that these agents all act to increase the synaptic concentration of the monoamines norepinephrine (NE), dopamine (DA), and serotonin (5-HT) has been a major reason for the focus on monoamines in ADDH (Cooper, Bloom, & Roth, 1986). Recent work has implicated particular aspects of monoamine neurotransmission in the therapeutic effects of sympathomimetics in ADDH.

Brain levels of NE are typically inferred from the urinary concentration of its metabolite 3-methoxy-4-hydroxyphenylglycol (MHPG). Studies have shown that approximately 60% of urinary MHPG derives from central NE metabolism (Maas et al., 1979). In hyperactive children treated for 2 weeks with 0.5 mg/kg/day d-amphetamine 24-hr urinary MHPG levels were reduced by approximately 50% relative to pre-treatment values (Shekim et al., 1977). When corrected for body weight and age by expressing this as a ratio to 24-hr creatinine excretion, an approximate 20% reduction was found. These results have been confirmed by others (Brown et al., 1981) and furthermore the reduction in urinary MHPG has been correlated to the clinical effectiveness of d-amphetamine (Shekim et al., 1979). A recent comparison of the effects of d-amphetamine and methylphenidate on urinary NE metabolites in ADDH children has, however, shown that methylphenidate does not appear to have a significant effect on urinary MHPG (Zametkin et al., 1985). The effects of methylphenidate on noradrenergic receptor sensitivity in ADDH children was explored in a recent study (Hunt et al., 1986). In this study, noradrenergic receptor sensitivity was tested pharmacologically by measuring growth hormone levels in response to a single-dose of clonidine both before and after treatment. During treatment, this index decreased by approximately 50%, and was still reduced by 30% one day after treatment. Thus, the possibility exists that a common mechanism of action for d-amphetamine and methylphenidate might be a reduction in NE receptor sensitivity.

Levels of homovanillic acid (HVA), a metabolite of dopamine (DA), have been measured in the urine of children with ADDH treated with either d-amphetamine or methylphenidate. No change in urinary HVA has been observed (Shekim et al., 1977; Wender et al., 1971). However, urine HVA derives from both central and peripheral DA stores. A more accurate measure of central DA is CSF HVA. CSF HVA was reduced by 33% in children treated with d-amphetamine (Shetty & Chase, 1976). In summary, evidence to date suggests that d-amphetamine reduces urinary MHPG levels in ADDH children and this effect correlates with therapeutic effectiveness. However, methylphenidate does not appear to produce a significant change in urinary MHPG. HVA and 5-HIAA, metabolites of NE and 5-HT respectively, are unaltered by d-amphetamine and methylphenidate treatment. d-Amphetamine also appears to down-regulate NE receptors. The effect of methylphenidate and d-amphetamine on DA receptors in ADDH children also deserves study; the importance of this latter point is discussed when reviewing an animal model for ADDH. First, data concerning basal monoamine metabolite levels in ADDH is reviewed.

Studies have shown that baseline urine MHPG levels in ADDH children are significantly lower than in control children (Shekim et al., 1977, 1979). However, levels of normetanephrine, a metabolite of peripheral NE was also reduced raising the possibility that the changes in NE seen in ADDH are peripheral rather than central. Also, some investigators have found increased MHPG levels in ADDH children (Kahn & Dekirmerjian, 1981). Some investigators have suggested that dysregulation of monoamine metabolism (rather than an absolute increase or decrease in level) may underlie ADDH (Raskin et al., 1984). Hunt et al. (1986) have shown that untreated ADDH children demonstrate an augmented growth hormone response to clonidine compared to control children. This suggests that children with ADDH may have augmented NE receptor sensitivity.

Urinary HVA levels do not appear to be significantly altered in ADDH (Shekim et al., 1977, 1979). ADDH children do, however, demonstrate decreased CSF HVA compared to control children following probenecid loading (Shaywitz et al., 1977).

No consistent differences have been found in the levels of serotonin or 5-HIAA in whole blood and platelets of ADDH children (Raskin et al., 1984). Further-more, 5-HIAA levels in CSF following probenecid loading also appears to be unaltered in ADDH (Shetty & Chase, 1976). Platelet monoamine oxidase levels, a monoamine catabolic enzyme, are reduced in ADDH; this reduction has fur-thermore been correlated with objective measures of impulsivity and distractability (Shekim et al., 1986).

Thus, central DA and possibly NE may be decreased in ADDH. Augmented postsynaptic NE receptor sensitivity has been demonstrated pharmacologically in ADDH children. DA receptor sensitivity remains to be delineated in ADDH. We will now review data concerning an animal model for ADDH based on a reduction in central DA neurotransmission.

The ontogeny of locomotion in the rat is biphasic, with activity increasing during the first two weeks of life and then decreasing over the next week or two to nor-mal adult levels (Bolles & Woods, 1964; Campbell, Lytle, & Fibiger, 1969; Erinoff, MacPhail, Heller, & Seiden, 1979). On the basis of the parallel ontoge-ny of central catecholaminergic systems and locomotor behavior and also the ability of amphetamine to increase locomotion within the first two weeks, Campbell, Lytle and Fibiger (1969) inferred that this ascending phase of locomotor develop-ment was related to the development of CNS catecholamine function. However, work in this and other laboratories demonstrated that CNS dopaminergic trans-mission may also play an important role in suppression of locomotion and the eventual achievement of normal adult low levels of activity.

In these experiments, large selective depletions of brain dopamine were achieved using intraventricular (ivt) injections of the catecholamine neurotoxin 6-hydroxydopamine (6-OHDA) following systemic pretreatment with desmethyl-imipramine (DMI) (Breese & Traylor, 1970). Erinoff et al. (1979), using DMI and 6-OHDA (100 ug, ivt) on days 3 and 6, achieved greater than 90% deple-tions of striatal DA with minimal depletion of brain NE in the rat. While the ascending phase of locomotor development was unaltered, the 6-OHDA treated rats showed no evidence of the normal behavioral suppression (Fig. 1). The abil-

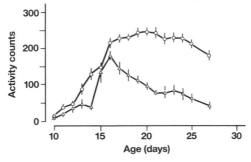

FIG. 1.   Locomotor activity of 6-OHDA/pargyline-treated rats compared to vehicle-treated rats. Activity represents counts per 55 min. Differences are statistically significant by Wilcoxon test for two samples from days 17–27. P < 0.01. 0 = 6- OHDA/pargyline, n = 15; = vehicle, n = 7. The bars represent the standard error of the mean.

ity of neonatal brain DA lesions to induce hyperactivity has also been reported by other investigators (Shaywitz et al., 1976; Stoof, Dijkstra, & Hillegers, 1978). These investigators also presented evidence for a critical phase in the effects of brain DA depletion on locomotor suppression. While rats treated with 6-OHDA and DMI on days 3 and 6, 11 and 14, and 20 and 23 all demonstrated locomotor hyperactivity relative to control levels, the locomotor activity of adult treated rats (46 and 48 days) was unaffected (Fig. 2). Treatment with 6-OHDA and DMI yielded similar losses of striatal DA (70-80%).

The magnitude and duration of the locomotor hyperactivity induced by the brain DA lesions has been shown to be dependent on the extent of the DA depletions induced. Miller et al. (1981) compared the development of locomotion in rats lesioned with various doses of 6-OHDA (ivt) following DMI pretreatment

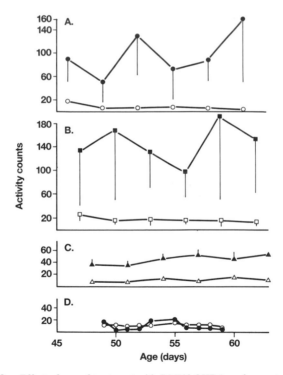

FIG. 2.   Effect of age of treatment with DMI/6-OHDA on locomotor activity. A: O = 6-OHDA/DMI 3.6; O = vehicle 3.6. B: = 6-OHDA/DMI 11.14: = vehicle 11.14; C: = 6-OHDA/DMI 20.23; = vehicle 20.23. D: O = 6-OHDA/DMI 46.48; O = vehicle 46.48. A: 6-OHDA/DMI significantly different from control on days 46, 52, 58, 61, P < 0.05 Wilcoxon. B: 6-OHDA/DMI significantly different from control on days 47, 50, 53, 56, 62, p < 0.05 Wilcoxon. C:6-OHDA/DMI significantly different from control on days 48, 63, P < 0.05 Wilcoxon. D: 6-OHDA/DMI not significantly different from control 49–59, p. 0.05, Wilcoxon. The bars represent the standard error of the mean.

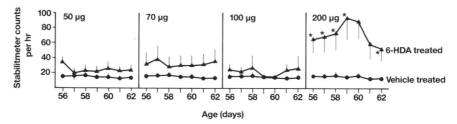

FIG. 3. Stabilimeter activity from day 56 through day 2 of life for rats treated on days 3 and 6 with 6-HDA, Or the 6-HDA vehicle solution following DMI treatment. Data for each 6-HDA treatment group is shown in a separate frame, while that for the 6-HDA vehicle group is shown in each frame. Each data point represents the mean for the following number of subjects: vehicle group, n = 7; 50 μg group, n = 7; 70 μg group, n = 6; 100 μg group, n = 8; 100 μg group, n = 7. Bars represent + 1 S.E.M. *p < 0.05, **p < .01 (t-test) compared to DMI-vehicle group.

on days 3 and 6 (Fig. 3). Groups of rats received total doses of either 50, 70, 100 or 200 μg 6-OHDA. Each group displayed 3- to 5-fold increases in locomotor activity on days 16 and 18 relative to vehicle control rats. However, rats given 50 or 70 μg displayed hypersensitivity that diminished during days 18-32, approaching the levels exhibited by the control group while the 100 and 200 μg groups continued to display high levels of locomotion during this time. When tested as adults, the 200 μg group continued to display hyperactivity. Also, the average increase in locomotor activity seen in groups of 6-OHDA treated rats was positively correlated to the extent of DA depletion in multiple brain nuclei.

Further studies have suggested impaired central DA neurotransmission without actual neuronal destruction may be sufficient to produce locomotor hyperactivity. Miller and Seiden (1983) demonstrated transient locomotor hyperactivity in neonatal rats treated chronically with the DA synthesis inhibitor α-methyl-tyrosine.

Two central DA pathways implicated in the control of locomotor behavior are the nigrostriatal and the mesocortical pathways. Investigations to determine the role of these pathways in the mediation of dopamine's effects on the development of locomotor suppression were conducted by Heffner et al. (1983). Nigrostriatal DA neurons were destroyed in 4-day old rats by bilateral electrolytic lesions of the substantia nigra according to the methods of Heller et al. (1979). The mesocortical projection was destroyed in two groups of 4-day old rats receiving either small or large electrolytic lesions of the ventral tegmental area. Representative projection tracings demonstrating the extent of the lesions for each group are shown in Fig. 4. The substantia nigra lesions yielded a 68% reduction in DA in the substantia nigra and minimal reductions in mesocortical DA, while the ventral tegmental lesions yielded 30-60% reductions in mesocortical DA and minimal reductions in nigrostriatal DA. When tested for locomotor activity during the fourth week of life, only the groups with ventral tegmental lesions demonstrated hyperactivity (Fig. 5).

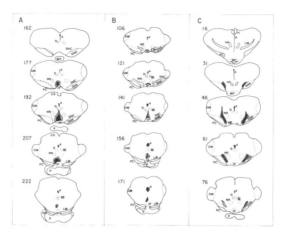

FIG. 4. Projection tracings of brain sections showing brain lesions in representative animals from each of the 3 groups. A: a typical lesion from the large VTA lesion group. B: a typical lesion from the small VTA lesion group. C: typical bilateral lesion from the SN group. Numbers at the upper left of each section denote the position within the serial sections, numbered rostrally to caudally. Darkened areas correspond to the cavity of the lesion: stippled areas correspond to the area around each lesion which was devoid of cells. A. cerebral aqueduct; CS, superior colliculus; D. nucleus of Darkschewitz; GM, medial geniculate body; HP, habenulo-interpeduncular tract; IP, interpeduncular nucleus; LM, medial lemniscus; MP, posterior mammillary nucleus; NR, red nucleus; P, pons; PC, cerebral peduncle; SNC, substantia nigra pars compacta; SNR, substantia nigra pars reticulate; III, nucleus of the oculomotor nerve. Horizontal bars represent 1 mm.

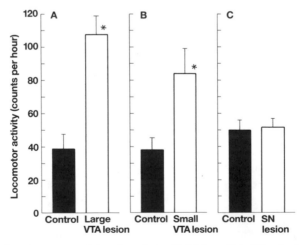

FIG. 5. Locomotor activity of rats during 22–24 days of age following brain lesions at 3 days of age. A: open bar, large VTA lesion (n = 9); shaded bar, control (n = 9). B: open bar, small VTA lesion (n = 10); shaded bar, control (n = 10). C: open bar, SN lesion (n = 12); shaded bar, control (n = 12). Each bar represents the mean + S.E.M. *P < 0.05, compared to control group.

The effect of d-amphetamine on the locomotor hyperactivity induced by the neonatal brain DA lesions was examined by Heffner and Seiden (1982). Rats treated on days 3 and 6 with a total of 200 μg 6-OHDA (ivt) following DMI pretreatment were used. As stated previously, this treatment caused large selective depletions of brain dopamine and a 7-fold increase in locomotor activity compared to control rats. d-Amphetamine (1 mg/kg) administered on days 21, 29, 39, and 46 days of age significantly reduced locomotor hyperactivity in the DA depleted rats while increasing locomotion in control rats (Table 1). This result is consistent with the work of other investigators (Shaywitz, Klopper, Yager, & Gordon, 1976; Sorenson, Vayer, & Goldberg, 1977). Methylphenidate similarly selectively reduced locomotion in the 6-OHDA lesioned rats. Curiously, this effect of d-amphetamine did not appear to be mediated by residual DA neurons, but rather via serotonergic neurons. The DA antagonist had no effect on d-amphetamine locomotor suppression while the 5-HT antagonist methysergide did reduce the effect of amphetamine (Table 1). The suppressive effects of the serotonin agonists quipazine and fenfluramine on the 6-OHDA induced locomotor hyperactivity were consistent with this notion (Table 2).

Investigators had previously hypothesized that the suppression of locomotion was cholinergically mediated based on the parallel development of locomotor suppression and the development of markers for forebrain acetylcholine (ACh) neurons (Campbell et al., 1969). The possibility existed that destruction of central DA neurons early in life resulted in a transneuronal degeneration of ACh neurons. Experiments dealing with the sensory systems have clearly demonstrated transneuronal degeneration in the neonatal brain (Kupfer & Palmer, 1964 (Miller's thesis); DeLong & Sidman, 1968). The integrity of central ACh mechanisms for behavioral suppression in the 6-OHDA lesioned rats was tested pharmacologically in our laboratory using the ACh antagonist atropine sulfate. As shown in Figure 6 both the vehicle treated group and the 6-OHDA treated group showed dose dependent increases in locomotion. This effect was clearly centrally mediated since atropine methylbromide, which acts only peripherally, had no effect on locomotion. Thus, pharmacological evidence suggests that central ACh systems are undamaged by the neonatal DA lesions. Further evidence for this was the fact that assays of the synthetic enzyme for ACh, choline acetyltransferase, in the caudate, nucleus accumbens, olfactory tubercle and septum demonstrated no reduction in this marker for ACh neurons following the neonatal brain DA lesions (Table 3). DA receptor sensitivity was tested pharmacologically using the DA precursor L-Dopa. Dose-response curves for the effects of L-Dopa on locomotion in rats treated on days 3 and 6 with 6-OHDA (2 x 100 μg ivt) were conducted (Fig. 7). The DA lesioned rats demonstrated marked sensitivity to a low dose of L-Dopa (2.5 mg/kg). Indeed, higher doses were associated with extreme stereotypy including self-mutilation in the DA lesioned rats (Fig. 8). These results are strongly suggestive of extreme DA post-synaptic receptor supersensitivity. Further work using DA antagonists is needed to confirm this hypothesis.

TABLE 1

Effect of D-amphetamine on locomotor activity in rats given DMI−6-OHDA or DMI-vehicle treatments at 3 and 6 days of age. Values represent mean ± S.E.M. locomotor activity counts per hours.

Group	n	Days of age			
		21	29	39	46
DMI-vehicle					
Saline	8	34.6 ± 4.0	34.1 ± 6.1	25.5 ± 2.4	23.2 ± 6.1
D-amphetamine (1 mg/kg)	8	299.9 ± 31.5*	179.3 ± 30.3*	121.3 ± 25.8*	142.0 ± 32.5*
DMI-6-OHDA					
Saline	8	210.4 ± 23.2	325.8 ± 45.3	321.2 ± 39.1	151.0 ± 29.9
D-amphetamine (1 mg/kg)	8	104.1 ± 18.4*	99.0 ± 38.6*	68.7 ± 27.8*	19.7 ± 8.9*

*$P < 0.01$, compared to saline treatment.

TABLE 2

Effects of Drug Treatments on Locomotor Hyperactivity
in Rats Given DMI-6-OHDA at 3 and 6 Days of Age[a]

Treatment[b]	Locomotor activity (counts per hour)
Saline	215 + 40
Saline-amphetamine (1 mg/mg)	33 + 12*
Spiroperidol (0.1 mg/kg)—amphetamine (1 mg/kg)	41 + 15
Methysergide (2 mg/kg)—amphetamine (1 mg/kg)	153 + 42**
Propranolol (5 mg/kg)—amphetamine (1 mg/kg)	35 + 13
Atropine (0.5 mg/kg)—amphetamine (1 mg/kg)	32 + 10
Naloxone (10 mg/kg)—amphetamine (1 mg/kg)	31 + 13
Quipazine (4 mg/kg)	63 + 18*
Fenfluramine (3 mg/kg)	22 + 10*

[a]Values represent the mean + S.E.M. results from 6–8 rats tested during days 37–46 of age.
[b]Rats received drug pretreatments 30 min prior to amphetamine and received amphetamine, quipazine or fenfluramine 30 min prior to the 1 hour locomotor test.

*$p < 0.05$, compared to saline treatment. **$p < 0.05$, compared to saline-amphetamine treatment.

TABLE 3

Regional Brain Choline Acetyltransferase Activity
in Rats Treated Neonatally with 6-OHDA/DMI[a]

Treatment	Brain Region			
	Caudate	Nucleus Accumbens	Olfactory Tubercle	Septum
6-HDA/DMI	113.1 ± 4.0	225.7 ± 7.7	210.4 ± 13.7	64.9 ± 1.9
Vehicle/DMI	104.6 ± 3.4	238.1 ± 12.0	198.2 ± 11.8	64.3 ± 4.1

[a]Data are presented as mean ± S.E.M.

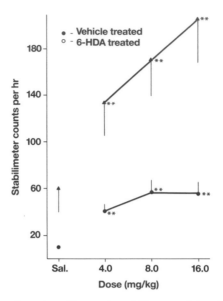

FIG. 6.   Effect of atropine sulfate on the stabilimeter activity of rats treated on days 3 and 6 of life with 6-OHDA or the vehicle solution following DMI treatment. Total dose of 6-OHDA used was 200 ug. Values represent the mean activity + 1 S.E.M. for nine 6-OHDA-treated rats, and 15 vehicle-treated rats. *p < .05.

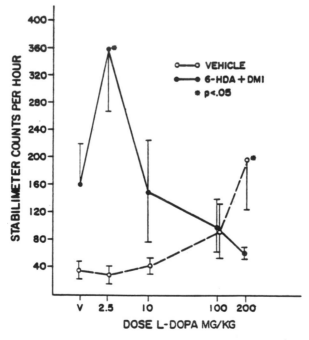

FIG. 7.   Effect of L-Dopa on the stabilimeter activity of rats treated on days 3 and 6 of life with a total dose of 200 ug 6-OHDA or the 6-OHDA vehicle solution following treatment with DMI. Values represent the mean activity + 1 S.E.M. for 5–6 rats. *p < .05.

232

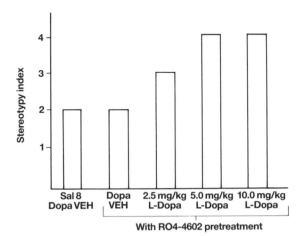

FIG. 8.   Stereotypic behavior produced by L-Dopa in rats treated on days 3 and 6 of life with a total dose of 200 ug 6-HDA following DMI pretreatment. Each column represents the mean response of 6 rats.

REFERENCES

Bolles, R. C., & Woods, P. J. (1964). The ontogeny of behavior in the albino rat. *Animal Behavior, 12*, 427–441.

Breese, G. R., & Traylor, T. D. (1970). Effect of 6-hydroxydopamine on brain norepinephrine and dopamine: Evidence for selective degeneration of catecholamine neurons. *Journal of Pharmacology and Experimental Therapeutics, 174*, 413–430.

Brown, G. L., Ebert, M.H., & Hunt, R. D. (1981). Urinary 3-methoxy-4-hydroxyphenylglycol and homovanillic acid response to d-amphetamine in hyperactive children. *Biological Psychiatry, 16*, 779.

Brunstetter, R. W., & Silver, L. B. (1985). Attention Deficit Disorder. In H. I. Kaplan & B. J. Sadock (Eds.) *Comprehensive textbook of psychiatry*. Baltimore, MD: Williams and Wilkins Press.

Campbell, B. A., Lytle, L. D., & Fibiger, H. C. (1969). Ontogeny of adrenergic arousal and cholinergic inhibitory mechanisms in the rat. *Science, 166*, 635–637.

Cooper, J. R., Bloom, F. C., & Roth, R. H. (1978). *The biochemical basis of neuropharmacology*. New York, NY: Oxford University Press.

DeLong, G. R., & Sidman, R. L. (1968). Effects of eye removal at birth on histogenesis of mouse super colliculus: An autoradiographic analysis with tritiated thymidine. *Developmental Biology, 16*, 513–531.

Erinoff, L., MacPhail, R. C., Heller, A., & Seiden, L. S. (1979). Age-dependent effects of 6-hydroxydopamine on locomotor activity in the rat. *Brain Research, 164*, 195–205.

Heffner, T. G., Heller, A., Miller, F. E., Kotake, C., & Seiden, L. S. (1983). Locomotor hyperactivity in neonatal rats following electrolytic lesions of mesocortical dopamine neurons. *Developmental Brain Research, 9*, 29–37.

Heffner, T. G., & Seiden, L. S. (1982). Possible involvement of serotonergic neurons in the reduction of locomotor hyperactivity caused by amphetamine in neonatal rats depleted of brain dopamine. *Brain Research, 244*, 81–90.

Heller, A., Hutchens, J. L., Kirby, M. L., Karapas, F., & Fernandez, C. (1979). Stereotaxic electrode placement in the neonatal rat. *Journal of Neuroscience Methods, 1*, 41–76.

Hunt, R. D., Cohen, D. J., Anderson, G., & Clark, L. (1986). Possible change in noradrenergic receptor sensitivity following methylphenidate treatment: Growth hormone response and MHPG response to clonidine challenge in children with attention deficit disorder and hyperactivity. *Life Science, 35*, 885-897.

Kahn, A. U., & Dekirmerjian, H. (1981). Urinary excretion of catecholamine metabolites in hyperkinetic child syndrome. *American Journal of Psychiatry, 138*, 108-110.

Kupfer, C., & Palmer, P. (1964). Lateral geniculate nucleus: Histological and cytochemical changes following afferent denervation and visual deprivation. *Experimental Neurology, 94*, 400-409.

Maas, J. W., Greene, N. M., & Hattox, S. E. (1979). Neurotransmitter metabolite production by human brain. In E. Usdin, I. J. Kopin, & J. Barchas (Eds.), *Catecholamines: Basic and clinical frontiers*. New York, NY: Pergamon Press.

Miller, F. E., Heffner, T. G., Kotake, C., & Seiden, L. S. (1981). Magnitude and duration of hyperactivity following neonatal 6-hydroxydopamine is related to the extent of brain dopamine depletion. *Brain Research, 229*, 123-132.

Miller, F. E., & Seiden, L. S. (1983). Locomotor hyperactivity following chronic alpha-methyltyrosine administration in the neonatal rat. *Developmental Brain Research, 6*, 91-92.

Raskin, L. A., Shaywitz, S. E., Shaywitz, B. A., Anderson, G. M., & Cohen, D. J. (1984). Neurochemical correlates of attention deficit disorder. *Pediatric Clinicians of North America, 31*, 387-396.

Shaywitz, B. A., Cohen, D. J., & Bowers, M. D. (1977). CSF monoamine metabolites in children with minimal brain dysfunction: Evidence for alteration in brain dopamine. *Journal of Pediatrics, 90*, 67.

Shaywitz, B. A., Klopper, J. H., Yager, R. D., & Gordon, J. W. (1976). Paradoxical response to amphetamine in developing rats treated with 6-hydroxydopamine. *Nature* (London), *261*, 153-155.

Shaywitz, B. A., Yager, R. D., & Klopper, J. H. (1976). Selective brain dopamine depletion in developing rats: An experimental model of minimal brain dysfunction. *Science, 191*, 305-307.

Shekim, W. O., Bylund, D. B., Alexson, J., Glaser, R. D., Jones, J. B., Hodges, K., & Perdue, S. (1986). Platelet MAO and measures of attention and impulsivity in boys with attention deficit disorder and hyperactivity. *Psychiatry Research, 18*, 179-188.

Shekim, W. O., Dekirmenjian, H., & Chapel, J. L. (1977). Catecholamine metabolites in hyperkinetic boys treated with d-amphetamine. *American Journal of Psychiatry, 134*, 1276.

Shekim, W. O., Dekirmenjian, H., & Chapel, J. L. (1979). Urinary MHPG excretion in minimal brain dysfunction and its modification by d-amphetamine. *American Journal of Psychiatry, 136*, 667.

Shetty, T., & Chase, T. N. (1976). Central monoamines and hyperkinesis of childhood. *Neurology, 26*, 1000-1002.

Smith, R. D., Cooper, B. R., & Breese, G. R. (1973). Growth and behavioral changes in developing rats treated intracisternally with 6-hydroxydopamine: Evidence for involvement of brain dopamine. *Journal of Pharmacology and Experimental Therapeutics, 185*, 609-619.

Sorenson, C. A., Vayer, J. S., & Goldberg, C. S. (1977). Amphetamine reduction of motor activity in rats after neonatal administration of 6-hydroxydopamine. *Biological Psychiatry, 12*, 133-137.

Stoof, J. C., Dijkstra, H., & Hillegers, J. P. M. (1978). Changes in the behavioral response to a novel environment following lesioning of the central dopaminergic system in rat pups. *Psychopharmacology, 57*, 163-166.

Weiss, G., & Hechtman, L. (1979). The hyperactive child syndrome. *Science, 205*, 1348-1354.

Wender, P., Epstein, R. S., & Kopin, I. J. (1971). Urinary monoamine metabolites in children with minimal brain dysfunction. *American Journal of Psychiatry, 127*, 147.

Zametkin, A. J., Karoum, F., Linnoila, M., Rapoport, J. L., Brown, G. L., Chuang, L. W., & Wyatt, R. J. (1985). Stimulants, urinary catecholamines and indoleamines in hyperactivity. *Archives of General Psychiatry, 42*, 251-255.

16

Issues Regarding Possible Therapies Using Cognitive Enhancers

H.J. Normile
H.J. Altman
S. Gershon
Department of Psychiatry,
Wayne State University School of Medicine and
Lafayette Clinic, Detroit, Michigan

Stimulants are the most frequently prescribed medication for children with ADDH. While stimulants produce positive behavioral changes in many, but not all children with ADDH, it is generally accepted that such changes are not accompanied by an improvement in overall academic performance. The nature of the academic underachievement with or without stimulant medication is not understood and remains an area of controversy. For example, it is not known if the poor academic achievement is solely due to arousal and attentional deficits, or result from a functional impairment in one or more specific cognitive (e.g., learning, memory) components.

In this chapter we discuss the various strategies employed to discover cognitive enhancers that may prove efficacious in the treatment of human cognitive disorders. The discussion focuses on preclinical (animal) research in the development of treatments for cognitive impairments ranging from ADD to Alzheimer's disease. General methodological issues and the basic preclinical strategies are discussed. In addition, an example of the application of these strategies is provided by reviewing the preclinical studies that support many of the clinical attempts to treat the cognitive deficits associated with Alzheimer's disease. Important issues regarding the development of cognitive enhancers to treat ADDH are presented.

INTRODUCTION

Since Bradley (1937) first described the positive effect of amphetamine on hyperactive children, CNS stimulants such as methylphenidate and dextroamphetamine

235

have become the drugs of choice for the treatment of ADD with hyperactivity (ADDH). Stimulants have been shown to produce short-term improvement on home and classroom behavior, as well as enhanced performance on specific laboratory tests of vigilance and memory (e.g., Barkley, 1977a; Evans, Gualtieri & Amara, 1986; Rosenthal & Allen, 1978; Taylor, 1985).

ADDH and Academic Performance

Children with ADDH have been shown to have a high rate of academic failure. Given the positive effects of stimulants on behavior and manageability, it was expected that the stimulant-induced reductions in these target symptoms would produce a concurrent improvement in academic performance. However, there is little evidence to support any positive, long-term effect of stimulants on scholastic progress (Barkley & Cunningham, 1978; Charles & Schain, 1981; Gadow, 1983).

The nature of the academic underachievement associated with ADDH is unclear and remains, like many other issues relating to the disorder, an area of controversy. Several different explanations have been offered to account for the lack of relation between symptom reduction and enhanced academic performance. For example, the child may fail to develop fundamental academic skills or learning strategies prior to the onset of therapy (Barkley & Cunningham, 1978). Therefore, the child lacks the prerequisites necessary to incorporate new and more difficult academic material. An alternative explanation suggests that stimulant drugs may actually retard learning by making the child less focused and inquisitive (Barkley, 1977b; Rie, Rie, Stewart, & Ambuel, 1976; Robbins & Sahakian, 1979). Another possibility is that stimulant drugs fail to affect those variables which are directly responsible for or contribute to academic failure (Adams, 1982; Barkley, 1977a; Weingartner, Rapoport, Ebert, & Caine, 1980; Weiss, Kruger, Danielson, & Elman, 1975). Thus, while affecting certain extrinsic components of cognitive function (e.g., attention), the drugs may not affect higher cortical operations (e.g., memory) required for normal information processing.

Alternative Treatment Strategies

The continued deficits in academic performance following stimulant therapy have led to: (a) the search for alternative clinical and educational treatments, either alone or in combination with stimulant medication, and (b) further characterization of the specific cognitive processes affected in the disorder. In addition, there is a continued effort to derive information concerning etiologic factors and possible treatment strategies from animal behavioral studies. The focus of the preclinical studies range from the development of cognitive enhancers that may prove efficacious in the treatment of a number of disorders, including ADDH, to the development of specific animal models that may reflect some of the cognitive deficits observed clinically.

Animal Research and ADDH Psychopharmacology

There are a number of important conceptual and pragmatic issues that should be considered in the development of specific animal models of ADDH-related cognitive deficits, as well as the assessment of the effects of drugs on those deficits. For instance, the cause of the disorder is not known, with the possible existence of multiple etiologies. Moreover, various subgroups (based on multiple etiologies or variable clinical manifestations) may exist. In addition, it is not clear which cognitive components underlie the deficits in academic performance.

The development of appropriate animal models may lead to significant advances in the treatment of the academic failure associated with ADDH. In addition, it may be possible to derive information from current animal behavioral studies which do not target this specific disease. That is, deficits in information processing are not restricted to children with ADDH. Rather, such deficits are a prominent feature of any one of a number of disorders that may occur through the life span of the individual (Bowen & Davison, 1986; Corkin et al., 1985). Accordingly, animal behavioral studies directed toward the discovery of drugs that treat the clinical manifestations, rather than etiology or specific neurochemical disturbances, may be relevant to ADDH. Therefore, the major theme of this chapter is to discuss the role of animal behavioral studies in the development of compounds to treat human cognitive disorders. The first part of the chapter examines a few important methodological issues that should be considered in such studies. The second part summarizes three strategies employed to identify agents that may be of potential therapeutic value in humans. The discussion does not focus on any specific disease since the purpose is to provide a general overview of the rationale for each strategy. In the third part of the chapter we discuss the application of these strategies in the search for a treatment of the progressive decline in memory and global cognitive impairment associated with Alzheimer's disease (AD). Alzheimer's disease was selected as an example because: (a) like ADDH, its etiology is unknown, (b) unlike ADDH, extensive information exists concerning the behavior and pathology of AD, (c) animal behavioral models have been developed that mimic some of the symptomatology of the disease, and (d) several pharmacotherapies have been examined based on either the CNS deficits observed in the disease, or on drug effects produced in animal behavioral studies. This is followed by a summary of some possible explanations for the discrepancies between animal behavioral studies and clinical trials. The final part of the chapter is a discussion of important issues relevant to the use of these strategies in the discovery of compounds to treat ADDH-related deficits in information processing.

GENERAL METHODOLOGICAL CONSIDERATIONS IN THE USE OF ANIMAL BEHAVIORAL STUDIES

There are many methodological considerations in the use of animal behavioral studies for the discovery of drugs to treat human learning-memory disorders (see Olton, 1984; Olton, 1985; Wolkowitz, Tinklenberg, & Weingartner, 1985, for reviews).

Non-Specific Processes

Animal behavioral studies require the assessment of the animals' performance in specific tasks. Drugs could alter task performance by affecting processes such as perception, arousal, and motivation. While these extrinsic processes may modulate or be an integral part of certain aspects of information processing, they are generally not considered the target variables in animal learning-memory studies. Many animal studies attempt to determine whether the drug-induced changes in performance are due to direct effects on learning-memory processes or result from an influence on extrinsic processes. However, perception, arousal and motivation are rather vague concepts and their role in or influence on different cognitive operations is not well understood and cannot be easily assessed.

Distinct Cognitive Components

Many different theories or models have been proposed to describe the various components that underlie information processing in humans and animals. Acquisition, consolidation, storage and retrieval are terms often used to delineate specific mnemonic components. Each of these may be temporally related, and may be under the control of distinct neurophysiological mechanisms. Consequently, a pharmacological agent may alter performance by affecting one or more of these components. Assuming that some of the components operate in a specific order, it may be possible to differentiate which are affected by the design of the experiment (e.g., post-train vs. pre-test drug administration). This type of analysis is critical in attempts to develop effective strategies for the treatment of human cognitive dysfunctions, since the human disorder may be related to an impairment in the operation of a specific cognitive component (Weingartner, 1984, 1985).

Behavioral Task

Many methodological considerations exist with respect to the nature of the task employed to assess the performance of the animal. First, and most obvious, is that the task must be sensitive to memory; meaning that changes in memory will produce measurable changes in the performance of the animal. Second, the task should be, as much as possible, selective to changes in memory, so that drug-induced changes in extrinsic processes will not be a major contributing factor to the change in the performance of the animal. For example, a food reinforced discrimination task may not be the ideal task to examine a drug with known effects on appetite. Third, some consideration should be given to the type of process that is reflected by the change in performance. That is, many different types of processes have been proposed for certain aspects of memory (see Kesner, 1986; Squire, 1986, for reviews). Certain tasks may be selective or may differentiate various types of processing which may be relevant to the human disorder.

With these methodological considerations in mind, the following section will summarize three basic strategies employed in the discovery of drugs to treat human cognitive disorders. The operative word "memory" is used throughout most of the discussion since space limitations do not allow for any inference regarding the specific cognitive component involved or the contribution of extrinsic variables to the change in behavior.

GENERAL STRATEGIES OF ANIMAL BEHAVIORAL STUDIES

It is possible to group animal behavioral studies into one of three broad approaches: (a) effects of drugs in normal animals, (b) effects of drugs on naturally occurring or artificially induced memory deficits, and (c) effects of drugs on memory deficits exhibited by specific models thought to reflect certain psychological and/or neurological aspects of the disease state.

Normal Animals

The aim of this approach is to identify drugs that facilitate memory in normal animals. The major assumption of this approach is that memory can be enhanced in animals thought to be operating at maximal levels of processing (Gamzu, 1985). For example, most of us have learned to avoid inserting a finger into an electrical outlet. It is unlikely this avoidance response could be enhanced by any drug. However, a number of behavioral tasks are used that are thought to be sensitive to drug-induced enhancement of performance. Such tasks may involve many trials or days for the animal to acquire the new behavior, thus allowing inferences about drug effects on the rate of learning or the rate of normal forgetting.

Naturally Occurring or Artificially Induced Memory Deficits

This approach examines the ability of drugs to prevent or ameliorate memory deficits normally exhibited by animals, or which are artificially induced by any one of a number of manipulations. This approach does not attempt to make comparisons between the cause of the deficit condition in the animal and the cause (which in many cases is unknown) of the memory dysfunction in the human. On the other hand, a parallelism is made between the memory deficit observed in the animal and the human condition.

Examples of naturally-occurring deficits include differences between certain genetic strains, slow vs. fast learners, and aged vs. young animals. However, the use of aged animals may fall into the latter category if it is assumed that the memory deficits exhibited by aged animals and aged humans share common etiologies or specific neurological/neurochemical deficiencies.

There are many methods of experimentally inducing memory deficits in animals. Probably the two most popular methods are electroconvulsant shock (ECS) and anoxia/hypoxia. Others methods used to disrupt memory include administration of pharmacological agents, and neurochemical or neuroanatomical lesions. As in the case of the aged animal, the artificially induced deficit may fall into the next category if it is thought that the animal model mimics specific functional disturbances of the human disease.

Pathology-Related Animal Models

In this approach, the behavioral parallelism between the animal model and the human disease is extended to include a concordance between one or more biochemical or physiological abnormalities. Consequently, this approach requires some theoretical assumptions regarding the etiology of the human condition, or more commonly, some knowledge of the CNS deficiencies associated with the disease. For example, attempts have been made to develop an animal model of the memory deficits associated with AD by destroying cholinergic neurons in the nucleus basalis magnocellularis (NBM), which results in a reduction of cortical choline acetyltransferase (CAT) and acetylcholinesterase (AChE), as well as memory impairments in specific tasks (e.g., Altman, Crosland, Jenden, & Berman, 1985; Flicker, Dean, Watkins, Fisher, & Bartus, 1983; Friedman, Lerer, & Kuster, 1983). This model is based, in part, on evidence indicating that the cells in this region of the basal forebrain may be selectively degenerated in patients with AD, which in turn may be responsible for the loss of cortical CAT activity observed in these patients (see Bartus, Dean, Pontecorvo, & Flicker, 1985; Hardy et al., 1985, for reviews).

The development of pathology-related animal models requires the investigator to make some decisions regarding the extent to which the model approximates the human condition. This point is illustrated by Shaywitz (1976) who suggests that a suitable animal model for minimal brain dysfunction-hyperactivity should satisfy the following criteria: (a) specific cardinal features (hyperactivity, cognitive difficulties, attentional difficulties) should be replicated in the animal, (b) the human and animal syndromes must have similar pathogeneses, (c) the syndrome must follow the same developmental course (evident in young developing animals, not so evident in the adult animal), and (d) the response to medication (stimulants and other drugs) in the animal must parallel the response observed clinically. Obviously, these criteria represent the ideal condition. If you were to substitute minimal brain dysfunction-hyperactivity with your favorite psychopathological disease, a suitable animal model most likely does not exist which fulfills all the criteria. From a practical perspective, pathology-related models do not model all the physiological and behavioral aspects of the disease. Consequently, such models offer incomplete representations of the human condition.

ALZHEIMER'S DISEASE PHARMACOTHERAPY

The ultimate goal of the animal behavioral studies described above is to discover or develop pharmacological interventions that may prove effective in the treatment of human memory disorders. Therefore, the validity of the studies lie in their ability to predict clinical utility.

A number of agents have been used in an attempt to treat the severe memory disturbances associated with AD. The basis or support for these various treatment approaches stem, in part, from the demonstrated effects of the drugs on memory in animals. The following section reviews some of these treatment strategies, focusing on drugs that enhance cholinergic activity, neuropeptides (ACTH and vasopressin analogues), and nootropics.

Enhancement of Cholinergic Activity

While the etiology of AD is unknown, a considerable amount of biochemical and behavioral data have suggested that a reduction in cholinergic activity may underlie the memory impairment in AD (Bartus et al., 1985). For instance, a reduction in the activities of CAT and AChE have been shown in many studies (see Hardy et al., 1985, for review). The reduction in CAT has been correlated with the extent of neuropathological changes, as well as with the degree of memory/cognitive dysfunction (Perry et al., 1978). Moreover, in normal subjects, drugs that impair cholinergic function appear to mimic the memory deficits associated with AD (Caine, Weingartner, Ludlow, & Cudahy, 1981; Drachman & Leavitt, 1974). This "cholinergic hypothesis" is further supported by a number of animal studies which implicate the cholinergic nervous system in normal memory processes (e.g., Deutsch, Hamburg, & Dahl, 1966; Whitehouse, 1964).

Animal Studies. While numerous studies have examined the effects of altered cholinergic activity on learning and memory in normal animals, the combined results do not provide a clear picture as to the precise role of the cholinergic system in information processing (see Deutsch & Rogers, 1979, for review). The results of studies which examined the effects of enhanced cholinergic activity have not been consistent. The effects appear to be highly dose-, time-, and task-dependent. In normal animals, less variable effects are observed when the cholinergic drugs are administered following training. For example, most, but not all experiments, have shown that post-training administration of direct- (arecoline, oxotremorine) or indirect- (physostigmine, tetrahydroaminoacridine) acting cholinergic agonists facilitate performance in a number of memory tasks (e.g., Baratti, Huygens, Mino, Merlo, & Gardella, 1979; Bartus, Dean, & Beer, 1980; Flood, Smith, & Cherkin, 1983).

In contrast to the variable effects observed in normal animals, interventions thought to enhance cholinergic activity have produced more consistent results in animals with naturally-occurring or artificially-induced memory deficits. For example, dietary loading of choline has been reported to facilitate avoidance memory in aged mice (Bartus, Dean, Goas, & Lippa, 1980). Anticholinesterase treatment has been shown to improve memory in aged monkeys (Bartus, 1979; Bartus, Dean, & Beer, 1983), attenuate the memory deficits induced by NBM lesions in the rat (Haroutunian, Barnes, & Davis, (1985), and reduce scopolamine-induced amnesia in monkeys (Bartus, 1978). In addition, direct acting agonists (arecoline and oxotremorine) have been shown to attenuate age-related memory deficits in monkeys (Bartus, Dean, & Beer, 1980; Bartus et al., 1983).

Clinical Studies. The biochemical evidence indicating a cholinergic deficit in AD, in addition to the animal studies demonstrating the ability of enhanced cholinergic activity to attenuate naturally occurring or artificially induced deficits, provides strong support for "cholinergic replacement therapy" in the treatment of AD. Unfortunately, the various treatment approaches (i.e., precursor loading, cholinesterase inhibitors, and receptor agonists) have not resulted in any substantial and consistent clinical benefit. For example, it is generally accepted that precursor loading (either choline salts or lecithin) fails to produce any reliable positive response in AD (see Bartus, Dean, & Beer, 1984; Etienne, 1983; Fovall, Dysken, & Davis, 1983, for reviews). While subtle (but variable) positive results have been reported using cholinesterase inhibitors and muscarinic agonists (e.g., Christie, Shering, Ferguson, & Glen, 1981; Wettstein & Spiegel, 1984), there are clear limitations (short half life, narrow therapeutic window, adverse side effects) in the use of these drugs for the treatment of AD (Bartus, Dean, & Fisher, 1986). Consequently, the therapeutic potential of existing cholinergic agents appears to be rather small. However, intraventricular infusion of cholinomimetics (Harbaugh, Roberts, Coombs, Sanders, & Reeder, 1984) may circumvent many of these problems and thereby improve the therapeutic effect of these agents.

Some studies have tried to combine precursor loading and postsynaptic activation. The result of these clinical studies, although inconsistent (Wettstein, 1983), are promising. For example, precursor loading in combination with physostigmine (Peters & Levin, 1982; Thal, Fuld, Masur, & Sharpless, 1983) or tetrahydroaminoacridine (Kaye et al., 1982) has been reported to produce positive (but modest) results.

Nootropics

The term "nootropic" was coined to describe a group of metabolic enhancers thought to activate "higher" functions of the brain (e.g., learning and memory), with no sedative, stimulant or analgesic effects. The drugs in this group include piracetam, amiracetam, pramiracetam, and oxiracetam. Piracetam is the prototypic nootropic, which in addition to its effect on ATP synthesis, may enhance acetylcholine release (Wurtman, Masil, & Reinstein, 1981).

Animal Studies. In normal animals, piracetam or its analogues have been shown to facilitate learning and retention in different types of tasks and in different species (e.g., Giurgea & Salama, 1977; Rigter, Janssens-Elbertse, & van Riezen, 1976; Wolthius, 1971). Certain nootropics have also been shown to be effective in attenuating naturally occurring or artificially induced memory deficits. Thus, amiracetam and/or piracetam has been shown to facilitate performance in "poor learners," aged rats and monkeys, as well as to protect against memory disruption caused by non-convulsant electrobrain shock, ECS, protein synthesis inhibitors, scopolamine, hemicholinium, and CO_2 hypoxia (e.g., Bartus et al., 1983: Franklin, Sethy, & Tang, 1986; Gamzu et al, 1986; Sara & David-Remacle, 1974; Vincent, Verderese, & Gamzu, 1985; Wolthius, 1971).

Clinical Studies. In a review of the literature on piracetam, Ferris (1981) concluded that evidence for the therapeutic efficacy of the drug in SD is equivocal. In general, piracetam therapy does not appear to produce a consistent effect in AD (Schneck, 1983). The subtle positive effects which have been reported are questioned as to their clinical significance. For example, in a double-blind, placebo-controlled crossover study of 40 patients diagnosed as having AD, piracetam produced a significant improvement on only 2 of 37 cognitive test measures evaluated (Ferris et al., 1982).

Some studies have tried to combine piracetam with either choline or lecithin. The rationale for these trials was based, in part, on the report that combined choline and piracetam treatment attenuated the memory deficits normally exhibited by aged rodents (Bartus, Dean, & Sherman, 1981). However, the combination of choline and piracetam did not yield any significant improvements in AD (Growdon, Corkin, & Huff, 1985). The combination of lecithin and piracetam did not produce any significant treatment effect when compared with piracetam alone or placebo (Pomara et al., 1984). Another study that involved the combination of lecithin plus piracetam for several months provided some evidence for a positive treatment effect (Smith, Vroulis, Johnson, & Morgan, 1984).

Neuropeptides: ACTH and Vasopressin Analogues

A number of peptides have been shown to be present in the brain and active in the central nervous system. These neuropeptides, which are either synthesized by the brain or transported there from the hypothalamus, may act as neurotransmitters, neuromodulators or neurohormones. Neuropeptides related to ACTH and vasopressin have been extensively examined for their behavioral effects in animals, and their potential for use in the treatment of AD.

Animal Studies. N-terminal ACTH fragments (e.g., $ACTH1_{4-10}$, $ACTH_{4-10}$, $ACTH_{4-9}$) and vasopressin (arginine-, lysine-vasopressin) have been reported to enhance the performance of normal animals in a variety of learning and memory tasks (see De Wied & Jolles, 1982; Tinklenberg & Thornton, 1983; Van Ree, Hijman, Jolles, & De Wied, 1985, for reviews). Likewise, the peptides have been reported to attenuate artificially induced memory deficits produced by a variety of methods (e.g., Judge & Quartermain, 1982; Rigter, van Riezen, & De Wied, 1974; Rigter et al., 1976; Tinklenberg & Thornton, 1983).

Vasopressin and ACTH analogues also produce modest effects on aged-related memory impairments in monkeys (Bartus, Dean, & Beer, 1982; Bartus et al., 1983). While the peptide-induced improvement in performance was not consistent or robust enough to produce significant differences between group means, there was a significant enhancement of performance in the majority of animals. However, even in responders, no clear dose-response functions were observed.

The mode of action of the vasopressin and ACTH analogues in modifying performance is a matter of debate. It has been suggested that the behavioral effects may result from peptide-induced changes in extrinsic processes such as attention, arousal, and motivation (see Born, Fehm, & Voigt, 1986; Wolkowitz et al., 1985, for reviews).

Clinical Studies. Clinical trials to assess the role of ACTH and vasopressin analogues in the treatment of AD have not been too rewarding (Chase, Durso, Fedio, & Tamminga, 1982; Tinklenberg & Thornton, 1983). For example, Chase et al. (1982) failed to find any effects of lysine-vasopressin on learning or memory of verbal and non-verbal material. However, the peptide produced a small reduction in reaction time latency. Similar negative results have been reported for the vasopressin analogue desmopressin (Jenkins, Mather, & Coughlan, 1982). In a recent study with $ACTH_{4-9}$, no significant effect of the peptide on cognitive function was observed during six months of treatment (Soininen, Koskinen, Helkala, Pigache, & Riekkinen, 1985). In another study (Ferris, 1983), a two week $ACTH_{4-9}$ treatment period produced some changes in verbal memory. The greatest effects, however, appeared to be on mood and attention.

In summary, the drugs discussed above appear to have limited utility in the treatment of the cognitive deficits associated with AD. Moreover, clinical studies using other investigational drugs not reviewed (e.g., vasodilators, stimulants, opiates) have also failed to establish any clinically effective agent for AD. A number of factors may account for these disappointing results, a summary of which is beyond the scope of this chapter. However, it should be emphasized that the treatment strategies per se may be valid. The negative clinical effects may be due to the nature or properties of the drug. For example, cholinergic replacement therapy may prove to be a viable strategy when a more suitable (i.e., longer lasting, less-side-effects) cholinomimetic agent is discovered.

LACK OF CORRELATION BETWEEN ANIMAL
AND HUMAN STUDIES

The discrepancies between the positive preclinical studies and the negative results in AD patients have important implications with respect to the use of animal behavioral studies for the discovery of drugs to treat human cognitive disorders. A number of factors may account for the discrepancies, which should be kept in mind when attempting to extrapolate from animal data to clinical trials.

Design

Animal and human studies rarely have similar designs. Differences in a number of variables, including dose, dose schedules, and route of administration, may contribute to the discrepancies in the results. For example, the use of animals often allows sampling of a wide range of doses to establish an effective dose range. Most human studies, however, do not offer this latitude, allowing a sampling of only a few doses. Another source of variability may be differences in dose schedules. Thus, it is difficult to compare the results of clinical studies that often administer drugs repeatedly, to animal studies that often administer the drug once. This point is illustrated by a study (Loullis et al., 1983) which found that chronic administration of a cholinomimetic impaired retention, while chronic administration of an anticholinergic enhanced retention in rats. These chronic effects are opposite to those seen following the acute administration of the drugs (see Bartus, Dean, Beer, & Lippa, 1982, for review).

Behavioral Measures

The various components of cognitive processes may be differentially affected by a drug. The component which is sensitive to drug action in animal studies may not be the component that underlies the memory dysfunction in the human. Animal studies that assess the effect of an agent on "memory" often fail to provide information regarding the component processes involved in the drug-induced change in performance. Therefore, it may be difficult to predict the effect of a drug on a distinct and specific human cognitive component based on the drug-induced performance change in the animal.

Another factor that should be included in this category is the possible existence of differences in the complexity of cognitive processes between animals and humans. Thus, examination of the effect of a drug on the animal's ability to remember not to cross from a illuminated chamber to a shocked darkened chamber is inherently different from many of the behavioral measures commonly used to assess drug effects on memory in humans.

Anatomical/Neurochemical Variables

Another factor that may contribute to performance discrepancies is the existence of anatomical and/or neurochemical differences between animals and humans. These may include interspecies differences in the anatomical substrates which underlie information processing, as well as differences in blood-brain permeability, cell membrane permeability, enzymatic activity, receptor availability, and ultradian rhythms. Whether these differences contribute to drug-related behavioral variability is unclear.

RELEVANCE OF ANIMAL RESEARCH TO PHARMACOTHERAPY FOR ADDH

The preceding two sections illustrate the difficulties in extrapolating from animal behavioral research to the effects of drugs in patients with AD. Despite the plethora of information regarding drug effects in animals, as well as the symptomatology and pathology of AD, a treatment strategy has not been developed which either arrests or ameliorates the primary symptoms of the disease.

Animal Research and ADDH

A number of additional factors must be considered in attempting to extrapolate from animal behavioral studies to drug effects in ADDH. For example, by far the majority of research concerning the effects of drugs on performance of normal animals in learning and memory tasks have employed mature subjects. Similar, artificially induced performance deficits usually involve animals with mature nervous systems. Given that ADDH is a developmental disorder, some degree of caution must be exercised in predicting drug effects in various adult age groups which exhibit behavioral and neurochemical differences.

Attempts to develop pathology-related animal models for ADDH are severely hampered since the cause of the disorder is not known, and the data from clinical neurochemical studies have not been consistent (Anderson et al., 1983; Hunt, Cohen, Shaywitz, & Shaywitz, 1982). Therefore, a number of "animal models" that have been proposed for ADDH fall in the category of the artificially-induced models. Thus, prefrontal cortical lesions, caudate nucleus lesions, lead poisoning, carbon monoxide exposure, undernourishment, and depletion of brain DA have been shown to produce overactivity and/or learning impairments (e.g., Anderson et al., 1983; Culver & Norton, 1976; Dean & Davis, 1959; Michaelson, Bornschein, Loch, & Ratales, 1977; Millichap, 1972; Sildergeld & Goldberg, 1974). However, inferences concerning the etiology or pathology of the human disorder are made depending on how closely the model mimics the symptomatology and developmental course of the disease, and its response to treatments known to be effective in the clinical disorder. For example, Shaywitz and colleagues (Shaywitz, 1976; Shaywitz, Yager, & Klopper, 1976) have shown that depletion of brain DA in the rat pup by 6-hydroxydopamine administration resulted in hyperactivity and poor avoidance learning. Following maturation, the hyperactivity disappeared while the learning deficits persisted. Moreover, the hyperactivity could be decreased by injections of d-amphetamine or methylphenidate. The authors conclude that the dopamine-depleted rat pup produces an animal model that closely parallels the human condition. In as much as some clinical studies have indicated a deficit in dopaminergic function associated with ADDH (e.g., Cohen, Shaywitz, Young, & Bowers, 1980; Shaywitz, Cohen, & Bowers, 1977), the behavioral effects induced by dopamine depletion may indicate that disturbances in brain dopaminergic systems are linked to the behaviors observed in ADDH.

Non-Stimulant Treatment of ADDH

The failure of some ADDH children to respond to stimulants, as well as the continued academic underachievement despite stimulant medication, have led to a search for alternative drug treatments. Clinical trials have been conducted with tricyclic antidepressants, phenothiazines, dopamine agonists, monoamine oxidase inhibitors, and ACTH analogues (e.g., Gittelman Klein, Klein, Katz, Saraf, & Pollack, 1976; Langer, Rapoport, Brown, Ebert, & Bunney, 1982; Rapoport, Quinn, Bradbard, Riddle, & Brooks, 1974; Rapoport, Zametkin, Donnelly, & Ismond, 1985). Since stimulant medication still remains the drug of choice, it should not be surprising that the effects observed with the alternative drugs have not produced a replacement for stimulant therapy. For example, trials with ACTH analogues were without effect on several psychomotor and mental performance tests including memory (Butter et al., 1983; Rapoport, Quinn, Copeland, & Burg, 1976). These negative results are of particular interest since it has been suggested that the effects of ACTH peptides on learning and memory may operate through extrinsic processes such as attention, arousal and motivation.

In general, the results of trials with many non-stimulant drugs have been disappointing, producing effects less than that observed following stimulant medication. On the other hand, the positive effects produced by some agents (e.g., tricyclic antidepressants) may warrant their use in clinical populations that are unresponsive to stimulants. However, it should be emphasized that most clinical trials with non-stimulant drugs are short-term. Consequently, their long-term effects (such as on academic performance) have not been extensively assessed.

With respect to nootropics, we are unaware of any controlled clinical trials with these agents in ADDH. However, nootropics, either alone or in combination with other agents, may eventually prove to be a treatment strategy for the cognitive disorders associated with ADDH. That is, piracetam has been shown to produce positive results in the treatment of certain childhood learning disabilities, particularly dyslexia (see Wilsher, 1986, for review). In addition, a recent animal study (Sansone, Ammassari-Teule, & Oliverio, 1985) has shown that ox-iracetam and piracetam, given alone, had no effect on avoidance acquisition in C57 mice, but strongly enhanced acquisition when given in combination with methamphetamine. The two nootropic drugs did not effect the locomotor stimulation induced by methamphetamine.

CONCLUSIONS

Given the methodological problems associated with the use of animals in the development of compounds to treat human cognitive disorders, as well as the often negative results observed in attempts to treat the disorders despite positive preclinical data, the question arises as to the value of animal behavioral studies in the development of drugs to treat ADDH. While there is little argument that preclinical research is important in the understanding of the pathological basis of the disorder and its treatment, more productive outcomes will be realized when the discontinuity between animal research and human clinical research is reduced. In terms of animal research, this will be accomplished by identifying the role of extrinsic processes in the drug-induced changes in performance, and/or identifying which cognitive components underlie the performance change. In addition, further characterization of the neurobiological basis of normal learning and memory processes will no doubt lead to a better understanding of the neurobiological basis of cognitive disorders. Parallel developments in clinical research also include an understanding of the specific cognitive processes or operations that may underlie the academic underachievement associated with ADDH. Can the apparent cognitive deficits be explained totally by defective extrinsic mechanisms such as arousal and attention, or do defective intrinsic mechanisms (e.g., acquisition, storage, retrieval) play a significant role? Such knowledge may help to explain the continued academic difficulties observed following stimulant medication, as well as identify the primary and secondary processes that may then be targeted for pharmacological treatment. Moreover, clinical sources of ambiguity and confusion must be addressed. These include: (a) the various subjective diagnostic criteria employed by different clinicians, (b) confusion and overlap in the use of terms such as sustained attention, selective attention, distractibility, arousal, alertness, inhibitory control and impulsivity, and (c) the different methodological procedures (e.g., drug dosage, length of treatment, criteria for judging drug effects) used in clinical trials. Clarification of these issues will not only lead to a better understanding of the clinical manifestations of the disorder, but also greatly assist in the development and use of animal models of ADDH.

REFERENCES

Adams, W. (1982). Effect of methylphenidate on thought processing time in children. *Developmental Behavioral Pediatrics, 3*, 133–135.

Altman, H. J., Crosland, R. D., Jenden, D. J., & Berman, R. F. (1985). Further characterization of the nature of the behavioral and neurochemical effects of lesions to the nucleus basalis of Meynert. *Neurobiology of Aging, 6*, 125–130.

Anderson, G. M., Shaywitz, B. A., Leckman J. F., Hunt, R. D., Shaywitz, S. E., & Cohen, D. J. (1983). Developmental and pharmacological aspects of attention deficit disorder (ADD). *Progress in Clinical Biological Research, 135*, 207–223.

Baratti, C. M., Huygens, P., Mino, J., Merlo, A., & Gardella, J. (1979). Memory facilitation with posttrial injection of oxotremorine and physostigmine in mice. *Psychopharmacology, 64*, 85–88.

Barkley, R. A. (1977a). Review of stimulant drug research with hyperactive children. *Journal of Child Psychology and Psychiatry, 18*, 137–165.

Barkley, R. A. (1977b). The effects of methylphenidate on various types of activity level and attention in hyperactive children. *Journal of Abnormal Child Psychology, 5*, 361–369.

Barkley, R. A., & Cunningham, C. E. (1978). Do stimulant drugs improve the academic performance of hyperkinetic children? *Clinical Pediatrics, 17*, 85–92.

Bartus, R. T. (1978). Evidence for a direct cholinergic involvement in the scopolamine-induced amnesia in monkeys: Effects of concurrent administration of physostigmine and methylphenidate with scopolamine. *Pharmacology Biochemistry and Behavior, 9*, 833–836.

Bartus, R. T. (1979). Physostigmine and recent memory effects in young and aged nonhuman primates. *Science, 206*, 1087–1089.

Bartus, R. T., Dean, R. L., & Beer, B. (1980). Memory deficits in aged Cebus monkeys and facilitation with central cholinomimetics. *Neurobiology of Aging, 1*, 145–152.

Bartus, R. T., Dean, R. L., & Beer, B. (1982). Neuropeptide effects on memory in aged monkeys. *Neurobiology of Aging, 3*, 40–45.

Bartus, R. T., Dean, R. L., & Beer, B. (1983). An evaluation of drugs for improving memory in aged monkeys: Implication for clinical trials in humans. *Psychopharmacology Bulletin, 19*, 168–184.

Bartus, R. T., Dean, R. L., & Beer, B. (1984). Cholinergic precursor therapy for geriatric cognition: Its past, present and a question of its future. In M. M. Ordy, D. Harman, & R. Alfin-Slater (Eds.), *Nutrition in gerontology* (pp. 191–225). New York: Raven Press.

Bartus, R. T., Dean, R. L., Beer, B., & Lippa A. S. (1982). The cholinergic hypothesis of geriatric memory dysfunction: A critical review. *Science, 217*, 408–417.

Bartus, R. T., Dean, R. L., & Fisher, S. K. (1986). Cholinergic treatment for age-related memory disturbances: Dead or barely coming of age? In T. Crook, R. Bartus, S. Ferris, & S. Gershon (Eds.), *Treatment development strategies for Alzheimer's disease* (pp. 421–450). New Canaan, CT: Mark Powley.

Bartus, R. T., Dean, R. L., Goas, J. A., & Lippa, A. S. (1980). Age-related changes in passive avoidance retention: Modulation with dietary choline. *Science, 209*, 301–303.

Bartus, R. T., Dean, R. L., Pontecorvo, M. J., & Flicker, C. (1985). The cholinergic hypothesis: A historical overview, current perspective, and future directions. In D. S. Olton, E. Gamzu, & S. Corkin (Eds.), *Memory dysfunctions: An integration of animal and human research from preclinical and clinical perspectives* (Vol. 444, pp. 332–358), Annals of the New York Academy of Sciences.

Bartus, R. T., Dean, R. L., & Sherman, K. A. (1981). Profound effect of combining choline and piracetam on memory enhancement and cholinergic function in aged rats. *Neurobiology of Aging, 2*, 105–111.

Born, J., Fehm, H. L., & Voigt, K. H. (1986). ACTH and attention in humans: A review. *Neuropsychobiology, 15*, 165–186.

Bowen, D. M., & Davison, A. N. (1986). Can the pathophysiology of dementia lead to rational therapy? In T. Crook, R. Bartus, S. Ferris, & S. Gershon (Eds.), *Treatment development strategies for Alzheimer's disease* (pp. 35–66). New Canaan, CT: Mark Powley.

Bradley, C. (1937). The behavior of children receiving Benzedrine. *American Journal of Psychiatry, 2*, 127–140.

Butter, H., Lapierre, Y., Leprade, K., Firestone, P., Cote, A., & Pierre-Louis, F. (1983). A comparative study of the efficacy of ACTH 4–9 analogue (ORG 2766) and methylphenidate on hyperactive behavior. *Journal of Clinical Psychopharmacology, 3,* 226–230.

Caine, E. D., Weingartner, H., Ludlow, C. L., & Cudahy, E. A. (1981). A qualitative analysis of scopolamine-induced amnesia. *Psychopharmacology, 74,* 74–80.

Charles, L., & Schain, R. (1981). A four-year follow-up study of the effects of methylphenidate on the behavior and academic achievement of hyperactive children. *Journal of Abnormal Child Psychology, 9,* 495–505.

Chase, T. N., Durso, R., Fedio, P., & Tamminga, C. A. (1982). Vasopressin treatment of cognitive deficits in Alzheimer's disease. *Aging* (Vol. 19, pp. 457–461). New York: Raven Press.

Christie, J. E., Shering, A., Ferguson, J., & Glen, A. I. M. (1981). Physostigmine and arecoline: Effects of intravenous infusions in Alzheimer's presenile dementia. *British Journal of Psychiatry, 138,* 46–50.

Cohen, D. J., Shaywitz, B. A., Young, J. G., & Bowers, M. B. (1980). Cerebrospinal fluid monoamine metabolites in neuropsychiatric disorders of childhood. In J. Wood (Ed.), *Neurobiology of cerebrospinal fluid* (pp. 665–683). New York: Plenum Press.

Corkin, S., Cohen, N. J., Sullivan, E. V., Clegg, R. A., Rosen, T. J., & Ackerman, R. H. (1985). Analyses of global memory impairments of different etiologies. In D. S. Olton, E. Gamzu & S. Corkin (Eds.), *Memory dysfunctions: An integration of animal and human research from preclinical and clinical perspectives* (Vol. 444, pp. 10–40). Annals of the New York Academy of Sciences.

Culver, B., & Norton, S. (1976). Juvenile hyperactivity in rats after acute exposure to carbon monoxide. *Experimental Neurology, 50,* 80–98.

Dean, W. H., & Davis, G. D. (1959). Behavioral changes following caudate lesions in rhesus monkeys. *Journal of Neurophysiology, 22,* 524–537.

Deutsch, J. A., Hamburg, M. D., & Dahl, H. (1966). Anticholinesterase-induced amnesia and its temporal aspects. *Science, 151,* 221–223.

Deutsch, J. A., & Rogers, J. B. (1979). Cholinergic excitability and memory: Animal studies and their clinical applications. In K. L. Davis & P. A. (Eds.), *Acetylcholine and neuropsychiatric disease* (pp. 175–204). New York: Plenum Press.

De Wied., & Jolles, J. (1982). Neuropeptides derived from proopiocortin: Behavioral, physiological, and neurochemical effects. *Physiological Reviews, 62,* 976–1059.

Drachman, D. A., & Leavitt, J. (1974). Human memory and the cholinergic system. *Archives of Neurology, 30,* 113–121.

Etienne, P. (1983). Treatment of Alzheimer's disease with lecithin. In B. Reisberg (Ed.), *Alzheimer's disease: The standard reference* (pp. 353–354). New York: Free Press.

Evans, R. W., Gualtieri, C. T., & Amara, I. (1986). Methylphenidate and memory: Dissociated effects in hyperactive children. *Psychopharmacology, 90,* 211–216.

Ferris, S. H. (1981). Empirical studies in senile dementia with central nervous system stimulants and metabolic enhancers, In T. Crook & S. Gershon (Eds.), *Strategies for the development of an effective treatment for senile dementia* (pp. 173–187). New Canaan, CT: Mark Powley.

Ferris, S. H. (1983). Neuropeptides in the treatment of Alzheimer's disease. In B. Reisberg (Ed.), *Alzheimer's disease: The standard reference* (pp. 369–373). New York: Free Press.

Ferris, S. W., Reisberg, B., Crook, T., Friedman, E., Schneck, M. K., Mir, P., Sherman, K., Corwin, J., Gershon, S., & Bartus, R. T. (1982). Pharmacologic treatment of senile dementia: Choline, L-DOPA, piracetam, and choline plus piracetam. *Aging* (Vol. 19, pp. 475–481). New York: Raven Press.

Flicker, C., Dean, R. L., Watkins, D. L., Fisher, S. K., & Bartus, R. T. (1983). Behavioral and neurochemical effects following neurotoxic lesion of a major cholinergic input to the cerebral cortex in the rat. *Pharmacology Biochemistry and Behavior, 18,* 973–982.

Flood, J. F., Smith, G. E., & Cherkin, A. (1983). Memory retention: Potentiation of cholinergic drug combinations in mice. *Neurobiology of Aging, 4,* 37–43.

Fovall, P., Dysken, M. W., & Davis, J. M. (1983). Treatment of Alzheimer's disease with choline salts. In B. Reisberg (Ed.), *Alzheimer's disease: The standard reference* (pp. 346–352). New York: Free Press.

Franklin, S. R., Sethy, V. H., & Tang, A. H. (1986). Amnesia produced by intracerebroventricular injections of hemicholinium-3 in mice was prevented by pretreatment with piracetam-like compounds. *Pharmacology Biochemistry and Behavior, 25*, 925–927.

Friedman, E., Lerer, B., & Kuster, J. (1983). Loss of cholinergic neurons in the rat neocortex produces deficits in passive avoidance learning. *Pharmacology Biochemistry and Behavior, 19*, 309–312.

Gadow, K. D. (1983). Pharmacotherapy for learning disabilities. *Learning Disabilities, 2*, 127–140.

Gamzu, E. (1985). Animal behavioral models in the discovery of compounds to treat memory dysfunction. In D. S. Olton, E. Gamzu & S. Corkin (Eds.), *Memory dysfunctions: An integration of animal and human research from preclinical and clinical perspectives* (Vol. 444, pp. 370–393). Annals of the New York Academy of Sciences.

Gamzu, E., Vincent, G., Verderese, A., Boff, E., Lee, L., & Davidson, A. B. (1986). Pharmacological protection against memory retrieval deficits as a method of discovering new therapeutic agents. In A. Fisher, I. Hanin & C. Lackman (Eds.), *Alzheimer's and Parkinson's disease: Strategies in research and development, Advances in behavioral biology* (Vol 29, pp. 375–391). New York: Plenum Press.

Gittelman-Klein, R., Klein, D. F., Katz, S., Saraf, K., & Pollack, E. (1976). Comparative effects of methylphenidate and thioridazine in hyperkinetic children. *Archives of General Psychiatry, 33*, 1217–1231.

Giurgea, C., & Salama, M. (1977). Nootropic Drugs. *Progress in Neuropsychopharmacology, 1*, 235–247.

Growdon, J. H., Corkin, S., & Huff, F. J. (1985). Clinical evaluation of compounds for treatment of memory dysfunction. In D. S. Olton, E. Gamzu, & S. Corkin (Eds.), *Memory dysfunctions: An integration of animal and human research from preclinical and clinical perspectives* (Vol 444, pp. 437–449). Annals of the New York Academy of Sciences.

Harbaugh, R. E., Roberts, D. W., Coombs, D. W., Sanders, R. L., & Reeder, T. M. (1984). Preliminary report: Intracranial cholinergic drug infusion in patients with Alzheimer's disease. *Neurosurgery, 15*, 514–518.

Hardy, J., Adolfsson, R., Alafuzoff, I., Bucht, G., Marcusson, J., Nyberg, P., Perdahl, E., Wester, P., and Winblad, B. (1985). Transmitter deficits in Alzheimer's disease. *Neurochemistry International, 7*, 545–563.

Haroutunian, V., Barnes, E., & Davis, K. L. (1985). Cholinergic modulation of memory in rats. *Psychopharmacology, 87*, 266–271.

Hunt, R. D., Cohen, D. J., Shaywitz, S. E., & Shaywitz, B. A. (1982). Strategies for study of the neurochemistry of attention deficit disorder in children. *Schizophrenia Bulletin, 8*, 236–252.

Jenkins, J. S., Mather, H. M., & Coughlan, A. K. (1982). Effect of desmopressin on normal and impaired memory. *Journal of Neurology and Neurosurgical Psychiatry, 45*, 830–831.

Judge, M. E., & Quartermain, D. (1982). Alleviation of anisomysin-induced amnesia by pre-test treatment with lysine vasopressin. *Physiology Biology and Behavior, 16*, 463–466.

Kaye, W. H., Sitaram, N., Weingartner, H., Ebert, M. H., Smallberg, S., & Gillin, J. C. (1982). Modest facilitation of memory in dementia with combined lecithin and anticholinesterase treatment. *Biological Psychiatry, 17*, 275–280.

Kesner, R. P. (1986). Neurobiological views of memory. In J.L. Martinez & R.P. Kesner (Eds.), *Learning and memory: A biological view* (pp. 399–438). Orlando: Academic Press.

Langer, D. H., Rapoport, J. L., Brown, G. L., Ebert, M. H., & Bunney, W. E. (1982). Behavioral effects of cardidopa/levodopa in hyperactive boys. *Journal of the American Academy of Child Psychiatry, 21*, 10–18.

Loullis, C. C., Bean, R. L., Lippa, A. S., Meyerson L. R., Beer, B., & Bartus, R. T. (1983). Chronic administration of cholinergic agents: Effects on behavior and calmodulin. *Pharmacology Biochemistry and Behavior, 18*, 601–604.

Michaelson, I. A., Bornschein, R. L., Loch, R. K., & Ratales, L. S. (1977). Minimal brain dysfunction hyperkinesis: Significance of nutritional status in animal models of hyperactivity. In I. Hanin & E. Usdin (Eds.), *Animal models in psychiatry and neurology* (pp. 37–49). New York: Pergamon Press.

Millichap, J. G. (1972). Neuropharmacology of hyperkinetic behavior: Response to methylpheni-date correlated with degree of activity and brain damage. In A. Vernadakis and N. Weiner (Eds.), *Drugs and the developing brain* (pp. 475–488). New York: Plenum Press.

Olton, D. S. (1984). Animal models of human amnesias. In L. R. Squire & N. Butters (Eds.), *Neuropsychology of memory* (pp. 367–373). New York: Guilford Press.

Olton, D. S. (1985). Strategies for the development of animal models of human memory impairments. In D. S. Olton, E. Gamzu, & S. Corkin, (Eds.), *Memory dysfunctions: An integration of animal and human research from preclinical and clinical perspectives* (Vol. 444, pp. 113–121). Annals of the New York Academy of Sciences.

Perry, E. K., Tomlinson, B. E., Blessed, G., Bergman, K., Gibson, P. H., & Perry, R. H. (1978). Correlation of cholinergic abnormalities with senile plaques and mental test scores in senile dementia. *British Medical Journal, 2*, 1457–1459.

Peters, B. H., & Levin, H. S. (1982). Chronic oral physostigmine and lecithin administration in memory disorders of aging. *Aging* (Vol 16, pp. 421–426). New York: Raven Press.

Pomara, N., Block, R., Moore, N., Rhiew, H. P., Berchou, R., Stanley, M., & Gershon, S. (1984). Combined piracetam and cholinergic precursor treatment for primary degenerative dementia. *IRCS Medical Science, 12*, 388–389.

Rapoport, J. L., Quinn, P. O., Bradbard, G., Riddle, K. D., & Brooks, E. (1974). Imipramine and methylphenidate treatments of hyperactive boys. *Archives of General Psychiatry, 30*, 789–793.

Rapoport, J. L., Quinn, P. O., Copeland, A. P., & Burg, C. (1976). ACTH 4–10: Cognitive and behavioral effects in hyperactive, learning disabled children. *Neuropsychobiology, 24*, 291–296.

Rapoport, J. L., Zametkin, A., Donnelly, M., & Ismond, D. (1985). New drug trials in attention deficit disorder, *Psychopharmacology bulletin, 21*, 232–236.

Rie, H. E., Rie, E., Stewart, S., & Ambuel, J. P. (1976). Effects of methylphenidate on under-achieving children. *Journal of Consulting Clinical Psychology, 44*, 250–260.

Rigter, H., Janssens-Elbertse, R., & van Riezen, H. (1976). Reversal of amnesia by orally active ACTH 4–9 analog (Org 2766). *Pharmacology Biochemistry and Behavior, 5*, 53–58.

Rigter, H., van Riezen, H., & De Wied, D. (1974). The effects of ACTH and vasopressin analogues on CO_2-induced retrograde amnesia in rats. *Physiology and Behavior, 13*, 381–388.

Robbins, T. W., & Sahakian, B. J. (1979). Paradoxical effects of psychomotor stimulant drugs in hyperactive children from the standpoint of behavioral pharmacology. *Neuropharmacology, 18*, 931–950.

Rosenthal, R. H., & Allen, T. W. (1978). An examination of attention, arousal, and learning dysfunctions of hyperactive children. *Psychological Bulletin, 85*, 689–715.

Sansone, M., Ammassari-Teule, M., & Oliverio, A. (1985). Interaction between nootropic drugs and methamphetamine on avoidance acquisition but not on locomotor activity in mice. *Archives internationales de Pharmacodynamie et de Therapie, 278*, 229–235.

Sara, S. J., & David-Remacle, M. (1974). Recovery from electroconvulsive shock-induced amnesia by exposure to the training environment: Pharmacological enhancement by piracetam. *Psychopharmacology, 36*, 59–66.

Schneck, M. K. (1983). Nootropics. In B. Reisberg (Ed.), *Alzheimer's disease: The standard reference* (pp. 362–368). New York: Free Press.

Shaywitz, B. A. (1976). On minimal brain dysfunction: Dopamine depletion. *Science, 194*, 452–453.

Shaywitz, B. A., Cohen, D. J., & Bowers, M. B. (1977). CSF monoamine metabolites in children with minimal brain dysfunction-Evidence for alteration of brain dopamine. *Journal of Pediatrics, 90*, 67–71.

Shaywitz, B. A., Yager, D., & Klopper, J. H. (1976). Selective brain dopamine depletion in developing rats: An experimental model of minimal brain dysfunction. *Science, 191*, 305–308.

Sildergeld, E. K., Goldberg, A. M. (1974). Lead induced behavioral dysfunction: An animal model of hyperactivity. *Experimental Neurology, 42*, 146–157.

Smith, R. C., Vroulis, G., Johnson, R., & Morgan, R. (1984). Comparison of therapeutic response to long term treatment with lecithin versus piracetam plus lecithin in patients with Alzheimer's disease. *Psychopharmacology Bulletin, 20,* 542–545.

Soininen, H., Koskinen, T., Helkala, E. L., Pigache, R., & Riekkinen, P. J. (1985). Treatment of Alzheimer's disease with synthetic ACTH 4–9 analog. *Neurology, 35,* 1384–1351.

Squire, L. R. (1986). Mechanisms of memory. *Science, 232,* 1612–1619.

Taylor, E. (1985). Drug treatment. In M. Rutter & L. Hersov (Eds.), *Child and adolescent psychiatry: Modern approaches* (pp. 780–793). Oxford: Blackwell.

Thal, L. J., Fuld, P. A., Masur, D. M., & Sharpless, N. S. (1983). Oral physostigmine and lecithin improve memory in Alzheimer's disease. *Annals of Neurology, 13,* 491–496.

Tinklenberg, J. R., & Thornton, J. E. (1983). Neuropeptides in geriatric psychopharmacology. *Psychopharmacology Bulletin, 19,* 198–211.

Van Ree, J. M., Hijman, R., Jolles, J., & De Wied, D. (1985). Vasopressin and related peptides: Animal and human studies. *Progress in Neuro-psychopharmacological and Biological Psychiatry, 9,* 551–559.

Vincent, G., Verderese, A., & Gamzu, E. (1985). The effects of aniracetam (Ro 13-5057) on the enhancement and protection of memory. In D. S. Olton, E. Gamzu, & S. Corkin (Eds.), *Memory dysfunctions: An integration of animal and human research from preclinical and clinical perspectives* (Vol 444, pp. 489–491). Annals of the New York Academy of Sciences.

Weingartner, H. (1984). Psychobiological determinants of memory failures. In L. R. Squire & N. Butters, (Eds.), *Neurophysiology of memory* (pp. 203–212). New York: Guilford Press.

Weingartner, H. (1985). Models of memory dysfunctions. In D. S. Olton, E. Gamzu, & S. Corkin (Eds.), *Memory dysfunctions: An integration of animal and human research from preclinical and clinical perspectives* (Vol 444, pp. 359–369). Annals of the New York Academy of Sciences.

Weingartner, H., Rapoport, J. L., Ebert, M. H., & Caine, E. D. (1980). Cognitive processes in normal and hyperactive children and their response to amphetamine treatment. *Journal of Abnormal Psychology, 89,* 25–37.

Weiss, G., Kruger, E., Danielson, U., & Elman, M. (1975). Effect of long-term treatment of hyperactive children with methylphenidate. *Journal of the Canadian Medical Association, 112,* 158 164.

Wettstein, A. (1983). No effect from double-blind trial of physostigmine and lecithin in Alzheimer's disease. *Annals of Neurology, 13,* 210 212.

Wettstein, A., & Spiegel, R. (1984). Clinical trials with cholinergic drug RS 86 in Alzheimer's disease (AD) and senile dementia of the Alzheimer type (SDAT). *Psychopharmacology, 84,* 572–573.

Whitehouse, J. M. (1964). Effects of atropine on discrimination learning in the rat. *Journal of Comparative and Physiological Psychology, 57,* 13–15.

Wilsher, C. R. (1986). The nootropic concept and dyslexia. In The Orton Dyslexia Society (Eds.), *Annals of dyslexia* (pp. 118–137). Baltimore: The Orton Dyslexia Society.

Wolkowitz, O. M., Tinklenberg, J. R., & Weingartner, H. (1985). A psychopharmacological perspective of cognitive functions: I. Theoretical overview and methodological considerations. *Neuropsychobiology, 14,* 88–96.

Wolthius, L. (1971). Experiments with UCB 6215, a drug which enhances acquisition in rats: Its effects compared with those of methamphetamine. *European Journal of Pharmacology, 16,* 283–297.

Wurtman, R. J., Masil, S. G., & Reinstein, D. K. (1981). Piracetam diminishes hippocampal acetylcholine levels in rats. *Life Sciences, 28,* 1091–1093.

Model Experiments of Attention Deficit Disorder and Hyperkinetic Syndrome

Trevor Archer
Department of Behavioral
Pharmacology
AB Astra Alab Södertälje
and Department of Psychology
University of Umeå

Terje Sagvolden
Institute of Neurophysiology
University of Oslo

The chapters dealing with model experiments of Attention Deficit Hyperactivity Disorder (ADHD), by definition requiring a psychobiological approach, encompass a vast collection of procedures, techniques and methods that may, either explicitly or implicitly, be applicable eventually as animal models for the derivation of new therapeutic agents. A basic assumption is that model experiments must bear an intimate relationship to animal models of disease states, whether it be as the initial step or as the consequence of the problem, and the two terms will henceforth be used synonymously. Animal models involve some need to describe/understand the etiology of the disease state. In the following chapters it is noted that the terms animal models and model experiments are used analogously to some extent. The chapters by Sagvolden and coworkers, Archer, Beninger and Thompson offer us animal experiments that address either the hyperactive state or the cognitive deficiencies or both. In ADHD research there appears to be a special requirement for the consideration of the animal models (in the loose usage of the term) currently available. A few of these models (and/or model experiments) are described in the following chapters by Terje Sagvolden and coworkers, Trevor Archer, Richard Beninger and Richard Thompson while the chapter by Bennett and Sally Shaywitz (this volume, see chapters on clinical aspects) centers upon the more fundamental issues of how, when and where to apply an animal model of ADHD. This latter orientation leads to questions regarding both the generality and sufficiency of the procedures described by the former three chapters. Thus, it seems fruitful and necessary to review other animal models of the ADHD syndrome.

Hilakivi (1987) has reviewed evidence relating the ADHD syndrome to prenatal alcohol exposure. The children of mothers that abused alcohol during pregnancy were found to show marked problems of academic achievement together with enhanced activity and attentional deficits (Shaywitz, Cohen, & Shaywitz, 1980). These behavioral alterations appear to be related, at least in part, to disturbances of the sleep cycles of the developing infant (e.g., Havlicek & Childiaeva, 1982; Rosett, Snyder, Sander, Lee, Cook, Weiner, & Gould, 1979). Animal studies of alcohol administration, prenatally or neonatally, have demonstrated a wide range of abnormalities, several of which may be clearly relevant to the ADHD problem including instrumental learning deficits (Martin, Martin, Sigman, & Radow, 1977; Shaywitz, Klopper, & Gordon, 1976), hyperactivity (Bond & DiGiusto, 1976, 1977; Branchey & Friedhoff, 1976; Martin, Martin, Sigman, & Radow, 1978), a failure to suppress responding in both taste-aversion and passive avoidance learning (Riley, Lochry, & Shapiro, 1979), an enhanced perseveration of responding (Riley, Lochry, Shapiro, & Baldwin, 1979), and increased aggressive behavior (Krsiak, Elis, Pschlova, & Masek, 1977). These and other findings concerning behavioral dysfunctions of the Fetal Alcohol Syndrome (FAS) offer tempting reasons for sometimes to link some aspects of the ADHD condition to maternal alcohol consumption during pregnancy (Shaywitz, 1978).

A wide range of other chemical agents have been shown to produce some or all of the components of the ADHD syndrome. These include the Fetal hydantoin syndrome (Hanson & Smith, 1976) as a result of prenatal exposure to the hydantoin anticonvulsants, methyl mercury poisoning (Takeuchi & Matsumoto, 1969), maternal cigarette smoking (Denson, Nanson, & McWatters, 1975; Dunn, McBurney, Ingram, & Hunter, 1977; Saxton, 1978), prenatal heroin and/or methadone (Wilson, Desmond, & Verniand, 1973). The barbiturates are both used and abused quite excessively such that among pregnant women 24 to 32 percent use sedative drugs including barbiturates (Forfar & Nelson, 1973). Long-lasting functional defects have been obtained as a result of barbiturate usage (Wolf & Forsythe, 1978). In animal studies, learning deficits as well as other behavioral changes have been shown in rats prenatally treated with barbiturates (Murai, 1966). Behavioral and neurochemical changes have been obtained in mice following prenatal phenobarbital exposure (Middaugh, Santos, & Zemp, 1975; Middaugh, Thomas, Simpson, & Zemp, 1981). Pick and Yanai (1982) tested juvenile mice that had been exposed to phenobarbital, either prenatally or neonatally, on a spontaneous alternation task and in the acquisition of the Olton radial arm maze task. Whereas only neonatal treatments produced deficits in the spontaneous alternation task, both neonatal and prenatal treatment disrupted acquisition in the radial arm maze. The effects of the prenatal barbiturate exposure on behavioral paramenters could be of consequence in the quest for suitable animal models. In the light of all the evidence involving some dopaminergic involvement in hyperactivity it should be noted that prenatal exposure to phenobarbital induces long-term supersensitivity of the postsynaptic dopamine receptors, as shown by both an increase in locomotor activity and a decrease in apomorphine induced hypothermia (Feigenbaum & Yanai, 1982; Yanai, 1983).

In any consideration of animal models for the ADHD syndrome, the role of environmental variables is important for both a theoretical and clinical perspective and is possibly integral to an adequate foundation for assuming construct validity. Several sources of environmental influence upon the fetus and neonate have been investigated. Similar to rats subjected to neonatal dopamine lesions in the forebrain, the offspring of pregnant mice subjected to immobilization restraint stress is retarded in the development of startle onset, cliff avoidance and air-righting (free-fall) behavior (Barlow, Knight, & Sullivan, 1978). The administration of diazepam during immobilization was found to counteract the behavioral effect seen in the offspring (Barlow, Knight, & Sullivan, 1979). Prenatal/neonatal hypoxia induced both learning impairments and hyperactivity in the offspring (Hedner, Lundborg, & Engel, 1979; Martin & Becker, 1971; McCullough & Blackman, 1976). Over crowding and/or malnutrition during the preweaning stage of development led also to learning deficits accompanied by neurochemical changes (e.g. Leathwood, Bush, Berent, & Mauron, 1974; Shoemaker & Wurtman, 1971). Finally, a variety of functional and neuromorphological changes have been observed following rearing in enriched or deprived environments (e.g., Cummins & Livesey, 1979; Rosenzweig, Bennet, & Diamond, 1972). The differential rearing effect appears to be defined by marked hyperactivity and learning deficits in the deprived/isolated rats (Einon & Morgan, 1976; Sahakian, Robbins, & Iversen, 1977). Furthermore, an important interaction between environment rearing conditions and perinatal drug effects has been obtained whereby the offspring of imipramine treated dams were fostered at birth to non-treated females (Coyle & Singer, 1975 a, b). At weaning, the pups were separated into differential rearing conditions, enricher or deprived. Imipramine offspring and control offspring raised in the deprived condition were equally poor in maze learning performance whereas, of the animals raised in the enriched environment, the imipramine offspring performed significantly worse than control offspring. For the control condition, the enriched group performed significantly better than the deprived group. A similar interaction between environmental rearing conditions and 6-hydroxydopamine induced noradrenaline lesions has been obtained (O'Shea, Saari, Pappas, Ings, & Stange, 1983). Thus, taken together the effects of drug treatments and environemental manipulations during prenatal and postanatal development serve to illustrate a major necessity for achieving construct validity in animal models of the ADHD syndrome, i.e., the multidimensional approach.

REFERENCES

Barlow, S. M., Knight, A. F., & Sullivan, F. M. (1978). Delay in postnatal growth and development of offspring produced by maternal restraint stress during pregnancy in the rat. *Teratology*, *18*, 211–218.

Barlow, S. M. Knight, A. F., & Sullivan, F. M. (1979). Prevention by diazepam of adverse effects of maternal restraint stress on postnatal development and learning in the rat. *Teratology, 19,* 105–110.

Bond, N. W., & DiGiusto, E. L. (1976). Effects of prenatal alcohol consumption on open-field behaviour and alcohol preference in rats. *Psychopharmacology, 46,* 163–168.

Bond, N. W., & DiGiusto, E. L. (1977). Prenatal alcohol consumption and open-field behaviour in rats: Effects of age at time of testing. *Psychopharmacology, 52,* 311–312.

Branchey, L., & Friedhoff, A. J. (1976). Biochemical and behavioral changes in rats exposed to alcohol in utero. *Annals New York Academy of Sciences, 273,* 328–330.

Coyle, I. R., & Singer, G. (1975). The interaction of post-weaning housing conditions and prenatal drug effects on behaviour. *Psychopharmacology, 41,* 237–244. (a)

Coyle, I. R., & Singer, G. (1975). The interactive effects of prenatal imipramine exposure and postnatal rearing conditions on behavior and histology. *Psychopharmacology, 44,* 253–256. (b)

Cummins, R. A., & Livesey, P. J. (1979). Enrichment-isolation, cortex length and the rank order effect. *Brain Research, 178,* 89–98.

Denson, R., Nanson, J. L., & McWatters, M. A. (1975). Hyperkinesis and maternal smoking. *Canadian Psychiatric Association Journal, 20,* 183–187.

Dunn, H. G., McBurney, A. K., Ingram, S., & Hunter, C. M. (1977). Maternal cigarette smoking during pregnancy and the child's subsequent development. II. Neurological and intellectual maturation to the age of 6 1/2 years. *Canadian Journal of Public Health, 68,* 43–50.

Einon, D. F., & Morgan, M. J. (1976). A critical period for social isolation in the rat. *Developmental Psychobiology, 10,* 123–132.

Feigenbaum, J. J., & Yanai, J. (1982). Lessened sensitivity to apomorphine hypothermia is associated with postsynaptic dopaminergic receptor supersensitivity. Proceedings of the 13th CINP Congress, p. 211.

Forfar, J. O., & Nelson, M. N. (1973). Epidemiology of drugs taken by pregnant women: Drugs that may affect the fetus adversely. *Clinical Pharmacological Therapeutics, 14,* 632–642.

Hanson, J. W., & Smith, D. W. (1976). Fetal hydantoin syndrome. *Lanset, i,* 692.

Havlicek, V., & Childiaeva, R. (1982). Sleep EEG in newborns of mothers using alcohol. In E. E. Abel (Ed.), *Fetal alcohol syndrome* (Vol. 2, pp. 149–178). Boca Raton: CRC press.

Hedner, T., Lundborg, P., & Engel, J. (1979). Brain biochemical and behavioral changes in 4 week old rats after neonatal oxygen deprivation. *Pharmacology, Biochemistry and Behavior, 10,* 647–650.

Hilakivi, L. (1987). Adult alcohol consumption after pharmacological intervention in neonatal sleep. *Acta Physiologica Scandinavica, 130 (Suppl. 562),* 1–58.

Krsiak, M., Elis, J., Poschlova, N., & Masek. (1977). Increased aggressiveness and lower brain serotonin levels in offspring of mice given alcohol during gestation. *Journal of Studies of Alcohol, 38,* 1696–1704.

Leathwood, P., Bush, M., Berent, C., & Mauron, J. (1974). Effects of early malnutrition on Swiss white mice: Avoidance learning after rearing in large litters. *Life Sciences, 14,* 157–162.

Martin, J. C., & Becker, R. F. (1971). The effects of maternal nicotine absorption or hypoxic episodes upon appetitive behavior of rat offspring. *Developmental Psychobiology, 4,* 133–147.

Martin, J. C., Martin, D. C., Radow, B., & Sigman, G. (1976). Growth, development and activity in rat offspring following maternal drug exposure. *Experimental Aging Research, 2,* 235–251.

Martin, J. C., Martin, D. C., Sigman, G., & Radow, B. (1977). Offspring survival, development, and operant performance following maternal alcohol consumption. *Developmental Psychobiology, 10,* 435–446.

Martin, J. C., Martin, D. C., Sigman, G., & Radow, B. (1978). Maternal ethanol consumption and hyperactivity in cross-fostered offspring. *Physiological Psychology, 6,* 362–365.

McCullough, M. L., & Blackman, D. E. (1976). The behavioral effects of prenatal hypoxia in the rat. *Developmental Psychobiology, 9,* 335–342.

Middaugh, L. D., Santos, III, C. A., & Zemp, J. W. (1975). Phenobarbital during pregnancy alters operant behavior of offspring in C57BL/6J mice. *Pharmacology, Biochemistry and Behavior, 3*, 1137–1139.

Middaugh, L. D., Thomas, T. N., Simpson, L. W., & Zemp, J. W. (1981). Effect of prenatal maternal injections of phenobarbital on brain neurotransmitters and behavior of young C57 mice. *Neurobehavioral Toxicology and Teratology, 3*, 271–275.

Murai, N. (1966). Effect of maternal medication during pregnancy upon behavioral development of offspring. *Tohuku Journal of Experimental Medicine, 89*, 265–272.

O'Shea, L., Saari, M., Pappas, B. E., Ings, R., & Stange, K. (1983). Neonatal 6-hydroxydopamine attenuates the neural and behavioral effects of enriched rearing in the rat. *European Journal of Pharmacology, 92*, 43–47.

Pick, C. G., & Yanai, J. (1982). Changes in hippocampal behaviors after early exposure to phenobarbital in mice. *Proceedings of the International Society for Developmental Neuroscience*, p. 182.

Riley, E. P., Lochry, E. A., & Shapiro, N. R. (1979). Lack of response inhibition in rats prenatally exposed to alcohol. *Psychopharmacology, 62*, 47–52.

Riley, E. P., Lochry, E. A., & Shapiro, N. R., Baldwin, J. (1979). Response perseveration in rats exposed to alcohol prenatally. *Pharmacology, Biochemistry and Behavior, 10*, 255–259.

Rosett, H. L., Synder, P. A., Sander, L. W., Lee, A., Cook, P., Weiner, L., & Gould, J. (1979). Effects of maternal drinking on neonate state regulation. *Developmental and Medical Child Neurology, 21*, 464–473.

Rosenzweig, M. R., Bennett, E. L., & Diamond, M. C. (1971). Chemical and anatomical plasticity of brain: Replications and extensions. In J. Gaito (Ed.), *Macromolecules and behaviour* (pp. 205–278). New York: Appleton Century Crofts.

Sahakian, B. J., Robbins, T. W., & Iversen, S. D. (1977). The effects of isolation on exploration in the rat. *Animal Learning and Behavior, 5*, 193–198.

Saxton, D. W. (1978). The behaviour of infants whose mothers smoke in pregnancy. *Early Human Development, 24*, 363–369.

Shaywitz, B. A. (1978). Fetal alcohol syndrome: An ancient problem rediscovered. *Drug Therapy, 10*, 53–60.

Shaywitz, B. A., Klopper, J. H., & Gordon, J. W. (1976). A syndrome resembling minimal brain dysfunction in rat pups born to alcoholic mothers. *Pediatric Research, 10*, 451.

Shaywitz, S. E., Cohen, J. D., & Shaywitz, B. A. (1980). Behaviour and learning difficulties in children of normal intelligence born to alcoholic mothers. *Journal of Pediatrics, 96*, 978–982.

Shoemaker, W. J., & Wurtman, R. J. (1971). Perinatal undernutrition: Accumulation of catecholamines in rat brain. *Science, 171*, 1017–1019.

Takeuchi, T., & Matsumoto, H. (1969). Minamata disease of human fetuses. In H. Nishimura & R. W. Miller (Eds.), *Methods for teratological studies in experimental animals and man* (pp. 280–283). Tokyo: Igaku Shoin.

Wilson, G. S., Desmond, M. M., & Verniand, V. M. (1973). Early development of infants of heroin-addicted mothers. *American Journal of Disorders of Children, 126*, 457–462.

Wolf, S. M., & Forsythe, A. (1978). Behavioral disturbance, phenobarbital and febrile seizures. *Pediatrics, 61*, 728–731.

Yanai, J. (1983). Possible dopaminergic involvement in early phenobarbital induced changes in sensitivity to barbiturate. *Teratology, 27*, 86 A.

Results from a Comparative Neuropsychological Research Program Indicate Altered Reinforcement Mechanisms in Children with ADD

Terje Sagvolden
Boaz Wultz
Edvard I. Moser
May-Britt Moser
Institute of Neurophysiology
University of Oslo

Lars Mørkrid
Dikemark Hospital,
Solberg, Norway

Children with ADD (attention deficit disorder) are supposed to have attention problems as one of their main dysfunctions: They often fail to finish things started on, often do not seem to listen, are easily distracted, have problems with concentrating on tasks requiring sustained attention, have difficulty with sticking to play activities; and, they may be hyperactive (APA, 1987; for reviews see Rutter; Taylor; Shaywitz & Shaywitz; Sergeant & van der Meere, all this volume).

When testing attention in ADD children and other children with attention problems, it is important that the hyperactivity factor does not interfere. As argued by Douglas (1983), ADD children may respond poorly to material presented automatically at a pace set by the experimenter, but not when they are able to set their own pace. Thus, a self-paced task where the subject itself determines when stimuli are going to be presented might be a better choice than an experimenter-paced one like e.g., the Continuous Performance Test of Rosvold, Mirsky, Sarason, Bransome, and Beck (1956). We have for some time been using self-paced vigilance tasks based on methods from operant psychology (Sagvolden & Saebø, 1986; Sagvolden, Saebø, Schiørbeck, & Rugland, 1985; Sagvolden, Wultz, Mørkrid, & Saebø, 1987; Saebø, 1984). The operant vigilance tasks originally described by Jim Holland (Holland, 1958) seem to be capable of measuring sustained attention and should thereby differentiate between ADD children and other children. These tasks were designed according to the principles of operant psychology (Ferster & Skinner, 1957; Harnad & Catania, 1984). During the last few years there have been a considerable number of studies of human operant behavior, partly further developing Holland's tasks (e.g., Matthews, Shimoff, Catania, & Sagvolden, 1977). These methods not only allow within-session replications, but make it possible to use the same type of tests for describing both human and animal behavior. In other words, these methods allow us to test aspects of human behavioral dysfunctions on animal models, a feature that in general is important for the advancement of medical knowledge.

The main problem addressed in the present chapter is an analysis of aspects of the sustained-attention behavior of ADHD children. These results are contrasted with results from relevant comparative, model experiments. Some of our previous results showed systematic within-session increases in the baseline response rate in ADHD children, but not in controls (Sagvolden et al., 1985, 1987; Sagvolden & Saebø, 1986; Saebø, 1984). Such changes might indicate that basic reinforcement mechanisms are altered in some ADHD children. Therefore, the reinforcement schedule controlling the presently used vigilance task (see below) was varied in a systematic fashion.

When discussing ADHD children's performance on tasks involving a continuous (CRF or 100%) schedule of reinforcement for choosing correct answers versus the performance on a partial (50%) reinforcement schedule, Virginia Douglas concluded that there seems to be a "production problem" more than a cognitive problem since the hyperactive children had no difficulty as long as their behavior was reinforced according to an optimal schedule (Douglas, 1983, p. 316). In other words, there seems to be an output problem more than an input or attention problem in these children.

Gorenstein and Newman (1980) as well as Virginia Douglas and her co-workers (Douglas, 1983; Douglas & Parry, 1983; Douglas & Peters, 1979; Parry & Douglas, 1983) have presented evidence that when compared to other children's behavior, reinforcers may work differently on ADHD children's behavior. ADHD children seem to be unusually sensitive both to the presence of reward and to the loss of anticipated rewards, have problems with "delayed gratification", an impaired ability to inhibit "impulsive responding", as well as "an impaired ability to modulate arousal or alertness to meet situational demands" (Parry & Douglas, 1983, p. 328). Such problems may warrant experimental analyses of reinforcement mechanisms.

CLINICAL DATA

Methods

Subjects are illustrative cases selected from a population of normal children and children with various attention problems. One, R.E., an ADD child, was a 14 1/2 year old boy that scored more than 47 points on the Norwegian translation of the Swanson DSM III Check List. The maximum score is 69. He had a low sympathetic arousal as indicated by a low skin-conductance baseline level and few spontaneous electrodermal responses. Another ADD child was H.H., a 8 1/2 year old somewhat *anxious* boy with a high sympathetic arousal. He was rated as having attention problems and being hyperactive by both of his parents (Swanson DSM III score > 42), but not to the same degree by two of his teachers (Swanson DSM III score > 18). The results of these children will be compared to the ones of a child with phenylketonuria (Følling's disease; A.S., a 12 year old girl) and a control child without any neurological or psychiatric problems (E.S., a 12 1/2 year old boy). The reason for presenting single cases, not group data, is that ADD children constitute a heterogeneous group and we feel that individual data at present might be more informative.

Procedure. The child was seated in front of a 11" monochrome, Sony CVM-111E TV monitor. There were two small, white push buttons between the child and the monitor. These buttons were situated on a slightly slanted, blue panel without any text or cues. The distance between the buttons was 10 cm. Curtains and various laboratory equipment surrounded the child. The entire experiment was controlled by a microcomputer.

The child was told that she/he was going to play a video game and that she/he was out in a forest where there were some trees (Fig. 1). Now and then a monster, a "troll", would appear among the trees. The monster's face, consisting of two periods, one comma, one hyphen and two parentheses, was then pointed out to the child. It was told that when the monster appeared, an alarm had to be sounded, then the monster would explode. Further, the child was told that the picture on the screen would disappear when the game started and that she/he had to find out her-/himself how to get the picture to reappear on the screen and how to sound the alarm. "Thus", the child was told, "your task is two-fold: look for the monster when you think it has returned; and, sound the alarm if it has".

Notice that the stimulus presentation was paced by the child itself and that the child had to find out what the two push buttons in front of her/him were used for. In addition, the monster was quite difficult to detect, not only because its face consisted of few and simple elements, but also because the child was not told that the monster may appear at different places on the screen and that each stimulus presentation was brief, only about 0.2 s.

Baseline/"Continuous Reinforcement (CRF) Schedule." The test had altogether five different parts. Figure 1 shows a flow chart of the baseline condition occurring as the first, third and fifth of these parts. Presses on the right button (P1, not marked as such on the panel) were recorded as "observing responses". If less than 30 s (T < 30 sec) had elapsed since the start of the session, stimulus 1 was shown for approximately 0.2 s following an observing response. Stimulus 2, with the monster somewhere on the screen, was presented for approximately 0.2 s if more than 30 s had elapsed. After the monster had been presented, the child had to find out how to sound the alarm. Most children localized the alarm button (P2) quite easily. The monster "exploded" (stimulus 3) and the response was recorded as an "alarm response". The response was recorded as a "false" alarm if the child pressed P2 before the 30-s fixed interval had elapsed. Notice that since each presentation of any of the stimuli on the screen was very brief, the actual stimulus was not present when the child sounded the alarm.

"Fixed-Interval (FI) Schedule." Previously, we used the baseline condition only (Sagvolden et al., 1985, 1987; Sagvolden & Saebø, 1986; Saebø, 1984) and found that ADD children sometimes showed systematic within-session increases in the rate of observing responses. These results made us suspect that some kind of basic reinforcement mechanism might be altered in ADD children. In order to test whether such mechanisms were changed, we had to vary systematically stimuli that may be reinforcing, "rewarding", and thereby maintaining the child's button-pressing behavior, "vigilance".

The possibility that every presentation on the screen, not only the ones where the monster exploded, reinforced ADD children's behavior while only the ex-

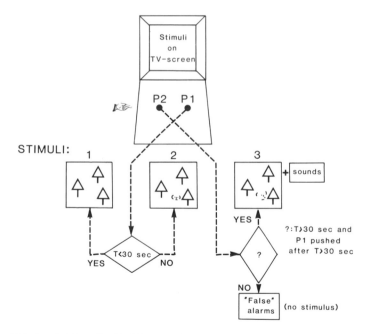

FIG. 1.   A "flow chart" of the events in the procedure. During the "continuous reinforcement schedule", and only then, activation of push button P1 leads to the presentation of stimulus 1 if less than 30 s of the interval had elapsed. If more than 30 s had elapsed when P1 was operated, stimulus 2 was presented. P1 activations were recorded as "observing responses". For the case of the "continuous reinforcement" and "fixed interval" schedules, stimulus 3 was always presented when P2 was activated after a presentation of stimulus 2. The same was the case in 8 of the 14 intervals the "variable interval" schedule was in effect. P2 activations were recorded as "alarm responses" when stimulus 2 had just been presented and "false" alarms, when not. For details see text.

plosions reinforced the control children's behavior, is the reason why the baseline condition is called the "CRF schedule" even if the "monster" only appeared after 30 s. The "FI" schedule, the second part, was introduced following the four initial intervals with the baseline condition (first part): Observing responses produced no stimulus on the screen until 30 s had elapsed, i.e., stimulus 1 was never presented following observing responses in any of the 30-s intervals. Similarly, "false" alarms had no consequence, but were recorded. When the 30-s fixed interval had elapsed, stimulus 2 was presented, i.e., there was always a monster somewhere, and an alarm response produced an "explosion" (stimulus 3). The "FI" schedule was run for 14 intervals. Then followed four intervals with the "CRF" schedule for reestablishment of the baseline (the third part).

"Variable-Interval (VI) Schedule." The fourth part of the test investigated the reinforcement value of stimuli associated with the monster's explosion. During this part, just as when the "FI" schedule was in effect, observing responses produced no stimulus until 30 s had elapsed. Then stimulus 2 was presented. But, in difference from the "FI" schedule, the alarm button worked in only 8 of the 14 intervals. This schedule, tentatively called the "VI" schedule, was run for 14 intervals. Finally followed the last four intervals, the fifth part, with the "CRF" schedule for reestablishment of the baseline.

Timing of the observing responses were recorded as a function of fixed-interval segment. Responses occurring within 5 s of the last explosion of the monster were placed in the first bin, the ones occurring between 5 and 10 s since the last explosion within the second 5-s bin and so on. Because the different conditions need some time to change the behavior under control, the first four intervals with the "CRF" schedule have been deleted from the figure, the same is the case with the four initial "FI" and "VI" intervals. Note that the responses actually producing stimulus 3, with the monster, occurred in a seventh bin. The timing of these responses are not shown because this final bin by necessity will vary from interval to interval and therefore is difficult to compare with the other bins always lasting 5s.

Results and Discussion

In general, the behavior of the two hyperactive children differed both from that of the normal child and from that of the child with phenylketonuria. The results presented below are from the second and the third sessions.

During his second session, the control child emitted few observing responses during the "CRF", "FI" and "VI" conditions (Fig. 2A). The alarm responses were few, adequate and well timed. With the exception of the "VI" condition, the few observing responses were placed late in the intervals (Fig. 3A). Thus, there is no reason to suspect that the "CRF" and "FI" conditions affected the behavior of this child differently, i.e., acted as different schedules of reinforcement. In this connection it should be added that not all control children time their responses equally well.

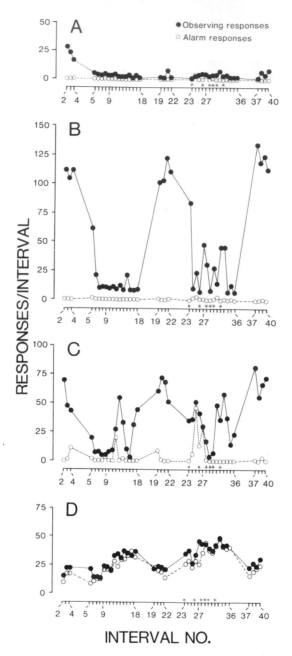

FIG. 2.　Number of observing and alarm (real as well as false) responses as functions of 60-s intervals. Asterisks (*) mark the intervals where stimulus 3 was unavailable during the "variable interval schedule". The "continuous reinforcement schedule" operated during intervals 2-4, 19-22 and 37-40, the "fixed interval schedule" during intervals 5-18 and the "variable interval schedule" operated during intervals 23-36. Child A was a normal control child, B and C ADD children and D a child with phenylketonuria.

The first of the ADD children, R.E., had a low sympathetic arousal and was clinically judged hyperactive. The results shown are from his third session. Therefore this child had had more time to learn the task than the control child above. The pattern of emitting observing responses was quite different: The overall rates of observing responses, especially the "CRF" rates, were considerably higher than those of the control child above (Fig. 2B). There were pronounced differences between the three schedules: Responding sky-rocketed during the "CRF" condition, but fell drastically when the "FI" condition was in effect. Although the "VI" condition produced more responding than the "FI" condition, these rates were lower than the "CRF" rates. Figure 3B shows that this child did not time his responses. On face value, one could perhaps suspect that timing was a too difficult discrimination for this child, but there were almost no false alarms (Fig. 2B), indicating that there was no profound attention deficit!

The second hyperactive, somewhat anxious, ADD child, H. H., had a high sympathetic arousal. Figure 2C shows that the results from this child's third session were more variable than that of the previous ADD child. But, also in this case, the rates of observing responses were quite high, especially during "CRF" conditions. Also this child showed no time discrimination (Fig. 3C). Except for the "VI" condition, false alarms were almost nonexistent, again indicating no profound discrimination deficit in an ADD child.

In general, it seems as if the stimuli that reinforced the ADD children's button pressing ("vigilance" behavior) were different from the ones maintaining the control child's behavior. His behavior was almost not affected by the presentations of stimulus 1; the child waited for the appearance of the monster (stimulus 2). The ADD-children's response rates were affected substantially by the presentations of stimulus 1. Thus, simply flashing stimuli on the screen acted as a reinforcer in much the same way as getting the monster to explode. Notice that when the opportunity to shoot the monster was changed to a "VI" schedule, the behavior became quite variable. Just like the first ADD child, the second showed few indications of an attention deficit. The lack of time discrimination during the "CRF" condition may be explained as a schedule effect rather than a discrimination problem: all stimuli presented on the screen had reinforcing properties, not only the explosion. Similarly, the reduced response rates during the "FI" and "VI" condition may be schedule-induced.

In order to show the behavior of a child with pronounced attention problems, the results of the control and the ADD children are contrasted with those of children with phenylketonuria, Følling's disease, which could have substantial attention problems. In our experience, some of these children need considerable help for getting started on the task and show substantial discrimination problems. Figure 2D shows that even during the second session, this child did not discriminate between the observing button and the alarm button. This discrimination was just as poor during the "CRF" conditions, where there was response feedback (observing responses produced stimulus 1 while false alarms produced no stimu-

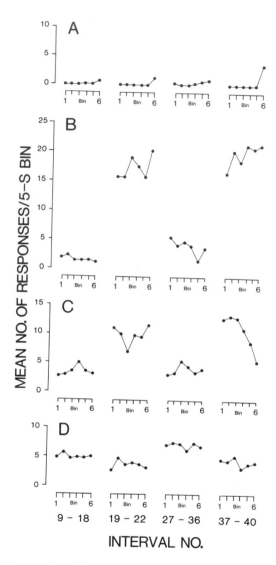

FIG. 3. Mean number of observing responses in consecutive 5-s bins of the 30-s interval. Intervals 9-18 were from the "fixed interval schedule", 19-22 and 37-40 from the second and third presentations of the "continuous reinforcement schedule" and 27-36 from the "variable interval schedule". For details see text. Child A was a normal control child, B and C ADD children and D a child with phenylketonuria.

lus), as during the "FI" and "VI" conditions where there is no such feedback. There were no obvious schedule effects and no evidence of timing (Fig. 3D).

MODEL STUDIES

We have initiated a comparative neuropsychological research programme in order to advance our understanding of clinical results. There are several reasons for this, including better control over environmental factors influencing the behavior, good control over the rearing conditions including feeding regimes, and more time available for testing than is possible with humans. When investigating effects of pharmacological interventions like drug therapy, model studies have several advantages: it is possible not only to study a large range of doses in a systematic and balanced fashion, but to do this both in experimental and control groups. Further, it is difficult to do neurochemical assays on human beings, and one is forced to deal with often less reliable and less valid indirect measures. Direct neurochemical interventions and assays are possible with animals. However, the most important advantage is probably that an animal model provides a simpler system than a human being. One could aim for modelling only one or a few of the symptoms at a time rather than all. Such a strategy will give results that probably are easier to understand than those one might get if there was a model that had all the problems of ADD children (but cf. Shaywitz, 1976).

In the present context, the following problems are among the ones that need to be modelled: fixed-interval operant behavior, effects of reinforcers, interactions between reinforcers, drug effects on behavior, hyperkinesis; and, the central-nervous substrate(s) for these effects and for hyperkinesis. The models needed for the different problems are obviously not the same.

Fixed-Interval Behavior

In the video game presented in the first part of this chapter, fixed-interval schedules were programmed in two ways: one without any response feedback during the 30-s interval (the "true" FI) and one with response feedback that could possibly act as a second reinforcer (the "CRF" schedule). It is therefore important to analyze behavioral characteristics of FI schedules.

A reinforcer acts not only on responses immediately preceding it; but, although to a lesser degree, retroactively on responses emitted earlier (Catania, 1971). The retroactive effect on a particular response decreases by increasing interval between this response and the reinforcer. This phenomenon is called the delay-of-reinforcement gradient. The characteristic fixed-interval scallop frequently seen may be a behavioral expression of the delay gradient (Dews, 1960, 1962). Catania, Sagvolden and Keller (1988) show that the retroactive effect of a reinforcer, the delay gradient, is terminated by the reinforcer immediately preceding it (Fig. 4, upper).

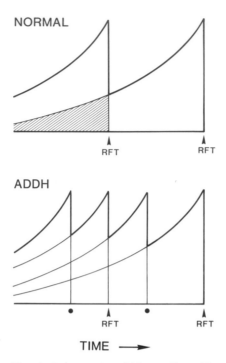

FIG. 4. *Upper:* Hypothetical truncation of delay gradients. The two reinforcers (RFT) both act retroactively. The early reinforcer cuts off the tail of the delay gradient of the later reinforcer (shaded area). *Lower:* Scheduled reinforcers (at arrows) and hypothetical extra reinforcers (dots) occurring in ADD children (and possibly SHR rats). Each reinforcer cuts off the tail of the delay gradient of the later reinforcer (not shown, but cf. above). The total area below the heavy curves are larger than the one in the upper half of the figure, implying that more responding is maintained as a consequence of the increased number of reinforcers.

Methylphenidate Effects on FI Behavior

Methylphenidate (Ritalin) may be one of the most effective drugs for treating the problems of ADHD children (Gittelman Klein & Abikoff, this volume). Although d-amphetamine as well as methylphenidate facilitate release and reduce reuptake of dopamine and noradrenaline from the synaptic cleft (Chiueh & Moore, 1975; Ferris, Tang, & Maxwell, 1972), the pharmacological actions of methylphenidate are different from those of d-amphetamine (Braestrup, 1977; Shaywitz & Shaywitz, this volume). Psychomotor stimulants can be grouped into two types: the ''d-amphetamine group'' and the ''methylphenidate group''. Among other things, the former decreases brain DOPAC (a dopamine metabolite) while the latter increases DOPAC (Braestrup, 1977). The behavioral effects are different as well. Both d-amphetamine and methylphenidate have response stimulatory actions. While the d-amphetamine effect depends on newly synthesized dopamine, the methylphenidate effect is qualitatively different and may act through a reserpine-sensitive pool of catecholamines (Scheel-Krüger, 1971; Thornburg & Moore, 1973). In addition, it seems that the reinforcing properties of amphetamines and methylphenidate are different (Mithani, Martin-Iverson, Phillips, & Fibiger, 1986). The latter authors suggest that methylphenidate "may produce its rewarding effects via actions on presently unspecified, non-dopaminergic neuronal systems" (p. 251).

In rats, low doses of methylphenidate are response stimulatory, e.g., they increase responding throughout the entire fixed interval (Sagvolden, Jenssen, & Brorson, 1983; Sagvolden, Slåtta, & Arntzen, 1988; Fig. 5). One way of interpreting such results is that the low doses of this drug lengthen the delay gradient and/or enhance the reinforcing effects of the reinforcer. Somewhat higher doses produce rate-dependent (rate-related) responding (Dews, 1958; Lyon & Robbins, 1975; Robbins, Jones, & Sahakian, this volume; Sagvolden et al., 1983; Fig. 5). Rate-related effects mean that the behavioral consequences are related to the frequency of behavior during control conditions: low response rates increase and high response rates decrease following administration of psychomotor stimulants. Following even higher doses, stereotyped and perseverative responding dominate. The rate of correct responses starts to fall when perseverations begin to appear (Sagvolden et al., 1988). A clinical consequence of such a result is that one ought to be aware that reductions in (hyper)activity may be caused by interferences from stereotyped behavior rather than reflecting any "improvement" of behavior.

Fixed-interval schedules are quite appropriate for testing rate-related effects since responding changes systematically from a low frequency, or rate, to a high one over and over again within each session. Such analyses are important because even in cases where the rate-related effects are pronounced, the effects of the drug on the total response output might be quite small (Fig. 5).

Eckerman, Segbefia, Manning, and Breese (1987) used a mixed FI 60-s EXTinction 120-s procedure in order to test rate-related effects as well as "time discrimination" following methylphenidate and following d-amphetamine injections. "Time discrimination" is reflected by the point in time when the maximum ("peak") responding occurred during the unsignalled EXT component. Just as in our studies (Sagvolden et al., 1983, 1988), the response-stimulatory effect early in the interval was the most pronounced rate-related effect. Further, Eckerman and co-workers showed that the peak responding in the EXT 120-s component occurred earlier in the interval following the drug injections than following no injection or vehicle. These results are in accordance with the lengthened-delay-gradient hypothesis.

It seems that the behavioral effects of the drug change by increasing dose (Sagvolden et al., 1983, 1988). Such results might mean that brain structures are affected in a qualitatively different manner by low, medium and high doses. Porrino

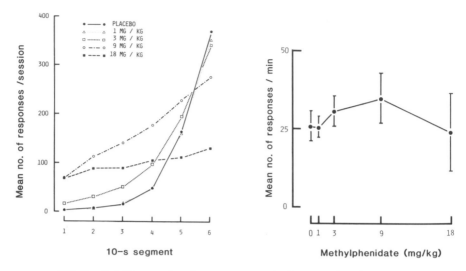

FIG. 5. *Left:* Mean number of responses per session in consecutive 10 s-segments of the 60-s fixed interval schedule as functions of methylphenidate dose. *Right:* Mean ± s.e.m. number of responses per minute as a function of methylphenidate dose.

and Lucignani (1987) measured brain energy metabolism following several doses ranging from 1.25 to 15 mg/kg of methylphenidate in rats. The local cerebral glucose utilization showed dose-dependent changes that differed between the different brain structures: following low and medium, but not high, doses, increased metabolism was recorded only in the olfactory tubercle and the nucleus accumbens septii; in contrast, inreasing doses elevated metabolism in the substantia nigra pars reticulata, the entopeduncular and the subthalamic nuclei. The increased metabolism in nucleus accumbens following low and medium doses are of particular significance for the lengthened-delay-gradient hypothesis since this brain structure seems to play a primary role in mediating the rewarding effects of amphetamine (Carr & White, 1986; Lyness, Friedle, & Moore, 1979; Taylor & Robbins, 1984, 1986), although this might be different for the case of methylphenidate (cf., Mithani et al., 1986).

Hyperkinetic Rats

Spontaneously hypertensive rats (SHR) may be used as an animal model of hyperkinesis. Wistar-Kyoto rats (WKY) of the same progenitor serve as controls. These rats were developed by Okamoto for research on hypertension (Okamoto & Aoki, 1963). SHR are pervasively hyperactive, but only when they have been in the novel environment for some time (Knardahl & Sagvolden, 1979; Moser, Moser, Wultz, & Sagvolden, 1988; Sagvolden, Schiørbeck, & Rugland, 1985). When first encountering a novel situation, these rats may even be hypoactive (Fig. 6, lower). Their hyperactivity is stimulus-induced and of obvious advantage in some tasks (Knardahl & Sagvolden, 1982).

In general, SHR have reduced brain weight and reduced brain volume when compared to WKY (Nelson & Boulant, 1981). There are histological differences as Golgi-Cox impregnations show a different dendritic arborization in the noradrenergic locus coeruleus in SHR compared to WKY (Felten, Rubin, Felten, & Weyhenmeyer, 1984). There are neurochemical differences as dopamine β-hydroxylase activity (reflecting noradrenaline synthesis) in locus coeruleus and hypothalamus are reduced in SHR compared to WKY, although tyrosine β-hydroxylase activity (reflecting both dopamine as well as noradrenaline synthesis) in both dopaminergic (nucleus caudatus) and noradrenergic (locus coeruleus) regions are similar in SHR and WKY (Nagatsu et al., 1976). Substantially less binding of the α_2 agonist (3)para-aminoclonidine has been noted in locus coeruleus of SHR compared to WKY (Gehlert & Whamsley, 1987). A nonsignificant reduction in binding was measured in the hippocampus as well. Further, Low, White-horn and Hendley (1984) found reduced noradrenergic uptake rates in the hippocampal synaptosomes of SHR. Also, unpublished results from our labora-

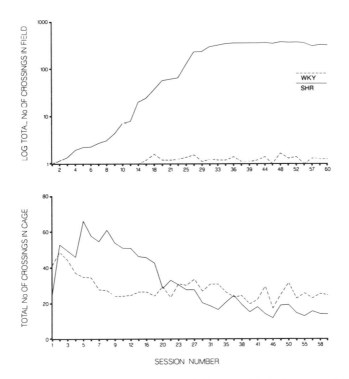

FIG. 6. Total number of crossings in the field (top) and in the home cage (bottom) of a two-compartment (free-exploration) open field across sessions for SHR and WKY rats.

tory (Wultz, Moser, Sagvolden, Moser, & Archer, in prep.) indicate that the SHR has a reduced noradrenaline content in the hippocampus ($t(12) = 2.31$, $p < 0.04$, two-tailed), but not in the neocortex or the hypothalamus ($ts(12) < 0.75$, $ps > 0.40$). This might be a little surprising because neocortex, like the hippocampus, receives its noradrenergic afferents exclusively from locus coeruleus (Moore & Bloom, 1979). In accordance with the anatomical and neurochemical results, Olpe, Berecek, Jones, Steinmann, Sonnenburg and Hofbauer (1985) found reduced spontaneous firing rates in the SHR locus coeruleus. The strain differences in noradrenergic characteristics are of clinical relevance as altered functions of this neurotransmitter may be central in the genesis of ADHD (cf., Shaywitz & Shaywitz, this volume; and the changed sympathetic activities of the ADHD children described above).

SHR have reduced hippocampal noradrenaline functions. Following Scoville and Milner's (1957) observations, it is generally assumed that damage of temporal-lobe structures could cause severe learning dysfunctions. Learning-like changes in hippocampal synapses, long-term potentiation (LTP), were originally shown by Terje Lømo (Lømo, 1966; Bliss & Lømo, 1973; for a recent review, see Andersen & Hvalby, 1986). Reduced monoamine levels, serotonin and to some extent also noradrenaline, affect LTP (Andersen & Hvalby, 1986). Skelton, Scarth, Wilkie, Miller and Phillips (1987) showed that both appetitively-motivated operant behavior as well as LTP changed the efficacy of synaptic transmission from the perforant path to the granule cells of the hippocampal dentate gyrus in rats. It is therefore not unreasonable to suggest that reduced levels of hippocampal neurotransmitters such as noradrenaline (and dopamine) in SHR could somehow interfere with learning processes.

Dopamine input to the hippocampus has not been shown until recently and the input is believed to be concentrated to its dorsal regions (Itoh, Fukumori, & Suzuki, 1984). To the extent that the low dopamine concentrations measured in our study permit generalization, they suggest that also dopamine levels are reduced in the SHR hippocampus ($t(12) = 2.30$, $p < 0.04$, two-tailed). The dopamine levels in neocortex and hypothalamus were similar in the two strains. Unfortunately, the dopamine levels in nucleus accumbens were not measured.

Fixed-Interval Behavior of Hyperkinetic Rats

Methylphenidate therapy alleviates some of the problems of ADHD children (Gittelman Klein & Abikoff; Shaywitz & Shaywitz, both this volume). A logical step is now to investigate how this drug acts on SHR behavior. Methylphenidate might normalize some of the SHR behavior by elevating their reduced catecholamine levels.

SHR show somewhat elevated response rates on a so-called "simple" FI 60-s schedule (Rugland & Schiørbeck, 1984; Sagvolden, Schiørbeck, & Rugland, 1985;

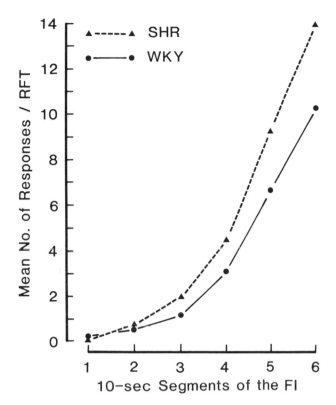

FIG. 7. Mean number of lever presses per 60-s fixed interval in SHR and WKY rats.

Fig. 7). Whatever the source, the pervasive hyperactivity of SHR has to be taken into account when interpreting such results. The reason for this is that the curve describing SHR behavior may have two components: One consisting of generally increased responding, a second consisting of a changed slope. A steeper FI scallop may reflect a shorter-than-normal delay gradient. One important consequence of this is that only responding rather late in the interval would be maintained by the programmed reinforcer. Responding early in the interval may then be maintained by other, unscheduled reinforcers which would disrupt the normally regular behavior maintained by FI schedules. Thus, one way of detecting such extra reinforcers would be inspections of cumulative records. These records show more erratic responding with multiple "breaks and runs" in SHR than in WKY rats' behavior (Fig. 8). Such extra reinforcers would, per definition, increase the total response output and might not easily be detected without instruments like cumulative recorders. The extra reinforcers may give rise to behavior that might be misinterpreted as discrimination/ attention problems. The latter point is of special interest in relation to the suggestion by Sergeant and van der Meere

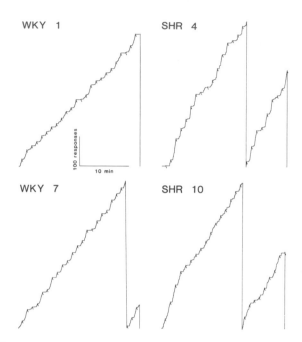

FIG. 8.   Representative cumulative records showing the entire sessions of two
SHR (nos. 4 and 10) and two WKY control rats (nos. 1 and 7). Lever presses move
the pen a small step upwards. Reinforcements are marked by short diagonal strokes.
Vertical lines correspond to the resetting of the pen after 500 responses.

(this volume) that the seemingly impaired attention of ADHD children may be
due to malfunctioning motor energizing mechanisms and the results from the video
game showing that the two ADD children had grossly elevated response rates
during the "CRF" conditions compared to the "FI" condition.

Methylphenidate affects SHR and WKY FI behavior differently. In Figure 9,
the surface representing the control rats' behavior twists and becomes parallel
to the z (segment) axis at lower doses than the surface describing the SHR behavior. This means that SHR are less sensitive to the drug than WKY are. Response
stimulation is seen in both groups following low doses. The lack of a "paradoxical" effect of the drug is in accordance with current clinical knowledge (Kløve;
Rutter, both this volume). Clinically, SHR's reduced sensitivity to methylphenidate could mean that a response stimulatory effect, and possibly a lengthening
of the delay gradient, could be obtained with higher doses than is the case with
the controls.

The Behavior of Hyperkinetic Rats "Improves"
Following Methylphenidate Administration, But
There is No "Paradoxical" Effect

The results from another study (Sagvolden, Rugland, & Schiørbeck, unpublished)
used a two-component multiple FI 60-s EXTinction schedule where reinforcers

could be obtained only when the house light was on (the FI component), but not when the light was off (the EXT component). Figure 10 shows that, when unmedicated, SHR differentiated poorly between the two components signalled by light on and light off! This indicates either a severe attention deficit or, alternatively, that other, unscheduled reinforcers contribute to the control of the hyperactive rats' behavior, i.e., that reinforcement mechanisms are altered in these rats. Following 1 to 6 mg/kg methylphenidate, responding during the EXT component virtually disappeared in the SHR although the characteristic poor differentiation between schedule components was unaltered in drug-free sessions run in between drug sessions. Following 1 mg/kg, the behavior of the two groups was quite similar. WKY rats started to leverpress during the EXT component when they were given 3 or 6 mg/kg methylphenidate. A pronounced response-stimulatory effect was seen in the control animals following 6 mg/kg. When 9 mg/kg was administered, both groups' behavior was quite stereotyped. Just like the results in Figure 9, this study shows that, by and large, methylphenidate changes the behavior of SHR and WKY in the same way. The main difference is that SHR's behavior is less sensitive to methylphenidate than WKY rats' behavior. Clinically, it is important to notice that if this study had used saline and 6 mg/kg only, the effect might easily have been misinterpreted as "paradoxical": response stimulation in the WKY and "improved performance" without response stimulation in SHR following 6 mg/kg.

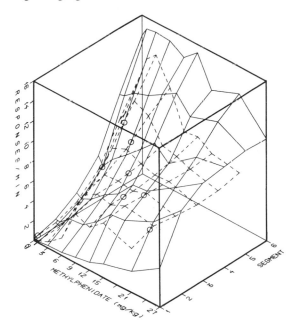

FIG. 9.   Number of water-reinforced responses in SHR (continuous lines) and in WKY rats (dashed lines) in a three-dimensional plot as functions of 10-s segments of the fixed interval and methylphenidate dose.

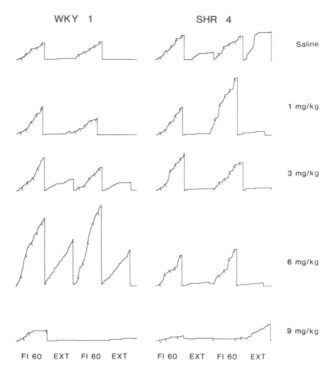

WKY 1   SHR 4

Saline

1 mg/kg

3 mg/kg

6 mg/kg

9 mg/kg

FI 60   EXT   FI 60   EXT   FI 60   EXT   FI 60   EXT

FIG. 10.   Representative cumulative records showing the entire sessions of one SHR (no. 4) and a WKY (no. 1) rat. The schedule used was a multiple fixed interval 60 s with houselight on (FI 60) extinction with houselight off (EXT). The records shows effects of various doses of methylphenidate. The magnification and details are the same as in Figure 8.

Effects of Methylphenidate on Hyperkinetic Rats' Exploratory Behavior

The two-compartment (free-exploration) open field described by Knardahl and Sagvolden (1979) may be used for studying general behavioral effects of reduced central noradrenaline levels. Behaviors recorded in the field seem to reflect active exploration by approaching novel stimuli, whereas activity in the cage, particularly the frequency of rearings, are indicative of another, qualitatively different, kind of exploration where the rat orients toward the distant stimuli without leaving the safe home cage (Moser et al., 1988). SHR actively explore by the former strategy, whereas WKY mostly use the latter strategy (Fig. 6). On a stable-state baseline, systematic tests of methylphenidate-induced behavior were undertaken (Wultz et al., in prep). d-Amphetamine administration produces a large stimulatory effect especially on rearing (Sanberg, Henault, Hagenmeyer-Hauser, & Russell, 1987). Similarly, our results show large stimulatory effects of 1 to 9 mg/kg doses of methylphenidate on ambulation and rearing. WKY rearings in the cage increased by 200% (Fig. 11). A stimulatory effect following the same doses is observed in the SHR as well, but in these animals the effect as measured on rearings in the field, is only about 70% (Fig. 12). This agrees with findings showing that amphetamine-induced locomotor activity is attenuated in the SHR (Hynes, Langer, Hymson, Pearson, & Fuller, 1985). Since exploratory behavior may be under the control of noradrenergic neurons (Berridge & Dunn, 1987), these results do not necessarily indicate an effect mediated by dopamine.

Effects of Neurochemical Lesions on Hyperkinetic Rats' Exploratory Behavior and Reactivity to Methylphenidate

The possible role of the previously described noradrenergic differences between SHR and WKY animals' behavioral differences and differential reactivity to methylphenidate was investigated by DSP4-induced depletion of central noradrenaline (Wultz, Moser, Sagvolden, Moser, & Archer, in prep.). DSP4 (N-(2-chloroethyl)-N-ethyl-2-bromobenzylamine) is a neurotoxin which selectively depletes central noradrenergic projections, particularly those originating in the locus coeruleus (Ross, 1976; Archer, this volume). Peripheral noradrenergic neurons recover within 2 weeks (Archer, Øgren, Johansson, & Ross, 1982). In our study, behavioral testing was resumed 2 weeks after the neurotoxic intervention. The biochemical results confirmed that the depletion was selective. Noradrenaline was heavily depleted ($ts(11) > 3.6$, $ps < 0.004$, two-tailed), particularly in the ne-

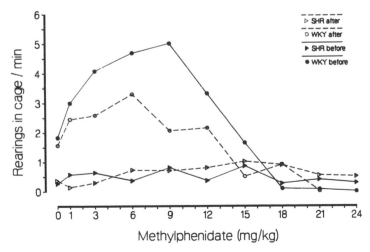

FIG. 11.   Effects of methylphenidate on rearings in the cage of a 2–compartment open field before and after neurotoxic noradrenergic lesions (DSP4) in SHR and WKY rats.

ocortex and the hippocampus, the two main projection areas of locus coeruleus noradrenergic neurons. Dopamine levels were left untouched in all areas except in the hippocampus of control rats, where some reduction in dopamine content was seen, a result that is difficult to evaluate and might be spurious due to the normally low dopamine levels in this structure.

The neurotoxic lesion did not alter non-drugged rearings in the cage in WKY (Fig. 11), only rearings in the field in SHR (Fig. 12). But the stimulatory effect following low to medium doses of methylphenidate was attenuated in both groups. This attenuation seems to be most pronounced in the WKY, in which the pre-lesion stimulatory effect of the drug appears to have been larger. Rearings were particularly sensitive to the intervention. In the WKY, the stimulatory effect following methylphenidate is only about half of what it was before.

The attenuation of the methylphenidate-induced stimulatory effect indicates that some of this effect is mediated by ascending noradrenergic projections. This might be quite general for psychomotor stimulants. DSP4 treatment produces a similar attenuation of d-amphetamine-induced increase in rearings (Archer, Fredriksson, Jonsson, Lewander, Mohammed, Ross, & Søderberg, 1986) and in locomotion (Bruto, Beauchamp, Zacharko, & Anisman, 1984). In addition, following low doses of d-amphetamine, locomotion was attenuated by 6-OHDA-lesions of either the dorsal noradrenergic bundle or locus coeruleus (Archer et al., 1986; Mohammed, Danysz, Øgren, & Archer, 1986). This does not mean, however, that dopamine is of no importance in the control of activity induced by psychomotor stimulant drugs (for reviews see, Archer; Beninger; Normile, Altman, & Gershon; Robbins et al.; Seiden, Miller, & Heffner, all this volume). Most likely, noradrenaline and dopamine control somewhat different functions (see Robbins, 1984).

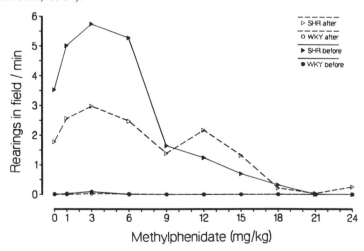

FIG. 12.   Effects of methylphenidate on rearings in the field of a 2–compartment open field before and after neurotoxic noradrenergic lesions (DSP4) in SHR and WKY rats.

AN ALTERED-DELAY OF REINFORCEMENT
HYPOTHESIS FOR SOME ADHD BEHAVIOR

Repeatedly, it has been suggested that some of the problems of ADD children may be linked to malfunctioning catecholaminergic systems (see e.g., Wender, 1971; Shaywitz & Shaywitz, this volume; Shaywitz, Shaywitz, Cohen, & Young, 1983). There are now several lines of evidence suggesting that output rather than input mechanisms might be malfunctioning in the ADHD child. Sergeant and van der Meere (this volume) report thorough and systematic investigations of the input mechanisms. Their findings were not as predicted by an attentional-process dysfunction, rather, it turned out, these children suffer from a disorder in the energetical regulation mechanisms of motor control. Further, Robbins and co-workers (this volume) argue that changes in attention may be secondary to response processes. Similarly, Beninger (this volume) hints that reinforcement mechanisms might be altered. Previously, Virginia Douglas and her co-workers have presented evidence that reinforcers may work differently on ADHD children's compared to other children's behavior (Douglas, 1983; Douglas & Parry, 1983; Parry & Douglas, 1983). She suggested that the primary effect of stimulant medication on hyperactive children's behavior might be to decrease ''the impact of immediate reward on their behavior'' (Douglas, 1983, p. 322).

Thus, it seems worthwhile to analyze reinforcement mechanisms in ADHD children. Reinforcers act retroactively on the behavior preceding the reinforcer (Catania, 1971). This retroactively-acting reinforcing effect, the delay gradient, decays as a function of time. Catania et al. (1988) have shown that the retroactive effect is terminated by the reinforcer preceding the present (Fig. 4). This interactive effect between reinforcers, combined with the shape of the delay gradient, predicts that response output will be a monotonically increasing, negatively accelerated function of the rate of reinforcement (Catania et al., 1988; Catania & Reynolds, 1968). The most parsimonious explanation of the hyperactivity of ADHD would be that their behavior is maintained by an unusually high density of reinforcement. In Figure 4, the increased reinforcement effect in ADHD is illustrated by the increased total area under the ADHD curves compared to the normal curves. Thus, the reason for the increased reinforcement effect is not that each reinforcer has a larger effect, but that there might be more reinforcers acting on their behavior. These extra reinforcers will cut the tail of the delay of reinforcement gradient of the ordinary reinforcers and thereby isolate behavior occurring before the extra reinforcer from the influence of the programmed reinforcer (cf. the cumulative records in Fig. 8 showing erratic responding in SHR). Relevant to this argument is the observation that these children are not good at accepting delayed gratification (Douglas, 1983; Douglas & Parry, 1983; Parry & Douglas, 1983). According to the present analysis, this may be due to putative extra reinforcers acting on other behavior than the intended. Similarly, these children have problems whenever they have to delay their responding as is the case when the behavior is maintained by differential reinforcement of low response rates (DRL schedules, see Douglas, 1983).

The behavior of the ADHD child will depend on the availability of extra reinforcers, not on the schedule itself. In the present investigation there were lots of stimulus presentation on the monitor during the CRF condition, but not during the "FI" or "VI" conditions. In other experimental investigations this situation may be different. In the tasks discussed by Douglas (1983) involving a CRF (100%) schedule of reinforcement for choosing correct answers versus a partial (50%) schedule, the ADD children had problems with the partial reinforcement schedule rather than the CRF schedule.

Responses have to be present in order for reinforcers to change their probabilities. This means that there should be little or no hyperactivity the first time the child encounters a situation. As the probability of the behavior is changed by reinforcement, the behavior may take the form of hyperactivity if ambulation happens to be reinforced. Such a process, involving a higher than normal number of reinforcers, predicts that the behavior occurring may at times get frequencies totally out of proportion. The behavioral results of altered reinforcement processes should be quite variable because which behavior that happen to be reinforced may to some degree be a random process. Thus, the prevalence of the (secondary) symptoms of ADD depends on which responses happen to occur and be reinforced.

According to the altered-reinforcement hypothesis, increased impulsivity is a behavioral manifestation of an increased number of reinforcers: if stimuli ordinarily not having reinforcement properties start to control behavior at times not expected by other people, the behavior might be perceived as increased distractability and impulsivity and be misinterpreted as the result of an attention deficit. Thus, the altered reinforcement hypothesis explains among other things the lack of hyperactivity in novel situations, the increased distractability, the increased impulsivity and the hyperactivity seen in various combinations in ADD children as secondary to altered reinforcement mechanisms. It even explains why the symptoms should be highly variable.

Pharmacological treatment strategies of ADD have included the use of d-amphetamine and methylphenidate (Ritalin) as well as other compounds (for a review see Gittelman Klein & Abikoff, this volume). Low doses of methylphenidate seem to affect reinforcement mechanisms by increasing the reinforcing properties of the scheduled reinforcer and thereby lengthening the delay gradient of the scheduled reinforcers (Sagvolden, Slåtta, & Arntzen, 1988). It is conceivable that increased reinforcer effects might be one of the mechanisms behind the therapeutic effect of methylphenidate.

Rachel Gittelman Klein and Howard Abikoff (this volume) argue that a combination of methylphenidate treatment and behavioral therapy is the most effective treatment strategy for the problems of the ADD child. The altered-reinforcement hypothesis would accommodate these results the following way: ADD children have inborn neurochemical, probably catecholaminergic, changes.

These changes modify the characteristics of stimuli in such a way that more stimuli get reinforcing properties. The reinforcers will change the long-term probabilities of the various responses in the person's behavioral repertoire. Central-stimulant therapy may normalize the reinforcing properties of stimuli, but the previous learning history, including changed probabilities of some responses, will not be altered by the medication. Although these probabilities may be changed temporarily as side effects of the drug therapy (see Robbins, Jones, & Sahakian, this volume), permanent effects can best be obtained by behavioral therapy reversing the earlier learning history. Each of these therapies reduce some of the child's problems, but the best effect should be obtained by having them operating synergistically (see also the final chapter of the present volume). Other psychological therapies not reversing the learning history should not have the same effect because it is not simply a question of simply "understanding" one's own behavior.

CONCLUSION

We still have a long way to go before the riddles of ADD and related disorders are solved. However, the explosive development within the neurosciences is promising as at least some pieces of the puzzle seem to fall in place. In the future, there is reason to believe that model experiments on animals will be of utmost importance because one is then able to study specific aspects of behavior, neurochemistry, neuropharmacology etc., in organisms and systems that are simpler than humans.

In the future one might have to look for defective reinforcement mechanisms possibly linked to catecholaminergic systems that are not in proper balance with other neurotransmitter systems. Such a view may explain many of the characteristics of ADD, and at the same time put these in new perspectives. This disorder might perhaps be called RD ("reinforcement disorder"). The main diagnostic criterion should be altered reinforcement mechanisms, secondary behavioral criteria may be the same as the ones used for ADD. The altered-reinforcement hypothesis may be submitted to experimental testing. Presently, the reigning attention deficit hypothesis does not seem to stand experimental testing and we need alternatives to gain more insight into the riddles of what is malfunctioning in the children we now label "ADD".

REFERENCES

American Psychiatric Association (1987). *Diagnostic and Statistical Manual of Mental Disorders.* (3rd ed.-rev. ed.), Washington, DC: Author.

Andersen, P., & Hvalby, Ø. (1986). Long-term potentiation. Problems and possible mechanisms. In R. L. Isaacson & K. H. Pribram (Eds.), *The hippocampus* (Vol. 3, pp. 169–186). New York: Plenum Press.

Archer, T., Fredriksson, A., Jonsson, G., Lewander, T., Mohammed, A. K., Ross, S. B., & Søderberg, U. (1986). Central noradrenaline depletion antagonizes aspects of d-amphetamine-induced hyperactivity in the rat. *Psychopharmacology, 88,* 141–146.

Archer, T., Øgren, S.-O., Johansson, G., & Ross, S. B. (1982). DSP4-induced two-way active avoidance impairment in rats: Involvement of central and not peripheral noradrenaline depletion. *Psychopharmacology, 76,* 303–309.

Berridge, C. W., & Dunn, A. J. (1987) α_2-Noradrenergic agonists and antagonists alter exploratory behavior in mice. *Neuroscience Research Communications, 1*, 97–103.

Bliss, T. V. P., & Lømo, T. (1973). Long-lasting potentiation of synaptic transmission in the dentate area of the anaesthetized rabbit following stimulation of the perforant path. *Journal of Physiology (London), 232*, 331–356.

Braestrup, C. (1977). Biochemical differentiation of amphetamine vs. methylphenidate and nomifensine in rats. *Journal of Pharmacy and Pharmacology, 29*, 463–470.

Bruto, V., Beauchamp, C., Zacharko, R. M., & Anisman, H. (1984). Amphetamine-induced perseverative behavior in a radial arm maze following DSP4 or 6-OHDA pretreatment. *Psychopharmacology, 83*, 62–69.

Carr, G. D., & White, N. M. (1986). Anatomical disassociation of amphetamine's rewarding and aversive effects: An intracranial microinjection study. *Psychopharmacology, 89*, 340–346.

Catania, A. C. (1971). Reinforcement schedules: The role of responses preceding the one that produces the reinforcer. *Journal of the Experimental Analysis of Behavior, 15*, 271–287.

Catania, A. C., & Reynolds, G. S. (1968). A quantitative analysis of the responding maintained by interval schedules of reinforcement. *Journal of the Experimental Analysis of Behavior, 11*, 327–383.

Catania, A. C., Sagvolden, T., & Keller, K. J. (1988). Reinforcement schedules: Retroactive and proactive effects of reinforcers inserted into fixed-interval performances. *Journal of the Experimental Analysis of Behavior, 49*, 49–73.

Chiueh, C. C., & Moore, K. E. (1975). Blockade by reserpine of methylphenidate-induced release of brain dopamine. *Journal of Pharmacology and Experimental Therapeutics, 193*, 559–563.

Dews, P. B. (1958). Studies on behavior. IV. Stimulant actions of methamphetamine. *Journal of Pharmacology and Experimental Therapeutics, 122*, 137–147.

Dews, P. B. (1960). Free-operant behavior under conditions of delayed reinforcement. I. CRF-type schedules. *Journal of the Experimental Analysis of Behavior, 3*, 221–234.

Dews, P. B. (1962). The effects of multiple S⁻ periods on responding on a fixed-interval schedule. *Journal of the Experimental Analysis of Behavior, 5*, 369–374.

Douglas, V. I. (1983). Attentional and cognitive problems. In M. Rutter (Ed.), *Developmental neuropsychiatry* (pp. 280–329). New York: Guilford Press.

Douglas, V. I., & Parry, P. A. (1983). Effects of reward on delayed reaction time task performance of hyperactive children. *Journal of Abnormal Child Psychiatry, 11*, 313–326.

Douglas, V. I., & Peters, K. G. (1979). Toward a clearer definition of the attentional deficit of hyperactive children. In G. A. Hale & M. Lewis (Eds.), *Attention and cognitive development (pp. 173–247).* New York: Plenum Press.

Eckerman, D. A., Segbefia, D., Manning, S., & Breese, G. S. (1987). Effects of methylphenidate and d-amphetamine on timing in the rat. *Pharmacology, Biochemistry & Behavior, 27*, 513–515.

Felten, D. L., Rubin, L. R., Felten, S. Y., & Weyhenmeyer, J. A. (1984). Anatomical alterations in locus coeruleus neurons in the adult spontaneously hypertensive rat. *Brain Research Bulletin, 13*, 433–436.

Ferris, R. M., Tang, F. L. M., & Maxwell, R. A. (1972). A comparison of the capacities of isomers of amphetamine, deoxypipradrol and methylphenidate to inhibit the uptake of tritiated catecholamines into the rat cerebral cortex slices, synaptosomal preparations of rat cerebral cortex, hypothalamus and striatum and into adrenergic nerves of the rabbit aorta. *Journal of Pharmacology and Experimental Therapeutics, 181*, 407–416.

Ferster, C. B., & Skinner, B. F. (1957). *Schedules of reinforcement.* New York: Appleton-Century-Crofts.

Gehlert, D. R., & Whamsley, J. K. (1987). Quantitative autoradiography of alpha-2 agonist binding sites in the spontaneously hypertensive rat brain. *Brain Research, 409*, 308–315.

Gorenstein E. E., & Newman, J. P. (1980). Disinhibitory psychopathology: A new perspective and a model for research. *Psychological Review, 87*, 301–315.

Harnad, S., & Catania, A. C. (Eds.). (1984). Canonical papers of B. F. Skinner (Special issue). *The Biological Psychiatry, 22*, 126–138.

Behavioral and Brain Sciences, 7(4).

Holland, J. G. (1958). Human vigilance. *Science, 128*, 61–67.

Hynes, M. D., Langer, D. H., Hymson, D. L., Pearson, D. V., & Fuller, R. W. (1985). Differential effects of selected dopaminergic agents on locomotor activity in normotensive and spontaneously hypertensive rats. *Pharmacology, Biochemistry and Behavior, 23*, 445–448.

Itoh, K., Fukumori, R., & Suzuki, Y. (1984). Effect of methamphetamine on the locomotor activity in the 6-OHDA dorsal hippocampus lesioned rat. *Life Sciences, 34*, 827–833.

Knardahl, S., & Sagvolden, T. (1979). Open-field behavior of spontaneously hypertensive rats. *Behavioral and Neural Biology, 27*, 187–200.

Knardahl, S., & Sagvolden, T. (1982). Two-way active avoidance behavior of spontaneously hypertensive rats: Effects of intensity of discontinuous shock. *Behavioral and Neural Biology, 35*, 105–120.

Low, W. C., Whitehorn, D., & Hendley, E. D. (1984). Genetically related rats with differences in hippocampal uptake of norepinephrine and maze performance. *Brain Research Bulletin, 12*, 703–709.

Lømo, T. (1966). Frequency potentiation of excitatory synaptic activity in the dentate area of the hippocampal formation. *Acta Physiologica Scandinavica, 68*, (Suppl. 277), 128

Lyness, W. H., Friedle, N. M., & Moore, K. E. (1979). Destruction of dopaminergic nerve terminals in nucleus accumbens: Effect on d-amphetamine self-administration. *Pharmacology, Biochemistry and Behavior, 11*, 553–556.

Lyon, M., & Robbins, T. W. (1975). The action of central nervous system stimulant drugs: A general theory concerning amphetamine effects. In W. B. Essman & L. Valzelli (Eds.), *Current Developments in Psychopharmacology* (Vol. 2, pp.79–163). New York: Spectrum.

Martin-Iverson, M. T., Ortmann, R., & Fibiger, H. C. (1985). Place preference conditioning with methylphenidate and nomifensine, *Brain Research, 332*, 59–67.

Matthews, B. A., Shimoff, E., Catania, A. C., & Sagvolden, T. (1977). Uninstructed human responding: Sensitivity to ratio and interval contingencies. *Journal of the Experimental Analysis of Behavior, 27*, 453–467.

Mithani, S., Martin-Iverson, M. T., Phillips, A. G., & Fibiger, H. C. (1986). The effects of haloperidol on amphetamine- and methylphenidate-induced conditioned place preferences and locomotor activity. *Psychopharmacology, 90*, 247–252.

Mohammed, A. K., Danysz, W., Øgren, S. O., & Archer, T. (1986). Central noradrenaline depletion attenuates amphetamine-induced locomotor behavior. *Neuroscience Letters, 64*, 139–144.

Moore, R. Y., & Bloom, F. E. (1979). Central catecholamine neuron systems: Anatomy and physiology of the norepinephrine and epinephrine systems. *Annual Reviews of Neuroscience, 2*, 113–168.

Moser, M. B., Moser, E. I., Wultz, B., & Sagvolden, T. (1988). Component analyses differentiate between exploratory behavior of SHR and WKY in a free-exploration (choice) open field. (Submitted).

Nagatsu, T., Ikuta, K., Numata Y., Kato, T., Sano, M., Nagatsu, I., Umezawa, H., Matsuzaki, M., & Takeuchi, T. (1976). Vascular and brain dopamine β-hydroxylase activity in young spontaneously hypertensive rats. *Science, 191*, 290–291.

Nelson, D. O., & Boulant, J. A. (1981). Altered CNS neuroanatomical organization of spontaneously hypertensive (SHR) rats. *Brain Research, 226*, 119–130.

Okamoto, K., & Aoki, K. (1963). Development of a strain of spontaneously hypertensive rats. *Japanese Circulation Journal, 27*, 282–293.

Olpe, H. R., Berecek, K., Jones, R. S. G., Steinmann, M. W., Sonnenburg, Ch., & Hofbauer, K. G. (1985). Reduced activity of locus coeruleus neurons in hypertensive rats. *Neuroscience Letters, 61*, 25–29.

Parry, P. A., & Douglas, V. I. (1983). Effects of reinforcement on concept identification in hyperactive children. *Journal of Abnormal Child Psychology, 11*, 327–340.

Porrino, L. J., & Lucignani, G. (1987). Different patterns of local brain energy metabolism associated with high and low doses of methylphenidate - Relevance to its action in hyperactive children.

Robbins, T. W. (1984). Cortical noradrenaline, attention and arousal. *Psychological Medicine, 14*, 13–21.

Ross, S. B. (1976). Long-term effect of N-2-chloroethyl-N-ethyl-2-bromobenzylamine hydrochloride on neurons in the rat brain and heart. *British Journal of Pharmacology, 58*, 521–527.

Rosvold, H. E., Mirsky, A. F., Sarason, I., Bransome, E. D., & Beck, L. H. (1956). A continuous performance test of brain damage. *Journal of Consulting Psychology, 20*, 343–350.

Rugland, A. L., & Schiørbeck, H. K. (1984). *Spontaneously hypertensive rats (SHR) as an experimental model of behavioral hyperactivity: Effects of methylphenidate (Ritalin) on fixed-interval responding and adjunctive behaviors*. Dissertation, University of Oslo, Norway.

Sagvolden, T., Jenssen, J. R., & Brorson, I. W. (1983). Rate-dependent effects of methylphenidate (Ritalin) on fixed-interval behavior in rats. *Scandinavian Journal of Psychology, 24*, 231–236.

Sagvolden, T., Schiørbeck, H. K., & Rugland, A. L. (1985). An experimental model for behavioral hyperactivity: Effects of methylphenidate hydrochloride (Ritalin) on fixed-interval responding. *Neuroscience Letters, Supplement 22*, S264. (abstract).

Sagvolden, T., Slåtta, K., & Arntzen, E. (1988). Low doses of methylphenidate (ritalin) may alter the delay-of-reinforcement gradient. *Psychopharmacology, 95*, 303–312.

Sagvolden, T., Saebø, S., Schiørbeck, H. K., & Rugland, A. L. (1985). Ritalin effects on hyperactivity and attention. Paper presented at European Brain and Behaviour Society: Workshop on Clinical Neuropsychology. Zürich, April 9–11, 1985.

Sagvolden, T., Wultz, B., Mørkrid, L., & Saebø, S. (1987). Are changed reinforcement mechanisms the key for understanding some of the behavioral problems of children with MBD/ADD? *Behavioural Brain Research, 26*, 234–235.

Sagvolden, T. & Saebø, S. (1986). A comparative research program testing children with attention deficit disorder with hyperactivity (ADD(H)). *Behavioural Brain Research, 20*, 142–143.

Sanberg, P. R., Henault, M. A., Hagenmeyer-Hauser, S. H., & Russell, K. H. (1987). The topography of amphetamine and scopolamine-induced hyperactivity: Toward an activity print. *Behavioral Neuroscience, 101*, 131–133.

Scheel-Krüger, J. (1971). Comparative studies of various amphetamine analogues demonstrating different interactions with the metabolism of the catecholamines in the brain. *European Journal of Pharmacology, 14*, 47–59.

Scoville, W. P., & Milner, B. (1957). Loss of recent memory after bilateral hippocampal lesions. *Journal of Neurology, Neurosurgery and Psychiatry, 20*, 11–21.

Shaywitz, B. A. (1976). On minimal brain dysfunction: Dopamine depletion. *Science, 194*, 452–453.

Shaywitz, S. E., Shaywitz, B. A., Cohen, D. J., & Young, J. G. (1983). Monoaminergic mechanisms in hyperactivity. In M. Rutter (Ed.), *Developmental neuropsychiatry* (pp. 330–347). New York: Guilford Press.

Skelton, R. W., Scarth, A. S., Wilkie, D. M., Miller, J. J., & Phillips, A. G. (1987). Long-term increases in dentate granule cell responsivity accompany operant conditioning. *The Journal of Neuroscience, 7*, 3081–3087.

Saebø, S. R. (1984). *Learning in hyperactive and other children with special reference to attentional processes*. Dissertation, University of Oslo.

Taylor, J. R., & Robbins, T. W. (1984). Enhanced behavioural control by conditioned reinforcers following microinjections of d-amphetamine into the nucleus accumbens. *Psychopharmacology, 84*, 405–412.

Taylor, J. R., & Robbins, T. W. (1986). 6-Hydroxydopamine lesions of the caudate nucleus, attenuate enhanced responding with reward-related stimuli produced by intra-accumbens d-amphetamine. *Psychopharmacology, 90*, 390–397.

Thornburg, J. E., & Moore, K. E. (1973). The relative importance of dopaminergic and noradrenergic neuronal systems for the stimulation of locomotor activity induced by amphetamine and other drugs. *Neuropharmacology, 12*, 853–866.

Wender, P.H. (1971). *Minimal brain dysfunction in children*. New York: Wiley.

Neurotoxin-Induced Cognitive and Motor Activity Modifications: A Catecholamine Connection

Trevor Archer

AB Astra Alab, R&D Laboratories, S-151 85 Södertälje, and Department of Psychology, Umeå University, 902 47 Umeå, Sweden

The Attention Deficit Disorder (ADD) and hyperkinetic syndrome are manifested to varying degrees of severity by notable and indiscriminate hyperactivity, a limited attention span, low frustration tolerance and poor concentration accompanied by a high degree of distractibility and impulsiveness (APA, 1980). In DSM III, ADD is characterised by developmentally inappropriate inattention and impulsivity. Since the incidence may vary from 1 to 3 percent to 4 to 10 percent of elementary school children, there has been some considerable interest by teachers, school administrators, some parents and even physicians for effective drug therapy to alleviate the problems arising from handling these children (Wender, 1975). Current therapy includes stimulants, antianxiety and antipsychotic agents, antidepressants, antihistamines and anticonvulsants (Millichap, 1973). Indeed, a sufficient treatise on the dangers of the present status of drug therapy would require several volumes. Readers interested in the behavioral and neurobiological correlates of ADD and hyperkinetic syndrome, as well as issues relating to treatment practices, are referred to the excellent review by Oades (1987). Thus, the major problem is: If we must use drug therapy, how do we best maximise drug safety and selectivity of action and minimise deterious side-effects? how do we define and eludicate the basic mechanism of action of potentially suitable therapeutic agents? One tactic involves the use of animal models. A major requirement in the utility of animal models in psychopharmacological research is consideration of three characteristics: validity, reliability and predictability. Unlike pain or antiviral research, it is a difficult task to obtain validity for models of MBD and the present state of therapeutic alternatives does not realistically permit any analysis of predictability. Therefore, behavioral and psychopharmacological evidence concerning the reliability of four animal models of the ADD condition is considered.

ANIMAL MODELS

The animal models encompassed here include neurochemical or behavioural models.

Neurochemical Models

Four neurochemical models will be described:

Forebrain Noradrenaline Depletion. Recent proposals of NA function in learning and memory utilise some type of attentional hypothesis to describe Noradrenaline (NA) function (Robbins, Everitt, Fray, Gaskin, Carli & De La Riva, 1982). Forebrain NA depletions are most satisfactorily produced by either systemic administration of the NA neurotoxin, N-(2-chloroethyl)-N-ethyl-2-bromobenzylamine (DSP4) which causes a severe and sustained reduction of several neurochemical markers of NA function in the central nervous system (Archer, Jonsson, & Ross, 1984; Jaim-Etcheverry & Zieher, 1980; Jonsson, Hallman, Ponzio, & Ross, 1981; Ross, 1976), or bilateral microinjections of the catecholamine (CA) neurotoxin, 6-hydroxydopamine (6-OHDA) into the ascending fibers of the dorsal noradrenergic bundle (DNAB). DNAB lesions produce a most selective forebrain NA depletion of comparable severity to the DSP4 lesion (see Mason, 1981, 1983; Mason & Iversen, 1975; Mason & Iversen, 1979).

Methylazoxymethanol (MAM) Model. MAM is an antimitotic agent which, after administration to pregnant rats on Days 14 or 15, causes a marked telencephalic hypoplasia in the offspring (Fisher, Welker, & Waisman, 1972; Rabe & Haddad, 1972; Spatz & Laguer, 1968). The neurochemical evidence indicates that several brain regions are associated with a considerable hyperinnervation of monoamine and acetylcholine nerve terminals (Johnstone & Coyle, 1979, 1980; Johnstone, Grzanna, & Coyle, 1979; Matsutani, Nagayoshi, & Tsukada, 1980).

Environmental Housing Conditions and Neonatal NA Depletion. Housing and rearing conditions modulate to varying degrees both behavioral plasticity and neurochemical changes in the CNS (Diamond, Krech, & Rosenzweig, 1964; Diamond, 1967; Rosenzweig, Bennet, & Diamond, 1971; Smith, 1972). NA involvement in mediating behavioural plasticity has been demonstrated quite consistently (e.g., Kasamatsu, 1983; Kasamatsu, & Pettigrew, 1979; Kasamatsu, Pettigrew, & Ary, 1979; Horn, & McCabe, 1985) and most recently in instrumental learning tasks by O'Shea, Saari, Pappas, Inge and Stange (1983).

Neonatal 6-OHDA Induced Dopamine (DA) Depletions.   The involvement of forebrain DA neurons in cognitive functioning has been consistently demonstrated (e.g., Simon, Scatton, & Le Moal, 1980). The destruction of DA terminals in the CNS as a result of either intracerebroventricular or intracisternal neonatal microinjections of 6-OHDA caused severe and marked DA depletions in several forebrain regions (Heffner & Seiden, 1983; Shaywitz, Yager, & Kloper, 1976; Smith, Cooper, & Breese, 1973). Systemic injections of desipramine (DMI), the NA uptake inhibitor, provide an almost complete protection of NA neurons. The functional alterations, following DA depletion after neonatal 6-OHDA, are consistently induced by considerable changes in motor activity and learning performance of both juvenile and adult rats (Erinoff, MacPhail, Heller, & Seiden, 1979; Miller, Heffner, Kotake, & Seiden, 1981; Shaywitz & Pearson, 1978).

Behavioral Models

Some attempts must be made to utilise comparable behavioral procedures to those used to measure perceptual and cognitive function in children with ADD and hyperkinetic syndrome (for review, see Steinhausen & Goebel, 1985). Thus, continuous performance tasks have been used to measure attention span and performance (Thorley, 1984) and other methods for studying information processing have been applied (Naylor, Halliday, & Callaway, 1985; Rapoport, Bucksbaum, Zahn, Weingartner, Ludlow, & Mikkelsen, 1978; Weingartner, Langer, Grice, & Rapoport, 1982), although the hyperactivity condition seems to be a marked defining characteristic (Jackson & Pelton, 1978; Weiss, 1985; Weiss & Hechtman, 1979). Generally, it seems that ADD and hyperkinesis problems dissipate into adulthood but follow-ups of this type are not common (Buchsbaum, Haier, Sostek, Weingartner, Zahn, Siever, Murphy, & Brody, 1985).

Compound Stimulus Conditioning in Taste-Aversion Learning.   The utility of stimulus relations in the compound stimuli used in taste-aversion conditioning has been established in a long series of experiments (Archer, Sjöden, Nilsson, & Carter, 1979; Archer, Sjöden, & Nilsson, 1985). These compound stimuli consisted of a taste stimulus in combination with odor, housing and drinking bottle elements, all of which were novel at the time of conditioning. For the procedures described below, *latent inhibition* and *sensory preconditioning*, a taste stimulus (saccharin) and a particular type of drinking bottle (noisy bottle) were employed. These noisy bottles differed from the rats' ordinary bottles (silent bottles with 2mm apertures at the nozzles) by having 6mm apertures at the tips of the nozzles which contained two ball-bearings that caused some considerable noise each time a rat licked the tip of the nozzle.

Sensory preconditioning involves the initial unreinforced paired presentation of two stimuli (e.g., CS_1 and CS_2), and later one of the stimuli is paired with a reinforcer (the US). Still later, the response of the animal to the non-reinforced stimulus is tested. Thus, CS_1-CS_2 pairings are followed by CS_1-US pairings and the strength of the conditioning to the CS_2 tested later on.

A convenient and reliable procedure for investigating sensory preconditioning was offered by presenting saccharin, as the CS_2, in the noisy bottles, as the CS_1, during the preconditioning trials. Later, during the conditioning trials, the noisy bottles were established as an aversive stimulus through association with an illness-inducing agent, lithium chloride, the US. The sensory preconditioning of a saccharin (CS_2) aversion was then tested in the silent (normal) bottles. Latent inhibition is a useful procedure for any analysis of attentional processes (Lubow, 1965; Lubow & Moore, 1959). Within a taste-aversion paradigm a variant of the usual latent inhibition theme is provided through use of the taste stimulus and the noisy bottle. During the preexposure trials, saccharin was presented either in the novel noisy bottles or in the silent bottles. Later, during the conditioning trials, saccharin was presented in noisy bottles for all the rats and followed by lithium chloride injections. At testing, saccharin intake from the noisy bottles was measured.

Spontaneous Motor Activity.   Obviously, measures of motor activity are central to any analysis of ADD and hyperkinetic syndrome and two basic procedures were adopted: automated test boxes and a specially adapted Olton radial arm maze. Each rat was placed alone in the automated test cage (within two series of infrared beams (low and high level) and three parameters were measured: *Locomotion* counts occurred when the rats moved around the test cage horizontally, showing predominantly locomotor behavior. *Rearing* was registered when rats raised their front legs and/or rested on their haunches with the upper part of the body breaking the high level infra-red beams. *Total activity* was registered by a pick-up (mounted on a lever with a counterweight) with which the test cage was in contact. The pick-up registered all types of vibrations within the test cage, e.g. those caused by rat movements, shaking (tremors), grooming, sniffing and scratching. In a specially adapted radial arm maze each of the 8 arms (54 cm long and 10 cm wide) was divided into three units (each 18 cm long and 10 cm wide) which gave a total of 25 units (counting the central hub) for registering ambulation counts within the maze. The food cups, on the floor of the maze at the extremity of each arm, were not accessible during activity testing due to the presence of a special back wall hiding the food cup. *Ambulation* was defined as the passage of a rat's body from one unit to another. *Rearings*, when the rat raised itself onto its hindlegs, were counted and registered also. Ambulations and rearings were measured over 10-min periods on each test occasion.

Instrumental Learning Procedures.   Three maze learning techniques were used to study the acquisition of instrumental learning: the Olton radial arm maze, the Morris swim maze and the Hebb-Williams maze. The radial arm maze (Olton, Becker & Handelmann, 1979; Olton & Werz, 1978) was adopted to evaluate cognitive functions of the neonatally DA depleted rats and MAM treated rats. Forty-eight hours prior to testing all the food was removed from the rats' cages. At testing, the food cups at the extremity of each arm were exposed by removal of the false walls and a single food pellet was placed in each cup in each of the eight arms. At the start of each test, each rat was placed in the central hub and then monitored for its performance in taking all eight pellets. Two measures of performance were taken: Latency to take all eight food pellets and the number of arms visited in taking all eight pellets.

The swim maze test was performed essentially as described by Morris (1984). The maze consisted of a circular pool (diameter 140 cm) containing water to a depth of 30 cm, and a plexiglass platform that could be placed anywhere in the pool but always at a depth 1 cm below the level of the water. One day prior to testing each rat was given a swim test without the platform. At testing, on each consecutive day 5 trials were presented to each animal. For each trial, each rat was placed at the same point in the pool and allowed to swim around to find and escape from the water onto the platform. On reaching the platform each rat was allowed to remain upon it for 30 s before being placed in the water again for the next trial. After the fifth trial each animal was placed in a 'drying cage' confronted by a blow dryer which blew warm air towards it. In addition to a drawing of the swim path of each rat on each trial, two measures of performance were noted: (1) the latency to reach and climb onto the platform, (2) the number of trials on which the animal failed to reach the platform during a 65-s swimming period.

For the Hebb-Williams procedure each rat was maintained at 85 percent of free-food body weight for one week prior to testing. The task consisted of a number of different problems posed by the positioning of the walls of the labyrinth through which the rat was required to find a path from the start box to the goal box in order to receive a food pellet. Each problem in the Hebb-William maze confronted the rats with a task of varying complexity so that for each animal a particular pattern of performance was obtained over eight particular problems one of which was presented on each of eight consecutive days.

The empirical findings from the four neurochemical models are described below.

I A. *The effects of forebrain NA depletion on compound conditioning*

In the sensory conditioning experiments reliable first-order CS_2-US) conditioning (noisy bottle - lithium chloride pairings) was obtained and neither the DSP4 nor the DNAB lesions affected this phase. The test phase (see Fig 1 and 2) indicated that the sensory preconditioning of a saccharin (CS_2) aversion was established with a first-order stimulus consisting of the noisy bottle (the CS_1). Severe forebrain NA depletion, following either systemic DSP4 treatment or the 6-OHDA DNAB treatment, blocked or strongly antagonized sensory preconditioning. The demonstration of sensory preconditioning in each experiment is concluded from the occurrence of a significantly greater saccharin (CS_2) aversion by the PP groups

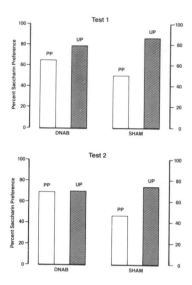

FIG. 1. Percent saccharin preference by DNAB and the sham-operated control rats during Tests 1 and 2 (testing for aversions to the CS² only). All the rats received one silent bottle with saccharin and one silent bottle with water in the 8-h saccharin preference test. The sham-operated rats received microinjections of the vehicle (0.9 % saline containing 0.02 % ascorbic acid) into the DNAB whereas DNAB rats received 6-OHDA (2 $\mu g/1\mu l$).

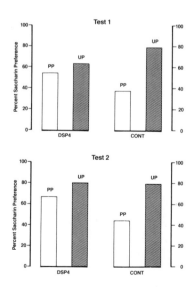

FIG. 2. Percent saccharin preference by DSP4-treated and saline- treated control rats during Tests 1 and 2 (testing aversions to CS² only). DSP4 was injected once (50 mg/Kg, intraperitoneally) two weeks prior to the start of the experiment.

292

in comparison with the UP groups. It has been shown previously that the UP control group was most critical for demonstrating sensory preconditioning (Archer & Sjödén, 1982; Rescorla, 1980; Rizley & Rescorla, 1972). Neurochemical assays indicated severe NA depletions in the forebrain regions of DNAB and DSP4 rats (Archer, Mohammed, Danysz, Järbe, & Jonsson, 1986).

In the latent inhibition experiments, the amount of latent inhibition to saccharin was shown to be dependent on the noisy bottle cue. Rats were given pre-exposure trials in which the taste stimulus, saccharin, was presented either together with the contextual cue, the novel type of drinking bottle (the noisy bottle), or in its absence (i.e. in the silent bottles). Later, during the conditioning trials, saccharin was presented in the noisy bottles followed by lithium chloride. Aversion testing to the saccharin + noisy bottle compound was performed with both single and two-bottle preference tests (see Fig. 3 and Fig. 4). In the control conditions the rats that had received the pre-exposure trials in the absence of the noisy bottle showed substantially more saccharin-aversion during testing, i.e., they demonstrated latent inhibition to saccharin dependent upon the presence or absence of the noisy bottle stimulus. We have termed this effect "context-dependent latent inhibition" (Archer, Mohammed, & Järbe, 1983, 1986; Mohammed, Callenholm, Järbe, Swedberg, Danysz, Robbins, & Archer, 1986). Biochemical analyses confirmed drastic NA depletions in the DSP4 and DNAB groups. NA depletions did not systematically alter saccharin intake but water intake was slightly decreased. The latent inhibition and sensory preconditioning experiments indi-

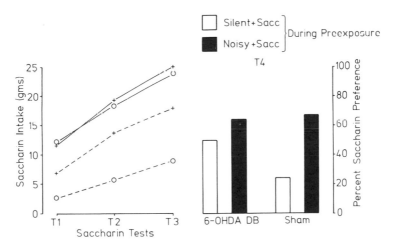

FIG. 3.   Absolute saccharin intake (Tests 1 to 3) and percent saccharin preference (test 4) by DNAB (6-OHDA DB) and the sham- operated control groups during the testing phase. +———+ = DNAB-NS; o———o = SHAM-NS; +---+ = DNAB-SS; o---o = Sham-SS. NS = both *novel* noisy bottle and *novel* saccharin during the preexposure phase, SS = *familiar* silent bottle and *novel* saccharin. At testing saccharin was presented in noisy bottles for all groups.

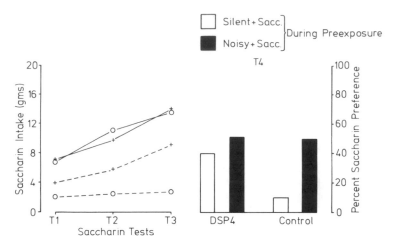

FIG. 4.   Absolute saccharin intake (Tests 1 to 3) and percent saccharin preference (Test 4) by DSP4-treated and control rats during the testing phase. +———+
= DSP4-NS; o———o = CONT-NS; +---+ = DSP4-SS; o---o = CONT-SS.

cate that NA-depletion disrupts rats' ability to attend to all aspects of a given
compound stimulus (taste-bottle) presentation.

I B. *The effect of NA depletion on amphetamine induced activity*

Differential effects upon amphetamine induced motor activity were produced
by the DSP4 and DNAB lesions. DSP4 treatment antagonized the increase in rearing behavior produced by a 2 mg/Kg dose of amphetamine, and to a lesser extent, the increase in total activity at the same dosage (see Fig. 5). Otherwise,
fairly typical dose- and time-dependent effects were obtained. No effects of the
NA depletion as a result of DSP4 treatment per se was observed. 6-OHDA induced DNAB lesions did not depress amphetamine (2 mg/Kg) stimulated rearing
behavior but rather enhanced it slightly but significantly (p < 0.05). Alternatively, the DNAB lesion antagonised the increase in locomotory behavior induced
by acute amphetamine (see Fig. 6). In this respect, note the noradrenergic involvement in methylphenida-te-treated children with ADD and hyperkinetic syndrome (Hunt, Cohen, Anderson, & Clark, 1986). The DNAB lesions did not affect
any of the three parameters of motor activity to any extent. Table 1 demonstrates the pattern of NA depletion produced by the DSP4 and DNAB lesioning techniques.

II A. *Effect of MAM treatment of compound conditioning*

Similar to NA-depleted rats, MAM treatment abolished the context dependent
latent inhibition effect in both male and female rats. No significant effects of the
treatment were observed on either water or saccharin intake, or on simple taste-

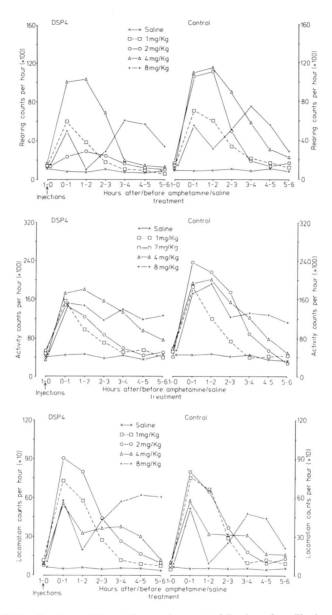

FIG. 5.   Rearing, activity and locomotion counts following a 2 mg/Kg dose of
d-amphetamine to DNAB (6-OHDA dorsal bundle) lesioned and sham-operated
rats. Each rat was exposed to the automated test cage for 60 min (1-0) prior to
d-amphetamine administration, and the motor activity measurements were continued
at the 1(0-1), 2(1-2), 3(2-3), 4(3-4), 5(4-5) and 6(5-6) h intervals following injection.

295

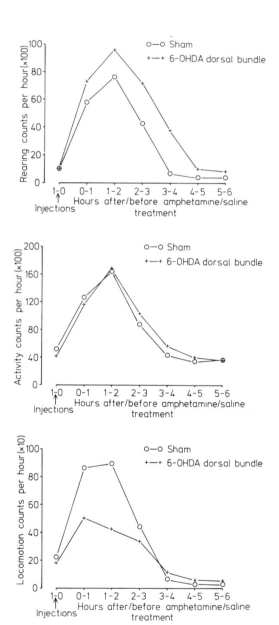

FIG. 6. Rearing, activity and locomotion counts following various doses of d-amphetamine (1-8 mg/Kg) to DSP4-treated and control rats.

Table 1.

The effects of DNAB lesions and DSP4 treatment upon catecholamine concentrations in various brain regions. Values are expressed as medians ± quartiles ng/g tissue wet weight. Vehicle, 0.9% NaCl containing 0.02% ascorbic acid. Control 0.9% NaCl.

	n	Frontal cortex		Hippocampus		Striatum	
		NA	DA	NA	DA	NA	DA
DNAB	16	38 ± 39[a]	61 ± 7	51 ± 30[a]	4.5 ± 3	6 ± 3[a]	9660 ± 1011
(%)		(9)	(115)	(11)	(100)	(17)	(102)
SHAM	16	401 ± 16	53 ± 8	476 ± 132	4.5 ± 2	36 ± 21	9442 ± 1814
DSP4	8	31 ± 16[a]	59 ± 13	23 ± 9[a]	4 ± 2	67 ± 39[b]	9563 ± 1070
(%)		(11)	(123)	(5)	(89)	(62)	(102)
Control	8	287 ± 34	48 ± 15	441 ± 47	4.5 ± 2	108 ± 51	9353 ± 981

[a] $p < 0.01$.
[b] $p < 0.05$.

aversion conditioning. The results of the latent inhibition context-dependent experiments (see Fig. 7) indicate that MAM rats (like DSP4 and DNAB rats) fail to attend to both the saccharin and the noisy bottle stimuli during either the pre-exposure phase or the conditioning, or both (Mohammed, Jonsson, Söderberg, & Archer, 1986; Mohammed, Jonsson, Sundström, Minor, Söderberg, & Archer, 1986).

II B. *Effect of MAM treatment on the acquisition of maze learning*

MAM treated rats showed a considerable impairment of acquisition performance in the swim maze task although both the MAM and control rats were observed to demonstrate an effective swimming technique using the characteristic adult swimming posture (Schapiro, Salas, & Vukovitch, 1970). The MAM treatment caused severe disruptions both in the mean daily latency to reach and climb onto the platform (A) and the number of failures (B) to reach the platform (see Fig. 8). A rank order correlation comparing the latency variable with the number of failures variable was performed: correlation coefficients were 0.98 for MAM rats and 0.97 for control rats (n = 26).

In the radial arm maze learning task, the MAM treated rats once again showed a severe impairment of acquisition, as measured by the latency to take all eight pellets and the number of arms visited by each animal in acquiring all eight pellets (see Fig. 9) over both of the tests. Table 2 demonstrates the effect of prenatal MAM-treatment on the catecholamine and metabolite levels of different brain regions.

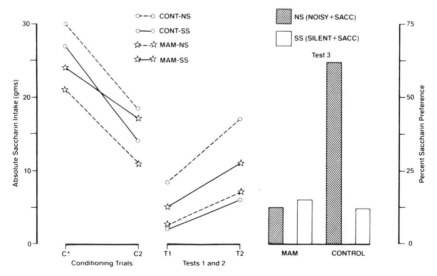

FIG. 7.   Absolute saccharin intake in noisy bottles by MAM-treated and control rats during the conditioning trials and Tests 1 and 2. Percentage saccharin preference during Test 3. o- - -o = CONT-NS; o————o CONT-SS; *- - -* = MAM-NS; *————* = MAM-SS. (For NS/SS details see above).

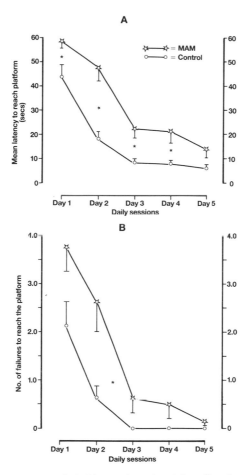

FIG. 8.   Performance of MAM-treated rats (stars) (n = 8) and controls (circles) (n = 8) on the Morris swim maze, expressed as (A) mean latency to reach platform and (B) number of failures to reach the platform.

II C. *The effect of MAM treatment on spontaneous and amphetamine/methylphenidate induced activity*

The MAM-treated rats demonstrated significantly more locomotor activity and motility (total activity) through the period of testing of spontaneous motor activity extending from 61 days of age to 106 days of age. For the rearing behavior, the MAM-treated rats did not consistently differ from the control rats until 79 days of age onwards (see Fig. 10). It should be noted that the most considerable degree of hyperactivity by the MAM rats, in comparison with controls, for all three activity parameters was shown also from 79 days of age onwards.

Table 2.
Effect of prenatal methylazoxymethanol treatment on monoamine and metabolite concentrations in brain regions. Methylazoxymethanol was administered to pregnant dams (25 mg/kg, i.v.) on gestation day 15 (see Jonsson & Hallman, 1982).

		ng/g wet weight of the tissue		
		Frontal Cortex	Striatum	Hippocampus
DA	Control	34.1 ± 3.2**	12955 ± 801**	58.9 ± 17.8
	MAM	150.7 ± 12.9	23368 ± 933	68.7 ± 6.2
	(%)	(442)	(180)	(117)
NA	Control	488.1 ± 23**	- - -	575.5 ± 58.6*
	MAM	1217.9 ± 21	- - -	891.5 ± 14.4
	(%)	(250)		(155)
DOPAC	Control	12.6 ± 1.3**	2440 ± 216*	32.5 ± 8.6
	MAM	80.3 ± 18.3	3791 ± 291	44.9 ± 5.1
	(%)	(637)	(155)	(138)

HVA	Control	11.8 ± 3.2**	949 ± 141*	38.2 ± 5.1
	MAM	63.0 ± 15.8	1441 ± 227	49.1 ± 8.1
	(%)	(534)	(152)	(129)
5-HT	Control	516.3 ± 25.3**	405.0 ± 34.0**	408.3 ± 12.6**
	MAM	1045.4 ± 61.8	1087.6 ± 99.8	737.4 ± 23.0
	(%)	(203)	(269)	(181)
5-HIAA	Control	253.5 ± 15.5**	426.3 ± 42.7**	554.1 ± 32.6*
	MAM	519 ± 66.6	891.2 ± 99.3	765.1 ± 65.0
	(%)	(205)	(209)	(138)

The values are expressed as means $\pm$ s.e.m.

(%) = percent of control values.

** $p < 0.001$, * $p < 0.01$, Student's t-test.

The MAM treatment potentiated drastically the stimulatory effects of amphetamine or methylphenidate at both doses used (0.25 and 1 mg/Kg). Although rearing behavior was also potentiated, the effect was not consistently significant. Otherwise, a dose and time dependency was obtained for both MAM and control rats (see Fig. 11). It will be observed that the MAM hyperativity is not quite evident. There are two obvious reasons: (1) the MAM hyperactivity is not always evident during the initial exposures to the test cages, i.e., control rats habituate to the novelty of the test cage and show less activity (exploration) whereas MAM rats often show increases in activity over time and fail to habituate, (2) the massive stimulatory effects of amphetamine masked the spontaneous activity effects during the first 60 min.

III A. *Effect of environmental housing conditions on instrumental learning*
Neonatal male rat pups were treated at birth (on Day 1) with either 6-OHDA (100 μg/gm, s.c.), vehicle (saline containing 0.1 % ascorbic acid) or DMI (25 μg/gm, s.c.) 30 min before 6-OHDA. On Day 21 (after weaning) the rats in each

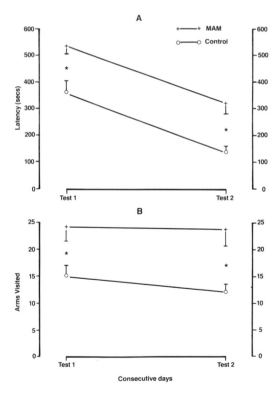

FIG. 9.   Mean latency to take all eight food pellets and mean number of arms visited in taking all eight food pellets by MAM and vehicle treated rats in a radial-arm maze on Tests 1 and 2.

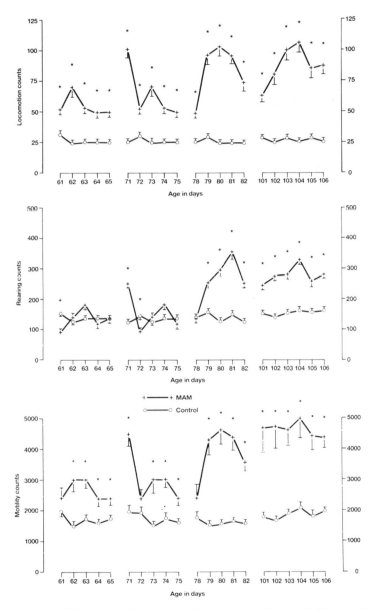

FIG. 10. Mean locomotion, rearing and motility counts by MAM offspring and control rats during 30-min periods i the automated 37 activity tests boxes. The rats were tested at 61-65, 71-75, 78-82, 101-106 days of age. *p < 0.01, Tukey's test.

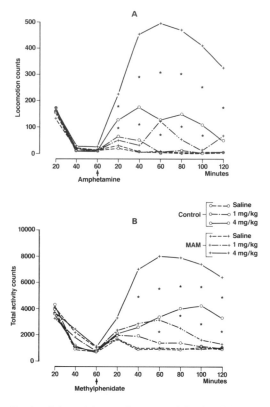

FIG. 11.   Total activity and locomotion counts following 0.25 and 1.0 mg/Kg doses of d-amphetamine to MAM-treated and control. Each rat was exposed to the automated test cage for 60 min prior to d-amphetamine administration, and the motor activity measurements were continued for a further 120 min following injection. *p < 0.01, Tukey's test.

treatment condition were placed in either a *Complex* or *Isolated* housing environment for 35 days. On Days 71 to 78 all the rats were tested on the first eight problems of the Hebb-Williams maze task and on Days 81 and 82 spontaneous motor activity was measured. In the vehicle and DMI plus 6-OHDA treatment conditions the *Complex* housing condition caused a significant overall improvement in performance, as measured by errors per problem, whereas no improvement was obtained for the 6-OHDA treatment condition (see Fig. 12). The rats from the *Isolated* condition showed more significant increases in spontaneous motor activity than those from the *Complex* housing condition. This hyperactivity was not affected by 6-OHDA treatment (see Fig. 13). NA depletion, therefore, antagonized the cognitive (maze learning) but not the hyperactivity aspect of the behavioural changes resulting from *Complex* or *Isolated* rearing conditions. The neurochemical analysis (See Table 3) indicated selective depletions of NA and

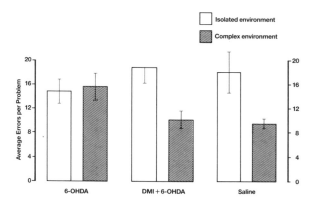

FIG. 12.   Median ($\pm$ quartiles) number of errors per problem in the Hebb-Williams maze for 6-OHDA, DMI plus 6-OHDA and saline treated rats housed in an Isolated (IC) or a Complex (EC) environment for 35 days following weaning. Saline and DMI plus 6-OHDA treated rats housed in th EC made significantly fewer errors than those housed in IC, Mann-Whitney U-tests, p < 0.01. Both 6-OHDA groups (EC and IC) made more errors than the EC groups of the saline and DMI plus 6-OHDA conditions.

the metabolite 3,4-dihydroxyphenylethylene glycol (DOPEG) in the 6-OHDA condition, whereas DMI antagonized the neurotoxic effects of 6-OHDA. Taken together, these results demonstrate an unique interaction between the housing conditions of juvenile rats and NA neurons in the CNS in the functional analysis of a cognitive task and spontaneous motor activity (Mohammed, Jonsson & Archer, 1986).

IV A. *Effect of neonatal DA depletion on instrumental learning*

Neonatal DA lesions were induced by intracerebroventricular administrations of 6-OHDA (200 μg/5 μl, bilaterally) on Days 3 and 6 postnatally. Protection of NA terminals was provided by DMI (20 mg/Kg) pretreatment. The control rats received DMI followed by vehicle. 6-OHDA treated rats demonstrated a clear impairment of acquisition of the radial arm maze task. These rats registered longer latencies to take all eight pellets and needed to visit significantly more arms in order to acquire all eight pellets, i.e., they made more errors, than the control rats (see Fig. 14).

IV B. *Effects of neonatal DA depletion on spontaneous motor activity*

6-OHDA rats with DA depletions showed long-lasting increases in motor activity as measured by the ambulation parameter but decreases as measured by the rearing parameter in the modified Olton maze. The 6-OHDA rats showed a greater number of ambulations but a lesser number of rearings on Days 30, 45, 52 and 60 after birth (see Fig. 15). In another experiment, the spontaneous

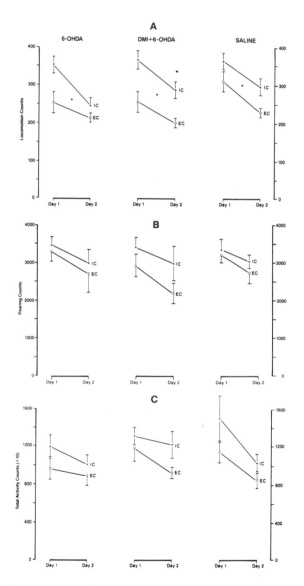

FIG. 13. Mean locomotion, rearing and total activity counts for the 6-OHDA, DMI plus 6-OHDA and saline treated rats housed in either an *Isolated* (IC) or a *Complex* (EC) environment for 35 days following weaning. *p < 0.01, Tukey's test.

Table 3.

Catecholamine and catecholamine-metabolite levels in the frontal cortex of 6-OHDA-, DMI plus 6-OHDA and saline-treated rats housed in a Complex (EC) or Isolated (IC) environment. ng/g wet assayed according to Durkin et al. (1985).

Treatment	NA	DOPEG	$\frac{\text{DOPEG}}{\text{NA}}$	DOPA	A	DA	DOPAC	$\frac{\text{DOPAC}}{\text{DA}}$
NaCl-IC	346 ± 18	27 + 1.6	0.078	12 + 1.2	2.2 + 0.5	52 + 1.5	41 + 1.9	0.79
NaCl-EC	372 + 9.1	25 + 0.9	0.067	9.8 + 0.3	1.1 + 0.2	35 + 2.6	35 + 1.6	0.60
6-OHDA-IC	154 + 61**	13 + 0.9***	0.084	6.3 + 0.3***	1.3 + 0.5	72 + 2.2***	40 + 1.6	0.56
	(45)	(48)	(108)	(53)	(59)	(138)	(98)	(71)
6-OHDA-EC	193 + 33***	17 + 2***	0.088	7.4 + 0.5**	1.2 + 0.3	69 + 2.5	38 + 2.0	0.55
	(52)	(68)	(131)	(76)	(109)	(119)	(109)	(92)
DMI+6-OHDA-IC	367 + 50	24 + 2.5	0.065	8.7 + 0.6*	2.5 + 0.7	63 + 3.8	38 + 2.2	0.60
	(106)	(89)	(83)	(73)	(114)	(121)	(93)	(76)
DMI+6-OHDA-EC	347 + 23	26 + 2.1	0.070	8.5 + 0.5*	1.7 + 0 5	53 + 3.9	33 + 2.5	0.62
	(101)	(96)	(104)	(87)	(155)	(91)	(94)	(103)

Values are expressed as Mean ± S.E.M.

(%) = percent of appropriate control (IC) or (EC).

Student's t-test: *** p<0.001,   ** p<0.01,   * p<0.05.

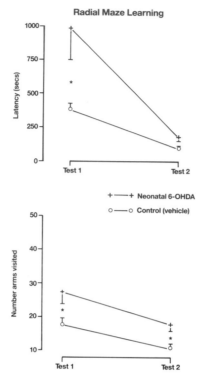

FIG. 14.   Mean latency to take all eight food pellets and mean number of arms visited in taking all eight food pellets by 6-hydroxydopamine and vehicle treated rats in a radial arm maze. At the start of each test, each rat was placed in the central hub and then monitored for its performance in taking all eight pellets. Body weights at the onset of testing were: 6-hydroxydopamine $= 228 \pm 18$, vehicle $= 249 \pm 11$ gm. *$p < 0.01$, Tukey's test.

motor activity of 6-OHDA and vehicle rats was measured in an automated device at 12-min intervals over 60 min during five consecutive days. The hyperactivity effect was confirmed on the locomotion (consistent with ambulation data) and total activity parameters whereas the hypoactivity effect was confirmed on the rearing parameter during the first twenty-four min of each session (see Fig. 16). However, towards the end of the 60-min periods at the later sessions (4 and 5) 6-OHDA showed more rearing behavior suggesting important within-session and between-sessions interactions with the lesioning treatment. The measures of motor activity in the Olton maze and automated test boxes demonstrated a reassuring degree of reliability: (1) Increased locomotion confirmed the increased ambulation effect; (2) Decreased rearing was confirmed in each instance. The latter increases in rearing in the test boxes are entirely understandable since activity in the radial arm maze was measured during a 10-min period only on each occasion. Table 4 presents the catecholamine assays of 6-OHDA and vehicle treated rats indicating drastic DA depletions in several forebrain regions.

IV C. *Effect of a low dose of amphetamine on DA lesion induced hyperactivity*

Rats with neonatal 6-OHDA induced DA depletions and vehicle rats were placed in the activity test boxes and all three parameters were measured at 12-min intervals over 60 min. Marked hyperactivity was observed for locomotion and total activity by 6-OHDA rats whereas for rearing behavior a considerable hypoactivity was noted followed by hyperactive rearing at the 36-, 48- and 60-min intervals (see Fig. 17). After the 60-min habituation phase, 6-OHDA and vehicle rats were injected with either d-amphetamine (0.25 mg/Kg) or saline. For the vehicle treated rats, d-amphetamine caused a significant increase in rearing and total activity counts at the 24- and 36-min intervals after injection; the increase in locomotion was not significant. For the 6-OHDA treated rats d-amphetamine caused significant decreases of locomotion, at the min interval, rearing, at the 12-, 24- and 36-min intervals, and total activity, at the 12- and 24-min intervals.

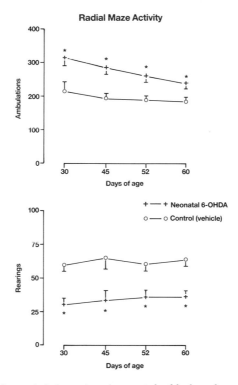

FIG. 15. Mean ambulation and rearing counts by 6-hydroxydopamine and vehicle treated rats in a radial-arm maze on Days 30, 45, 52 and 60 after birth. Ambulations and rearings were measured over 10-min periods on each test occasion. *p < 0.01, Tukey's test.

Table 4.
Regional changes in noradrenaline and dopamine concentrations in the CNS of adult rats treated intraventricularly with 6-OHDA neonatally. Catecholamine assays were performed as described previously (Keller, Ore, Mefford, & Adams, 1976).

Region	Noradrenaline			Dopamine		
	Control	6-OHDA	%	Control	6-OHDA	%
Frontal cortex	388 ± 16	338 ± 74	-13	37 ± 3	9 ± 2***	-76
Nucleus Accumbens	404 ± 198	249 ± 60	-39	10063 ± 914	1580 ± 419***	-84
Septum	829 ± 44	1005 + 818	+21	1148 ± 221	131 ± 39**	-89
Striatum	not detectable	not detectable		12726 ± 384	542 ± 226***	-96
Amygdala	871 ± 35	667 ± 32**	-23	398 ± 31	137 ± 32***	-66
Hypothalamus	2547 ± 208	2174 ± 264	-15	488 ± 46	671 ± 89	+37
A9	223 ± 22	259 ± 36	+16	632 ± 43	227 ± 24***	-64

6-OHDA (100 μg / 5 μl) was administered at 3 and 6 days in the right and left ventricle, respectively, and the animals were killed in the adult stage (2 1/2 months old).

The data are expressed as ng/g; mean ± SEM of 6–9 determinations, male animals only. % = percent change compared to control. Statistical comparison by Student's t-test [4].

** = 0–01 > P > 0.001; *** = P < 0.001.

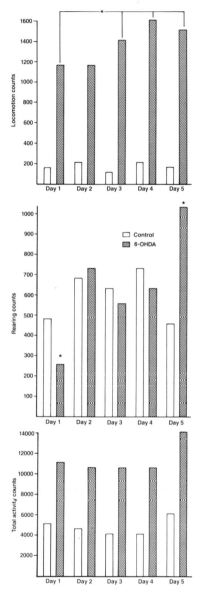

FIG. 16. Mean locomotion, rearing and total activity counts by 6-hydroxydopamine and vehicle treated rats on five consecutive days at Days 31 to 35 after birth. On each test occasion motor activity was measured over a 60-min period. *p < 0.01, Tukey's test.

In each case d-amphetamine treatment reduced the hyperactivity of the 6-OHDA rats to the level of the vehicle treated animals. Already 60-min after d-amphetamine administration had the hyperactivity of the 6-OHDA rats been completely reinstated (see Fig. 17).

Common Aspects of the Animal Models

Compound Stimulus Conditioning in Taste-Aversion Learning.   The latent inhibition phenomenon was studied in both NA depleted and MAM treated rats. Notable disruptions of context-dependent latent inhibition were obtained for both models. For the sensory preconditioning phenomenon, the forebrain NA depleted rats (DSP4 and DNAB) failed to demonstrated sensory preconditioning whereas MAM treated were at least as effective as the controls animals. This is an interesting discrepancy for it has been reasoned that latent inhibition may reflect selective attentional processes whereas sensory preconditioning may provide a unique measure of associative learning (Archer, Cotic, & Järbe, 1986; Archer, Mohammed, Danysz, Järbe, & Jonsson, 1986). Thus, by this yardstick it may be that forebrain NA depletion may disrupt some associative processes underlying Pavlovian conditioning while the MAM model results in attentionally defective rats. Unfortunately, it has not been possible yet to test the Complex/Isolated housed and DA depleted rats in the latent inhibition and sensory preconditioning models.

Spontaneous Motor Activity.   Three of the neurochemical models described above caused profound alterations, generally increases, of motor activity whether measured in the modified Olton maze or the automated test boxes. MAM treatment, *Isolated* housing and 6-OHDA induced DA lesions all caused considerable increases in spontaneous motor activity, forebrain NA did not affect motor activity in any consistent manner. However, some differences emerged: (1) MAM treated rats showed generalized activity increases as did the *Isolated* rats whereas the 6-OHDA rats consistently showed hyperactivity for the locomotion/ambulation parameter and hypoactivity for the rearing parameter, at least for the initial 20-30 min of each session. (2) The hyperactivity induced by prenatal MAM or postnatal intracerebroventricular 6-OHDA treatment appears to increase as a function of age and/or frequency and duration of exposure to the test situation whereas the *Isolated* housing effect on junenile rats involves a lessening of hyperactivity over time and testing, but the rate of increase is much faster for the 6-OHDA than the MAM rats.

Interactions with d-Amphetamine. Forebrain NA depletion enhanced d-amphetamine induced rearing behavior (DNAB but not DSP4) slightly but the most consistent effect is an antagonism of either the rearing or locomotion parameter stimulated by d-amphetamine (Archer, Fredriksson, Jonsson,

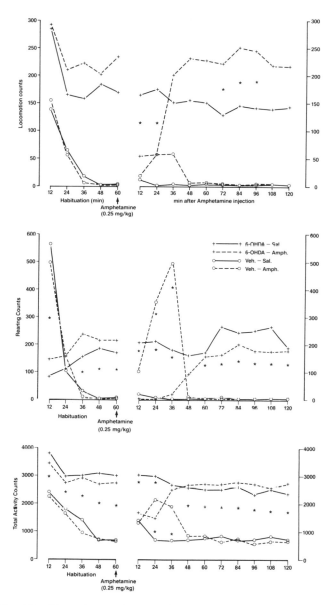

FIG. 17. Mean locomotion, rearing and total activity counts by 6-hydroxydopamine and vehicle treated rats following a 0.25 mg/Kg dose of d-amphetamine. Each rat was exposed to the automated test cage for 60 min prior to d-amphetamine or saline administration, and the motor activity measurements were continued for a further 120 mins following injection. *p < 0.01, Tukey's test.

313

Lewander, Mohammed, Ross & Söderberg, 1986; Mohammed, Danysz, Øgren, & Archer, 1986; Øgren, Archer, & Johansson, 1983). MAM treatment caused a drastic potentiation of d-amphetamine induced motor activity and this effect obtained for the stimulant effects of methylphenidate. On the other hand, the effects of the dose of d-amphetamine (0.25 mg/Kg) potentiated by MAM treatment were completely different in the 6-OHDA rats. Thus, 0.25 mg/Kg d-amphetamine abolished the hyperactivity of the 6-OHDA rats for a period of 20-30 min. The interactions of d-amphetamine and Isolated-Complex housing were not assessed.

Instrumental Learning Procedures

Forebrain NA depletion does not cause any robust effects on the acquisition of either the Morris swim maze task or the Olton radial arm maze task (e.g., Chrobak, DeHaven, & Walsh, 1985; Pang, Chavez, & Pos, 1985; Archer, unpublished data). MAM treatment caused clear and consistent impairments in the acquisition of both the Morris and Olton maze tasks. The 6-OHDA induced DA lesions caused an impairment of acquisition of the Olton maze but have not been tested as yet in the Morris maze. An *Isolated* housing environment produces reliable and marked deficits in the Hebb-Williams maze.

ADD, Hyperactivity, and Animal Models: Validity, Reliability, and Predictability

The validity of the neurochemical models described above may be assessed on the basis of two criteria: An attentional deficit and a state of general hyperactivity. In each case it is preferable that more than one method be available before making any claim. How valid are the models? Forebrain NA depletion certainly produces an attentional deficit but there is no evidence to suggest a state of hyperactivity. The inattention of ADD children is manifested by failure to terminate tasks, easy distractibility, apparent poor listening skills and other activities requiring sustained concentration. All these observations suggested a greatly increased span of attention whereby too many stimuli are attended to and too many activities indulged in. It has been suggested that rats with forebrain NA depletions may have a 'narrowed' span of attention with difficulty in attending to more than one or two stimuli (Archer, 1982) but note that the opposite interpretation has been offered also (Mason, 1981). Whatever the case, the forebrain NA model does not offer high validity but does remain useful in this connection. The *Isolated-Complex* environment housing model may have much potential validity: some attentional deficit is apparent and the hyperactivity is well documented (e.g. Smith, 1972), but the model remains to be tested adequately using classical conditioning techniques and d-amphetamine interactions. Furthermore, recent evidence suggests that forebrain NA may mediate the cognitive effects of differential housing but not the changes in motor activity (Mohammed et al., 1986c) which seems to implicate the involvement at least one other neurotransmitter pathway, possibly dopaminergic. The MAM model may have potential validity also: there is a clear and consistent attentional deficit from both classical conditioning and instrumental learning tasks, robust and probably permanent hyperactivity, inability to habituate and considerable increases in resistance to extinction to conditioned responding (Archer et al., submitted). The major stumbling block is that MAM hyperactivity is massively potentiated by both d-amphetamine and methylphenidate. However, the use of some neuroleptics on hyperactive children (e.g., Werry, Weiss, Douglas, & Martin, 1966) seems to suggest that a sedative-like indication may be considered also in the clinical therapeutic action.

At present, it would appear that the neonatal 6-OHDA induced DA lesion is quite a valid model of ADD and hyperactivity. The hyperactivity is complex, marked, is manifested immediately i.e., at the initial test instances, seems to be long-lasting, and is convincingly antagonised by d-amphetamine. Sahakian and Robbins (1977) have postulated that the improved "attention" shown by hyperactive children following treatment with amphetamine or methylphenidate may be related to the action of these compounds in causing 'stereotyped' behaviour (e.g., Lyon & Robbins, 1975), rather than any sedative effect. Sahakian and Robbins (1977) suggest that these stereotyped activities may enhance the "focusing" of attention by narrowing the range of different activities that would otherwise be initiated. This hypothesis is most interesting not least because it predicts that amphetamine-like compounds " . . . would be expected to aid performance in tasks involving sustained concentration of attention, but impair performance on tasks involving reversals in cognitive strategy" (p 154). This prediction may be tested quite straightforwardly in the rats with neonatally incurred DA depletions, utilising a complex procedural variant in either the Olton radial arm or the Morris swim maze. Whatever the result, the consensus of much clinical and experimental evidence appears to be that ascending dopaminergic pathways must somehow be involved in the ADD and hyperactive condition (Iversen & Creese, 1975; Shaywitz, Cohen, & Bowers, 1977). Some attentional deficit of the neonatal lesion is evident although a number of classical conditioning experiments must be performed. Thus, although a degree of validity may be attained from the neonatal DA depletion model the best preclinical results may require a combination of some if not all of the neurochemical models discussed above. However, as indicated by Robbins, Jones and Sahakian (this volume), the direct evidence linking hyperactivity to the catecholamine malfunctioning in these children is tenuous at best and further more critical biological markers are awaited.

Reliability does not appear to pose an insurmountable conceptual problem, rather one of a more practical nature. The procedures employed to assess possible attentional deficits as a consequence of the neurochemical and/or experimental changes of the treatments included classical conditioning phenomena and instrumental learning tasks. All four neurochemical models caused some type of cognitive dysfunction and the apparent replicability of the acquisition impairments from one maze learning task to another should provide a good index of reliability. Measures of hyperactivity usually provide a more straightforward means of studying reliability. If one is prepared to measure spontaneous motor activity with a sufficient number of direct observational and automated techniques with up to four parameters of motor activity, a satisfactory index of reliability will be obtained. Thus, it is no great issue to postulate that the hyperactivity resulting from prenatal MAM treatment or postnatal 6-OHDA intracerebroventricular administration is of good reliability.

The predictive value of the neurochemical models is dependent upon the testing of a sufficient number of potentially therapeutic or clinically proven therapeutic drugs. Of the variety of psychoactive drugs applied to alleviate the ADD and hyperactive state, the stimulant drugs including d-amphetamine and methylphenidate, and magnesium pemoline (note that this compound is much more slow acting and generally not as effective as the former two) appear to be the most effective. In this connection, the consensus of the evidence presented here and by others (e.g., Heffner & Seiden, 1982) appears to be that the intracerebroventricular 6-OHDA neonatal DA depletion technique may provide a useful model for studying both the attentional dysfunction and the hyperactivity syndrome in rats (but see also Seiden, Miller, & Heffner, this volume). Although the neuroleptic compounds chlorpromazine and thioridazine can alleviate the hyperactivity problem (Greenberg, Deem, & McMahon, 1972; Whitehead & Clark, 1970), the efficacy of this type of medication upon attention and performance is doubtful. It should be repeated here that the ADD with hyperactivity subdivision of the general disorder is under consideration here. It is possible that the stimulant drugs affect the hyperactivity component first and, perhaps as a consequence of the "calming" effect of the treatment, attentiveness and the production of schoolwork is increased (McDaniel, 1986), but the amphetamine-induced stereotypy hypothesis requires serious consideration. Note however, that although attention and performance of stimulant-treated children improves, achievement tests after a few years indicate that real differences from untreated groups are apparent. It seems that the therapeutic effects of stimulants must be supplemented by a regime of behavior modification (Pelham & Bender, 1982). Thus, the predictive value of potential therapeutic agents will be most effectively optimised by analyses employing valid neurochemical models and encompassing separate and reliable test procedures directed at both the attentional and the hyperactivity components.

CONCLUSION

Three criteria for assessing the utility of animal models of the ADD and hyperactivity syndrome in children were discussed: Validity, reliability and predictability. Experimental evidence from neurochemical models, including forebrain NA depletion, prenatal MAM treatment, differential environmental housing of juvenile rats and postnatal DA depletion with intracerebroventricular 6-OHDA, was analysed in the context of several behavioral models, including compound stimulus conditioning, spontaneous motor activity, instrumental maze learning and amphetamine-induced activity. Table 5 presents a summary of the available results on the animal models discussed. It should be noted, however, that clinicians and diagnosticians describe broad variations in the cognitive abilities and incidence of ADD children with or without hyperactivity, aggression or in retarded or gifted children that provide implications for the therapeutic value of any treatment regime (for reviews, see Sergeant & van der Meere, this volume; Shaywitz & Shaywitz, this volume). The available research on catecholamine functional models may be optimistically interpreted to allow us to use valid models of sufficient reliability to screen potentially viable therapeutic agents with acceptable predictability

TABLE 5
Animal Models: Validity, Reliability and Predictability

Concept and Criteria	DNAB DSP4	MAM	Juvenile Housing	DA-depletion
Validity:				
Attention deficit	+	+	+	+
Hyperactivity	–	+	+	+
Reliability:				
Latent inhibition	+	+	0[3]	0[4]
Sensory preconditioning	+	–	0	0
Motor activity	–	+	+	+
Radial arm maze	–	+	0[5]	+
Morris swim maze	#	+	0[6]	+
Hebb-Williams maze	0[7]	0	+	0
Predictability:				
Amphetamine	–[1]	–[2]	0[8]	+
Methylphenidate	+[1]	–[2]	0	+

+ = criterion fulfilled, – = not fulfilled, 0 = not tested here.
[1]no hyperactivity effect obtained therefore not applicable.
[2]hyperactivity potentiated.
[3]Impaired LI after non-handling isolation: Weiner, Feldon & Ziv-Harris, 1987; in preparation.
[4]DA-blockade improved LI: Weiner and Feldon, 1987.
[5]Impairment: Einon, 1980.
[6]Impairment: Unpublished results.
[7]No effect: Unpublished results.
[8]Interaction effects: see Robbins and Sahakian, this volume.

ACKNOWLEDGMENTS

I am grateful to my colleagues Anders Fredriksson, Abdul Mohammed, Johan Luthman, Erik Sundström, Wojciech Danysz, Torbjörn Järbe and Gösta Jonsson for the collaborations which form the basis of this review. May-Britt and Edvard Moser, and Terje Sagvolden gave comments to improve the manuscript.

REFERENCES

American Psychiatric Association (1980). Diagnostic and statistical manual of mental disorders (3rd ed.). Washington, DC: Author.

Archer, T. (1982). The role of noradrenaline in learned behaviours: Studies using DSP4. *Scandinavian Journal of Psychology, Suppl. 1*, 61–71.

Archer, T., Cotic, T., & Järbe, T. U. C. (1986). Noradrenaline and sensory preconditioning in the rat. *Behavioral Neuroscience, 100*, 704–711.

Archer, T., Fredriksson, A., Jonsson, G., Lewander, T., Mohammed, A. K., Ross, S. B., & Söderberg, U. (1986). Central noradrenaline depletion antagonizes aspects of d-amphetamine-induced hyperactivity in the rat. *Psychopharmacology, 88*, 141–146.

Archer, T., Jonsson, G., & Ross, S. B. (1984). A parametric study of the effects of the noradrenaline neurotoxin DSP4 on avoidance acquisition and noradrenaline neurones in the CNS of the rat. *British Journal of Pharmacology, 82*, 249–257.

Archer, T., Mohammed, A. K., Danysz, W., Järbe, T. U. C., & Jonsson, G. (1986). Attenuation of sensory preconditioning by noradrenaline depletion in the rat. *Behavioural Brain Research, 20*, 47–56.

Archer, T., Mohammed, A. K., & Jonsson, G. Altered extinction and long-lasting hyperactivity following prenatal treatment with methylazoxymethanol, submitted.

Archer, T., Mohammed, A. K., & Järbe, T. U. C. (1983). Latent inhibition following systemic DSP4: Effects due to presence and absence of contextual cues in taste-aversion learning. *Behavioral and Neural Biology, 38*, 287–306.

Archer, T., Mohammed, A. K., & Järbe, T. U. C. (1986). Context-dependent latent inhibition in taste aversion learning. *Scandinavian Journal of Psychology, 27*, 277–284.

Archer, T., & Sjödén, P. O. (1982). Higher-order conditioning and sensory preconditioning of a taste-aversion with an exteroceptive CS_1. *Quarterly Journal of Experimental Psychology, 34B*, 1–17.

Archer, T., Sjödén, P. O., & Nilsson, L. G. (1985). Contextual control of taste-aversion conditioning and extinction. In P. D. Balsam and T. Tomic (Eds.), *Context and learning* (pp. 225–271). Hillsdale, New Jersey: Lawrence Erlbaum Associates.

Archer, T., Sjödén, P. O., Nilsson, L.-G., & Carter, N. (1979). Role of exteroceptive background context in taste-aversion conditioning and extinction. *Animal Learning and Behavior, 7*, 17–22.

Buchsbaum, M. S., Haier, R. J., Soster, A. J., Weingartner, S., Zahn, T. P., Siever, L. J., Murphy, D. L., & Brody, L. (1985). Attention dysfunction and psychopathology in college men. *Archives of General Psychiatry, 42*, 354–360.

Chrobak, J. J., DeHaven, D. L., & Walsh, T. J. (1985). Depletion of brain norepinephrine with DSP4 does not alter acquisition or performance of a radial-arm maze task. *Behavioral and Neural Biology, 44*, 144–150.

Davies, D. C., Horn, G., & McCabe, B. J. (1985). Noradrenaline and learning: Effects of the noradrenaline neurotoxin DSP4 and imprinting in the domestic chick. *Behavioral Neuroscience, 99*, 652–660.

Diamond, M. C. (1967). Extensive cortical depth measures and neuron size increases in the cortex of environmentally enriched rats. *Journal of Comparative Neurology, 131*, 357–364.

Diamond, M. C., Krech, D., & Rosenzweig, M. R. (1964). The effects of enriched environments on the histology of the rat cerebral cortex. *Journal of Comparative Neurology, 123*, 111–119.

Durkin, T. A., Caliguri, E. J., Mefford, I. N., Lake, D. M., McDonald, I. A., Sundström, E., & Jonsson, G. (1985). Determination of catecholamines in tissue and body fluids using microbore and high pressure liquid chromatography with amperometric detection. *Life Sciences, 37*, 1803–1810.

Einon, D. F. (1980). Spatial memory and response strategies in rats: Age, sex and rearing differences in performance. *Quarterly Journal of Experimental Psychology, 32*, 473–489.

Erinoff, L., MacPhail, R. C. Heller, A., & Seiden, L. S. (1979). Age-dependent effects of 6-hydroxydopamine on locomotor activity in the rat. *Brain Research, 164*, 195–205.

Fisher, M. H., Welker, C., & Waisman, H. A. (1972). Generalized growth retardation in rats induced by prenatal exposure to methylazoxymethanol acetate. *Teratology, 5*, 223–232.

Greenberg, L. M., Deem, L. A., & McMahon, S. (1972). Effects of dextroamphetamine, chlorpromazine and hydroxyzine on behavior and performance in hyperactive children. *American Journal of Psychiatry, 129*, 532–539.

Heffner, T. G., & Seiden, L. S. (1982). Possible involvement of serotonergic neurons in the reduction of locomotor hyperactivity caused by amphetamine in neonatal rats depleted of brain dopamine. *Brain Research, 244*, 81–90.

Heffner, T. G., & Seiden, L. S. (1983). Impaired acquisition of an operant response in young rats depleted of brain dopamine in neonatal life. *Psychopharmacology, 79*, 115–119.

Hunt, R. D., Cohen, R. J., Anderson, G., & Clark, L. (1986). Possible change in noradrenergic receptor sensitivity following methylphenidate treatment: growth hormone response and MHPG response to clonidine challenge in children with attention deficit disorder and hyperactivity. *Life Sciences, 35*, 885–897.

Iversen, S. D., & Creese, I. (1975). Behavioral correlates of dopaminergic supersensitivity. *Advances in Neurology, 9*, 81–92.

Jackson, R. T., & Pelton, E. W. (1978). L-DOPA treatment of children with hyperactive behavior. *Neurology, 28*, 331–334.

Jaim-Etcheverry, G., & Zieher, L. M. (1980). DSP4: A novel compound with neurotoxic effects on noradrenergic neurons of adult and developing rats. *Brain Research, 188*, 513–523.

Johnstone, M. V., & Coyle, J. T. (1979). Histological and neurochemical effects of fetal treatment with methylazoxymethanol on rat neocortex in adulthood. *Brain Research, 170*, 135–155.

Johnstone, M. V., & Coyle, J. T. (1980). Ontogeny of neurochemical markers for noradrenergic, GABAergic, and cholinergic neurons in neocortex lesioned with methylazoxymethanol acetate. *Journal of Neurochemistry, 34*, 1429–1441.

Johnstone, M. V., Grzanna, R., & Coyle, J. T. (1979). Methylazoxymethanol treatment of fetal rats results in abnormally douse noradrenergic innervation of neocortex. *Science, 203*, 369–371.

Jonsson, G., & Hallman, H. (1982). Effects of prenatal methylazoxymethanol treatment on the development of central monoamine neurons. *Developmental Brain Research, 2*, 510–530.

Jonsson, G., Hallman, H., Ponzio, F., & Ross, S. B. (1981). DSP4-(N-2-chloroethyl-N-ethyl-2-bromobenzylamine) - a useful denervation tool for central and peripheral noradrenaline neurones. *European Journal of Pharmacology, 72*, 173–188.

Kasamatsu, T. (1983). Neuronal plasticity maintained by the central norepinephrine system in the cat visual cortex. In J. M. Sprague and A. N. Epstein (Eds.), *Progress in Psychobiology and Physiological Psychology,* (Vol. *10*, 1–112). City: Publisher.

Kasamatsu, T., & Pettigrew, J. D. (1976). Depletion of brain catecholamines: Failure of ocular dominance shift after monocular occlusion in kittens. *Science, 194*, 206–209.

Kasamatsu, T., Pettigrew, J. D., & Ary, M. (1979). Restoration of visual cortical plasticity by local microperfusion of norepinephrine. *Journal of Comparative Neurology, 185*, 163–182.

Keller, R., Oke, A., Mefford, I., Adams, R. N. (1976). Liquid chromatographic analysis of catecholamines - routine assay for regional brain mapping. *Life Sciences, 19*, 995–1004.

Lubow, R. E. (1965). Latent inhibition: Effect of frequency of nonreinforced preexposure of the CS. *Journal of Comparative and Physiological Psychology, 60,* 454–457.

Lubow, R. E., & Moore, A. V. (1959). Latent inhibition: The effect of nonreinforced preexposure of the CS. *Journal of Comparative and Physiological Psychology, 52,* 415–419.

Lyon, M., & Robbins, T. W. (1975). The action of central nervous system stimulant drugs: A general theory concerning amphetamine effects. In W. Essman & L. Valzelli (Eds.), *Current developments in psychopharmacology, Vol. 2* (pp. 79–163). New York: Spectrum.

Mason, S. T. (1981). Noradrenaline in the brain: Progress in theories of behavioral function. *Progress in Neurobiology, 16,* 263–303.

Mason, S. T. (1983). The neurochemistry and pharmacology of extinction behavior. *Neuroscience and Biobehavioral Review, 7,* 325–347.

Mason, S. T., & Iversen, S. D. (1975). Learning in the absence of forebrain noradrenaline. *Nature, 258,* 422–424.

Mason, S. T., & Iversen, S. D. (1979). Theories of the dorsal bundle extinction effect. *Brain Research Reviews, 1,* 107–137.

Matsuatani, T., Nagayoshi, M., & Tsukada, T. (1980). Elevated monoamine levels in the cerebral hemispheres of microencephalic rats treated prenatally with methylazoxymethanol or cytosine arabinoside. *Journal of Neurochemistry, 34,* 950–956.

McDaniel, K. D. (1986). Pharmacologic treatment of psychiatric and neurodevelopment disorders in children and adolescents. *Clinical Pediatrics, 25,* 65–71.

Miller, F. E., Heffner, T. G., Kotake, C., & Seiden, L. S. (1981). Magnitude and duration of hyperactivity following neonatal 6-hydroxydopamine is related to the extent of brain dopamine depletion. *Brain Research, 229,* 123–132.

Millichap, J. G. (1973). Drugs in the management of minimal brain dysfunction. *Annals New York Academy of Sciences, 205,* 321–334.

Mohammed, A. K., Callenholm, N. E. B., Järbe, T. U. C., Swedberg, M. D. B., Danysz, W., Robbins, T. W., & Archer, T. (1986). Role of central noradrenaline neurons in the contextual control of latent inhibition in taste aversion learning. *Behavioral Brain Research, 21,* 109–118.

Mohammed, A. K., Danysz, W., Øgren, S. O., & Archer, T. (1986). Central noradrenaline depletion attenuates amphetamine-induced locomotion behavior. *Neuroscience Letters, 64,* 139–144.

Mohammed, A. K., Jonsson, G., & Archer, T. (1986). Selective lesioning of forebrain noradrenaline neurons at birth abolishes the improved maze learning performance induced by rearing in complex environment. *Brain Research, 398,* 6–10.

Mohammed, A. K., Jonsson, G., Söderberg, U., & Archer, T. (1986). Impaired selective attention in methylazoxymethanol-induced microencephalic rats. *Pharmacology, Biochemistry and Behavior, 24,* 975–981.

Mohammed, A. K., Jonsson, G., Sundström, E., Minor, B. G., Söderberg, U., & Archer, T. (1986). Selective attentional and place navigation in rats treated prenatally with methylazoxymethanol. *Developmental Brain Research, 30,* 145–155.

Morris, R. G. M. (1984). Development of a water maze procedure for studying spatial learning in the rat. *Journal of Neuroscience Methods, 11,* 47–60.

Naylor, H., Halliday, R., & Callaway, E. (1985). The effect of methylphenidate on information processing. *Psychopharmacology, 86,* 90–95.

Oades, R. D. Attention Deficit Disorder with Hyperactivity (ADDH): The contribution of catecholaminergic activity. (1987). *Progress in Neurobiology, 29,* 365–391.

Øgren, S. O., Archer, T., & Johansson, C. (1983). Evidence for a selective brain noradrenergic involvement in the locomotor stimulant effects of amphetamine in the rat. *Neuroscience Letters, 43,* 327–331.

Olton, D. S., Becker, J. T., & Handelmann, G. E. (1979). Hippocampus, space, and memory. *Behavioral Brain Science, 2,* 313–365.

Olton, D. S., & Werg, M. A. (1978). Hippocampal function and behavior: Spatial discrimination and response inhibition. *Physiology and Behavior, 20*, 597–605.

O'Shea, L., Saari, M., Pappas, B. A., Ings, R., & Stange, K. (1983). Neonatal 6-hydroxydopamine attenuates the neural and behavioral effects of enriched rearing in the rat. *European Journal of Pharmacology, 92*, 43–47.

Pang, K., Chavez, A., & Pos, G. (1985). Effect of central depletion of norepinephrine or serotonin upon memory tasks using the radial maze. *Neuroscience Abstracts, 15*, 534.

Pappas, B. A., Gallivan, J. V., Dugas, T., Saari, M., & Ings, R.(1980). Intraventricular 6-hydro-xydopamine in the newborn rat and locomotor responses to drugs in infancy: No support for the dopamine depletion model of minimal brain dysfunction. *Psychopharmacology, 70*, 41–46.

Pelham, W. E., & Bender, M. E. (1982). Peer relationships in hyperactive children: Description and treatment. In *Advances in Learning and Behavioral Disabilities* (Vol. 1, pp. 365–576). JAI Press.

Rabe, A., & Haddad, R. K. (1972). Methylazoxymethanol induced microencephaly in rats: Behavioral studies. *Federal Proceedings, 31*, 1536–1539.

Rescorla, R. A. (1980). Simultaneous and successive associations in sensory preconditioning. *Journal of Experimental Psychology: Animal Behavior Process, 6*, 207–216.

Rizley, R. C., & Rescorla, R. A. (1972). Associations in second-order conditioning and sensory preconditioning. *Journal of Comparative and Physiological Psychology, 81*, 1–11.

Robbins, T. W., Everitt, B. J., Fray, P. J., Gaskin, M., Carli, M., & De La Riva, C. (1982). The roles of central catecholamines in attention and learning. In A. Levy & M. W. Y. Spiegelstein (Eds.), *Behavioural models and the analysis of drug actions* (pp. 109–134). Amsterdam: Elsevier.

Rosenzweig, M. R., Bennet, E. L., & Diamond, M. C. (1971). Chemical and anatomical plasticity of brain: replications and extensions. In J. Gaito (Ed.), *Macromolecules and behavior*, New York: Appleton Century Crofts.

Ross, S. B. (1976). Long-term effects of N(2-chloroethyl)-N-ethyl-2-bromoben-zylamine hydrochloride on noradrenergic neurons in the rat brain and heart. *British Journal of Pharmacology, 58*, 521–527.

Sahakian, B. J., & Robbins, T. W. (1977). Are the effects of psychomotor stimulant drugs on hyperactive children really paradoxical. *Medical Hypothesis, 3*, 154–158.

Shapiro, S , Salas, M., & Vukovitch, K. (1970). Hormonal effect on ontogeny of swimming ability in the rat: Assessment of central nervous system development. *Science, 168*, 147–150.

Shaywitz, B. A., Cohen, D. J., & Bowers, M. G. (1977). CSF monoamine metabolites in children with minimal brain dysfunction evidence for alteration of brain dopamine. *Journal of Pediatrics, 90*, 67–71.

Shaywitz, B. A., Klopper, J. H., Yager, R. D., & Gordon, J. W. (1976). Paradoxical response to amphetamine in developing rats treated with 6-hydroxydopamine. *Nature, 261*, 153–155.

Shaywitz, B. A., & Pearson, D. A. (1978). Effects of phenobarbital on activity and learning in 6-hydroxydopamine-treated rat pups. *Pharmacology, Biochemistry and Behavior, 9*, 173–179.

Shaywitz, B. A., Yager, R. D., & Klopper, J. H. (1976). Selective brain dopamine depletion in developing rats: An experimental model of minimal brain dysfunction. *Science, 191*, 305–308.

Simon, H., Scatton, B., & Le Moal, M. (1980). Dopaminergic A10 neurones are involved in cognitive functions. *Nature, 286*, 150–151.

Smith, H. W. (1972). Effects of environmental enrichment on open-field activity and Hebb-Williams problem solving in rats. *Journal of Comparative and Physiological Psychology, 80*, 163–186.

Smith, R. D., Cooper, B. R., & Breese, G. R. (1975). Growth and behavioral changes in developing rats treated intracisternally with 6-hydroxydopamine: Evidence for involvement of brain dopamine. *Journal of Pharmacological and Experimental Therapeutics, 185*, 609–619.

Spatz, M., & Laguer, G. L. (1968). Transplacental chemical induction of microencephaly in two strains of rats. *Proceedings of the Society for Experimental Biology and Medicine, 129*, 705–710.

Steinhausen, H. C., & Goebel, D. (1985). The validity of the hyperkinetic syndrome: A study in child psychiatric clinical attenders. *European Archives of Psychiatry and Neurology, 235*, 122–128.

Thorley, G. (1984). Hyperkinetic syndrome of childhood: Clinical characteristics. *British Journal of Psychiatry, 144,* 16–24.

Vorhees, C. V., Fernandez, K., Dumas, R. M., & Haddad, R. K. (1984). Pervasive hyperactivity and long-term learning impairments in rats with induced microencephaly from prenatal exposure to methylazoxymethanol. *Developmental Brain Research, 15,* 1–10.

Weiner, I., & Feldon, J. (1987). Facilitation of latent inhibition by haloperidol in rats. *Psychopharmacology, 91,* 248–253.

Weiner, I., Feldon, J., & Ziv-Harris, D. (1987). Early handling and latent inhibition in the conditioned suppression paradigm. *Developmental Psychobiology, 20,* 233–240.

Weingartner, H., Langer, D., Grice, J., & Rapoport, J. L. (1982). Acquisition and retrieval of information in amphetamine-treated hyperactive children. *Psychiatric Research, 6,* 21–29.

Weiss, G. (1985). Follow-up studies on outcome of hyperactive children. *Psychopharmacological Bulletin, 21,* 169–177.

Weiss, G., & Hechtman, L. (1979). The hyperactive child syndrome. *Science, 205,* 1348–1354.

Wender, P. H. (1975). The minimal brain dysfunction syndrome. *Annual Review of Medicine, 26,* 45–61.

Werry, J. S., Weiss, G., Douglas, V., & Martin, J. (1966). Studies on the hyperactive child. III The effect of chlorpromazine upon behavior and learning ability. *Journal of American Academy of Child Psychiatry, 5,* 292–

Whitehead, P., & Clark, L. (1970). Effect of lithium carbonate, placebo and thioridazine on hyperactive children. *American Journal of Psychiatry, 127,* 124–

20

Dopamine and Learning: Implications for Attention Deficit Disorder and Hyperkinetic Syndrome

Richard J. Beninger
Department of Psychology,
Queen's University,
Kingston, Canada

There is now evidence from a number of areas of research that suggests that the central neurotransmitter, dopamine (DA) may be decreased in the brains of children with attention deficit disorder and hyperkinetic syndrome (ADDH). The evidence includes the positive response to medications (c.g., amphctaminc) known to enhance dopaminergic neurotransmission (see Gittelman Klein & Abikoff, this volume), the observation of decreases in biochemical markers for DA in children diagnosed with ADDH (see Shaywitz & Shaywitz, this volume) and the finding that animals undergoing neonatal DA denervation develop a hyperkinetic syndrome that is ameliorated by amphetamine (for a review see Seiden, Miller & Heffner, this volume). It is important to note that other neurotransmitters, for example norepinephrine and serotonin, may also be involved in ADDH (for a recent review, see Oades, 1987, and this volume). It is not the purpose of this chapter to review the evidence for or against the possible role for various neurotransmitters in ADDH. That has already been done, for example by Seiden et al. (this volume). The purpose of this chapter is to discuss the possible role of DA in locomotor activity and learning. To the extent that a DA decrease is found to be involved in ADDH, the present discussion may assist in understanding how a hypofunctioning of DA may lead to some of the symptoms of this disorder.

In a previous review of the role of DA in locomotor activity and learning (Beninger, 1983), it was concluded that DA may be involved in both of these phenomena. Thus, systemic treatments that led to decreases in DA neurotransmission resulted in hypoactivity whereas those that led to increases in DA neurotransmission led to increased activity or stereotypy. When specific DA terminal

323

regions were considered, data suggested that DA neurons projecting to basal fore-brain regions including the caudate, putamen, nucleus accumbens and olfactory tubercle may enhance locomotor activity whereas mesocortical DA neurons may inhibit locomotion (but see below). Further results suggested that mesolimbic DA neurons may be primarily involved in increased locomotion produced by DA agonists whereas nigrostriatal DA neurons may be more involved in stereotypy (cf. Robbins, Jones, & Sahakian, this volume). DA was also implicated in reward-related learning, termed incentive motivational learning, but shown to be less involved in the learning of associations among stimuli.

The data supporting this general scheme have been extensively reviewed (Beninger, 1983, 1988a,b; Willner, 1983) and will not be covered again here. This chapter is concerned with new developments that further the understanding of the role of DA in locomotor activity and learning. These include studies of the possible role of DA receptor subtypes in phenomena involving DA; the sub-types are D1 receptors that are linked in an excitatory manner to the enzyme adeny-late cyclase and D2 receptors that are not (Kebabian & Calne, 1979). Another approach that has yielded important new results involves the use of regional microinjections of DA agonists and antagonists. It will be shown that DA projec-tions to the frontal cortex, like mesolimbic and nigrostriatal DA projections prob-ably exert an excitatory influence on locomotor activity. Evidence suggests that this effect may be mediated by D2 receptors in the frontal cortex. The results of studies of place conditioning support a role for DA in this phenomenon and suggest that stimulation of D2 receptors but not D1 receptors produces the ef-fect. The results of studies investigating the effects of DA receptor blockers on food-rewarded operant responding showed that both D1 and D2 blockers produced a gradual decline in responding. Intrasession declines in food-rewarded operant responding were seen following bilateral microinjections of a DA receptor blocker into the dorsal striatum. These findings are discussed in further detail below.

Frontocortical Dopamine and Circling

The results of previous studies have led to the conclusion that DA neurons project-ing to the frontal cortex may normally inhibit locomotion. This conclusion was based on the finding that bilateral depletion of frontal cortical DA by intracorti-cal injections of 6-hydroxydopamine (6-OHDA) led to hyperactivity after a peri-od of 7-10 days (Carter & Pycock, 1980; Robinson & Stitt, 1981; Joyce, Stinus, & Iversen, 1983). Further support for this hypothesis was provided by the find-ing of a high correlation between the increase in locomotor activity and decrease in frontal cortical DA levels 30 days after bilateral electrolytic destruction of the ventral tegmental area (Tassin, Stinus, Simon, Blanc, Thierry, LeMoal, Cardo, & Glowinski, 1978). However, biochemical data demonstrated that, 4 weeks af-ter frontal cortical DA denervation, there was an increase in DA function and utilization in subcortical areas (Pycock, Kerwin, & Carter, 1980). This result raised the possibility that locomotor hyperactivity seen following depletions of frontal cortical DA may have been the consequence of time-dependent increases in DA function in subcortical DA-innervated regions known to contribute to the control of locomotor activity.

One way to systematically test this possibility was to employ acute manipulations of frontal cortical DA using microinjections and thereby avoiding long term compensatory changes in the function of subcortical systems. Robert J. Stewart, Michel A. Morency and Patricia R. Dickson, working in my laboratory, have conducted an extensive series of studies investigating the effects of unilateral microinjections of dopaminergic agents into the medial prefrontal cortex on the circling behaviour of rats. As animals characteristically circle away from (contralateral to) the side of higher DA activity, results suggested that increased stimulation of DA receptors in the frontal cortex leads to increased activity. Results further suggested that this effect may have been mediated by D2 DA receptors.

The experimental protocol was as follows. Groups of rats (n = 18) were surgically prepared with chronic indwelling unilateral guide cannulae. After recovery from surgery, each rat was tested in a circular arena a total of seven times with 72 hours separating tests. The test sessions were as follows: (1) no central injection; (2) central injection of vehicle; (3), (4) and (5) each of three drug doses with order of central administration (in 0.5 or 1.0 μl) counterbalanced across rats over three sessions; (6) replication of vehicle; (7) replication of no central injection. All complete turns (360°), ipsiversive and contraversive to the side of the cannula, were counted during four observation periods that occurred at 0-5, 15-20, 30-35 and 45-50 min into the session. The following compounds were tested in separate groups of rats: the indirect-acting DA agonists (+)-amphetamine sulphate (6, 12, 25 μg) and cocaine hydrochloride (25, 50, 100 μg), the local anesthetic procaine hydrochloride (10, 100, 1000 μg), the D1 and D2 antagonist cis -flupenthixol (1, 10, 25 μg), the specific D1 agonist SKF 38393 (2,4,8 μg), the specific D2 agonist quinpirole (3, 6, 12 μg) and the specific D2 antagonists metoclopramide hydrochloride (6, 25, 100 μg) and sulpiride (.001, .01, .1 μg). The ability of sulpiride (1.0 μg) to antagonize the effects of cocaine (50 μg) also was tested in a separate group. Whenever an antagonist was tested, the rats always received an intraperitoneal (ip) injection of amphetamine (1.5 mg/kg) 15 min prior to every test session to increase overall activity.

After histological verification of cannulae placements and discarding rats that had defective cannulae during the conduct of the experiments, groups numbered from 8-14 rats. For each rat the total number of ipsiversive turns was summed over the four observation periods and similarly for contraversive turns. For each rat these sums were then used to calculate a ratio of ipsiversive turns to the total number of turns (ipsiversive plus contraversive). Ratio values of 0.5 indicated equal turning in both directions; values greater or less than 0.5 indicated ipsiversive or contraversive circling, respectively. The total number of turns per session (ipsiversive plus contraversive) served as the second dependent variable.

Comparisons of the turning ratio data for the first and second no-injection sessions, as well as the first and second vehicle sessions, never revealed any significant differences in any of the experiments. Consequently, the data for the two no-injection sessions and those for the two vehicle sessions were averaged for each rat. The results from the no-injection sessions illustrate the acute nature of the manipulations being made in these experiments as the animals returned to baseline circling ratios after drug sessions. Vehicle scores were found never to differ from no-injection scores further showing that intrafrontocortical saline did not systematically produce a directional bias.

The results for the combined no-injection sessions, combined vehicle sessions and each of the three doses of each drug are shown in Figure 1. Both amphetamine (Fig. 1A) and cocaine (Fig. 1B), but not procaine (Fig. 1C), dose-dependently produced contraversive circling, suggesting that stimulation of DA neurotransmission in the frontal cortex led to an enhancement of motor activity (Morency, Stewart, & Beninger, 1987; Stewart, Morency, & Beninger, 1985). The cocaine effect could not be attributed to a local anesthetic effect of the drug as procaine was without significant effect (Morency et al., 1987). The expected opposite effect of a DA receptor blocker was produced by *cis*-flupenthixol (Fig. 1D) that resulted in dose-dependent ipsiversive circling (Beninger & Dickson, 1987). The D1 agonist SKF 38393 (Fig. 1E) was without significant effect (Beninger & Dickson, 1987) whereas the D2 agonist quinpirole (Fig. 1F) produced contraversive circling (Beninger & Dickson, 1987) and the D2 antagonists metoclopramide (Fig. 1G) and sulpiride (Fig. 1H) produced ipsiversive circling (Morency et al., 1987; Stewart et al., 1985). Finally, the contraversive circling produced by cocaine was blocked by co-injection of sulpiride (Fig. 1I) further suggesting that the cocaine effect was a result of its action at DA synapses (Morency et al., 1987).

Total turns for each group are shown in Table 1. The much higher total turns of the groups given ip amphetamine can be seen clearly. With the exception of flupenthixol and quinpirole, all groups showing significant dose effects on turning ratios also showed significant changes in total turns over doses. In general, with increasing drug dose there was an increase in total turns. This might indicate the increase in directional bias, whether ipsiversive or contraversive, leading to more completed turns and fewer partial turns in either direction (only total turns were counted). The quinpirole group was an exception, showing a non-significant decrease in total turns with increasing dose. The explanation of this effect awaits further study, however, it is noteworthy that in spite of this drug's opposite effect on total turns, it, like amphetamine and cocaine, produced a dose-dependent increase in the proportion of contraversive circling.

The results of these and related studies (Morency, Stewart, & Beninger, 1985) suggest that DA in the frontal cortex, like DA in the dorsal and ventral striatum, may be excitatory in its influence on motor behaviour. If this hypothesis is supported by further research, it would suggest that DA in all of the terminal regions

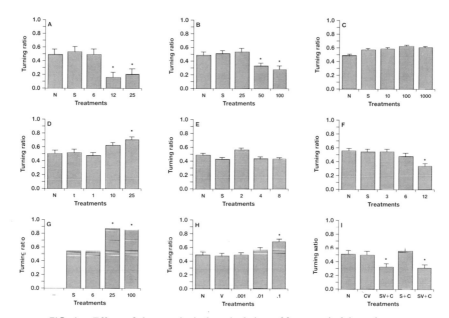

FIG. 1.   Effects of pharmacological manipulations of frontocortical dopamine on circling behavior of rats. Each bar graph shows the mean ($\pm$ SEM) turning ratios [total ipsiversive turns/(total ipsiversive + contraversive turns)] for one experiment for the combined no-injection sessions (N), the combined saline sessions (S), and each of the three doses of each drug. A: (+)-amphetamine; B: cocaine; C: procaine; D: *cis*-flupenthixol; note that the inactive geometric isomer, *trans*-flupenthixol (t), instead of saline, was used for control injections; E: SKF 38393; F: quinpirole; G: metoclopramide; H: sulpiride; I: sulpiride vehicle and cocaine (SV+C) or sulpiride and cocaine (S+C). Asterisks indicate doses that differed significantly from their respective saline conditions. (Adapted from Beninger & Dickson, 1987; Morency et al., 1987; Stewart et al., 1985.)

tested is similarly involved in the control of motor activity, increases in DA neurotransmission leading to increases in locomotor activity and decreases in DA neurotransmission leading to decreases in locomotor activity.

Dopamine and Place Conditioning

Besides being involved in the control of locomotor activity, DA also appears to be involved in reward related incentive motivational learning (Beninger, 1983). The place conditioning task provides one paradigm for studying this type of learning. In one version of this task, rats receive several daily exposures to a rectangular box, the stimuli associated with the two sides differing (e.g., floor texture, pattern on the walls, odour and/or illumination). The time spent on each side is recorded. A partition is then installed between the two sides and over a series of conditioning days, the rats consistently receive a rewarding stimulus (e. g., food) in one side and an equal amount of exposure to the other side but reward

TABLE 1
Total Number of Turns for Each Group of Rats Included in
the Frontocortical Dopamine and Circling Section

Drug	n	no-injection	vehicle	low	medium	high
			Phase			
(+)-amphetamine	13	14.3 ± 1.5	14.4 ± 1.6	17.6 ± 1.6	21.2 ± 2.2	20.9 ± 2.4
cocaine	12	10.5 ± 1.1	13.8 ± 0.6	14.3 ± 1.1	20.7 ± 1.1	21.1 ± 1.6
procaine	12	14.5 ± 1.4	16.8 ± 2.4	15.6 ± 2.0	15.9 ± 1.7	15.6 ± 2.4
cis-flupenthixol	10	20.2 ± 2.5	22.2 ± 2.0	23.7 ± 4.4	24.6 ± 4.0	28.0 ± 4.0
SKF 38393	8	13.6 ± 1.3	12.8 ± 2.2	10.1 ± 1.3	10.3 ± 1.9	12.4 ± 1.9
quinpirole	10	10.4 ± 1.4	9.9 ± 1.4	9.2 ± 1.3	8.9 ± 1.3	8.6 ± 2.1
metoclopramide	12		76.7 ± 7.0	88.4 ± 6.2	102.0 ± 8.8	98.6 ± 6.1
sulpiride	11	58.6 ± 6.3	56.4 ± 5.8	56.6 ± 4.2	61.0 ± 7.3	74.4 ± 6.6
cocaine & sulpiride	14	13.8 ± 1.5	14.9 ± 1.3	20.1 ± 1.6	13.6 ± 1.7	19.1 ± 2.3

Doses corresponding to "low", "medium" and "high" were different for different drugs as indicated in the text. Also indicated in the text is the protocol for the cocaine & sulpiride experiment which differed from the others.

is never presented there. On subsequent test days with the partition again removed and no reward given on either side, animals are observed to spend significantly more time on the side previously associated with reward (Spyraki, Fibiger, & Phillips, 1982a). A role for DA in this type of learning was suggested by the finding that treatment with the DA receptor blocker haloperidol on conditioning days, although not affecting feeding, led to a significant attenuation of place conditioning based on food (Spyraki et al., 1982a).

A number of related studies have shown that place conditioning can be established with the stimulant drugs amphetamine (Spyraki et al., 1982b) and cocaine (Spyraki et al., 1982c) and with the opiate compound heroin (Spyraki et al., 1983). DA was implicated in the effects of amphetamine and heroin by the finding that DA receptor blockers or destruction of the mesolimbic DA system blocked place conditioning in these groups (Spyraki et al., 1982b, 1983) but, surprisingly, neither the DA antagonists pimozide and haloperidol nor 6-OHDA lesions of the DA terminal region, nucleus accumbens, blocked cocaine produced place conditioning (Spyraki et al., 1982c). One possibility suggested by Spyraki et al. (1982c) was that cocaine might have a peripheral local anesthetic effect (Bedford, Turner, & Elsohly, 1984) that in some way resulted in place conditioning, a suggestion that was supported by the observation that the local anesthetic procaine also produced place conditioning.

Recently, Michel A. Morency, working in my laboratory, replicated the Spyraki et al. (1982c) finding of cocaine-produced place conditioning and also found that pimozide failed to block the effect (see Fig. 2A). He reasoned that if conditioning based on cocaine was attributable to its peripheral local anesthetic effects as Spyraki et al. (1982c) suggested, it might be possible to establish place conditioning following intracerebroventricular (icv) administration of cocaine that did not have a local anesthetic effect and that, therefore, could be blocked by pimozide. Results supported this hypothesis. Thus, icv cocaine produced place conditioning that was blocked by pimozide (Fig 2B). In addition, icv administration of procaine produced no significant effect on place learning (Morency & Beninger, 1986).

These results provide further support for the hypothesis that DA plays a role in mediating reward-related learning. They provide no clear basis for understanding the apparent reward effect following peripheral injections of procaine or cocaine in animals with central DA function reduced. One intriguing possibility is that the local anesthetic properties of cocaine or procaine reduced the putative discomfort resulting from the ip injection. As the animals were always injected with saline on control days when they were placed into the opposite side of the place conditioning chamber, the two sides may have had different levels of peripheral discomfort associated with them. On test sessions, animals may then have been seen to spend significantly more time in the side associated with the

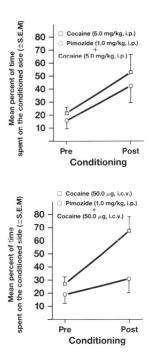

FIG. 2. Effects of pimozide on cocaine-produced place conditioning. Mean (±SEM) percent of time spent on the conditioning side by cocaine and pimozide + cocaine groups during pre- and postconditioning test sessions following intraperitoneal (i.p.) cocaine (upper panel) or intracerebroventricular (i.c.v.) cocaine (lower panel). Both i.p. and i.c.v. cocaine produced significant place conditioning but pimozide only blocked the latter effect. (From Morency & Beninger, 1986.)

(putative discomfort-reducing) local anesthetic. Although this account is speculative, the observation that icv administrations of procaine failed to lead to place conditioning and that icv cocaine-produced place conditioning was blocked by pimozide can be seen to be consistent with it (Morency & Beninger, 1986).

A new line of investigation concerns the possible differential involvement of D1 and D2 DA receptors in place conditioning. Diane C. Hoffman and Patricia R. Dickson have investigated the effects of the D1 agonist SKF 38393 (0.01, 0.1, 1.0 and 10.0 mg/kg ip) and the D2 agonists quinpirole (0.01, 0.025, 0.05, 0.1, 0.25, 1.0 and 5.0 mg/kg ip) or bromocriptine (0.01, 0.1, 0.5, 1.0, 5.0 and 10.0 mg/kg ip) in place conditioning. Results (Fig. 3) revealed that both quinpirole and bromocriptine but not SKF 38393 produced a significant place preference. In fact, the highest dose of SKF 38393 was seen to produce a place aversion (Hoffman, Dickson, & Beninger, 1988; Hoffman & Beninger, 1987). These results continue to support the hypothesis that DA is involved in reward-related learning and provide preliminary evidence that stimulation of D2 receptors may be important for this effect; a similar conclusion has been reached by others studying different reward paradigms, e.g., drug self-administration (Woolverton, Goldberg, & Ginos, 1984).

Dopamine and Food-Rewarded Operant Responding

Some of the earliest work that formed the foundation of the hypothesis that DA may form a critical link in the neurocircuitry that mediates the effects of reward on behaviour involved the observation that operant responding for rewarding

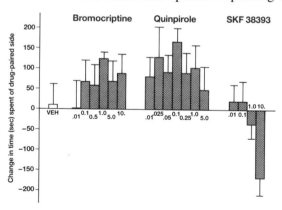

FIG. 3.   Ability of the D1 agonist SKF 38393 or the D2 agonists bromocriptine and quinpirole to produce place conditioning. Each bar indicates the mean ($\pm$SEM) change in time spent on the drug-paired side from pre- to postconditioning for vehicle (VEH) or one dose (mg/kg) of the drug. Both bromocriptine (1.0 mg/kg) and quinpirole (0.1 mg/kg) produced a significant place preference and SKF 38393 (10.0 mg/kg) produced an aversion. (Adapted from Hoffman & Beninger, 1987; Hoffman et al., 1988.)

stimulation of the brain was significantly reduced by manipulations that decreased central DA neurotransmission (see reviews by Fibiger & Phillips, 1979; Wise, 1982). It was subsequently reported that DA receptor blockade also affected responding for food, pimozide producing an extinction-like day-to-day decline (Wise, Spindler, deWit, & Gerber, 1978). Although this has been a highly controversial area of research, the basic finding has often been replicated (cf., Beninger, 1983, 1988a,b).

One approach to the question concerning the possible role of D1 and D2 receptors in reward-related learning has been to investigate the effects of receptor-subtype specific DA antagonists on operant responding for food. In a recent study the effects of the D1 antagonist SCH 23390 (0.01, 0.05 and 0.1 mg/kg ip) and the D2 antagonist metoclopramide (1.0, 5.0 and 10.0 mg/kg ip) were tested. Rats were trained to lever-press on a variable interval (VI) 30-sec schedule for food for 10 training days. Groups then received one of the doses of the drug or saline or extinction for 5 consecutive sessions. Results revealed that the highest doses of SCH 23390 (Fig. 4C) and metoclopramide (Fig. 4D) produced a significant day-to-day decline in responding similar to that seen in extinction (Beninger, Cheng, Hahn, Hoffman, Mazurski, Morency, Ramm, & Stewart, 1987). Others have similarly found that appetitive operant responding underwent an extinction-like decline following treatment with SCH 23390 (Nakajima & McKenzie, 1986) or D2 blockers (Gallistel & Davis, 1983). These data suggested that both D1 and D2 receptors may participate in the control of behaviour by food reward.

It has also been possible to seek the DA terminal region that may participate in food reward by locally administering microinjections of DA receptor blockers to animals trained to lever-press for food. Catherine M. D'Amico and Laura Suzuki have investigated the effects of bilateral microinjections of the DA receptor blocker *cis*-flupenthixol into the dorsal striatum on rats trained to lever-press on a VI 30-sec schedule of food reward. Results (Fig. 5) revealed that *cis*-flupenthixol (25.0 μg in 1.0 μl on each side) produced a significant intrasession decline in responding. No significant effect was seen following saline or the inactive geometric isomer, *trans*-flupenthixol (Beninger & D'Amico, 1986). Spread of the drug to other regions was unlikely (cf. Ahlenius, Hillegaart, Thorell, Magnusson, & Fowler, 1987) and control studies have shown no significant effects with injections into the cortex dorsal to the striatum or into the amygdala (Beninger & Suzuki, in preparation). Although this work is preliminary and other structures and drugs will be tested, results suggest that regional microinjections of DA antagonists to animals lever-pressing for food may eventually reveal the sites in the brain that mediate this type of reward-related learning.

Dopamine and Learning: Implications for ADDH

As already discussed, there is some evidence suggesting that DA may hypofunction in the brains of children with ADDH. This includes the positive response to amphetamine, a drug that enhances DA neurotransmission (see Gittelman Klein

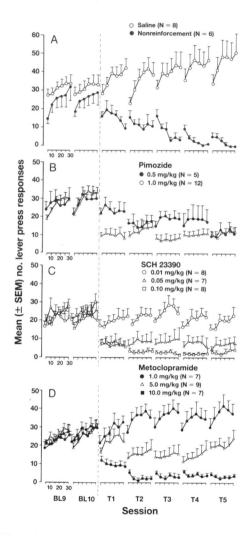

FIG. 4. Effects of D1 and D2 dopamine receptor blockers on food-rewarded variable interval operant responding. Each panel shows the mean ($\pm$ SEM) responses per min for each 5-min segment of two 30-min baseline sessions (BL9 and BL10) and five test days (T1–T5) for groups treated with saline or receiving nonreinforcement (A), groups receiving the D1 and D2 blocker pimozide during the test (B), groups receiving the D1 blocker SCH 23390 in the test (C), and groups receiving the D2 blocker metoclopramide in the test (D). (From Beninger et al., 1987.)

& Abikoff, this volume) and decreased biochemical markers for DA in children with ADDH (see Shaywitz & Shaywitz, this volume). It has been found that neonatal rats subjected to treatments that significantly reduce central DA levels show a hyperkinetic response that is ameliorated by amphetamine, providing an animal model, with some similarities to ADDH, that results from decreased DA (see Seiden et al., this volume). As reviewed elsewhere (Beninger, 1983, 1988a, b), there is good evidence that DA is involved in the control of locomotor activity and reward-related learning. The present chapter has provided an update of this position including the possible excitatory influence of frontal cortical DA on locomotor activity, the possibility that D2 receptors in the frontal cortex mediate this effect, the role of DA in cocaine reward in place conditioning, the possibility that D2 receptors are primarily involved in place conditioning, the possible role of striatal DA in food-rewarded operant responding and the possibility that both D1 and D2 receptors are involved in this phenomenon. For the purposes of this section, the most relevant aspect of DA's role in behaviour is that there is good evidence that DA participates in two separable phenomena: (1) the control of locomotor activity and (2) reward-related learning.

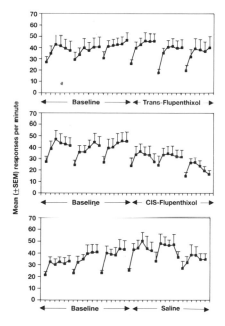

FIG. 5.   Effects of intrastriatal microinjections of the dopamine receptor blocker cis-flupenthixol (25.0 μg in 1.0 μl on each side) on operant variable interval responding for food. Baseline sessions were the last three 30-min sessions prior to the three test sessions that were separated by 72 hours. Mean (+SEM) responses per min for each 5-min segment of each session are shown. cis-flupenthixol but not saline or the inactive geometric isomer trans-flupenthixol produced a significant intrasession decline. (Adapted from Beninger & D'Amico, 1986.)

With regards to the involvement of DA in the control of locomotor activity, there is good evidence that in adult animals there is a positive correlation between the level of DA neurotransmission and the level of locomotor activity. There is also good evidence that in *neonatal* animals, this positive correlation is not found. To the contrary, it appears that neonatal animals depleted of DA are hyperactive (see Seiden et al., this volume). How can this empirical difference in the role of DA in adult versus neonatal locomotor activity be understood? In answering this question, only speculation is possible at present. It is well known that novel stimuli have an unconditioned ability to elicit approach responses. Perhaps the mechanism by which novel stimuli produce this effect is independent of DA. According to this speculation, locomotor activity in neonatal animals depleted of DA might fail to decrease because of the activating effects of relatively novel stimuli. In adult animals with a history of learning about a variety of stimuli in different environments, the relative novelty of most stimuli would be reduced. In the absence of the putative activating effects of novel stimuli, the reliance of locomotor activity on DA can be seen clearly. Of course, this speculation does not explain why animals neonatally depleted of DA are seen to be more active than controls. However, it may be possible to understand the hyperactivity with reference to the other phenomenon that may involve DA, reward-related learning.

Rewarding stimuli, often biologically important stimuli including, for example, food, water, thermal comfort, sexual contact and other social stimuli, produce learning. Empirically, they change behaviour by leading to an increase in the frequency of responses that preceded their presentation in a particular environment. Theoretically, they change neutral environmental stimuli associated with reward into conditioned incentive motivational stimuli that, by definition, acquire an enhanced ability to elicit approach and transactional responses (cf. Beninger, 1983; Bindra, 1978). It is well documented that this type of learning is impaired by treatments that reduce DA neurotransmission. For example, in place conditioning, stimuli on the side associated with food would be said to become conditioned incentive stimuli, leading to an increase in time spent in their presence. As already discussed, treatment with DA antagonists during conditioning trials, while not affecting eating, blocks learning. The acquisition of a lever press response for food can be understood as another example of incentive learning and it has similarly been shown to be impaired by DA antagonists (Wise & Schwartz, 1981). Animals undergoing neonatal DA depletions may show a similar impairment in incentive learning. Thus, Seiden (personal communication) has shown that water-rewarded lever press acquisition was significantly impaired in animals receiving neonatal DA depletions.

The effects of reward on behaviour could be said to change attention. A rat that has been rewarded for pressing a lever spends a great deal of time interacting with (paying attention to) the lever in comparison to a rat with a similar history of being fed in the test chamber independently of lever pressing. A rat in a place conditioning study is seen to spend significantly more time in the presence of (paying attention to) environmental stimuli signalling reward. Following this line of reasoning, rats undergoing lever press acquisition training or place conditioning while treated with DA receptor blockers and observed to be impaired in learning, could be said to have an attentional deficit.

The following speculation is an attempt to understand ADDH and its response to amphetamine as a consequence of DA hypofunction in the light of what is known about the role of DA in locomotor activity and learning. Thus, the child with ADDH, although possibly having reduced DA, may not be hypoactive because of the activating effects of novel environmental stimuli. The child may show an attention deficit because of an impairment in reward-related learning. The usual effects of reward on behaviour are to increase the incentive properties of environmental stimuli that signal reward leading to an increase in the ability of those stimuli to produce approach and transactional responses or, for present purposes, to command attention. As a result of the putative impairment of this usual learning process, the child with ADDH may move more frequently from stimulus to stimulus leading to an apparent *hyper*activity. It is perhaps worth adding that there is at least one other type of learning, the learning of associations among stimuli, which has been shown to be relatively independent of DA (cf., Beninger, 1983, 1988a, b). This finding might suggest that children with ADDH may show intact associative learning but impaired incentive learning. Finally, treatment with amphetamine would lead to enhanced DA neurotransmission which might, in turn, lead to better incentive learning, more attention to stimuli signalling reward and a resultant reduction in activity.

In conclusion, there is now an extensive literature suggesting an involvement of DA in the control of locomotor activity and incentive learning. Current studies seek to identify the possible involvement of DA terminal regions and receptor subtypes. There is some evidence that ADDH may result from a hypofunction of DA neurotransmission. It may, therefore, follow that children with ADDH are impaired in incentive learning. The development of these relationships requires considerable speculation and existing uncertainties about the etiology of ADDH (see Rutter, this volume) only make this task more difficult. However, the treacherous waters between basic research and clinical phenomena must be forded if the former is to contribute to an understanding of the latter.

ACKNOWLEDGMENTS

This chapter is dedicated to Rachal and Adam. I would like to thank Michel A. Morency for his helpful comments on the manuscript. The author was supported by a grant from the Ontario Ministry of Health.

REFERENCES

Ahlenius, S., Hillegaart, V., Thorell, G., Magnusson. O., & Fowler, C. J. (1987). Suppression of exploratory locomotor activity and increase in dopamine turnover following the local application of cis-flupenthixol into limbic projection areas of the rat striatum. *Brain Research, 402,* 131–138.

Bedford, J. A., Turner, C. E., & Elsohly, H. N. (1984). Local anesthetic effects of cocaine and several extracts of the coca leaf (E. coca). *Pharmacology, Biochemistry and Behavior, 20,* 819–821.

Beninger, R. J. (1983). The role of dopamine in locomotor activity and learning. *Brain Research Reviews, 6,* 173–196.

Beninger, R. J. (1988a). Methods for determining the effects of drugs on learning. In A. A. Boulton, G. B. Baker & A. J. Greenshaw (Eds.), *Neuromethods: Psychopharmacology.* Clifton, New Jersey: Humana Press Incorporated. In press.

Beninger, R. J. (1988b). The role of serotonin and dopamine in learning to avoid aversive stimuli. In T. Archer & L.-G. Nilsson (Eds.), *Perspectives on aversively motivated behaviour.* Hillsdale, New Jersey: Lawrence Erlbaum Associates. In press.

Beninger, R. J., Cheng, M., Hahn, B. L., Hoffman, D. C., Mazurski, E. J., Morency, M. A., Ramm, P., & Stewart, R. J. (1987). Effects of extinction, pimozide, SCH 23390 and metoclopramide on food-reinforced operant responding in rats. *Psychopharmacology, 92,* 343–349.

Beninger, R. J., & D'Amico, C. M. (1986). Effects of intrastriatal microinjections of cis-flupenthixol on lever pressing for food in rats. *Neuroscience Letters, Supplement 26,* 431.

Beninger, R. J., & Dickson, P. R. (1987). Rats circle following unilateral stimulation of D2 but not D1 dopamine receptors in the frontal cortex. *Neuroscience, Supplement 22,* 54–97.

Bindra, D. (1978). How adaptive behavior is produced: A perceptual-motivational alternative to response-reinforcement. *Behavioral and Brain Sciences, 1,* 41–91.

Carter, D. J., & Pycock, C. J. (1980). Behavioural and biochemical effects of dopamine and noradrenaline depletion within the medial prefrontal cortex of the rat. *Brain Research, 192,* 163–176.

Fibiger, H. C. and Phillips, A. G. (1979). Dopamine and the neural mechanisms of reinforcement. In A. S. Horn, J. Korf, & B. H. C. Westerink (Eds.), *The neurobiology of dopamine* (pp. 597–615). London: Academic Press.

Gallistel, C. R., & Davis, A. J. (1983). Affinity for the dopamine D2 receptor predicts neuroleptic potency in blocking the reinforcing effect of MFB stimulation. *Pharmacology, Biochemistry and Behavior, 19,* 867–872.

Hoffman, D. C., & Beninger, R. J. (1987). Selective D1 and D2 dopamine receptor agonists produce opposing effects in the place conditioning paradigm. *Canadian Psychology, 28,* 265.

Hoffman, D. C. Dickson, P. R., & Beninger, R. J. (1988). The dopamine D2 receptor agonists, quinpirole and bromocriptine produce conditioned place preferences. *Progress in Neuro-psychopharmacology and Biological Psychiatry, 12,* 315–322.

Joyce, E. M., Stinus, L., & Iversen, S. D. (1983). Effect of injections of 6-OHDA into either nucleus accumbens septi or frontal cortex on spontaneous and drug-induced activity. *Neuropharmacology, 22,* 1141–1145.

Kebabian, J. W., & Calne, D. B. (1979). Multiple receptors for dopamine. *Nature, 277,* 93–96.

Morency, M. A., & Beninger, R. J. (1986). Dopaminergic substrates of cocaine-induced place conditioning. *Brain Research, 399,* 33–41.

Morency, M. A., Stewart, R. J., & Beninger, R. J. (1985). Effects of unilateral microinjections of sulpiride into the medial prefrontal cortex on circling behaviour of rats. *Progress in Neuro-Psychopharmacology and Biological Psychiatry, 9,* 735–738.

Morency, M. A., Stewart, R. J., & Beninger, R. J. (1987). Circling behavior following unilateral microinjections of cocaine into the medial prefrontal cortex: Dopaminergic or local anesthetic effect? *Journal of Neuroscience, 7,* 812–818.

Nakajima, S., & McKenzie, G. B. (1986). Reduction of the rewarding effect of brain stimulation by a blockade of dopamine D1 receptor with SCH 23390. *Pharmacology, Biochemistry and Behavior, 24,* 919–923.

Oades, R. D. (1987). Attention deficit disorder with hyperactivity (ADDH): The contribution of catecholaminergic activity. *Progress in Neurobiology, 29,* 365–391.

Pycock, C. J., Kerwin, R. W., & Carter, C. J. (1980). Effect of lesion of cortical dopamine terminals on subcortical dopamine receptors in rats. *Nature, 286,* 74–77.

Robinson, R. G., & Stitt, T. G. (1981). Intracortical 6-hydroxydopamine induces an asymmetrical response in the rat. *Brain Research, 213*, 387–395.

Spyraki, C., Fibiger, H. C., & Phillips, A. G. (1982a). Attenuation by haloperidol of place preference conditioning using food reinforcement. *Psychopharmacology, 77*, 379–382.

Spyraki, C., Fibiger, H. C., & Phillips, A. G. (1982b). Dopaminergic substrates of amphetamine-induced place preference conditioning. *Brain Research, 253*, 185–193.

Spyraki, C., Fibiger, H. C., & Phillips, A. G. (1982c). Cocaine-induced place preference conditioning: Lack of effects of neuroleptics and 6-hydroxydopamine lesions. *Brain Research, 253*, 195–203.

Spyraki, C., Fibiger, H. C., & Phillips, A. G. (1983). Attenuation of heroin reward in rats by disruption of the mesolimbic dopamine system. *Psychopharmacology, 79*, 278–283.

Stewart, R. J., Morency, M. A., & Beninger, R. J. (1985). Differential effects of intrafrontocortical microinjections of dopamine agonists and antagonists on circling behavior of rats. *Behavioral Brain Research, 17*, 67–72.

Tassin J. P., Stinus, L., Simon, H., Blanc, G., Thierry, A. M., LeMoal, M., Cardo, B., & Glowinski, J. (1978). Relationship between the locomotor hyperactivity induced by A10 lesions and the destruction of the frontocortical dopaminergic innervation in the rat. *Brain Research, 141*, 267–281.

Willner, P. (1983). Dopamine and depression: A review of recent evidence. II Theoretical approaches. *Brain Research Reviews, 6*, 225–236.

Wise, R. A. (1982). Neuroleptics and operant behavior: The anhedonia hypothesis. *Behavioral and Brain Sciences, 5*, 39–88.

Wise, R. A., & Schwartz, H. V. (1981). Pimozide attenuates acquisition of lever-pressing for food in rats. *Pharmacology, Biochemistry and Behavior, 15*, 655–656.

Wise, R. A., Spindler, J., deWit, H., & Gerber, G. J. (1978). Neuroleptic-induced 'anhedonia' in rats: Pimozide blocks reward quality of food. *Science, 201*, 262–264.

Woolverton, W. L., Goldberg, L. I., & Ginos, J. Z. (1984). Intravenous self-administration of dopamine receptor agonists by rhesus monkeys. *Journal of Pharmacology and Experimental Therapeutics, 230*, 678–683.

The Cerebellum: Motor Skills, Procedural Learning, and Memory and Hyperactivity

Richard F. Thompson
Department of Psychology,
Stanford University, Stanford, CA 94305

> We can say that normally our most complex muscle movements are car-
> ried out subconsciously and with consummate skill. . . . It is my thesis that
> the cerebellum is concerned in this enormously complex organization and
> control of movement, and that throughout life, particularly in the earlier
> years, we are engaged in an incessant teaching program for the cerebel-
> lum. As a consequence, it can carry out all of these remarkable tasks that
> we set it to do in the whole repertoire of our skilled movements in games,
> in techniques, in musical performances, in speech, dance, song and so on.
> —John C. Eccles, 1977, p 328

There is general agreement that the cerebellum is involved in the production
and control of movements, including skilled, learned movements, but less agreement regarding possible loci of memory storage for learned movements. On one
side are the now-classic theories of how the cerebellar cortex might serve as the
site for storage of memory traces that code learned movements or motor programs (Marr, 1969; Albus, 1971; Eccles, 1971; Ito, 1972). The opposing view
holds that the cerebellum is a computational network involved in the control and
regulation of movement, including skilled movements, but that the memory traces
are not stored there (Llinas, 1981).

Evidence for the involvement of the cerebellum in skilled movements is in-
controvertible. Particularly impressive are studies using primates trained to make
highly skilled, precise movements. This literature has been reviewed in depth
(Brooks & Thach, 1981; Ito, 1984). In general, when a monkey performs an ''in-
tentional'' skilled movement, as in moving a lever rapidly in a particular manner
following a visual or auditory stimulus, one of the earliest signs of neuronal ac-

tivity is in the dentate nucleus; lateral Purkinje cells show alterations at about this time or a bit later. Next are neural changes in interpositus and in motor cortex. These statements are, of course, based on means of samples with considerable overlaps. The majority of dentate neurons fire in relation to the stimulus onset and a smaller proportion fire in relation to the onset of movement, whereas interpositus neurons, while often preceding the movement in terms of onset latencies, tend to fire more in relation to the movement itself. Interestingly, the "stimulus evoked" dentate response occurs in the trained animal and *disappears* if the learned behavior is extinguished. Cooling of the dentate nucleus in monkeys trained to perform a prompt arm-wrist flexion task causes the execution of the task to be delayed by 90 to 250 msec. Furthermore, cooling of the dentate in a monkey that has just learned a new variation of an arm-wrist task reverts the animal's arm movement back to prelearning levels of performance (see Chapman et al., 1986; Brooks et al., 1973; Brooks, 1979; Meyer-Lohman, 1977).

A common hypothetical functional description would have the 'intention" to move possibly originate in association areas of the cerebral cortex, which activate the striatum and the pontine nuclei. Neurons in the pontine nuclei project to the cerebellum as mossy fibers. In so far as the cerebellum is concerned, the next event is activation of dentate neurons by mossy fibers, and also activation of Purkinje neurons, which act in turn to modulate dentate neurons. The dentate neurons then activate motor cortex via the thalamus, which in turn activates descending pathways to motor neurons and also pontine mossy fibers to cerebellum. Interpositus neurons are also activated by mossy fibers, and influenced by Purkinje cells, although it is not clear at exactly what points in the above sequence. Once behavioral movement begins, feedback from the periphery is, of course, provided to these central systems. The climbing fiber system is not thought to play a direct role in movement initiation or control because of the very slow discharge frequency of inferior olivary neurons (1-2/sec). Instead, it may play some role as a "corrective" signal when errors occur or it may provide some other kind of information. The motor cortex and the interpositus provide two descending motor systems, the interpositus by way of the magnocellular red nucleus and rubral pathways. This schema is, of course, greatly oversimplified; most regions that connect have reciprocal connections, e.g., the nucleocortical fibers in the cerebellum, and other neuronal systems are also involved (see Brooks & Thach, 1981, for detailed discussion). Where the motor program memory traces for such skilled movements are located in these networks is not yet known, but the possibility they are stored in cerebellar cortex seems a reasonable working hypothesis and is not contradicted in any strong manner by current evidence.

The Cerebellum is the Essential Substrate for Classical Conditioning of the Eyeblink and Other Discrete Behavioral Responses

Some years ago we adopted the general strategy of recording neuronal unit activity in the trained animal (rabbit eyelid conditioning) as an initial survey and sampling method to identify putative sites of memory storage. A pattern of neuronal activity that correlates with the behavioral learned response, specifically one that precedes the behavioral response in time within trials, predicts the form of the learned response within trials and predicts the development of learning over trials, is a necessary (but not sufficient) requirement for identification of a storage locus.

We mapped a number of brain regions and systems thought to be involved in learning and memory. Neuronal activity of pyramidal cells in the hippocampus exhibited all the requirements described above (Berger et al., 1983). But the hippocampus itself is not necessary for learning and memory of such discrete behavioral responses (Thompson et al., 1983). Recent evidence argues strongly that long-lasting neuronal plasticity is established in the hippocampus in these learning paradigms (Disterhoft et al., 1986; Mamounas et al., 1984; Weisz et al., 1984). Thus, "memory traces" are formed in the hippocampus during learning but these "higher order" traces are not necessary for learning of the basic association between a neutral tone or light CS and the precisely timed, adaptive behavioral response. However, the hippocampus can become essential when appropriate task demands are placed on the animal, even in eyelid conditioning (Thompson et al., 1983). But the hippocampus is not a part of the memory trace circuit essential, i.e., necessary and sufficient, for basic associative learning and memory of discrete responses. Indeed, decorticate and even decerebrate mammals can learn the conditioned eyelid response (Norman et al., 1974; Oakley & Russel, 1977) and animals that are first trained and then acutely decerebrated retain the learned response (Mauk & Thompson, 1987). The essential memory trace circuit is below the level of the thalamus.

In the course of mapping the brain stem and cerebellum we discovered localized regions of cerebellar cortex and a region in the lateral interpositus nucleus where neuronal activity exhibited the requisite memory trace properties—patterned changes in neuronal discharge frequency that preceded the behavioral learned response by as much as 60 msec (minimum behavioral CR onset latency approximately 100 msec), predicted the form of the learned behavioral response (but not the reflex response) and grew over the course of training, i.e., predicted the development of behavioral learning (McCormick et al., 1981, 1982a; McCormick & Thompson, 1984; Thompson, 1986).

We undertook a series of lesion studies—large lesions of lateral cerebellar cortex and nuclei, electrolytic lesions of the lateral interpositus-medial dentate nuclear region and lesions of the superior cerebellar peduncle ipsilateral to the learned response all abolished the learned response completely and permanently, had no effect on the reflex UR and did not prevent or impair learning on the contralateral side of the body (McCormick et al., 1981, 1982a,b; Lavond et al., 1981; Lincoln et al., 1982; Thompson et al., 1984; Clark et al., 1984). After our initial papers were published, Yeo, Glickstein and associates replicated our basic lesion result for the interpositus nucleus, using light as well as tone CSs and a peri-orbital shock US (we had used corneal airpuff US), thus extending the generality of the result (Yeo et al., 1985).

Electrolytic or aspiration lesions of the cerebellum cause degeneration in the inferior olive—the lesion abolition of the learned response could be due to olivary degeneration rather than cerebellar damage, per se. We made kainic acid lesions of the interpositus—a lesion as small as a cubic millimeter in the lateral anterior interpositus permanently and selectively abolished the learned response with no attendant degeneration in the inferior olive (Lavond et al., 1985). Additional work suggests that the lesion result holds across CS modalities, skeletal response systems, species, and perhaps with instrumental contingencies as well (Yeo et al., 1984; Donegan et al., 1983; Polenchar et al., 1985). Electrical microstimulation of the interpositus nucleus in untrained animals elicits behavioral responses by way of the superior cerebellar peduncle, e.g., eyeblink, leg-flexion, the nature of the response being determined by the locus of the electrode (McCormick & Thompson, 1984). Collectively, these data build a case that the memory traces are afferent to the efferent fibers of the superior cerebellar peduncle, i.e., in interpositus, cerebellar cortex or systems for which the cerebellum is a mandatory efferent.

The basic interpositus lesion effect we first described—complete and permanent abolition of the CR with no effect on the UR—has been replicated in subsequent studies in our laboratory (Clark et al., 1984; Lavond et al, 1984a; 1985; Lincoln et al., 1982; Mauk et al., 1987; McCormick et al., 1984; Steinmetz et al., 1986; Woodruff-Pak et al., 1985) and in several studies in other laboratories (Polenchar et al., 1985; Yeo et al., 1985).

To our knowledge, this is the first demonstration that a very discrete and localized central brain lesion can completely and permanently abolish a learned response without any effect on ability to perform the response (reflex UR) and without impinging on classical sensory systems. The effect is dramatic, as schematized in Figures 1 and 2. Before lesion the CR is about 10 mm, using standard training conditions, e.g., 350 msec, 85 db, 1 KHz CS and a coterminating 100 msec corneal airpuff US (2.1 N/cm²). Following the effective lesion of the anterior lateral interpositus nucleus, the CR is completely abolished on both paired trials and CS alone test trials (see Figure 2).

The effects of partial lesions of the interpositus are particularly interesting (Clark et al., 1984). As schematized in Figure 2, the CR is markedly reduced in amplitude, the onset latency is increased and, most importantly, the frequency of occurrence of the CR is markedly reduced. The correlation between amplitude and frequency of CR in partially lesioned animals is extremely high: $r = 0.93$. Schematics in Figure 2 (bottom three traces) are of an individual CS-US trial on which the CR occurs, an individual CS alone test trial on which the CR occurs and an average of ten successive test trials. The much reduced amplitude of this last is due to the marked reduction in frequency of occurrence of the CR.

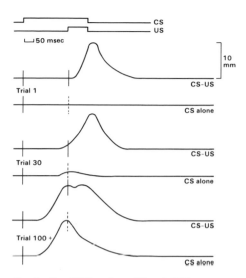

FIG. 1. Schematic of reflex (UR) and conditioned (CR) responses of the nictitating membrane (or eyelid). Top two traces — first trial before any learning has occurred. Upper trace, UR, bottom trace, CS alone trial showing no response. Middle two traces, paired trial (above) and CS alone trial (below) early in training. Bottom two traces, the same when the CR has been learned. Solid vertical lines indicate CS and US onsets, dashed lines indicate time of US onset on trials when US not presented (here and in Figures 2 and 3).

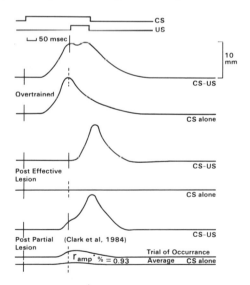

FIG. 2. Top two traces, well learned response. Middle two traces, effective lesion of the interpositus nucleus completely and permanently abolishes the CR on both paired and CS alone trials, but has no effect on the UR. Bottom three traces, effect of a substantial but incomplete lesion. Middle trace is a single trial on which a CR occurred, bottom trace is the average amplitude CR. See text for details.

343

The CR following partial lesion closely resembles the CR early in training (Figure 1). As Gormezano (1972) showed, the CR begins to develop at about the point in time where US onset occurs within trials. Over training the CR onset latency gradually moves toward the CS onset, asymptoting at about 100 msec after CS onset. But the peak amplitude of the CR zeroes in on the time of the US onset over the range of CS-US onset intervals where learning occurs, as noted above.

This fact of permanently reduced frequency and amplitude of the CR with partial lesions has interesting implications. (In the Clark et al., 1984 study, we saw a very small numerical, but not significant, increase in CR amplitude with post-lesion training in the partial lesion animals.) The lesion is causing either partial damage to the sensory afferent (CS) projection system to the memory trace, partial damage to the memory trace itself, or partial damage to the CR pathway efferent from the memory trace. But partial damage to the afferent CS pathway does not cause permanent reduction of the CR. Thus, using an auditory CS we have found repeatedly that partial lesions of the auditory pathway, e.g., lateral lemniscus, causes only temporary reduction in the amplitude and percent of the CR (Steinmetz et al., 1987). It is just as though the properties of the CS have been altered, e.g., intensity reduced. With a marked reduction in CS intensity, additional training is required to reestablish the normal amplitude and percentage of CR (Kettner & Thompson, 1985). Therefore, we argue that the interpositus lesion is either to the memory trace itself or to the efferent CR pathway. Recovery of CR amplitude with additional training would not be expected if the damage is efferent from the trace, i.e., beyond the site of the neuronal plasticity that codes the memory trace. By the same token, if the population of neurons that constitutes the trace for a particular CR is fixed, then little or no recovery from partial lesion of this population of neurons would be expected.

The Essential Memory Trace Circuit

The essential efferent CR pathway appears to consist of fibers exiting from the interpositus nucleus ipsilateral to the trained side of the body in the superior cerebellar peduncle, crossing to relay in the contralateral magnocellular division of the red nucleus and crossing back to descend in the rubral pathway to act ultimately on motor neurons (Lavond et al., 1981; McCormick et al., 1982; Haley et al., 1983; Madden et al., 1983; Chapman et al., 1985; Rosenfield et al., 1985) (see Figure 3). Possible involvement of other efferent systems in control of the CR has not yet been determined, but descending systems taking origin rostral to the midbrain are not necessary for learning or retention of the CR, as noted above.

A somatosensory stimulus (as in our corneal airpuff US) activates both mossy fibers and climbing fibers that converge in their projection to the cerebellum. When we set out to identify the essential US pathway we decided to focus on the climbing fiber system, guided by the classic theories of cerebellar learning, but recognizing that both mossy and climbing fibers are coactivated by the US.

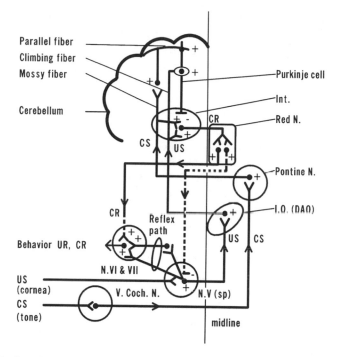

Parallel fiber
Climbing fiber
Mossy fiber

Cerebellum

Purkinje cell

Int.

CR — Red N.

CS   US

Pontine N.

CR   Reflex   I.O. (DAO)
        path

Behavior UR, CR

US   CS

N.VI & VII

US
(cornea)

V. Coch. N.   N.V (sp)

CS
(tone)

midline

FIG. 3.   Simplified schematic of hypothetical memory trace circuit for discrete behavioral responses learned as adaptations to aversive events. The US (corneal airpuff) pathway seems to consist of somatosensory projections to the dorsal accessory portion of the inferior olive (DAO) and its climbing fiber projections to the cerebellum. The tone CS pathway seems to consist of auditory projections to pontine nuclei (Pontine N) and their mossy fiber projections to the cerebellum. The efferent (eyelid closure) CR pathway projects from the interpositus nucleus (Int) of the cerebellum to the red nucleus (Red N) and via the descending rubral pathway to act ultimately on motor neurons. The red nucleus may also exert inhibitory control over the transmission of somatic sensory information about the US to the inferior olive (IO), so that when a CR occurs (eyelid closes), the red nucleus dampens US activation of climbing fibers. Evidence to date is most consistent with storage of the memory traces in localized regions of cerebellar cortex and possibly interpositus nucleus as well. Pluses indicate excitatory and minuses inhibitory synaptic action. Additional abbreviations: N V (sp), spinal fifth cranial nucleus; N VI, sixth cranial nucleus; N VII, seventh cranial nucleus; V Coch N, ventral cochlear nucleus. (From Thompson, 1986; Reprinted by permission of *Science*, 1986). Supported by grants from the National Science Foundation (BNS 8117115), the Office of Naval Research (N00014-83) the McKnight Foundation and the Sloan Foundation.

345

Our evidence to date argues strongly that the essential US reinforcing pathway, the necessary and sufficient pathway conveying information about the US to the cerebellar memory trace circuit, is climbing fibers from the dorsal accessory olive (DAO) projecting via the inferior cerebellar peduncle (see Figure 3). Thus, lesions of the appropriate region of the DAO prevent acquisition and produce normal extinction of the behavioral CR with continued paired training in already trained animals (McCormick et al., 1985). Electrical microstimulation of this same region elicits behavioral responses and serves as an effective US for normal learning of behavioral CRs; the exact behavioral response elicited by DAO stimulation is learned as a normal CR to a CS (Mauk, Steinmetz & Thompson, 1986).

Lesion and microstimulation data suggest that the essential CS pathway includes mossy fiber projections to the cerebellum via the pontine nuclei (see Figure 1). (As noted later, approximately 60% of the Purkinje cells we have studied in the untrained animal, from H VI, Crus I and Crus II, show clear evoked responses, usually an increase in frequency of discharge, to the tone CS stimulus.) Sufficiently large lesions of the middle cerebellar peduncle prevent acquisition and immediately abolish retention of the eyelid CR to all modalities of CS (Solomon et al., 1986b) whereas lesions in the pontine nuclear region can selectively abolish the eyelid CR to an acoustic CS (Steinmetz et al., 1986). Consistent with this result is current anatomical evidence from our laboratory for a direct contralateral projection from the ventral cochlear nucleus to this same region of the pons (Thompson, Lavond, & Thompson, 1986) and electrophysiological evidence of a "primary-like" auditory relay nucleus in this pontine region (Logan, Steinmetz, & Thompson, 1986).

Electrical microstimulation of the mossy fiber system serves as a very effective CS, producing rapid learning, on average more rapid than with peripheral CSs, when paired with, e.g., a corneal airpuff US (Steinmetz et al., 1985a). If animals are trained with a left pontine nuclear stimulation CS and then tested for transfer to right pontine stimulation, transfer is immediate (i.e., 1 trial) if the two electrodes have similar locations in the two sides, suggesting that at least under these conditions the traces are not formed in the pontine nuclei but rather in the cerebellum, probably beyond the mossy fiber terminals (Steinmetz et al., 1986). Finally, appropriate forward pairing of mossy fiber stimulation as a CS and climbing fiber stimulation as a US yields normal behavioral learning of the response elicited by climbing fiber stimulation (Steinmetz et al., 1985b). Lesion of the interpositus abolishes both the CR and the UR in this paradigm and backward presentation of US and CS or simultaneous presentation of CS and US produce no learning. All of these results taken together would seem to build an increasingly strong case for localization of the essential memory traces to the cerebellum, particularly in the "reduced" preparation with stimulation of mossy fibers as the CS and climbing fibers as the US.

Recordings from Purkinje cells in the eyelid conditioning paradigm are consistent with the formation of memory traces in cerebellar cortex. Prior to training, a tone CS causes a variable evoked increase in frequency of discharge of simple spikes in many Purkinje cells (Foy & Thompson, 1986; Donegan et al., 1985). Following training, the majority of Purkinje cells that develop a change in frequency of simple spike discharge that correlates with the behavioral response (as opposed to being stimulus evoked) show decreases in frequency of discharge of simple spikes that precede and "predict" the form of the behavioral learned response, although increases in "predictive" discharge frequency also occur fairly frequently.

Prior to training, the onset of the corneal airpuff US evokes a complex spike (signaling a climbing fiber volley) in the great majority of Purkinje cells that are influenced by the US (e.g., in H VII, Crus I and Crus II). However, the tone CS does not evoke complex spikes before or after training. These results are strongly supportive of our general hypothesis (Figure 1) that climbing fibers are the essential US pathway and mossy fibers the CS pathway. After training, complex spikes are rarely evoked by US onset, a result that has interesting implications for the nature of "reinforcement" in classical conditioning (see Thompson, 1986).

Conjoint electrical stimulation of mossy fibers and climbing fibers can yield normal learning of behavioral responses, as noted above (Steinmetz et al., 1985b). The properties of these learned responses appear identical to those of the same conditioned responses learned with peripheral stimuli (e.g., eyelid closure, leg flexion). The temporal requirements for such conjoint stimulation that yields behavioral learning are essentially identical to those required with peripheral stimuli: no learning at all if CS onset does not precede US onset by more than 50 msec, best learning if CS precedes US by 200-400 msec, and progressively poorer learning with increasing CS precedence (Gormezano, 1972). Further, normal learning occurs if the mossy fiber CS consists of only 2 pulses, 5 msec apart, at the beginning of a 250 msec CS-US onset interval (Logan et al., 1985).

Collectively, the evidence reviewed above demonstrates that the cerebellum is essential for the category of procedural memory we have studied. It also builds a very strong case that the essential memory traces are stored in very localized regions of the cerebellum.

Cerebellum: Hyperactivity and Procedural Learning

In view of the fact that a major aspect of hyperactivity is movement, it would not be entirely surprising if the cerebellum plays some role in hyperactivity. There is very recent evidence that cerebellar pathology can produce a syndrome of hyperactivity in mice (Crnic & Pizer, 1987). In brief, neonatal mice (e.g., day 2) were injected (subcutaneous, shoulder) with a mutant herpes simplex type 1 virus (012180C 3V2-BU-AU5). This virus is considerably weaker than the wild type. Controls were injected with heat inactivated virus. Those that survived were tested in development and as adults on measures of activity, passive avoidance learning and learning of a radial arm maze.

The infected animals showed marked increases in activity in the light portion of the 24 hour activity cycle, the period when they are normally least active. Consistent with this, infected mice took significantly longer to learn the passive avoidance task — they were slower to learn to inhibit responses. Interestingly, however, the infected animals learned the radical arm maze as did controls.

In terms of cerebellar involvement in the infected animals, the authors note damage to the cerebellar vermis and the deep nuclei and to structures connected with the cerebellum, e.g., colliculi and lateral thalamus. In some cases, the virus delayed and prevented completion of migration of cerebellar granule cells.

In the context of hyperactivity in children, the authors note that the human condition involves soft neurological signs of cerebellar pathology, particularly in attention deficit disorder (see also Nahmias & Visintine, 1976).

Study of humans with anterograde amnesia suggest a dichotomy between two types of learning and memory. HM is the classic case. Following bilateral removal of the medial regions of the temporal lobe, including large portions of the hippocampus and amygdala, HM developed severe anterograde amnesia. He is unable to remember his own experiences following the operation, although he remembers his life experiences quite normally prior to a year or two before the operation. He also has great difficulty learning new verbal- factual material. This has been termed declarative memory — learning what. Of equal importance are the kinds of memory that are entirely normal in HM: motor skills, including very complex "cognitive" tasks like learning to read mirror English (text reflected in a mirror). With practice he learned to become quite skilled at mirror reading, as much so as a normal person. But, he cannot remember what he has read. This kind of memory is termed procedural or learning how.

Classical conditioning of discrete behavioral responses (e.g., eyelid closure, limb flexion) is a clear case of procedural learning. As noted above, the cerebellum is essential for this form of learning and the evidence strongly suggests that the memory traces are, in fact, stored in the cerebellum. On the other hand, the hippocampus is not essential for this form of learning. Much has been made of the deficits in declarative memory exhibited by humans with anterograde amnesia; being unable to remember one's own experience seems a devastating loss. On the other hand, the kinds of learning and memory deficits exhibited by children with various learning disabilities, including those classed as hyperactive, are much more in the nature of procedural skills. Reading and writing are largely procedural tasks.

It is therefore not beyond the realm of possibility that hyperactivity and its attendant behavioral problems relate in some fundamental way to dysfunction of the cerebellum. At least our work, and that of Crnic (see above) raise this possibility.

REFERENCES

Albus, J. S. (1971). A theory of cerebellar function. *Mathematical Bioscience, 10*, 25–61

Berger, T. W., Rinaldi, P., Weisz, D. J., & Thompson, R. F. (1983). Single unit analysis of different hippocampal cell types during classical conditioning of the rabbit nictitating membrane response. *Journal of Neurophysiology, 450,* 1197–1219.

Brooks, V. B. (1979). Control of intended limb movements by the lateral and intermediate cerebellum. In H. Asanuma, & V. J. Wilson (Eds.), *Integration in the nervous system* (pp. 321–357). Tokyo: Igaku Shoin.

Brooks, V. B., Kozlovskaya, I. B., Atkin, A., Horvath, F. E., & Uno, M. (1973). Effects of cooling dentate nucleus on tracking-task performance in monkeys. *Journal of Neurophysiology, 36,* 974–995.

Brooks, V. B., & Thach, W. T. (1981). Cerebellar control of posture and movement. In J. M. Brookhart, V. B. Mountcastle, V. B. Brooks & S. R. Geiger (Eds.), *Handbook of physiology* (Vol. 2, pp. 877–946). Bethesda, MD: American Physiological Society.

Chapman, C. E., Spidalieri, G., & Lamarre, Y. (1986). Activity of dentate neurons during arm movements triggered by visual, auditory, and somesthetic stimuli in the monkey. *Journal of Neurophysiology, 55,* 203–226.

Chapman, P. F., Steinmetz, J. E., & Thompson, R. F. (1985). Classical conditioning of the rabbit eyeblink does not occur with stimulation of the cerebellar nuclei as the unconditioned stimulus. *Society for Neuroscience Abstracts, 11,* 835.

Clark, G. A., McCormick, D. A., Lavond, D. G., & Thompson, R. F. (1984). Effects of lesions of cerebellar nuclei on conditioned behavioral and hippocampal neuronal responses. *Brain Research, 291,* 125–136.

Crnic, L. S., & Pizer, L. I. (In Press). Behavioral effects of neonatal Herpes Simplex Type 1 infection of mice. *Neurobehavioral Toxicology and Teratology.*

Disterhoft, J. F., Coulter, D. A., & Alkon, D. L. (in press). Conditioning-specific membrane changes of rabbit hippocampal neurons measured in vitro. *Proceedings of the National Academy of Sciences.*

Donegan, N. H., Foy, M. R., & Thompson, R. F. (1985). Neuronal responses of the rabbit cerebellar cortex during performance of the classically conditioned eyelid response. *Society for Neuroscience Abstracts, 11,* 835.

Donegan, N. H., Lowry, R. W., & Thompson, R. F. (1983). Effects of lesioning cerebellar nuclei on conditioned leg-flexion responses. *Neuroscience Abstracts, 9,* (No. 100.7), 331.

Eccles, J. C. (1977). An instruction-selection theory of learning in the cerebellar cortex. *Brain Research, 127,* 327–352.

Foy, M. R., & Thompson, R. F. (1986). Single unit analysis of Purkinje cell discharge in classically conditioned and untrained rabbits. *Society for Neuroscience Abstracts, 12, 518.*

Gormezano, I. (1972). Investigations of defense and reward conditioning in the rabbit. In A. H. Black, & W. F. Prokasy, (Eds), *Classical conditioning II: Current research and theory* (pp. 151–181). New York: Appleton-Century-Crofts.

Haley, D. A., Lavond, D. G., & Thompson, R. F. (1983). Effects of contralateral red nuclear lesions on retention of the classically conditioned nictitating membrane/eyelid response. *Society for Neuroscience Abstracts, 9,* 643.

Ito, M., (1972). Neural design of the cerebellar motor control system. *Brain Research, 40,* 81–84.

Ito, M. (1984). *The cerebellum and neural control.* New York: Raven.

Kettner, R. E., & Thompson, R. F. (1985). Cochlear nucleus, inferior colliculus, and medial geniculate responses during the behavioral detection of threshold-level auditory stimuli in the rabbit. *Journal of the Acoustical Society of America, 77,* 2111–2127.

Lavond, D. G., Hembree, T. L., & Thompson, R. F. (1985). Effect of kainic acid lesions of the cerebellar interpositus nucleus on eyelid conditioning in the rabbit. *Brain Research, 326,* 179–182.

Lavond, D. G., Lincoln, J. S., McCormick, D. A., & Thompson, R. F. (1984). Effect of bilateral lesions of the denate interpositus cerebellar nuclei on conditioning of heart-rate and nictitating membrane/eyelid responses in the rabbit. *Brain Research, 305,* 323–330.

Lavond, D. G., McCormick, D. A., Clark, G. A., Holmes, D. T., & Thompson, R. F. (1981). Effects of ipsilateral rostral pontine reticular lesions on retention of classically conditioned nictitating membrane and eyelid response. *Physiological Psychology, 9,* 335–339.

Lavond, D. G., McCormick, D. A., & Thompson, R. F. (1984b) A nonrecoverable learning deficit. *Physiological Psychology*, *12,* 103–110.

Lavond, D. G., Steinmetz, J. E., Yokaitis, M. H., Lee, J., & Thompson, R. F. (1986). Retention of classical conditioning after removal of cerebellar cortex. *Society for Neuroscience Abstracts*, *12*, 753.

Lincoln, J. S., McCormick, D. A., & Thompson, R. F. (1982). Ipsilateral cerebellar lesions prevent learning of the classically conditioned nictitating membrane/eyelid response of the rabbit. *Brain Research*, *242*, 190–193.

Llinas, R. (1981). Electrophysiology of the cerebellar networks. In J. M. Brookhart, V. B. Mountcastle, V. B. Brooks, & S. R. Geiger (Eds.), *Handbook of physiology* (Vol. 2, pp. 831–876). Bethesda, MD: American Physiological Society.

Logan, C. G., Steinmetz, J. E., Woodruff-Pak, D. S., & Thompson, R. F. (1985). Short-duration mossy fiber stimulation is effective as a CS in eyelid classical conditioning. *Society for Neuroscience Abstracts*, *11*, 835.

Logan, C. G., Steinmetz, J. E., & Thompson, R. F. (1986). Acoustic related responses recorded from the region of the pontine nuclei. *Society for Neuroscience Abstracts*, *12*, 754.

Madden, J., IV, Haley, D. A., Barchas, J. D., & Thompson, R. F. (1983). Microinfusion of picrotoxin into the caudal red nucleus selectively abolishes the classically conditioned nictitating membrane/eyelid response in the rabbit. *Society for Neuroscience Abstracts*, *9*, 830.

Mamounas, L. A., Thompson, R. F., Lynch, G., & Baudry, M. (1984). Classical conditioning of the rabbit eyelid response increases glutamate receptor binding in hippocampal synaptic membranes. *Proceedings of the National Academy of Sciences*, *83*, 2548–2552.

Marr, D. (1969). A theory of cerebellar cortex. *Journal of Physiology*, *202*, 437–470.

Mauk, M. D., Steinmetz, J. E., & Thompson, R. F. (1986). Classical conditioning using stimulation of the inferior olive as the unconditioned stimulus. *Proceedings of the National Academy of Sciences*, *83*, 5349–5353.

Mauk, M. D., & Thompson, R. F., (1987). Retention of classically conditioned eyelid responses following acute decerebration. *Brain Research*, *403*, 89–95.

McCormick, D. A., Clark, G. A., Lavond, D. G., & Thompson, R. F. (1982a). Initial localization of the memory trace for a basic form of learning. *Proceedings of the National Academy of Sciences*, *79*, 2731–2742.

McCormick, D. A., Guyer, P. E., & Thompson, R. F. (1982b). Superior cerebellar peduncle lesions selectively abolish the ipsilateral classically conditioned nictitating membrane/eyelid response in the rabbit. *Brain Research*, *244*, 347–350.

McCormick, D.A., Lavond, D. G., Clark, G. A., Kettner, R. E., Rising, C. E., & Thompson, R. F. (1981). The engram found? Role of the cerebellum in classical conditioning of nictitating membrane and eyelid responses. *Bulletin of the Psychonomic Society*, *18*, 103–105.

McCormick, D. A., & Thompson, R. F. (1984a). Cerebellum: Essential involvement in the classically conditioned eyelid response. *Science*, *223*, 296–299.

McCormick, D. A., & Thompson, R. F. (1984b). Neuronal responses of the rabbit cerebellum during acquisition and performance of a classically conditioned nictitating membrane-eyelid response. *Journal of Neuroscience*, *4*, 2811–2822.

Meyer-Lohmann, J., Hore, J., & Brooks, V. B. (1977). Cerebellar participation in generation of prompt arm movements. *Journal of Neurophysiology*, *40*, 1038–1050.

Nahmias, A. J., & Visintine, A. (1976). Herpes simplex. In J. Remington & J. Klein (Eds.), *Infectious diseases of the fetus and newborn infant* (pp. 156–190). Philadelphia: Saunders Co.

Norman, R. J., Villablanca, J. R., Brown, K. A., Schwafel, J. A., & Buchwald, J. S. (1974). *Classical conditioning in the bilaterally hemispherectomized cat. Experimental Neurology*, *44*, 363–380.

Oakley, D. A., Russel, I. S. (1977). Subcortical storage of Pavlovian conditioning in the rabbit. *Physiology and Behavior*, *18*, 931–937.

Polenchar, B. E., Patterson, M. M., Lavond, D. G., & Thompson, R. F. (1985). Cerebellar lesions abolish an avoidance response in rabbit. *Behavioral and Neural Biology*, *44*, 221–227.

Rosenfield, M. E., Devydaitis, A., & Moore, J. W. (1985). Brachium conjunctivum and rubrobulbar tract: Brainstem projections of red nucleus essential for the conditioned nictitating membrane response. *Physiology and Behavior, 34*, 751–759.

Solomon, P. R., Lewis, J. L., LoTurco, J. J., Steinmetz, J. E., & Thompson, R. F. (1986). The role of the middle cerebellar peduncle in acquisition and retention of the rabbits classically conditioned nictitating membrane response. *Bulletin of the Psychonomic Society, 24*, 75–78.

Steinmetz, J. E., Lavond, D. G., & Thompson, R. F. (1985a). Classical conditioning of the rabbit eyelid response with mossy fiber stimulation as the conditioned stimulus. *Bulletin of the Psychonomic Society, 23*, 245–248.

Steinmetz, J. E., Lavond, D. G., & Thompson, R. F. (1985b). Classical conditioning of skeletal muscle responses with mossy fiber stimulation CS and climbing fiber stimulation US. *Society for Neuroscience Abstracts, 11*, 982.

Steinmetz, J. E., Logan, C. G., Rosen, D. J., Thompson, J. K., Lavond, D. G., & Thompson, R. F. (1987). Initial localization of the acoustic conditioned stimulus projection system to the cerebellum essential for classical eyelid conditioning. *Proceedings of the National Academy of Science, 84*, 3531–3535.

Steinmetz, J. E., Rosen, D. J., Woodruff-Pak, D. S., Lavond, D. G., & Thompson, R. F. (1986). Rapid transfer of training occurs when direct mossy fiber stimulation is used as a conditioned stimulus for classical eyelid conditioning. *Neuroscience Research, 3*, 606–616.

Thompson, R. F. (1986). The neurobiology of learning and memory. *Science, 233*, 941–947.

Thompson, R. F., Berger, T. W., & Madden, J., IV (1983). Cellular processes of learning and memory in the mammalian CNS. *Annual Review of Neuroscience, 6*, 447–491.

Thompson, R. F., Clark, G. A., Donegan, N. H., Lavond, D. G., Madden, J., IV, Mamounas, L. A., Mauk, M. D., & McCormick, D. A. (1984). Neuronal substrates of basic associative learning. In L. Squire, & N. Butters (Eds.), *Neuropsychology of memory* (pp. 424–442). New York: Guilford Press.

Thompson, J. K., Lavond, D. G., & Thompson, R. F. (1986). Preliminary evidence for a projection from the cochlear nucleus to the pontine nuclear region. *Society for Neuroscience Abstracts, 12*, 754.

Weisz, D. J., Clark, G. A., & Thompson, R. F. (1984). Increased activity of dentate granule cells during nictitating membrane response conditioning in rabbits. *Behavioral Brain Research, 12*, 145–154.

Woodruff-Pak, D. S., Lavond, D. G., & Thompson, R. F. (1985a). Trace conditioning: Abolished by cerebellar nuclear lesions but not lateral cerebellar cortex aspirations. *Brain Research, 348*, 249–260.

Woodruff-Pak, D. S., Lavond, D. G., Logan, C. G., Steinmetz, J. E., & Thompson, R. F. (1985b). The continuing search for a role of the cerebellar cortex in eyelid conditioning. *Society for Neuroscience Abstracts, 11*, 333.

Yeo, C. H., Hardiman, M. J., & Glickstein, M. (1984). Discrete lesions of the cerebellar cortex abolish the classically conditioned nictitating membrane response of the rabbit. *Behavioral Brain Research, 13*, 261–266.

Yeo, C. H., Hardiman, M. J., & Glickstein, M. (1985). Classical conditioning of the nictitating membrane response of the rabbit: I. Lesions of the cerebellar nuclei. *Experimental Brain Research, 60*, 87–98.

Attention Deficit Disorder and Hyperkinetic Syndrome: Biological Perspectives

Robert D. Oades
Department of Human Physiology,
Finders University Medical Centre,
Bedford Park, Australia

INTRODUCTION: THE CONDITION

What is the nature of the condition, referred to as attention deficit disorder (ADD) or childhood hyperkinesis in this chapter? Recent categorical descriptions in diagnostic manuals are widely felt by clinicians to be misleading (e.g. ADD, minimal brain dysfunction, childhood hyperkinesis). Indeed in contrast to conditions like Parkinsonism, there is little clear knowledge of the underlying disorder. There are symptoms. But no single one is indispensable for diagnosis and the number necessary varies with the authority.

The measurable items of interest include motor activity, attentional strategies, context dependent motivation and psychostimulant responsiveness. An arbitrary degree of deviation from the norm for several of these items currently forms the basis for diagnosis (e.g., from fidgetiness to pervasive hyperkinesis) and hence leads to the rather different estimates of the incidence of the condition around the world (Weiss & Hechtman, 1979; Thorley, 1984).

If we seek biological concomitants or symptoms to model we cannot overlook the questions raised by differences of clinical opinion. For example, at the mild end of the scale, is there a symptom in ''underachievement'' (cf. Shaywitz & Shaywitz, this volume)? This is a question for society and for the laboratory investigator. Is it relevant that after a given intervention an animal learns more slowly or that learning one task interferes with learning another? At the severe end of the scale, should the investigator be more concerned with pervasive hyperkinesia and/or autistic behaviour, mental handicap and/or responsiveness to psy-

353

chostimulants? Clearly biological correlates for each of these symptom pictures should be sought separately, and if possible, sometimes in combination. With a symptom-oriented strategy, there will remain doubts about the interpretation of the biological correlates in terms of the underlying cause of the disorder. But eventually one hopes that such studies will clarify the relationships between the components of a potential category, of the condition under consideration.

However there are some sobering caveats for the exclusive use of a symptom-oriented strategy without reference to knowledge about categories of symptoms and their epidemiology. For example, whilst classical childhood autism may improve slightly after neuroleptic treatment, autism associated with the fragile X chromosomal condition can benefit from psychostimulant treatment. The reverse is more usually true for childhood hyperkinesis, given that there is a response to treatment at all.

Nonetheless, let us concentrate on the symptoms and consider what indicators of changed biological function, associated with the symptoms of ADD, might be useful and then look for correlations with the behavioral items of interest from animal studies.

BIOLOGICAL INDICATORS

There are different requirements of biological indicators in diagnosis and treatment on the one hand and for providing clues to those investigating the biological bases underlying any symptom on the other. For instance there is a high incidence of subtle brain damage in hyperactive children (Taylor, this volume). Whilst the use of major neurological soft signs is felt not to be useful in diagnosis and management, more reports of refined and intelligent use of soft signs (e.g., multiple measures of cognitive performance) would be most welcome for the laboratory investigator of hyperactive children or animal models (cf. Milner, 1971; Carpenter, Strauss, & Bartko, 1981; Kolb & Whishaw, 1983). To illustrate the point, it is only through such reports that a rational argument for measuring frontal cerebral blood flow can be advanced to confirm anomalous biological function.

Electrophysiology. Electrophysiological investigations also illustrate the dichotomy between the value of diagnostic and investigatory tools. The main clinical use of the EEG lies not in diagnosis per se, but in the separation of a subgroup for pharmacotherapy (e.g., methylphenidate vs valproate; Morag, Frank, & Myslobodsky, paper presented at the Workshop on Attention Deficit Disorder, Oslo, 1987). But averaging the EEG after stimuli or events in a task situation (event-related potential, ERP) has not received appropriate or intensive study. Such studies may provide a useful investigatory tool, despite methodological difficulties.

Children with attentional problems are reported to show larger negative slow waves over frontal sites (CPT, Friedman, Cornblatt, Vaughan, & Erlenmeyer-Kimling, 1986) and a well-controlled group of ADD (both with and without hyperactivity) showed smaller P3b and late positive components over posterior sites (auditory odd-ball task, Holcomb, Ackerman, & Dykman, 1986). In this context it is of interest to discover that cerebral glucose utilization has been studied (Shaywitz & Shaywitz, this volume). A decreased utilization is reported in frontal regions and increased utilization in posterior regions. What might be the relation between ERPs, glucose utilization and mental (attention or response) effort?

Mental effort or the evaluation of events, as indexed by P3b latency, is said not to be influenced by methylphenidate (Callaway & Halliday, 1982). But others have shown and replicated an enhancement of the evaluation process (P3b latency) under such medication in certain forms of the Sternberg memory scanning task (Brumaghim, Klorman, Strauss, Lewine, & Goldstein, 1987). What is the fine distribution of these ERP changes (mapping) and their sensitivity to treatment in ADDH-subjects who respond and not respond to psychostimulant therapy? Does the severity of performance deficits correlate with ERP changes and are ERP changes subject to manipulation of the motivational interest of ADD subjects? Is the decrease in amplitude of late positive components in autistic children performing an auditory odd-ball task (Oades, Walker, Geffen, & Stern, 1988) related to the similar phenomenon in ADD children? Results of such studies will inform us about the nature of the attention-related phenomenon, its locus and the sub-group showing such changes.

Stimulants and Arousal. It may be that psychostimulant responsiveness should form a part of the diagnostic process (Rutter, this volume). It cannot be doubted that the separation of subjects for further study into those responding and not responding to amphetamine or methylphenidate treatment is crucial for progress in understanding the biology of the hyperkinetic syndrome. (Although the use of this type of separation should not exclude under-used methods for group separation, e.g. on the basis of mental or developmental retardation, autonomic arousal, peptide excretion or "food allergy").

Are hyperactive children under—or over-aroused? Is the therapeutic effect of psychostimulant medication paradoxical? What happens to catecholamine (CA) metabolism in underaroused and psychostimulant responders? Kløve (this volume) has capably summarised the conflicting literature on the arousal hypothesis. But Pandora's box has been opened. The measures (heart rate, skin conductance inter alia) not only vary between individuals and medication status (Brand & van der Vlugt, this volume), but according to stimulus salience, anticipatory set, motivation, stimulus consequence, age, institutional status and a host of other factors. To define the effect of medication requires the study of the individual as his/her own control and a truly enormous investigation controlling for each situational factor. More tellingly one must have reservations on the predictive power of such investigations of a global construct.

Resolution of the so-called paradoxical effect of psychostimulants does not lie in the determination of the status of a global construct such as arousal and its change with treatment. The effect of stimulant treatment is the sum of the numerous changes it induces in a wide range of measures. Some of these changes appear on the surface to be paradoxical. Psychostimulants can decrease urinary/plasma MHPG levels (metabolite of noradrenaline (NA), increase HVA levels (metabolite of dopamine (DA) or simply decrease HVA levels in hyperkinetic subjects with low MHPG (Shekim, Javaid, Dekirmenjian, Chapel, & David, 1982; see also Table 2, Oades, 1987). They can increase the prolactin response without affecting growth hormone levels (Shaywitz & Shaywitz, this volume). Behaviorally, as Robbins, Jones, and Sahakian (this volume) indicate, methylphenidate treatment of hyperactive children may increase perseverative errors in a Wisconsin card sorting task yet improve visual search on the Lafayette battery.

Some of these paradoxes rest on an assumption about the underlying substrate treated. For example, the neurophysiological effect of amphetamine is inhibitory, yet it stimulates the release and activity of CAs. Resolution of the conflict lies in separating pre- and post-synaptic mechanisms. Again, the beneficial effect of amphetamine was first seen in hyperactive subjects suffering from von Economo's encephalitis. In hindsight one can say that this was not paradoxical, for these subjects showed some Parkinsonian symptoms and post-mortem study showed some degeneration of the substantia nigra.

The "paradox" of hyperactivity being attenuated by stimulant treatment receives only partial solution by consideration of the rate-dependent effects of psychostimulants on behaviour (c. 30%, Robbins & Sahakian, 1979). Global effects of the stimulants on behavioural activity reflect baselines of transmitter activity. Low baselines increase after stimulant treatment. High baseline transmitter activity is relatively unaffected or often reduced by stimulant drugs. More important will be the neuronal innervation patterns in regions governing specific and separately organised responses (e.g., response and error monitoring, the search for a stimulus relevant for task solution and the control of vegetative activities such as hormone production). For example, as amphetamine can inhibit electrically induced DA release, but facilitate electrically induced NA release (Langer & Arbilla, 1984), behavioral activities depending on the neostriatum (mainly DA innervation) will be affected differently from those depending on active contributions from the prefrontal cortex or nucleus accumbens (related DA and NA innervation).

The true paradox of psychostimulant therapy yet presents itself when the biochemical and behavioral changes resulting from treatment are interpreted exclusively in terms of the known effects of these agents on blocking CA reuptake, stimulating CA release and attenuating monoamine oxidase (MAO) activity. Why are treatments with CA precursors and MAO inhibitors disappointing in the long term? It is curious that neurological soft signs, where present, do not predict stimulant responsiveness. Even where psychostimulants effectively reduce hyperactivity, such a decrease is a poor predictor of the ultimate outcome. Even where it is found that stimulants or MAO inhibitors do improve behavior and there is a behavioral rebound after drug withdrawal, MHPG levels remain as low as ever. These are some of the paradoxes and uncomfortable issues that need to be addressed. Elsewhere I have elaborated on the possibility that these issues point to a third "non-catecholamine" etiological factor in the hyperkinetic syndrome (Oades, 1987). These issues recall Baldessarini's remark (1977) that an understanding of the action of thiazide diuretics would not necessarily lead to an important insight into the pathophysiology of congestive heart failure.

Metabolism. Issues that have been addressed all too infrequently concern metabolites as biological indicators. Of interest are the breakdown products of the conventional monoamine transmitters (e.g., HVA, MHPG, 5-HIAA) of the neuropeptides (e.g., opioids) and of certain dietary constituents (e.g., casein).

Considering the relative and non-invasive ease with which urinary and plasma specimens may be obtained, it is regrettable that this practice is not more routine. Particularly taking into account that it is possible to increase the proportion of metabolites of central origin by prior use of debrisoquin, a mild monoamine oxidase inhibitor with largely peripheral action (Shaywitz & Shaywitz, this volume). The technique could provide valuable epidemiological data and illustrate more clearly the relevance of stimulant treatment. It could also highlight productive avenues for further study by providing correlations with some of the anomalous developmental or behavioural features of hyperactive children.

Why, amongst stimulant-responders, are MHPG levels low and not improved by pharmacotherapy? Do these levels reflect low turnover, low sympathetic arousal and a reduced ability to tune central neural processing to task relevant stimuli (cf. Oades, 1985)? Certainly there is evidence supporting enduring low "arousal" in hyperkinetic children (cf. Kløve, this volume) and the reduced P3 amplitude of the ERP (Holcomb et al., 1986) is modulated by locus coeruleus activity (Foote, personal communication). But the answer may be "No" to all three questions. MHPG levels may not be a good indicator of NA neural activity (Commissiong, 1985). Sympathetic and central arousal levels are likely to be reflected by other metabolites (e.g., VMA) and other transmitters (e.g., the amino acids). The P3 component is affected by many other neurotransmitters (e.g., acetylcholine; Hammond, Meador, Aung-Din, & Wilder, 1987).

In any case what are the behavioral differences between stimulant responders and the non-responders who show normal levels of MHPG? Why is the urinary HVA/MHPG ratio 50-100% higher in both responders and non-responders than in healthy controls? Perhaps these changes reflect an imbalance, not of the transmitter-CAs, but of the trophic-CAs. An imbalance of trophic properties might explain anomalous regional innervation patterns, some functional retardation and the progress, development and amelioration of different symptoms with maturity. It is not clear to what extent metabolite imbalance attenuates with age and if this is related to symptom changes.

The excretion of a range of N-substituted peptides and their relation to diet and psychiatric disorder was touched on by Reichelt et al. (paper presented at the Workshop on Attention Deficit Disorder, Oslo, 1987). They claim to be able to distinguish subjects with ADD, ADDH, conduct disorder and autism according to the pattern of peptide excretion (e.g., Reichelt, Saelid, Lindback, & Boeler, 1986). These results are provocative, suggesting perhaps a range of peptidase insufficiencies. The potential causes are legion. They range from the reduced availability of nutrients necessary as enzymic cofactors (e.g., zinc) to changed levels of neuropeptides which inhibit enzymes such as enkephalinase and angiotensin converting enzyme (e.g., beta endorphin and substance P; McGeer & Singh, 1979; Hui, Graf, & Lajhta, 1982). The functional relevance is hinted at by McGaugh (paper presented at the Workshop on Attention Deficit Disorder, Oslo, 1987). NA release is modulated by opioid activity. Thus changes of learning abilities, dependent on adrenergic activity, may be influenced by abnormal central opioid activity (Izquierdo, Dias, Souza, Carrasco, Elisabetsky, & Perry, 1980).

Challenges have been made. The metabolic pathways need to be examined. I have already raised the question of an involvement of angiotensin on the basis of hypertensive animal models and the psychological profile of some hypertensive people (Oades, 1987). More circumstantial evidence can be derived from the claim that a large proportion of hyperactive children show unusual thirsts (I. Colquhoun, personal communication). Are these items all merely coincidental? Are other neuropeptides such as cholecystokinin and neuropeptide Y involved? These peptides are associated with DA and NA neurons respectively: they can also modulate motor activity and hypertension.

ANIMAL MODELS

Two main types of model are used to illuminate ADDH. The first one draws on the implied CA dysfunction and describes the effects of interfering with CA function on the major symptoms of attention and behavioural activity. Symptoms relating to impulsivity and motivation have received less study. The second draws more broadly on the symptom picture and arguably can be said to attempt to model the disorder. Here I refer to spontaneously hypertensive animals and manipulations during the development of animals. I briefly mention a third category of model that seems to have been neglected, namely that of other childhood disorders with features in common with ADD.

Symptom Models

Noradrenaline (NA): The problem has been and remains that it is difficult to show or describe attentional or learning impairments that animals have when depleted of central NA. They are quite capable of learning: it is just in some situations that they are less efficient and less adaptive. Is this not remarkably similar to the situation with hyperactive children?

Burning the midnight oil in Södertälje and Cambridge has been rewarded by interesting findings (see the chapters by Archer and Robbins et al. for details). Firstly, performance on sensory preconditioning and latent inhibition - two tasks that experimental psychologists have proposed as indicators of attentional and selective learning ability - is impaired after the reduction of forebrain NA. I believe such studies have succeeded (e.g., Archer, Mohammed, Danysz, & Jonsson, 1986; Mohammed, Callenholm, Järbe, Swedberg, Danysz, Robbins, & Archer, 1986; Lorden, Rickert, & Berry, 1983) where others have failed (e.g., Tsaltas, Preston, Rawlings, Winocur, & Gray, 1984; Robbins & Everitt, 1985) because of the use of multiple cues. As I have suggested (Oades, 1985), only where demands are placed on NA to tune the relative importance between *several* potentially relevant stimuli will behavioural impairments be demonstratable after NA depletion. But for the sake of the model one must go further. Would non-sedative doses of pharmacological agents that result in low MHPG excretion produce similar results?

The second finding of interest is that animals depleted of forebrain NA can take an unusually long time in reaching strict learning criteria on some forms of discrimination task. In this context it is not surprising that agents of ''arousal'' that might be expected to challenge CA systems (e.g., white noise before presentation of discriminanda or amphetamine treatment of the nucleus accumbens) can impair the discrimination performance of lesioned animals (Robbins et al., this volume; Robbins & Everitt, 1985).

In connection with these results it is perhaps pertinent to note that intact animals respond to mild stressors or novel stimuli by releasing NA transiently in the terminal regions (c. 20%, Gold & Zornetzer, 1983; Svensson & Ahlenius, 1983). Such a neural response seems designed to control inappropriate reactions. One would expect that such neural and behavioural responses would not only be absent in lesioned animals, but perhaps reduced in children with low levels of MHPG. The lesson surely is that NA activity is important for cognitive performance to be appropriate and adaptive. It might prove instructive to examine further the strategies of exploration of *novel* objects in *novel* environments, - preferably structured to facilitate a comparison of studies of performance in lesioned animals and hyperactive children.

Dopamine (DA): Attention-related information processing is anomalous in a number of human conditions where DA activity is significantly altered. This has been shown by ERP studies of schizophrenia (for review see Oades, 1982), Parkinsonism (Wright, 1988), childhood autism (Oades, Stern, Walker, & Kapoor, submitted) and ADD/ADDH (Holcomb et al., 1986). Shaywitz and Shaywitz (this volume) has pointed out that a group of hyperactive children do show changes of HVA levels in samples of CSF, urine and plasma. Changed DA activity is a factor in the attentive processes (e.g., effort) of healthy students where neuroleptic effects are reversed by methylphenidate (Clark, Geffen, & Geffen, 1986). The role of DA activity in hyperactive children is also shown by the relative success of psychostimulant treatment and the fact that the effects can be blocked by neuroleptic pretreatment (Levy, personal communication). The efficacy of very low doses of neuroleptics in such children (Werry & Aman, 1975; Gittelman Klein & Abikoff, this volume), receives support from animal studies. Very low doses of sulpiride (like amphetamine treatment) eliminate latent inhibition (Feldon, Weiner & Ben-Shahar, 1987). In animal studies a variety of DA manipulations affect both latent inhibition and conditioned blocking (Weiner, Lubow, & Feldon, 1984; Crider, Blockel, & Solomon, 1986; Oades, Rivet, Taghzouti, Kharouby, Simon, & Le Moal, 1987). Yet it remains unclear just what the contribution of DA might be.

The chapters by Robbins et al. and Beninger (this volume) imply, respectively, that changes in DA activity could partly be responsible for the impulsivity and altered motivational control seen in many hyperactive children. Robbins et al. describes a 9-hole box where rats have to wait for the correct stimulus, then respond to the correct hole and pick up a reward elsewhere. Commission, omission and premature errors are recorded. He draws an analogy with the continuous performance task in which hyperactive children perform poorly on signal detection measures. The analogy is plausible. Amphetamine treatment increases premature responses, apparently decreasing beta, the response criterion of signal detection theory. This impairment is attenuated by chemical lesion of the DA innervation of the nucleus accumbens. This is an elegant demonstration implicating the role of DA activity. However as an explanation for the behavior of hyperactive children, it is ''upside down''. The performance of hyperactive children that show a low response criterion can be improved by amphetamine treatment. Of course there are many examples whereby the nature of the change is altered by training before or after a manipulation or by altering the sequence of events in the protocol. But although it may be worthwhile exploring these alternatives, it may be better to look at the role of another DA-innervated region such as the septal nuclei or the frontal cortex.

Intact innervation of the frontal cortex exerts an inhibitory control over the innervation of the nucleus accumbens (Pycock, Kerwin, & Carter, 1980; Tassin, Reibaud, Blanc, Studler, & Glowinski, 1984). The increase of limbic DA activity induced by frontal damage may be attenuated by the rate dependent action of amphetamine. One notes from studies of hyperactive children that glucose utilization is lower in the frontal regions of some subjects (Shaywitz & Shaywitz, this volume). Further, in the context of a putative frontal impairment and the so-called paradoxical action of psychostimulants, a recent result from Robertson (1986) is provocative. Unilateral cortical damage or chronic amphetamine treatment downgrades neostriatal DA receptors by between a fifth and a third. But together the treatments result in the upgrading of DA receptors by 50%.

The study of impulsivity in a 9-hole box after manipulation of DA-projection regions may yet prove productive in modelling human impulsivity, as could further study of both NA and DA influences on the nature of task-solving strategies. For example, hippocampal and DA activity can differentially affect errors and sequences of holevisits in a 16-holeboard (Oades & Isaacson, 1978). The technique, in the form of a pegboard, has been used for studying schizophrenic performance (Oldigs, Ulardt, & Rey, 1981). It could be useful in the study of hyperactive children.

Disorder Models

A model is an experimental compromise, a simplified preparation created to help understand a larger, more complex phenomenon (McKinney & Moran, 1981). With this in mind, the use of icv 6-hydroxydopamine (6-OHDA), environmental deprivation and the spontaneously hypertensive rat will be briefly discussed. But it should not be forgotten that similar behaviors in various species (or in separate situations) may exist for different reasons and therefore have different meanings (Kornetsky & Markowitz, 1978). The question must continually be raised whether the simplification or comparison is appropriate and relevant.

icv 6-OHDA.   At first sight the investigations of Seiden, Miller and Heffner (this volume) of the behavioral effects of the chemical toxin 6-OHDA in the cerebral ventricles of neonatal rats seem attractive. They showed that hyperactivity may be induced and, depending on the dose, may gradually disappear in adulthood. The hyperactivity was attenuated by amphetamine treatment and increased by water deprivation (cf. the frequent incidence of thirst in hyperactive children, see above). Further, his animals were slower to acquire a simple lever press task.

But one must ask what DA parameters are being changed by the different doses of 6-OHDA and amphetamine? Breese, Baumeister, McCown, Emerick, Frye, Crotty, and Mueller (1984) depleted DA levels neonatally and treated the adults with DA agonists. They suggest that this is a model for the Lesch-Nyhan syndrome (including self-mutilation, choreoathetoid movements). In their hands both neonatal and adult treatment with 6-OHDA depleted DA and DOPAC levels by a factor of 10, but altered neither D1 nor D2 receptor binding in the nucleus accumbens (Breese, Duncan, Napier, Bondy, Iorio, & Mueller, 1987). After neonatal lesions they stimulated locomotion in adults with selective D1 rather than D2 agonist treatment. But opposite results were obtained by varying the age for 6-OHDA treatment and by administering the agonists systemically or to the nucleus accumbens.

As exciting as this approach is, it is generating more than its fair share of questions. Before this type of treatment can be claimed as a model for any condition, one must study the potential bases for how behavioral supersensitivity is achieved without receptor upgrading (cf. Fleming, 1988). Under what conditions does icv-6-OHDA induce receptor supersensitivity? What mechanisms are the various direct and indirect agonists affecting? What constitutes the significant difference between various routes of administration and how do D1 and D2 receptors interact during development and in the adult?

Developmental Environment.   The role of the environment in development is often studied by following the effects of three types of influence: isolation vs social housing, regular vs no handling and simple vs enriched (object) environment. The simple and isolated environments are often similar. It is assumed that early deprivation could lead to a hyperactive syndrome in development. There is very little evidence for this supposition (Taylor, this volume). Let's suppose it is true. What happens after using the different rearing conditions?

Rats reared in isolation tend to show increased motor activity (Robbins et al., this volume). Intriguingly this is attenuated by treatment with amphetamine. Could this imply increased DA activity and a rate-dependent action of the stimulant? For rats, enriched housing is an advantage in learning mazes (Archer, this volume). Depletion of central NA reduces the advantage. So different housing conditions may affect CA activity and behavioural abilities differentially. Certainly NA and amphetamine can enhance sensory function in the cortices of deprived animals at a neurophysiological level. But to what extent are the effects due to neurotransmitter function, the trophic effects of CA agents and/or compensatory action for other numerous and perhaps more important structural changes? Extremes of developmental housing conditions have been correlated with the numbers of dendritic spines and cortical morphology (Diamond, Greer, York, Lewis, Barton, & Lin, 1987).

Feldon and colleagues have reported at the ADD workshop in Oslo and elsewhere that non-handled male rats (in contrast to females) did not show latent inhibition (an index of attentive capability: Weiner et al., 1985). This was counteracted by isolation experience. These results are intriguing for pointing out potential complex interactions between various experiential factors and in particular pointing to the difference in sensitivity between the sexes. They are valuable for advancing our knowledge of developmental processes. But they may be too preliminary to provide a model in the absence of an underlying hypothesis or evidence for a phenomenon to be paralleled. Far too little is understood of the far reaching biological changes wrought by these environmental manipulations. Further, not enough is known about the interactions of neurotransmitter activity, hormone secretion and heterogenic brain development between the ages of 3 and 8 in children.

The Spontaneously Hypertensive Rat (SHR).   As reported by Sagvolden and colleagues (this volume) the appeal of SHRs lies with their behavioral hyperactivity, hyperreactivity and performance on certain tasks. SHRs show changed central NA and DA activity and reactivity (Hellstrand & Engel, 1980; Ikeda, Hirata, Fujita, Shinzato, Takahashi, Yagyu, & Nagatsu, 1984; Koulu, Saavedra, Niwa, & Linnoila, 1986).

Questions about the appropriateness of the comparison of SHRs with childhood hyperkinesis arise when the motor activity increase is by day and not by night and task performance may vary as a function of sensitivity to electric shock (Knardahl & Sagvolden, 1979, 1982; Knardahl & Karlsen, 1984). Adding to the problems are a number of conflicting reports on the behavioral reactivity of SHRs (Sutterer, DeVita, & Rykaszewski, 1981; Hard, Carlsson, Jern, Larsson, Lindh, & Svensson, 1985). Here one of the major problems may be the choice of the Wistar-Kyoto control for the Okamoto strain of SHR. In some studies the control animals have been hypoactive and/or emotional (Sutterer et al., 1981; Hard et al., 1985; Sutterer, Stoney, & Sanfillipo, 1984; Delini-Stula & Hunn, 1985). Recent investigations include Sprague-Dawley normotensive rats as a second control group. (Of course the parallel problem for studies of childhood hyperkinesis exists. Should one use control groups comprising, say, conduct disorder or dyslexia as well as healthy children?)

Sagvolden et al. (this volume) have taken these problems into account and with careful and persistent work shown that an analysis of the response patterning of SHRs and hyperactive children does hold promise. Both groups show deviant responding, the nature of which depends on the schedule of reinforcement (e.g., interval schedules). It is stimulating and relevant that Sergeant and van der Meere (this volume) reported that the performance of hyperactive children is particularly sensitive to variable interval schedules. Here there is clearly a phenomenon that is modelled and one eagerly awaits the results of investigations of the biological variables controlling this type of appropriate response organization.

Crucial investigations of the future on the role of psychostimulants in the model must take into account regional as well as general changes of CA metabolism. Biochemical changes may be region specific and some relevant changes may be specific to a particular developmental period (cf. Sutterer et al., 1984; Oades, 1987). The comparison of these regional and developmental changes with situation-specific task performance is one of the exciting challenges for the development of the SHR model.

Yet there remains plenty of scope for comparative study of the SHR with other hypertensive animals (e.g., Bareggi, Becker, Ginsberg, & Genovese, 1979; Denoroy, Sautel, Schlager, Sacquet, & Sassard, 1985) and non-hypertensive strains of rats (e.g., Naples excitable strains, Sadile, Cerbone, & Cioffi, paper presented at the Workshop on Attention Deficit Disorder, Oslo, 1987). Such comparisons might help to distinguish the relevant from the irrelevant features of the hypertensive model.

Comparative Models

The comparative approach to the study of the underlying biological mechanisms has seldom been invoked for childhood psychiatric disorders. More often a range of disorders is cited for the distinguishing features. To be sure, for example, in Tourette's syndrome there are tics and language problems and in the Lesch-Nyhan syndrome there is self mutilation, in addition to involuntary motor impairments. But children with such syndromes often show learning disabilities and have difficulty in maintaining vigilance, motivation and effort (see Messiha & Carlson, 1983; Kelley & Wyngaarden, 1983 for reviews).

In Tourette's syndrome there can be both hyperactivity and reduced attention span (Fisarova, 1976). Certainly there have been comparative studies which showed no overt brain damage and impairments in path tracing, distractibility and performance of the digit-symbol sub-test of the WISC-R (Harcherik, Cohen, Ort, Paul, Shaywitz, Volkmar, Rothman, & Leckman, 1985; Harcherik, Carbonari, Shaywitz, Shaywitz, & Cohen, 1982). On the whole the problems were present in a milder form than in ADD. Reminiscent of ADD - DA, NA and opioid dysfunctions are implicated (see reviews, Sandyk, 1985; Caine, 1985; Haber, Kowall, Vonsattel, Bird, & Richardson, 1986). But reminiscent of childhood autism and the mirror image of ADD, - neuroleptics (and clonidine) are helpful in 80% of cases, whilst methylphenidate is likely to precipitate the condition (Sandyk, 1985).

The waxing and waning of behavioral symptoms in Tourette's syndrome may have more in common with Parkinsonism and striatal dysfunction than ADD. But potential dysfunctions of the mid-brain tegmentum (Devinsky, 1983), amyg- and cerebellar cortices (Haber et al., 1986) suggest closer comparisons with ADD and autistic subjects than has yet been sought. As I have suggested elsewhere (Oades, 1987), such comparisons would serve to sharpen our perception of the relationships between anatomical projection systems and their function or dysfunction.

CONCLUSIONS

In looking at the present understanding of the biological features associated with the "hyperactive syndrome" and the way experimental manipulations of animals illuminate these changes, one must remark that progress has been made in the last ten years. Two important changes have been the rejection of the concept of minimal brain dysfunction and the study of hypertensive animals. Yet an understanding of what features make up the important symptoms and how the relative efficacy of psychostimulant therapy can be explained remains woefully inadequate.

Studies of the hyperactive syndrome have been blinkered by giving inadequate attention to the detailed biochemical and behavioural differences between the responders and non-responders to psychostimulant treatment. As argued by Sagvolden et al. (this volume) new behavioural studies would be well advised to look at situations that can be structured for both children and animals to facilitate the type of dissection that is only appropriate for animals (e.g., correlates of learning strategies and learned inattention). For studies of children and of animals the adequacy of comparison groups should be more seriously questioned.

Studies of the effects of psychostimulants on monoamines and resultant behaviour require both methodological and quantitative refinement. They should be extended to include interactions of monoamines with brain damage (e.g., neo/archicortex) and other neuromodulators (e.g., peptides). In animal models there is scope for expanded studies of region specific differences and the trophic effects of CAs and CA agents. Within the next ten years both a broadening and a refinement of our knowledge of the biology of childhood hyperactivity and the attention-related problems is likely to be achieved.

REFERENCES

Archer, T., Mohammed, A. K., Danysz, W., Järbe, U. C., & Jonsson, G. (1986). Attenuation of sensory preconditioning by noradrenaline depletion in the rat. *Behavioural Brain Research, 20*, 47–56.

Baldessarini, R. J. (1977). Schizophrenia. *New England Journal of Medicine, 297*, 988–995.

Bareggi, S. R., Becker, R. E., Ginsberg, B. E., & Genovese, E. (1979). Neurochemical investigation of an endogenous model of the hyperkinetic syndrome'' in a hybrid dog. *Life Sciences, 24*, 481–488.

Breese, G. R., Baumeister, A. A., McCown, T. J., Emerick, S., Frye, G. D., Crotty, K., & Mueller, R. A. (1984). Behavioral differences between neonatal and adult 6-hydroxydopamine treated rats to dopamine agonists: Relevance to neurological symptoms in clinical syndromes with reduced brain dopamine. *Journal of Pharmacology and Experimental Therapeutics, 231*, 343–353.

Breese, G. R., Duncan, G. E., Napier, T. C., Bondy, S. C., Iorio, L. C., & Mueller, R. A. (1987). 6-Hydroxydopamine treatments enhance behavioral responses to intracerebral microinjection of D1 and D2-dopamine agonists into nucleus accumbens and striatum without changing dopamine antagonist binding. *Journal of Pharmacology and Experimental Therapeutics, 240*, 167–176.

Brumaghim, J. T., Klorman, R., Strauss, J., Lewine, J. D., & Goldstein, M. G. (1987). Does methylphenidate affect information processing? Findings from two studies on performance and P3b latency. *Psychophysiology, 24*, 361–373.

Caine, E. D. (1985). Gilles de la Tourette's syndrome. *Archives of Neurology, 42*, 393–397.

Callaway, E., & Halliday, R. (1982). The effect of attentional effort on visual evoked potential N1 latency. *Psychiatry Research, 7*, 299–308.

Carpenter, W. T., Strauss, J. T., & Bartko, J. J. (1981). Beyond diagnosis: The phenomenology of schizophrenia. *American Journal of Psychiatry, 138*, 948–953.

Clark, C. R., Geffen, G. M., & Geffen, L. B. (1986). Role of monoamine pathways in the control of attention: Effects of droperidol and methylphenidate in normal adult humans. *Psychopharmacology, 90*, 28–34.

Commissiong, J. W. (1985). Monoamine metabolites: Their relationship and lack of relationship to monoaminergic neuronal activity. *Biochemical Pharmacology, 34*, 1127–1131.

Crider, A., Blockel, L., & Solomon, P. R. (1986). A selective attention deficit in the rat following induced dopamine receptor supersensitivity. *Behavioral Neuroscience, 100*, 315–319.

Delini-Stula, A., & Hunn, C. (1985). Neophobia in spontaneous hypertensive (SHR) and normotensive control (WKY) rats. *Behavioral and Neural Biology, 43*, 206–211.

Denoroy, L., Sautel, M., Schlager, G., Sacquet, J., & Sassard, J. (1985). Catecholamine concentrations in discrete brain nuclei and sympathetic tissues of genetically hypertensive mice. *Brain Research, 340,* 148–150.

Devinsky, O. (1983). Neuroanatomy of Gilles de la Tourette's syndrome. *Archives of Neurology, 40,* 508–514.

Diamond, M. C., Greer, E. R., York, A., Lewis, D., Barton, T., & Lin, J. (1987). Rat cortical morphology during crowded-enriched living conditions. *Experimental Neurology, 96,* 241–248.

Feldon, J., Weiner, I., & Ben-Shahar, O. (1987). Dopaminergic system and attention: The effects of amphetamine, haloperidol and sulpiride on latent inhibition in rats. *Proceedings, 6th International Catecholamine Symposium,* p. 29.

Fisarova, M. (1976). Gilles de la Tourette's disease. In F.S. Abuzzahab & F.O. Anderson (Eds.), *Gilles de la Tourette's Syndrome* (pp. 89–98). St Paul, Minn: Mason.

Fleming, W. W. (in press). Adaptive supersensitivity. In U. Trendelenburg (Ed.), *The Handbook of Pharmacology.* Heidelberg: Springer Verlag.

Friedman, D., Cornblatt, B., Vaughan, H., & Erlenmeyer-Kimling, L. (1986). Event-related potentials in children at risk for schizophrenia during two versions of the continuous performance test. *Psychiatric Research, 18,* 161–177.

Gold, P. E., & Zornetzer, S. F. (1983). The mnemon and its juices: Neuromodulation of memory processes. *Behavioral and Neural Biology, 38,* 151–190.

Haber, S. N., Kowall, N. W., Vonsattel, J. P., Bird, E. D., & Richardson, E. P. (1986). Gilles de la Tourette's syndrome: A post-mortem neuropathological study. *Journal of the Neurological Sciences, 75,* 225–241.

Hammond, E., Meador, K., Aung-Din, R., & Wilder, B. (1987). Cholinergic modulation of human P3 event-related potentials. *Neurology, 37,* 346–350.

Harcherik, D. F., Carbonari, C. M., Shaywitz, S. E., Shaywitz, B. A., & Cohen, D. J. (1982). Attentional and perceptual disturbances in children with Tourette's syndrome, attention deficit disorder, and epilepsy. *Schizophrenia Bulletin, 8,* 356–359.

Harcherik, D. F., Cohen, D. J., Ort, S., Paul, R., Shaywitz, B. A., Volkmar, F. R., Rothman, S. L. G., & Leckman, J. F. (1985). Computed tomographic brain scanning in four neuropsychiatric disorders of childhood. *American Journal of Psychiatry, 142,* 731–734.

Hard, E., Carlsson, S. G., Jern, S., Larsson, K., Lindh, A-S., & Svensson, L. (1985). Behavioral reactivity in spontaneously hypertensive rats. *Physiology and Behavior, 35,* 487–492.

Hellstrand, K., & Engel, J. (1980). Locomotor activity and catecholamine receptor binding in adult normotensive and spontaneously hypertensive rats. *Journal of Neural Transmission, 48,* 57–63.

Holcomb, P. J., Ackerman, P. T., & Dykman, R. A. (1986). Auditory event-related potentials in attention and reading disabled boys. *International Journal of Psychophysiology, 3,* 263–273.

Hui, K. S., Graf, L., & Lajhta, A. (1982). Beta-endorphin inhibits metenkephalin breakdown by a brain amino-peptidase. Structure-activity relationship. *Biochemical and Biophysical Research Communications, 105,* 1482–1487.

Ikeda, M., Hirata, Y., Fujita, K., Shinzato, M., Takahashi, H., Yagyu, S., & Nagatsu, T. (1984). Effects of stress on release of dopamine and serotonin in the striatum of spontaneously hypertensive rats: An in vivo voltammetric study. *Neurochemistry International, 6,* 509–512.

Izquierdo, I., Dias, R. D., Souza, D. O., Carrasco, M. A., Elisabetsky, E., & Perry, M. (1980). The role of opioid peptides in memory and learning. *Behavioural Brain Research, 1,* 451–468.

Kelley, W. N. & Wyngaarden, J. B. (1983). Clinical syndromes associated with hypoxanthine guanine phosphoriribosyl transferase deficiency. In J. B. Stanbury, J. B. Wyngaarden, & D. S. Frederickson (Eds.), *The Metabolic Bases of Inherited Disease* (pp. 1115–1143). New York: McGraw-Hill.

Knardahl, S., & Karlsen, K. (1984). Passive avoidance behavior of spontaneously hypertensive rats. *Behavioral and Neural Biology, 42,* 9–22.

Knardahl, S., & Sagvolden, T. (1979). Open-field behavior of spontaneously hypertensive rats. *Behavioral and Neural Biology, 27,* 187–200.

Knardahl, S., & Sagvolden, T. (1982). Two-way active avoidance behavior of spontaneously hypertensive rats: Effect of intensity of discontinuous shock. *Behavioral and Neural Biology, 35,* 105–120.

Kolb, B., & Whishaw, I. Q. (1983). Performance of schizophrenic patients on tests sensitive to left or right frontal, temporal or parietal function in neurological patients. *Journal of Nervous and Mental Disease, 171*, 435–443.

Kornetsky, C., & Markowitz, R. (1978). Animal models of schizophrenia. In M. Lipton, A. Dimascio & K. Killam (Eds.), *Psychopharmacology: A generation of progress* (pp. 583–593). New York: Raven Press.

Koulu, M., Saavedra, J. M., Niwa, M., & Linnoila, M. (1986). Increased catecholamine metabolism in the locus coeruleus of young spontaneously hypertensive rats. *Brain Research, 369*, 361–364.

Langer, S. Z., & Arbilla, S. (1984). The amphetamine paradox in dopaminergic transmission. *Trends in Pharmacological Sciences, 5*, 387–391.

Lorden, J. F., Rickert, E. J., & Berry, D. W. (1983). Forebrain monoamines and associative learning: 1. Latent inhibition and conditioned inhibition. *Behavioural Brain Research, 9*, 181–199.

McGeer, E., & Singh, E. A. (1979). Inhibition of angiotensin converting enzyme by substance P. *Neuroscience Letters, 14*, 105–108.

McKinney, W. T., & Moran, E. T. (1981). Animal models of schizophrenia. *American Journal of Psychiatry, 138*, 478–483.

Messiha, F. S., & Carlson, J. C. (1983). Behavioral and clinical profiles of Tourette's disease: A comprehensive overview. *Neuroscience and Biobehavioral Reviews, 11*, 195–204.

Milner, B. (1971). Interhemispheric differences in the localisation of psychological processes in man. *British Medical Bulletin, 27*, 272–277.

Mohammed, A. K., Callenholm, N. E., Järbe, T. U., Swedberg, M. D., Danysz, W., Robbins, T. W., & Archer, T. (1986). Role of central noradrenaline in the contextual control of latent inhibition in taste aversion learning. *Behavioral Brain Research, 21*, 109–118.

Nauta, W. J. H. (1982). Limbic innervation of the striatum. In A. J. Friedhoff & T. N. Chase (Eds.), *Gilles de la Tourette's Syndrome* (pp. 41–43). New York: Raven Press.

Oades, R. D. (1982). *Attention and schizophrenia: Neurobiological bases.* London: Pitman.

Oades, R. D. (1985). Role of noradrenaline in tuning and dopamine in switching between signals in the CNS. *Neuroscience and Biobehavioral Reviews, 9*, 261–282.

Oades, R. D. (1987). Attention deficit disorder with hyperactivity (ADDH): Contribution of catecholaminergic activity. *Progress in Neurobiology, 29*, 365–391.

Oades, R. D., & Isaacson, R. L. (1978). The development of food search behavior by rats: Effects of hippocampal damage and haloperidol treatment. *Behavioral Biology, 24*, 327–338.

Oades, R., Rea, M., & Taghzouti, K. (1985). Modulation of selective processes in learning by neocortical and limbic dopamine: Studies of behavioural strategies. In B. Will, P. Schmitt & J. Dalrymple-Alford (Eds.), *Brain plasticity, learning and memory* (pp. 241–251). New York: Plenum Press.

Oades, R. D., Walker, M. K., Geffen, L. B., & Stern, L. M. (in press). Event-related potentials in healthy and autistic children on an auditory choice reaction time task. *International Journal of Psychophysiology.*

Oades, R. D., Rivet, J-M., Taghzouti, K., Kharouby, M., Simon, H., & Le Moal, M. (1987). Catecholamines and conditioned blocking: Effects of ventral tegmental, septal and frontal 6-hydroxydopamine lesions in rats. *Brain Research, 406*, 136–146.

Oldigs, J., von Ulardt, I., & Rey, E-R. (1981). Denkstoerung bei Schizophrenie: Eine experimentelle Untersuchung. *Tagung Experimentell Arbeitender Psychologen, 23*, 138.

Pycock, C., Kerwin, R., & Carter, C. (1980). Effect of lesion of cortical dopamine terminals on subcortical dopamine in rats. *Nature, 286*, 74–77.

Reichelt, K. L., Saelid, G., Lindback, T., & Boeler, J. B. (1986). Childhood autism: A complex disorder. *Biological Psychiatry, 21*, 1279–1290.

Robbins, T. W., & Everitt, B. J. (1985). Noradrenaline and selective attention. In B. Will, P. Schmitt & J. Dalrymple-Alford, (Eds.), *Brain plasticity, learning and memory* (pp. 219–226). New York: Plenum Press.

Robbins, T. W., & Sahakian, B. J. (1979). "Paradoxical" stimulant effects of psychomotor stimulant drugs in hyperactive children from the standpoint of behavioural pharmacology. *Neuropharmacology, 18*, 931–950.

Robertson, H. A. (1986). Cerebral decortication reverses the effect of amphetamine on striatal D2 dopamine binding site density. *Neuroscience Letters, 72*, 325–329.

Sandyk, R. (1985). The endogenous opioid system in neurological disorders of the basal ganglia. *Life Sciences, 37*, 1655–1663.

Shekim, W. O., Javaid, J., Dekirmenjian, H., Chapel, J. L., & David, J. M. (1982). Effects of d-amphetamine on urinary metabolites of dopamine and norepinephrine in hyperactive boys. *American Journal of Psychiatry, 139*, 485–488.

Sutterer, J. R., DeVito, W. J., & Rykaszewski, I. (1981). Developmental aspects of 2-way shuttlebox avoidance in the spontaneously hypertensive and normotensive rat. *Developmental Psychobiolgy, 14*, 405–414.

Sutterer, J. R., Stoney, C. M., & Sanfillipo, M. (1984). Is the hypertensive rat really hyperreactive? *Hypertension, 6*, 868–876.

Svensson, L., & Ahlenius, S. (1983). Suppression of exploratory locomotor activity by the local application of dopamine or l-noradrenaline to the nucleus accumbens of the rat. Pharmacology, *Biochemistry and Behavior, 19*, 693–699.

Tassin, J-P., Reibaud, M., Blanc, G., Studler, J. M., & Glowinski J. (1984). Regulation of the sensitivity of D1 receptors in the prefrontal cortex and the nucleus accumbens by non-dopaminergic pathways. In E. Usdin, A. Carlsson, A. Dahlström, & J. Engel (Eds.), *Catecholamines: Neuropharmacology and central nervous system - theoretical aspects* (pp. 103–111). New York: Alan Liss.

Thorley, G. (1984). Hyperkinetic syndrome of childhood: Clinical characteristics. *British Journal of Psychiatry, 144*, 16–24.

Tsaltas, E., Preston, G. C., Rawlings, J. N. P., Winocur, G., & Gray, J.A. (1984). Dorsal bundle lesions do not affect latent inhibition of conditioned suppression. *Psychopharmacology, 84*, 549–555.

Weiner, I., Lubow, R. E., & Feldon, J. (1984). Abolition of the expression but not the acquisition of latent inhibition by chronic amphetamine in rats. *Psychopharmacology, 83*, 194–199.

Weiner, I., Schnabel, I., Lubow, R. E., & Feldon, J. (1985). The effect of early handling on latent inhibition in male and female rats. *Developmental Psychobiology, 18*, 291–297.

Weiss, G., & Hechtman, L. (1979). The hyperactive child syndrome. *Science, 205*, 1348–1354.

Werry, J. S., & Aman, M. G. (1975). Methylphenidate and haloperidol in children. *Archives of General Psychiatry, 32*, 790–795.

Wright, M. (1988). Event-related potential indices of monoamine function in Parkinson's disease. Unpubl. doctoral dissertation: Flinders University.

23

Future Perspectives on ADD Research: An Irresistible Challenge

Terje Sagvolden
Institute of Neurophysiology
University of Oslo
Norway

Trevor Archer
Department of Behavioural
Pharmacology,
Astra ALAB, Södertäje, and
Department of Psychology,
Umeå University, Umeå, Sweden

There is general agreement among clinicians that Attention Deficit Disorder (ADD) constitutes a syndrome. Still, one of the most important future problems is to reach agreement on how to diagnose ADD, so that, for example, not only all ADHD children are identified as such, but also that non-ADHD children are excluded from this group. It seems that the present ADD diagnosis leads us to consider attention in broad and imprecise terms. This penchant has led investigators and clinicians to include as ADHD, children with other disorders also encompassing attention problems and hyperactivity. But it is hard to see why these *other* children should be diagnosed as ADHD. Attention deficit and hyperactivity should be regarded as necessary, but not sufficient criteria for being diagnosed as ADHD. The main argument for this is, of course, that the underlying dysfunctions are different and that such lumping together of different disorders would hamper our understanding of *all* of these disorders, not only ADHD. If this perspective is agreed upon, the data and arguments brought forward in the present volume, i.e., strongly implicating catecholaminergic dysfunctions in ADHD, suggest that a favorable response to drugs like methylphenidate (Ritalin) ''normalizing'' the catecholaminergic systems could be included as a diagnostic criterion. Another, more expensive to fulfill, but possible, criterion could be levels of catecholaminergic metabolites in urine or plasma outside normal values.

A precise and reliable nosology is important for new advances in the understanding and treatment of this disorder. Sally and Bennett Shaywitz (this volume) argue in favor of a new terminology: ADDnoH may be used for children with ADD without any other complicating feature, ADD-Plus indicates that ADD is present in association with some other complicating factor, e.g., ADHD for children with ADD that are also hyperactive, ADDRT (ADD Residual Type) for older adolescents with a history of ADHD at a younger age, but who no longer exhibit hyperactivity though the inattention and impulsivity persists. As discussed by them (Shaywitz & Shaywitz, this volume), a future challenge is a group of children that might be grossly undertreated for their problems: ADDnoH. It is all too easy to overlook the quiet, non-hyperactive, non-aggressive child with ADD, some of which are very gifted, while this is less likely to happen with the hyperactive ADHD child. The gifted ADDnoH children may be trying hard, but still have problems because of their attentional incapacity. They are at high risk for academic difficulties and poor self concept partly because educators often fail to recognize the symptoms and do not know how to help these children. Some of these children are even now succeeding through intelligence and hard work, but many more could.

It may be timely at this point to insert a further note concerning diagnosis in ADD. Recently, Gordon (1986) discussed the pros and cons regarding microcomputer-based assessment of ADD in comparison with the Gordon Diagnostic system (GDS; Gordon & McClure, 1973, 1984), indicating certain advantages with the GDS. The system appears to have been developed from a study by Gordon (1979) involving 20 hyperactive and 20 clinic-referred nonhyperactive children on a differential reinforcement of low rates of responding (DRL) schedule test that showed much promise (cf. Milich & Kramer, 1984). The GDS was originally built around a differential-reinforcement-of-low-rates (DRL) schedule. In view of the relatively high costs involving the GDS system, Milich and coworkers (Milich, Pelham, & Hinshaw, 1986) have made a cost-benefit analysis of the system and questioned the validity, normative data (i.e., the problem of gender differences) and the response to stimulant compounds. For example, Barkley (1985) found that none of the three measures of the DRL schedule (i.e., rewards, responses, or efficiency ratio) differentiated between the placebo and methylphenidate (0.3 and 0.5 mg/kg) treatments, whereas most of the other measures employed showed evidence of a response to the stimulant compounds. But also rating scales and structured interviews may have questionable reliability and validity (Loney, 1981; Sandoval, 1977). Thus, although the GDS is innovative and remains an exciting prospect, the issues raised concerning the possible generality of its application serve to illustrate the growing pains that are a necessary part of the common ADD endeavor (but see also Gordon, 1987; Sack, 1986; for further discussions on the utility of the system).

THE NATURE OF THE DYSFUNCTION

Any diagnosis represents only a summary of diagnosticians' knowledge at a certain time and as new knowledge is acquired, diagnostic criteria will be altered. Our understanding of ADD is under constant development, causing the diagnosis to change. In the future, the diagnosis of this disorder has to evolve from a structural to a process model. Several chapters in the present volume indicate that we might be on our way not only of abandoning the outdated MBD concept, but also the current ADD concept, because it gives inaccurate predictions of what is wrong (see e.g., Rutter, this volume).

There are now several lines of evidence suggesting that output rather than input mechanisms might be malfunctioning in the ADHD child. Sergeant and van der Meere (this volume) report thorough and systematic investigations of the input mechanisms. Their findings were not in accordance with predictions from an attentional-process dysfunction, rather, it appears that these children suffer from a disorder in the energetical regulation of motor control. These data may well be accommodated by the discussions of Robbins, Jones and Sahakian (this volume). These authors not only review the literature on how central stimulants affect neurotransmitter systems, but have also tried to extrapolate results from animal studies to clinical findings. Robbins and his co-workers argue that changes in attention may be secondary to response processes.

In line with this reasoning, Sagvolden and co-workers (this volume, Sagvolden, Schiørbeck, & Rugland, 1985; Sagvolden & Saebø, 1986; Sagvolden, Wultz, Mørkrid, & Saebø, 1987) argue in favor of analyses of reinforcement mechanisms in ADHD children, mechanisms that are the most likely ones to explain Sergeant's energetical regulation mechanisms of motor control. Sagvolden et al. (this volume) have a detailed presentation of an altered-reinforcement hypothesis. This hypothesis explains among other things the lack of hyperactivity in novel situations, the increased distractibility, increased impulsivity and the hyperactivity seen in various combinations in ADD children as secondary to changed reinforcement mechanisms. It may even explain the highly variable symptoms. Responses have to be present in order for reinforcers to increase the frequency of these responses. For example, there might be little or no hyperactivity the first time the child encounters a novel situation, but as the probability of the behavior is changed by reinforcement, hyperactivity may develop if ambulation happens to be the behavior reinforced. Such a process, involving an increased number of reinforcers, predicts that the behavior elicited may acquire frequencies totally out of normal proportions. Thus, the prevalence of the (secondary) symptoms of ADD is dependent on which behaviors happen to be reinforced by the (now increased) number of stimuli with reinforcing properties. According to the altered-reinforcement hypothesis, increased impulsivity is a result of the increased number of reinforcers. One reason for advocating the altered-reinforcement hypothesis is that it provokes us to view existing data in new perspectives and may generate new research hopefully advancing our knowledge and understanding of these disorders.

Treatment in Relation to the Altered-Reinforcement Hypothesis

Any brain damage or dysfunction is to varying degrees influencing the functioning of the rest of the highly complex central nervous system (CNS). Since the CNS constantly adjusts in order to cope with the varying nature of the interactions between its structures, such interactions will by necessity involve the neurobiological, structural and chemical bases underlying a vast multitude of possible functions. Thus, when there is malfunction or damage, one is studying and describing what the undamaged parts of the brain, in their new equilibrium, are able to perform, and not the functions of the malfunctioning or damaged parts.

Intuitively, one could speculate that a localization of the various components of the ADD syndrome could allow researchers to tackle each component directly and thereby obtain a treatment response. For example, and at a very simplified level, if the central locus of the dysfunction turns out to be an imbalance in catecholaminergic levels relative to the levels of other neurotransmitters, one could alleviate the problem by normalizing these levels (note well that any 'normalized' undertaking of catecholamine/metabolite levels could by itself prove to be an extremely complex and difficult enterprise). At this stage we have not even considered the involvement of the serotonergic system which some lines of evidence do implicate (e.g., Blue & Molliver, 1987; Seiden et al., this volume, but see also, Shaywitz & Shaywitz, this volume). The nature of the interactions in the extremely complex CNS remains so that even following such "normalization", one cannot expect a good treatment response simply because administering a drug cannot reverse the person's and his/her environment's past learning history (i.e., within the ontogenetic perspective). This is one consideration that might be a contributory reason why some therapeutic strategies have failed.

Pharmacological treatment strategies of ADD have included the use of d-amphetamine, methylphenidate as well as other compounds (for a review see Gittelman Klein & Abikoff, this volume). Relevant in this connection are results showing that therapeutic doses of methylphenidate and d-amphetamine differ in their action on brain catecholaminergic systems (for detailed reviews see, Sagvolden et al., or Shaywitz & Shaywitz, both this volume). Behaviorally, low doses of methylphenidate seem to affect reinforcement mechanisms by increasing the reinforcing properties of the scheduled reinforcer and thereby lengthening the delay gradient (Sagvolden, Slåtta, & Arntzen, 1988). It is conceivable that increased reinforcer effects might be one of the mechanisms behind the therapeutic effect of methylphenidate. McGaugh's data (McGaugh, Introini-Collison, Nagahara, & Cahill, 1988) are also relevant: Retention of a large variety of behaviors is enhanced by post-trial increased noradrenaline levels (one way of obtaining such an increase would be by methylphenidate administration). The exact mechanism behind these well documented findings is not well-understood, but the catecholamine connection in ADD has decided clinical potential.

Rachel Gittelman Klein and Howard Abikoff (this volume) show that both treatment with methylphenidate and behavioral therapy is effective and does to some extent alleviate the problems of the ADHD child, but, they argue, the best results are seen following a combination of methylphenidate treatment and behavioral therapy, as has been shown previously (e.g., Brown, Wynne, & Medenis, 1985; Hinshaw, Henker, & Whalen, 1984). This outcome may be predicted from the altered-reinforcement hypothesis: One assumption is that probably from birth onward, there are neurochemical, maybe catecholaminergic, changes in ADD children. These neurochemical changes may modify the characteristics of environmental stimuli in such a way that stimuli ordinarily not having reinforcing properties become reinforcers. Both ordinary and extra reinforcers will alter the long-term probabilities of the various responses in the individual's behavioral repertoire. Methylphenidate therapy may normalize the reinforcing properties of stimuli, but the previous learning history, including altered probabilities of some responses, should not be influenced by the medication. Although these probabilities may be altered temporarily as side effects of drugs (see Robbins et al., Sagvolden et al., both this volume), permanent effects should best be obtained by behavioral therapy procedures reversing the earlier learning history. Each of these therapies may obtain an effect, but the best result should be obtained by having them operate synergistically. These arguments are not necessarily valid for situationally-hyperactive children, because Taylor (this volume) shows that pervasively-hyperactive children are distinctly different from situationally-hyperactive children that are hyperactive in one setting exclusively. Only the former showed a marked response to methylphenidate medication.

The altered-reinforcement hypothesis provides us with an optimistic perspective: Following (at least partially) a "normalization" of the catecholaminergic levels, one should be able to alleviate the symptoms and problems by using behavioral therapy. Even if the reinforcement mechanisms are not entirely normalized, ingenious clinicians should be able to turn this dysfunction to the individual's advantage by structuring his/her environment in such a way that the altered-reinforcement mechanisms help, and not hamper, behavioral (and personal) development. Thus, the enormous personal loss of resources represented by each ADD individual, may be reversed and brought to the eventual benefit of a society in need of all its capacities.

Practical Implications

What are the practical implications of the altered-reinforcement hypothesis for ADD? More than ever, thorough behavioral analyses will be needed and thus the relevance of the earlier discussions concerning diagnosis. This necessity is not only the case for analyzing home and school behavior, but we should also analyze the tests used clinically. The reason for this is that participation in behavioral testing, at least when it takes some time, requires either that aspects of the test reinforces the behavior involved in testing, or that "quitting" leads to aversive consequences of some sort (e.g., the "doctor" gets angry or upset).

Thus, the apparent inattentiveness of ADD children at home, in the class room or when tested, may be associated with changed reinforcement properties of stimuli, not an attention disorder. In addition, there might be altered effects of social reinforcers in these children. The frequent observation that these children grow up to be lonely people with no or few friends supports such a notion.

DIETARY CONTROL

Some of the problems of ADD children with or without hyperactivity may have a dietary origin (see Arnold, 1984; Taylor, 1984; Varley, 1984). Something so obvious that it might easily be overlooked, is that neurotransmitters, neuromodulators, neuropeptides, etc. all are synthesized from amino acids that are broken down from foods and other substances, like sweets and candy, ingested. Up to now it seems that the arguments on dietary control have not suspected the catecholamines in particular (for a review see Graham, this volume). But the information brought forward in this volume points to the possible role of foods and food-related substances that are influencing the synthesis, release and reuptake of catecholamines. If the results from such analyses are shown to be negative, one may have rather strong case against the use of unrestricted dietary control in the treatment of ADHD.

In fact, some ADD children may suffer from a hyperpeptidergic disorder affecting the monoamines: Different peptides and their concentrations may be measured in urine. When gel filtrated, the urinary fractions of ADD children differ both from those of psychiatric and neurological patients, and those of controls (Hole, Lingjaerde, Mørkrid, Bøler, Saelid, Diderichsen, Ruud, & Reichelt, 1988; Reichelt, Mørkrid, Krogh & Pedersen, presentation at the workshop on Attention Deficit Disorder and Hyperkinetic Syndrome, Oslo, 1987). In addition, the urinary fractions of the different ADD subgroups were different. ADHD was associated with increases in the late peaks consisting of proteins, uric acid and peptides in noncovalent complexes. Control experiments showed that high physical activity per se could not produce such urinary fractions. Data indicated that one of the urinary peptides increased blood platelet uptake of serotonin. Thus, it is possible that monoamine activity may be affected by these fractions. The origin of these peptides is not known, it could be the CNS, but it could also be the intestine. The peptides from milk and from gluten may increase the level of peptides in blood due to insufficient breakdown or to peptidase insufficiency. Peptides generally inhibit the breakdown of other peptides (LaBella, Geiger, & Glavin, 1985). Therefore, exogenous peptides could prevent endogenous peptides from being broken down. Hole et al. (in press) suggest that ADD syndromes may be associated with alterations in peptidase levels signifying that the formation of peptides overrides the breakdown. This hyperpeptidergic condition may affect CNS as in coeliac disease functions and therefore the behavior of these patients. Such behavioral changes may interact with the environment and thereby produce a conditioning history giving rise to new behavioral dysfunctions.

Another common assumption is that the hyperkinetic syndrome, at least, is related to blood levels of sugar and that the removal of sugar from the child's diet would reduce, at any rate, the hyperactive state; this type of reasoning would imply an important role for all manner of food preservatives, coloring, flavors, etc., in the condition. Thus, Feingold (1975) performed a major analysis of the various factors involved and proposed that an alleviation of the symptoms of at least 30% to 50% of hyperactive children was possible. Unfortunately, this evidence has not been convincingly confirmed, partially because the nourishing and wholesome "food plan" of Feingold is not easy to maintain in these children. Also, on those occasions when positive reports were obtained, no difference to the improvement rates of placebo-maintained children was obtained (Conners, 1980; Harley & Mathews, 1980).

It would be foolhardy to neglect the possible importance of an insufficient and/or unhealthy diet in the problem of ADHD, even though it is stated by the National Advisory Committee on Hyperkinesis and Food Additives (1980) that much evidence refutes claims that artificial food colorings, artificial flavorings and salicylates increase the probability of learning disorders and hyperactivity; and, this particular body is certainly mistaken in suggesting that there is no continued need for high priority, specially funded programs for further investigation. The prenatal evidence concerning drug intake by pregnant mothers (whether human or animal) is not inconsiderable (see animal models chapter, Archer & Sagvolden, this volume).

STIMULANT MEDICATION
AND STATE-DEPENDENT EFFECTS

Stimulant medications have been, and probably still are, the most commonly applied type of medical treatment for ADDH. These compounds, including d-amphetamine, methylphenidate and pemoline, have been shown frequently to reduce levels of activity and assist in the focusing and sustaining of attention (e.g., Gittelman Klein & Abikoff, this volume; Rapport, Stoner, DuPaul, Brimingham, & Tucker, 1985; Ullman & Sleator, 1985). Unfortunately, side effects of these compounds, both the short-term, including anorexia and insomnia, and long-term, including growth impairment, tics and hallucinations, loss of spontaneity and cognitive perseveration, are serious limitations (Cantwell, 1975; Young, 1981; but see also Sprague & Sleator, 1977). In addition, there are a number of other considerations that are not always readily apparent: (1) The comparison of results between studies employing stimulant and other drug or placebo therapies are complicated by the lack of agreement on operational definitions. (2) There are variations in individual responses to drug/dosage, and thus overmedication problems have arisen (Ross & Ross, 1982). (3) In some instances children have problems recalling information acquired under drug influence or vice versa, i.e., the phenomenon of State-Dependent Learning (cf. Overton, 1964) may be in operation and interfere with performance (but see also Eich & Birnbaum, 1982; Stephens, Pelham, & Skinner, 1984).

State-dependent effects of drugs and contextual control of behavior may have far-reaching consequences. For instance, state-dependent effects can cause apparently complete forgetting of responses learned under drug conditions different from testing conditions (Bliss, Sledjeski, & Leiman, 1971; Sachs, Weingarten, & Klein, 1966), but in other cases represent at most a weak effect (e.g., Eich, 1977, 1980; Overton, 1968, 1971). In addition, the strength of state-dependent effects is extremely dependent upon drug and dosage employed (Mayse & DeVietti, 1971; Overton, 1982). However, those investigations that have compared the extent of response control by drug stimuli with that exerted by sensory stimuli, have generally obtained weaker control by the former (Balster, 1970; Kilbey, Harris, & Aigner, 1971; Spear, Smith, Bryan, Gordon, Timmons, & Chiszar, 1980; but see also Overton, 1985). In relation to ADD, it should be noted that there are two general phenomena to consider in assessing therapeutic efficacy: drug-state dependent and sensory (contextual)-state dependent learning.

The problem of state-dependency may be quite relevant to the outcome of any given treatment strategy in cases of ADHD, and, there is an interesting case at hand. A twelve-year-old girl who had received methylphenidate medication during a 5-year period was studied over a 2-month period by M. Klevstrand (unpublished thesis, University of Oslo). Four main classes of behavior were monitored: (1) vocal interruptions; (2) interruptions resulting from excessive erasions ('rubbing out'); (3) nonvocal disturbing behavior (foot-tapping, turning around, etc.); (4) problem solving tasks. The monitoring was initiated during a 5-day baseline period under methylphenidate medication followed by a 5-day baseline period without medication, after which behavior modification procedures in the classroom were implemented. Figure 1 presents the frequencies of the undesirable behaviors (1, 2 and 3) as well as the desired behaviors (4) during the initial methylphenidate (R) baseline, the no-medication (N) baseline and during the period of behavior modification. At least in this case the beneficial outcome of behavior modification procedures seems quite clear. Thus, it is interesting to consider the parental assessment of desirable/undesirable behaviors in the home - no change from the former baseline periods. Even as a most rudimentary analysis, this case serves to demonstrate the very real problem of context/state dependency in the treatment of ADHD.

THE SEARCH FOR OTHER THERAPEUTIC DRUGS

Pemoline is a compound structurally dissimilar to methylphenidate that has been

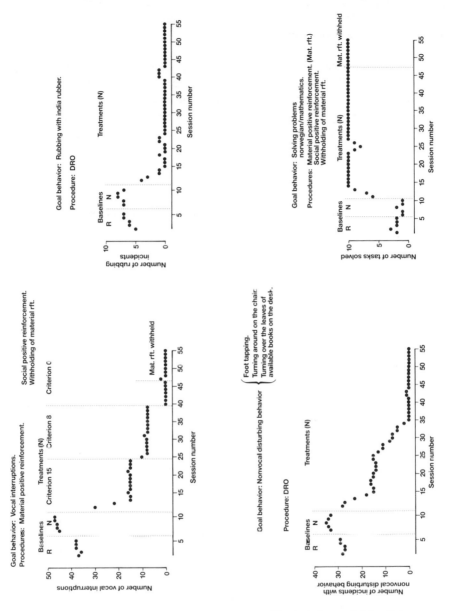

FIG. 1. *Top, left:* Number of interruptions per 30 min during methylphenidate baseline (R), no-drug baseline (N), and a maximum of 15, 8 and 0 interruptions allowed before the reinforcer (three glossy children's pictures) was lost. From session 47 on, the only reinforcer was vocal praise from the teacher and the class. *Top, right:* Number of times the child rubbed with an eraser, during baselines and during reinforcement of other behavior (DRO). *Bottom, left:* Number of nonvocal disturbances during baselines and during reinforcement of other behavior. *Bottom, right:* Number of mathematics of norwegian problems solved during baseline sessions when glossy children's pictures, and just praise (social positive reinforcement) were used as reinforcers. (Redrawn from Klevstrand, 1983).

377

shown to elicit similar changes in CNS function with minimal adverse effects on the cardiovascular system. Its usage in the treatment of ADHD is facilitated by its long half-time, i.e., bioavailability, which means that it is administered once daily. On the other hand, it appears that clinical improvement is delayed by 3 to 4 weeks which is a clear disadvantage (cf., Barkley, 1985; Gittelman Klein & Abikoff and Shaywitz & Shaywitz, this volume). Pure dopaminergic agents such as l-DOPA (Langer, Rapoport, Brown, Ebert, & Bunney, 1981) and the dopamine agonist piribedil appear not to be clinically effective (Brown, Ebert, & Mikkelsen, 1979).

Bearing in mind these problems, it is of some interest to note that other types of medication could prove efficacious. Recently, Hunt et al. (Hunt, Cohen, Anderson, & Clark, 1984; Hunt, Minderaa, & Cohen, 1985) reported a double-blind, placebo crossover comparison of clonidine, an antihypertensive agent possessing primarily α_2-adrenergic agonistic properties (e.g., Brody, 1981; DeTong, Zandberg, & Bohus, 1975), in 10 children with ADHD. Both teacher's and parent's ratings were used. Clonidine treatment was compared with methylphenidate treatment (see Fig. 2). The results of Hunt et al. (1985) do suggest that clonidine may be an alternative therapy, although the effects of this compound on the cardiovascular system remain problematic. Guanfacine, which has similar pharmacological properties to clonidine, but a longer bioavailability, may be a suitable alternative (Hedner, Nyberg, & Mellstrand, 1984). Clonidine affects noradrenergic neurotransmission (cf. Starke & Altman, 1973) and it is now well established that noradrenergic mechanisms mediate certain aspects of selective attention and the reactions to novel stimuli (e.g., Archer, Mohammed, Forsberg, & Siddigui, 1983; Aston-Jones & Bloom, 1981; but see also Archer, this volume; Robbins et al., this volume). In ADHD children, a pathophysiology of the noradrenergic system is suggested from the metabolite, 3-methoxy-4-hydroxyphenylglycol (MHPG), levels in urine (Shekim, Dekirmenjian, & Chapel, 1979). Thus, Hunt (1987) makes an interesting case for the possible therapeutic value of compounds affecting noradrenergic neurotransmission.

Another class of compounds with possible efficacy, has been the tricyclic antidepressants that have been demonstrated to improve attention. But their effect is inferior to the stimulants and their usefulness is limited through the incidence of anticholinergic and cardiac side effects (Fox, 1982; Garfinkel, Wender, Sloman, & O'Neill, 1983). In addition, the efficacy of tricyclic antidepressants appears limited (Winsberg, Kupietz, Yepes, & Goldstein, 1980). However, it is not certain whether or not atypical antidepressants, such as mianserin and trazadone, have been studied in this respect. Bupropion hydrochloride is a novel antidepressant of the aminoketone class (Preskorn & Othmer, 1984) which appears to have weak dopamine-agonist activity. Recently, Casat et al. (Casat, Pleasants, & Van Wyck Fleet, 1987) performed a 6-week parallel design study with a randomized double-blind comparison of hypropion versus placebo in 30 outpatient children aged 6 to 12 fitting the DSM-III criteria. The children studied were either naive or nonresponsive to conventional stimulant therapy. Although limited, the results indicated that the children tolerated the medication well and adverse effects were minimal. However, though an improvement appears to have been obtained for some measures, this was not so for all the parameters. The conclusion drawn by Casat et al. (1987) suggests that, though promising, more definitive investigations on the efficacy and safety of bupropion as a therapy for ADHD remain to be conducted.

Notwithstanding the potential therapeutic values of other classes of centrally-acting compounds, it is well established that methylphenidate is effective in the treatment of ADD with or without hyperactivity (e.g., Gittelman, 1983; Gittelman Klein & Abikoff, this volume; Shaywitz, Heint, Jatlow, Cohen, Young, Pierce, Anderson, & Shaywitz, 1982; Shaywitz & Shaywitz, this volume; Solanto, 1986) in spite of troubling side effects such as headache, stomachache, dysphoria and negative long-term impact on growth (Matles & Gittelman, 1983). On the other hand, the effect of methylphenidate upon cognitive skills and academic achievement are not promising (e.g., Gittelman, Klein, & Feingold, 1983; Pelham, Bender, Caddell, Booth, & Moorer, 1985). In fact, O'Brian and Obrzut (1987) recently suggested "There are so many problems associated with drug therapy that it seems as if any alternative treatment would be preferred" (p. 286). Therefore, it may be of some benefit to consider three aspects of the clinical usage of methylphenidate: (1) The possible development of tolerance, (2) the salivary levels of the drug (and compliance) in children, and (3) the issue of rate-dependency.

Children with ADD, or ADHD, who respond to methylphenidate sometimes lose their initial response, temporarily or permanently (Winsberg, Yepes, & Bialer, 1976). Uncontrolled observations on the long-term effectiveness of stimulant therapy using clinical case follow-up methods have not revealed a loss of drug effectiveness (e.g., Charles, Schain, & Guthrie, 1979; Quinn & Rapoport, 1975; Riddle & Rapoport, 1976). In a short-term placebo-controlled experimental study, Gualtieri, Hicks, Mayo and Schroeder (1984) showed that hyperactive children treated chronically (1 to 5 years) with methylphenidate, were still effectively controlled by the drug. On the other hand, Winsberg, Bialer, Kupietz, Botti and Balka (1980) found that although tolerance was not common, neither was it rare. One problem is that plasma levels of methylphenidate do not always show a better relation to the behavioral measures than do the oral dosages (e.g., Gualtieri, Hicks, Patrick, Schroeder, & Breese, 1984; Winsberg, Kupietz, Sverd, Hungund, & Young, 1982). Both the oral dose and the plasma concentration measures of methylphenidate are required as comparable predictors of the behavioral outcome in order to provide evidence for the development of tolerance (e.g., Adler & Geller, 1984). Thus, Winsberg, Matinsky, Kupietz and Richardson (1987) demonstrated recently that tolerance may develop in chronic methylphenidate treatment at higher doses.

The relevance of measuring salivary levels in ADD children treated with

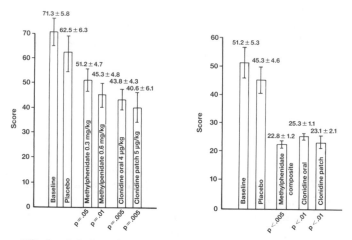

FIG. 2.   *Left:* Parent's ratings (Conners Child Behavior Checklist) of children with attention deficit disorder with hyperactivity in response to methylphenidate and clonidine (oral or transdermal/patch). *Right:* Teacher's ratings (Conners Teaching Rating Scale-Revised) of children with attention deficit disorder with hyperactivity in response to methylphenidate and clonidine. (Redrawn from Hunt, 1987).

methylphenidate relates to the problem of compliance (e.g., Brown, Borden, & Clingerman, 1985). Subjects may skip doses and thereby reduce real differences between placebo and active drug phases, or, take the active drug during placebo periods. Since other psychotropic agents such as nortriptyline (Virtanen, 1980), appear to maintain steady saliva/plasma concentrations, Greenhill, Cooper, Solomon, Fried, and Cornblatt (1987) have developed a stable and reliable technique for measuring salivary levels of methylphenidate, thereby facilitating compliance control in drug-treated ADD groups. The saliva measures could provide another dimension of validation, especially when patients show substantial concentrations when maintained on the active compound and negligible levels when maintained on placebo.

In spite of the widespread use of methylphenidate (and d-amphetamine) in treatment of ADD (Safer & Krager, 1983, 1985), there is limited information regarding underlying mechanisms and the specific overt variables which may contribute to their effectiveness (cf. Robbins & Sahakian, 1979; Sahakian & Robbins, 1977). At the same time, animal studies have shown consistently that the behavioral effects of psychomotor stimulants are *rate-dependent* or rate-related, i.e., the drug effect depends on the rate of occurrence of a given behavior in a drug-free state (Dews, 1977). Recent demonstrations of rate-dependency have included the operant key-pressing behaviors of ADD children (Rapport, DuPaul, & Smith, 1985). Later, Rapport and DuPaul (1986) studied the rate-related effects of methylphenidate on the behavior of a group of 20 ADHD children with chronic problems of inattention, impulsivity and overactivity by examining the relationship between the control response rate (i.e., response rate under placebo) and the output ratio (i.e., the ratio of response rate after medication to control response rate) (cf. Dews & Wenger, 1977). Rapport and DuPaul's (1986) results established this relationship by indicating drug-induced proportional changes in the attention of the ADHD children. These findings are of a fundamental nature since there have been no prospective empirical investigations in the psychopharmacological research on ADD that systematically assess whether or not a child's drug-free rate of behavior contributes to drug responsiveness (Reatig, 1984). Sagvolden, Slåtta and Arntzen (1988) suggest that rate-related effects may indicate altered delay-of-reinforcement gradients. Drug treatment is *not* a cure for hyperactivity, but might contribute to the reduction of some of the problems of these children (cf. the discussion of altered reinforcement processes above).

MODEL EXPERIMENTS

Although many contributing factors have been advanced, the etiology of ADD is as yet unknown (e.g., Bloomingdale, Davies, & Gold, 1984; Corbuz & Cuenod, 1984). Model experiments are necessary in ADD research both to provide inferences concerning etiology and to derive potential drug screens to obtain possible novel therapeutic agents. The animal model does not have to be one with all the symptoms and intricacies of an ADD child; quite the contrary, since animal models are notoriously difficult to validate. It is without any doubt an uphill job to provide and evaluate animal models of ADD for a number of reasons: Firstly, because the disorder itself is poorly understood (cf. Rutter; Sergeant & van der Meere; Shaywitz & Shaywitz; Taylor, all this volume), not least with regard to cause and classification (Rutter, Chadwick, & Schachar, 1983). Secondly, because it might seem impossible to find or create an animal model of this disorder even if it were well understood (cf. Oades, this volume). But, if an animal preparation models all aspects of a disease, little or nothing is gained by using the model, which then will be as complex as the disease itself. Models ought to simplify the problem in question so that it could be brought into the laboratory for systematic investigation. The results of the experiments on animals could then be tested clinically in order to improve our understanding of the disease/disorder (cf. Sagvolden et al., this volume). Thirdly, the range of efficacious compounds for the treatment of ADD is notably limited (see above), which complicates the quest for predictive validity in the potential animal models available. However, any new understanding derived from the drug-screens or animal models will give rise to new problems that may be tested either on (other) animals model or clinically.

A substantial proportion of normal and deviant human behavior depends on reinforcement and punishment of various kinds. The basic principles were discovered by systematically investigating the behavior of pigeons and rats. The results were described in the classical work of Ferster and Skinner (1957). In the present volume, Sagvolden and co-workers have applied some of the same behavioral analyses on ADHD children and their model system: the spontaneously hypertensive rat (SHR). In this research programme, it has been possible see the budding of a comparative neuropsychology where experiments on the animal model had its roots in clinical problems and the methods were designed to be similar. Similar attempts have been seen in the research of Sally and Bennett Shaywitz (see above).

It is likely that the neurochemical, endocrinological and morphological compositions of the neonatal and juvenile organism are quite different from those of the adult organism and that some of the riddles of ADD are buried in such differences. Answers to such problems may best be found by investigating animal models (see Archer; Robbins et al.; Seiden, Miller, & Heffner, all this volume).

COGNITION AND BEHAVIOR MODIFICATION

The possible therapeutic value of behavior therapy as well as procedures developing cognitive abilities should be considered also. Generally, the former approach does not take very much account of the child's history or diagnostic category. Typically, treatment involves the monitoring of observable behaviors, followed by modification of these behaviors through contingency-management (reinforcement) techniques. The efficacy of these procedures has been shown with regard to hyperactivity reduction, task-related behavior increase, and facilitation of academic exercises. Note however, that the benefits seem to be mainly in a short-term perspective (e.g., Gittelman Klein & Abikoff, this volume; Taylor, 1985; Brown, 1986; Ross & Ross, 1986). *Active-participation* programs, involving self-instruction, self-monitoring and self-reinforcement, provide a further development on the simple reinforcement theme since the emphasis is on self-control strategies by which the child assumes control over his/her own behavior through consideration of self-directed verbal commands (cf. Luria, 1966). Thus, cognitive behavior modification (CBM) was used successfully by Douglas, Parry, Marton, and Garson (1976) to improve measures of oral reading and comprehension in hyperactive boys. Recently, however, a comparison was made between the efficacy of cognitive training and stimulant drug treatment (Abikoff & Gittelman, 1985; Brown et al., 1985) and the results were not encouraging: the training program plus medication did not improve academic performance nor the behavior of the children or allow stimulant dosages to be lowered, although some improvement on certain measures of attention was obtained in the Brown et al. (1985) study. It may be as Campione, Brown, and Ferrara (1982) suggest, that the children should first experience problem-solving activities in the presence of others, and then slowly participate themselves. Thus, they outlined four principles that could serve as valuable guidelines to the entire issue of behavior modification: (1) the instructions must be appropriate to each particular child's level of understanding; (2) provision must be made and reminders given of the child's prior, related knowledge; (3) their attention must be focused on the salient features of each problem, task, or fact; and, (4) comprehension, understanding and attention will require continual monitoring. Finally, two other factors must not be overlooked: A good, working pupil-teacher relationship is invaluable (Kaufman & Kaufman, 1983), and children who receive essential support from both family and school usually show good performance in their late teens and young adulthood (Safer & Allen, 1976). Also, the case of the 12-year-old girl (described above) offers some hope for the possible therapeutic value of behavior modification.

CONCLUSION

This chapter was meant to be a little provocative in order to generate new investigations and hopefully new insights. There seems to be good reason and powerful need to get rid of the minimal brain dysfunction, MBD, concept. It was based on circular reasoning of various kinds and has not stood the test of time. The attention deficit disorder, ADD, concept is more descriptive and is really more parsimonious, but we still have a long way to go before the riddles of ADD and related disorders are solved. However, the explosive development one sees within the neurosciences is promising as at least some pieces of the puzzle seem to fall in place. In the future, there is reason to believe that model experiments on animals will be of utmost importance because one is then able to study specific aspects in organisms and systems that are far simpler than humans.

Another important future perspective to which we hope this book contributes, is that the diagnosis of this disorder has to evolve from a structural model to a process model. We have to realize that the diagnosis is only a summary of our knowledge at a certain time, as new knowledge is acquired the diagnosis has to change. The material presented at, and the discussions during, the ADD conference, together with the chapters incorporated into this volume, indicate that we might be in the process not only of abandoning the outdated concept MBD, but also ADD, because it gives inaccurate predictions of what is not functioning. In the future, one might have to look for defective reinforcement or energizing mechanisms of behavior, possibly linked to catecholaminergic systems that are not in proper balance with other neurotransmitter systems (for example, there is some evidence for serotonergic involvement (Seiden et al., this volume) and neuropeptide/hormonal (McGaugh et al., 1988) interactions). Such a view may explain many of the characteristics of ADD, and at the same time put these in new perspectives. This disorder might be called RD (reinforcement disorder), which points to the necessity of functional, behavioral analyses of the disorder.

The main diagnostic criterion could be changed reinforcement mechanisms, secondary behavioral criteria may be the same as the ones used for ADD, the pharmacological one should probably be a favorable response to medication normalizing catecholaminergic functions. It is important to realize that just as is the case with ADD where the ultimate measure has to be one of attention, if altered reinforcement mechanisms turn out to be the critical feature of this disorder, the ultimate measure has to be one of reinforcement mechanisms. But one has to realize that changing the name, i.e., putting a new label, on this disorder, does not help the children. The important point is to advance our knowledge and understanding of the disorder.

It might be a reasonable research policy to concentrate on the ADD type we seem to understand best: ADDH with a good methylphenidate response, probably associated with a catecholaminergic dysfunction. This is a disorder that might be associated with changed reinforcement mechanisms. By advancing our understanding of this disorder even more, we might in the process learn more about other, related disorders with attention and/or hyperactivity problems. In this connection, it might also be reasonable to predict that diets or specific food regimens normalizing catecholaminergic functions relative to the other neurotransmitters and neuromodulators may be found.

It was our intention that this volume should document the need for, and the essential requirement of, cooperation between scientists from different areas of research, such as clinical diagnoses, clinical and experimental neuropsychology, neuropharmacology and modern technology, in order to bring about fast advances in ADD research as well as neuropsychiatry in general. In the future, one should give priority to such multidimensional research groups as it is probable that the real break-throughs will occur in such "expensive-to-run" institutions.

It is our hope that this volume (and the preceding conference) has shown us some research paths that may be followed. Let us not be paralyzed by the enormous problems research on ADD still has to face. The hope is that some more pieces of the puzzle will fall into place as we work on some of the seemingly easier (sub)problems. We expect that clinical and basic researchers will join forces in order to alleviate the problems of those unfortunate individuals suffering form these disorders whether it is diagnosed as MBD, ADD or even RD.

REFERENCES

Abikoff, H., & Gittelman, R. (1985). Hyperactive children treated with stimulants. *Archives of General Psychiatry, 42,* 953–961.

Adler, M. W., & Geller, E. B. (1984). Contributions of neuropharmacology to understanding mechanisms of tolerance and dependence. *National Institute of Drug Abuse Research and Monographs Services, 54,* 27–38.

Archer, T., Mohammed, A., Forsberg, B., & Siddigui, A. (1983). Neophobia to novel taste and novel exteroceptive stimulus following DSP4 administration. *Experimental Animal Behaviour,* *2,* 19–36.

Arnold, L. E. (1984). Diet and hyperkinesis. *Integrative Psychiatry, 2,* 188–200.

Aston-Jones, G., & Bloom, F. E. (1981). Norepinephrine-containing locus coeruleus neurons in behaving rats exhibit pronounced responses to non-noxious environmental stimuli. *Journal of Neuroscience, 1,* 887–900.

Balster, R. L. (1970). *The effectiveness of external and drug produced internal stimuli in the discriminative control of operant behavior.* Doctoral dissertation, University of Houston.

Barkley, R. A. (1985). Assessment of stimulant drug responding in ADD-H children. Paper presented at the 93rd annual meeting of the American Psychological Association, Los Angeles, CA.

Bliss, D. K., Sledjeski, M., & Leiman, A. (1971). State dependent choice behavior in the rhesus monkey. *Neuropsychologia. 9,* 51–59.

Bloomingdale, L. M., Davies, R. K., & Gold, M. S. (1984). Some possible neurological substrates in Attention Deficit Disorder. In L. M. Bloomingdale (Ed.), *Attention deficit disorder: Diagnostic, cognitive, and therapeutic understanding* (pp. 37–66). New York: Spectrum Publications.

Blue, M. E., & Molliver, M. E. (1987). 6-Hydroxydopamine induces serotonergic axon sprouting in the cerebral cortex of newborn rat. *Developmental Brain Research, 32,* 255 269.

Brody, M. J. (1981). New developments in our knowledge of blood pressure regulation. *Federal Proceedings, 40,* 2257–2261.

Brown, G. (1986). Attention deficit disorder. *Current Pediatric Therapy, 12,* 44–48.

Brown, R. T., Borden, K. A., & Clingerman, S. R. (1985). Adherence to methylphenidate therapy in a pediatric population: A preliminary investigation. *Psychopharmacology Bulletin, 21,* 28–36.

Brown, R. T., Wynne, M. E., & Medenis, R. (1985). Methylphenidate and cognitive therapy: A comparison of treatment approaches with hyperactive boys. *Journal of Abnormal Child Psychology, 13,* 68–88.

Campione, J., Brown, A., & Ferrara, R. (1982). Mental retardation and intelligence. In R. Sternberg (Ed.), *Handbook of human intelligence* (pp. 392–490). Cambridge University Press.

Cantwell, D. P. (1975). *The hyperactive child: Diagnosis, management and current research.* New York: Spectrum.

Casat, C. D., Pleasants, D. Z., & Van Wyck Fleet, J. (1987). A double-blind trial of bupropion in children with attention deficit disorder. *Psychopharmacology Bulletin, 23,* 120–122.

Charles, L., Schain, R. J., & Guthrie, D. (1979). Long-term use and discontinuation of methylphenidate with hyperactive children. *Developmental Medicine and Child Neurology, 21,* 759–764.

Conners, C. (1980). *Food additives and hyperactive children.* New York: Plenum

Corbuz, R. J., & Cuenod, M. (1984). Biological correlates of ADD. In L. M. Bloomingdale (Ed.), *Attention deficit disorder: Diagnostic, cognitive, and therapeutic understanding* (pp. 11–36). New York: Spectrum Publications.

DeTong, W., Zandberg, P., & Bohus, P. (1975). Central inhibitory noradrenergic cardiovascular control. *Progress in Brain Research, 209,* 196–204.

Dews, P. B. (1977). Rate-depending hypothesis. *Science, 198,* 1182–1183.

Dews, P. B., & Wenger, G. A. (1977). Rate-dependency of the behavioral effects of amphetamine. In T. Thompson & P. B. Dews (Eds.), *Advances in behavioral pharmacology* (pp. 169–227). New York: Academic Press.

Douglas, V., Parry, P., Marton, P., & Garson, C. (1976). Assessment of a cognitive training program for hyperactive children. *Journal of Abnormal Child Psychology, 4,* 389–410.

Eich, J. E. (1977). State-dependent retrieval of information in human episodic memory. In I. M. Birnbaum, & E. S. Parker (Eds.), *Alcohol and human memory* (pp. 141–157). Hillsdale, N.J.: Lawrence Erlbaum Associates.

Eich, J. E. (1980). The cue-dependent nature of state-dependent retrieval. *Memory and Cognition, 8,* 157–173.

Eich, J. E., & Birnbaum, I. M. (1982). Repetition, cuing and state-dependent memory. *Memory and Cognition, 10,* 103–114.

Feingold, B. (1975). *Why your child is hyperactive.* New York: Random House.

Ferster, C. B., & Skinner, B. F. (1957). *Schedules of reinforcement.* New York: Appleton-Century-Crofts.

Fox, W. H. (1982). An indication for use of imipramine in attention deficit disorder. *American Journal of Psychiatry, 139,* 1059–1060.

Garfinkel, B. D., Wender, P. H., Sloman, L., & O'Neill, I. (1983). Tricyclic antidepressants and methylphenidate treatment of attention deficit disorder in children. *Journal of the American Academy of Child Psychiatry, 22,* 343–348.

Gittelman, R. (1983). Experimental and clinical studies of stimulant use in hyperactive children with other behavioral disorders in stimulants. In I. Creese (Ed.), *Neurochemical behavioral and clinical perspectives* (pp. 205–226). New York: Raven Press.

Gittelman, R., Klein, D., & Feingold, I. (1983). II. Effects of methylphenidate in combination with reading remediation. *Journal of Child Psychology and Psychiatry, 24,* 193–212.

Gordon, M. (1979). The assessment of impulsivity and mediating behaviors in hyperactive and non-hyperactive children. *Journal of Abnormal Child Psychology, 7,* 317–326.

Gordon, M. (1986). Microprocessor-based assessment of attention deficit disorders. *Psychopharmacology Bulletin, 22,* 288–290.

Gordon, M. (1987). Errors of omission and commission: A response to Milich and colleagues regarding the Gordon Diagnostic system. *Psychopharmacology Bulletin, 23,* 325–328.

Gordon, M., & McClure, F. D. (1983). The objective assessment of attention deficit disorder. Paper presented at the 91st annual meeting of the American Psychological Association, Anaheim, CA.

Gordon, M., & McClure, F. D. (1984). Assessment of attention deficit disorders using the Gordon Diagnostic System. Paper presented at the 92nd annual meeting of the American Psychological Association. Toronto, Canada.

Greenhill, L. L., Cooper, T., Solomon, M., Fried, J., & Cornblatt, B. (1987). Methylphenidate salivary levels in children. *Psychopharmacology Bulletin, 23,* 115–119.

Gualtieri, T. C., Hicks, R. E., Mayo, J. P., & Schroeder, S. R. (1984). The persistence of stimulant effects in chronically treated children: Further evidence of an inverse relationship between drug effects and placebo levels of response. *Psychopharmacology, 83,* 44–47.

Gualtieri, T. C., Hicks, R. E., Patrick, K., Schroeder, S. R., & Breese, G. R. (1984). Clinical correlates of methylphenidate blood levels. *Therapeutic Drug Monitors, 6,* 379–392.

Harley, J., & Mathews, C. (1980). Food additives and hyper-activity in children: Experimental investigations. In R. Knights, & D. Bakker (Eds.), *Treatment of hyperactive and learning disabled children* (pp. 229–247). Baltimore: University Park Press.

Hedner, T., Nyberg, G., & Mellstrand, T. (1984). Guanfacine in essential hypertension: Effects during rest and isometric exercise. *Clinical Pharmacological Therapeutics, 35,* 604–609.

Hinshaw, S. P., Henker, B., & Whalen, C. K. (1984). Cognitive-behavioral and pharmacologic interventions for hyperactive boys. Comparative and combined effects. *Journal of Consultive and Clinical Psychology, 57,* 739–749.

Hole, K., Lingjaerde, O., Mørkrid, L., Bøler, J. B., Saelid, G., Diderichsen, J., Ruud, E., & Reichelt, K. L. (1988). Attention deficit disorders: A study of peptide-containing urinary complexes. *Developmental and Behavioral Pediatrics, 9,* 205–212.

Hunt, R. D. (1987). Treatment effects of oral and transdermal clonidine in relation to methylphenidate: An open pilot study in ADD-H. *Psychopharmacology Bulletin, 23,* 111–114.

Hunt, R. D., Cohen, D. J., Anderson, G. M., & Clark, L. (1984). Possible change in noradrenergic receptor sensitivity with attention deficit disorder and hyperactivity: Response to chronic methylphenidate treatment. *Life Sciences, 35,* 885–897.

Hunt, R. D., Minderaa, R. B., & Cohen, D. J. (1985). Clonidine benefits children with attention deficit disorder and hyperactivity: Report of a double-blind placebo-crossover therapeutic trial. *Journal of the American Academy of Child Psychiatry, 5,* 617–629.

Kaufman, N., & Kaufman, A. (1983). Remedial intervention in education. In G. Hynd (Ed.), *The school psychologist, an introduction* (pp. 132–148). Syracuse, N.Y.: Syracuse University Press.

Kilbey, M. M., Harris, R. T., & Aigner, T. G. (1971). Establishment of equivalent external and internal stimulus control of an operant behavior and its reversal. *Proceedings of the American Psychological Association, 6*, 767-768.

Klevstrand, M. *Atferdsanalytisk behandling av overaktiv atferd i en klassesituasjon som alternativ til ritalin-behandling.* (Behavior therapy of hyperactivity in the classroom as an alternative to ritalin treatment). Dissertation for the degree of candidatus psychologiae, University of Oslo, 1983. (In Norwegian).

LaBella, F. S., Geiger, J. D., & Glavin, G. B. (1985). Administered peptides inhibit the degradation of endogenous peptides. The dilemma of distinguishing direct from indirect effects. *Peptides, 6*, 645-660.

Langer, D. H., Rapoport, J. L., Brown, G. L., Ebert, M. H., & Bunney, W. E. (1981). Questioning of a dopaminergic hypothesis. *American Journal of Psychiatry, 138*, 537-538.

Loney, J. (1981). Evaluating treatments for childhood hyperactivity: Some methodological considerations. In K. D. Gadow, & J. Loney (Eds.), *Psychosocial aspects of drug treatment for hyperactivity* (pp. 77-103). Boulders, CO.: Westview Press, Inc.

Luria, A. (1966). *Higher cortical functions in man.* New York: Basic books.

Matles, J. A., & Gittelman, R. (1983). Growth of hyperactive children on maintenance regimen of methylphenidate. *Archives of General Psychiatry, 40*, 317-321.

Mayse, J. F., & DeVietti, T. L. (1971). A comparison of state-dependent learning induced by electroconvulsive shock and pentobarbital. *Physiology and Behavior, 7*, 717-721.

McGaugh, J. L., Introini-Collison, I. B., Nagahara, A. H., & Cahill, L. (1988). Involvement of the amygdala in hormonal and neurotransmitter interactions in the modulation of memory storage. In T. Archer, & L.-G. Nilsson (Eds.), *Aversion, avoidance and anxiety: Perspectives on aversively motivated behavior*, Hillsdale, N.J.: Lawrence Erlbaum Associates.

Milich, R., & Kramer, J. (1984). Reflections on impulsivity: An empirical investigation of impulsivity as a construct. In K. D. Gordon (Ed.), *Advances in learning and behavioral disabilities* (pp. 57-94). Greenwich, CT: JAI Press.

Milich, R., Pelham, W. E., & Hinshaw, S. P. (1986). Issues in the diagnosis of Attention Deficit Disorder: A cautionary note on the Gordon Diagnostic System. *Psychopharmacology Bulletin, 22*, 1101-1104.

National Advisory Committee on Hyperkinesis and Food Additives. (1980). New York: The Nutrition Foundation.

O'Brian, M. A., & Obrzut, J. E. (1986). Attention deficit disorder with hyperactivity: A review and implications for the classroom. *The Journal of Special Education, 20*, 281-297.

Overton, D. A. (1964). State-dependent or "dissociated" learning produced with pentobarbital. *Journal of Comparative and Physiological Psychology, 57*, 3-12.

Overton, D. A. (1968). Visual cues and shock sensitivity in the control of T-maze choice by drug conditions. *Journal of Comparative and Physiological Psychology, 66*, 216-219.

Overton, D. A. (1971). Discriminative control of behavior by drug states. In T. Thompson, & R. Pickens (Eds.), *Stimulus properties of drugs* (pp. 87-110). New York: Appleton-Century-Crofts.

Overton, D. A. (1982). Memory retrieval failures produced by changes in drug state. In R. L. Isaacson, & N. E. Spear (Eds.), *The expression of knowledge, neurobehavioral transformations of information into action* (pp. 113-139). New York: Plenum Press.

Overton, D. A. (1985). Contextual stimulus effects of drugs and internal states. In P. D. Balsam, & A. Tomie (Eds.), *Context and learning* (pp. 357-384). Hillsdale, N.J.: Lawrence Erlbaum Associates.

Pelham, W., Bender, M., Caddell, J., Booth, S., & Moorer, S. (1985). Methylphenidate and children with attention deficit disorder. *Archives of General Psychiatry, 42*, 948-952.

Preskorn, S. H., & Othmer, S. C. (1984). Evaluation of bupropion hydrochloride: The first of a new class of atypical antidepressants. *Pharmacotherapy, 4*, 20-34.

Quinn, P. Q., & Rapoport, J. L. (1975). One-year follow-up of hyperactive boys treated with imipramine or methylphenidate. *American Journal of Psychiatry, 132*, 241-245.

Rapport, M. D., & DuPaul, G. J. (1986). Methylphenidate: Rate-dependent effects on hyperactivity. *Psychopharmacology Bulletin, 22*, 223–228.

Rapport, M. D., DuPaul, G. J., & Smith, N. F. (1985). Rate-dependency and hyperactivity: Methylphenidate effects on operant responding. *Pharmacology, Biochemistry and Behavior, 13*, 1–7.

Rapport, M. D., Stoner, G., DuPaul, G. J., Birmingham, B. K., & Tucker, S. (1985). Methylphenidate in hyperactive children: Differential effects of dose on academic, learning and social behavior. *Journal of Abnormal Child Psychology, 2*, 227–243.

Reatig, N. (1984). Attention deficit disorder: A bibliography. *Pharmacological Bulletin, 20*, 693–718.

Riddle, D. K., & Rapoport, J. L. (1976). A 2-year follow-up of 72 hyperactive boys. *Journal of Nervous and Mental Disorders, 162*, 126–134.

Robbins, T.W., & Sahakian, B.J. (1979). "Paradoxical" effects of psychomotor stimulant drugs from the standpoint of behavioural pharmacology. *Neuropharmacology, 18*, 931–950.

Ross, D., & Ross, S. (1982). *Hyperactivity, current issues, research, and theory* (2nd ed.). New York: John Wiley & Sons.

Rutter, M., Chadwick, O., & Schachar, R. (1983). Hyperactivity and minimal brain dysfunction: Epidemiological perspectives on questions of cause and classification. In R. Tarter (Ed.), *The child at psychiatric risk* (pp. 80–107). New York: Oxford University Press.

Sachs, E., Weingarten, M., & Klein, N.W. (1966). Effects of chlordiazepoxide on the acquisition of avoidance learning and its transfer to the normal state and other drug conditions. *Psychopharmacologia, 9*, 17–30.

Sack, S.A. (1986). "The pivotal role of the Gordon Diagnostic System in the assessment of attention deficit disorder: A practitioner's view from the trenches". Paper presented at the 94th annual convention of the American Psychological Association. Washington, D.C.

Safer, R., & Allen, D. (1976). *Hyperactive children: Diagnosis and management.* Baltimore: University Park Press.

Safer, D.J., & Krager, J.M. (1983). Trends in medication treatment of hyperactive school children: Results of six biannual surveys. *Clinical Pediatrics, 22*, 500–504.

Safer, D.T., & Krager, J.M. (1985). Prevalence of medication treatment for hyperactive adolescents. *Psychopharmacological Bulletin, 21*, 212–215.

Sagvolden, T., Schiørbeck, H.K., & Rugland, A.-L. (1985). An experimental model for behavioral hyperactivity: Effects of methylphenidate hydrochloride (Ritalin) on fixed-interval responding. *Neuroscience Letters, Supplement 22*, S264. (abstract).

Sagvolden, T., Slåtta, K., & Arntzen, E. (1988). Low doses of methylphenidate (ritalin) may alter the delay-of-reinforcement gradient. *Psychopharmacology, 95*, 303–312.

Sagvolden, T., & Saebø, S. (1986). A comparative research program testing children with attention deficit disorder with hyperactivity (ADD(H)). *Behavioural Brain Research, 20*, 142–143.

Sagvolden, T., Wultz, B., Mørkrid, L., & Saebø, S. (1987). Are changed reinforcement mechanisms the key for understanding some of the behavioral problems of children with MBD/ADD? *Behavioural Brain Research, 26*, 234–235.

Sahakian, B.J., & Robbins, T.W. (1977). Are the effects of psychomotor stimulant drugs on hyperactive children really paradoxical? *Medical Hypotheses, 3*, 154–158.

Sandoval, J. (1977). The measurement of the hyperactive syndrome in children. *Review of Educational Research, 47*, 293–318.

Shaywitz, S.E., Heint, R.D., Jatlow, P., Cohen, D., Young, G.J., Pierce, R.N., Anderson, G.M., & Shaywitz, B.A. (1982). Psychopharmacology of attention deficit disorder: Pharmacokinetic, neuroendocrine and behavioral measures following acute and chronic treatment with methylphenidate. *Pediatrics, 69*, 688–694.

Shekim, W.O., Dekirmenjian, H., & Chapel, J.L. (1979). Urinary catecholamine metabolites in hyperactive children treated with d-amphetamine. *American Journal of Psychiatry, 134*, 1276–1279.

Solanto, M.V. (1986). Behavioral effects of low dose methylphenidate in childhood attention deficit disorder: Implications for a mechanism of stimulant drug action. *Journal of the American Academy of Child Psychiatry, 25*, 96–101.

Spear, N.W., Smith, G.J., Bryan, R.G., Gordon, W.C., Timmons, R., & Chiszar, D.A. (1980). Contextual influences on the interaction between conflicting in the rat. *Animal Learning and Behavior, 8*, 273–281.

Sprague, R.L., & Sleator, E.K. (1977). Methylphenidate in hyperkinetic children: Differences in dose effects on learning and social behavior. *Science, 198*, 1274–1276.

Starke, K., & Altman, K.P. (1973). Inhibition of adrenergic neurotransmission by clonidine: An action on prejunctal alpha-receptors. *Neuropharmacology, 12*, 339–349.

Stephens, R., Pelham, W., & Skinner, R. (1984). State-dependent and main effects of methylphenidate and pemoline on paired-associate learning and spelling in hyperactive children. *Journal of Consulting and Clinical Psychology, 52*, 104–112.

Taylor, E. (1984). Diet and Behavior. *Archives of the Disorders of Childhood, 59*, 97–98.

Taylor, E. (1985). Syndromes of overactivity and attention deficit. In M. Rutter, & L. Herrov (Eds.), *Child and adolescent psychiatry, modern approaches* (pp. 113–147). New York: Plenum Press.

Ullman, R.K., & Sleator, E.K. (1985). Attention deficit disorder children with or without hyperactivity. Which behaviors are helped by stimulants? *Clinical Pediatrics, 10*, 547–551.

Varley, C.K. (1984). Diet and the behavior of children with Attention Deficit Disorder. *Journal of the American Academy of Child Psychiatry, 23*, 182–185.

Virtanen, R. (1980). Excretion of nortriptyline into salvia. *International Journal of Clinical Pharmacological and Therapeutic Toxicology, 18*, 78–81.

Winsberg, B.G., Bialer, I., Kupietz, S.S., Botti, E., & Balka, E.B. (1980). Home vs. hospital care of children with behavior disorders: A controlled investigation. *Archives of General Psychiatry, 37*, 413–418.

Winsberg, B.G., Kupietz, S.S., Sverd, T., Hungund, B.L., & Young, N.L. (1982). Methylphenidate oral dose plasma concentrations and behavioral response in children. *Psychopharmacology, 7*, 81–84.

Winsberg, B. G., Kupietz, S. S., Yepes, L. E., & Goldstein, S. (1980). Ineffectiveness of imipramine in children who fail to respond to methylphenidate. *Journal of Autism and Developmental Disorders, 10*, 129–137.

Winsberg, B.G., Matinsky, S., Kupietz, S.S., & Richardson, E. (1987). Is there dose-dependent tolerance associated with chronic methylphenidate therapy in hyperactive children: Oral dose and plasma concentrations. *Psychopharmacological Bulletin, 23*, 107–110.

Winsberg, B.G., Yepes, L.E., & Bialer, I. (1976). Pharmacologic management of children with hyperactive/aggressive behavior disorder. *Clinical Pediatrics, 15*, 471–477.

Young, J.G. (1981). Methylphenidate-induced hallucinosis: Case histories and possible mechanisms of action. *Journal of Developmental and Behavioral Pediatrics, 2*, 35–38.

Author Index

Subject Index